MARKETING: THEORY AND PRACTICE

efore

Other books by Michael J. Baker include

MARKETING STRATEGY AND MANAGEMENT (2nd edn)
MARKETING: AN INTRODUCTORY TEXT (5th edn)
RESEARCH FOR MARKETING

MARKETING THEORY AND PRACTICE

Third Edition

Edited by

Michael J. Baker

with Olivier Badot, Ken Bernard, Stephen Brown, Douglas Brownlie, Sara Carter, K. C. Chan, Bernard Cova, Keith Crosier, Adamantios Diamantopoulos, Bill Donaldson, Sean Ennis, Pervez Ghauri, Susan J. Hart, Peter Leeflang, Dale Littler, Michael C. McDermott, Lyn McGregor, Shan Rajagopal, Daniel Tixier, John Webb

MACMILLAN
Business

First edition 1976
Reprinted 1979 (twice, 1981)
Second edition 1983
Reprinted 1987, 1988, 1990 (twice), 1993, 1994
Third edition 1995

Published by
MACMILLAN PRESS LTD
Houndmills, Basingstoke, Hampshire RG21 2XS
and London
Companies and representatives
throughout the world

ISBN 0–333–64181–7 hardcover
ISBN 0–333–64182–5 paperback

A catalogue record for this book is available
from the British Library.

10 9 8 7 6 5 4 3 2 1
04 03 02 01 00 99 98 97 96 95

Printed in Great Britain by
The Bath Press, Avon

Contents

List of Tables

List of Figures

Preface to the Third Edition

As the publishing history reveals *Marketing: Theory & Practice* first appeared in 1976 with a second edition following in 1983. During this period the book has been continuously available and reprinted on numerous occasions. For the Editor this performance is itself an interesting example of the inextricable link between theory and practice as well as a salutary reminder that in the domain of marketing the unexpected is often the norm. Normally, in the face of very much increased competition and rapid development in a product category, one would anticipate that a product would rapidly become obsolescent and move into the decline phase of its life-cycle. But, for *Marketing: Theory & Practice* this has not been the case.

Given such a track record it goes without saying that one should be very clear about one's objectives before considering tinkering with a tried and tested formula. Equally, it is clear that given the extensive and dynamic growth which has occurred over the past decade or so some reappraisal of both the market and the product is called for. As can be seen from the Prefaces to the earlier editions the original intention was to provide a synoptic but authoritative overview of both theory and practice on the major marketing topics a student (or practitioner) would be likely to encounter on first acquaintance with the subject. No particular assumptions were, or are, made about the age or experience of the prospective reader simply that they were either coming completely new to the subject or, perhaps, wished to remind themselves of principles or practices which they had not considered or used for some time. So it is with the Third Edition – this book is both an introduction to the subject of marketing as well as a work of reference to which the reader may return for revision or reminder about key concepts and issues which underpin successful marketing practice.

However, while the objectives remain the same the growth of the subject itself, as well as the enormous expansion of the number of students pursuing both broadly based and specialised courses, calls for both revision and extension of the earlier editions. Accordingly, in discussions with the publishers it was decided that this third edition would be even more comprehensive than its predecessors and that, given the creation of an enlarged European Union, the recruitment of authors would be extended to include experts from other centres of marketing excellence. The results are readily apparent from a comparison of the contents of the second and third editions. The second edition comprised 13 Chapters and contained 426 pages; this edition comprises 22 Chapters and 442 pages – a major development of the earlier editions.

Of the original authors only three remain – Baker (Chapters 1, 2 and 9), Brownlie (Chapter 14), and Crosier (Chapter 13). Six of the remaining seventeen chapters cover the same subjects as in the second edition but are by new authors:

Chapter 3	Sources and Status of Marketing Theory	Stephen Brown
Chapter 4	Consumer Behaviour	Lyn McGregor
Chapter 5	Organisational Buyer Behaviour	Shan Rajagopal
Chapter 10	New Product Development	Susan J. Hart
Chapter 12	Channel Management	Sean Ennis

Chapter 16 Retailing   Sara Carter
            (in place of the chapter
            'The Distributive Trades')

It follows that eleven chapters (50%) are completely new. These are:

Chapter 6   Market Segmentation   Dale Littler
Chapter 7   Marketing Research   John Webb
Chapter 8   Modelling Markets   Peter Leeflang
Chapter 11 Pricing   Adamantios
                                   Diamantopolous
Chapter 15 Business to   Ken Bernard
            Business Marketing
Chapter 17 Customer Care   Bill Donaldson
Chapter 18 Consumerism   Daniel Tixier
Chapter 19 International   Michael C.
            Marketing   McDermott and
                                   K.C. Chan
Chapter 20 Marketing to   Pervez Ghauri
            Eastern Europe
Chapter 21 Beyond Relationship   K.C. Chan
            Marketing   and Michael C.
                                   McDermott
Chapter 22 Marketing Theory   Bernard Cova
            and Practice in a   and Olivier
            Postmodern Era   Badot

While all the authors worked to the same brief there are, inevitably, differences in the way in which they interpreted this. That said, it is the Editor's view that the contributing authors have provided authoritative overviews of their areas of expertise and so achieved the primary objective of creating a work of reference which will be of value to both newcomers and those wishing to up-date themselves on current thinking. We hope it meets with your approval.

MICHAEL J. BAKER

■ Chapter 1 ■

Evolution of the Marketing Concept

Michael J. Baker

■ Introduction

In this chapter we seek to provide some answers to the frequently posed question 'What is marketing?' We will argue that, essentially, marketing is concerned with exchange relationships between producers and users, suppliers and customers, and will suggest that uncertainty, confusion or misunderstanding as to the scope and nature of this exchange relationship would seem to stem from the fact that all of us have participated in such interchange and have formulated our own interpretation of its nature.

However, despite the multiplicity of definitions that are bound to arise from such a process, we propose that consensus is possible by distinguishing between marketing as a philosophy of exchange between persons and/or organisations and marketing as it has emerged as a business function. To establish this proposition we describe briefly the evolution of exchange from its early beginning in the form of barter to the sophisticated operation of a modern market economy. Against this background we identify the three managerial orientations which have characterised the development of the modern business organisation – production, sales and marketing – and argue that the recent development of a marketing orientation reflects a return to the original basis of exchange 'consumer sovereignty'.

Finally, some reference will be made to the relevance of a marketing orientation in the changing economic and social conditions which seem likely to obtain during the final years of the present century.

■ Marketing = exchange

It is universally accepted that the lowest (and simplest) form of economic organisation is the subsistence economy in which each individual family unit is wholly dependent upon its own productive resources to satisfy its consumption needs. For our purposes it is unimportant to inquire into the precise social organisation of subsistence economies, for while this is of fundamental interest to the anthropologist, the distinction between gathering, hunting and/or pastoral nomadism is irrelevant in the absence of exchange, for, as Kotler has noted, 'it is a stage (of economic development) devoid of a concept of marketing'.[1]

Exchange first comes about where a producer creates a surplus in excess of the immediate needs of himself and his family, a surplus which he is willing to trade for some other good. Clearly, the potential for exchange is limited by the availability of other producers of different goods (or services) with surplus units which are intrinsically

1

more attractive to the first producer than increased consumption of his own output (in the language of the economist they have a greater 'marginal utility'). In turn, the owners of these surpluses must seek supplies of the first producer's surplus. Assuming, therefore, that two producers of different products are brought into contact, each of whom has a desire for units of the other's surplus, it is logical to assume that any exchange effected by them is to their mutual satisfaction. In my opinion this is the essence of marketing – a mutually satisfying exchange relationship.

However, if we were to suggest this as our definition of marketing, that is 'Marketing is a process of exchange between individuals and/or organisations which is concluded to the mutual benefit and satisfaction of the parties', then clearly this proposition would go far beyond what most people consider to be the scope of the subject. In no small measure such rejection would arise from the modern interpretation of marketing as a business function which has evolved in its most extreme form in the sale of mass-consumption, packaged convenience products. As such it is appropriate to stress the point in the preceding paragraph that the essence of an exchange relationship is freedom to decide how much of one's own surplus of any good or service, or title to any good or service, one is prepared to commute into supplies of some other good or service. Whether in fact this constitutes 'marketing' in the modern idiom can only be established by tracing the development of exchange relationships from their first beginnings in barter.

As a result of chance, application or natural aptitude most persons develop a particular skill in some aspect of life. If such skill yields an output of goods or services in demand by other persons, then the benefits of specialisation are immediately apparent. Increased productivity arising out of task specialisation results in a concomitant growth in the potential for exchange and this stage of economic development is generally associated with the genesis of the marketplace. The need for an agreed meeting place where exchanges might be effected is obvious, for otherwise much productive time will be lost in seeking out potential customers for one's output who also possess supplies of desired goods or services. Similarly, as the degree of specialisation increases so does the assortment of goods, which further complicates the problem of bringing together two parties with a mutual interest in exchange.

To facilitate barter, at least two interrelated problems must be resolved – the problem of timing and the problem of value. Value is an essentially subjective concept and, like beauty, lies in the eye of the beholder. However, for an exchange to meet our criterion that it be 'mutually satisfying' it is clear that the parties to the exchange must agree on the basis for a subjective opinion as to 'value'. In formulating this value judgement the parties are bound to be guided by the more generalised value system evolved by the social grouping of which they are members. However, it would seem that there are certain concepts fundamental to most value systems among which may be numbered scarcity, utility and skill.

While scarcity must result from a natural deficiency, as is the case with precious metals, or from the time and effort required to create a unit of supply, physical scarcity in and of itself is insufficient to invest an object with value. Only if it is perceived as possessing utility in the widest sense of the word will people prize its ownership. Thus utility is inextricably linked with concepts of value, as it is with concepts of skill, that is the scarcity value of a skill is also proportionate to its perceived utility.

Given that one has developed generalised criteria for judging value, it is obvious that agreement on a unit of measurement will greatly facilitate comparative judgements on the exchange value of widely differing goods and services. Such a unit of measurement may take any form so long as it is universally recognised and accepted within the community which wishes to use it, and has been expressed in terms of cattle, shells, beads, and so forth, as well as its modern equivalent, money.

Evolution of a standard unit of exchange goes a long way to solving the problems of barter, for it provides a common denominator for estimating the value of goods and services as well as mitigating problems of timing. These latter are bound to arise as a result of disequilibrium between supply and demand, and, in the case of barter, are exacerbated by differences in the value and divisibility of different outputs. Universally acceptable units of exchange act as a store of value and so alleviate these timing problems.

Clearly the evolution of a money economy greatly encouraged increased specialisation and led to the development of sophisticated institutions for facilitating exchange both nationally and internationally. However, while increased specialisation led to enormous improvements in productivity in the manufacture of products, primary and tertiary activities – mining and farming, distribution and personal services – were less amenable to improvement through specialisation and the division of labour.

Eventually the benefits of the division of labour were subject to diminishing returns in manufacturing industry too and the next step forward had to await the application of technology to the productive process. With the development of steam power an industrial revolution was set in train which enabled man's productive capacity to break through the plateau which it had reached when limited by natural power sources – wind and water – and the slow increase in population.

The history of the Industrial Revolution is familiar to us all and does not bear repetition here. Suffice it to say that increased productivity enabled a rapid increase in population which provided both the need for more sophisticated marketing institutions as well as the means of supplying them. However, it is important to recognise that while we speak of an industrial 'revolution' the actual process was more evolutionary and extended over a much longer period of time than is consistent with the connotations of revolution. Certainly there was no immediate solution to the grinding poverty which the working classes had endured since time immemorial, and the critical problem remained that of increasing the supply of the basic necessities of life. It was this emphasis which has led to the era being characterised as production orientated.

From production to marketing orientation

Nowadays it is fashionable to distinguish different managerial approaches to the conduct of business and to suggest that there are fundamental differences between a production, a sales and a marketing orientation.[2] The validity of such a proposition must of course depend upon how one defines a production, a sales and a marketing orientation, and it is necessary to put forward and examine such definitions before passing judgement.

As indicated in the preceding section, the endemic problem of mankind was (and still is in many developing countries) a basic disequilibrium between supply and demand. In the face of such disequilibrium the concept of homeostasis predicates the action of natural forces to restore balance in the system. Clearly, the restoration of balance may arise or be brought about by either increasing supply, through increased productivity, or by reducing demand. In the nature of things man is a wanting animal and so seeks to increase supply, although in the case of warfare this is pursued in a negative manner more akin to demand reduction. Generally, however, demand reduction results from natural causes beyond man's immediate control, such as famine and disease, and history clearly demonstrates that population growth has been checked or declined when demand has caught up with or has overtaken available supply.

Because of the unpredictable incidence of the natural population controls of famine and disease, and recognising the need to increase the labour supply to maintain or improve production, most human societies have encouraged fertility. Indeed many religions contain a positive invocation to 'go forth and multiply' which has not been challenged seriously until very recent times. Thus, although Malthus warned in his *Essay on Population* that if the population continued to expand geometrically while production expanded in an arithmetic progression there would develop a major disequilibrium between supply and demand which could only be resolved by the natural controls, his warning fell into disrepute due to its failure to come into early effect. With the benefit of hindsight we can now see that supply did not expand arithmetically in the nineteenth century – it grew exponentially and more rapidly in the industrialised economies than did population, thus giving rise to a very significant improvement in the standards of living enjoyed by the members of those economies.

Today, however, there has been a Malthusian revival which has received perhaps its greatest support from the work of Jay Forrester[3] at the Massachusetts Institute of Technology (MIT) and from the project sponsored by the Club of Rome which developed from this, reports of which were contained in *The Limits to Growth*.[4] The thesis underlying neo-Malthusianism is essentially that the world is a finite resource which will be rapidly exhausted if present consumption trends are allowed to continue, being reinforced by the multiplier effect of a rapidly expanding population.

In the medium term of three or four generations it is not too difficult to reject the pessimism of the Meadows model which predicts catastrophe long before this, by pointing out that Meadows, like Malthus, has fallen into the trap of extrapolating population and consumption geometrically and technological innovation and production arithmetically. However, for the longer term, even if one assumes that the means of sustaining life are available, it is clear that this planet can only physically accommodate a certain level of population. In recognition of this fact, as well as the validity of many of the arguments of the neo-Malthusians, the case for stabilising demand by population control is considered a much more viable and realistic solution to the human predicament than are attempts to increase supply. If, therefore, a production orientation is considered synonymous with efforts to increase supply, we can readily understand why it should have occupied a central place in the thinking of entrepreneurs from time immemorial. Further, given that the capacity to create over-supply only exists in a limited number of the world's economies it is not difficult to see why it should remain the focus of immediate effort in those

countries with a supply deficiency *vis-a-vis* their present population.

King summarises the period of production orientation as 'an era of managerial concern with problems of capacity creation, work methods, and volume production'.[5] However, as he continues to point out, 'Although it is not suggested that corporate management gave no consideration during this period to the markets for which they produced, it appears that, generally, problems related to manufacturing assumed greater significance than did those related to identification and development of markets.'

While King is confining his discussion to the twentieth century, it is quite obvious, for the reasons discussed above, that his comments are equally applicable to preceding centuries. It seems to me, therefore, that we render entrepreneurs a grave disservice if we use 'production oriented' in a pejorative sense and with overtones which imply that such an orientation ignores consumer needs. Rather, it seems to me that the production-orientated manager got his priorities right, in that demand for basic goods and services was clearly identifiable and that an emphasis upon volume rather than differentiation or choice was eminently sensible in that it went a long way towards maximising total satisfaction. Certainly, by achieving the economies of mass production, Henry Ford made his model-T available to vast segments of the population who otherwise would never have had the opportunity to own the basic product – a car – which they sought, the colour of which was essentially irrelevant. Yet today we cite 'You can have any colour of car as long as it's black' as the antithesis of marketing – a review that it is difficult if not impossible to sustain if one adopts the definition proposed earlier that marketing is concerned with mutually satisfying exchange relationships. As more than 60 per cent of American car sales in 1920 were Fords, we must accept that two-thirds of American car buyers felt this to be a more satisfying situation than buying (or not being able to afford to buy) the products of the myriad producers who collectively accounted for the remaining third of the market.

The situation that was to bring the production orientation into disrepute was what I have referred to elsewhere as 'the creation of "excess" supply'.[6] Excess supply is of course a comparative state and applies only to certain categories of products under very limited conditions, foremost among which is a presumption of available discretionary consumer purchasing power that is only satisfied, and then only partially, in the most affluent societies. However, from the firm's point of view, a state of excess supply begins to become apparent when the market ceases to absorb all of its output and exhibits price inelasticity of demand within the range which would be acceptable to the firm. In other words, to stimulate increased consumption, it would be necessary to sell at an unacceptably low price.

Faced with price inelasticity of demand for its output, and a situation in which the joint potential supply of the firm and its immediate competitors exceeds effective demand, managements immediate reaction tends to be to maintain volume through non-price competition and especially by means of product differentiation, promotion and selling effort.

In the short term it is easiest to increase the sales effort, and for this reason there was a transitional period which King identifies as the sales-management orientation between the production-management orientation and the present emphasis upon marketing. Simplistically, the sales-management orientation, which prevailed between 1930 and 1950 in the United States, may be characterised as 'selling what we can make' in contradistinction to 'making what we can sell' which is considered a central feature of the marketing concept. However, these catch phrases do scant justice to the philosophical difference between a sales-management and marketing approach.

From the sales manager's standpoint, products and services are given and potential customers must be persuaded to see them as the solution to a generalised consumption need. From the marketer's standpoint customers are given and potential products must be developed or modified to match specific consumption needs. Thus, where the production- or sales-orientated manager would tend to ask himself 'What do customers want?', the marketer would ask the customers themselves and then proceed to organise a supply of the desired objects.

One of the first firms to embrace a marketing approach was the American General Electric Company, and King cites two quotations which help spell out this fundamental difference between selling and marketing:

> Under the traditional 'sales' concept, engineering designed a product, manufacturing produced it – and then the sales people were expected to sell it. Under the modern 'marketing' concept, the whole business process starts with marketing research and sales forecasting to provide a sound, factual customer-oriented basis for planning all business operations, and the business function which has sales responsibility now participates in all the stages of the business planning process.[7]

> [the marketing concept] introduces the marketing man at the beginning rather than the end of the production cycle and would integrate marketing into each phase of the business. Thus marketing, through its studies and research, will establish for the engineer, the designer and the manufacturing man what the customer wants in a given product, what price he is willing to pay, and where and when it will be wanted. Marketing would have authority in product planning, production scheduling and inventory control, as well as in the sales, distribution and servicing of the product.[8]

Similarly, Robert J. Keith's description of the role of marketing in the Pillsbury Company serves to reinforce this point:

> Marketing is viewed in our company today as the function which plans and executes the sale – all the way from the inception of the idea, through its development and execution, to the sale to the customer. Marketing begins and ends with the consumer. The idea for a new product is conceived after careful study of her wants and needs, her likes and dislikes. With the idea in hand, the marketing department functions as a universal joint in the corporation, marshalling all the forces of the corporation to translate the idea into product and the product into sales.[9]

■ Full circle

In describing the evolution of the marketing concept it appears that we have been guilty of considerable arrogance in presuming it to be of recent origin. In reality it seems to me that if our early definition of marketing as 'a process of exchange between individuals and/or organisations which is concluded to the mutual benefit and satisfaction of the parties' is acceptable, then marketing is as old as exchange relationships themselves. However, as society has developed, and has harnessed the power of science and technology to assist it in meeting the apparently insatiable demand for goods and services, so it has been necessary to evolve new institutions and new mechanisms to cope with the complexity which has accompanied this development.

It follows that if the criterion to be used to judge or measure the effectiveness of a single exchange relationship is the mutual satisfaction derived from it, then, in the aggregate, marketing (exchange?) will be at its most efficient when it maximises aggregate satisfaction. If this is so, then, as we have already argued, the much despised production orientation with its emphasis upon manufacturing and volume of output may be the most appropriate to conditions of chronic under-supply. Under such conditions the nature of demand is likely to be as self-evident to the entrepreneur responsible for setting up and controlling a factory with an output measured in millions of identical units as it was and is to the supplier who engaged in a direct one-to-one relationship with his customer.

Thus it would seem more accurate to speak not of the emergence of the marketing concept in the 1950s but rather to talk about the need to reappraise the precise nature of consumer demand due to the changes brought about by the physical separation of producer and customer (accompanied by the potential to create excess supply in some sectors of production) in order to ensure that we maximise aggregate satisfaction. Asking customers what they want can hardly be as revolutionary a step as some writers would have us believe! More likely it reflects the basic and continuing nature of exchange, that is consumer sovereignty.

It is gratifying that since the First Edition of *Marketing: Theory & Practice* appeared in 1976 considerable support has appeared to reinforce our view that while the 'three eras' approach (production, sales, marketing), popularised by Keith[10] is a useful device for highlighting the change of emphasis in the relationship between supply and demand, it is an over-simplified explanation which promotes marketing as a 20th-century innovation. In reality, of course, marketing is as old as exchange itself and much of what has been characterised as a recent development is, in fact, of considerable antiquity.

In an article entitled 'How Modern is Modern Marketing?' Ronald A. Fullerton[11] challenges the three eras conceptualisation. As noted, the three-stage evolutionary model has been useful to both authors and teachers alike in highlighting major changes in the dominant orientation of business. However, it doesn't analyse in detail the much more complex processes which underlay and resulted in these changes. Such an analysis is properly the domain of the business historian following the requirements of rigorous historical research. Based on such research Fullerton argues that there is considerable evidence to deny the existence of a production era. In his words:

1. It ignores well established historical facts about business conditions – competition was intense in most businesses, over-production common, and demand frequently uncertain.
2. It totally misses the presence and vital importance of conscious demand stimulation in developing the advanced modern economies. Without such stimulation revolution in production would have been stillborn.
3. It does not account for the varied and vigorous marketing efforts made by numerous manufacturers and other producers.
4. It ignores the dynamic growth of new marketing institutions outside the manufacturing firm. (p. 111)

Each of these arguments is examined in detail and substantial evidence is marshalled to support them.

A particularly telling point concerns the need for active demand stimulation and the need for production and marketing to work in tandem.

> Some of the famous pioneers of production such as Matthew Boulton and Josiah Wedgwood were also pioneers of modern marketing, cultivating large-scale demand for their revolutionary inexpensive products with techniques usually considered to have been post-1950 American innovations: market segmentation, production differentiation, prestige pricing, style obsolescence, saturation advertising, direct mail campaigns, reference group appeals, and testimonials among others. (p. 112)

In Fullerton's view 'demand enhancing marketing' spread from Britain to Germany and the USA. In the USA it was adopted with enthusiasm and Americans came to be seen as 'the supreme masters of aggressive demand stimulation' a fact frequently referred to in contemporary marketing texts in the early 1900s. Numerous examples support Fullerton's contention that producers of the so-called production era made extensive use of marketing tools and techniques as well as integrating forward to ensure their products were brought to the attention of their intended customers in the most effective way. That said, the examples provided (with one or two possible exceptions) do not, in my view, invalidate the classification of the period as the 'production era' in the sense that it was the producer who took the initiative and differentiated his product to meet the *assumed* needs of different consumer groups based on economic as opposed to sociological and psychological factors. In other words, producers inferred the consumer's behaviour but they had not yet developed techniques or procedures which would enable them to define latent wants and design, produce, and market products and services to satisfy them. Similarly, while the period 1870–1930 saw the emergence and development of important marketing institutions in terms of physical distribution, retailing, advertising and marketing education, which are still important today, it does not seem unreasonable to argue that all these institutions were designed to sell more or what was being produced. This is not to deny the 'rich marketing heritage' documented by Fullerton but to reinforce the point that the transition to a 'marketing era' was marked by a major change in business philosophy from a producer-led interpretation of consumer needs to a consumer-driven approach to production.

As to the existence of a sales era (rejected by Fullerton) this seems as convenient a label as any to give to the transitional period between a production and marketing orientation. In addition to the reality of a depressed world economy in the 1930s, which required large-scale producers to sell more aggressively to maintain economies of scale, the period saw the migration of many behavioural scientists from a politically unstable Europe to the safety of the USA. In retrospect it appears that it was this migration which led to the more rigorous analysis of consumer behaviour which was to underpin the emergence of a new 'marketing era'.

Combined with this greater insight into consumer behaviour were a period of great economic growth and prosperity following the Second World War, together with a major increase in the birth rate which was to result in a new generation of consumers brought up in a period of material affluence (the baby boomers). It was this generation which sought to re-assert consumer sovereignty and so initiated the change in the balance of power between the producer and consumer which heralded the 'marketing era'.

While Fullerton proposes an alternative 'complex flux model' this is seen as extending rather than dismissing the three eras model. In our view the latter seeks to distinguish between marketing as a practice which was clearly present in both the production and sales eras and marketing as a philosophy of business which shifts the emphasis from the producer's pursuit of profit as the primary objective to the achievement of customer satisfaction which, in the long run, is likely to receive the same financial reward. It is not without significance that as we move towards the millennium many US academics are beginning to advocate the importance of the relationship rather than the transaction as the basis of marketing exchange. This emphasis has been evident in European circles for some 20 years or more now and takes a quite different approach to the marketing exchange process than is the case with the American's emphasis upon the transaction under-pinned by the implementation of a marketing mix emphasising the 4 P's first proposed by McCarthy.[12]

Marketing – philosophy or function?

Unfortunately, while the philosophy of marketing is firmly rooted in the principle of consumer sovereignty, even if only out of enlightened self-interest, there is a growing body of criticism which believes and argues to the contrary. It would be naive to deny that this criticism has foundation for there are sufficient well-established examples[13] to warrant a case against modern marketing practices. However, to establish that some members of a community are criminals is not to prove that all are. Similarly, to identify some misleading advertisements or malpractices such as pyramid selling (albeit that the latter only thrives on the greed of the victims who want something for nothing) is not to substantiate a case that marketing as a whole is against the consumer interest.

Further, it seems to me that most criticism is directed at the practice, or perhaps it would be nearer the truth to say the malpractice, of marketing and not against the philosophy or principles as we have outlined them above. Indeed, given our definition of marketing it is difficult to see how anyone could ever take exception to it. On the other hand, it is not difficult to understand how ordinary consumers can become dubious about marketing when they have no clear definition of what the marketing concept is supposed to be, save possibly a cliché such as 'the customer is always right', and so can only judge from their own direct experience at the hands of marketers.

However, while one is forced to acknowledge defects in the function of marketing arising from certain marketing practices, it would be unwise to accept all of the criticism directed against it by consumerists. Because consumerists are intelligent, articulate and often highly vocal one should not automatically assume that they have a monopoly of the truth nor that one must accept their point of view. Accordingly, while most advertisers, and certainly all responsible ones, would agree with the desirability of truth in advertising, this is not to concede that all advertising should be purely factual and devoid of any subjective associations or connotations.

Where the consumerists go wrong in their condemnation of marketing is in their insistence upon a concept of objective rationality the origin of which would seem to be a simplifying assumption necessary to make early price theory work. As economics has become more sophisticated it has become possible to relax such rigid assumptions as homogeneity of demand and supply and to admit, as Lawrence Abbott[14] has pointed out, that 'What people really desire are not products but satisfying experiences.' Thus, as Abbot comments,

> what is considered satisfying is a matter for individual decision: it varies according to one's tastes, standards, beliefs and objectives – and these vary greatly, depending on individual personality and cultural environment. Here is a foundation for a theory of choice broad enough to embrace Asiatic as well as Eastern cultures, nonconformists as well as slaves to convention, Epicureans, stoics, cynics, roisterers, religious fanatics, dullards, and intellectual giants alike.

In fact, a theory of choice founded on consumer sovereignty.

To criticise 'Admass' (mass advertising) for treating all consumers as the same, and mindless automatons to boot, would seem contradictory to say the least when reinforced by an all-embracing demand that we all buy on the basis of price and product specification while ignoring all aesthetic and/or subjective associations.

But merely to deny the consumerists' case against marketing is insufficient. Rather it is necessary to show that marketing too possesses a theoretical foundation which, without claiming it to be a better theory than any other theory of how people behave, at least deserves equal consideration. Only if marketers can raise the argument above the trivial of the rights and wrongs

of specific marketing actions does it seem to me
that we may be able to persuade our critics that
marketing is a subject worthy of serious study,
and an honourable profession as well. Further, I
believe that it is essential to establish that marketing is not merely another transitional phase, like
the sales-management orientation of the 1930s
and 1940s, to be characterised as one of 'demand
stimulation' and 'conspicuous consumption' and
wholly inappropriate to the growing awareness of
the need to conserve our limited resources, but a
social philosophy of increasing relevance.

To this end, in the next two chapters we
examine the need for a theory of marketing, and
its likely nature and sources before considering
how theory can improve our understanding of
specific areas such as marketing communications
and distribution. Finally, we broaden our review
once again to discuss the role marketing has to
play in the changing social and economic conditions likely to obtain in the final years of the
century.

■ Notes and references

1. Kotler, P., *Marketing Management*, 2nd edn,
   Englewood Cliffs, N.J.: Prentice-Hall, 1972, p. 6.
2. This follows a trichotomy suggested by Robert L.
   King in 'The Marketing Concept', in *Science in
   Marketing*, ed. George Schwartz, New York:
   Wiley, 1965. The discussion on these different
   orientations draws extensively on this source.
3. See *World Dynamics*, Cambridge, Mass.: Wright-
   Allen Press, 1971.
4. Meadows, D., *et al.*, *The Limits to Growth*,
   London: Earth Island, 1972.
5. King, 'The Marketing Concept'.
6. *Marketing*, 2nd edn, London: Macmillan, 1974,
   pp. 26ff.
7. Quoted from an unpublished paper, 'The
   Marketing Concept in General Electric', by
   Edward S. McKay.
8. General Electric Company, *Annual Report*, 1952.
9. 'An Interpretation of the Marketing Concept',
   Advancing Marketing Efficiency, Proceedings
   of the 41st National Conference, American
   Marketing Association (Chicago, 1959), cited in
   King, 'The Marketing Concept'.
10. Keith, R. J., 'The Marketing Revolution', *Journal
    of Marketing* (January 1960), pp. 35–38.
11. Fullerton, R. A., 'How Modern is Modern
    Marketing?', *Journal of Marketing* (1988).
12. McCarthy E. Jerome, *Basic Marketing: A
    Managerial Approach*, Homewood Ill: Unwin,
    1960.
13. See, for example, Vance Packard's books, *The
    Hidden Persuaders*, London: Longmans, Green,
    1957, and *The Waste Makers*, London:
    Longmans, Green, 1961. Also Ralph Nader's
    Unsafe at any Speed, New York: Grossman, 1963.
14. Abbott, L., *Quality and Competition*, Columbia
    University Press, 1955.

■ Chapter 2 ■

The Need for Theory in Marketing

Michael J. Baker

■ Introduction

The purpose of this chapter is to establish why it is considered essential that the study and practice of marketing should be founded upon a sound theoretical base.

To do this one must first specify what one means by 'theory' and then identify its role. Equipped with a definition of theory we may then enquire into its nature, which in turn will allow us to focus attention upon its function. This consideration suggests that theory is essential to the development of an integrated body of knowledge and raises the question as to how theory evolves or is developed.

A basic distinction is frequently drawn between 'art' and 'science' and we review what appears to us to be the difference between the two prior to a fuller consideration of the nature of science and the scientific method in the context of its possible relevance to marketing.

■ The definition of theory

The word 'theory' is normally associated in people's minds with the development of ideas or conjectures about the manner or ways in which part of the world works. From the Oxford dictionary we find that one derivation of theory is from the Greek θεωρία which was used in the sense of 'pertaining to or connected with public spectacles, religious functions and solemn embassies', which we presume were looked at by spectators as an attempt on the part of actors or participants to interpret one way of looking at part of the real world. With the passage of time the meaning of theory became more generalised and the Latin root *theoria* was used to mean 'a looking at or a speculation or a contemplation'. Today, however, we have endowed the word 'theory' with a more specific meaning and for our purposes will adopt the working definition suggested in the Oxford dictionary which defines a theory as being 'a scheme or system of ideas or statements held as an explanation of a group of facts or phenomena'.

■ The nature of theory

A review of human progress would seem to suggest that the main catalyst is a change in emphasis in the orientation of critical thought from a 'descriptive' basis to a basis which may be defined as primarily 'analytical'. For example, in the field of medicine early developments were confined to general descriptions of the human body and the naming of its various parts. In turn this descriptive base permitted the transference of ideas concerning the nature and causes of disease from one case to another. However, with Harvey's discovery of how the blood circulated the orientation of medicine changed from being one of description to one of analysis based upon a theory which satisfies the definition advanced earlier.

Just as Harvey's discovery provided the foundation for the modern profession of medicine so too have similar breakthroughs provided the basis for the development and extension of other fields of human endeavour. At the same time it must be recognised that many breakthroughs in thought and practice have occurred without the application of developed theory. Thus most early innovations were developed by inventors whose approach could be defined as pragmatic, as was the case when James Watt designed the first rudimentary steam-engine based upon his observations of the pressure exerted upon the lid of a kettle as a result of the build up of steam which took place when it boiled upon an open fire. The thermodynamic theory of heat transfer had not been developed, yet steam-engines were constructed and worked successfully for over a century before this theory was evolved. But, with the development of a theory of thermo-dynamics the design of the steam-engine underwent a revolutionary change, and from that time onwards they were designed largely according to theoretical principles rather than by studying and applying empirical data concerning the past design and operation of steam-engines. As a result of this application of theory the efficiency of the steam-engine increased geometrically by contrast with the arithmetic rate of progress which had characterised it prior to a statement of theory concerning its operation.

This same process of development from applied art to analytical or theoretical knowledge has held good in many fields of human activity. When these activities first developed they were essentially based upon the application of skill or technique and characterised as 'arts'. However, with the formulation and statement of a sound theoretical base a whole new insight into the activity began to emerge and the transition took place from art to science.

However, before going on to consider the nature of the differences between art and science it will be helpful if we delineate three basic requirements which any theorist must satisfy.

A basic requirement of any theory are definitions which state clearly the meaning of the various terms which will be used in that theory. The need for clear and precise definitions is obvious, for without them we will be uncertain as to what constitutes a relevant observation and how to interpret it in order to test the theory. In addition to defining the terms that are to be used, an area of science frequently termed 'semantics', the statement of an adequate theory also requires that we define the conditions or assumptions under which the theory will hold. The third requirement of a theory is that it should be built upon hypotheses about the way in which things actually behave or about relationships between things in the real world. In essence hypotheses are working guesses to which we attach a high antecedent probability that they will be validated by the collection and analysis of evidence or data. Thus a hypothesis differs from a theory in that it has not been demonstrated to yield predictions with an accuracy greater than that which could be achieved if predictions were made by some random device. However, once a hypothesis has been shown to be able to yield predictions with greater accuracy than would arise from such a random process, then we will term it a 'theory'. In turn, if a theory can be demonstrated to yield perfectly accurate predictions every time it is used, then that theory will take on the status of a 'law'.

The usefulness and quality of marketing theory will depend upon the way in which definitions, assumptions and hypotheses are combined together. The theory or model which is produced may be regarded as a simplification of a part of reality which usually fits the observed facts approximately rather than exactly. Thus the role of a researcher in any field is to try and impose order upon the observation he makes of that part of the real world which is his area of interest, for otherwise these observations will be little more than a confused jumble of facts and ideas. The statement of a theory demands that these facts and ideas should be brought together in a related and meaningful way. Thus in many respects a valid theory is very similar to a road map. A valid theory, like a valid road map, requires to be based on facts if it is to be realistic and useful. If it is too detailed and incorporates every hedge and post upon the road it will be confusing and of little use to the driver using it as a means of getting from one place to another. On the other hand, if it is insufficiently detailed, it will be inadequate as a guide to real-life situations.

To be useful, then, a theory, like a road map, must satisfy certain functions, functions which to some degree are dependent upon the structure of the theory itself. Until now, researchers in the field of marketing have tended to limit the functions of theory to those of description and prescription, that is the ability to give direction. These two functions are basic to all theory but in addition there are others which should be performed by any theory with pretensions to adequacy, namely the functions of delimitation, generation and integration.

□ *Delimitation function*

While the basic function of any theory is to describe part of reality such description must operate selectively. This selection is the delimiting function and means in effect that the theory cannot include everything in the world of reality. Thus a theory which does not delimit in this fashion would break under its own excess of explanation. The process of deciding what to include and exclude from a theory through this process of delimitation depends very much upon the purpose for which the theory is being constructed.

□ *The generative function*

The generative function may be defined as the capacity to create testable hypotheses and encompasses the processes which we otherwise describe as theoretical speculation, creativity, or even

'hunch'. Thus as well as being founded upon tested hypotheses a theory must also generate new hypotheses which will permit us to extend our understanding and knowledge.

When a theory is used to stimulate empirical investigation we speak of using the theory 'heuristically'. The heuristic use of theory is often made by analogy, for example Freud used the physical concept of hydraulic fluid to express mental states.

□ *The integrative function*

This function of theory refers to the ability to bring together the various constructs and propositions which have been elucidated by the researcher into a more or less consistent and useful whole. Thus the objective of theorists working in an area such as marketing must be to endeavour to integrate and pull together their ideas into a coherent and interdependent unit which warrants identification as a formal theory.

However, such a process of formalisation can have side-effects such as confusion and inconsistency. For example, in the field of marketing a number of independent researchers have attempted to construct complex theories of consumer behaviour in order to explain the buying process. Often, however, these theories contradict as much as confirm one another.

The integrative function is of prime importance in the development of theory. In many ways marketing like psychology has been going through a period in which the emphasis has been upon a number of micro or miniature theories which constitute an adequate explanation of some part or parts of the subject (the 'piecemeal' approach). Thus some observers are of the opinion that the first priority in developing theory in marketing must be the integration of these various pieces of emerging theory into a consistent whole (a 'holistic' approach).

▋ The need for a theory in marketing

As we indicated in Chapter 1, the practice of marketing has existed since the first exchange relationship. However, in tracing the evolution of marketing from the early days of barter through to the statement of the modern marketing concept in the early 1950s, it became apparent that the need for a formal restatement of the basis upon which such relationships exist arose out of the separation which had occurred between buyer and seller. In turn the degree and extent of this separation reflects the development of a very complex and sophisticated system for matching highly specific wants with supplies of goods and services capable of satisfying these wants.

In recent years it has been fashionable to decry the operation of the marketing system and to give great attention to its deficiencies rather than to its achievements. In large degree it is felt that many of the deficiencies which exist in the marketing system arise out of a lack of understanding as to its actual operation. It is recognition and acceptance of the need to improve our understanding of the manner in which the system works which underlies the need to develop a workable theory of exchange. It must be stressed that the key word in the preceding sentence is 'workable' for clearly there are well-developed theories of exchange in economics and in the behavioural sciences. However, from our point of view these are inadequate for they are an oversimplified and stylised representation of real-world behaviour. Further, it is our opinion that a theory of marketing demands a synthesising of concepts from both the economic and the behavioural sciences if it is to constitute an adequate explanation of the true nature of exchange.

In many senses the practice of marketing today is in a very similar situation to that which obtained prior to the statement of the law of thermo-dynamics in terms of the development of the steam-engine. Thus, as Halbert has pointed out,[1] marketing needs to develop a theory both to improve operational performance as well as to satisfy an intellectual desire to evolve an explanation of a confused world. With the formulation and statement of a theory of marketing we could look forward to the more effective solution of immediate operating problems and so could concentrate our attention on the more important and basic problems which underlie them. Further, increased operational efficiency would also free

practitioners from 'fire-fighting' activities and so leave them with more time in which to solve these problems. Thus the increasing complexity of business makes the need for theory even more pressing than hitherto in order to speed up and improve our decision-making capability. At the same time it appears that developments in other sciences have created the intellectual and analytical tools necessary to the statement of a theory of marketing.

▌ Marketing and the scientific method

At a number of places in the preceding pages we have referred to science and scientific method and it is appropriate that we should now consider the relevance that these may have for the formulation of a theory of marketing.

As hinted earlier, the factor that tends to differentiate science from art or applied skill is that science goes beyond mere description and seeks to provide an explanation of why things are what they are. Thus one of the main objectives of science has been that of spelling out the interrelationship between the parts of the structure in order to derive laws or principles which may serve as a basis for prediction, decision and action. Prediction in any field of study is possible only to the extent that uniformity exists in the phenomena under study. Indeed it is probably because the conditions and events of a physical nature are found to have a relatively higher degree of uniformity that predictions regarding them can be thought of as comparatively reliable with the result that the methods by which such phenomena have been studied have become the standards for scientific research and the basis of what has been termed 'the scientific method'.

In an article entitled 'Is Marketing a Science?' Robert D. Buzzell[2] suggests that a science is 'a classified and systemized body of knowledge...organized around one or more central theories and a number of general principles...usually expressed in quantitative terms, knowledge which permits the prediction and, under some circumstances the control of future events'. Invariably science that conforms to this definition is the outcome of a process known as 'the scientific method' which is usually recognised as possessing a number of clearly defined steps: (i) observation and measurement, (ii) experimentation, (iii) classification, and (iv) accurate generalisation.

■ Is marketing a science?

The question posed by Buzzell has long been debated by marketing academics being originally sparked off by Converse[3] in 1945 and raged in the 1950s and 1960s fuelled by such authors as Alderson and Cox (1948),[4] Vaile (1949),[5] Bartels (1951),[6] Hutchinson (1965),[7] Jueck (1953),[8] Baumol (1957),[9] Buzzell (1963),[10] Halbert (1965)[11] and Taylor (1965).[12] Three definite schools of thought can be identified:

1. Those who say marketing is not and never will be a science.
2. Those who believe marketing is a science.
3. Those who presuppose the attainment of science is possible and who either do not concern themselves with justifying their position or suggest that as marketing matures it will become worthy of the title 'science'. Others who may be included in this school are those who point out marketing's use of scientific method as justification of its evolving status.

Vaile[13] was one of the earliest critics of the 'marketing is a science' school. In answer to Alderson and Cox's[14] attempt at a single theory in 1948, he said 'When all is said and done, marketing will remain an art in which innovation and extravaganza will continue to play an important, albeit unpredictable part.'[15] Hutchinson[16] similarly eloquently dismisses marketing as a science. He too believes that marketing should be considered as an art or practice, more closely resembling engineering, medicine and architecture and that marketers should follow the medical profession whose members are called practitioners and whose work it is, 'as it is of any practitioner, to apply the findings of many sciences to the solution of problems'.[17] Levitt suggests science is only

used as a limited background to help marketers make decisions and reduce risks, but their objective must always be the practical application and thus 'The highest form of achievement is always art, never science.'[18] He further believes that marketing will probably never be a science because little day-to-day guidance is possible. Taylor is also of the opinion that 'the act of marketing is an art'. He does, however, admit that in the course of the marketing practitioner's work 'he may publish observations and conduct experiments. To the extent that he does so and contributes to the field of conceptual schemes that are fruitful and that extend the range of theory in marketing, he functions as a scientist.'[19] Weiss[20] is perhaps the most scathing, suggesting that the Marketing Science Institute in the United States should drop 'science' from its title for all social sciences are merely disciplines and 'undisciplined disciplines at that'. Since behaviour can never be 'average', to develop diagnostic tools to analyse it, he insists, is irrelevant.

The 'marketing is a science' school is less polemic. Bartels[21] suggests one commonly held view is that 'Marketing thought is ... seen beginning as simple inquiry and findings, progressing to the status of a discipline and emerging as science.'[22] Most marketers, however, are more cautious and fall into the third category, believing marketing will be worthy of the title of science eventually, provided marketers do not concentrate on borrowing theories from other disciplines without validating them, but stick instead to building up theory from observation and the measurement of raw data.

Whether marketing is classified as a science or art is largely dependent upon the author's perspective and approach. If he is a practitioner, or favours the view that marketing should be approached in a managerial or institutional way, he is likely to insist that marketing is an art. The academic and researcher are more likely to believe that marketing is, or has the potential of being, a science. Numerous definitions of science have consequently been quoted to prove or disprove that marketing is a science. For example, Buzzell says that since science is 'a classified and systematic body of knowledge...organised around one or more central theories and a number of general principles' and since marketing lacks the requisite central tendencies, it cannot be termed a science. In addition, he suggests its ability to predict (another of science's criteria) is limited. However, even the critics have to admit that marketing uses science and scientific techniques. Hutchinson[23] seeks to resolve the problem by drawing a distinction between the scientist pushing back the frontiers of knowledge and the practitioner applying that knowledge. Ramond[24] suggests the linkage is much closer, 'using science is an art'. He goes on to show how scientific knowledge and methods can help practitioners operate most effectively. 'Marketing, like medicine and engineering, requires the practice of many arts, important among which is the use of science.'

The supporters of marketing being a science frequently quote Homans,[25] 'What makes a science are its aims, not its results', while others have taken dictionary definitions of science, for example, 'any distinct branch or department of systematized knowledge considered as a distinct field of investigation or object of study, it is concerned with observation and the classification of facts and with the establishment of general laws, chiefly by induction and hypotheses'[26] and matched the function of marketing accordingly. They point out that science is built up through the scientific method – the selection, registration and rearranging of facts into some workable form from which conclusions can be derived – and since marketing already uses this process it must be at least a potential science, but may not yet be science because it is still a young discipline. They refer to the fact that physics achieved the status of science before psychology, and psychology before sociology. Since marketing has not progressed very far along the evolutionary spectrum, it is only a matter of time before it arrives.

The battle tends to focus on one or two controversial areas. One is whether marketing meets the objectives of science. Most accept that science's objectives are to derive laws and principles from studying underlying uniformities to serve as the basis for prediction. The 'marketing is an art' school argue that marketing phenomena are different from those in the physical sciences and do not therefore have a sufficient degree of uniformity to serve as the basis for prediction. The 'marketing is a science' school argue that there is sufficient uniformity and stability for making valid and reliable predictions, and measurement can be used in marketing equally well as it is used in physics or chemistry – the only difference being that 'precision is a relative matter'.[27] Also, while it is true that marketing is a complex discipline with numerous variables interacting within a wider dynamic framework, complexity is also common in physical sciences, but here it is often assumed away.

Another point of disagreement is whether the scientific approach is inductive or deductive. The 'marketing is an art' school say that true science is made up of laws that are empirically derived (and therefore more objective) while the social sciences have tended to rely on theoretical laws (i.e. rules of inference). Supporters of the 'marketing is a science' school are prepared to accept either or both types, for even subjective factors, they say, can be reduced to scientific statement in law.[28]

Perhaps Bartels sums up the definition of science debate the best by showing how marketing can be described to fit the definition of an art, a discipline or a science. The only reason for one's choice is one's approach. To define marketing as an art puts the emphasis on doing. To define marketing as a discipline stresses the academic side. To define marketing as a science is to see it as a body of knowledge with concepts, theories, principles and laws.

It would seem that to consider marketing solely as an art is myopically to deny the utility and function of science and restrict marketing's development in the future. Despite the fact that most marketers will always be concerned with the discipline's practical application, all effective practice is dependent upon evolving theory. Without better theory practice cannot become more effective and to regard theory as the opposite end of the continuum from practice is to exemplify the misunderstanding portrayed by many of the 'marketing is an art' school. The purpose of science as a problem-solving tool for society should be sufficient reason to regard marketing as a science, and theory, an integral part of science, therefore has an essential role.

■ Science and marketing

While we have suggested that the basic distinction between art and science rests on the fact that the latter goes beyond description to explanation, none the less it is clear that the first step in the scientific method must be the collection and description of facts. Based upon observation the first distinction which a person is likely to make is qualitative, for example *A* is bigger than *B* and *A* is bigger than *C*. It is immediately apparent that such qualitative statements severely limit our ability to make inferences about the relationship between *B* and *C*. For this reason science lays great emphasis upon precise measurement and quantification and so enables us to make much more accurate and elaborate statements about the relationship between objects.

If we assume that the first step in the evolution of scientific methods is the chance or random observation of objects and events, then it is clear that our knowledge and understanding will be greatly improved if these observations are undertaken in a systematic manner. Even greater progress becomes possible when such systematic observation is complemented by experimentation. Experiments may be conceived of and undertaken for a variety of reasons but all rest upon the principle that every natural event is a consequence of preceding and ascertainable conditions of its physical environment. It follows, therefore, that if one changes the conditions in the physical environment then one will produce corresponding changes in the event. Amongst the various types of experiment may be distinguished exploratory investigations in which one varies input in a controlled manner in order to determine the effect upon the outputs; experiments to test accepted principles, for example Galileo's experiments with weights whereby he disproved the Aristotelian law that material bodies fall with velocities proportional to their weights; experiments to check on chance observations; and experiments to test hypotheses.

Clearly, experimentation results in a great improvement in both the quantity and quality of data available to scientists. However, to be meaningful this data must now be classified as a basis for analysis and a statement of accurate generalisations. This process whereby one develops generalisations from particular instances and events is known as 'induction' and, irrespective of the name given to them, all models, principles, laws and theories possess the common property that they are generalisations about an area of reality arrived at by the process of abstracting from reality.

Good representations of phenomena abstracted from reality can also be used to explain occurrences or even to make predictions. This method is known as 'deduction' – a process of reasoning from general assumptions or statements to particular conclusions. It is clear that deductive methods permit the verification of conclusions arrived at by inductive reasoning, and thus the cycle of induction, deduction and verification constitutes the framework of the scientific method.

The need for a scientific approach to the solution of marketing problems was well exemplified in a paper delivered by Colin McDonald at the Market Research Society's Seminar on Strategic Advertising Decisions in November 1974.[29] Given the magnitude of advertising expenditures (£874 million in 1973 in the United Kingdom at the time at which McDonald was writing and now (1992) estimated at £8,769 million including Direct Mail), it is not surprising that marketers have long sought for some measure of the return on this outlay but, so far, with a singular lack of success. In McDonald's view this lack of success is due to speculative theorising which fails to observe the rules of the scientific method, and especially its failure first to observe and describe the phenomenon. Thus he comments:

I find myself very much in agreement with David Berdy[30] when he categorises most of the approaches to advertising as ideological, or fundamentalist, and for that reason sterile, and complains of its failure to adopt a true scientific approach in spite of trying: Outside the pure sciences...there is an inverse relationship between preoccupation with theoretical structures and the understanding of practical techniques or processes. You cannot observe a theory without observing facts; such short cuts are a negation of the scientific method.

In deciding just what one should observe, McDonald cites three basic questions posed by advertisers:

1. How should we decide the size of the advertising appropriation?
2. How should we decide the media mix?
3. How should we decide whether to have continuous or burst advertising?

He goes on to say that 'The second and third of these questions are subsidiary to the first one. The first question involves *what* advertising is trying to do (objectives) and how we measure that it is doing it; the other two questions are about how to achieve what is determined by the first.'

But, after reviewing the advertisers' viewpoint, McDonald is forced to conclude that an approach based upon measuring advertising's success (or lack of it) in achieving predetermined objectives is doomed to failure. As he trenchantly points out, 'The trouble is that, *because* there is ignorance of advertising effect, people have no basis on which to *set* objectives in the first place. Thus the objectives they do set (when indeed they propose any) tend to be circular; they reflect their existing preconceptions'. Accordingly, it follows that one must first observe, record and measure what actually happens as a result of advertising in terms of perception, awareness, attitude and behavioural change. In turn, as we are concerned with people, we must study them as individuals and over time, which militates against the type of aggregate and cross-sectional studies which have predominated in the past.

Once we have built up a sound base of observations, McDonald feels that we should not be so constrained by the true scientific method as to become heavily involved in experimentation. This opinion is predicated on the belief that the high level of interdependence between many marketing variables (for example distribution and promotion) makes it very difficult to separate out their effects and that attempts to do so may be sterile

and self-defeating (as they often have been in the past). Thus experimentation should be used where feasible and appropriate but should not be regarded as a *sine qua non* of progression to the stages of classification and generalisation.

Throughout his paper McDonald returns again and again to the need for a sound empirical basis to theory founded upon observation and testing of these observations, for otherwise there is a considerable danger of falling into the trap of circular reasoning. As an example of this he cites the DAGMAR model which is postulated on a premise that this is how advertising 'should' work and validated by data or evidence which proves the point – in other words a self-fulfilling prophecy.

▌ The development of marketing theory

Much of what McDonald has to say about the measurement of advertising effectiveness would seem to be equally true of many other areas of marketing. Perhaps marketers lack sufficient humility to get back to first principles and collect raw data as the basis for developing their own theory, or perhaps we place too much reliance upon the theories which we have borrowed from other disciplines without validating them. Whatever the reason we are inclined to subscribe to the general view that while marketing is not yet worthy of the title 'science', there is no reason why it should not become so. However, to achieve scientific status we must accept the rigour implicit in the scientific method and begin at the beginning with observation and measurement and not jump into experimentation, classification and generalisation without this essential foundation.

Assuming then that we accept the desirability of committing effort and resources to the development of marketing theory, and are prepared to adopt a scientific approach, what criteria should we seek to satisfy? On this issue we can do no better than reproduce Leslie Rodger's statement of the requirements of good theory.[31]

(a) it must provide the means of classifying, organising, and integrating information relevant to the factual world of business;

(b) it must provide a technique of thinking about marketing problems, and a perspective for practical action;

(c) it must make available an analytical tool-kit to be drawn on as appropriate in the solution of marketing problems;

(d) it should provide a basis for the explanation, prediction, and perhaps even the control of marketing processes and events;

(e) it should, in time, permit the derivation of a number of principles, possibly even laws, of marketing behaviour.

If we adopt these criteria then it is apparent that there are at least some ideas and concepts which enjoy currency among both academics and practitioners that go a long way towards satisfying them. Thus, while this chapter has been concerned primarily with establishing the need for theory and the benefits of a scientific approach to its formulation, in the process of which we have been critical of non-scientific methods, this is not to say that marketing lacks any theoretical foundations at all.

To date, however, theory is poorly developed in marketing. It can be evaluated in terms of (i) integration or cohesion, (ii) consistency of approach, (iii) practical applicability, (iv) sophistication, and (v) origin. While its role and function have varied through time – from a means of identifying problems to facilitating solutions and today helping to organise a much wider social system to explain the exchange relationship-theory on both the overall and the specific levels remains relatively unintegrated and its practical utility is limited in scope, lacking in sophistication, and its foundations lie largely within other disciplines. In terms of its inconsistency of approach, nowhere is this more clearly seen than in early attempts to develop a marketing 'theory'.

Early approaches to marketing theory on the overall level

By considering the historical evolution of marketing theory on the broad level, it is obvious how disparate, eclectic and inconsistent in approach

attempts at such a theory were. Marketing was conceived, or discovered, according to Bartels, between 1900 and 1910. Previously it had been incorporated into macroeconomic theory but at the beginning of the century the scientific study of management practice was developing. Attention thus turned from the public to private economic problems. Economic theory was seen to be inadequate and marketing began to borrow theory from other disciplines. Overall, however, marketing theory received little interest before 1941. Between 1940 and 1950, and closely associated with the 'is marketing a science?' debate, it was felt that there was an insufficient theoretical basis in marketing. The most significant contributions to emerge were those developed by Alderson and Cox[32] and Bartels.[33]

Cox and Alderson suggest that two factors promoted the call for a new theoretical perspective – first, dissatisfaction with the numbers and kinds of generalisations thus far achieved through sedulous accumulation of innumerable facts; and secondly, and perhaps more importantly, dissatisfaction with the adequacy of individual theories already incorporated within marketing, notably economic theory. Nevertheless, they believe that marketing is not doomed to a 'fragmentary, superficial and inaccurate' future, but that 'the accumulating elements for at least a rudimentary theory of marketing are scattered throughout the literature of the social sciences'. Thus, while they dismiss the idea that a definitive theory of marketing can be developed immediately, they suggest certain insights and borrowing from such fields as group behaviourism and ecological studies, could, using a creative approach, help to develop some basic overall theory.

Wroe Alderson attempts his own creative approach through functionalism. Functionalism, first introduced into marketing by Shaw[34] in 1912, is defined as an approach to science which first identifies some system of action and then tries to determine how and why it works as it does. Alderson's normative theory of marketing systems examines the way organised groups function in continuous adjustment to an operating environment. The normative aspect of his discussion specifies how decision-makers (problem-solvers) ought to behave if they want to achieve their goal – which is seen as survival. The economic, social and ecological environments offer various choices on both the supply and demand sides. Problem-solving is seen as an attempt to reduce the uncertainty. Thus the theory resolves problem-solving by decision-makers in different operating environments. It suffers several limitations. For example, Alderson assumes marginal utility theory in consumer behaviour, suggesting that two-thirds of all American consumers are rational problem-solvers, but to justify its claim to being a first step in marketing theory, it should not have to mirror reality in all its complexity. Such an approach, says Alderson, can be applied to all types of commodities and firms on the individual level, and will help explain how an entire marketing system continues to evolve through the activities of its components on the macro-marketing level. Thus Alderson provides a perspective for future model-building directed at either the general interpretation of marketing or the solution of individual problems.

Alderson is not the only writer who has attempted to use functionalism. McGary[35] in 1953, identifying six marketing functions (contractual, propaganda, merchandising, physical distribution, pricing and termination), attempted to develop a theory of marketing. It is a deductive, speculative approach that envisages marketing as a social mechanism that develops with the growth of an economy and aids the adjustment of man to his environment. McGary, unlike Alderson, believes the consumer is imperfectly rational. While such controversies are inherent in a subject-matter with so many unknown variables, both McGary and Alderson provide the beginnings of an overall theory which simplifies, explains, may eventually predict, and which would seem to be of great potential value today.

Bartels, the other major contributor to general marketing theory, is concerned about the cohesiveness of marketing. He believes a holistic theory is necessary to bind together the proliferation of facts and the various viewpoints, concepts and approaches, which are constantly changing as marketing becomes more people-oriented and more subject to public and environmental constraints.

Bartel's perspective of marketing is summarised by his statement 'Marketing is the process whereby society, to supply its consumption needs, evolves distribution systems composed of participants, who, interacting under constraints – technical (economic) and ethical (social) – creates the transactions or flows which resolve marketing separations and result in exchange and consumption.'[36] He then attempts to expand this into a general theory summarised in Figure 2.1.

Figure 2.1. *Bartels's summary of marketing theory*

Source: R. Bartels, 'The General Theory of Marketing', *Journal of Marketing* 32 (January 1968), p. 32.

Whether such a diagram can be regarded as an overall theory is open to debate. Certainly it serves to epitomise the lack of sophistication associated with theory at this level. Bartels is the only author to call his work 'a general theory'. Others readily admit that their suggestions are merely perspectives that might form the beginnings of general theory.

▋ Problems involved in the use and development of theory

Many of the major problems involved in using and developing theory are interrelated with the acceptability of marketing as a science. The youth of the discipline and the nature of marketing phenomena are obvious initial handicaps. If it is assumed that any science starts with curiosity and that it is first necessary to understand and explain in order to predict and eventually control the future, marketing's progression along this path has been hindered from the early stages. Curiosity and inspection of marketing phenomena calls for definition, since it is difficult to predict without some precision of language. Unfortunately the essential step of formulating a language is still underway. The problem of definition revolves around three areas of controversy: (i) what kinds of phenomena and issues are perceived to be in the scope of marketing, (ii) what kinds of phenomena and issues should be included in the scope of marketing, and (iii) how can marketing be defined so as to encompass systematically all the phenomena and issues that should be included, while at the same time systematically excluding all other phenomena and issues.[37] Since the scope of marketing is very broad, and the phenomena are complex, interacting and dynamic, responding to a much wider system, it is not surprising that the definition of marketing's boundaries and functions has varied according to individuals' perspectives.

Major perspectives adopted can be identified by using three dichotomies – micro/macro, descriptive/decision-oriented, profit/non-profit. By examining the various approaches and allocating authors to these categories, it is easy to understand why marketing is considered a science by some and not by others, and why theoretical development and agreement is more difficult. The practitioners like Levitt, Buzzell, Vaile and Taylor would suggest that marketing should be restricted to the profit/micro/normative definition, which can be traced to the 1920s, but received greatest emphasis in the early 1960s when the managerial approach to marketing was in fashion. Since marketing is purely evaluative and prescriptive if this approach is adopted, not unnaturally the authors regarding it in this light see marketing as an art. However, it is unnecessary, unrealistic and undesirable to restrict the definition of marketing to this extent. Marketing also includes positive di-

mensions which can be understood, explained and predicted, and therefore involves science. Furthermore, because marketing deals with the real world which is constantly changing, corresponding changes in foci and priorities are essential. The growth of the public sector, social and societal issues and other new values and priorities are now forcing the traditional definitions of marketing like 'the performance of business activities that directs the flow of goods and services from producer to consumer or user in order to satisfy customers and accomplish company objectives'[38] to be broadened. Thus profit/macro/normative and non-profit macro/ and micro/normative approaches to marketing are the most fashionable today.

In the past the problems of definition and the widening scope and changing foci of marketing have been exacerbated by the lack of interaction between academic marketers and marketing practitioners. The practitioner has tended to dismiss marketing theory as irrelevant, or an impossible dream, since (i) the various assumptions made by the theorist can always be disputed, (ii) marketing models are often seen as reductionistic and therefore useless, concentrating on the individual as opposed to aggregate factors like market demand, and (iii) static equilibrium models are worthless in the dynamic real world.

Yet, even the practitioner has 'rules of thumb' which could be seen as models to help him predict. Furthermore, his function of setting goals, analysing, planning, implementing and control corresponds to normative prescriptions given by the theoretician. Therefore, while the idea that theory and practice are separate is clearly wrong, at the same time, because the academic has in the past been of little help with his theories, which seek to explain the variables originating from other disciplines or which incorporate *ceteris paribus* assumptions, the gap between theorist and practitioner has been maintained. In an increasingly dynamic, unpredictable and complex world, new models, even if simple, are essential to allow the decision-maker to identify correctly the basic structure of the environment in which his organisation operates and allow him to predict relationships, for example, that between advertising outlays and company demand.

Certainly some cohesion within the discipline is necessary and some framework which will be accepted by marketers must be developed. The answer would seem to lie in using criteria sufficiently broad to enable both schools of thought to regard marketing as a science. Since marketing has (i) a distinct subject-matter, being centred on transactional relationships, (ii) can be described and classified (as well exemplified by the marketing literature), (iii) has underlying uniformities and regularities on both *a priori* and empirical grounds, and (iv) can be studied by using the methodology of science, it should be regarded as a science. Such criteria overcome the criticism like lack of central theories, while the focus of the transaction provides some solution to the problems of definition. Through reconciling the two schools of thought in this manner, the way ahead to develop better theory specifically suited to marketing's needs rather than reliance on theories borrowed from other disciplines is open. The purpose of theory in broad terms is to increase understanding through systematised structure but the practitioner's cooperation will ensure that theory is developed in the right direction to maximum utility. It may be that some business practitioners are already coming round to this way of thinking if Newman[39] is to be believed. He suggests that dating from the 1960s there has been a shift from the 'seat of the pants' type of decision-making to a new era of professional management based on regularly sought, expertly interpreted information. The practitioners' acceptance of marketing as a science can also be witnessed by the establishment of associations like the United States's Marketing Science Institute which has the specific aim of contributing to the emergence of science in marketing, stimulating increased applications of scientific techniques.

The case for accepting marketing as a science is clearly a good one. It diverts energy spent on arguing over the criteria of what is science to more fruitful application elsewhere and ensures a more integrated approach towards marketing from both the academics and the practitioners.

■ Notes and references

1. Halbert M., *The Meaning and Sources of Marketing Theory*, New York: McGraw-Hill, 1975.
2. Buzzell, D., 'Is Marketing a Science?', *Harvard Business Review* (January–February 1963).
3. Converse, P. D., 'The Development of the Science of Marketing – An Exploratory Survey', *Journal of Marketing* (July 1945), pp. 14–23.
4. Alderson, W., and Cox, R., 'Towards a Theory of Marketing', *Journal of Marketing* (October 1948), pp. 137ff.
5. Vaile, R., 'Towards a Theory of Marketing', *Journal of Marketing* (April 1949), pp. 520–522.
6. Bartels, R., 'Can Marketing Be a Science?', *Journal of Marketing* (January 1951), pp. 319–328.
7. Hutchinson, K. D., 'Marketing as a Science: An Appraisal', *Journal of Marketing* (January 1952), pp. 286–293.
8. Jueck, J. E., 'Marketing Research, Milestone or Millstone?', *Journal of Marketing* (January 1953), pp. 16ff.
9. Baumol, W. J., 'On the Role of Marketing Theory', *Journal of Marketing* (April 1957), pp. 413–418.
10. Buzzell, 'Is Marketing a Science?'.
11. Halbert, *The Meaning and Sources of Marketing Theory*.
12. Taylor, W. J., 'Is Marketing a Science Revisited?', *Journal of Marketing* (July 1965), pp. 49–53.
13. Vaile, 'Towards a Theory of Marketing'.
14. Alderson and Cox, 'Towards a Theory of Marketing'.
15. Vaile, 'Towards a Theory of Marketing', p. 522.
16. Hutchinson, 'Marketing as a Science: An Appraisal'.
17. *Ibid.*, p. 290.
18. Levitt, T., *Innovation in Marketing*, New York: McGraw-Hill, 1962.
19. Taylor, 'Is Marketing a Science Revisited?'
20. Weiss, E. B., 'Will Marketing Ever become a Science?', *Advertising Age*, vol. 33 (August 1962), pp. 64–65.
21. Bartels, 'Can Marketing Be a Science?'
22. Bartels in *Science in Marketing*, ed. George Schwartz, New York: Wiley, 1965, p. 47.
23. Hutchinson, 'Marketing as a Science: An Appraisal'.
24. Ramond, C., *The Art of Using Science in Marketing*, New York: Harper & Row, 1974.

25. Homans, G. C., *The Nature of Social Science*, New York: Brace & World, 1967.
26. *Webster's 7th Collegiate Dictionary*, London: G. Bell & Sons, 1971.
27. Lee, C. E., 'Measurement and the Development of Science and Marketing', *Journal of Marketing Research*, 2 (February 1965), pp. 20–25.
28. Bartels, 'Can Marketing Be a Science?'; Ehrenberg, A. S. C., *Data Reduction*, London: Wiley, 1978.
29. 'The Hunting of Advertising Effectiveness', *Admap* (February 1975).
30. 'Towards an Alternative Advertising Theory', *Admap* (January 1974).
31. *Marketing in a Competitive Economy*, London: Hutchinson, 1965.
32. Alderson and Cox, 'Towards a Theory of Marketing'.
33. Bartels, 'Can Marketing Be a Science?'.
34. Shaw, A. W., 'Some Problems in Marketing Distribution', *Quarterly Journal of Economics* (1912).
35. McGary, E., 'Some Viewpoints in Marketing', *Journal of Marketing* (July 1953).
36. Bartels, R., 'The General Theory of Marketing', *Journal of Marketing* (January 1968), p. 32.
37. Hunt, S. D., 'The Nature and Scope of Marketing', *Journal of Marketing* (July 1976), pp. 17–28.
38. *Marketing Definitions: A Glossary of Marketing Terms*, compiled by the Committee on Definitions of the American Marketing Association, Chicago, 1960.
39. Newman, J. W., 'Marketing Science: Significance to the Profession of Marketing', in *Science in Marketing*.

■ *Chapter 3* ■

Sources and Status of Marketing Theory

Stephen Brown

■ Introduction

Few would deny that marketing occupies a central position in the business environment of the late twentieth century and is becoming increasingly pervasive in non-business contexts. There is ample evidence, after all, that a marketing orientation is the key to long-term business success.[1,2] Innumerable surveys of senior management attest to its continuing importance.[3,4] The marketing concept is being enthusiastically embraced in fields as diverse as health care, public administration and the not-for-profit sector.[5,6,7] It is rapidly colonising the erstwhile command economies of eastern Europe, where the market is supplanting marxism as the societal touchstone, albeit not without privation.[8,9] And, as the proliferation of publications, professorships, degree programmes and professional societies clearly testifies, marketing is in the ascendant as an academic discipline.

Despite the undeniable achievements of modern marketing, an undercurrent of concern is also discernible. Many latter-day commentators on the marketing condition have concluded that something is amiss, that the concept is deeply, perhaps irredeemably, flawed, that its seemingly solid foundations are by no means secure and that the discipline is teetering on the brink of a serious intellectual crisis.[10,11,12] Piercy, for example, commenced his recent best-selling book with the assertion that 'the traditional marketing concept assumes and relies on the existence of a world which is alien and unrecognisable to many of the executives who actually have to manage marketing for real'.[13] Gummesson states that 'the present marketing concept...is unrealistic and needs to be replaced'.[14] Rapp and Collins contend that 'the traditional methods...simply aren't working as well anymore'.[15] Brownlie and Saren argue that 'it is questionable whether the marketing concept as it has been propagated can provide the basis for successful business at the end of the twentieth century'.[16] McKenna maintains that 'there is less and less reason to believe that the traditional approach can keep up with real customer wishes and demands or with the rigours of competition'.[17] And, Professor Michael Thomas, one of Britain's most respected marketing academics, has recently made the frank, and frankly astonishing, confession that after thirty years of propagating the marketing message he is having serious doubts about its continuing efficacy.[18]

As on the previous occasions when marketing scholars felt it necessary to cry 'crisis',[19] this sense of uncertainty is largely attributable to unanticipated events in the external environment – the rise of strategic alliances, the fragmentation of mass markets, the collapse of eastern Europe etc – which have exposed the inadequacies of extant assumptions and precipitated a period of academic introspection. It is compounded, however, by the growing disaffection over marketing's apparent lack of theoretical progress.

For many people, admittedly, marketing theory is an oxymoron, a contradiction in terms. Marketing, they argue, is a practice, an enormously powerful practice which impinges on almost everyone's daily existence. It is intuitive, creative, spontaneous and iconoclastic, where success is achieved by breaking rather than adhering to the rules.[20] This argument, of course, is not exactly new. Variants of the 'art versus science' debate have been a mainstay of marketing thought for nigh on fifty years.[21,22] Nevertheless, it has been revived in recent years thanks to the emergence of a new and enormously influential generation of management thinkers, most notably Tom Peters, who elevate gut feel and instinct over 'scientific' management perspectives.[23,24] As Foxall rightly notes, 'questions of theory and metatheory are still widely considered to be irrelevant to, or even obstructive of, useful market research and the effective practice of marketing'.[25]

Another widely held perspective on the marketing condition concedes that theory development is a necessary and worthwhile pursuit but concludes that marketing has been held back by its undue reliance on the conceptual insights of other academic disciplines and a failure to formulate its own theoretical constructs.[26] Apologists for academic marketing usually attribute this dependency culture to the comparative youth of the subject area – though at *c.*100 years of age, it's hardly a babe in arms – and assert that theoretical achievements will occur as the discipline matures. Others are less convinced. Shelby Hunt, perhaps the foremost academic commentator on marketing theory

and thought, appears to have reached the depressing conclusions that, in its current state, marketing *cannot* make a genuine contribution to knowledge.[27] In a similar vein, George Day has recently denounced marketing for squandering its lead in the field of strategic management theory and for failing fully to exploit its own, original conceptual accomplishments.[28]

The growing concern over marketing's purported lack of theoretical achievements is not solely due to an inability to capitalise on conceptual innovations and excessive reliance on hand-me-down principles. There is also the issue of the deepening philosophical schism within marketing itself. Albeit largely confined to the sub-discipline of consumer research, recent years have witnessed a serious challenge to the 'positivist' orthodoxy by naturalistic, interpretive and humanistic researchers.[29] Although both sides are at pains to point out their open-mindedness and their support for a multiplicity of epistemological perspectives, to the uncommitted it looks very much like a debilitating and potentially ruinous civil war. At one extreme, 'post-positivists' like Holbrook and Hirschman are advocating the secession of consumer research and an abandonment of the long-standing managerial orientation.[30] At the other extreme, Hunt is happy to dismiss all interpretive approaches as 'postmodern episto-babble' (though, coming from someone who takes enormous care to position marketing scholarship in relation to positivism, such blanket dismissals are rather ironic, to say the least).[31]

The unedifying sight of prominent academic authorities indulging in mud-slinging and name-calling contests, coupled with the discipline's conceptual dependency culture and an apparent anti-theory undercurrent among applied researchers and practitioners, could be construed as the clearest possible indication of marketing's mid-life crisis. A closer examination, however, reveals that things are not quite so bleak as they appear. The anti-theorists' position is demonstrably false; marketing is by no means the second-hand rose of scholarship; and, internecine epistemological struggle is not necessarily unhealthy or indicative of an intellectual impasse.

■ Theory über alles

Referring to theory construction in his recent book on consumer behaviour, Gordon Foxall noted that 'applied researchers and marketing practitioners often avoid what appears to be no more that academic speculation, preferring to "let the facts speak for themselves"'.[32] There are at least three reasons why this apparent aversion to marketing theory is mistaken. The first is the theory-ladenness of observation; the second concerns theory-in-use; and, the third pertains to the reflexivity of knowledge.

□ *Theory-ladenness of observation*

Although the rise of post-positivism has provoked derision and hostility from mainstream marketing academics (I once heard the celebrated Consumer Odyssey[33] described as 'what we did on our holidays'), its emergence has also served to highlight the theory-ladenness of observation. According to the conventional wisdom of positivism, theories and hypotheses are tested against an observable, empirical reality. If the hypothesis or theory corresponds with a researcher's observation of the facts, its truth is taken to be established or, if it fails to correspond, the theory or hypothesis is abandoned as erroneous. This 'correspondence theory of truth' has many advantages – logic, commonsense appeal and the basis it provides for evaluating rival hypotheses – but it is premised on the prior assumption that the facts of the external world can be observed in an objective and neutral fashion by the application of rigorous research procedures.[34]

Dominant though it remains, the positivist perspective does not recognise the possibility that an observer's (highly selective) perceptual apparatus and (implicit) theoretical preconceptions may in some way shape or influence what is 'seen'. It is well known, however, that the same events are often viewed and interpreted differently by different people and it follows that observation is neither neutral nor objective. The world, in other words, is not composed of brute facts waiting to be discovered or observed. Facts only become meaningful within the context of an existing theory. They are not antecedent to theory, they are determined by it.[35] The upshot of this state of affairs is that a theory or hypothesis can never be 'proved' or 'disproved' by empirical analysis alone. As Kuhn, Lakatos, Feyerabend and several other post-positivist philosophers of science have shown, empirical evidence is *never* decisive when it comes to theory testing (hence the survival of oft-refuted concepts like the product life-cycle, wheel of retailing and stages theory of internationalisation). The fact of the matter, therefore, is that facts do *not* speak for themselves.[36]

□ *Theory-in-use*

The close interrelationship between theory, observation and behaviour is amply illustrated by the day-to-day activities of marketing practitioners. Albeit quick, in some cases, to condemn theory building, their own actions are invariably shaped by implicit theoretical constructs. Most retailers, for example, believe that sales will peak in the week before Christmas, that price-cutting helps clear unwanted stock, that car-parking restrictions discourage potential customers, that impulse goods should be displayed where customer flows are heaviest and that people who slink around the store in the middle of summer wearing loose, bulky overcoats with many inside pockets, are up to no good. All of these beliefs rest upon theoretical assumptions concerning human behaviour.[37] As theories, admittedly, they are implicit rather than explicit and would fail to pass muster with the majority of philosophers of science. Nevertheless, they start from the premise that the world contains many continuing regularities and meet Baker's definition of a marketing theory, namely, a 'meaningful generalisation'.[38]

Marketing theory, in other words, *is* being put into practice, but it is not always the formal theory that is contained in the journals and textbooks. According to Heffring,[39] there are four factors which inhibit the use of marketing theories by practitioners: first, marketing theories describe the world as seen by the theory builder rather than the theory user; second, marketing theory provides complex answers to marketing problems when simple guidelines are required; third, marketing theories may be logically correct but lack external validity; and, fourth, theory-builders believe that theory is useful in itself, whereas marketing managers maintain that additional theory only serves to confuse the issue. In an attempt to close the gap between theorists and practitioners, Heffring posits a procedure for exploiting managers' 'theory-in-use', that is the accumulated knowledge, developed through experience, reflection and experimentation, that determines their marketing decisions and which can be distilled into meaningful guidelines or 'maps' for others (Figure 3.1). This approach has recently been applied, with some success, by Jaworski and Kohli to the issue of marketing orientation.[40]

□ *Reflexivity of knowledge*

If, on occasion, marketing theorists stand accused of failing to formulate concepts that are meaning-

ful for practitioners, it is wrong to conclude that marketing theories do not impinge upon the consciousness of practising managers. On the contrary, such is the wealth of marketing textbooks, periodicals, short-courses, degree programmes, consultancy services and so on now on offer, and so insistent are the providers of start-up finance and venture capital on the preparation of meaningful marketing plans, it is fair to assume that most practitioners have been exposed to marketing's conceptual apparatus in some shape or form. Indeed, entire generations of managers have been inculcated into the mores of marketing and, if truth be told, they have readily embraced some of its concepts such as the product life-cycle and the Boston matrix.[41] The managing director of Signet, the troubled retailing mini-conglomerate, recently described Ratners and Salisbury as the 'problem children' of the group, a clear indication of the influence of BCG's time-honoured strategic framework.[42] Unfortunately, however, a recent academic evaluation of the concept concluded that 'it is a real worry that the original matrix is seductively simple and the temptations and risk of using it off the shelf are real...It is a

Figure 3.1.   *Theory-in-use development cycle*

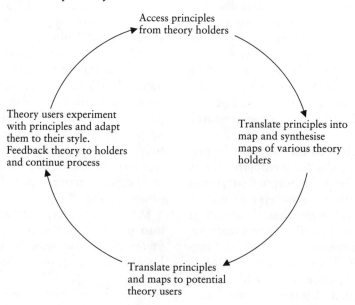

Source: Heffring (1985).

badly taught, outmoded and discredited orthodoxy, which is seductive and dangerous for our young managers of tomorrow.'[43]

Practising managers, it would appear *are* employing certain marketing concepts and acting on their predictions, yet the concepts themselves are far from firmly established. Although theoretical constructs can hardly be held responsible for the failings, or indeed the successes, of marketing managers *per se*, theory undoubtedly influences how managers 'view' their competitive environment and the strategic decisions they take. It is not unknown, after all, for perfectly sound products to be killed off because of management's belief in the existence of a product life-cycle.[44] The codification of the retail hierarchy concept has given rise to decades of conflict between retail organisations and urban planning authorities, and impeded the introduction of innovative retailing formats.[45] Consider also the innumerable marketing practitioners who were exhorted to think in terms of marketing warfare and competitive advantage, a worldview that has since been superseded by the 'co-operative' rhetoric of relationships, strategic alliances, boundaryless corporations and the like.[46] Marketing theories, in short, do not simply *reflect* events in the marketing environment, they *affect* marketplace behaviour. Theory is not neutral, it influences and alters the phenomena to which it pertains, in the human sciences at least. As Giddens points out, 'concepts...are not merely handy devices whereby agents are somehow more clearly able to understand their behaviour than they could do otherwise. They actively constitute what that behaviour is and inform the reasons for which it is undertaken'.[47]

■ Sources of theory

Just as misconceptions continue to circulate concerning the place and importance of theoretical constructs, so too discussions of the sources of marketing theory tend to present a slightly distorted picture. Introductory overviews, such as those of Williams,[48] Chisnall,[49] Bartels[50] and Sheth *et al.*,[51] almost invariably commence with a

summary of the debt owed by marketing to adjacent academic disciplines, principally economics, psychology and sociology. This is followed with what can be termed either the 'optimistic' or 'pessimistic' scenarios. The former maintains that, although marketing is reliant on the theoretical constructs of other disciplines, it has strengths that cognate academic specialisms lack and thus acts as a much-needed bridge between them and the real world of the practising manager. The latter, by contrast, holds that marketing's dependence on exogenous concepts serves to inhibit indigenous theory development and, whereas marketing is open to the ideas of outsiders, the reverse process does not obtain. Needless to say, neither scenario is entirely accurate. The situation is not as rosy as the optimists suppose, nor is it as bleak as the pessimists believe. What is more, the traditional emphasis on the economics-psychology-sociology axis serves to overshadow some of the more innovative and interesting extra-disciplinary theoretical intrusions of recent years.

□ *Extra-disciplinary intrusions*

It is generally recognised that marketing is heavily dependent on the theoretical achievements (and methodological apparatus) of adjacent subject areas. Most commentators on the emergence of marketing as a separate academic discipline emphasise that it grew from the rib of economics.[52,53] Indeed, the influence of economic theory is evident throughout the marketing literature in concepts such as perfect and imperfect competition, price elasticity, utility maximisation, equilibrium, functional specialisation, game theory, countervailing power, the business cycle, marginal analysis, economies of scale, the theory of the firm and so on. Much of modern marketing theory, as Baker[54] points out, also rests upon the notion of 'economic man', the perfectly rational, profit maximising individual with full and complete information about the decision under consideration. Besides its debt to economics, marketing has drawn heavily upon concepts and procedures developed in psychology, cognitive psychology in particular. Examples include cognitive dissonance, bounded rationality, operant conditioning, satisficing behaviour, attitude formation, motivation research, the hierarchy of needs, decision theory, stimulus-response models and the techniques of group discussion and laboratory experimentation.[55] Sociology, similarly, has had a significant influence in the shape of opinion leadership, innovation diffusion, the family life-cycle, social stratification, conspicuous consumption and, not least, questionnaire design and social survey methodology.[56]

Although economics, psychology and sociology are usually (and rightly) cited as the primary sources of marketing theory, a host of other academic specialisms have also contributed to a greater or lesser degree.[57] The influence of mathematics, statistics and informatics is all pervasive. The management sciences have added much ranging from the linear programming preoccupations of operations research and the Chandler/Mintzberg/Aldrich models of organisational development, to the strategic matrices of Ansoff, Porter and their numerous imitators. Geography's emphasis on spatial organisation is manifest in manifold models of retail and warehouse location, analyses of international markets and, increasingly, the growing interest in 'green' and environmental issues. Recent years, moreover, have witnessed the intrusion of disciplines from the 'qualitative' end of the social science spectrum. Thanks to the rise of post-positivist marketing research, concepts and techniques derived from anthropology, history and literary studies have had considerable impact. Sherry, McCracken and several other anthropologically inclined scholars, have endeavoured to explore, through a variety of ethnographic techniques, the deeply felt beliefs, emotions and meanings that inhere in the rituals, myths and symbols of consumption behaviour.[58,59] Hollander and Rassuli note the appearance of 'new marketing history' and, as their two volume study amply illustrates, the 'stunning growth' of academic interest in the sub-discipline.[60] Holbrook *et al.* moreover, have argued that works of art – literature, the cinema, music, performance etc. – can provide meaningful

Table 3.1. *Literature and consumption behaviour: an example*

Your Feet's Too Big
I do not like buying new shoes: there is the bit where you walk up and down the window outside gazing at the gleaming ranks of these somewhat comic things and vainly attempting to imagine them poking out of the end of your trousers, there is the bit where you enter and engage in the unsettling intimacy of being unshod by someone you have never met, there is the bit where the shoes come out of their boxes and you limp up and down in one of them, very carefully so as not to crack it and therefore totally unnaturally and therefurthermore totally uselessly for assessing its comfort, and there is the bit where you go out of the shop carrying the only pair of shoes you hated when you first saw them in the window. Since all these bits precede the bit where you get them home and try walking about in them the way you normally walk about, only to discover that they seem to be made of teak, you will understand why I hang on to the old ones.

Source: A. Coren, *A Year in Cricklewood*, London: Robson Books (1991), pp. 179–180.

insights into the nature and characteristics of marketplace behaviour.[61] It would be hard, for instance, to find a better description of the shoe buying process than that outlined in Table 3.1.

☐ *The optimistic scenario*

The optimistic interpretation of marketing's conceptual legacy openly acknowledges its dependence upon propinquitous disciplines, but maintains that, thanks to its focus on the concerns of practising managers, marketing is ideally placed to curb their scholarly excesses and act as a much-needed intermediary between the groves of academe and the real world.[62] It seeks to avoid the unreal, laboratory based ethos of psychology, eschews the oversimplified assumptions that characterise much of economic model building and treats with disdain the marxian turn which has done so much to undermine people's willingness to entertain the insights of sociology. Although this argument is not without merit, it can lead to blinkered thinking and the propagation of academic stereotypes. One suspects that few economists, psychologists and sociologists would welcome marketing's offer to act as a bridge to the real world, especially as marketers appear to possess dated and distorted perceptions of the disciplines concerned. Indeed, it is ironic to note how marketing academics can become upset when their specialism is misrepresented as cynical, manipulative and possessed of powerful techniques with which to milk the hapless public, yet they are content to perpetuate caricatures of cognate disciplines.

In economics, for example, the *homo oeconomicus* stereotype is decades out of date and ignores manifold recent advances in the subject area such as uncertainty reduction, rational expectations, the introduction of increasingly 'realistic' assumptions into economic models and a growing awareness of influence of rhetoric and language in the dissemination of theoretical constructs.[63] The depiction of psychology as laboratory bound is also dangerously close to distortion. To cite but a single instance, there has been a marked movement towards what is termed 'ecological validity' (i.e. real world applications) in the sub-field of memory research.[64] At the same time, marketing has also seen a rapid growth of research into memory effects in consumer decision taking. The bulk of these studies, however, are laboratory (i.e. classroom) based and employ unrepresentative (student) samples.[65] It is arguable therefore that the most 'relevant' work in memory research is not taking place in marketing but in mainstream psychology. Marxian sociologists, moreover, have undertaken many perceptive if disconcerting analyses of marketing artifacts, advertising especially, though comparatively few academic marketers appear to be aware of the conceptual opportunities provided by critical theory.[66,67]

□ *The pessimistic scenario*

If, on occasion, certain marketing commentators stand accused of recycling antiquated and over-simplified pictures of proximate academic disciplines, this does not imply that our endeavours to develop indigenous marketing theory should immediately be abandoned for a heightened appreciation of the current conceptual concerns of our academic elders and betters (though wider reading never hurt anyone). Nor, for that matter, does it follow that endemic theoretical advances are inhibited, as Sheth[68] has suggested, by marketing's open-door policy towards individuals trained in other disciplines. On the contrary, it is arguable that marketing can only benefit from the infusion of outside ideas. After all, numerous studies of the innovation process, whether it be new products or concepts, have shown that the most original ideas often come from outsiders, rebels, individuals who are not part of the establishment or trained to think in the conventional manner.[69,70]

More fundamentally perhaps, those clamouring for conceptual protectionism not only fail to appreciate marketing's value-added function but they assume that marketing theories cannot compete in the open marketplace of ideas, that they are ignored or overlooked by adjacent disciplines. Nothing could be further from the truth. Although it is undeniable that the constructs of cognitive psychology underpin the various models of buyer behaviour, it is equally true to say that, for example, the EKB model (Figure 3.2) represents a significant and much cited contribution to knowledge.[71] Likewise, the roots of the product life-cycle lie outwith marketing, but Lambkin and Day's recent reformulation remains no mean achievement.[72] Furthermore, despite its continuing conceptual balance of payments deficit, marketing theories and research techniques have had, and are having, an impact on adjacent academic disciplines. The 'law of retail gravitation' has spawned literally thousands of papers in the fields of economic geography, town planning and regional science, yet it was formulated some sixty years ago by William J. Reilly, a marketing researcher.[73] The marketing literature on product positioning is regularly referred to in the mainstream economics journals,[74] Day has described the debt owed to marketing by strategic management[75] and Baker's model of consumer behaviour

Figure 3.2. *The Engel, Kollat and Blackwell model of consumer behaviour*

INFORMATION PROCESSING — DECISION — VARIABLES INFLUENCING DECISION PROCESS

Exposure — Problem Recognition — Individual Characteristics: Motives, Values, Life-style, Personality

Stimuli: Marketer Dominated, Other — Attention — Internal Search — Search — Memory

Comprehension/Perception — Beliefs — Social Influences: Culture, Reference Group, Family — Attitude

Yeilding / Acceptance — Alternative Evaluation — Intention

Retention — Purchase — Situational Influences

External Search — Outcomes

Dissatisfaction — Satisfaction

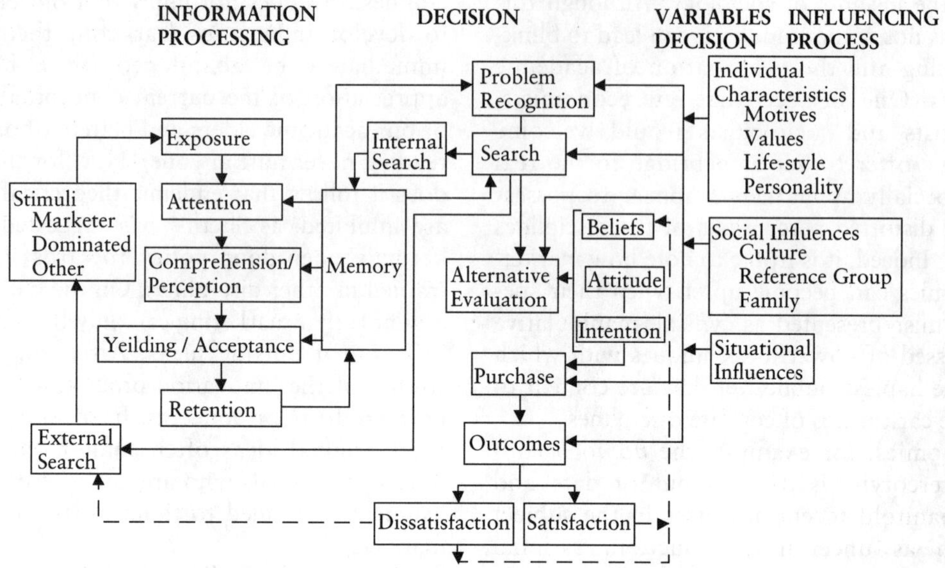

Source: Engel *et al.* (1991).

has attracted a small but enthusiastic following among cultural theorists.[76] Discussing the latter-day intellectual crisis in marxian sociology, moreover, Dick Hebdige acknowledged that 'marketing has provided the dominant and most pervasive classifications of social types in the 1980s'.[77] Hebdige, admittedly, considered this state of affairs to be both morally repugnant and indicative of the bankruptcy of radical sociology, nevertheless it illustrates the extent to which marketing thought is being disseminated and the seriousness, if not respect and admiration, with which it is now treated.

■ Status of marketing theory

It is apparent from the foregoing discussion that marketing is not in an unhealthy state conceptually. As the specialist chapters in section two of this book amply demonstrate, marketing's theoretical cupboard is by no means completely bare. The discipline is not entirely dependent on the scraps from the tables of its conceptual superiors. Nor, for that matter, are marketing theories treated with total disdain by cognate academic disciplines. Encouraging though it undoubtedly is, however, this position does not mean that all is well with marketing thought. Marketing remains beset by unprincipled principles and philosophical discord, though the former is common to all human sciences and the latter can be interpreted as a sign of strength rather than weakness, healthy conflict as opposed to debilitating debate.

□ *Unprincipled principles*

Although marketing is not short of theories, be they imported or home produced, few if any can withstand detailed scrutiny. Despite decades of research, the validity, reliability, universality and predictive power of the product life-cycle, innovation diffusion theory, Howard-Sheth model of consumer behaviour, fashion cycle, classification of goods theory, hierarchy of advertising effects, stages of internationalisation theory, models of the marketing development of the firm and so on, are far from firmly established. Indeed, even the strongest advocates of prominent marketing (or quasi-marketing) principles acknowledge that, when put to the test, the performance of the wheel of retailing, Porter's generic strategies model, Fishbein's behavioural intentions theory and many more, is far from perfect.[78] Dignity, of course, is usually preserved through allusions to the peda-gogic utility of the concept concerned and an asser-tion that with a modicum of additional research and in the fullness of time superior versions of the theory will become available. It is equally arguable that the process of diminishing returns has already set in and that the bulk of latter-day conceptual contributions comprise minor – and arguably worthless – variations of well worn themes (for example, does the 'market maven' construct add anything of substance to what is already known about the diffusion of innovations?).

The impression that marketing theories lack robustness, and the impoverishment implied by minor modifications to long-standing but unproven concepts, has been compounded in recent years by the materialisation of a host of vigorously pro-moted marketing cure-alls. These solutions to the discipline's apparent ills come in a variety of forms, though a suitably snappy, dynamic, macho, evangelical or alliterative title is common to all – maxi-marketing,[79] turbo-marketing,[80] micro-mar-keting,[81] after-marketing,[82] value-added market-ing,[83] relationship marketing[84] and so on. Granted,

the marketing of marketing nostrums has always gone on to some degree – after all, it is only through the identification of latent shortcomings and the provision of an appropriate, albeit expen-sive, remedy that management gurus and market-ing consultants can reap the rich financial rewards that are their due. However, the academics in-volved are so prominent and highly respected that the current proliferation of marketing panaceas appears to be more indicative of conceptual aporia that a cynical money-grubbing exercise.

☐ *Philosophical discord*

Just as the multiplication of marketing catho-licons and minor me-too additions to established principles are suggestive of conceptual dis-functionalism, so too the growing sense of un-certainty is attributable to the deepening philosophical discord within the discipline. Traditionally, marketing has been dominated by the positivist paradigm, which seeks to apply the methods of the natural sciences to the study of social beings. As Table 3.2 indicates, positivism rests on the assumption that a single, external world exists, that this social reality can be meas-

Table 3.2. *Positivist and post-positivist paradigms: key features*

	Positivist paradigm	Post-positivist paradigm
Basic beliefs:	The world is external and objective	The world is socially constructed and subjective
	Observer is independent	Observer is part of what observed
	Science is value-free	Science is driven by human interests
Researcher should:	Focus on facts	focus on meanings
	Look for causality and fundamental laws	try to understand what is happening
	Reduce phenomena to simplest elements	look at the totality of each situation
	Formulate hypotheses and then test them	develop ideas through induction from data
Preferred methods include:	Operationalising concepts so that they can be measured	using multiple methods to establish different views of phenomena
	Taking large samples	small samples investigated in depth or over time

Source: adapted from M. Easterby-Smith, R. Thorpe and A. Lowe, *Management Research: An Introduction*, London: Sage (1991), p. 27.

ured by independent observers using objective procedures and, not least, that this world can be explained and predicted through the identification of universal laws. Many active marketing researchers, admittedly, may be unaware that they are part of the positivist tradition and others have challenged the 'positivist' label, thereby effectively deflecting some of the criticism. Nevertheless, it is undeniable that the 1980s witnessed the emergence, initially from the sub-discipline of consumer research, of an alternative to the positivist orthodoxy of marketing science. This 'post-positivist' challenge has been accorded a variety of appellations – naturalistic, interpretive, humanistic, phenomenological, postmodernism etc. – but, as depicted in Table 3.2, it is premised on the presupposition that the world is not objective and external to the observer but socially constructed and given meaning by people. Hence, the aim of social research is not to explain, predict and develop law-like generalisations but to understand and describe the different constructions and meanings that people place upon their individual experiences.[85,86]

The recent philosophical schism within marketing is usually portrayed as a two-way split, with the quantitatively orientated positivist monolith on one hand and a range of qualitatively orientated, post-positivist perspectives on the other. Albeit useful for the purposes of explication, the situation is rather more complicated than this. Qualitative techniques, for example, are often used for essentially positivist purposes and, as Venkatesh et al have recently argued,[87] a distinction can be drawn between post-positivist (interpretive, naturalistic, humanistic) research and postmodernism, the so-called 'new perspective on life and the human condition that is sweeping across the globe'.[88] A useful way of demonstrating these differences is by means of a basic and admittedly over-simplified four-cell matrix. Illustrated in Figure 3.3, this distinguishes between epistemology (the nature of knowledge) and ontology (the nature of the world) and arbitrarily subdivides these continua along objective and subjective dimensions. The top left-hand cell, which embraces the vast bulk of traditional, positivist academic marketing research, assumes that individuals have direct, unmediated access to the real world and that, notwithstanding the problems associated with sampling, questionnaire design and suchlike, it is possible to obtain hard,

Figure 3.3. *Philosophical discord in marketing: epistemology and ontology*

	EPISTEMOLOGY	
	OBJECTIVE	SUBJECTIVE
ONTOLOGY OBJECTIVE	'Traditional' Marketing Research	'Traditional' Qualitative Research
SUBJECTIVE	Naturalistic and Interpretive Research	Postmodern Marketing Research

secure, objective knowledge about this external reality. The top right-hand cell also assumes direct, unmediated access to external reality but assumes that people's knowledge of this world is highly individual, subjective, unquantifiable and best illuminated through the use of 'traditional' qualitative research procedures like depth interviews and group discussions. The bottom left-hand cell presupposes that individuals do not have direct access to the real world – language, culture, theory and other distortions are interposed – but that their knowledge of this perceived world is meaningful in its own terms and can be understood through careful use of appropriate naturalistic, interpretive and ethnographic research methods. The final, bottom right-hand cell represents the postmodern position which not only rejects the notion that individuals have unmediated access to external reality, but it also questions the very existence of the free-thinking human 'subject'. It maintains that the knowledge people imagine they possess is unreliable, dispersed, fragmented, pre-existing and an epiphenomenon of language. In other words, it demotes the human subject from a constitutive to a constituted status.

Debilitating debate or healthy conflict?

However many sub-divisions of marketing philosophy are identified, the process of fragmentation has not been without incident. Apart from the rebarbative exchanges between positivists and post-positivists, in the broadest sense, energetic debate is also evident between quantitative and qualitative positivists, and mainstream interpretative-cum-naturalistic researchers and postmodern fundamentalists. These differences of opinion have generated a rich brew of metaphorical descriptors, all of which emphasise conflict. For example, the long-running dispute between the respective champions of realism and relativism, Hunt and Anderson, has been depicted as a sixteen-round boxing march.[89] A religious analogy – true believers versus heretics – has also been employed[90] (a prayer for the 4Ps of peace has even been proffered[91]). And Sherry, a pro-

minent post-positivist, has variously described the situation of interpretive researchers as being equivalent to the accused in a court case and the defenders of an isolated frontier outpost surrounded by positivists on the warpath.[92]

Few would deny that the challenge to positivist hegemony has led to a degree of disagreement, antagonism and recrimination among theorists. It can be argued, however, that such epistemological altercations are not necessarily unhealthy. In the first instance, they raise the profile of philosophical issues. One of the great strengths (and weaknesses) of positivism is that its emphasis on empirical observation enables researchers effectively to ignore philosophical issues in the pursuit of their specific research objectives. Unfortunately, this can also lead to 'the primacy of technique over problems', and over-emphasis on applying the latest research method (e.g. LISREL) rather than addressing meaningful marketing issues.[93] Philosophical mud-slinging may be unseemly but it certainly draws a crowd, particularly when such prominent scholars are involved, and if the performance persuades onlookers to examine their own assumptions, the overall standards of academic marketing research can only be improved. Second, and somewhat ironically, the childish squabbling is actually a sign of the growing maturity of the discipline. As interpretive perspectives, broadly defined, are long established in cognate academic specialisms like sociology, psychology and, to a lesser extent, economics, their eventual diffusion into marketing is only to be expected. Bruised egos are a small price to pay for the wider range of research opportunities that are now available and the potential value of the links forged with like-minded scholars in other subject areas. Some of the most innovative research in marketing, as noted earlier, is being conducted by non-marketers. Third, it is arguable that conflict is not an unfortunate occurrence, nor an unedifying sideshow, but *vitally necessary*, for the post-positivists in particular. Because it is only through conflict and the antipathy of the establishment that the (disparate) challenging group can generate a sense of cohesion, shared purpose and commitment to their 'subversive' cause. In these circumstances, therefore, the more vitriolic the attacks of mainstream marketing academics the better is it for post-positivists. It is in the latter's interest to antagonise the establishment. Fourth, and most importantly perhaps, this conflict is likely to prove a temporary phenomenon. Many studies of avant-garde movements in the arts, academic disciplines and most walks of life, demonstrate that hostility between the establishment and outsiders is the first stage of a development process which eventually leads to accommodation and mutual tolerance.[94,95] For instance, the emergence of structuralism in literary studies, cognitivism in psychology and spatial science in geography were characterised initially by bitter conflict and schismatic tendencies, only to be replaced in due course by grudging respect and a search for common ground. Indeed, Foxall,[96] after Feyerabend,[97] maintains that it is only through the interplay of various tenaciously held theoretical perspectives that scientific progress can be attained.

■ Metaphor and meta-theory

The rise of post-positivism, and the associated internecine conflict, has not only encouraged many mainstream marketing academics to step back and take stock of their own philosophical assumptions, but it also illustrates the importance and pervasiveness of metaphorical thinking. Whereas positivist epistemology regards figurative language in general and metaphor in particular to be 'deviant and parasitic',[98] most post-positivist philosophers and postmodern literary theorists maintain that knowledge claims are inherently metaphorical.[99,100] Tropes, they argue, lie at the very heart of our understanding of the world and figurative thinking is central to the process of theory articulation. This point is amply demonstrated by extant marketing theories, the most frequently cited of which rely on metaphorical reasoning – the product life-cycle (biological), the marketing mix (cooking), information pro-

Figure 3.4. *The wheel of marketing thought*

cessing (computational), wheel of retailing (mechanical), channels of distribution (environmental), relationship marketing (marriage), marketing warfare etc.

Even theories about marketing theory (i.e. meta-theory[101]) are often couched in figurative language. Hunt and Goolsby, for example, have employed the product life-cycle concept to frame the rise and fall of the functional school of marketing research[102] and a similar cycle has been identified for the various theoretical constructs of the regional (locational) school.[103] Bartels' model of the development of marketing thought is premised on a construction/building trope and underpinned by the western world's metaphysical assumption of ineluctable 'progress' and the ascent of man.[104] Likewise, Sheth *et al.'s* identification of twelve schools of marketing theory is an excellent example of figurative reasoning, though their framework actually relies on metonymy (where the part stands for the whole) rather than metaphor as such.[105] Indeed, it is arguable that the entire trajectory of modern marketing can be described in terms of an expanded wheel of retailing theory (Figure 3.4).

As described in the previous chapters of this book, the modern marketing concept emerged in the 1950s, when environmental conditions were conducive, as a simple, radical and (at that time) counterintuitive approach to doing business, which proved to be enormously appealing and highly successful. Through time, marketing progressively broadened its domain and, as a consequence of inter-academic rivalry, it became increasingly sophisticated both methodologically and philosophically. This very success, however, led to disciplinary status, academic esotericism and, some would say, delusions of scholarship. Most importantly, it was characterised by failure to keep in touch with marketing's principal constituents, practising managers and prospective managers, who faced a business environment which bore little or no relation to that encountered by their predecessors forty years beforehand. Marketing scholarship, in short, became increasingly divorced from reality and this gave rise to the fragmentation of the discipline into a multiplicity of hostile and unco-ordinated fac-

tions. It also appears to have precipitated another turn of the wheel with the recent emergence of back-to-basics reformulations which eschew esoterism and appear to be more relevant to the needs of the current generation of practising marketing managers (relationship marketing, micro-marketing, etc.).

Although the wheel metaphor can be applied to the trajectory of marketing thought, and although tropes are all-pervasive in marketing generally, metaphorical thinking is not without its weaknesses. In particular, it can result in a suppression of some aspects of the figurative relationship and an overemphasis on others. This point is exemplified by the differences in perspective that can occur when two contrasting metaphors are applied to the same phenomena. As noted earlier, the emergence of post-positivism has spawned a host of conflict based tropes (boxing contests, religious schism and so on), all of which emphasise the differences between the two opposing sides. The current state of marketing scholarship, however, could just as easily be compared to the cinema, where the monolithic, slightly down-at-heel 'picture palace' of positivism is in the process of being replaced by a glittering, multi-paradigmatic, multi-screen complex offering a wide choice of research programmes.[106] These marketing research programmes vary considerably in their content and certification, with some suitable for a mainstream audience and others reliant on art-house appeal. What is more, as many of the programmes are incommensurable, they cannot be viewed simultaneously, though they are at least showing under the same roof, which we term 'marketing'. The multiplex metaphor, in other words, retains the differences that are central to the warfare analogy, but replaces conflict and estrangement with shared values, complementarity and mutual understanding.

Regardless of the preferred metaphor – even the metaphor that marketing thought is non-metaphorical – the essential points about the sources and status of marketing theory are as follows: first, the contention that 'marketing should focus on effects application research, problem orientation research and the like without being concerned with explanatory theory', is mistaken.[107] The very act of observation is theory laden, practitioners continually employ theoretical constructs, albeit implicitly, and, as concepts affect not simply reflect marketing activities, theory development is of the utmost importance. Second, marketing owes an enormous debt to theoretical developments in its parent disciplines, but, contrary to the claims of some conceptual protectionists, marketing can only benefit from exposure to ideas in adjacent academic specialisms. Marketing, moreover, is not entirely dependent on theoretical hand-me-downs; its own concepts are being appropriated and utilised by outsiders. Finally, marketing's lack of *firm* and *proven* principles is common to most social sciences. More importantly, the current bout of internecine conflict is not only a necessary and temporary phenomenon, but it is also partly a function of the warfare metaphor itself.

■ Notes and references

1. Baker, M. J., and S. Hart, *Marketing and Competitive Success*, Hemel Hempstead: Philip Allan, 1989.
2. Kheir-El-Din, A., 'The Contribution of Marketing to Competitive Success', in *Perspectives on Marketing Management*, vol. 1, ed. M. J. Baker, Chichester: John Wiley, 1991, pp. 1–28.
3. Narver, J. C., and Slater, S. F., 'The Effect of a Marketing Orientation on Business Profitability', *Journal of Marketing*, 54 (4) (1990), pp. 20–35.
4. Wong, V., 'Marketing's Ascendancy and Transcendance: Is This What it Takes for Business to Succeed?', in *Rethinking Marketing*, eds D. Brownlie *et al.*, Coventry: Warwick University Business School, 1993, pp. 71–85.
5. Doyle, P., 'Marketing Planning: Rethinking the Core', in *Rethinking Marketing*, eds D. Brownlie *et al.*, Coventry: Warwick University Business School, 1993, pp. 86–90.
6. Jennings, D., and Saunders, J., 'Can the Church Look out the Window? Marketing the Church in England Today', in *Emerging Issues in Marketing*, eds M. Davies *et al.*, Loughborough: MEG Proceedings, 1993, pp. 527–533.
7. Walsh, K., 'Marketing and the New Public Sector Management', in *Rethinking Marketing*, eds D. Brownlie *et al.*, Coventry: Warwick University Business School, 1993, pp. 124–133.
8. Hooley, G., Cox, T., and Shipley, D., 'A Comparative Study of Marketing in Hungary, Poland and Bulgaria', in *Developments in Marketing Science* 16, eds M. Levy and D. Grewal, Miami: Academy of Marketing Science, 1993, pp. 655–657.
9. Miller, C., Toth, A., and Priboda, M., 'The Question of Marketing in Central and Eastern Europe', in *Developments in Marketing Science* 16, eds M. Levy and D. Grewal, Miami: Academy of Marketing Science, 1993, pp. 658–662.
10. Marion, G., 'The Marketing Management Discourse: What's new Since the 1960s?', in *Perspectives on Marketing Management* 3, ed. M. J. Baker, Chichester: John Wiley, 1993, pp. 143–168.
11. Cova, B., and Svanfeldt, C., 'Marketing Beyond Marketing in a Post-modern Europe: The Creation of Societal Innovations', in *Marketing for Europe – Marketing for the Future*, eds K. G. Grunert and D. Fuglede, Aarhus: EMAC Proceedings, 1992, pp. 155–171.
12. Hunt, S. D., 'For Reason and Realism in Marketing', *Journal of Marketing* 56 (2) (1992), pp. 89–102.
13. Piercy, N., *Market-led Strategic Change*, Oxford: Butterworth-Heinemann, 1992.
14. Gummesson, E., 'The New Marketing – Developing Long-term Interactive Relationships', *Long Range Planning* (4) (1987), pp. 10–20.
15. Rapp, S. and Collins, T., *The Great Marketing Turnaround*, New York: Prentice-Hall, 1990.
16. Brownlie, D. and Saren, M., 'The Four Ps of the Marketing Concept: Prescriptive, Polemical, Permanent and Problematical', *European Journal of Marketing* 26 (4) (1992), pp. 34–47.
17. McKenna, R., 'Marketing is Everything', *Harvard Business Review* 69 (1) (1991), pp. 65–69.
18. Thomas, M. J., 'Marketing – In Chaos or Transition?', in *Rethinking Marketing*, eds D. Brownlie *et al.*, Coventry: Warwick University Business School, 1993, pp. 114–123.
19. For example, the spate of 'marketing in crisis' papers in the early 1970s probably reflects the general economic malaise, concerns over sustainable development and periodic oil crises of the time.
20. Economist, 'Management Brief – Still Trying', *The Economist* 313 (7623) (1989), pp. 112–113.

21. Converse, P. D., 'The Development of the Science of Marketing – An Exploratory Survey', *Journal of Marketing* 9 (3) (1945), pp. 14–23.

22. Sheth, J. N., Gardner, D. M. and Garrett, D. E., *Marketing Theory: Evolution and Evaluation*, New York: John Wiley, 1988.

23. Peters, T., *Liberation Management: Necessary Disorganisation for the Nano-second Nineties*, Basingstoke: Macmillan, 1992.

24. Kay, J., *Foundations of Corporate Success*, Oxford: Oxford University Press, 1993.

25. Foxall, G. R., *Consumer Psychology in Behavioural Perspective*, London: Routledge, 1990.

26. Sheth, J. N. *et al.* (1988).

27. Hunt, S. D., 'On Rethinking Marketing: Our Discipline, Our Practice, Our Methods', *European Journal of Marketing*, 28 (3) (1994), pp. 13–25.

28. Day, G. S., 'Marketing's Contribution to the Strategy Dialogue', *Journal of the Academy of Marketing Science* 20 (4) (1992), pp. 332–330.

29. Although the terms 'positivist' and 'positivism' are widely used in discussions of marketing theory, they are slightly misleading as very few marketers would be considered positivists in the strict Carnap/Vienna Circle sense of the word. In practice, however, the terms are employed in a fairly loose sense – as they are in this chapter – to refer to marketing's traditional emphasis on empirical research and hypothesis testing. 'Positivism' as practised in marketing is actually a mix of positivism, realism, pragmatism, instrumentalism and conventionalism (for an excellent discussion of these issues see O'Shaughnessy, n. 56 below).

30. Hirschman, E. C., and Holbrook, M. B., *Postmodern Consumer Research: The Study of Consumption as Text*, Newbury Park: Sage, 1992.

31. Hunt, S. D. (1994).

32. Foxall, G. R. (1990).

33. Belk, R. W., Wallendorf, M., and Sherry, J. F., 'The Sacred and the Profane in Consumer Behaviour: Theodicy on the Odyssey', *Journal of Consumer Research* 16 (June 1989), pp. 1–38.

34. Hunt, S. D., *Modern Marketing Theory*, Cincinnatti: South-Western Publishing, 1991.

35. Hughes, J., *The Philosophy of Social Research*, Harlow: Longman, 1990.

36. Easterby-Smith, M., Thorpe, R., and Lowe, A., *Management Research: An Introduction*, London: Sage, 1991.

37. Hollander, S. C., 'Retailing Theory: Some Criticism and Some Admiration', in *Theory in Retailing: Traditional and Non-traditional Sources*, eds R. W. Stampfl and E. C. Hirschman, Chicago: American Marketing Association, 1980, pp. 84–94.

38. Baker, M. J., 'Editorial', *Journal of Marketing Management* 7 (2) (1991), pp. 101–103.

39. Heffring, M., 'A Theory-in-use Approach to Developing Marketing Theories', in *Changing the Course of Marketing: Alternative Paradigms for Widening Marketing Theory*, eds N. Dholakia and J. Arndt, Greenwich: JAI Press, 1985, pp. 105–117.

40. Jaworski, B. J., and Kohli, A. J., 'Market Orientation: Antecedents and Consequences', *Journal of Marketing* 57 (3) (1993), pp. 53–70.

41. Heffring, M. (1985).

42. Blackwell, D., 'Renamed Ratners Loses £27m in Dull First Half', *Financial Times* (Saturday 1 September 1993), p. 10.

43. Morrison, A., and Wensley, R., 'Boxing up or Boxed in: A Short History of the Boston Consulting Group Share/Growth Matrix', *Journal of Marketing Management* 7 (2) (1991), pp. 105–129.

44. Van Rossum, R., 'Is the Theory of Life Cycles Pure Humbug?', *Financial Times* (Thursday 23 August 1984), p. 14.

45. Brown, S., 'Retail Location Theory: Retrospect and Prospect', *Irish Marketing Review* 5 (2) (1991), pp. 52–60.

46. Stoltman, J. J., Gentry, J. W., and Morgan, F., 'Marketing Relationships: Further Consideration of the Marriage Metaphor With Implications for Maintenance and Recovery', in *Enhancing Knowledge Development in Marketing Vol. 4*, eds D. W. Cravens and P. R. Dickson, Chicago: American Marketing Association, 1993, pp. 28–35.

47. Giddens, A., *The Consequences of Modernity*, Cambridge: Polity Press, 1990.

48. Williams, K. C., *Behavioural Aspects of Marketing*, London: Butterworth-Heinemann, 1981.

49. Chisnall, P. M., *Marketing: A Behavioural Analysis*, Maidenhead: McGraw-Hill, 1985.

50. Bartels, R., *History of Marketing Thought*, Columbus: Grid, 1988.

51. Sheth, J. N. *et al.* (1988).

52. Bartels, R., 'Influences on the Development of Marketing Thought, 1900–1923', *Journal of Marketing*, 16 (1) (1951), pp. 1–19.

53. Jones, D. G. B. and D. D. Monieson, 'Early Development of the Philosophy of Marketing

Thought', *Journal of Marketing* 54 (1) (1990), pp. 102–113.

54. Baker, M. J., 'The Sources of Marketing Theory', in *Marketing: Theory and Practice*, M. J. Baker *et al.*, London: Macmillan, 1983, pp. 33–51.

55. Sheth, J. N. *et al.* (1988).

56. O'Saughnessy, J., *Explaining Buyer Behaviour: Central Concepts and Philosophy of Science Issues*, New York: Oxford University Press, 1992.

57. Halbert, M., *The Meaning and Sources of Marketing Theory*, New York: McGraw-Hill, 1965.

58. Sherry, J. F., 'Postmodern Alternatives: The Interpretative Turn in Consumer Research', in *Handbook of Consumer Behaviour*, eds T. S. Robertson and H. H. Kassarjian, Englewood Cliffs, NJ: Prentice-Hall, 1991, pp. 548–591.

59. McCracken, G., *Culture and Consumption: New Approaches to the Symbolic Character of Consumer Goods and Activities*, Bloomington: Indiana University Press, 1988.

60. Hollander, S. C., and Rassuli, K. M. *Marketing*, Brookfield: Edward Elgar, 1993.

61. Holbrook, M. B., Bell, S., and Grayson, M. W., 'The Role of the Humanities in Consumer Research: Close Encounters and Costal Disturbances', in *Interpretive Consumer Research*, ed. E. C. Hirschman, Provo: Association for Consumer Research, 1989, pp. 29–47.

62. Baker, M. J. (1983).

63. Hutchison, T., *Changing Aims in Economics*, Oxford: Blackwell, 1992.

64. Gruneberg, M., and Morris, P., *Aspects of Memory*, London: Routledge, 1992.

65. Alba, J. W., Hutchinson J. W., and Lynch, J. G., 'Memory and Decision Making', in *Handbook of Consumer Behaviour*, eds T. S. Robertson and H. H. Kassarjian, Englewood Cliffs, NJ: Prentice-Hall, 1991, pp. 1–49.

66. Rogers, E. M., 'The Critical School and Consumer Research', in *Advances in Consumer Research Vol 14*, eds R. Belk and M. Wallendorf, Provo: Association for Consumer Research, 1986, pp. 7–11.

67. Morgan, G., 'Marketing Discourse and Practice: Towards a Critical Analysis', in *Critical Management Studies*, eds M. Alvesson and H. Willmott, London: Sage, 1992, pp. 136–158.

68. Sheth, J. N., 'Is Academic Marketing Really Relevant?', paper presented at the 1993 Academy of Marketing Science conference Miami, May 1993.

69. Dickson, R., 'Innovations in Retailing', *Retail Control* 51 (June–July 1983), pp. 30–54.

70. Kirton, M. J., *Adaptors and Innovators: Styles of Creativity and Problem Solving*, London: Routledge, 1989.

71. Engel, J. F., Blackwell, R. D., and Miniard, P. W., *Consumer Behaviour*, Hinsdale, The Dryden Press, 1991.

72. Lambkin, M., and Day, G. S., 'Evolutionary Processes in Competitive Markets: Beyond the Product Life Cycle', *Journal of Marketing* 53 (3) (1989), pp. 4–20.

73. Brown, S., 'The Wheel of Retail Gravitation', *Environment and Planning A* 24 (10) (1992), pp. 1409–1429.

74. Hjorth-Anderson, C., 'Evidence on Agglomeration in Quality Space', *Journal of Industrial Economics* 37 (3) (1988), pp. 209–223.

75. Day, G. S. (1992).

76. Tomlinson, A., *Consumption, Identity and Style*, London: Routledge, 1990.

77. Hebdige, D., 'After the Masses', in *New Times: The Changing Face of Politics in the 1990s*, eds S. Hall and M. Jacques, London: Lawrence and Wishart, 1989, pp. 76–93.

78. Brown, S., 'Postmodern Marketing?', *European Journal of Marketing* 27 (4) (1993), pp. 19–34.

79. Rapp, S., and Collins, T., *Maxi-marketing*, New York: Plume, 1988.

80. Caruso, T. E., 'Kotler: Future Marketers Will Focus on Customer Data-base to Compete Globally', *Marketing News* 26 (12) (1992), pp. 21–22.

81. Schlossberg, H., 'Packaged Goods Experts: Micro-marketing the Only Way to Go', *Marketing News* 26 (14) (1992), p. 8.

82. Vavra, T. G., *After-marketing*, Homewood, Ill.: Business One, Irwin, 1992.

83. Nilson, T. H., *Value-added Marketing*, Maidenhead: McGraw-Hill, 1992.

84. Christopher, M., Payne, A., and Ballantyne, D., *Relationship Marketing*, Oxford: Butterworth-Heinemann, 1992.

85. Ozanne, J. L., and Hudson, L. A., 'Exploring Diversity in Consumer Research', in *Interpretive Consumer Research*, ed. E. C. Hirschman, Provo: Association for Consumer Research, 1989, pp. 1–9.

86. Peter, J. P., 'Philosophical Tensions in Consumer Inquiry', in *Handbook of Consumer Behaviour*,

eds T. S. Robertson and H. H. Kassarjian, Englewood Cliffs, NJ: Prentice-Hall, 1991, pp. 533–547.

87. Venkatesh, A., Sherry, J. F., and Firat, A. F., 'Postmodernism and the Marketing Imaginary', *International Journal of Research in Marketing* 10 (3) (1993), pp. 215–223.

88. Firat, A. F., and Venkatesh, A., 'Postmodernity: The Age of Marketing', *International Journal of Research in Marketing* 10 (3) (1993), pp. 227–249.

89. Kavanagh, D., 'Hunt v. Anderson: Round 16', in *Rethinking Marketing*, eds D. Brownlie *et al.*, Coventry: Warwick University Business School, 1993, pp. 36–49.

90. Brown, S., 'Postmodernism … the End of Marketing?', in *Rethinking Marketing*, eds D. Brownlie *et al.*, Coventry: Warwick University Business School, 1993, pp. 1–11.

91. Hirschman, E. C., and Holbrook, M. (1992).

92. Sherry, J. F. (1991).

93. O'Shaughnessy, J. (1992).

94. Burger, P., *Theory of the Avant-Garde*, Manchester: Manchester University Press, 1984.

95. Benjamin, A., *Art, Mimesis and the Avant-Garde*, London: Routledge, 1991.

96. Foxall, G. R. (1990).

97. Feyerabend, P., *Against Method*, London: Verso, 1988.

98. Ortony, A., 'Metaphor: A Multi-dimensional Problem', in *Metaphor and Thought*, ed. A. Ortony, Cambridge: Cambridge University Press, 1979, pp. 1–16.

99. Norris, C., *Deconstruction: Theory and Practice*, London: Routledge, 1991.

100. Sarup, M., *An Introductory Guide to Post-structuralism and Postmodernism*, Hemel Hempstead: Harvester Wheatsheaf, 1993.

101. In the marketing literature, the term 'meta-theory' is used in a variety of ways (cf. refs. no. 22 and 54 above). Strictly speaking, it means theory about theory. Just as 'meta-marketing' means marketing marketing, 'meta-memory' refers to memory of memory and 'meta-fiction' pertains to fiction about fiction, so too the term 'meta-theory' alludes to the science of science, the investigation of investigation, theory about theory.

102. Hunt, S. D. and Goolsby, J., 'The Rise and Fall of the Functional Approach to Marketing: A Paradigm Replacement Perspective', in *Historical Perspectives in Marketing: Essays in Honour of Stanley C. Hollander*, eds T. Nevett and R. A. Fullerton, Lexington, Mass.: Lexington Books, 1988, pp. 35–51.

103. Brown, S., 'Retail Location Theory: Evolution and Evaluation', *International Review of Retail, Distribution and Consumer Research* 3 (2) (1993), pp. 187–229.

104. Bartels, R. (1988).

105. Sheth, J. N., *et al.* (1988).

106. Brown, S., 'Marketing as Multiplex: Screening Postmodernism', *European Journal of Marketing*, 28 (8/9) pp. 27–51.

107. O'Shaughnessy, J. (1992).

■ *Chapter 4* ■

Consumer Behaviour

Lyn McGregor

▌ Why study consumer behaviour?

To some people consumer behaviour is one of the underlying basic theories of marketing; I hope not only to demonstrate its relevance to the modern practice of marketing, but also to suggest that, in the dynamic business environment of the 1990s, an understanding of such fundamental theories may be more important to the practising marketer than a knowledge of the tools and techniques which worked effectively in the past.

The contention that an understanding of the theories of consumer behaviour may be more important to those involved in marketing is based upon the belief that marketers should acquire transferable knowledge and skills, which will result in a flexibility in approach and outlook that will enable them to identify problems and develop innovative solutions in a rapidly changing environment. The knowledge and skills developed by a study of consumer behaviour can easily be transferred to many of the current preoccupations of marketing professionals such as the analysis of internal marketing, the role of quality within organisations, relationship marketing and services marketing.

This chapter will examine the key theories of consumer behaviour and their application to the practice of marketing. The chapter seeks to answer questions such as What is consumer behaviour? Why should we study consumer behav-

iour? How will a knowledge of consumer behaviour theory benefit in the development of more effective marketing strategies?

▯ *Consumer behaviour and marketing strategy*

In his recent text, *Marketing Strategy and Management*, Baker points out that 'the marketing concept is concerned with **exchange relationships** in which parties to the exchange are seeking to maximise their personal satisfaction'. Baker proceeds to quote Lawrence Abbott who contended in 1955 that 'what is considered satisfying is a matter for individual decision: it varies according to one's tastes, standards, beliefs and objectives – and these vary greatly depending on individual personality and cultural environment'.

The marketing concept stresses that the motivating force in the exchange relationship should be the consumer, not the supplier. Levitt (1960) in the classic paper, *Marketing Myopia* describes this as 'Management must think of itself not as producing products but as providing customer-creating value satisfactions.'

This focus on the consumer emerged as the number, variety and range of goods produced exceeded the limited resources of consumers, resulting in efforts by firms to compete more effectively, or gain competitive advantage. As a result of increasing competition, firms sought to compete by differentiating products, rather than offering homogeneous products to a hetero- geneous market.

Market segmentation

According to a review by Tynan and Drayton (1987), this is a technique which 'divides total demand into relatively homogeneous segments which are identified by some common character- istics. These characteristics are relevant in ex- plaining and in predicting the response of consumers, in a given segment, to marketing stimuli.'

A variety of ways exist for segmenting markets and it is up to the manager to determine the most appropriate basis. The market can be subdivided by geographic, demographic, psychological, psy- chographic, or behavioural variables. In order to effectively segment the market we must be able to analyse the behaviour of the market to identify the variables which are most useful in segmenting the market.

It should be noted that a range of organisations have adopted the marketing concept. These include organisations in the private and public sectors, profit-making and non-profit making. The terminology used here may appear to be more applicable to those commercial organ- isations producing fast-moving consumer goods, but most of the principles may be applied effect- ively, with modification, to other organisations involved in exchange relationships.

Strategic marketing planning

This is defined by Baker (1992) as: 'The establish- ment of the goal or purpose of a strategic busi- ness unit and the means by which this is to be achieved.' There are four basic ingredients which the marketer may combine in different ways to achieve different effects, product, price, promo- tion and distribution; these are often referred to as the *marketing mix*.

Borden (1975) identified that the list of forces which influence the marketing mix are: consumer attitudes and habits; trade attitudes and methods; competition; and government controls. Few – if any – strategy decisions do not involve thinking about consumer behaviour. As a result, greater understanding of consumer behaviour increases the chances of developing successful marketing strategies.

In terms of the practical application of the mar- keting concept, and the theoretical development of marketing thought, it is therefore vital that we develop an understanding of the differences between individuals, and the similarities which may occur among groups of consumers. Not only does such an analysis make it possible to segment the total market, but the greater understanding achieved will also enable a more effective design of the various marketing mix elements:

Product: the specific nature of the product or service, and ele- ments of packaging which will appeal to the target segment(s);

Promotion: the most effective means of communicating the benefits to these consumers;

Distribution: the most appropriate points of distribution which would meet consumer expectations, and/or match existing behaviour pat- terns enabling the consumer to be made aware of the product, or reminded of his/her need for the product;

Price: the pricing of a good or service in line with the consumer's per- ception of value for money, or price-quality associations.

Consumer behaviour and dynamic marketing environments

Individual consumers, homogeneous segments of consumers, and society as a whole are evolving and changing all the time. John Brady and Ian Davis in the McKinsey Quarterly last year are quoted as saying: 'The environment has changed so dramatically that marketers are simply not picking up the right signals any more.'

Brand building

This assumed great importance in marketing during the eighties. The recognition of a need to develop sustainable competitive advantage which is not solely based on price led to the perceived need for brand-building activities. Attention has been focussed on developing points of differentiation. Practitioners such as Larry Light, an American Advertising Research professional, are quoted as saying that: 'The marketing battle in the future will be a battle of brands, a competition for brand dominance.' Doyle (1989) described a successful brand as 'a name, symbol, design, or some combination which identifies the "product" of a particular organisation as having a sustainable competitive advantage'. In other words, customers have a reason for preferring the brand, and the advantage is not easily copied by competitors. Branding simplifies the selection of stimuli, and recall from memory, which enable the consumer to make evaluations with relative ease by developing brand loyalty. During the eighties great faith was placed in the development of the brand by marketers, in the belief that a premium price could be charged for a successful brand.

The nineties have begun during a period of recession in most of the Western world which has affected consumer confidence and behaviour; as a result, the consumer is thought to be more discerning about value for money, and price is playing a more important role in choice decisions. In 1991 Stephen King in his review of *Brand-Building in the 1990s* suggests that success will depend critically on brand-building, but constant innovation will reduce timescales for demonstrable product or service advantages. King also predicts that brands in the 1990s will be *company brands* which encapsulate and communicate what an organisation is, and what it stands for.

The rise of *company brands* results in a proliferation of audiences. Where traditionally the company may have been concerned about the opinions of its customers, the need to communicate effectively, and satisfy the expectations of others, such as employees and shareholders, and those who influence opinions such as journalists, is increasing in importance. The knowledge of consumer behaviour theory can be transferred to these new tasks with ease.

Positioning

In 1969, Jack Trout introduced the idea of *positioning*. Ries and Trout (1986) suggests that although positioning starts with the product 'positioning is not what you do to a product. Positioning is what you do to the mind of the prospect. That is, you position the product in the mind of the prospect.'

Aaker (1991) notes that positioning is closely related to the concepts of *brand association* and brand image. Brand association is anything 'linked' in memory to a brand. A brand image is defined by Aaker as a *set* of associations, usually organised in some meaningful way. The difference is that positioning implies a frame of reference, the reference point usually being competition.

The ability of a potential buyer to recognise or recall that a brand is a member of a certain product category is defined as *brand awareness* by Aaker. The *brand position* is based upon associations, and how these differ from the association generated by the competition. Within these associations we are interested in the perception of quality, and the creation of positive thoughts and feelings. According to Doyle, *brand images* are based upon cultural, social, and personality factors, as well as commercial stimuli like advertising, public relations and prominence of distribution, and we form attitudes to brands even if we have no actual experience of them.

To identify the competitors for a particular brand, we need to identify those brands the consumer is aware of, and perceives to be similar enough to be worthy of comparison (the evoked set); the perceptions and associations related to the brands; and the relative positioning of each brand along the most important decision dimensions. This reference point will be subject to change as new competitors enter the market and existing ones alter their marketing mix to compete more effectively for market segment(s).

Brand names, symbols and slogans are central to brand recognition and brand associations. As consumer analysts we need to understand how these associations work, and we need to appreciate the interactions between beliefs and knowledge and our emotions or feelings. Positioning may be based upon associations with a tangible product attribute, or an intangible attribute such as overall quality, or a combination of rational and emotional benefits, or the relative pricing position. Other association types suggested are use applications, product users, celebrities, life-styles and personalities, product class, competitors, and country or geographic area.

In the 'overcommunicated society' that Ries and Trout identified, the consumer uses selective perception to cope. The individual has a limited capacity for comparing alternatives. Motivation to consider the available alternatives is affected by the level of involvement an individual experiences in the specific choice situation. The effects of this specific choice situation upon consumers strengthens the need to view consumer behaviour as a dynamic process.

If we accept the predictions that the development of successful brands will be the key factor of success in many markets, it is evident that an understanding of consumer behaviour is vital to the analysis of brand images, and the way in which the target market positions the brands perceived to be in competition with one another. Furthermore, given the dynamic nature of the market environment, the analysis of consumer behaviour must be an ongoing activity.

We have identified in this section, that marketing involves exchange relationships, and the marketing concept places emphasis on the consumer as the focus of attention in determining marketing strategy. Furthermore, this section has examined the dynamic environment for marketing, the importance of branding, and the development of a perception of the company as the brand, which results in a need to understand the motivations and perceptions of different groups of individuals, not simply the ultimate consumer. It is suggested that an understanding of the theories of consumer behaviour is transferable to the understanding of the behaviour of these different groups.

Consumer behaviour is transferable

A recent article by Alan Mitchell in *Marketing Business*, the magazine of the Chartered Institute of Marketing, concludes that:

> When all the branding, pricing and new product development is done, it's that ability to make contact with consumers, to communicate, to adapt, to learn, to seize opportunities, that matters – what really counts is not the brilliant application of the 4Ps, but the ability to repeat these feats of imagination and application in rapidly shifting circumstances. That requires a new emphasis on new Ps like people, personality, philosophy and process.

The high levels of competition in today's environment mean that marketers are faced with constant change. In this situation, success will be determined by the ability to analyse the situation, and adapt the company's response. An essential part of the analysis, for those who support a marketing philosophy, is an understanding of the interactions between the consumer and the environment, and the resulting effects on consumer behaviour.

The rest of this chapter is devoted to a brief description of some of the key theories utilised in the process of understanding consumer behaviour. The descriptions are brief and the reader who discovers an interest in this subject is strongly recommended to consult the many books and journals devoted to this subject.

■ What is consumer behaviour?

To quote a recent text by Peter and Olson (1993), the American Marketing Association defines consumer behaviour as: 'the dynamic interaction of affect and cognition, behavior, and environmental events by which human beings conduct the exchange aspects of their lives.' Consumer Behaviour involves interactions between *affect* (emotions, specific feelings, moods and overall evaluations) and *cognitions* (interpretation of the environment to create meanings which guide behaviour), *behaviour*, and *environmental events*. As a result, Consumer Behaviour has drawn upon theories developed in related fields of study of human behaviour such as psychology, sociology, economics, behavioural economics, and anthropology, to develop a theoretical framework for the analysis of the behaviour of consumers.

This author supports the view of Peter and Olson (1993) that the relationships among the elements of affect and cognition, behaviour, and the environment, should be viewed as a continuous set of interactions, which may be referred to as *reciprocal determinism*. Peter and Olson point out that this approach has four important points: firstly, any comprehensive analysis of consumer behaviour must consider all three elements, affect and cognition, behaviour, and the environment; secondly, any of these three may form the starting point for consumer analysis; thirdly, the framework is designed to recognise that consumer behaviour is dynamic; and fourth, this framework may be applied at the level of the individual, the group, or society as a whole.

A comprehensive analysis of consumer behaviour involves an understanding of affect and cognition, attitudes and behaviour, and the environment; that these elements interact; and that the whole process is dynamic. Subsequent sections will be devoted to examining some of the key theories concerning these elements and their dynamic interaction.

☐ *Affect and cognition*

This section will examine the roles of affect and cognition in influencing consumer behaviour.

Affect

Affect is generally defined as including moods, emotions, specific feelings and evaluations. The affective system is viewed as being reactive, in that it responds immediately and automatically to the stimulus. People appear to have little voluntary control over these reactions; our bodies often give us away when we try to conceal our reactions.

Moods

Moods have been a subject of interest for several consumer researchers in the late eighties. Gardner (1985) suggests that mood-state knowledge may be particularly relevant for understanding consumer behaviour as it is affected by service encounters, point-of-purchase stimuli, the content of marketing communications and the context in which these communications appear.

Aaker talks about the difference between 'rational' benefits and 'psychological' benefits. Rational benefits are those closely linked to a product attribute, and part of a 'rational' decision process, whereas 'psychological benefits relate to what feelings are engendered when buying and/or using the brand. A research study by Stuart Agres of the Marschalk Company (1986) found that in 168 television commercials, all of which were judged to contain a rational appeal, only 47 were judged also to contain a psychological benefit. According to a previous test of effectiveness, the 47 providing both types of benefit had a higher effectiveness rating (136 to 86) than those which relied upon rational appeals.

Emotional responses

Emotional responses are necessary to arouse a perception of product category need, to develop a brand attitude, to induce brand purchase intention, and to communicate the ease of purchase to the consumer. Rossiter and Percy (1987) point out that all communication effects except brand awareness have an attitudinal basis, and emotional responses are necessary whenever an element relates to a motivation, and thus to an attitude.

Emotions are strong affective responses such as joy, love, fear, guilt, or anger. Strong emotions and specific feelings such as warmth, satisfaction, disgust, or sadness, often involve the activation of various physiological reactions in the body (sweating, increases in heart rate, the feeling of 'butterflies in the tummy', etc.).

Research has examined the motivational effects of fear in communications designed to encourage a change in consumer behaviour, such as anti-smoking communications. A study that manipulated subjects' degree of anxiety about AIDS found that ads for condoms were evaluated more favourably when a moderate amount of fear was induced. If the level of fear induced is too high members of the audience tend to defend themselves by denying the existence of the threat, or refusing to think about it. It is most effective to raise a degree of fear and combine this with a solution to the problem.

Evaluations

Evaluations involve lower levels of arousal, and concern liking or dislike of a product or brand, or an overall evaluation that it is good or bad. This takes us into the area of attitudes and what these are composed of. According to Baron and Byrne (1987) an attitude is a lasting, general evaluation of people (including oneself), objects or issues.

Researchers differ in their definition of an attitude; most agree that it has three components: **affect** or feelings about the object, **behaviour** or the *intention* to do something with regard to the attitude object, and **cognition** or the beliefs a consumer has about the attitude object.

Recently researchers have argued that the affect, or the consumer's overall evaluation of the product, should be considered to be the core of an attitude. This viewpoint has evolved as the brands within the marketplace have chosen to compete on intangible attributes such as the creation of a brand image, which is based upon feelings towards the brand, rather than a rational evaluation of the tangible attributes of the brand in question.

There are evident parallels with this definition of attitude, and the definition of consumer behaviour given above. The other important area for marketers is the awareness of a brand or product; a pre-condition for developing an attitude to a brand or product is that the consumer should be aware of that brand or product. With this in mind, we shall turn our attention to cognition, and the role of perception within the process of information processing.

Cognition

Cognition is a term used to group together mental processes such as understanding and interpreting the environment; evaluating or judging; planning or problem-solving; and comparing alternative solutions and deciding. All of these activities involve thinking. Many purchases do not involve elaborate thinking or cognitive processing, and consumers are not always aware or conscious of the processes.

For practical purposes, most aspects of the marketing mix of a given brand can be considered to be information which the consumer may choose to process, or not. An information processing model helps us to understand the processes involved. Mowen presents a simplified model. The diagram (see Figure 4.1) shows three stages of *perception*: the exposure stage, when consumers receive information via their senses; the attention stage when they allocate processing capacity to the stimulus; and the comprehension stage when they interpret the information.

First of all, we shall consider perception, then we shall examine the role of the other two elements in the diagram; involvement and memory.

Perception

According to Atkinson *et al.* (1990), information may enter our senses in bits and pieces, but we perceive the world as integrated wholes – a world of people and objects – not piecemeal sensations. The study of perception is concerned with how we integrate sensations, and how we use this process to enable us to cope with our environment. This generally involves a process of *recognition*, and what is referred to as *localisation*, or the means used to navigate through the environment. There are two important aspects to this process of perception: the first is that perception is *selective;* and the second is that it is *subjective.*

Recognition involves a process of categorisation; we interpret the environment by grouping

Figure 4.1. *Information Processing Model*

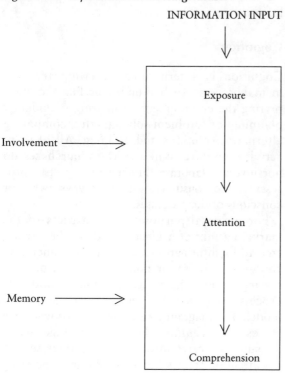

INFORMATION INPUT

Exposure

Involvement

Attention

Memory

Comprehension

PERCEPTION

objects. The shape of objects has been found to be the predominant means of assigning objects to the appropriate category. Recognition requires a matching process with knowledge stored in the individual's memory. We also use the context surrounding the object as information to help us work out what the object is. In this way we make judgements based upon the available information. This information may be ambiguous which may result in individuals forming different perceptions of the same object. We also use our expectations to help us form our perceptions, and this once again leads to differing *subjective* perceptions.

Localisation is the means of separating objects from one another and the context or background. Atkinson *et al.* point out that this process of segregation, and determining distance and move-

ment, is the process which enables us to *organise* the stimuli into objects. Researchers have demonstrated that different ways of grouping objects has a noticeable effect on our perceptions. Most renowed in this area of psychology is the work by Max Wertheimer (1923) the founder of Gestalt psychology, an approach which concentrated upon the way in which we organise or group objects.

Selective perception results from the fact that we are bombarded by stimuli and as a result we are unable to recognise all of them. The process by which we select stimuli for recognition is called *selective attention* (Atkinson *et al.*, 1990). There is some evidence that our perceptual system processes non-attended stimuli briefly even though the stimuli do not reach consciousness. In the past, this led to concerns that people could be influenced by stimuli that were subliminal. There is little evidence that such stimuli influence consumer behaviour after years of interest in the subject (Moore, 1982).

Marketers seeking to attract attention to their brands try to ensure that the brand provides the appropriate cues to aid in recognition and localisation. With regard to recognition package design is used to provide cues as to the category of product the brand should be assigned to. Failure to do so can lead to consumers confusing one brand for something else. An example cited by Solomon is confusion over the intended purpose of a yellow plastic bottle of washing-up liquid with lemon juice, and a similar yellow plastic bottle of pure lemon juice.

Colour and contrast is often used by advertisers to attract attention and to separate the brand from its background; for example, the use of colour adverts in a predominantly black and white newspaper, or the use of black and white ads on colour television. Intensity of stimuli – whether sound or vision – is used to attract attention. For instance, adverts are often louder than the accompanying television programme. The perfume industry often use intense colours in their advertising to evoke different emotional responses as well as attract attention. An example of using an unexpected cue which contrasts with its context, is the use of rough textured paper in a glossy magazine to attract attention to the brand Fenjal, a bath oil product which emphasises its ability to leave your skin 'silky smooth'.

The appeal to the sense of smell has been used by the perfume industry, who use scented strips in their magazine adverts. Recently, marketers have turned to our sense of smell to attract attention and stimulate moods within retail outlets. This approach is becoming increasingly sophisticated; instead of pumping a smell such as baking bread around the store, micro-encapsulation is used at the point where a purchasing decision is made. An article in Supermarketing (21 August 1992) about this approach considers that: 'A smell works in three ways. Firstly, it triggers a conditional response – that is, the smell of the food makes you salivate. Secondly, it can induce fond memories, such as the smell of cut grass, and thirdly it can have a drug effect which can relax or stimulate.' The managing director of a retail consultancy referred to in this article, considers that smells and music can be used to create the personality of a store. Given the increasing importance attached to the company as a brand, and the resultant importance of retail outlets, we may anticipate that increasing interest will be focused upon ways of attracting attention by retail outlets, and that this will lead to adoption of innovative ways of stimulating the senses.

An important concept for marketing is the *differential threshold* which refers to the ability of a sensory system to detect change or differences among stimuli. Ernst Weber found that the amount of change which is necessary to be noticed is related to the original intensity of the stimulus. This relationship is known as Weber's Law. At times marketers may not want consumers to notice a change; for example if reducing the size of a chocolate bar, or increasing the price, or updating the company logo, it may be advantageous to ensure that the change is not noticeable, that it does not exceed the JND or *just noticeable difference*.

Awareness of the JND is also important for advertisers who wish to combat *advertising wearout*. This results from the process of adaptation where familiarity leads to a reduction in attention. By altering the advert sufficiently the advertiser can revive the levels of attention paid to the advert. This has led to the practice of developing a central theme for a series of adverts such as the Guinness ads on television.

Subjective interpretation is the process by which individuals assign meaning to stimuli according to the associations which the stimuli evoke. In the process of interpretation, or recognition and localisation, the individual uses his/her own set of beliefs or *schema* which has evolved as a result of learning and experience.

The ability of the human species to develop abstract meanings or symbols, play an important role in the meanings people assign to stimuli. Symbols are powerful means of communicating meanings within a society, and as we shall see later in our discussion of the environment, each society differs in the meanings and symbols which apply. Consumers organise information at various levels of abstraction ranging from simple product attributes to complex personal values. For example, the perception of quality may be viewed as an overall attitude, a more abstract dimension, and not an attribute of the product (Zeithaml, 1988; Olshavsky, 1985; Holbrook and Corfman, 1985).

Perception may be viewed as the process by which stimuli are selected for attention, organised in a way which enables an individual to recognise and categorise, using previous knowledge and expectations in the process of assigning meaning or interpreting the stimulus. Our understanding of this process should be integrated with the discussion on memory processes which follows the next item of involvement: The role of involvement is to determine how much effort the consumer will assign to processing information; the role of memory helps us to understand the effects of knowledge stored in our memories on the subjective meanings the individual gives to the stimuli selected for further processing.

Involvement

The frequently cited definition of involvement is that of Celsi and Olson (1988) that it is a motivational state influenced by the perceived personal importance and/or interest evoked by a stimulus. Involvement is of great importance in discussion of information processing and decision making, and contrasts are drawn between high and low involvement, although it is more realistic to view involvement as a continuum rather than two extremes.

Two types of involvement which have been identified are: *situational* involvement, where the involvement is dependent upon the situation the consumer is in, such as the difference in attention and evaluation of alternatives between purchasing a bottle of wine to take to a dinner party given by your boss, to the purchase of one to be consumed at a large party; and the other type is *enduring* involvement, which describes a longer lasting interest in the product area, such as that of a hi-fi enthusiast who will read about products and new advances even when he/she is not contemplating a purchase.

Celsi and Olson point out that consumers' attention and comprehension processes are strongly influenced by their motivations, abilities and opportunities to process salient information in their environments.

The *ability to process* is influenced by the amount and type of knowledge the consumer has acquired through experience, and the ability to retrieve relevant material from memory in a given situation. This suggests that the ability of those individuals who have extensive experience with a product such as a personal computer would be more able to process information about PCs than a 'novice'. The effect of knowledge upon consumer search for product information and evaluation of information has been studied by several researchers. Brucks (1985) found that prior knowledge facilitates the acquisition of new information and increases search efficiency. Wilkie and Dickson (1985) found that consumer knowledge may reduce search activity in shopping for appliances.

The *opportunity to process* is dependent upon aspects of the immediate environment; the sheer amount of information available; the format and modality of the information presented. Information overload was alluded to in the opening discussion, and there is no doubt that consumers are faced with sensory overload in the modern environment. This overload results in selective perception; the consumer selects the information to be exposed to, and selects the information which is then given further attention and processing.

The *motivation to process* is dependent upon the individual's involvement with the stimuli; this may be described as the perceived personal relevance which the stimulus has for the individual: 'The personal relevance of a product is represented by the perceived linkage between an individual's needs, goals and values (self-knowledge) and their product knowledge (attributes and benefits)...In sum, motivation to process information is a function of the personally relevant knowledge that is activated in memory in a particular situation' (Celsi and Olson, 1988). The idea of perceived personal relevance is closely linked to the concept that each individual has a sense of 'Self'; an identity or attitude about who he/she is. The Self may be understood by combining various theories on individual motivation, personality and learned behaviour. We shall examine these ideas in greater detail later in this chapter.

Petty, Cacioppo and Schumann (1983) suggest that involvement plays a moderating role in advertising effectiveness; Greenwald and Leavitt (1984) develop this approach further by suggesting that there are four levels of involvement which are identified (from low to high) as preattention, focal attention, comprehension, and elaboration. In essence they are suggesting that the degree, or level, of processing is dependent upon the level of involvement, and that the extent to which the individual attempts to integrate new information with information already held in memory is dependent upon the involvement experienced by the individual in the purchase situation.

In other words, under conditions of high involvement, the consumer will process new information in more depth, allocating more processing capacity to understanding the new information, possibly by retrieving relevant information from memory, and attempting to integrate the new information with the existing information stored in long-term memory.

Memory

Many authors treat the memory process as if dealing with a computer; information is placed in the memory for storage, and subsequently retrieved as necessary. Two models of memory have been developed; one which considers that the memory has three distinct systems, the sensory memory, the short-term memory (STM) and the long-term memory (LTM) (Atkinson *et al.*, 1990); the other approach views memory processes from the point of view of levels of processing, considering that the individual will

Figure 4.2. *The three-memory system*

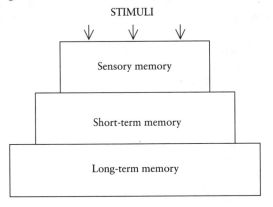

process some information in greater depth than others (Craik and Lockhart, 1972). These two approaches are not mutually exclusive, and for ease of conceptualisation we shall use the three store model in this chapter.

Sensory memory is the stage in the process where the individual determines whether to process the stimuli further. Storage in the sensory memory is very brief; this is the sorting house for all the stimuli we are constantly bombarded with. At this point we select stimuli for further *attention*.

Short-term memory is also referred to as the *working memory*, to indicate that this is the point

in the processing where incoming information is *chunked* into a unit of information which has meaning for the individual. The capacity of STM is limited and information is not stored here for more than a few seconds before the individual selects to store this information, or not. Other information stored in the long-term memory may be retrieved to aid in the process of interpretation and *elaboration*. The new information may be integrated with previously stored information and then stored in LTM.

Long-term memory is the system which allows us to store information for a long period of time. It is useful to think of the memory process in terms of three stages; encoding, storage, and retrieval. With regard to the LTM there are important interactions between encoding and retrieval. The dominant long-term memory representation is based on the meanings of items (Atkinson *et al.*). The more deeply, or elaborately the meaning is encoded, the better able is the individual to recall the information. This process is helped by the development of meaningful connections.

It is believed that many cases of forgetting from long-term memory result from the inability to *access* the information rather than the decay or loss of the information. Two factors have been identified as aiding retrieval; the organisation of the information at the time of encoding; and the similarity of the context in which the information is encoded and that in which it will be retrieved.

Much of marketing communication is involved in creating meanings and meaningful connections to aid in the process of elaboration. Cues are provided to aid the consumer in the retrieval process. The material is presented in a way which is designed to aid organisation, or to fit in with existing networks of information, referred to as *associative networks*, stored in the consumer's memory. Some adverts try to create a similar context as to the decision context to increase the chances that their information will be retrieved at the point of decision-making. Those brands recalled are referred to as the *evoked set*. The types of communication effects desired by marketers varies according to the decision situation which the consumer is most likely to encounter.

According to Rossiter and Percy (1987): 'Advertising and promotion cause action through the process of communication by establishing relatively enduring mental associations connected to the brand in the prospective buyer's mind, called communication effects.' They proceed to identify five communication effects; category need, brand awareness, brand attitude, brand purchase intention, and purchase facilitation. The first and last of these is generic to the product category, whereas the middle three are concerned with developing brand specific communication effects in competition with other brands.

Rossiter and Percy point out that with regard to brand awareness, the consumer must be able to identify (recognise or recall) the brand within the category in sufficient detail to make a purchase. This can be *recall* by brand name, colour of packaging, or location, or *recognition* such as the effect of seeing packaging in a supermarket which is recognised.

However, although brand awareness is essential if the brand is to be chosen, by itself it will not result in purchase; the consumer must develop a favourable brand attitude and intention to purchase.

☐ *Attitudes and behaviour*

Attitudes have been the subject of a great deal of research by consumer researchers and academics. Most notable in this area has been Fishbein, who has conducted extensive research in this area over the years. As Lutz (1991) points out, numerous researchers in both psychology and marketing have failed to document the attitude-behaviour relationship, leading some to question the utility of attitude in understanding behaviour.

Attitudes

Fishbein's early theory (1963), examined Attitude-toward-the-Object; this theory was subsequently extended to incorporate the attitude towards performing the behaviour in question. The later Theory of Reasoned Action (Ajzen & Fishbein, 1980) incorporates evaluations and beliefs about the consequences of the behaviour, and also a Subjective Norm; the beliefs about others' expectations and the motivation to comply with those expectations. These modifications to the theoretical models have been motivated by a desire to establish causal links between attitude and behaviour.

The concept of attitude has proved to be a useful tool for marketers in the segmentation of markets; in new product concept testing; and in the development of promotional strategies, particularly with regard to establishing current attitudes and developing strategies for changing the current attitudes.

The importance of direct personal experience in the formation of strongly learned attitudes is identified by Fazio *et al.* who base their process model of attitude-behaviour relations on principles of information processing. (Fazio, 1986; Fazio, Powell and Williams, 1989). Strongly held attitudes are more likely to be accessible in memory. Once retrieved from memory, this attitude guides the processing of further information about the attitude object; in other words, the

Figure 4.3. *Process models of attitude–behaviour relations*

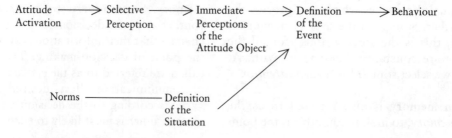

process of selective perception. This theory also allows for the influence of norms.

Rossiter and Percy define brand attitude as: 'Brand attitude refers to the buyer's overall evaluation of the brand with respect to its perceived ability to meet a currently relevant motivation.' Rossiter and Percy proceed to identify four important characteristics:

1. Brand attitude *depends upon the currently relevant motivation* – this is open to change.
2. Brand attitude consists of a *cognitive* component, which guides behaviour, and an associated *affective* component, which energises behaviour.
3. The cognitive component is made up of a number of specific *benefit beliefs*.
4. Brand attitude is a *relative* concept. In almost all product categories, it is a matter of which brand under consideration meets the motivation relatively better than alternative brands.

The brand purchase intention is the conscious decision to purchase the brand; it is the planning of the action step. This may occur when the consumer sees an advert for a product, or it may be delayed until the consumer is in the shop, and it may appear to be an impulsive choice. For example the consumer may have seen advertising for a new chocolate bar, but may not decide to purchase this bar until faced with the decision in a shop.

Motivation

Given the important role of the currently relevant motivation in transforming a positive brand attitude into a conscious decision to purchase the brand, it is worth examining one or two of the theories in the area of motivation, personality and self-concept.

The role of the unconscious

Freud emphasised the role of the unconscious in motivating behaviour. He believed that personality is composed of three major systems: the *id*, and the *ego*, and the *superego*. The id consists of basic biological impulses (or drives). Freud considered that the sexual and aggressive drives were the most important instinctual determinants of personality. It is certainly evident that advertisers have chosen to stimulate the strong sexual drives in much of the advertising used today. The ego develops as the child realises that many of the basic drives cannot be satisfied immediately. The superego is essentially the individual's conscience; the internalised set of values which society deem to be appropriate. These are learnt by the individual during interactions with parents, friends, school, and the Church.

There are many critics of Freudian theory, and the structural approach to personality outlined above has been the subject of particular criticism. Another area of Freudian theory which has fared better is the concept of *defence mechanisms* and the individual's use of *repression*, in which the ego pushes a threatening thought or forbidden impulse into the unconscious.

The use of projective techniques by market researchers in qualitative research studies in the commercial environment is widespread, as marketers seek to understand those motivations which people may be unaware of, or may choose not to reveal in open discussion in a group context.

Freud remained open to new ideas, and many of his followers have subsequently developed new theories of their own which are too numerous to be covered in this chapter.

A hierarchy of needs

Atkinson *et al.* maintain that motives can be categorised as survival needs, social needs and the need to satisfy curiosity. Maslow (1908–1970) proposed a *hierarchy of needs* which was based on the idea that there are basic needs which must be at least partially satisfied before the next level of need will determine the actions of the individual. These needs are ordered with physiological needs, followed by safety needs, belongingness and love needs, esteem needs, cognitive needs, aesthetic needs, and finally the need for self-actualisation.

This hierarchy has value in that it reminds marketers that the consumer may have different need priorities at different times, and in different situations. Some needs are often associated with particular products. For example, the purchase of a car may be associated with esteem needs for some consumers; for others, the need for safety may be paramount – indeed Volvo has used this to differentiate its products for many years, although we are now witnessing an 'explosion of airbags' in TV advertising for other makes of cars, which indicates that research has uncovered an increasing awareness of a need for safety features on our increasingly crowded roads!

However, the hierarchy is also rather a simplistic tool, and its limitations include the culture-bound nature of the rankings of the various needs which may not be so appropriate in cultures where group needs are deemed to be more important than those of the individual.

Self-concept

Self concept refers to the attitude an individual holds about him- or herself. Some theorists have used the concept of personality to explain the Self. Of these many studies in consumer research have attempted to link purchase behaviour with specific traits with mixed success. Sirgy (1982) suggests that individuals have several 'selves'; their 'actual' self, their *'ideal' self*, their social self, and their ideal social self.

Two important points emerge from this: firstly, there is often a 'gap' between how we perceive ourselves and how we would like to be; secondly, we use other people's opinions to form our perceptions of ourselves, as a type of mirror. The concept of multiple selves also helps us to play a range of different 'roles' in different situations; the calm efficient executive by day, and the sexy good fun person by night!

The self-concept is of value to marketing because people may purchase goods which they perceive to be compatible with their view of themselves, or they may purchase goods and services which will help them to achieve their 'ideal' selves, or to help them portray the role that they wish to portray.

By understanding the desire of many individuals to be slimmer, a whole industry of diet products has emerged. At times individuals may hold a negative view of their self which can be very damaging; for example a negative body image which leads to bulimia or anorexia. To some extent the views of the 'ideal' self may be learned as a result of the reactions of others; indeed it is like all attitudes in the respect that it is learned. The role of advertising is important in setting role models which form a type of learning known as vicarious learning.

Behaviour

We have touched on the role of behaviour in our discussion of attitudes, and the need to assess the intention to behave in a certain manner, as well as the predictions of the outcomes of such behaviour, rather than simply measuring attitudes to the brand. This emphasises the inter-related nature of these areas, and the somewhat artificial grouping of items under headings. In this section we shall deal quite briefly with the most important aspects of behavioural learning theory which helps to explain aspects of behaviour, which are not fully explained by the cognitive learning approach as it is often described in consumer behaviour texts.

Theories of learning include simple Stimulus-Response (S-R) models, the vicarious type of learning referred to above, as well as the view of consumers as complex problem-solvers who store abstract rules in their memories to aid in solving similar problems in the future. We shall concentrate on the S-R theories in this section.

This view of learning considers that learning takes place as a result of a response to external events, or stimuli. One of the major theories in this area which is of interest to marketers is that of classical conditioning.

Classical conditioning

Pavlov discovered this phenomenon when he paired a neutral stimulus (a bell) with a stimulus known to cause salivation (meat powder). The meat powder was the *unconditioned stimulus* because it could naturally produce the response.

After repetition, the bell became a *conditioned stimulus* because the dogs learnt to associate the bell with the meat powder. The salivation as a result of hearing the bell is termed the *conditioned response*.

This process has been used by marketers in an attempt to associate brands with basic drives in the hope that the brand will subsequently evoke a conditioned response. This process of classical conditioning is used to elicit positive emotional responses in advertising by the use of unconditioned stimuli, or even other previously conditioned stimuli. Even credit cards have been identified as a form of conditioned stimuli; as a result of prior conditioning, 'credit card stimuli acquire the ability to elicit spending behaviour as a conditioned response' (Feinberg, 1986). There are a number of factors which influence the effectiveness of efforts to induce conditioning. The interested reader is directed to a text such as Engel, Blackwell and Miniard for a fuller discussion.

Operant conditioning

The other type of conditioning we shall briefly examine is the idea of operant conditioning or instrumental learning. A very detailed examination of the merits of this approach may be found in the recent text by Professor Foxhall, *Consumer Psychology in Behavioural Perspective*. In this text Foxhall examines the work of B. F. Skinner who is most closely associated with this area of theory.

Responses in classical conditioning are thought to be involuntary, whereas those in operant conditioning are more deliberate and are designed to achieve a specific goal. The desired behaviour may be learnt over a period of time, a process referred to as *shaping*. The desired behaviour is learnt as a result of a reward received following the desired behaviour, which may take the form of a *positive reinforcement* or a *negative reinforcement*. A positive reinforcement is the reward of a positive stimulus as a result of a desired behaviour. A negative reinforcement is the removal of an adverse stimulus as a result of the behaviour. This is not to be confused with *punishment* which is the administering of an adverse stimulus, rather than removal of one.

Reinforcement is used by marketers extensively. Products may provide positive or negative reinforcement. Engel *et al.* point out that consumers are less likely to enjoy buying and using negative reinforcement products. Free samples and a variety of introductory promotions may be used to shape behaviour.

Discriminative stimuli are stimuli which result from prior association with reinforcers; they act as cues which indicate the likelihood that a reinforcer will be present if the behaviour is carried out. By this process marketers may hope to differentiate their brands from the competition. The use of company brands means that consumers use corporate names or logos as discriminative stimuli. Other discriminative stimuli used are the various elements of the marketing mix; price, packaging, advertising and distribution.

Stimulus generalisation is essentially the opposite process where consumers generalise the response; the purchase of one brand which rewards leading to the purchase of another similar brand. Obviously, marketers are generally hoping to avoid this effect.

□ The environment

In this section we shall consider the effects of the social contacts of the individual consumer; the influence of family, work associates, and friends. We shall also consider the effects of the wider environment, and the two-way influence which takes place between consumers and society.

Social influence

As we have pointed out above individuals determine their sense of Self partly by the reactions of others. We also identified the motivating role of social contact, belongingness, love and esteem. The earlier examination of attitude theory mentioned the attention which has been paid to the influence of others and the level of motivation to comply with this influence. The discussion of rewards and punishment of behaviour is also relevant to an understanding of the influence other people have on our behaviour.

Although many Western societies have advocated individualism, the influence of family and friends may be very strong in the purchase of certain products. Some individuals may exert more influence over the behaviour of their contacts than do others; these type are referred to as *opinion leaders* (Rogers, 1983). It is possible for opinion leadership to take place without personal contact, for example journalists may lead opinions in society by their writing.

A group of people that the individual uses as a point of reference to evaluate his/her choices or decisions is known as a reference group (Hyman, 1942). The group may be a group the individual belongs to, or it may be a group the consumer would like to belong to, known as an *aspirational group*. The greatest influence and impact is usually exerted by primary groups, or those which the consumer has face-to-face contact with.

Social visibility is an important factor determining the level of influence of others in decision making. Bearden and Etzel (1982) identify two factors which influence the strength of reference group influence; whether the product is a necessity or a luxury item, and whether it is publicly consumed or privately consumed. Furthermore, their analysis identifies the conditions under which the influence is upon the choice of product, and when it is upon the choice of brand (see Table 4.1).

Cultural influence

Our discussion of the environment is restricted; for instance, I have chosen not to include important topics such as social class, and the influence of the family upon the individual. Before concluding, I feel our understanding of consumer choice of products and brands would be helped by an examination of the cultural meaning of goods, and the transfer of cultural meanings via goods.

McCracken (1986) analysed the movement of cultural meaning theoretically from the culturally constituted world to consumer goods, then from those goods to the individual consumer. McCracken identified several instruments which were responsible for this process; advertising, the fashion system, and four consumption rituals. Advertising and the fashion system move meaning from the culturally constituted world to consumer goods, while consumer rituals move

Table 4.1. *Combining public–private and luxury–necessity dimensions with product and brand decisions*

	Publicly consumed	
Brand\Product	Weak reference group influence (–)	Strong reference group influence (+)
Strong reference group influence (+)	*Public necessities* Influence: Weak product and strong brand e.g. Wristwatch, automobile, man's suit	*Public luxuries* Influence: Strong product and brand e.g. golf clubs, snow skis, sailboat
Weak reference group influence (–)	*Private necessities* Influence: Weak product and brand e.g. mattress, floor lamp, refrigerator	*Private luxuries* Influence: Strong product and weak brand e.g. TV game, trash compactor, ice maker
	Privately Consumed	

Source: Adapted from W. O. Bearden and M. J. Etzel, 'Reference Group Influence on Product and Brand Purchase Decisions', *Journal of Consumer Research* 9 (September 1982).

Figure 4.4 *Movement of meaning*

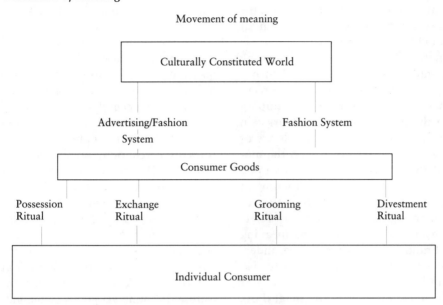

Movement of meaning

```
            ┌──────────────────────────────┐
            │   Culturally Constituted World │
            └──────────────────────────────┘

   Advertising/Fashion            Fashion System
       System
            ┌──────────────────────────────┐
            │       Consumer Goods          │
            └──────────────────────────────┘

 Possession    Exchange      Grooming      Divestment
 Ritual        Ritual        Ritual        Ritual

    ┌──────────────────────────────────────────┐
    │           Individual Consumer             │
    └──────────────────────────────────────────┘
```

Source: G. McCracken, 'Culture and Consumption', *Journal of Consumer Research* 13 (June 1986).

meaning from the consumer good to the consumer.

This movement of meaning enables the consumer to use goods to develop and communicate a sense of Self to others in his/her society by using meaning systems understood by other members of the society. Those involved in the advertising and fashion systems must be sensitive to the meanings which are associated with products, which will be suitable in communications designed to achieve a perception of a category need, or awareness and favourable brand attitude and intention to purchase. As Judith Williamson pointed out in 1978: 'Advertisements are selling us something else besides consumer goods: in providing us with a structure in which we, and those goods, are interchangeable, they are selling us ourselves.'

Williamson believed that advertising, by creating these structures of meaning, is replacing the role that was traditionally fulfilled by art or religion. Creative ad teams must have a highly developed sense of the culture they are operating in; this includes understanding the categories which operate such as social class, and the cultural principles which underlie these categories. We need these categories, and the sense of selves; it is part of our process to organise and understand our environment, including our perceptions of our own identities. In our modern consumer societies we use the purchase of products and the choice of brands to communicate our identities, where once we might have relied upon what we produced, and our role in the production process to communicate who we were.

Frequently advertisers use symbolism to communicate a similarity between an aspect of the culture which is understood by members of that culture, and the brand which they are promoting. Because cultures differ in terms of their structures and ideologies, it has proved to be rather difficult to transplant adverts from one culture to another, and expect the successful transfer of meanings to take place. If, and when, this similarity is accepted and understood, the brand is then associated with this aspect of the culture. Williamson cites the example of diamonds which may be marketed by likening them to 'eternal love' – 'a diamond is forever' – creating a symbolism where the mineral means something in human terms as a 'sign'. Once the connection has been made, we begin to translate the other way, and to omit the translation, accepting the sign for what it signifies, the thing for the feeling.

This explanation of the role of advertising within society integrates many aspects of theory previously examined: it uses the ideas of perception in terms of differentiating and grouping stimuli; the role of associative networks in memory; the role of involvement in the levels of information processing undertaken, and the motivating role of the sense of Self; it draws upon the ideas of classical and operant conditioning in creating associations; and it utilises the effect of social influence, and the individual's use of reference groups, in understanding that the meaning created for a brand or product must be understood by others in the relevant society. It also helps us to understand the important role of affect and the creation of brand images. As McCracken (1986) pointed out: 'so much of advertising has to do not with lists of information and descriptions of product benefits but with evocative images and text that appears to supply no obvious basis for rational product choice'.

Thus we have returned to the concept of the development of brand associations and brand images with which we began this chapter. I hope to have cast some light on the processes which are involved in the development of these associations and images within the individual consumer's mind. There are many more theories than this chapter allows us to explore, but I hope that the selection indicates the practical role which a knowledge of consumer behaviour theory can play in understanding behaviour, and developing appropriate marketing strategies in a dynamic environment.

■ In summary

We opened the chapter by examining the need for consumer behaviour theory and its role in explaining exchange relationships. An understanding of consumer behaviour enables us to segment markets and to develop effective marketing strategies. We acknowledged the dynamic marketing environment and the key role of brand building in the 1990s.

We have considered the dynamic interaction of *affect and cognition, behaviour, and the environment*. With regard to **affect**, we considered that individual moods, and complex emotional responses influence the evaluations of consumer goods. Our examination of **cognition** was more detailed, as we attempted briefly to explain the roles of perception, involvement, and memory processes. We discussed attitudes and behaviour and the motivating role of the Self. Our treatment of **behaviour** concentrated on the stimulus-response theories of classical conditioning, and operant conditioning. Finally, the chapter looked at two theories concerning the influence of **the environment** upon consumer behaviour; firstly the role of reference groups, and then the transfer of cultural meaning via goods to the individual. This view of cultural meaning transfer concluded in an attempt to draw together the many threads of theory explored in the chapter and link them to the earlier discussion of brand associations and brand images.

We have not included a comprehensive model of consumer behaviour in this chapter because it tends to convey a sense of separate units rather than the reciprocal determinism we hoped to convey. Those who would like to view a comprehensive model are directed to the most recent edition of the text *Consumer Behaviour*, by Engel *et al.*

■ References

Aaker, D. A. (1991), *Managing Brand Equity: capitalizing on the value of a brand name*, New York: The Free Press.

Abbott, L. (1955), *Quality and Competition*, New York: Columbia University Press.

Agres, S. (1986), *Emotion in Advertising: An Agency's View*, The Marshalk Company, quoted in Aaker, *Managing Brand Equity*, pp. 119–120.

Atkinson, R. L., Atkinson, R. C., Smith, E. E., Bem, D. J. and Hilgard, E. E. (1990), *Introduction to Psychology*, 10th edition, New York: Harcourt Brace Jovanovich, Inc.

Ajzen, I. and Fishbein, M., (1980) *Understanding Attitudes and Predicting Social Behaviour*, Englewood Cliffs, NJ: Prentice-Hall.

Baker, M. J. (1992), *Marketing Strategy and Management*, 2nd edition, London: Macmillan.

Baron, R. A. and Byrne D. (1987), *Social Psychology: Understanding Human Interaction*, 5th edition, Boston: Allyn & Bacon.

Bearden, W. O. and Etzel, M. J. (1982), 'Reference Group Influence on Product and Brand Purchase Decisions', *Journal of Consumer Research* 9 (September).

Borden, N. H. (1964) 'The Concept of the Marketing Mix', *Journal of Advertising Research*, Advertising Research Foundation, Inc. (June), pp. 2–7.

Brady, J. and Davis, I. (1993), *The McKinsey Quarterly,* quoted in 'New Generation Marketing', *Marketing Business, the magazine of the Chartered Institute of Marketing* (February 1994).

Brucks, M. (1985), 'The Effects of Product Class Knowledge on Information Search Behaviour', *Journal of Consumer Research* 12 (June), pp. 1–15.

Celsi, R. L. and Olson, J. C. (1988), 'The Role of Involvement in Attention and Comprehension Processes', *Journal of Consumer Research* 15 (September), pp. 210–224.

Craik, Fergus I. M. and Lockhart, Robert S. (1972), 'Levels of Processing: A Framework for Memory Research', *Journal of Verbal Learning and Verbal Behaviour* (December), pp. 671–684.

Doyle, P. (1991), *The Marketing Book*, 2nd edition, ed. M. J. Baker, London: Butterworth-Heinemann.

Engel, J. E., Blackwell, R. D. and Miniard, P. W. (1990), *Consumer Behaviour*, 6th edition, The Dryden Press International Edition.

Fazio, R. H. (1986), 'How Do Attitudes Guide Behaviour?', in *Handbook of Motivation and Cognition: Foundations of Social Behaviour*, eds R. M. Sorrentino and E. T. Higgins, New York: Guildford, pp. 204–243.

Fazio, R. H., Powell, M. C. and Williams, C. J. (1989), The Role of Attitude Accessibility in the Attitude-to-Behaviour Process', *Journal of Consumer Research* 16 (December), pp. 280–288.

Feinberg, R. A. (1986), 'Credit Cards as Spending Facilitating Stimuli: A Conditioning Explanation', *Journal of Consumer Research* 13 (December), pp. 348–356.

Fishbein, M. (1963), 'An Investigation of the Relationship between Beliefs about an Object and the Attitude toward that Object', *Human Relations*, pp. 223–240.

Fishbein, M. and Ajzen, I. (1975), *Beliefs, Attitudes, Intentions, and Behaviour: An Introduction to Theory and Research*, Reading, Mass.: Addison-Wesley.

Foxhall, G. (1990), *Consumer Psychology* in *Behavioural Perspective*, London: Routledge.

Gardner, M. P. (1985), 'Mood States and Consumer Behaviour: A Critical Review,' *Journal of Consumer Research* 12 (December), pp. 281–300.

Greenwald, A. G. and Leavitt, C. (1984), 'Audience Involvement in Advertising: Four Levels', *Journal of Consumer Research* 11 (June), pp. 581–592.

Holbrook, M. B. and Corfman, K. P. (1985), 'Quality and Value in the Consumption Experience: Phaedrus Rides Again', in *Perceived Quality*, J. Jacoby and J. Olson eds, Lexington, Mass.: Lexington Books, pp. 31–57.

Hyman, Herbert H. (1942), The Psychology of Status', *Archives of Psychology* 38.

Kassarjian, H. H. and Sheffet, M. J. (1991), 'Personality and Consumer Behaviour: An Update', in *Perspectives in Consumer Behaviour,* 4th edition, Englewood Cliffs, NJ: Prentice-Hall International Editions.

King, S. (1991), 'Brand Building in the 1990s', *Journal of Marketing Management* 7 (1).

Levitt, T. (1960), 'Marketing Myopia', *Harvard Business Review*, (July–August).

Light, L. (1991), quoted by D. A. Aaker in the preface to *Managing Brand Equity: capitalizing on the value of a brand name*, New York: Free Press.

Lutz, R. J. (1991), 'The Role of Attitude Theory in Marketing,' in *Perspectives in Consumer Behaviour*, 4th edition, Englewood Cliffs, NJ: Prentice-Hall International Editions.

McCracken, G. (1986), 'Culture and Consumption: A Theoretical Account of the Structure and Movement of the Cultural Meaning of Consumer Goods', *Journal of Consumer Research* 13 (June), pp. 71–84.

Mitchell, A. (1994), 'New Generation Marketing', *Marketing Business, the magazine of the Chartered Institute of Marketing* (February).

Moore, T. E. (1982), 'Subliminal Advertising: What you see is what you get', *Journal of Marketing* 46 (Spring), pp. 38–47.

Mowen, J. C. (1993), *Consumer Behaviour*, 3rd edition, London: Macmillan.

Olshavsky, R. W. (1985), 'Perceived Quality in Consumer Decision Making: An Integrated Theoretical Perspective', in *Perceived Quality*, eds J.Jacoby and J. Olson, Lexington, Mass.: Lexington Books, pp. 3–29.

Peter, J. P. and Olson, J. C. (1993), *Consumer Behaviour and Marketing Strategy*, 3rd edition, New York: Irwin.

Petty, R. E., Cacioppo, J. T., and Schumann, D. (1983), 'Central and Peripheral Routes to Advertising Effectiveness: The Moderating Role of Involvement, *Journal of Consumer Research* 10 (September).

Ries, A. and Trout, J., 'Positioning Cuts Through Chaos in Marketplace', *Advertising Age* (1 May 1972); 'The Positioning Era: A View Ten Years Later', *Advertising Age* (16 July 1979); *Positioning: The Battle for Your Mind*, New York: McGraw-Hill (1985; 1986 1st rev edition).

Rogers, E. M., *Diffusion of Innovation*, 3rd.edition, New York: Free Press, 1983.

Rossiter, J. R. and Percy, L. (1987), *Advertising and Promotion Management*, International Edition, New York: McGraw-Hill.

Sirgy, M. J. (1982), 'Self-Concept in Consumer Behaviour: A Critical Review', *Journal of Consumer Research* 9 (December), pp. 287–300.

Solomon, M. R. (1992), *Consumer Behaviour: Buying, Having and Being*, Boston: Allyn & Bacon.

Tynan, A. C. and Drayton, J. (1987), 'Market Segmentation', *Journal of Marketing Management* 2 (3) (Spring).

Wertheimer, M., in Atkinson *et al.* (1990), *Introduction to Psychology*, 10th edition, New York: Harcourt Brace Jovanovich, Inc.

Williamson, J. (1978), *Decoding Advertisements: Ideology and Meaning in Advertising*, London: Marion Boyers.

Zeithaml, V. A. (1988), 'Consumer Perceptions of Price, Quality and Value: A Means–End Model and Synthesis of Evidence, *Journal of Marketing* 52 (July), pp. 2–22.

Chapter 5

Organisational Buying Behaviour

Shan Rajagopal

■ Introduction

The competitive business environment of today has a major impact on marketing and procurement strategies. In order to develop these strategies effectively, it is important to understand as much as possible about the nature of the buyer-seller interaction which is changing with the influence of technology development, shortened product life-cycles, and the demands being placed on industrial customers by their customers. Thus an understanding of organisational buying behaviour (OBB) becomes fundamental not only for the development of appropriate industrial marketing strategies but also has significant implications for the development of procurement strategy within the buying organisation.

This chapter has three primary objectives. Firstly, the chapter reviews the most important theoretical and research contributions of the last three decades and attempts to provide a fairly comprehensive understanding of organisational buying behaviour, its decision process, the factors influencing the buying decisions together with a review of the various models proposed by academics. Secondly, the chapter will examine the application of OBB knowledge in developing marketing strategies and looks into the suppliers' marketing strategies. In addition, it also examines the applications of OBB knowledge in developing

procurement strategies for the buying organisation and its own interaction with marketing strategy. Finally, the chapter discusses future trends in the development of this knowledge. Figure 5.1 provides a simplified diagram of the dimensions of OBB knowledge and the buyer/seller strategy development. The flow of this chapter will be based on this diagram. It will become apparent through the course of this chapter that organisational buying is a complex process. Attempts to oversimplify this process ultimately result in a loss of understanding of the dynamics of the process and its constituent elements.

■ Factors influencing organisational buying behaviour

No buying decision is ever taken in isolation. Each decision is influenced by factors having to do with the buying company and the individuals who are involved. In this section, the forces are examined using an analysis model developed by Webster and Wind (1972) that has formed the basis of many later attempts to understand business buying. As shown in Figure 5.2, this model groups the various factors into four levels of buying influences: environmental (e.g. health of the economy); organisational forces (e.g. size of buying organisation); group forces (e.g. com-

Figure 5.1. *Dimensions of OBB knowledge and buyer/seller strategy development*

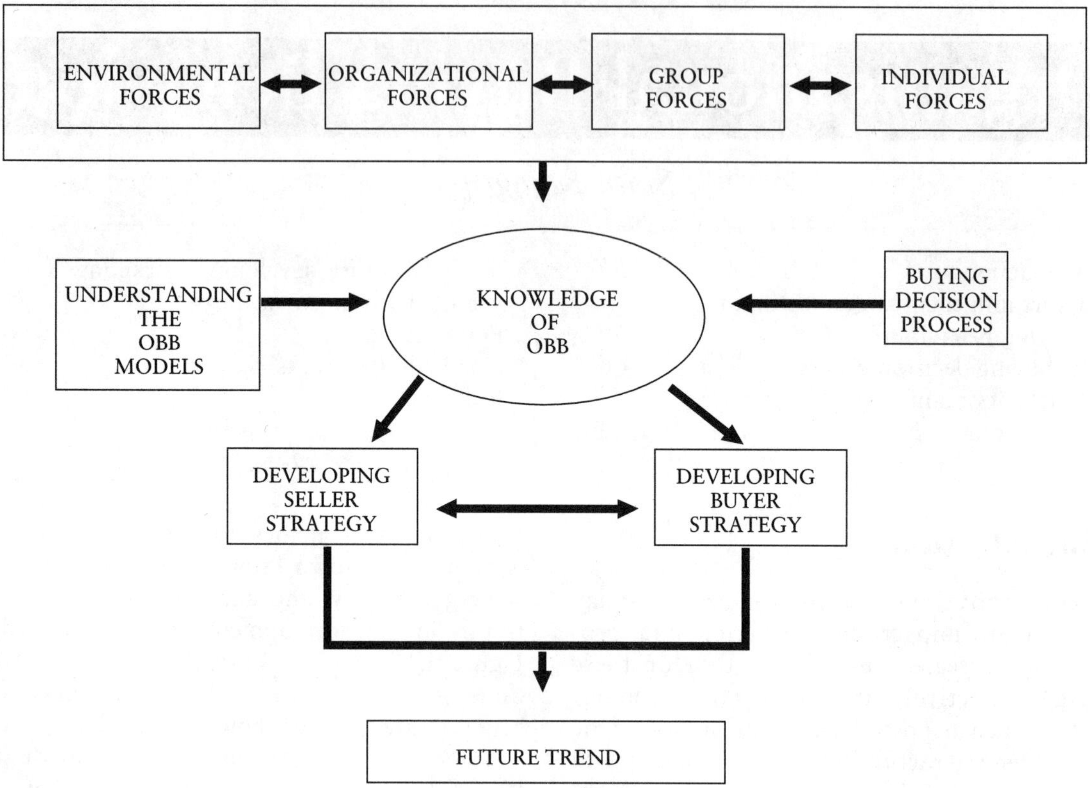

position and roles of members); and individual forces (e.g. preference of individual organisational members). Each of these areas constitutes a sphere of influence that encircles organisational buying decisions.

□ *Environmental forces*

Organisational buyers do not make decisions in isolation, but instead are influenced by a broad range of forces in the external environment. These environmental forces embody a set of constraints and opportunities that can significantly influence the nature, direction and timing of organisational buying decisions. A projected change in business conditions, a technological development, or a new piece of legislation can drastically alter organisational buying plans. Collectively, such environmental influences define the boundaries within which industrial buyers and sellers interact. Six

types of environmental forces influence organisational buying behaviour: economic, political, legal, cultural, physical and technological.

Economic influences

The general condition of the economy is reflected in the level of economic growth, employment, price stability and income as well as the availability of resources, money and credit. Because of the derived nature of demand in the industrial market, the marketer must also be sensitive to the strength of demand in the ultimate consumer market. The demand for many industrial products fluctuates more widely than the general economy.

Political and legal influences

The political environment includes tariffs and trade agreements with other countries, government funding of selected programmes and

Figure 5.2. *Factors influencing organisational buying behaviour*

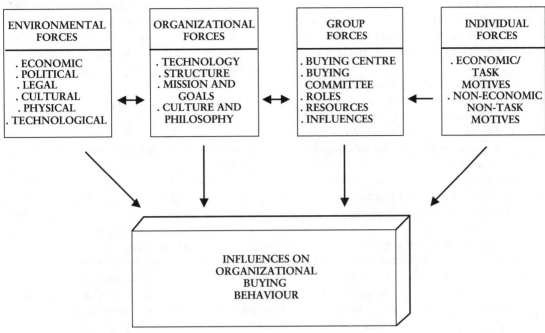

Source: Adapted from F. E. Webster and Y. Wind, 'A General Model of Organisational Buying Behaviour', *Journal of Marketing* 36 (1972), pp. 12–19.

government attitudes towards business and social activities.

Culture

Human decision making is greatly affected by the culture in which it operates. Culture can be thought of as the means and methods of coping with the environment that are shared by people as members of society and are passed from one generation to another. Culture as reflected in values, morals, customs, habits, norms, traditions and so on will influence the structure and functioning of the organisation and the way members of the organisation feel and act toward one another and various aspects of the environment (Webster and Wind, 1972).

Physical influences

The physical environment which also affects organisational buying decisions includes such factors as climate and geographical location of

the organisation. The availability of labour, selected raw materials, and the transportation services often play dominant roles in the initial selection of a location by an organisation. In turn, suppliers that are located in close proximity to the buying organisation often have an advantage in the vendor selection process, particularly when procurement requirements necessitate a close buyer-seller relationship. Thus, the physical environment defines the constraints and options that surround the specific buying tasks of an organisation.

Technological influences

Rapidly changing technology can restructure an industry and dramatically alter organisation buying plans and influences the composition of the decision making unit in the buying organisation (Bonoma and Zaltman, 1978). Existing and projected technological changes are given careful attention in the organisational buying process as they may affect the whole structure and competition in the industry. Technical and engineering personnel tend to play a more significant role and marketers also get more involved so as to adapt their marketing strategy to the new technological environment (Bright, 1970).

Researches by Spekman and Stern (1979) and Spekman (1979) identify the role of the purchasing agent as becoming more centrally co-ordinated in an uncertain environment. As purchasing is the 'eyes and ears' of the supply market, and has the ability to collect and analyse information for top management, the researchers highlight the importance of monitoring key environmental trends and tracing their impact on the organisational buying process.

Collectively, these environmental influences define the general business conditions, the political and legal setting, the availability of products and services, and the values and norms that encircle the specific buying actions of organisations. In addition, the environment provides a stream of information to the buying organisation. Marketing communications directed toward the buying organisation constitutes a particularly important information source.

☐ *Organisational forces*

Organisational factors affecting business buying behaviour relate to the buying organisation itself. The organisation's structure, its buying technology, its mission and goals, and its culture and philosophy. Insight into the domain of the decision makers can unravel the complex organisational forces that interplay within any given firm.

Organisational structure

The position of the purchasing function within the organisational structure strongly influences the nature and direction of buying behaviour, in particular to the management of the company's operations (Webster, 1991). An organisation that centralises procurement decisions at regional division, or headquarters level will approach purchasing differently from a company that is decentralised with purchasing decisions made at individual user locations. A marketer who is sensitive to these organisational influences can more accurately map the decision-making process, isolate buying influentials, identify salient buying criteria and target marketing strategy.

Centralisation v. decentralisation

Several important differences in buying behaviour emerge when centralised and decentralised procurement functions are compared. First, centralisation leads to purchasing specialisation. Purchasing specialists who concentrate their attention on selected items develop comprehensive knowledge of supply/demand conditions, vendor options, cost factors affecting the supply industry, and other relevant information concerning the supply environment. This knowledge, coupled with the significant volume of business that centralised procurement functions control, enhances their buying strength such as negotiating lower prices and standardising the products that are used across the whole company so as to obtain quantity discounts and improve their supplier options.

Second, the priority given to selected buying criteria is also influenced by the organisational location of the purchasing function. By identifying the organisational domain that the buyer represents, the marketer can generally identify the purchasing manager's objectives. Centralised purchasing units have placed more weight on long-term supply availability and the development of a healthy supplier base. Organisational buying behaviour is influenced to an important degree by the measures and regulatory system that an organisation employs in monitoring the performance of an organisational unit.

Third, the personal selling skills of the sales force and the brand preferences of users influence purchasing decisions to a greater degree at user locations than at centralised buying locations. Buyers in these local offices are likely to be very concerned with issues that are important to local managers, such as reliability of deliveries and ease of using products. The conflicting priorities that exist between central buyers and local users often lead to conflict in the buying organisation. In identifying demand at the user level, the marketer should assess the potential for such conflict and attempt to develop a strategy that can resolve the differences between the two organisational units.

The organisation of the marketer's selling strategy should parallel the organisation of the purchasing function of key accounts in the market. The marketer will interact with centralised purchasers that have plants in several different territories of the seller. Decisions made at a central level would involve and affect several organisational units in both the buying and selling firms. To avoid disjointed selling activities and internal conflict in the sales organisation, well-conceived policies and a carefully co-ordinated marketing strategy are required.

Buying technology

There are many dimensions to buying technology. Two dimensions of technological issues can be considered with specific reference to OBB. First, to a large extent a customer company is not simply buying products from a supplier, but buying the technologies on which that product is based. These include the suppliers' skill and knowledge in developing, designing, and manufacturing the product. No buying company can know everything about what goes into its products, and so it relies on the technology of the suppliers. For example, an automobile manufacturer relies on the technical knowledge of the makers to contribute to the road holding and safety of its vehicles. It also relies on the technology of fuel injection equipment manufacturers to ensure the performance and economy of its engines.

In contrast, when the automobile manufacturer buys steel, it may be quite confident in knowing exactly what type of steel is right for its particular applications, but it probably knows little about precisely how that steel is made. Thus the way in which a company buys a product, and indeed what it buys, are strongly affected by its level of knowledge of the technologies on which the product is based.

The way in which a company buys will also depend on whether the product has been designed by the company or by a supplier. When the buying company has developed its own design for a component, it will seek suppliers that are willing to make to its design (custom/tailor made) and are able to offer the best combination of quality, service, price and delivery. Under these circumstances, the buying company will not need, nor will it be willing to pay for, the design skills, or product technology, of the seller. Instead, it will be paying for the seller's skill in manufacturing the product to the appropriate standards and consistency, i.e. their process technology (Ford 1988). Some companies decide to rely as much as possible on their own technologies. Thereby they increase their research and development costs but hope to reduce the cost of what they buy. Others rely much more on the skill and inventiveness of their suppliers and develop close and long term relations with them.

Secondly, the buying technology employed by an organisation influences the nature of the organisational decision-making process. One of the most important technological developments in organisational purchasing is the application of electronic data processing (EDP) to the procurement function. The objective of these computer-based purchasing systems is to improve the quality of managerial purchasing decisions by improving the decision maker's ability to handle and process information. Essentially, the computer system expands the memory of the buying organisation by strong relevant data that may be retrieved and profitably applied to future purchasing decisions. Computers often provide management with the following information:

1. Vendor price and address files.
2. Purchase history data.
3. Purchase usage data.
4. Receiving and invoicing information.
5. Inventory control data.

The computer system is especially useful in straight rebuy situations. Such routine purchases can be handled faster and more economically by the computer than by the purchasing staff.

Further, computerised decision-making capability allows the purchasing agent to quickly dispense with routine purchases, thereby providing time for a more thorough evaluation of possible vendors in more complex buying situations. Likewise, the purchasing agent can devote more time to direct negotiation with potential suppliers and assume an expanded role in inter-departmental activities in the organisation.

Finally, the introduction of the computer into purchasing influences vendor selection decisions of buying organisation. The computer-assisted buyer engages in a more intensive search for potential suppliers but concentrates orders with fewer vendors. Thus the addition of the computer to the purchasing function leads to a reduction in the number of suppliers utilised by the buying organisation.

Mission and goals

Increasingly, business buyers are adopting an approach to suppliers that is much closer to that of the Japanese (Burt and Doyle, 1993; Christopher *et al.*, 1991). This approach involves making longer term commitment to suppliers to achieve value and quality improvement, as opposed to frequently changing suppliers to achieve a short term price advantage. These two different approaches have many implications for the relationship between selling and buying companies and mean that the business marketer must examine in great detail the strategy and the specific purchasing mission, goals and tasks of the particular buying company. Thus, business marketing is less about assembling a marketing mix that is then offered to a wide, undifferentiated and relatively passive market than it is about tailoring the marketer offering to the precise requirement of each customer company.

Culture and philosophy

The final organisational factor affecting buying decisions is the corporate culture, philosophy and motivation of the organisation and its individual personnel or 'actors' involved in the decision. Baker (1980), defined corporate culture as 'an interrelated set of beliefs, shared by most of an organisation's members, about how people should behave at work and what tasks and goals are important'.

While an organisation's corporate culture can be due to a company's development over a long period of time, the current emphasis of a company's top management may also go a long way in determining what things are more important or stressed by the organisation. A key element in the development of a corporate culture may be the backgrounds of key executives in the organisation. We can expect managers to have different attitudes to buying depending on whether they consider themselves technologists or marketers. Their attitudes will also be different if they are more concerned about the long term development of their company or its short term profit. Thus we may expect a very particular set of requirements from a buying company in which the attitude of the management is centred on product excellence, such as Mercedes-Benz. Individuals involved in making purchase decisions in such companies will tend to emphasise product reliability and performance rather than price. A study of the company's corporate culture by the purchasing personnel should enable them to respond and adapt to the dominant function or emphasis in their company allowing purchasing to shift to a strategic role and influence the buying decision.

□ Group forces

The organisation buying process typically involves a complex set of smaller decisions which are made or influenced by several individuals (Thomas, 1982; Wind, 1976). Multiple buying influences or group forces play a critical role in organisational buying decisions. The degree of involvement of group members in the procurement process varies from routine rebuys, where the purchasing agent takes into account the preference of others, to complex new task buying situations, where a group plays an active role throughout the decision process. The group force influencing business buying behaviour relates to the *buying centre* (Johnston and Spekman, 1982;

Johnston and Bonoma, 1981; Johnston, 1981; Wind, 1978).

The *buying centre*, consists of all organisation members involved in the purchase decision, either consciously or unconsciously. The size of the buying centre varies, but on the average, buying centres will include more than four persons per purchase (Van Der Most, 1976).

The marketer needs to know the *roles performed by different members* of the buying centre and the *resources* available to them to help make their purchase decision. The composition of the buying centre is affected by the purchase situation. Thus, the buying centre tends to evolve during the purchasing process, and it tends to vary from firm to firm.

A central task for the marketer is to identify the organisational members that will constitute the buying centre for the particular product. Such knowledge is crucial for well targeted personal selling and marketing communications. A marketer can also predict the composition of the buying centre by projecting the impact that the industrial product will have on different functional areas in the buying organisation (Corey, 1978). If the procurement decision will affect the marketability of a firm's product (e.g. product design, price), the marketing department will play an active role in the decision process.

Members of the buying centre assume several different roles throughout the procurement process. These roles, which are defined in Table 5.1 include users, influencers, buyers, deciders and gatekeepers. It is important to remember that one person could assume all roles in a purchase situation or each individual could assume a different buying role.

The buying centre's purchase decisions are influenced by the resources that the centre has available to aid in decision making. These resources include information and expertise. Some companies have a purchasing research department that is able to assist in the buying process by assessing supply markets, product trends, and the characteristics of individual suppliers and products. But in many companies purchase research is less well developed than is market research. When purchase research is undeveloped, the business buyer is likely to be more dependent on suppliers for information and will have more difficulty in evaluating different competing offerings (Hardwick and Ford, 1988).

Corey (1978a) and Thomas and Grashaf (1982) emphasise the influence of purchasing on the buying centre's procurement decisions. They state that purchasing assumes a relatively powerful position when the design of the purchased product is established and vendors have been qualified. Likewise, purchasing is dominant in repetitive buying situations through technical expertise, knowledge of the dynamics of the supplying industry, and close working relationships with individual suppliers. Factors that contribute to purchasing's strength include: (1) its level of technical competence and credibility, (2) its base of relevant information, (3) its base for top management support, and (4) its organisational status as an authority in selected procurement areas (Strauss 1962). Attention should centre on the relative importance of purchasing in a particular buying situation and in a particular organisational context.

□ *Individual forces*

Business purchases are not made by companies but by individuals within those companies. Thus, attention must ultimately centre on individual behaviour within the organisational context. This means that we need to understand the requirements and motivations of these individuals, as well as those that are stated by the company. These motives can be divided into two broad categories. *Economic* or *task* motives represent factors that are important to the firm and can usually be quantified and measured by the individuals. These include cost savings, productivity improvements, and motives related to the long-term well-being of the firm. *Non-economic* or *non-task* motives are factors that may be important to the firm and in most circumstances significant to the individuals making the purchase decision, but are difficult to quantify. They include status or prestige for the firm or buyer,

Table 5.1.   *Buying centre roles defined*

ROLE	DESCRIPTION
USER	As the role name implies, these are the personnel who will be using the product in question. Users may have anywhere from inconsequential to an extremely important influence on the purchase decision. In some cases, the users initiate the purchase action by requesting the product. They may even develop the product specifications.
GATEKEEPERS	Gatekeepers control information to be reviewed by other members of the buying centre. The control of information may be in terms of disseminating printed information or advertisements or though controlling which salesperson will speak to which individuals in the buying centre. To illustrate, the purchasing agent might perform this screening role by opening the gate to the buying centre for some sales personnel and closing it to others.
INFLUENCERS	These individuals affect the purchasing decision by supplying information for the evaluation of alternatives or by setting buying specifications. Typically, technical personnel, such as engineers, quality control personnel and research and development personnel and individuals outside of the buying organisation can assume this role (e.g. an engineering consultant or an architect who writes very tight building specifications.).
DECIDERS	Deciders are the individuals who actually make the buying decision, whether or not they have the formal authority to do so. The identity of the decider is the most difficult role to determine: buyers may have formal authority to buy, but the president of the firm may actually make the decision. A decider could be a design engineer who develops a set of specifications that only one vendor can meet.
BUYERS	The buyer has formal authority for selecting a supplier and implementing all procedures connected with securing the product. The power of the buyer is often usurped by more powerful members of the organisation. Often the buyer's role is assumed by the purchasing agent, who executes the clerical functions associated with a purchase order.

Source: Adapted from F. E. Webster and Y. Wind, *Organisational Buying Behaviour*, Englewood Cliffs, NJ: Prentice-Hall (1972), pp. 77–80.

career motives for the individuals, the organisational politics, ethics, friendship and social needs. Figure 5.3 depicts these motives affecting the individual buyers.

■ The buying decision process

Buying decisions do not just happen, they represent a complex set of activities engaged in by many members of the buying organisations and result in a commitment to purchase goods and services from a vendor. Buying is not an event. It is an organisational decision-making process, the result of which is a contracted obligation. As part of that

process, individual participants in the process must each arrive at their own conclusions and decisions with respect to the purchasing problem.

The buying decision process varies widely. Table 5.2 shows a simplified version of the Robinson, Faris and Wind *Buygrid* which helps categorise the process in different circumstances. The buygrid is widely used in business to make sense of different types of purchasing and the process which these purchases go through. The buygrid will be used to examine the categories of purchases, known as the 'buy classes' or 'buying situations' and the different types of products – and the stages in the buying process, known as the buy phases.

Figure 5.3. *Economic and non-economic motives influencing business buyer*

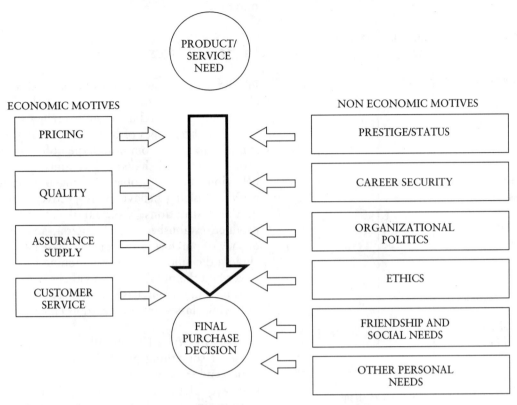

Derived in part from T. L. Power, *Modern Business Marketing*, St Paul, Minnesota: West Publishing Co. (1991).

□ *Buying decision phases*

The process of buying decision is not made in isolation by the buying company alone. Instead, it is a process of interaction between the buying company and potential suppliers, which will be seeking to influence the process to their advantage. These suppliers can be separated into the in-supplier, who is already supplying the company, and the out-suppliers who are trying to displace the in-supplier. One of the path breaking studies of the buying decision process in industrial organisations defined eight phases in the process (Robinson, Faris and Wind, 1967):

1. Need recognition.
2. Definition of characteristics and quantity needed.
3. Establishment of specifications to guide the procurement.
4. Identification of potential sources.
5. Evaluation of alternatives.
6. Selection of suppliers.
7. Select an order routine.
8. Performance feed back and evaluation.

In an actual purchase, however, the buy phases are not clear cut. The marketer who wishes to influence the buyer often faces the difficult task of finding out exactly which stage the buying company is at in the buying process. However, for the buying organisation, these activities are distinct phases in the purchasing process. For example, it was found that phase three, development of the specifications to guide the procurement, was a distinct step involving translating the

Table 5.2.   *The buying decision process by classes*

Buy Phases	Buy Classes		
	Straight Rebuy	Modified Rebuy	New Task
Need Recognition			
Defined Characteristics and quantity needed			
Establish Specification			
Identification of potential sources			
Evaluation of alternatives			
Selection of Suppliers			
Select order routine			
Performance feedback and evaluation			

Source: P. J. Robinson, C. W. Faris and F. Wind, *Industrial Buying and Creative Marketing*, Boston: Allyn & Bacon Inc. and Marketing Science Institute Series (1967), pp. 13–18.

defined need for purchased goods or services into a detailed and precise description of the desired characteristics for potential vendors. Also, this stage contains a specific opportunity for the industrial marketer to become involved in the procurement process in a way that gives it some competitive advantage, such as when the specifications are developed to include specific product features where a certain potential vendor has unique capability.

An analytical description of the buying decision process is potentially useful to the industrial marketer in developing a selling strategy, since it defines the target for its efforts, the steps through which it must respond to the buyer's needs for information. Figure 5.4 illustrates the buying phases and the various considerations to be given by the buyer and seller. It is the sequence of activities that must be completed before a buying commitment is made by the purchasing organisation

and then, perhaps, reaffirmed through repeat purchases.

☐ *Buy classes*

Purchases may be categorised into three buy classes according to the newness of the buying situation: straight rebuy, modified rebuy and new task. The three types of buying situation are very similar to the common type of consumer problem-solving behaviour – routinised response behaviour, limited problem solving and extensive problem solving behaviour, respectively. In each of these situations, risk, familiarity with the product, established choice criteria, and the frequency of purchase affect the purchase pattern including the amount of information needed by the buyer and the number of individuals who will be consulted in the purchase process. The three types of buying classes are compared in Figure 5.5.

Straight Rebuy: This usually involves the purchase of something purchased before, from the same vendor as before, although purchase terms may vary slightly. There will be little risk perception in these instances and the purchase decisions will be taken by lower management. Such purchases can be computerised and handled in a completely routine fashion with the triggering mechanism set at a specified inventory level or a certain day of the month.

Modified Rebuy: The company already has prior experience of the product but the particular purchase situation demands some degree of novelty. Thus it may include search for information about alternative sources of supply and terms, due to different specifications in a product or service that has been bought before, there will be less evaluation than when the buyer has no experience or skill in the purchase, as in a new task situation, but much more than in a straight rebuy.

New Task: This situation involves the purchase of something not purchased before, with all the stages of the buying decision process involved. In these more complex decisions, the earlier stages

Figure 5.4 *The buying process consideration*

Buying Phases	Buyer Consideration	Seller Consideration
Need Recognition ⬇	Identification of need by primary area	Need creation, understanding primary area motives
Need Definition ⬇	Definition of product or service to satisfy need	Presence with customer
Establishment of specifications ⬇	Firms specifications development. Involvement of other areas	Can influence specifications. Understanding secondary area motive
Identification of sources ⬇	Determination of possible vendors	Presence in market place. Ongoing contact with company
Evaluation of alternatives ⬇	Providing supplier with firm specifications request	Meeting or influencing specifications and requests
Selection of Suppliers ⬇	Determination of best overall solution	Continuing contact with buyer
Selection of order routine ⬇	Implementation by purchasing	Response as agreed upon; close contact
Performance feedback and evaluation	Evaluation of product and vendor	Corrections as required, or new opportunity not previously identified

of the buying process take on relatively greater importance, whereas the later stages receive more emphasis in straight and modified rebuy situations. Consequently perceived risk will be high and purchase decisions will be more likely to be made by senior management.

A more recent study by Anderson, Chu and Weitz (1987) provided empirical support for the buy class framework. They found a strong association of newness with the amount of information desired and processed by decision makers, but only a weak correlation of these two measures

with the tendency for the buyer to consider new sources. Thus, they concluded that task newness and information needs, but not consideration of alternatives, define the buy classes. They also found that sales forces that frequently encounter New Task buying situations observe the 'buying centre' (the collection of organisational actors involved in the purchase) to be:

- large
- slow to decide
- uncertain about its needs and the appropriateness of the possible solutions

Figure 5.5.   *Comparison of buying classes*

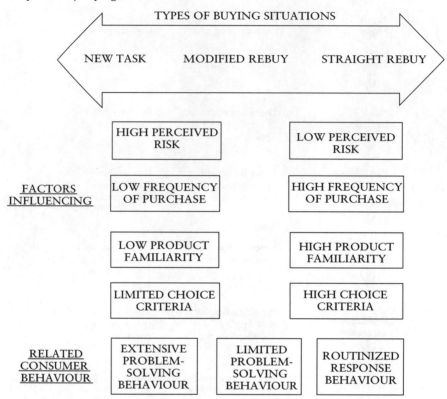

- more concerned about finding a good solution than getting a low price or assured supply
- more willing to entertain proposals from 'out' suppliers and less willing to favour 'in' suppliers'
- more influenced by technical personnel
- less influenced by purchasing agents.

In contrast, the sales forces commonly facing a more routine (straight and modified rebuy) buying situations described buying centres with just the opposite characteristics:

- small
- quick to decide
- confident in their appraisal of the problem and possible solutions
- concerned about price and supply
- satisfied with 'in' vendors
- more influenced by purchasing agents.

These findings tend to support the earlier conclusion of Robinson, Faris and Wind that the features of the buying situation are more important than the type of product in determining industrial buying behaviour. Although other researchers have come to the opposite conclusion (Bellizzi and McVey, 1983), for most observers, the buy class framework has a good deal of face validity. Table 5.3 shows in summary, the buying decision process in practice. The table comprises some of the distinctive features of fourteen different purchases in the new task, modified/rebuy, and straight rebuy classes (Doyle, Woodside and Michell, 1979). In these examples, a new task/ modified rebuy purchase took as long as five years to complete, there were as many as six people in the buying centre, different people were the initiators of the buying process, in the different buy classes, and different factors were critical in choosing among suppliers.

Table 5.3. *Characteristics of the business buying process for different buy class*

Characteristics of buying process	Buy class and number of purchases	
	New, Task/Modified, Rebuy (n = 7)	Straight Rebuy (n = 7)
Length of time	7 months–5 years	1 week–7 months
Number in buying center	3–6 members	2–3 members
Source of contact with suppliers	Buyer, plant or project manager, engineer	Buyer
Initiators of buying process	Manager, other suppliers, engineers	Buyer, user
Critical factors in purchase	Price, product, performance, delivery, guarantee	Delivery, price, terms of payment
Composition of buying center	Fluctuates	Buyer and fluctuates
Reasons for supplier contact by customers	Modifications desired, incapable suppliers, dissatisfaction	Depletion of stocks, dissatisfaction
Postpurchase evaluation	Informal	Informal

Source: P. Doyle, A. G. Woodside and P. C. Michell, 'Organisations Buying in New Tasks and Rebuy Situations', *Industrial Marketing Management* 8 (1979), pp. 7–11.

Types of buyer–seller relationships

One way to understand business marketing and characterising the purchase situation is to see it as establishing and developing relationships between buyers and sellers. This means, for example the business marketer has the task of managing this relationship, and each purchase and delivery of goods is just one, albeit very important, episode in such a relationship. Each episode is affected by the overall relationship with the supplier and in turn may affect the whole relationship. Webster (1991) stress the importance of time as a dimension in the buyer seller relationship. The concept of time was identified in a continuum of extremely short term orientation to very long term orientation (see Figure 5.6).

As buying relationships move along this continuum from pure transactions through increased buyer–seller interdependence to downward integration, there are three things to observe. First, the movement is from complete reliance on market forces in pure transactions, to achieve lower prices and to minimise cost, to the virtual absence of market forces in downward integration. Secondly, the buyer is incurring additional administrative costs and increased dependency in return for a set of benefits relating to quality, reliability, and service. Finally, it is interesting to consider that the movement is away from pure 'buy' toward the decision to 'make' the product or service within the customer organisation itself. However in recent times, due to high interest rates, high inflation and the need to map access to technology are influencing firms to form strategic relationship/partnerships with supplying companies. In the 1990s the emphasis is towards forming such partnerships. Ford (1989) assigned three dimensions to a buyer–seller relationship: width, depth and closeness.

The *width* signified the range of activities in the relationship. This in turn is a function of the capabilities which bring the parties together. For example, a narrow relationship may be built upon a single standardised component delivered regularly. A broader relationship may involve many different products, delivery patterns, service

Figure 5.6. *The continuum of industrial buying situations*

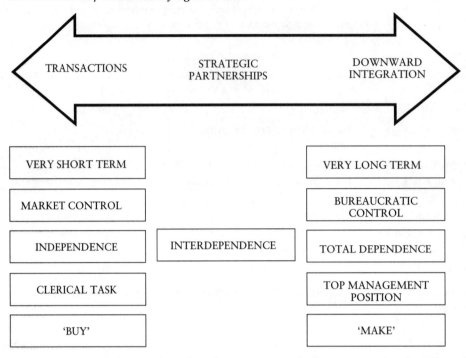

Source: Adapted in part from F. E. Webster, *Industrial Marketing Strategy,* 3rd edition, New York: John Wiley and Sons (1991), p. 34.

back up, etc. These aspects may or may not be specifically tailored to the requirements of either party. Some of these aspects may be basic technologies of either party, for example they may use the industry's normal production process or involve a generic product. Alternatively they may be distinctive and unique to the providing company. It is important to note that a relationship does not always require a distinctive technology. Very often, a seller company can be successful by assembling a package of basic product and process technologies which suit the requirements of particular partners and effectively delivering this tailored package (marketing technology).

The *depth* of a relationship is one where there is little separation into discrete or separate activities which are solely the responsibility of one or other partner. This has been referred to by Marrett (1971) as reciprocity. A deep relationship is one where interactions affects a considerable propor-tion of the decision making of both parties. Nevertheless, depth is multi-faceted. One party may welcome discussion in product specification but retain an absolute monopoly over decisions on the logistic flow between the components.

In a *close* relationship expectations of the likely behaviour of others are strongly held. This does not mean that the expected behaviour is desired – just that the parties 'know where they stand' in their dealings with the other. The relationship has a strong basis of shared meanings. Of course, strong expectations of undesired outcomes can quickly cause a relationship to disintegrate – unless an element of coercion is present. 'We have to put up with this supplier even though he is difficult, because he's the only one who can supply this product.' Perhaps more commonly, the shared expectations involve trust that the other party will provide what is required. Failure to live up to expectations of payment, or delivery timing can reduce closeness.

There are clear implications of the buyer/seller relationship model for the business marketer. The complexity of the buyer/seller relationship means that for a successful relationship to develop, a *relationship management* is needed. The marketer must develop and manage relationships with each customer company. As an out-supplier, the marketer must determine the nature of any inadequacies that a customer sees in its current supplier. On the other hand, the marketer must carefully measure and evaluate the sales effort, product, or production resources that it devotes to each of its customers, so that it can satisfy the customer's requirements while not allowing the customer to take those resources for granted. Even more important, a seller must not let its relationship with a customer become fixed and unresponsive, and hence provide the buyer with an incentive to seek another supplier. As well as the operational management of a single relationship, marketers have a strategic management task in dealing with all the company's portfolio of relationships. A sales person involved in detailed interaction with customers may have difficulty in seeing each relationship in a wider perspective. An overall marketing view must be taken of how the company will allocate its resources and efforts among different customers, including such decisions as for which customers it should use its limited product development facilities, for which it should change its production schedules and on which it should concentrate it's sales and service efforts. The basis of this strategy is an audit of the company's relationships.

The *relationship audit* as described by Gross *et al.* (1993) involves answers to the following questions:

- What is the likely sales and profit potential of this relationship?
- What resources are required to fulfil this potential?
- Does the likely return justify this investment when compared with the potential in other relationships?
- Where do the threats to one development of this relationship come from?
- What is the contribution of this relationship to the company's overall operations? Does it provide a strong cash flow, is it the source of joint product development that will enhance the company's general market position, and does it provide entry for other similar customers?
- Are the current efforts devoted to this relationship appropriate to the company's overall strategy?
- Are we too dependent on this customer?
- Are our ways of dealing with this customer appropriate both to its needs and our strategy, or are they dealing based on habit or history?

Source: A. Gross, P. Benting, L. Meredith and D. Ford, *Business Marketing*, Boston: Houghton Mifflin Co. (1993), p. 99.

Models of organisational buyer behaviour

The purpose of modelling buyer behaviour is to clarify and understand the interaction between buyer and seller in a business market. Several models of business buying decision process have been developed in complex economic organisations. The various models tend to emphasise *economic* or *task attributes* and *non-economic* or *non-task* attributes as well as models that focus on several factors, sometimes including both task and non-task objectives. Models that focus on economic or task objectives look at economic criteria that can be measured and evaluated. For example, there are models that emphasise minimum price or the lowest cost possible. These models are valid within the area that they examine, although they do not take into account more subjective non-economic influences, such as career security. The second category of models, which focus on the non economic or personal considerations, are likewise constrained by the variables that they are examining. More complex models take both of these factors into account and attempt to view the buying processes from a much broader perspective.

These models offer valuable insights into the buying decision process and are useful to the industrial marketing strategist by describing that process in analytical and conceptual terms. Like all models, those describing the organisational buying decision process are simplifications of the true process but gain their strength and relevance by focusing on the most important variables and relationships among them.

Five models are presented here that provide an overview of the buying process: the Sheth model, the Webster and Wind model, the Anderson and Chambers reward/measurement model, the Choffray and Lilien model and the dyadic exchange model. The following sections discusses each briefly.

Individual and group decision making: the Sheth model

The Sheth model is based on the Howard and Sheth model of consumer buyer behaviour, although it incorporates a number of different considerations applicable for business markets. As demonstrated before, the consumer buying process in primarily one of individual behaviour, which is the orientation of the Howard and Sheth model. The Sheth model of business buyer behaviour has as its focus decision making among a group of individuals within an organisation. As seen in Figure 5.7, several major considerations are made in the model. Inputs to the individual decision makers or influencers include sources of information or marketing stimuli. These can be actively searched for and can be distorted in meaning by the individuals receiving the stimuli. Also, the background of the individuals, including their education and role orientation, can impact on their expectations. Within buying firms, it is common for business marketers to find highly different expectations of individuals which this model accounts for.

Decision making is depicted as being exercised either individually or jointly between people. This process is determined by such factors as the product being purchased, time pressure, perceived risk and company-specific factors, such as the size of the organisation and degree of centralisation. In the case of individual decision making, there is usually a low degree of risk involved. In group decisions, it may be a situation where one group within the organisation is dominant.

Group decision making, which is more commonly found in high risk decisions or in larger organisations, is also accounted for by the model. In group decision making, several methods may be utilised including problem solving and persuasion, where there is a basic agreement about goals. In the absence of goal agreement, bargaining or 'politicking' may be utilised to reach a final decision. This overall process results in the final outcome of the model, which is the supplier or brand choice decision. Also impacting this final decision are situational factors beyond the control of the organisation or the individual buyer.

Roles of the buyer: the Webster and Wind model

The Webster and Wind model of organisational buyer behaviour adds several elements that increase the understanding of the buying process. It begins with a set of factors that determine the need of the firm and the situation that the firm is in. These factors include the technical, economic, cultural, legal and political environment and in combination influence what are termed as a buying situation. Based on the needs of the organisation, a buying centre is created that goes about the purchase decision. The nature of the buying centre is based on the task at hand and involves people within the organisation who perform differing roles, including users, influencers, deciders, buyers, and gate keepers. The Webster and Wind model (see Figure 5.8) adds a substantial amount of information about the interpersonal aspects of business buyer behaviour. The Sheth model and Webster and Wind model provide insight into the structure and process of business buying. The Sheth model provides an ordered sequence of events, whereas the Webster and Wind models focuses on the many variables that influence the buying process. Both models can assist the business marketer in identifying the complexity of the decision process and the influences on business buyer behaviour.

Figure 5.7. *The Sheth model of business buyer behaviour*

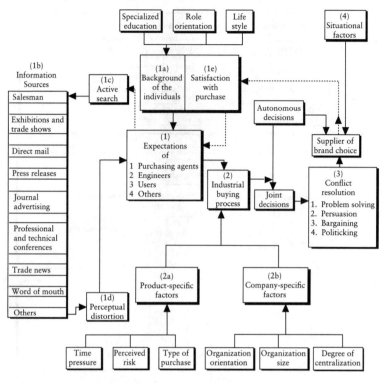

Source: J. N. Sheth, 'A Model of Industrial Buyer Behaviour', *Journal of Marketing* 37 (1973), pp. 50–56.

The Anderson Chambers reward measurement model

It is a central assertion of the Webster and Wind model that a key to understanding the functioning of the buying centre is to know how the measurement and reward systems of the organisation affect the behaviour of its members. Anderson and Chambers have developed a model of buying centre participants' motivation and decision involvement that extends this central idea more precisely (Anderson and Chambers, 1985). The reward/measurement model comprises two parts: the motivational component and the group consensus part. In the motivational component of the model, individual's job motivation and satisfaction are determined by both 'intrinsic' and 'extrinsic' rewards. With the intrinsic rewards, the nature of the work itself are im-

portant in satisfying oneself, like individual needs of a sense of accomplishment in completing a difficult task, self esteem and self actualisation.

The extrinsic rewards are determined by the performance measurement system of the organisation. This may be specific performance indexes which identify specific behaviours and outcomes that the organisation will consider when evaluating performance. A key issue is the extent to which such indexes are consistent with the person's view of how the job should be performed, whether all aspects of job performance are capture by the indexes, and the amount of error in the respective measurement. As a result, in the buying centre, there can be a major source of conflict as the participants will be using different criteria in evaluating product offerings and vendors, especially when the individuals come from different functions and departments within the organisation. In the group consensus part of

Figure 5.8. *The Webster and Wind model of organisational buyer behaviour*

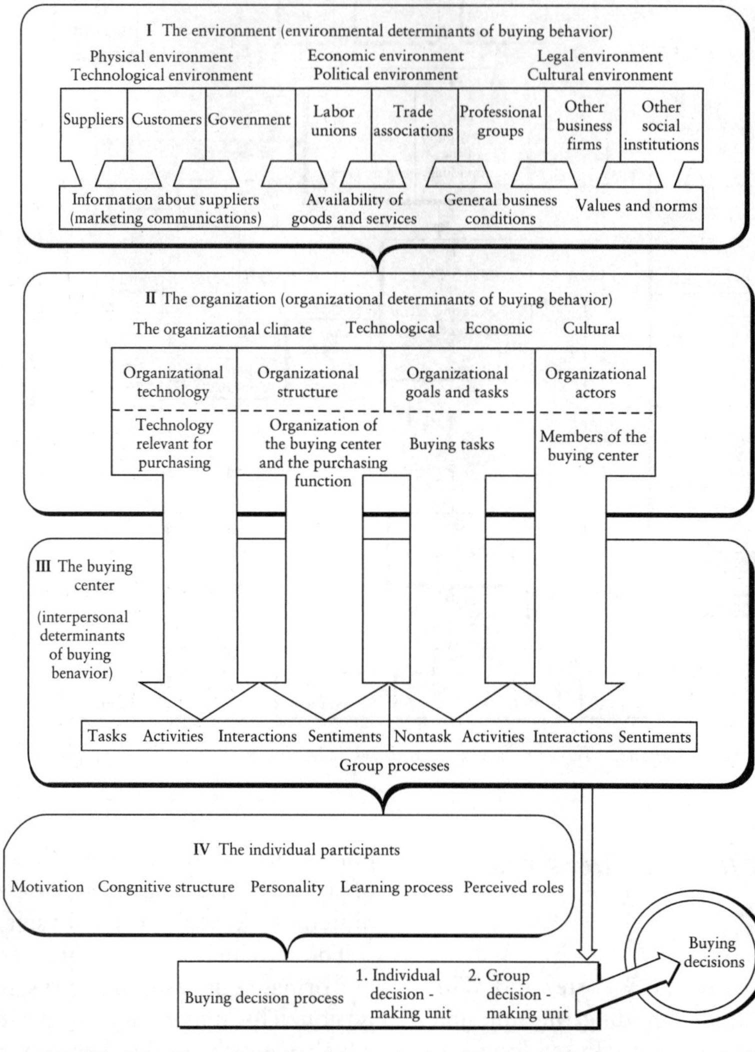

I The environment (environmental determinants of buying behavior)

Physical environment Economic environment Legal environment
Technological environment Political environment Cultural environment

| Suppliers | Customers | Government | Labor unions | Trade associations | Professional groups | Other business firms | Other social institutions |

Information about suppliers (marketing communications) Availability of goods and services General business conditions Values and norms

II The organization (organizational determinants of buying behavior)

The organizational climate Technological Economic Cultural

| Organizational technology | Organizational structure | Organizational goals and tasks | Organizational actors |

| Technology relevant for purchasing | Organization of the buying center and the purchasing function | Buying tasks | Members of the buying center |

III The buying center

(interpersonal determinants of buying behavior)

| Tasks | Activities | Interactions | Sentiments | Nontask | Activities | Interactions | Sentiments |

Group processes

IV The individual participants

Motivation Congnitive structure Personality Learning process Perceived roles

| Buying decision process | 1. Individual decision - making unit | 2. Group decision - making unit |

Buying decisions

Source: F. E. Webster and Y. Wind, 'A General Model of Organisational Buying Behaviour', *Journal of Marketing* 36 (1972), pp. 12–19.

the model, the individuals' 'preferred position' regarding a vendor's offering will be reflected back to the rewards and measurements offered by their primary work group (i.e. department or function). Participants bring these predisposition's into the group interaction and consensus formation process, which may take several forms, along the lines of the Sheth model described earlier. Another way of conceptualising the group decision process has been proposed by Choffray and Lilien.

☐ The Choffray and Lilien model

In the basic Choffrey and Lilien model (1978), the behaviour of the organisational buyers are influenced by environmental, organisational, group and individual factors. These spheres of influence have been discussed earlier. The Choffray and Lilien framework (Figure 5.9) focuses on the relationship between an organisation's buying centre and three major stages in the individual purchase decision process through:

i   The screening of alternatives which do not meet organisational requirements;
ii the formation of decision participants' preferences;
iii the formation of organisational preferences.

Further, Choffray and Lilien (1980) proposed seven formal models of the multi person decision making that produces organisational/group choices:

Model 1: The weighted probability model

The weighted probability model assumes that the buying centre is likely to adopt a given vendor-product alternative in proportion to the relative importance of the buying centre members. The weighted probability model is:

$$P_G(a_o) = \sum D_{d=1} W_d P_d(a_o)$$

Model 2: The equiprobability model

The equiprobability model is a special case of the weighted probability model. Each decision participant is given equal weight – for a three person group, each participant would be assigned a weight of 0.33 – and the weights sum to 1.0.

Model 3: The autocracy model

Another special case of the weighted probability model is the autocracy model. This is a 'key in-

Figure 5.9. *Major elements of organisational buying behaviour of Choffray and Lilien model*

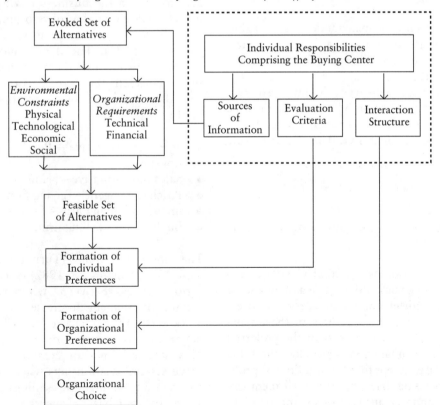

Source: J. M. Choffray and G. L. Lilien, 'Assessing Response to Industrial Marketing Strategy', *Journal of Marketing* 42 (1978), p. 22.

formant' model because the most important member of the buying centre is given a weight of 1.0 and other members are given a weight of 0.0. This model represents the current norm for industrial marketing research studies, i.e. that one individual's preferences represent those of the buying organisation.

Model 4: The voting model

The voting model does not include a weighting factor for buying centre members. It states that the probability that the group will choose a vendor product alternative $[P_G (A_o)]$ is the likelihood that the alternative (A_o) receives the highest preference score versus any other alternative in the set of vendor-product alternatives.

Model 5: The minimum endorsement model – majority rule

The minimum endorsement model assumes that in order to be accepted by a firm, a product alternative has to be the choice of a prespecified number (quota) of participants involved in the decisions. For a majority rule, at least two members of a three person buying centre must be in favour of a vendor-product before it can be assigned a choice probability. The majority rule model is:

$$P_G(a_o) = \Pi D_{d=1} P_d(a_o)/\Sigma J_{j=0} \Pi D \ d=1 \ P_d (a_j)$$

Model 6: The minimum endorsement model – unanimity rule

The unanimity model is a second version of the minimum endorsement model. The assignment of choice probabilities to vendor product alternatives requires that all members of the buying centre agree in their judgements of the preferred alternatives. The unanimity model has the same form as model 5 except that the conditional probability is now calculated based on all members reaching unanimity in vendor-product judgements rather than a simple majority.

Model 7: The preference perturbation model

The preference perturbation model assumes that if a group does not reach unanimity, it is most likely to choose the alternative that perturbs individual preferences least. The preference perturbation model is:

$$P_G (A_o) = \Sigma P_G (A_{o1} \ Yw) \times Pr \ [Yw]$$

Individual and organisation interaction: the dyadic exchange model and the interaction model

The dyadic approach to understanding business buyer behaviour focuses on the smallest interactions within the business buying framework, namely, the interaction of two units that should be individuals, firms, or businesses. (Bonoma and Johnston, 1978). The **dyadic model** of buyer behaviour also focuses on the exchanges that take place between the two parties. This model considers five basic dyadic relationship (Figure 5.10):

- Sales representative – Purchasing agent relationship.
- Sales representative – Selling firm.
- Purchasing agent – Buying firm.
- Images of buying firm – Images of selling firm.
- Buying firm – Selling firm.

The *interaction model* (Turnbull and Cunningham, 1981; Hakansson, 1982) is seen as an interaction process between two parties within a certain environment. It stresses the necessity that marketers are perceptive and flexible in the definition and satisfaction of customer needs. This is done by placing greater emphasis on the processes and relationships which occur between and within buying and selling organisations. There are four basic elements in the interaction model (Hakansson, 1982):

Figure 5.10. *A dyadic model of buyer behaviour*

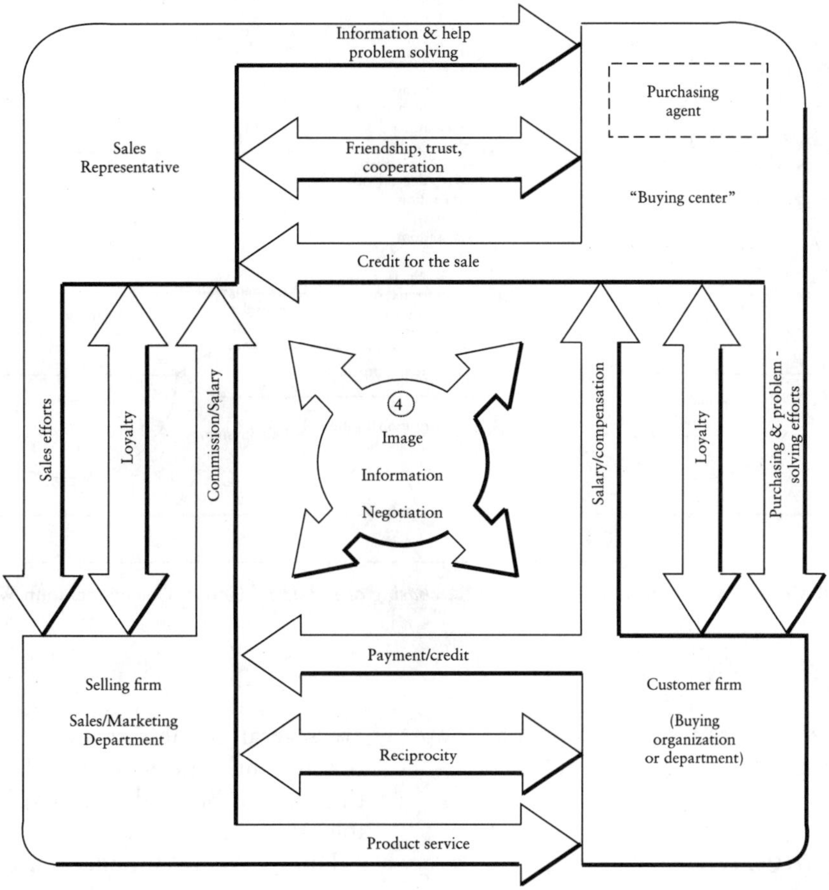

Source: T. V. Bonoma and W. J. Johnston, 'The Social Psychology of Industrial Buying and Selling', *Industrial Marketing Management* (1978), pp. 213–224.

- The interaction process
- The participants in the interaction process
- The environment within which interaction takes place
- The atmosphere affecting and affected by the interaction.

Figure 5.11 illustrates the different variables in the interaction model. The model shows the short-term and long-term aspects of the interaction process between buying and selling companies. The short-term exchange episodes involve product service, financial, information, and social exchange. These are separated from the longer term processes of adaptations and institutionalisation.

Implications for developing marketing and procurement strategy

The study of OBB is not purely a theoretical exercise. The knowledge of OBB's subject when applied can be a significant input to practice for both marketing and purchasing managers when designing their strategy. The following section

Figure 5.11.   *The interaction model*

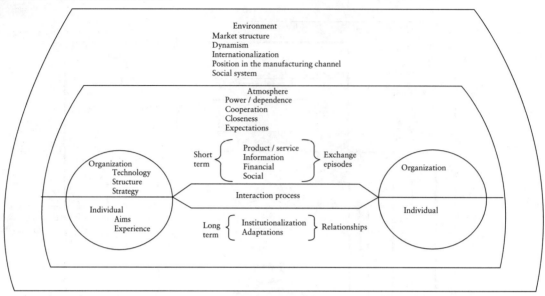

Source: The IMP Group, *International Marketing and Purchasing of Industrial Goods,* Chichester: John Wiley (1982).

will examine the practical implication of developing a marketing and purchasing strategy.

□ *Marketing strategy*

The marketing strategy for a firm in the business market is that of a supplier's strategy. There are two types of supplier to an organisation. The 'in' supplier, who is already supplying to a particular company. The other is the 'out' suppliers, who are trying to get into and sell to the buying organisation. At the outset, the 'in' supplier has more advantages than an 'out' supplier. These include, the knowledge of the buying organisation, knowing who's important and who's not and what motivates the purchase. The perceived risk felt by the buying organisation is less, and the cost of search is also minimal or none. Against these odds, the out supplier needs to compete. Their primary objective would be to get credibility with the buying organisation. When the business marketer is developing marketing strategies in the context of the buying situations, there

are several possible strategic responses for both the 'in' and 'out' suppliers. Table 5.4 (based on the original Buygrid research) indicates the possible strategic responses.

Firstly, the 'in' supplier must keep the buyer in a straight rebuy situation. It can do this, by dealing with the customer problems efficiently and making sure its performance is up to scratch. The buyer may go to modified rebuy situation, due to technological development that allows one product to be substituted for another one of better performance or a product can be made much more cheaply. In either situation, the 'in' supplier strategy will include, monitoring the competitors' moves, i.e. keep track of its own industry and what are being offered, ensuring that its product range is always competitive.

The 'in' supplier can take the initiative and suggest a new modified product, so as to 'shut the door' on rival 'out' suppliers. However, for the new buy situation, both 'in' and 'out' suppliers tend to start together, but 'in' supplier tend to be favoured because of perceived risk. On the other hand, buyers may have doubts on capability of

Table 5.4. *Seller's strategic responses to differing buying situations*

	Supplier Status	
Buying Situations	*In Supplier*	*Out Supplier*
New Task	Monitor changing emerging purchasing needs in organisation.	
	Isolate specific needs	Isolate specific needs
	If possible, participate actively in early phases of buying process by supplying information and technical advice.	If possible, participate actively in early phases of buying process by supplying information and technical advice.
Straight Rebuy	Reinforced buyer/seller relationship by meeting organisations expectations.	Convince organisation that the potential benefits of re-examining requirements and suppliers exceed the costs.
	Be alert and responsive to changing needs of customer	Attempt to gain a position on organisation's preferred list of suppliers, even as a second or third choice.
Modified Rebuy	Act immediately to remedy problems with customer	Define and respond to the organisation problem with existing supplier.
	Re-examine and respond to customer needs.	Encourage organisation to sample alternative offerings.

Source: P. J. Robinson, C. W. Faris and F. Wind, *Industrial Buying and Creative Marketing*, Boston: Allyn and Bacon, Inc. and Marketing Science Institute Series (1967).

'in' suppliers to meet new demand. So the 'in' supplier for a new task situation need to:

- demonstrate his capability to meet new demands and to solve problems brought by the new situation
- capitalise on his 'in' status by monitoring the change in circumstances which may give rise to the new product needs
- once needs identified, 'in' supplier can ensure early involvement.

Most firms stick to current suppliers because of the cost of search and perceived risk. So, the 'out suppliers' strategy is to encourage the buyer to reappraise the purchase situation. It needs to move the buyer into modified rebuy situations and convince the buyers that it's worth the risk to select a new vendor. Out suppliers must try to convince the buyer to switch sources either by psychological or rational influence. The psychological factors for the out supplier would be his credibility and reputation and it needs to understand the role of the buying centre and the decision process. Using the rational influence, the out supplier must convince the buyer that his firm's performance may be improved by reappraising the situation, i.e. with cheaper or better product. He must further convince the buyer that his needs have changed and that the performance factors outweigh the risk and cost to be experienced by the buying organisation. The out supplier can use risk reducers such as performance guarantees.

In a new task situation, due to lack of purchase experience, the buyer may have no predisposition to a particular situation. So both in and out suppliers will be on an equal footing. Thus, the out supplier strategy can be similar to the in suppliers, i.e. develop general image of problem solver and get involved in the decision making process early on.

In summary there are three main considerations for the business marketer to develop strategies based on the buying situation. These are information gathering, understanding 'creeping commitment' and the 'centre of gravity' influence (Robinson, Faris and Wind 1967).

First, *information requirements* greatly increase as purchase situations move towards a new task buy. Thus, a primary task of the business marketer is to identify the situation that the buyer is in and facilitate information needs relative to that situation. For a straight rebuy, limited amounts of information are needed, and the seller may concentrate on the other areas, such as increasing the number of potential customers contacted. For a new task purchase, the business marketer must spend great amounts of time collecting information on the company's needs from areas within the buying organisation and providing information to those areas on possible solutions that it has to offer.

Secondly, Robinson, Faris and Wind (1967) used the term *creeping commitment* to explain the tendency for reducing the committed range of product alternatives as the purchasing process continues. For example, if a firm is exploring alternative solutions to a particular problem, as it progresses through the state of identifying the characteristics of the needed item, it will eliminate some viable alternatives at this point. Likewise, as it begins to identify potential sources of supply, it will eliminate more vendors. This process, from the perspective of the seller, is in effect a process of elimination that can work against the seller. If, however, the seller is playing an active role with the customer in the buying process, it can help direct the choice of product and supplier in its favour.

The final consideration is that there will be different areas of influence during the decision process, based on the firm and the situation at hand. This is referred to as a *centre of gravity* (Robinson, Faris and Wind, 1967). For example, during the need recognition stage, the originating department has the primary influence. When the identification of possible product alternatives is developed, the centre of gravity may pass to engineering. Finally, when potential vendors are identified, the centre of gravity may move towards the purchasing area, which has expertise in vendor analysis.

☐ *Procurement strategy*

Over the past three decades, purchasing as a function has been growing in importance and it has become increasingly clear that purchasing may be crucial to the competitiveness of a firm. (Doyle, 1989; Speckman, 1988; Farmer, 1972; Adamson, 1980; Axelsson and Hakansson, 1984; Rajagopal and Bernard, 1993).

Axelsson and Hakansson (1984) gave a comprehensive view of the potential of purchasing to affect a company's strategic competition status. They distinguish three strategic roles in purchasing: the rationalisation role, the development role and the structural role as shown in Figure 5.12.

These strategic roles of purchasing influence the buying decision as their status gain recognition. Further in response to the buying situation, procurement's role tends to focus around three major purchasing issues:

- The balance between external purchasing and in-house production (rationalisation role).
- The design of the supplier structure (structural role).
- The development of relationships with individual suppliers (development role).

The first issue deals with the decision of what to produce in-house and what to purchase externally. This type of analysis (make or buy analysis) is firmly rooted in purchasing. It is a highly strategic question and is nothing new but has, over time, gained importance owing to specialisation of production and development. In a new task situation,

Figure 5.12. *The role of purchasing*

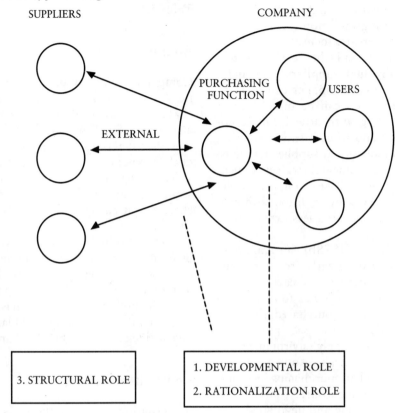

Source: E. L. Gadde and H. Hakansson, *Professional Purchasing*, London: Routledge (1993), p. 7.

the decision to produce in-house or to out source the material is a critical decision.

The second issue deals with the design of the supplier structure. (The number of suppliers and how they are organised in relation to one another.) A classical decision and a problem in purchasing strategy is the choice between single sourcing (one supplier per product) and multiple sourcing (several suppliers per product). Traditionally multiple sourcing was viewed as efficient purchasing, since competition among suppliers was given high priority (Puto *et al.*, 1985).

However, multiple sourcing as a purchasing strategy was on the rapid decline in the 1980s because increasing numbers of suppliers increased the need for co-ordination and this led to a rapid

rise in indirect costs. Newman (1988) found that there was a distinct trend towards single sourcing, or at least in the direction of a substantial reduction of the number of suppliers. The shift from multiple sourcing to single source was found to be highly advantageous especially with close cooperation with individual suppliers. (Raia, 1988; Deans and Rajagopal, 1991a). For this reason, many firms have begun to work actively towards changing their entire supplier structures, which has given the issue strategic significance for the first time. In the past it was not uncommon for management not even to know how many suppliers the firms used or who they were. The supplier structure as a whole was considered irrelevant. Because the main aim was to make every individual purchase as cheaply as possible, the structure was, as such, uninteresting. With the trend towards single sourcing the demand for evaluating and monitoring vendor performance receives greater focus.

The third issue deals with the development of relations with individual suppliers. The main question is what role each supplier can play for the purchasing firm. This can be broken down into sub-issues dealing with how intimate co-operation should be and what it should involve, and thus touches on quality in supplier relations. None of these three fundamental strategic dimensions is new. They have all been important elements of purchasing work by tradition, although the second and third have been less explicit than the first.

According to Corey (1978b), procurement strategies developed vary greatly from one purchase situation to another because each situation is unique. Thus, every strategy has to be tailored to the type of product being purchased, the stage of the procurement cycle, the past purchasing history, the nature of the supply environment and the buying company itself: its resources, its negotiation strength, and its purchasing policies. These procurement strategies are: routine purchasing, competitive bidding and negotiated contracts. Each strategy relates to the various buying situations as described earlier. The purchase strategy and the buying situation are summarised in Table 5.5.

Routine purchasing

Companies routinely purchase a wide variety of items. These items typically are frequently purchased and may have a low price with a low associated risk. The firm usually knows exactly what it is that it wishes to purchase and has a great deal of experience with the product. This type of situation has previously been referred to as a straight rebuy; the firm is simply repeating a purchase that it has made in the past. In this type of situation, there is little reason for the firm to re-evaluate products or suppliers. The purchase method is therefore routine and normally consists of simply notifying a supplier of the order. A few different methods of accomplishing this task exist, including straight purchase orders, automatic reorders, release against blanket orders and link with electronic data interchange.

Competitive bidding

In situations where there is a degree of uncertainty regarding the price or other aspect of a potential purchase, organisations use a some-

Table 5.5. *Purchasing strategy and the buying situation*

Purchase Strategy	Purchase Methods	Buying Situation
Routine Purchasing	• Straight purchase orders • Automatic reorders. • Blanket orders and releases • Electronic data interchange link.	Straight Rebuy.
Competitive Bidding	• Open bidding. • Closed bidding. • Fixed-price bids. • Cost-price bids.	Modified Rebuy.
Negotiated Contracts	• Cost-based price model. • Market-price based model.	New Task

what more complex method of purchasing. This is referred to as competitive bidding. The most important aspect of competitive bidding strategy is the selection of a sufficient number of qualified vendors. The buyer's primary objective is to have vendors enough to provide effective competition for his business but not more than would allow a meaningful sales potential to each vendor. There has to be a certain 'critical mass' of sales volume available to the vendor to induce low price quotations and to evoke high levels of service if a contract is awarded. On the other hand, a buyer that has too few suppliers could in time find he is dealing with a 'live-and-let live' attitude on the part of each, with the result that price competition is dulled and service levels deteriorate. As a result the key strategic issue here is how many 'qualified' suppliers will exist in a certain period of time. Competitive bidding is a common procedure that organisations utilise to make purchases, typically in a modified rebuy situation. Unlike routine purchasing method, this method allows the buyer to examine competitive offers. At the same time, it allows for standardisation by the buyer of the requirements desired.

Negotiated contracts

In purchase situations involving totally new products, buyers and sellers need to exchange a great deal of information. For this reason, firms usually meet face to face to negotiate a contract for the products required. Although the name of this type of purchasing procedure implies that intense negotiations are made on the price, the real exchange of information occurs on the needs of the buyer. Once the product configuration is determined and presented by the seller, the price may simply be presented, and a true negotiation process can take place.

The *cost-based price model* is the basis for a close working relationship, typically symbiotic in nature, between vendor and customer. The salient features of the strategy initially are: i) single supplier, ii) a single item being developed and purchased, iii) a time-and-material pricing arrangement, and iv) contracts initially negotiated for short durations and limited quantities. Then the price arrangement may evolve into a firm fixed price, other suppliers may be solicited, but negotiations may continue to be vendor-cost-based. The cost base strategy with single sourcing involves at the early stages of developmental work (value engineering) and this leads to:

- planning a narrow (one item) procurement
- work as a practical matter with one supplier rather than with several.

Much has been written about single sourcing benefits that accrue to the buying organisation (Trevelen, 1987; Farmer and MacMillan, 1976; Hahn *et al.*, 1983; Sheriden, 1988; Juran and Gryna, 1980; Deans and Rajagopal, 1991). Even when such a relationship foregoes the benefits of competitors, the cost-based price negotiation becomes appropriate as a way of assuring that the price is fair for the seller and optimal for the buyer.

In considering a *market-price-based* negotiation strategy, critical materials are sourced according to the following priority requirements:

- assurance of long-run availability of material
- assurance that the material will be of suitable quality
- obtainable at the lowest prices.

In this market-priced-based model, it is absolutely essential to have a multi-supplier sourcing system. While prices are essentially determined in strict conformity with published market prices and are the same for all customers in a using industry, the large buyer has some ability to influence overall price levels by introducing new competitive elements. Also, by working on price differences among suppliers at the lowest level, he can bring pressure to achieve price uniformity among them. Hence procurement planning calls for massing total requirements across one corporation and for buying a wide range of items for each supplier. Negotiations focus on longer-range considerations, such as adding new capacity and new product development. Further, significant bargaining strength derives from the ability of the large buyer to shift purchase volumes among suppliers.

Finally, the study of buying centre and buying situations has implications for improving buying centre decision making within the organisation. Some organisations have formal decision making procedures established which buying centres must observe.

Buying centres may be advised by organisational policy that given particular situations – choice schemes may be useful in reaching an efficient and satisfactory supplier choice. For example, when the buying centre is considering a new task purchase for a technically complex item requiring low/moderate financial commitment, members may more efficiently reach a majority of opinion about supplier choice compared to requiring unanimous agreement among members. While the decision outcome may not provide maximum utility to the organisation, it is likely to provide an acceptable level of utility, or satisfaction, to the organisation. In addition, time saved by not requiring extensive deliberations that usually accompany unanimous consensus may contribute to the utility gained. Similarly buying centres faced with rebuy situation for a simple technology product which requires low/moderate financial commitment may recognise that the most experienced member can efficiently and effectively make an autonomous decision. In general, a buying centre may assess individual preferences for real vendor-product decisions by developing decision evaluation forms using various evaluative criteria. Over time, particular decision schemes may consistently be favoured by buying centres or organisations in general. In addition, one or two decision schemes may emerge as effective for particular product categories over time.

■ Future trends

In order to foresee the future trend in organisational buying behaviour study, we have to understand the changes likely to occur in the industrial or business market. In 1987 representatives of ten major Japanese industries (sponsored by the Japan Machinery Federation and the Systems Science Institute of Waseda University) began a five-year project to explore the future of Japanese manufacturing (Manufacturing 21). Subsequently, in 1991, over 100 American manufacturing executives in coordination with the Department of Defense and the Iacocca Institute of Lehigh University formulated a structured manufacturing vision and strategy. These two studies believe that 'agile manufacturing' will be in place by the year 2006. The group agreed that:

● A new competitive environment for industrial products and services is emerging.
● Competitive advantage will belong to agile manufacturing enterprises, ones *capable of responding rapidly to demand for high quality, highly customised products*.
● Agility requires integrating flexible technologies, with the skill base of a knowledgeable work force, and flexible management structures that *stimulate cooperative initiatives within and between firms*.
● An agile enterprise has the flexibility to adapt for each project. Sometimes this will take the form of an internal cross-functional team with *participation by suppliers and customers*.

Based on these vision for 2006, one can understand the need for cross-functional teams for group decisions. The literature on OBB has dealt in depth and has provided insight into the structure, process and influencing variables of business buying. These have been depicted in various models.

However, what the subject lacks is empirical evidence and practical application of making buying decisions as a team. Further, the concept of relationship development within different functions and between buyer and supplier need to be investigated further. Thus a reasonable forecast for the 21st century is that matters relating to the management of internal and external relationships will be considered important to the productivity, development and competitiveness of an organisation.

■ Concluding remarks

Organisational buying is a complex process and any attempts to oversimplify this process will ultimately result in a loss of understanding of the dynamics of the process and its constituent elements. As the trend towards the year 2000 is a development of integrated strategy and formation of alliances, the challenge for academics is to lay aside their theoretical rectitude and consultants their quick fix and come to terms with the challenges of applying academic research of buying behaviour to the practical application in decision making and relationship management within and between organisations.

■ References

Adamson, J. (1980), 'Corporate Long-Range Planning Must Include Procurement', *Journal of Purchasing and Materials Management*, (Spring), pp. 25–32.

Anderson, P. F. and Chambers, T. M. (1985), 'A Reward/Measurement Model of Organisational Buying Behaviour', *Journal of Marketing* 49, (Spring), pp. 7–23.

Anderson, E., Chu, W. and Weitz, B. (1987), 'Industrial Purchasing: An Empirical Exploration of the Buyclass Framework', *Journal of Marketing* 51, (3) (July), pp. 71–86.

Axelsson, B. and Hakannson, H. (1984), *Inköp för Konkurrenskraft*, Stockholm: Liber.

Baker, E. L. (1980), 'Managing Organisational Culture', *Management Review* (July).

Bonoma, T. (1982), 'Major Sales: Who Really Does the Buying?', *Harvard Business Review* 60 (May–June), pp. 111–119.

Bonoma, T. and Johnston, W. (1978), 'The Social Psychology of Industrial Buying and Selling', *Industrial Marketing Management* 7 (July), pp. 213–224.

Bonoma, T. and Zaltman, G. (1978), *Organisational Buying Behaviour*, Chicago: American Marketing Association.

Bright, J. R. (1970), 'Evaluating signals of Technological Change', *Harvard Business Review* 48 (January–February), pp. 62–70.

Burt, D. N. and Doyle, M. F. (1993), *The American Keiretsu: A Strategic Weapon for Global Competitiveness*, New York: Irwin, Business One.

Choffray, J. M. and Lilien, G. L. (1978), 'Assessing Responses to Industrial Marketing Strategy', *Journal of Marketing* 42 (2) (April), pp. 20–31.

Choffray, J. M. and Lilien, G. L. (1980), *Marketing Planning for New Industrial Products*, New York: Wiley.

Corey, R. E. (1978a), *The Organisational Context of Industrial Buying Behaviour*, Cambridge, Mass: Marketing Science Institute.

Corey, R. E. (1978b), *Procurement Management: Strategy, Organisation and Decision-making*, Boston: CBI Publishing Company Inc.

Deans, K. R. and Rajagopal, S. (1991a), 'Comakership: A Worthwhile Word', *Journal of Purchasing and Supply Management*, published by CIPS (March), pp. 15–17.

Deans, K. R. and Rajagopal, S. (1991b), 'Competitive Purchasing Strategy: A Proactive Approach to Improve Firm's Competitive Position', *Proceedings of 76th International Purchasing Conference*, Research in Purchasing and Materials Management as Gateway to 1990s, NAPM, pp. 36–42.

Doyle, M. (1989), 'Strategic Purchasing Can Make or Break a Firm', Strategic Purchasing, Executive Viewpoint, *Electronic Business* (March), published by Cahners Publishing Co.

Doyle, P., Woodside, A. and Michell, P. (1979), 'Organisations Buying in New Task and Modified Rebuy Situations', *Industrial Marketing Management* 8, pp. 7–11.

Farmer, D. H. (1982), 'The Impact of Supply Markets on Corporate Planning', *Long Range Planning* (March), pp. 10–15.

Farmer, D. and MacMillan, K. (1976), 'Voluntary Collaboration vs. Disloyalty to Suppliers', *Journal of Purchasing and Materials Management* (Winter), pp. 3–8.

Ford, D. (1988), 'Develop Your Technology Strategy', *Long Range Planning* 21, pp. 85–95.

Ford, D. (1989), 'One More Time, What Buyer–Seller Relationships are All About', *Proceedings of the 5th IMP Conference* (September), eds David T. Wilson, Sang-Lin Han and Gary W. Holler, in *Research in Marketing: An International Perspective*, vol. II, pp. 814–836.

Gadde, L. E. and Hakansson, H. (1993), *Professional Purchasing*, London: Routledge.

Gross, A. C., Banting, P., M., Meredith, L. N. and Ford, D. I. (1993), *Business Marketing*, Boston: Houghton Mifflin Company.

Hahn, C. K., Pinto, D. A. and Bragg, D. J. (1983), 'Just-In-Time Production and Purchasing', *Journal of Purchasing and Materials Management* 19 (Fall), pp. 2–10.

Hakansson, H. (ed.) (1982), *International Marketing and Purchasing of Industrial Goods*, Chichester: John Wiley.

Juran, J. M. and Gryna, F. M. Jr. (1980), *Quality Planning Analysis*, New York: McGraw-Hill.

Hardwick, B. and Ford, D. (1988), 'Industrial Buyer Resources and Responsibilities and the Buyer–Seller Relationship', *Industrial Marketing Management* 1, pp. 3–26.

Hutt, M. and Speh, T. (1985), *Industrial Marketing Management: A Strategic View of Business Markets*, 2nd edition, Chicago: The Dryden Press.

IMP Group (1982), *International Marketing and Purchasing of Industrial Goods*, Chichester: John Wiley.

Johnston, W. J. and Bonoma, T. V. (1981), 'The Buying Centre: Structure and Interaction Patterns', *Journal of Marketing* 45 (2) (Summer), pp. 143–156.

Johnston, W. J. and Spekman, R. E. (1982), 'Industrial Buying Behaviour: A Need for an Integrative Approach', *Journal of Business Research* 10 (June), pp. 135–146.

Krapfel, R. Jr. (1985), 'An Advocacy Behaviour Model of Organisational Buyer's Vendor Choice', *Journal of Marketing* 49 (Fall), pp. 51–59.

Manufacturing 21 Report (1990), Wheeling, II: Association for Manufacturing Excellence, 2.

Marrett, C. B. (1971), 'On the Specification of Interorganisational Dimensions', *Sociology and Social Research* 56 (October), pp. 83–99.

Most, G. V. (1976), 'Purchasing Process: Researching Influence is Basic to Marketing Plan', *Industrial Marketing* (October), p. 120.

Newman, R. G. (1988), 'Single Source Qualification', *Journal of Purchasing and Materials Management* (Summer), pp. 10–17.

Puto, C., Patton, W. and King, R. (1985), 'Risk Handling Strategies in Industrial Vendor Selection Decisions', *Journal of Marketing* 49 (Winter), pp. 89–98.

Rajagopal, S. and Bernard, K. N. (1993), 'Strategic Procurement and Competitive Advantage', *International Journal of Purchasing and Materials Management* 29 (4), pp. 13–20.

Raia, E. (1988), 'JIT in Detroit', *Purchasing* 15 (September), pp. 68–77.

Robinson, P., Faris, C. and Wind, Y. (1967), *Industrial Buying and Creative Marketing*, Marketing Science Institute Series, Boston: Allyn & Bacon.

Sheridan, J. H. (1988), 'Strategic Manufacturing: Betting on a Single Source', *Industry Week* (6) (1 February), pp. 31–36.

Sheth, J. N. (1973), 'A Model of Industrial Buyer Behaviour', *Journal of Marketing* 37 (October), pp. 50–56, American Marketing Association.

Spekman, R. E. (1979), 'Information and Influence: An Exploratory Investigation of the Boundary Role Person's Basis of Power', *Academy of Management Journal* 22 (March), pp. 104–117.

Spekman, R. (1988), 'Strategic Supplier Selection: Understanding Long-Term Buyer Relationships', *Business Horizons* (July–August), pp. 75–81.

Spekman, R. E. and Stern, L. W. (1979), 'Environmental Uncertainty and Buying Group Structure: An Empirical Investigation', *Journal of Marketing* 43 (Spring), p. 56.

Thomas, R. J. (1982), 'Correlates of Interpersonal Purchase Influence in Organisations', *Journal of Consumer Research* (September), pp. 191–182.

Thomas, G. and Grashof, J. (1982), 'Impact of Internal and External Environmental Stability on the Existence of Determinant Buying Rules', *Journal of Business Research* 10 (June), pp. 159–168.

Trevelen, M. (1987), 'Single Sourcing: A Managerial Tool for the Quality Supplier', *Journal of Purchasing and Materials Management* (Spring), pp. 19–24.

Turnbull, P. (1987), 'Organisational Buying Behaviour', in *The Marketing Book*, ed. Michael J. Baker, London: Heinemann, pp. 147–164.

Turnbull, P. and Cunningham, M. T. (1981), *International Marketing and Purchasing*, London: Macmillan.

Webster, F. E. (1991), *Industrial Marketing Strategy*, 3rd edition, New York: John Wiley.

Webster, F. E. and Wind, Y. (1972a), 'A General Model of Organisational Buying Behaviour', *Journal of Marketing* 36 (2) (April), pp. 12–19, American Marketing Association.

Webster, F. E. and Wind, Y. (1972b), *Organisational Buying Behaviour*, Englewood Cliffs, NJ: Prentice-Hall.

Wilson, E. J. (1989), 'Group Choice Models in Organisational Buying: Implication for Purchasing Strategy', *Proceedings of 74th International Purchasing Conference*, Boston, April, (NAPM), pp. 327–334.

Wind, Y. (1976), 'Preference of Relevant Others and Individual Choice Models', *Journal of Consumer Research* 3 (August), pp. 50–57.

■ Chapter 6 ■

Market Segmentation

Dale Littler

Market segmentation – the disaggregation of markets into clusters of buyers with similar tastes, preferences and purchasing behaviour – is now firmly established in marketing theory and practice (Wind 1978). It is widely regarded as an essential component of the process of marketing strategy formulation, since it is the means of identifying and defining customer targets. In this way, market segmentation assists in structuring and focusing an organisation's marketing management activities. It is therefore not surprising that it 'is one of the most talked about and acted upon concepts in marketing' (Green and Kreiger, 1991). It can be regarded as a compromise between the convenience of mass marketing and the costly and generally impractical approach of marketing offerings suited to the idiosyncrasies of each individual buyer.

Although it has entered received wisdom in marketing that buyers can differ significantly in terms of one or more characteristics – attitudes, purchasing procedures employed, product usage, personality, resources and so on – there is still a tendency amongst some to regard markets as homogenous mass markets on which standard products could be unloaded; or as an aggregation of convenient but often large sub-markets to which a range of adapted versions of standard

products could be sold. However, it is clear that current trends are likely to encourage increasing fragmentation of markets, as a result of both economic and technological developments. For instance, increases in discretionary income permit the exercise of greater choice and the luxury of demanding product specifications suited to the satisfaction of psychological and social needs, as against just basic economic requirements, that can differ markedly between individuals. This puts the onus on suppliers aiming to secure a competitive advantage to tailor offerings to suit more closely the particular specifications of different customers, and is considerably assisted by the introduction of, for example, flexible manufacturing systems which permit lower cost customisation. Such developments may, however, have significant implications for market segmentation as traditionally perceived.

This chapter starts by examining what is meant by market segmentation and its role in the development of marketing strategy. It proceeds to analyse the advantages and disadvantages of segmentation and the appropriate criteria for effective segmentation. The various methodologies for segmenting markets are described. These range from approaches employing readily available demographic data to those based on 'softer', more subjective information, such as 'lifestyle'. The chapter concludes by noting some of the barriers to and problems with the implementation of market segmentation.

Segmentation of the market

The concept of product differentiation in itself involves an implicit recognition that customers may have different requirements since it is based on the premise that competitive advantage may be obtained by offering products with varying specifications. However, it is essentially producer driven, in that suppliers attempt to set themselves apart from their rivals in an increasingly competitive market. Wendell Smith (1956) was one of the first to suggest that product variation should be founded on an understanding of the differences in requirements of different groups of customers. He suggested that overall demand for a product class could be decomposed into several different demand schedules: 'segmentation is based upon developments on the demand side of the market and represents a rational and more precise adjustment of product and marketing effort to consumer or user requirements. In the language of the economist, segmentation is disaggregative in its effects and tends to bring about recognition of several demand schedules where only one was recognised before' (p. 5).

By clustering purchasers according to such variables as age, location, income, size of households, lifestyle and even personality, it may be possible to identify variations in demand between different groups of purchasers. This is the underlying principle of market segmentation. It can be defined as: *the process of clustering customers into groups with similar characteristics that are likely to exhibit similar purchasing patterns*. A market segment is then: 'a group of present or potential customers with some common characteristic which is relevant in explaining (and predicting) their response to a supplier's marketing stimuli' (Wind and Cardozo, 1974, p. 155).

Segmentation and strategy

Market segmentation is an important strategic tool. By dividing markets into sub sectors, and targeting marketing effort in such a way as to meet the technical and other requirements of each of these, organisations may be able to secure a superior competitive position than if they attempted to satisfy the general requirements of the market as a whole. The latter approach may end up not pleasing anyone fully: there will often be groups of buyers whose requirements are largely unmet so that they do not enter the market; other buyers may have some of their specific requirements largely unsatisfied, thereby creating opportunities for competitors to capture a greater market share or to enter the market by producing offerings tailored in some way to the requirements of the dissatisfied purchasers. The potential value of market segmentation can be seen by considering the example of the provider of health care insurance which instead of producing a standard and expensive insurance that covered the costs of private hospital care as well as a range of other services, including private consultant treatment, marketed a range of policies, including a basic, cheaper policy that covered only hospital care. In this way, it widened the market for healthcare insurance, by bringing it within the scope of those with less disposable income. Thus, differing sensitivities to marketing stimuli, such as product quality, pricing, service support and such like, constitute an important means of segmenting the market.

Organisations can adopt at least three broad approaches to strategic marketing. First, they can regard the market as homogeneous, market standard offerings and reap the advantages of economies of scale, with the aim of securing a high market share. As a result the marketer should because of its high level of relative experience have lower costs, thereby offering it the discretion to lower prices (to increase market share further); or maintain prices, and therefore increase profitability. However, the organisation leaves itself vulnerable to competitors which adopt a more specific marketing approach based on segmenting the market. Second, the organisation may adopt an approach aimed at marketing a range of offerings directed at several groups of customers. This multi-segment strategy could be aimed at maximising revenues, by covering those areas of the market with the highest potential, whilst minimising its exposure to competition through its wide coverage of the market. Nevertheless, rivals may be able to identify areas of customer dissatisfaction that can be exploited. Thirdly, the organisation may adopt a very focused strategy, concentrating on one or just a very few market segments which are defined relatively narrowly. Through detailed knowledge of the specific requirements of its target customers, it may develop the ability to anticipate and respond to the changing requirements of its target customers and through careful relationship management build up almost impenetrable customer loyalty.

The formulation of marketing strategy may involve a sequence of logical stages: the segmentation of the market; the selection of market targets; the development of appropriate market mixes; the assessment of the assumptions made; implementation; and control.

The first stage involves segmenting the market in several different ways; those segments that satisfy the organisation's criteria in terms of compatibility with its overall strategy, demand potential, ease with which the segments can be reached and so on will be selected as market targets. The development of the appropriate marketing mix will involve a detailed understanding of the sensitivity of the segments to different marketing variables (such as price) as well as knowledge of the purchasing behaviour of the constituents of the segment. The organisation may then 'test' the assumptions made, including the ease with which the segment can be reached and the response to the market mixes developed. After implementation, the organisation needs to monitor carefully whether or not its expectations are being realised and the responses, if any, of competitors and take appropriate action as necessary.

Criteria for market segmentation

There are at least four criteria that need to be satisfied in order for market segmentation to be effective. A market segment should be:

Identifiable, that is, there should be observable indicators which enable the segment to be defined and quantified.

Substantial, meaning that the segment should be of sufficient size to make the effort involved in segmentation worthwhile.

Accessible, that is, it should be possible to target specifically the segment using existing communication and distribution channels.

Stable, so that after identification of the segment there should be sufficient time to capitalise on the investment involved in segmentation.

Finally, as Frank *et al.* (1972) note the segment should be unique in its response to marketing stimuli.

One of the major difficulties is in being able to target the marketing stimuli specifically at a market segment. Often, for example, communication channels that give exclusive access to the target segment may not exist; instead they may cover a wide range of different purchaser types, or the profile of the audience of the communication channels is not defined according to the criteria used to define the market segments. Finally, it is clear that the value of segmentation may be somewhat diminished if intra-segment variation exceeds inter-segment differences, and practitioners need to pay particular regard to this.

Benefits and costs of market segmentation

The contribution of market segmentation to the development of strategy has already been noted. It is perhaps worth emphasising, though, that segmentation can have an important proactive role in helping to identify market gaps where existing customers are unsatisfied by existing offerings. It can also play its part in the development of innovative marketing strategies: by creatively combining different sets of variables, it enables the marketer to perceive the market in different ways, point not only to new product possibilities within existing markets, but also to the identification of totally new markets. In general, then, segmentation facilitates the more effective allocation of marketing resources through directing these to those areas where they are likely to yield the highest returns.

However, segmentation can incur higher costs of:

(a) Research and Development required in developing different product versions.
(b) Production, because of the disruption to the production process and the consequential time lost in changing from the production of one product version to another; the different plant and equipment that may be required to manufacture different product versions; and the inability to reap fully economies of scale.
(c) Marketing, because bulk discounts in advertising cannot be realised; there is a need for different packaging and so on.
(d) Inventory, as overall stock levels may increase the need to have minimum levels of stock for each product version.

Overall, there may be considerable additional time and effort involved in managing a more diverse and complex product range. However, advances in technology enable greater production flexibility and responsiveness to customers, thereby reducing if not eliminating some of the extra costs of segmentation.

■ Means of market segmentation

In general, segmentation is founded on the identification of a relationship between two or more independent variables and one or more dependent variables. There are at least two main approaches to segmentation, according to Wind (1978). The first, *a priori*, involves the selection of the particular variables that are to be used in segmenting the market and evaluating whether or not these discriminate between different groups of customers according to their consumption or purchasing behaviour. Alternatively, clustering starts without any preconceived notion of what the relevant discriminating variables are. Rather, data is collected on a range of variables and

through statistical analysis clusters which have similarities in terms of purchasing behaviour, for example, are identified and named. One methodology for identifying clusters is based on multidimensional scaling using the repertory grid technique.

The repertory grid can be employed to elicit from buyers the criteria they use in evaluating specific products. These may then be analysed to identify clusters of customers. The analyst will then attempt to discern whether or not each cluster has a distinctive pattern of behaviour which might form the basis or a marketing strategy.

The variables for segmenting the market can be categorised according to whether or not they are intuitive or observable; and general or specific to the purchase. The matrix in Figure 6.1 provides some indication of the various segmentation approaches possible.

Figure 6.1. *General approaches to market segmentation*

	Intuitive	*Observable*
General	Personality Lifestyle	Demographic Economic influences
Situation Specific	Attitudes Perceptions and preferences	Usage Purchasing behaviour

Source: Adapted from Frank, Massey and Wind (1972).

Practical market segmentation will generally involve combining two or more variables such as, for example, age and income; location and lifestyle. In Figure 6.2 there is one possible approach to the segmentation of the market for newspapers. In fact, newspaper publishers pay careful regard to the readership profiles, some aiming specifically at the 'female' market (such as the Daily Mail) or at the business market (such as the Financial Times). These profiles will be used in selecting the appropriate media to gain access to their target customers.

The major bases for segmentation are given in Table 6.1.

Figure 6.2. *Segmenting the newspaper market*

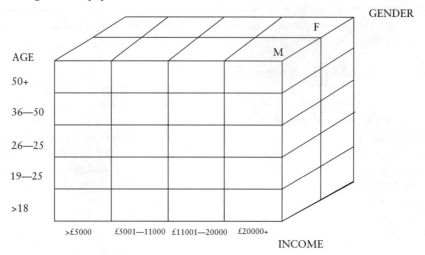

Table 6.1. *Major segmentation variables*

Geographic	Regional
	National
	Urban vs Rural
	Density
Demographic	Age
	Gender
	Household size
	Composition of household
	Social class
	Religion
	Occupation
	Ethnic origins
	Family lifecycle
	Marital state
	Income
Psychographic	Lifestyle
	Personality
Behavioural	Volume purchased
	Location of purchase
	Benefits sought

Source: Adapted from Thomas (1980).

□ *Geographic*

Geographical segmentation can be considered on at least three levels: national, regional and local,

each of which could be viewed as having one or more sub levels. National variations in buying behaviour can result from differences in cultures, infrastructure and government regulations. There can be significant variations in what is, for example, regarded as acceptable in terms of tastes, functions and such like between countries, although it may be possible to group countries according to common general features (for example, the Nordic countries) for certain purposes; and within these regional groupings, it may be possible to identify customer segments that transcend national barriers (Wind and Douglas, 1972).

National markets are not however homogenous, and within them there can be considerable regional diversity, such as might exist in food purchasing between the North East and the South East of England. Moreover, a nation may embrace several ethnic groups, such as Caribbean, Asian, and Chinese, which can form the basis of market segmentation.

On a more micro level, localities may exhibit common features because, according to the old adage, 'birds of a feather flock together'. This is the basis underpinning geodemographics, of which an example is ACORN (A Classification Of Residential Neighbourhoods). This categorises districts according to types of housing.

The approach of geodemographics is based on social research undertaken by Richard Webber

Table 6.2. *Major ACORN groups*

Group	Description
A	Modern housing for manual workers; tend to be younger families.
B	Up-market modern housing; tendency to be in traditional social classes C1 towards B.
C	Older housing of intermediate status, with a broad spectrum of traditional social classes, but with a trend towards C1.
D	Poor quality older terraced housing (the 'have nots' rather than 'haves'). Tend to be C2 and D.
E	Rural areas.
F	Urban local authority type housing; middle range to 'down' market housing.
G	Densely populated housing e.g. Scottish tenements (often council owned).
H	Low income areas with a high proportion of immigrants.
I	Inner city, student and high status non-family areas; residents tend to be well educated.
J	Up-market suburbia.
K	Areas for elderly people, often by the sea.

Source: Adapted from CACI information.

aimed at condensing census data into a form based on enumeration districts, that is, the voting districts that consist of around 150 households. Using a set of 40 variables (15 social and economic, 12 related to age and household consumption, and 13 concerned with household type) it was possible to cluster households to give 36 neighbourhood types which have been aggregated into 11 ACORN groups as given in Table 6.2.

Through surveys, it is possible to relate the propensity to purchase certain categories of goods and services to the neighbourhood type, which in turn can be related to postal codes. This then provides a valuable marketing tool, allowing the specific targeting by direct mail to selected segments; the assessment of market potential for selected products; and the definition of the features of areas with high tendency to use certain types of retail outlets. For example, a chain of off-licences may employ geodemographic information in formulating its branch location strategy. Through surveys, it might collect the post codes of the users of its existing branches and employ these to identify a profile of the most frequent users by ACORN type. Future branches could then be located in those areas with the appropriate ACORN profile. However, this approach would not necessarily lead to the optimum location since it is based on the continuation of an existing strategy. The company does not know whether or not a different marketing strategy, including the location of branches in areas which it does not traditionally use, would lead to increased profitability. There is then a possible disbenefit that methodologies for constructing strategies may be founded on static perspectives, involving responses to situations as they exist, rather than on encouraging experimentation and the development of approaches aimed at shaping markets in a manner appropriate to the continued future development of the organisation in a dynamic environment.

■ Demographic data

There is a wide range of demographic data which can be employed, ranging from age, social class and income to household size. Often two or more are combined to yield segments, such as that for the newspaper market referred to earlier. As will be indicated below, such observable data can be correlated with softer 'intuitive' means of segmenting the market, to facilitate the definition and measurement of segments which are primarily defined in terms of such 'softer' variables.

There are several widely quoted demographic based approaches to segmentation, including life-cycle analysis and social class.

□ *Life-cycle analysis*

This is based on the assumption that as individuals age they pass through a sequence of stages that can be matched with levels of discretionary income and their requirements for certain categories of goods and services. The major life-cycle phases range through newly marrieds to empty nesters (older married couples with no children living with them) to the solitary survivor status (Wells and Gubar, 1966).

Thus, according to this model the bachelor stage would probably live in rented accommodation and have a demand for essential household goods and single person prepared meals.

There are at least three criticisms of this approach. First, it is obvious that not all individuals will follow the deterministic sequence assumed, so that there are categories of consumers that are not described by the model, thereby giving rise to, for example, missed marketing opportunities. Secondly, there have been significant social changes, such as the substantial increase in the number of one parent households, which highlight the extreme simplicity of the model. Thirdly, any life-cycle category is unlikely to have the coherence that it apparently implies, if only because within any group there are likely to be considerable variations in income.

Practitioners have in any case found the model increasingly inappropriate. For example,

Summers and Smith (1994) have questioned its applicability in defining financial needs. They have developed an alternative approach which has seven different segments: young professionals; dual career families; up market empty nesters; mid-market empty nesters; new inheritors; self-employed; and high net worth individuals. Each of these has a number of sub-segments.

□ *Social class*

Social class is perhaps one of the most extensively employed demographically based approaches. It is founded on the premise that societies can be disaggregated into broad socio-economic groups each of which has consistent beliefs and attitudes, and common behaviour patterns. According to the Registrar General's classification, there are seven categories which although based on occupation are broadly related to the social class categories as defined by the Institute of Practitioners of Advertising (see Table 6.3).

The Registrar General has classified specific jobs according to its broad occupational categories.

The major disadvantage of social class is that the categories are not sufficiently refined so that each grouping could embrace a diverse range of sub-groups. Customer targeting is, then, likely to be at best extremely blunt. The schema fails to take into account, for example, that some members of a social group may have considerably higher incomes than other members of the same social group, and some higher income members of lower social groups in this implicit hierarchy may have greater incomes than members of 'higher' social groups. This can mean that there are 'over privileged' and 'under privileged' members of the same social group which may have different attitudes and spending patterns. As Coleman (1961) suggested, the most economical cars are not necessarily bought by the really poor, but by 'those who think themselves as poor relative to their status aspirations and to their needs for a certain level of clothing, furniture, and housing which they could not afford if they bought a more expen-

Table 6.3. *Occupation and social class categories*

Registrar General's Definition		Institute of Practitioners of Advertising	
I:	Professional occupations	A:	Higher managerial, administrative or professional
II:	Intermediate occupations (including most managerial and senior administrative occupations)	B:	Intermediate managerial, administrative or professional
IIIN:	Skilled occupations (non-manual)	C1:	Supervisory or clerical, and junior managerial, administrative or professional
IIIM:	Skilled occupations (manual)	C2:	Skilled manual workers
IV:	Partly skilled occupations	D:	Semi- and un-skilled manual workers
V:	Unskilled occupations	E:	State pensioners or widows (no other earner), casual or lowest grade workers
Other:	Residual group including, for example, armed forces, students, and those whose occupation cannot be easily categorised	Not applicable	

Sources: Registrar General's Classification *Social Trends* 14, HMSO (1984); Institute of Practitioners in Advertising Classification *JICNARS* (January/December 1983).

sive car'. The increase in the number of women in paid employment further obscures the distinction between social groups based on the occupation of the head of the household, since many households have at least two incomes. The net result is that in some instances intra-class variations can exceed inter-class differences, thereby making this far from being a subtle approach to segmentation. There are other trends that are blurring traditional social class boundaries, including an increasing general level of education. Yet despite its inadequate discriminatory power, social class still remains a common means of market segmentation, probably on the basis that it is easily comprehensible and usable.

■ Psychographics

Personality and lifestyle tend to be the two major approaches to segmentation included under the umbrella of psychographics.

□ *Lifestyle*

This is a general but ill defined composite notion that indicates an individual's general orientation and behaviour pattern. It is assumed that consumers tend to select offerings compatible with the way they live – their activities, interests and opinions (Craven *et al.*, 1987). Terms such as 'strivers', 'hedonistic', 'swingers' and such like are typical of the broad descriptors of 'lifestyles'. The significance of 'lifestyle' as a discriminatory variable in attitudes towards and usage of, in particular, mobile telecommunications products was highlighted in research undertaken by Leverick and Littler (1994). They found that there were significant differences in the attitudes and propensity to use mobile communications amongst different groups of consumers. Four clusters of consumers were identified (see Table 6.4) that ranged from the 'compulsive communicators' who wanted to have access to communications to both make and receive calls when 'out and about' to the 'reluctant communicators' who did not

Table 6.4.   *Consumer clusters for mobile communications*

COMPULSIVE COMMUNICATORS	Value making and receiving calls when out and about.
	Owners of communications products; Mercury subscribers; owners of high technology products; make frequent use of telephone boxes; positive attitudes towards new technology products; positive attitudes towards videophones; generally younger than average.
RELUCTANT COMMUNICATORS	Low disposition to want to make calls when out and about
	Do not own mobile communication products; low ownership of high technology products; use telephone boxes infrequently; negative attitudes towards new technology products; negative attitudes towards videophones; older than average.
ACTIVE COMMUNICATORS	Value making calls over receiving calls.
	Lead active/outdoor lifestyle; lead social lifestyle/prefer to socialise in large groups.
FAMILY-CONSCIOUS COMMUNICATORS	Value receiving calls over making calls
	Live in large households; likely to have children

Source: Leverick and Littler (1994).

have a strong desire to use mobile telecommunications services. The former are significantly more likely to be frequent users of telephone boxes, to be younger than average for the sample and have positive attitudes towards other new technology products, including communications products and videophones. The reluctant communicators, on the other hand, regard telephone calls as an intrusion into their lives; have negative attitudes towards videophones; believe that 'society was a better place before the advent of mobile communications'; sometime leave their telephone unanswered; are generally single; are less sociable than average and prefer to socialise in small groups; and tend not to take part in risky activities.

SRI International have developed a psychographics categorisation based on values attitudes and lifestyles (VALS) (Riche, 1989). The classification has two main dimensions: **consumer resources** (income, education, self-confidence, health, eagerness to buy, intelligence and energy level); and **self orientation**, which is divided into three groups: *principle oriented* consumers who

have set views; *status oriented* consumers who are influenced by what others think; and *action oriented* consumers who seek physical activity, variety and adventure.

Principle oriented consumers include *fulfillers* and *believers*. Fulfillers are mature, home oriented, well educated professionals with relatively high incomes. They are value oriented consumers who are open to new ideas. Believers are family and community oriented people of more modest means, They are brand loyal and favour American-made products.

Status oriented consumers include *achievers* and *strivers*. Achievers are work oriented and successful. They have high job satisfaction, respect authority and favour the status quo. Achievers like to demonstrate their success through their purchases. Strivers are lower income people with values similar to achievers.

The action oriented category consists of *experiencers* and *makers*. Experiences are the youngest group in VALS with a median age of 25. They are active in both physical and social activities, and they are also avid consumers who favour new products. Makers are the self-sufficient group. They are practical people who have little interest in most material possessions.

The two remaining groups are *strugglers* and *actualisers*. Strugglers are brand loyal; actualisers have both high income and self-esteem.

In the food industry, consumers have been classified by the NPD Group, according to their agreement or disagreement with a number of AIO (activities, interests and opinions) statements, into four major categories: traditional taste, health maintainers, busy urbanites and moderates.

In the US the 'Limited' store defined its position in terms of a lifestyle oriented language: It saw itself as a: 'fashion retailer, specialising in the sale of medium-priced fashion apparel tailored to the tastes and lifestyles of women 16–35 years of age'. It continued: 'She is educated, affluent, gregarious, fashion-oriented, and more often than not, she is a working woman who lives in or near a major metropolitan area. The Limited is here favourite place to shop because of our fashion and quality' (Blackwell and Talarzyk, 1983, p. 11).

There have also been attempts to identify segments which transcend national boundaries. One study (Anon, 1990) suggested that there are five global psychographic segments termed: strivers (young people who lead active lives), achievers (young people who have achieved success), the pressured (mainly women in all age groups who find it difficult to manage all the problems in their lives); adaptors (older consumers who live comfortably); and traditionals (those who embody the oldest values of their countries and cultures).

□ *Personality*

In theory at least one could expect personality type to be a powerful explanatory variable of purchasing behaviour. However, many of the accepted means of categorising individuals are unlikely to be sufficiently discriminating to be a meaningful way of segmenting the market. For example, extrovert and introvert personalities could be seen to embrace a wide variety of behaviour. A much quoted personality variable is

the degree of innovativeness. Five major categories have been defined (Rogers and Shoemaker, 1971). The *innovators* comprise the first 2.5% of adopters. These tend to be more cosmopolitan, relatively affluent and venturesome. The *early adopters* account for the next 13.5% of adopters. They tend to be integrated into their communities, unlike the innovators; have a high degree of opinion leadership; and be less risk averse. The *early majority* form 34% of the remaining adopters. There then follow the *late majority* (34% of adopters); and finally the *laggards* (16%), whose dominant characteristic is traditionalism.

Each of these groups of customers will have different requirements – the innovators, for example, are concerned with novelty and are relatively price insensitive – that can define the manner in which a marketing strategy may evolve through appealing to different segments over time.

The application of psychographic segmentation may pose some difficulty, if only because it may be problematic at least to identify clearly buyer types according to criteria which are in essence intuitive. This suggests that it may be necessary to correlate psychographic criteria with measurable demographic variables. Moreover, extensive studies have failed to identify unambiguous relationships between life styles and brand choices (Cosmas, 1982); or between personality and purchasing behaviour, with often only weak relationships between the two being identified (Tucker and Painter, 1961; Guen, 1960). For instance, Evans (1959) was not able to demonstrate a clear correlation between the purchase of certain types of vehicles and personality, and indeed he found that the more observable measures were more significant that personality variables.

■ Situation-specific criteria

Other approaches to segmentation are founded on specific features of the purchasing process, such as the benefits sought from the product. For example, in a much quoted study Haley (1968) categorised the market for toothpaste into groups of consumers according to the values they looked for: decay prevention; brightness of teeth; flavour and appearance; and price. He suggested that the resulting four segments would have the following features:

The decay prevention segment contains a disproportionately large number of families with children. They are seriously concerned about the possibility of developing cavities and show a definite preference for fluoride toothpaste. These individuals tend to be hypochondriacs. They are the worriers.

Brightness of teeth segment includes a significant number of young marrieds. They smoke more than average, and tend to be more active. These are more sociable.

Flavour and appearance segment is one where children tend to be influential in the choice of toothpaste. The use of spearmint toothpaste is well above average. This is the 'sensory segment'.

Price-oriented segment contains a high proportion of men. Consumers in this segment tend to be above average in terms of toothpaste usage. Brand loyalty is not a feature. In terms of personality, these people are more individualistic. This is referred to as the 'independent segment'.

Yankelovich (1964) segmented the market for watches as follows:

(1) people who want to pay the lowest possible price for any watch that works reasonably well;
(2) people who value watches for their long life, good workmanship, and superior styling;
(3) people who look not only for useful product features but also for meaningful emotional connotations (e.g. gift).

He argued that socio-economic data would not have led to the identification of these segments since high priced watches were purchased by both low and high income groups.

High income groups would often buy cheap watches which they would throw away when servicing was necessary. Timex, because all the major watch companies focused on segment three, decided to aim its marketing at segment one, but in the process also managed to attract segment two. The producers of the higher priced watches had associated product quality with water and shock resistance, but Timex was able to offer these features at a lower price. Moreover, Timex advertised all the year round, and since the other watch companies focused on the Christmas period, Timex obtained exclusive attention for ten months of the year. The company quickly grew to become the dominant force in the United States watch market.

Twedt (1964) suggested that a major proportion of the demand for products was accounted for by only 50% of the purchasers. This 'heavy half' as he termed it was likely to have particular characteristics. However, the implications for marketing of these situation oriented approaches remain unclear. Should the marketer accept the status quo and focus on for example the 'heavy half', or would it be more appropriate to attempt to convert some of the remainder, for which competition may be less intense, into higher volume users? Would it be more advantageous to attempt to educate potential purchasers into seeking new product values which the marketer has added to or associated with the product? It may in fact be more profitable to concentrate on the 'light half'; or it may be more appropriate to assess what benefits non-users are seeking. The approach also rests on the assumption that segments established according to situation specific criteria have distinctive characteristics, but as Haley (1968, p. 31) suggests, there is no reason to suppose that the 'heavy half' is uniform in its preferences, and if this is so, and there is no empirical evidence to suggest otherwise, the utility of this approach is considerably undermined.

■ Segmenting the business market

A two-stage approach to the segmentation of business markets has been suggested (Wind and Cardozo, 1974). First, what are termed macrosegments are identified, using such observable criteria as size of organisation, or geographical location. Second, these are divided into microsegments, defined in terms of the decision making features of the units which comprise each macrosegment. Macrolevel features might include:

Size of the buying organisation: a large organisation might be expected to have different, perhaps more formal and elaborate, procedures for example, compared with a small organisation.

Usage rate: for example, the difference between non-users and large users, which in turn might require different marketing approaches.

Structure of the procurement function: those with a highly centralised purchasing function would have different procedures to those with a more decentralised approach.

Application: the market can be divided according to end uses.

Purchase type: whether or not it is a new task, straight rebuy or a modified rebuy. For example, a first time buyer would have different requirements than a purchaser involved in a repeat purchase.

Within each macrosegment, there may be a number of subsegments differentiated in terms of different requirements and responses to marketing stimuli. Important criteria might be: service level, product quality, speed of delivery, price, technical support, all of which can have significant implications for the marketing strategy adopted.

Bonoma and Shapiro (1983) suggested that industrial markets might be segmented according to demographic (e.g. size, industry, location), purchasing procedures (e.g. criteria; organisational structure) and behavioural factors (e.g. attitude to risk).

■ Validity of segmentation

Various criticisms can be levelled at market segmentation. Some have suggested that the difficulties in its meaningful application are often underestimated, with the result that in practice it does not often appear to be frequently employed (Saunders, 1987). Others have argued this results more from an emphasis on the technique rather than on its implementation (Hooley, 1980; Bonoma and Shapiro, 1984; and Piercy and Morgan, 1993) suggest that more attention needs to be directed to the organisational environment in which the segmentation is to be applied. Issues, they believe, that need to be addressed include: whether or not the information systems are capable of gathering the necessary information; the receptivity of the organisational culture to the new approaches demanded; the compatibility of the existing structures to any new requirements resulting from the adoption of the new segmentation techniques; and so on. Overall, they stress that it is important for effective implementation to relate segmentation *criteria* and processes to the user environment.

Even if these conditions for effective implementation are fully satisfied, there are several other potential problems. For instance, buyers may not necessarily be consistent in their purchasing behaviour and segments may be unstable. It may be that many consumers in particular are promiscuous in their brand purchases, for example, because they desire innovation and variety, so that the proliferation of brands reflects suppliers' recognition of this reality (Reynolds, 1965).

There are of course several factors, some of which may not be easily detectable, that can distort the relationships between the dependent and independent variables, including information scarcity and unavailability of preferred product choices. In addition, one cannot conclude that the impetus to action is the same in all cases, thereby making it difficult to conclude with certainty that a particular segmentation measure, such as personality, leads to a specific form of action. Moreover, it may be difficult to satisfy the criterion of accessibility. As Bleda and Kassarjian note: 'Unfortunately those starved for self-esteem, the hypochondriacal types, or heavy users of toothpaste do not cooperate by differentially exposing themselves to specific media, purchasing from different outlets or necessarily being willing to pay different prices' (Bleda and Kassarjian, 1969, p. 250).

In essence, segmentation can be viewed as a means of imposing a structure on the market in order to simplify the formulation and implementation of marketing strategies. Whether or not there exist the clearly defined categories that emerge from the process of segmentation followed is in fact irrelevant as long as it leads to the practical end results desired, namely, the identification of customers whose requirements are unfulfilled, the securing of a competitive advantage by developing and marketing offerings that are perceived in some way as superior by selected customers, and the providing of a focus for and direction to marketing efforts. Market segmentation is then essentially creative and utilitarian; nothing more, but nothing less.

■ References

Anon. (1990), 'Ad Agency Finds 5 Global Segments', *Marketing News* 8 (January), pp. 9–17.

Bleda, J. C. and Kassarjian, H. H. (1969), 'An Overview of Market Segmentation', in Morin, B. A. (ed.), *Marketing in a Changing World*, Chicago: American Marketing Association, pp. 249–253.

Bonoma, T. V. and Shapiro, B. P. (1983), *Segmenting the Industrial Market*, Lexington, Mass: Lexington Books.

Bonoma, T. V. and Shapiro, B. P. (1984), 'Evaluating Market Segmentation Approaches', *Industrial Marketing Management* 13, pp. 257–268.

Coleman, R. P. (1961), 'The Significance of Social Stratification in Selling', *Marketing: A Maturing Discipline*, ed. M. L. Bell, Chicago: American Marketing Association, pp. 171–184.

Cosmas, S. (1982), 'Life Styles and Consumption Patterns', *Journal of Consumer Research* 8 (March), pp. 453–456.

Craven, D., Hills, G. and Woodruff, R. (1987), *Marketing Management*, Homewood, Ill.: Richard D. Irwin, pp. 297–300.

Evans, F. B. (1959) 'Psychological and Objective Factors in the Prediction of Brand Choice', *Journal of Business* 32 (October), pp. 340–369.

Frank, R. E., Massey, W. F. and Wind, Y. (1972), *Market Segmentation*, Englewood Cliffs, NJ: Prentice-Hall.

Green, P. E. and Kreiger, A. M. (1991), 'Segmenting Markets with Conjoint Analysis', *Journal of Marketing* (October), pp. 20–31.

Guen, W. (1960), 'Preference for New Products, and its Relationship to Different Measures of Conformity', *Journal of Applied Psychology* 44, pp. 361–366.

Haley, R. J. (1968), 'Benefit Segmentation: A Decision Oriented Research Tool', *Journal of Marketing* (July), pp. 30–35.

Hooley, G. (1980) 'The multivariate jungle: the academic's playground but the manager's minefield', *European Journal of Marketing* 14 (7), pp. 379–386.

Leverick, F. and Littler, D. A. (1994), *Communication on the Move: A Study of Consumers' Attitudes towards and Usage of Mobile Communications*, mimeo UMIST Manchester School of Management, p. 49.

Piercy, N. F. and Morgan, N. A. (1993), 'Strategic and Operational Market Segmentation: A Managerial Analysis', *Journal of Strategic Marketing* 1, pp. 123–140.

Reynolds, W. H. (1965), 'More Sense About Market Segmentation', *Harvard Business Review* (September/October), pp. 107–111.

Riche, M. F. (1989), 'Psychographics for the 1980s', *American Demographics* (July), pp. 24–26, 30–31, 53–54; quoted in Boone, L. E. and Kurtz, D. L. (1992), *Contemporary Marketing*, seventh edition, Orlando, Fl.: The Dryden Press.

Rogers, E. M. and Schoemaker, F. F. (1971), *Communication of Innovations*, second edition, London: Collier Macmillan.

Saunders, J. (1987), 'Marketing and Competitive Success', in Baker, M. J. (ed.), *The Marketing Book*, London: Macmillan.

Smith, W. (1956), 'Product differentiation and market segmentation as alternative marketing strategies', *Journal of Marketing* 21 (July), pp. 3–8.

Summers, D. and Smith, A. (1994), 'A brand new campaign', *Financial Times* (20 January), p. 15.

Thomas, M. J. (1980), 'Market Segmentation', *Quarterly Review of Marketing* 16 (1) (Autumn), pp. 25–28.

Tucker, W. T. and Painter, J. J. (1961), 'Personality and Product Use', *Journal of Applied Psychology* 45, pp. 325–329.

Twedt, D. W. (1964), 'How Important to Marketing Strategy is the Heavy User?', *Journal of Marketing* (January).

Wells, W. D. and Gubar, G. (1966), 'Life Cycle Concept in Marketing Research', *Journal of Marketing Research* 3 (November), pp. 355–363.

Wind, Y. (1978), 'Issues and advances in segmentation research', *Journal of Marketing Research* 15 (August), pp. 317–37.

Wind, Y. and Cardozo, R. N. (1974), 'Industrial Market Segmentation', *Industrial Marketing Management* 3 (March).

Wind, Y. and Douglas, S. (1972), 'International Market Segmentation', *European Journal of Marketing* 5 (1).

Yankelovich, D. (1964), 'New Criteria for Market Segmentation', *Harvard Business Review*, (March–April), pp. 83–90.

■ Chapter 7 ■

Marketing Research

John Webb

■ Introduction

It has become increasingly common, in recent years, for marketing to become accepted, primarily, as a process of exchange. Bagozzi (1975) writes: 'In order to satisfy human needs, people and organisations are compelled to engage in social and economic exchanges with other people and organisations... Social actors obtain satisfaction of their needs by complying with, or influencing, the behaviour of other actors. They do this by communicating and controlling the media of exchange, which in turn, comprise the links between one individual and another.' The process of communication, in a marketing context, comprises a two way exchange between the principal 'social actors': the producers and the consumers. The former communicates with the latter by means by the provision of goods and through advertisements and promotions. The consumer communicates with the producers of the goods and services by the purchase of their offerings.

In the earliest days of such an exchange process, what today would be called a barter system (where markets were physical entities rather than concepts) it can be seen that the process of communication would have been easily facilitated by the physical proximity of the two 'actors'. If the producer's current offerings were acceptable (in the sense of size, shape etc.) then the deal would be concluded, after haggling, with an agreement as to the price to be paid. A price which was acceptable to the consumer as representing 'value for money' and to the producer of the good as providing evidence of an acceptable level of financial return for the physical effort of producing the good and of the risk in bringing such a good to the market place. If the goods on display were not acceptable, then the prospective consumer could describe his/her requirements to the producer and, if a suitable price could be ageed, place an order for a bespoke item. Communications had again ensured that the exchange process had delivered mutual benefits; one side is guaranteed the price and profits that he/she wants, while the other side obtains the product to their exact specifications at a price with which they feel comfortable.

Currently, the communication process between consumers and producers has, however, evolved to a very high degree of sophistication. Unfortunately, while one side (advertising/promotions) would appear to have 'gone to the ball', the other – the way in which consumers communicate with suppliers of goods/services – would appear to have become the 'Cinderella' of management techniques. Fortunately, Marketing Research, the Cinderella of which we speak, appears, once more, to be regaining its rightful place in the armoury of the manager.

Certain factors have combined to facilitate such a rapprochement between managers and marketing research; the two major reasons being the increasing physical and 'psychic' distance between the two parties in the exchange process, the other being the amount of 'danger' that arises from operating in certain environments, 'danger' coming from such sources as the pervasive effects of technology, environmental turbulence, market segmentation and the effects of culture. The philosophy of marketing, as an exchange process, demands that the producer should place the consumer at the focus of their attempts to provide a stream of profitable goods. Implicit in such an idea is an acceptance that companies must listen to what their current and potential customers think of their current offerings and to what they aspire in the future.

Marketing research is that 'bundle' of techniques which have been developed, or appropriated from other subjects in the social, medical and/or physical sciences, to furnish a stream of valid, reliable and appropriate information such that managers will be able to manage better.

▌Definitions of the role of marketing research

Marketing research occupies a service function; it has as its raison d'être the role of supplying management with reliable, valid, timely, relevant and current information.

Factors already touched upon, e.g. technology, combined with higher levels of competition have had the effect of reducing a manager's ability to rely upon past experience as a guide to the future; the amounts of 'danger' in the system have increased, and change becomes the only constant. Managers have to take decisions with far reaching consequences, opportunities must be grasped, threats avoided, markets segmented, target markets selected, control exercised, marketing

plans implemented and monitored. But managers do not exist nor make decisions in a vacuum – there is an environment, outside their control, of which they must take due note. Marketing research can be viewed as a managed 'conduit' through which managers can link the steps over which they do have control, their internal environment(s), with the external environment(s).

The ability to identify, measure, evaluate and anticipate relevant change is becoming increasingly critical to the long-term success of organisations. Marketing research is a process by which data on which these decisions are based, may be collected. And collected in such a manner that the end result renders a true, like-like representation of the situation under regard and not some cartoon-like image with distorted features.

Many authors have provided definitions of the subject, here are a sample:

'Marketing research is the systematic and objective approach to the development and provision of information for the marketing decision making process' (Kinnear and Taylor 1991).

'Marketing research is the systematic and objective identification, collection, analysis and dissemination of information for the purpose of assisting management in decision-making related to the identification and solution of problems and opportunities in marketing' (Malhotra, 1993).

From these definitions two key words recur; systematic and objective:

Systematic means that the research process should be well planned and organised, with rules established for its implementation, the types of data to be collected, the way in which it is to be collected, the system of analysis to be employed, all being established in advance of the advent of the research.

Objective means that the research should be conducted in a way that eliminates (as far as possible) bias and the ingress of subjectivity/emotion, the research may not take place in a laboratory setting, but it should still strive for scientific objectivity.

■ Types of research

Kinnear and Taylor (1991) classify marketing research into three groups: exploratory research, conclusive research and performance monitoring (routine feed-back) research, with each stage in the decision-making process determining the appropriate class of research that is required.

Recognise/define
marketing objectives
Sense/define marketing } Exploratory research
problems/opportunities

Evaluate courses of action
Decide on appropriate } Conclusive research
responses

Implement responses } Performance monitoring research

Exploratory research is usually preferred in the initial stages of the investigation, when uncertainty/ignorance are at their highest. It is characterised by flexibility, a lack of formal structure and the desire to measure. It may be used to define the boundaries of the environment in which problems/opportunities are likely to exist, and to uncover those salient variables which are relevant to the successful completion of the project. Exploratory research may alert researches to any temporal/seasonal effects which may impinge upon the results; identify any dialects/jargon which may be the common currency in a particular situation; and, allow an estimation to be made as to how easy/difficult it will be to carry out the research. Data sources include, secondary sources of data, observation, mini-surveys, interviews with experts and case histories.

Conclusive research may be used to provide information to evaluate and select a course(s) of action; research is formal, objective and systematic. It will include a definition of the objectives of the research, sampling plans, decisions as to, for example, types of survey, possible systems of experimentation and ways in which the data is to be analysed. A clear link should be exhibited between the information that is sought and the possible alternatives courses of action under consideration.

Performance-monitoring research: a course of action, once selected, cannot merely be imple-

mented and then ignored; managers will need to be informed as to the results of its implementations. It is the way in which comparisons are made between what was planned and what is actually happening; marketing plans need to be controlled. Thus, not only should marketing mix variables and the situational variables be subjected to careful monitoring, but also such measures as sales, market share, profit and ROI.

Quantitative and qualitative research methods are not mutually exclusive methods of research, but complementary. Each having plus and minus points, which may be used to ameliorate the disadvantages inherent in one system of thought by the use of the other. The choice(s) of what system, or combination of systems, should be guided by the specific factors which are found in each research problem. Most contemporary research projects contain elements of both qualitative and quantitative research methods.

Gordon and Langmaid (1988) provide the following comparison between the two methods:

Qualitative	*Quantitative*
Open-ended, dynamic, flexible	Statistical and numerical measurement
Depth of understanding	Sub-group sampling or comparisons
Taps consumer creativity	Survey can be repeated in the future and results compared
Database – broader and deeper	Taps individual responses
Penetrates rationalised or superficial responses	Less dependent on research executive skills or orientation
Richer source of ideas for marketing and creative teams	

■ The process of marketing research

The sequence of steps for marketing research is shown below:

1. Set the objectives of the research programme
2. Define the research problem
3. Assess the value of the research
4. Construct the research proposal
5. Specify the data collection method(s)
6. Specify the technique(s) of measurement
7. Select the sample
8. Data collection
9. Analysis of the results
10. Presentation of the final report

■ Secondary data

Secondary data, which consists of previously published material, should always be consulted before commencing primary research.
Newsom-Smith (1988) says that secondary data can:

1. provide a background to primary research; if the research has already been conducted by a third party, then why repeat it, if it will serve the current research objectives? Even if it doesn't exactly fulfil what is required, then it may help determine key variables that any subsequent primary research will have to include; it may help determine sampling methods and sample sizes; alert researchers to key 'actors' in the environment, and illustrate active trends in that particular market.
2. act as a substitute for field research; tailor-made, primary research can be very expensive. Secondary data may help save such costly exercises in that previously published data may fully answer all the questions posed by the current research objectives. Even if not all questions are answered, then the need for primary research may be substantially reduced. A cost-benefit analysis should be made to weight the cost of further (possibly expensive) primary research against the advantages of less detailed/specific, but much cheaper, secondary research.
3. Baker (1991) shows how some types of research may only be carried out realistically by the use of secondary data, and cites the case of attempting to establish trends in market

behaviour. Longitudinal studies are unrealistic propositions for primary research, thus one must rely on published, historical data. Secondary data may also set the boundaries and establish the situation of the environment in which primary research will be set.
4. Acquisition studies; acquisition has been a popular strategy for companies to follow in recent years. Predator companies, not wishing to alarm their intended 'targets', could hardly mount large primary field studies without making themselves known to other interested parties. Thus secondary research may be used to gain information on other companies.

But before the wholesale acceptance of secondary data, researchers should ask themselves the following questions:

Is the secondary data relevant?
Is it too costly to acquire?
Is the secondary data available?
Is there a possibility that the data is biased?
Is the secondary data accurate?
Is the data sufficient for the current research project's purposes?

□ *Sources of secondary data*

With vast amounts of data currently available, it is all too easy to gather only peripherally relevant data. Sensible advice is given by Luck and Rubin (1987) 'a good rule in all research is parsimony; using only meaningful data'. The first place to start a search for 'meaningful data' is within the organisation itself. With the increasing use of Management Information Systems, functional departments are now more likely to hold data in a form readily accessible to research personnel.
Internal sources of data may be divided as follows:

Accounts: contain information on customers' names and address, types and quantities of products purchased, costs of sales, advertising, manufacture, salaries, etc., discounts, etc.

Sales records: contain information on markets, products, distribution systems

Other reports: contain information on trade associations/trade fairs, exhibitions, customers complaint letters, previous marketing research reports, conferences.

If such sources prove inadequate for the intended task, then external data sources should be consulted. Where, though, does one start to make sense of the vast amounts of externally published data?

A useful rule of thumb is to start with the general and then gradually to focus onto the specific. Thus, in an unfamiliar research setting, one should start with those guides, which render indications as to the general direction in which to proceed. From such 'directory of directories' type publications, one may begin with, for example, general industry data, and proceed through specific industry data, via market/category information down to specific company/product data.

Trained librarians offer an excellent way of finding a 'way in' to these huge data sources. they are especially useful when first consulting computer databases, which can be very complex – as mistakes in their operation can, in financial terms, be most costly.

■ Quantitative primary data

Primary data is that which is collected to fulfil the demands of the current research project, should secondary sources of data fail to provide the information necessary to meet the research objectives.

If it is determined that individuals hold the data necessary to answer the questions posed by the project's research objectives, then they can be asked questions, observed, or invited to become a member of a continuous research panel.

□ *Survey research*

Personal interviews, telephone interviews and mail questionnaires are known collectively as survey research. Each have their individual advantages and disadvantages and the optimum choice between them, or combination of them, is mostly dependent upon the skill of the research in matching individual methods with the situation-specific demands of the research objectives, taking into account the environment in which the research is to take place. Aaker (1990) says that the following are the main factors to be considered when making this choice: available budget, the nature of the problem, the complexity of the data requirements, the need for accuracy and the constraints of time. There is no formal rule which categorically states that only one method may be used for a particular research project. In many situations, a mixture of several (or even all) methods may be used.

Survey methods are particularly well suited to gathering data on: behaviour (past and present): attitudes and opinions: respondent variables: knowledge.

Personal interviews

The two factors which are used to classify interviews are structure and directness. The former refers to the degree of formality/rigidity of the interview schedule; the latter refers to the degree to which the respondent is aware of the purpose of the research.

Unstructured-indirect methods are rarely used in marketing research, being more the territory of psycho-analysis. Unstructured-direct and structured-indirect will be covered in the section on Qualitative Primary Research. Structured-direct is the method most often used in research surveys.

Its advantages are:

It allows the researcher: to reduce respondent anxiety (increasing rapport which may increase response rates); to guide respondents through complex questionnaires with difficult to comprehend routing instructions; and to ask for ambiguous/unclear answers to be clarified. Question wording and order are fixed with answers being recorded in a standard manner, thus reducing the effects of the interviewer – a potential problem when multiple interviewers are being employed. Standardised formats allow projects the use of less skilled interviewers, thus reducing costs. Also, pictures, products, sign etc. may be displayed to refresh respondents' memories or to demonstrate some action.

Its disadvantages are:
It is time-consuming and the cost per completed interview is high compared with mail questionnaires and telephone interviews. Because of the standardised/rigid format of the questionnaire, the data gathered may lack depth and richness. Questions usually have to be closed because of the problems associated with recording the answers to open-ended questions.

Telephone interviews

An administered questionnaire delivered via the telephone.

Its advantages are:
Low cost per completed questionnaire with the use of a central location reducing travel-times and costs and permitting tight administrative control of interviewers, thus reducing the opportunity for contamination by bias and error. The method can deliver quicker results, compared with mail questionnaires and face to face interviews, and it allows the sample to be drawn, very easily, from a wide geographical spread.

Its disadvantages are:
It is difficult, during a call's short duration, to establish a good, working rapport with respondents; this may result in their not being fully at ease in the interaction or in allowing them, easily, to terminate the interview. Thus questions must be short and able to engage, quickly, the attention/interest of the interviewees. Respondents may confuse a 'research' call with a cold-call telephone sales 'pitch' and terminate the call for fear of being sold something. The sample may not be fully representative of the population as not everyone is connected to the telephone system (though this reason grows less important as time passes). It is impossible to

show respondents signs, pictures or actual products to 'jog' their memories or to demonstrate some action.

Mail questionnaires

Mail questionnaires do not make use of an interviewer, so the interviewer, as a source of error, is removed, thus they may be used where the ingress of such error might cause serious problems.

Its advantages are:
It allows for the reduction of field staff to a minimum, resulting in a low cost per completed questionnaire if response rates are high. The relatively anonymous method of data collection may give certain respondents the confidence to answer what, to them, might otherwise be considered to be 'embarrassing' questions. They can cover, economically, wide geographical areas. They may 'open up' certain areas of the population for survey research which are denied personal interview and telephone interview techniques because of their problems in gaining access. Respondents may fill in the mail questionnaire using their own time-scale, thus removing the 'pressure' that some feel arises because of the physical presence of the interviewer. It also allows respondents to consult their files, notes, account records, etc.

Its disadvantages are:
Even though addressed to named individuals, there is no way of knowing who exactly made the responses. All questions may be read in advance, therefore the ability to control the sequence of questions is removed, respondents can see exactly where the questions are leading merely by turning to the last pages. There is no-one to explain/interpret to respondents complicated/ambiguous questions, resulting in the possibility that such questions are either guessed or omitted. Questionnaires which are long, or which are perceived to be long, will either not be answered at all or will have large numbers of questions unanswered. High non-response rates will mean that the cost per completed questionnaire can become prohibitively high.

☐ *Panel/syndicated research*

The panel, from whom the data is collected, may consist of individuals, households, industrial buyers, firms etc., who agree to provide data to research agencies on a regular basis.

Supplied data may include information concerning consumer and/or industrial products and store audits.

Data sources may be classified into six main groups: consumer, retail, wholesale, industrial, media/audience, and for advertising evaluation.

Advantages of panel research

Data is generated continuously, so trends such as market share and brand switching etc. may be established, and as there is a reduced need to keep on generating sample the potential effects of sampling error are lessened. Evidence suggests that higher response rates will be enjoyed when compared with rates from ad hoc surveys. The results are likely to be more accurate as panel members become experienced in recording their purchases. Data may be generated for a comparatively smaller outlay, when compared with the costs of mounting an ad hoc survey. Panels/syndicated research can provide data on competitor activities. Because of its continuous nature, it is likely to produce results quicker than with an ad hoc survey.

Disadvantages of panel research

The main disadvantages of panel research lie with the sample itself; once the initial sample has been selected, by whatever, though usually probability-based methods, selected panellists may refuse to join, thus 'upsetting' the representativeness of the sample. Of those panellists that do agree to joint, some, over time, may for whatever reason(s), drop-out, again 'upsetting' the sample's representativeness, and there might be difficulties in finding new panel members with equivalent characteristics. Some panel members may have to be 'retired' when they get too old. Old age itself is not a problem, but the research organisation has to maintain a panel representative of the population's demographic constitution. Panel members *may* change their purchasing habits as a result of being surveyed. This effect may be reduced by (i) a reasonably rapid turnover of panel members, and (ii) disregarding their diary entries for the first 2–3 months of membership.

☐ *Observation*

All members of a society are observers, but the adjective mostly used to describe such an act would be casual, subject, as it is, to large and unreliable amounts of subjectivity and bias on the part of the observer. Therefore, it must be made more objective and rigorous. Observation does not immediately spring to mind as a marketing research method but there are two situations where it may prove useful:

1. where it is the only way of gathering certain types of data, e.g. it would be difficult for a respondent to recall their exact path through a department store and the amount of time they spent in each section, but the results could be obtained by using a trained observer.
2. it may be employed to confirm that the results gathered by other methods are valid; here, it stands as half of a two-pronged investigation.

Tull and Hawkins (1993) give three conditions to be met if observation is to be used successfully:

1. the action must be overt, therefore the the measurement of such factors as feelings, motivation, attitdue, etc., are ruled out.
2. the action should be frequent, repetitive and predictable.
3. the action should encompass a reasonably short time span.

Modes of observation are classed according to four main factors; naturalness, openness, structure and directness.

Questionnaires and their design

A questionnaire is an ordered list of questions which may be used in a wide variety of research situations. They may vary in the amount of freedom which is allowed to the respondent in answering the questions. Highly structured questionnaires with rigid answer formats are usually easier to administer, answer and analyse; unstructured questionnaires are, in general, more difficult to administer, require more thought on the respondent's part and require considerable interpretative skills in their analysis. The situation-specifics of the research context will 'dictate', to a certain extent, the type of questionnaire to be employed.

The format of the questions may be dichotomous, which require only a yes/no type answer; multiple-choice, where respondents are invited to select one or a number of responses from a predetermined list; or open-ended, where the respondents are permitted to reply using their own words. Though these questions are more diffcult to interpret, they go some way in eliminating interviewer bias.

When deciding on the constituent questions, Webb (1992) suggest that the following questions be asked:

i.   is the question necessary?
ii. will the respondent comprehend the question?
iii. is the question sufficient to elicit the required data?
iv. does the respondent have the necessary data to answer the question?
v.   is the respondent willing /able to answer the question?

When phrasing the questions, one should ensure that the vocabulary employed is appropriate to the type of respondent being examined and that only the clearest and simplest words are used; vague/ambiguous questions should be avoided as should biased words or leading questions. Certain types of question also may prove difficult to administrate and/or analyse: those which contain estimates and those which rest on implicit assumptions. These types of question should only be asked if absolutely necessary. All questionnaires should undergo rigorous pre-testing on a sub-sample of potential respondents before their use.

Qualitative research methods

Not all research objectives may be met by the use of a question-and-answer format, good though these methods are at gaining information concerning factual data. There are other areas of human activity which do not fall into such convenient and relatively easily accessed categories. For respondents' attitudes, motivations, opinions, feelings, etc., as well as certain types of question with which respondents might experience heightened levels of anxiety or embarrassment, or where they might feel a difficulty in putting their answers into words, a different approach is required. Qualitative research is used to find ways of gaining access to such types of data; they seek to answer the 'why' and 'how' questions, rather then the 'what happened' or 'how many' types of enquiry.

Gordon and Langmaid (1988) say that qualitative research is used optimally in situations which increase understanding, expand knowledge, clarify use, generate hypotheses, identify a range of behaviours, explore/explain motivations and attitudes, highlight distinct behavioural groups and provide an input into future research. It may also be used for basic exploratory studies, new product development, creative development, diagnostic studies and tactical research projects.

□ *Group discussions*

The main 'motor' of this research tool is the dynamic interaction of the various group members. Group discussions usually last between one and three hours and employ between six to twelve respondents. Bellinger, Bernholdt and Goldstucke (1976) say that groups may be used to:

1. generate hypotheses subsequently to be tested quantitatively.
2. generate information useful in questionnaire construction.
3. provide background information on a product category.
4. gain reactions to new product concepts, for which there is no secondary data.
5. stimulate new ideas concerning the use of older products.
6. generate ideas for new creative concepts.
7. help interpret other qualitative results.

However, Gordon and Langmaid (1988) report that group discussions may be inappropriate under the following conditions:

a. in intimate/personal situations.
b. where there are strong pressures to conform to social norms.
c. where detailed case histories are required.
d. where the group is likely to be too heterogeneous with respect to the idea/product, etc. of interest.
e. where 'complex psycho-social issues' are involved.
f. where it is difficult to recruit the required sample, e.g. where people are physically widely separated.

The physical setting for the discussion required some thought, as pleasant surroundings are conducive to a free flow of ideas and help to reduce respondents' anxiety. The chair of the discussion (moderator), usually, a key member of the research team which set up the exercise and who will be pivotal in its analysis, should rapidly establish an easy going but workmanlike rapport with all the respondents.

As group discussions generate large amounts of data, which needs lengthy, hence expensive, analysis, it is vital that they are carefully planned and administered.

Malhortra (1993) gives the following guide for planning and conducting a group discussion:

1. set the objectives of the marketing research programme and problem definition.

2. specify objectives of the qualitative research.
3. state the objectives/questions to be answered by the group discussion.
4. write a screening questionnaire.
5. develop a moderator's outline.
6. conduct group discussion.
7. analyse the data.
8. summarise findings and plan follow-up research or action.

A screening questionnaire is used to eliminate those respondents who do not fulfil the requirements of the research brief. Developing the moderator's outline involves intense discussions between the client, research team and the moderator. This guide will ensure that all the required areas of interest are covered. It will also go some way to improve the reliability of the research method; a problem which may occur if multiple moderators are employed.

Advantages of group discussions

Cost and speed: since a large number of respondents are being 'processed' at the same time, data collection and the analysis of resultant data are quicker than for individual interviews. The social dimension: many individual decisions are made in a social context – groups provide that context. Society's requirements and perspectives are part of the discussion process and not a mere 'add-on'. The method allows for the observation of non-verbal communications, this will enable the trained moderator to make an assessment of the validity of the respondents' statements. Stimulation/synergism: a group of people will generate a far wider range of opinions, insights and information than they would have done when being examined as individuals. Some respondents may feel less exposed than they would have done in an individual interview, their anxiety being reduced, the method will enable them to produce more honest, valid and accurate responses. The unstructured or semi-structured nature of the discussion allows the moderator to probe behind respondents' answers which are vague and/or ambiguous. As many observers can become involved in the collection of the data and its analysis, a higher level of reliability should result.

Disadvantages of group discussions

As only a small number of respondents are involved, the question of unrepresentativeness arises, thus the ability to generalise about a population is constrained. This does not fully invalidate the method as a research tool as it is usually only used, as in exploratory research, where projections onto a population are not required. Some respondents may feel overawed/inhibited by the presence of the other respondents, thus causing them to act in an atypical manner, it may be that the shyer members of the group are allowed to be 'shouted down', by an ineffective moderator, by more dominant personalities. Thus the role of the moderator occupies a pivotal position in the research process and much will depend upon them. If the groups reacts, in a negative sense, against the moderator, then the chances of gaining valid, useful data are much reduced.

☐ *Individual depth interviews*

Between the interviewing poles of structured-direct and the unstructured-indirect, lies the individual depth interview, what Kinnear and Taylor (1991) call 'an unstructured personal interview which uses extensive probing to get a single respondent to talk freely and to express detailed beliefs and feelings on a topic'. Both group discussions and depth interviews are techniques whose main aim is to seek out, to delve, to try to understand and to explore, thus a flexibility of approach is essential – the interviewer must be able to alter and adapt to changing situations which may arise during the interaction.

Depth interviews have been found to be most beneficial where:

1. the situation being discussed has the potential to be embarrassing, stressful or of a confidential nature.
2. there is a need to uncover attitudes, motivations, beliefs and feelings.

3. peer pressure may cause respondents to act in an atypical manner (e.g. to say that they conform to certain societal norms when, in reality, they do not so do).
4. the interviewer needs to determine the chronology or case history of a decision process.
5. the situation is new and/or complex and exploration of the subject matter, rather than measurement, is the prime objective.

In depth interviews it is not too strong to claim that the nature of the relationship between interviewer and subject is of prime importance. Thus the establishment of a good rapport should be the first of the interviewer's functions and questions aimed at carrying this out should come first. Then it is recommended that the general questions gradually give way to the specific, where the heart of the interview lies.

Advantages of individual interviews

Great depth/richness of data, with the ability to attach, directly, an opinion to single individual; something which is not so easy in a group discussion. The lack of peer pressure allows for the expression of unconventional sentiments without fear of any sanction, mockery or embarrassment. The close rapport between interviewer and subject encourages a freer flow of valid and useful information.

Disadvantages of individual interviews

Costly in terms of time/money both to conduct the interview and to analyse the results, and because of this high cost, it is usual only to work with small samples, thus limiting the ability of the research to generalise about the results. There may be problems in gaining access to interviewers with the requisite skills. Because of the highly personal nature of the interchange between the two parties and because of the unknowable amounts of subjectivity which will colour the proceedings, it may be difficult to compare the information gathered by one interviewer with that from another.

□ *Projective techniques*

Appropriated from psychology/psychiatry, projective techniques rely on the principle that the way people organise and respond to relatively ambiguous stimuli will tell trained observers something about the respondent's perceptions of the outside world and their reactions to it. Kidder (1981) says that projective techniques are useful in:

> encouraging in respondents a state of freedom and spontaneity of expression where there is reason to believe that respondents cannot easily evaluate or describe their motivations or feelings or where topics on which a respondent may hesitate to express their opinions directly for fear of disapproval by the investigator or when respondents are likely to consider direct questions as an unwarranted invasion of privacy or to find them threatening for some reason.

Classed as structured-indirect techniques, they receive their name from the way in which respondents 'project' their feelings, attitudes, beliefs etc. onto a third party or object. Emotions which would have remained covert if the chosen investigative technique had tried to gain access to them by means of more direct questioning, etc. It is not intended to be a system by which measurements are made, but more one where those emotions which the majority of the population have difficulty in articulating, are uncovered. They may be used:

a. to explore and generate hypotheses, which may then be tested by more quantitative methods.
b. to reveal feelings, beliefs, behaviour patterns which would have remained hidden if a more quantitatively based method had been employed.

Techniques used in this research method may be conveniently grouped under the following headings: completion, association, construction, choice ordering and expressive techniques.

Advantages of projective techniques

Useful in exploratory studies where emotional guidance, feelings etc. are sought and where inputs useful in generating hypotheses are required. They enable researchers to gain access to data which they might have been denied if a more direct, interrogative technique had been employed. They may be used to 'break the ice', and help in establishing rapport in the initial stages of qualitative studies.

Disadvantages of projective techniques

Expensive: to be of use, the services of highly skilled research workers need to be used; also it is only possible to employ small samples using these methods, so the ability to generalise about the results is severely restricted. It is time-consuming to administer and to analyse the results. Some respondents may be too shy and refuse to join in – therefore, non-response may be a problem. There are many opportunities for the results to become 'contaminated' by measurement error; the role of the researcher thus becomes of great importance as a way of reducing such error.

▍ Measurement in the research process

Having made a choice as to the style of data collection method, market researchers now have to opt for system(s) of measurement to be used. Measurement is part of everyday life; food is bought by weight, petroleum/cooking oil/beer is bought by volume, fabric by length – each product being dispensed by using a characteristic, weight, volume, length, etc., by which certain amounts of it may be isolated.

In marketing research measurements are common too; the research objectives might be, for example, to ascertain the number of people in a certain age group who buy a certain brand of instant coffee. Such measurements are relatively easy to make as the characteristics of interest are overt, easily accessed and of a unitary status, i.e. they only have one dimension – number, age grouping, etc. However, some other measurements are far more complicated because of the ambiguous nature of the answer to the question 'what is to be measured?'

Torgerson (1958) said that measurement is 'the assignment of numbers to objects to represent amounts of degrees of a property possessed by all of the objects'. Now while it is a relatively simple process to see how such a definition applies, say, to age (number of years since inception), or weight (number of units of gravitational attraction), it is not such a straight forward process when it come to the measurement of those factors, important in a social research setting, which are more covert. For example, there is no universally agreed (as there is with metres, etc.) system 'of the assignment of numbers' to a respondent's attitude towards hunting for pleasure, or their motivation in purchasing one specific brand of soap.

When measuring such abstract constructs as motivations, attitudes etc. in marketing research they may have to be expressed 'in terms of still other concepts whose meaning is assumed to be more familiar to the inquirer' (Green, Tull and Albaum, 1988). To make an evaluation of a stipulated situation there is a need to measure factors/variables (both overt and covert) which are relevant, but there is also a need to know *what* to measure. Attitude, for example, can be defined in many ways, some of which have more and some less relevance to a specific situation. It is not a unidimensional concept – there are many components. In making a definition of attitude, some of these components are excluded. Thus measurement is never fully able to translate reality into sets of numbers – representation can only ever be incomplete.

A variable is a factor relevant to a research situation which is capable of varying and in doing so affects the state of that situation. For example, many research studies are concerned with consumer responses to proposed changes in a product's price. The dependent variable is thus the consumer response, and it is affected by movements in the independent variables; such as packaging, the price of competing brands/products and brand loyalty. The research objectives will have stipulated what the outcome of interest is – in the above case, consumer response. There will also have been an implicit assumption as to what the independent variables are – but implicit assumptions cannot be used as a basis for

research: the implicit needs to be made explicit. One way to accomplish this is to construct a model of the research situation. If there is insufficient information to do this, then exploratory research will be required. It may also be possible to determine the significant variables by means of a thorough search of the literature.

Southern (1988) writes that there are three important components of the measurement process:

1. Measurement is a process; it is controlled and open, not arbitary or intuitive.
2. Measurement translates qualities into quantities, the numbers then being capable of manipulation. However, numbers in themselves have no meaning and those that manipulate them must exercise care if the validity of the relationship between number and characteristic is to be preserved.
3. Measurement has formal rules which may vary depending upon the manipulation, but once set, they must be followed consistently if reliability of data is to be guaranteed.

□ Scales in marketing research

There are four main levels of measurement: nominal, ordinal, interval, and ratio, and each makes different assumptions regarding the way in which the numbers reflect the situation under measurement.

Nominal scales assign numbers to objects, variables or people to show that they belong to some stipulated category; categories which are mutually exhaustive and mutually exclusive. Numbers here have no mathematical value, they merely show that the objects, etc., belong to a nominated group. Thus *Guardian* readers might be assigned the value 7 and *The Times* readers the value 456. The only mathematical function operable is to count the number of objects inside each category. Bus numbers, bank accounts and football team shirt numbers are examples of nominal scales.

Ordinal scales rank order objects/people, etc., according to the amount of a property which they possess. But to be useful, respondents in a research programme must be able to discriminate between items of interest with respect to an attribute, i.e. they must have the ability to say, for example, that this pizza tastes better than that pizza. In effect, they are saying that this pizza, the better one, has more of the attribute 'good taste' than the other pizza, their second choice. Ordinal scales do not enable researchers to know, or to infer, by how much one item is preferred over the others in the same category. Thus it is not possible to say if the difference between the first and second and between the second and third is the same, more, or less.

Interval scales possess order and distance, but do not have a unique origin, i.e. their zero point is arbitrary. Thus meaningful statements concerned with the distance between two objects may be made. It is permissible with an interval scale to say that the difference between scale points five and six is the same as the difference between scale points fifty five and fifty six. However, interval scales do not allow a researcher to make meaningful statements about the value of a scale point being a multiple of another value on the same scale.

Ratio scales possess order, distance and a unique origin indicated by zero. All mathematical operations are allowed here, so one can say that a reading of sixty on a scale is three times a reading of twenty on the same scale. Measures such as height, weight, volume are examples of ratio scales.

■ Attitudes and their measurement

Marketing research is constantly seeking to measure respondents' attitudes towards, for example, a change in price, etc. But an attitude is rather a difficult type of concept marketing research has to come to terms with. How have attitudes been defined?

Allport (1935) say that an attitude is 'a mental and neural state of readiness to respond that is organised through experience and exerts a directive and/or dynamic influence on behaviour'. Fishbein and Ajzen (1975) say that is 'a learned predisposition to respond in a consistently favourable or unfavourable manner with respect

to a given object'. There are many other definitions, but all seem agreed that an attitude is a learned mental state of readiness, a way in which an individual has constructed their own world such that when confronted with a certain stimulus they act in a certain manner.

Attitudes are not held to be the sole cause of human behaviour, there are many other factors at play at the moment at which the behaviour under investigation becomes manifest. Attitudes, though internal to the subject, are conditioned through external experience; experience which is not a random process, but organised through the process of learning.

☐ *The components of attitude*

It is generally agreed that attitudes have three components:

1. *Cognitive*: represents an individual's awareness and knowledge about an object, person, etc. They say 'I have heard about Brand X' or 'I believe that Brand X will carry out this function.'
2. *Affective*: represents an individual's feelings – good/bad, etc. – towards an object, etc., and is usually expressed as a preference. They say 'I do not like Brand C', or 'I like Brand D better than Brand F.'
3. *Behavioural*: represents an individual's predisposition to action prior to the actual decision being made or their expectations of possible future actions towards an object, etc.

In investigating the link between attitude and behaviour, research may try to use the information in one of two ways:

1. by measuring the cognitive and affective components to predict possible future behaviour.
2. by altering the cognitive and affective components in order to influence future behaviour.

□ *The measurement of attitudes*

Cook and Sellitz (1964) put forward, among others methods, the following way in which measured responses may give an indication as to an individual's attitude, by using techniques which rest on a relatively direct style of question which respondents answer in a way which enables an inference to be made as to the strength and direction of the attitude towards the research's object.

Measurement scales may be divided into two groups; rating scales and attitude scales.

Rating scales measure a single component of an attitude, respondent typically indicating their attitude to an object by means of a placement along a continuum of numerical values or of ordered categories. Scales may be labelled with verbal or numerical descriptors. In using the former, the researcher should be aware that some respondents may not place the same psychological distances between a 'very' and an 'extremely' as does the scale's constructor; a pre-test should check on this. By allocating a numerical value to the object depending on the strength with which they hold a given attribute, they can be used to measure:

1. a respondent's overall attitude towards something.
2. the degree to which something possesses a certain attribute.
3. a respondent's feeling towards a certain attribute.
4. the importance a respondent invests in a certain attitude.

Non-comparative rating scales: respondents are asked to assign a number, to the object of interest in isolation, there being no standard against which measurements are made. Respondents mark their attitude position on a continuum – a graphic scale – or they may choose a response from a limited number of ordered categories – an itemised scale.

Comparative rating scales: respondents make an assessment of the object of interest against a stated standard.

Rank order scales: respondents are asked to rank order a list of items against a stated criterion, e.g. taste, power etc. These are ordinal scales, thus respondents are able to show the order of their preferences. But it is not possible to say by how much the first item is preferred to the second, etc.

Constant sum rating scales: this method overcomes the drawbacks of rank order scales. The respondent is allocated a constant sum, usually a round number, 100, etc., and asked to allocate it between the given items in a way which reflects the object's attributes under investigation. This shows the rank order of the items and also the size of the preference distances.

Attitude scales, which combine many single rating scales, are an attempt to overcome the unrepresentativeness that may arise from inferring an individual's overall response to some object, etc., by measuring the attitude to only one aspect of that object; attitude scales try to measure several facets of an individual's attitude. The three most popular attitude scales will now be described.

Likert or summated scales require respondents to indicate their degree of agreement or disagreement with a number of statement concerning the attitude being measured. Their responses are given a numerical value and/or sign to reflect the strength and direction of the respondent's reaction to the statement. So, statements with which the respondent agrees are given positive or high values, while those with which they disagree are given negative or low marks. Scales may run, for example, from 1 to 5, from 5 to 1 or from +2 to –2. Statements should give the respondent the opportunity to express unambiguous statements, rather then neutral, ambiguous ones.

Semantic differential scales are probably the most widely used of all attitude scales. Respondents show the position of their attitude to the research object on a 7-point itemised scale, thus revealing both the strength and direction of the attitude. The extremities of the continuum are 'secured' by a pair of polarised adjectives or adjectival statements.

Example: Respondents are asked to record their attitude towards a certain law firm:

Unfriendly .... Friendly
Modern .... Old fashioned
Efficient .... Inefficient
Slow .... Fast
Pleasant .... Unpleasant

Osgood, Suci and Tannenbaum (1957) who invented the scale, developed some 50 pairs of bipolar adjectives grouped to measure three fundamental components of attitude: evaluative, activity, and potency.

If phrases, rather than words are used, then the scale will have more meaning for respondents, Dickson and Albaum (1977). Luck and Rubin (1987) recommend that no side of the scale should be exclusively reserved for either the positive or the negative aspect of the pairs, as this may encourage respondents to tick only down one side – the 'halo' effect.

Semantic differential scales may be analysed in two main ways.

Aggregate analysis: score are summed for each respondent for all pairs of words/statements, resulting in a numerical value of their attitude. Individual aggregate scores may then be compared with other individuals with respect to the same object, or two or more objects may be compared with respect to the same individual or group of individuals.

Profile analysis: involves calculating the arithmetic median or mean value for each pair of adjectives for an object for each respondent or respondent group. The profile so derived can then be compared with the profile of another object.

The principle disadvantage of semantic differential scales lies in their construction. For valid results, scales need to be made of truly bipolar pairs of adjectives/phrases, but some of the pairs chosen may not be true opposites in the respondents' minds.

The *Stapel scale* is a modified semantic differential scale, and uses a unipolar 10-point verbal rating scale with values from +5 to −5 which measures both the strength and direction of the attitude simultaneously. Stapel scales are easy to administer and do not require that adjectives be tested to ensure true polarity.

■ Sampling

Without the ability to extract a sample from a population, as opposed to conducting a census, many marketing research projects could not take place. There are four main reasons for this:

Cost: except where populations are very small, it is usually much cheaper to take a sample, rather than conduct a census.

Time: a census, generally, is a large undertaking, thus by the time the results had been collected and analysed, the situation under investigation might have changed. Samples may be extracted and analysed much quicker than a census.

Accuracy: i.e. the degree to which a measure of a characteristic in a sample compares with the measure of the characteristic in the population from which the sample was drawn. In sampling accuracy is affected by; 1. sampling error – caused by selecting a probability sample from a population which is not representative of that population; such error can be reduced by increasing the size of the sample; 2. non-sampling error – all other errors in a marketing research project whose origin is not based in sampling error.

The destructive nature of measurement: one cannot carry out a census on a box of fireworks and still have any product for sale. Thus sampling is the only alternative if an assessment of quality is required. Some forms of measurement destroy. For example, one can only measure a populations' initial reaction to an advertisement once. But, by extracting non-overlapping samples, such an evaluation may be repeated.

□ *Probability sampling techniques*

Probability samples are selected randomly, with each unit having a known chance of selection. Thus before a probability sample can be drawn, the research needs to define a sampling 'frame' for the population to ensure that each unit is included only once, and that no unit should be excluded – thus all units have an equal likelihood of selection; the frame should cover the entire population and be convenient to use.

A probability sample should be representative of the entire population – however, it can never be an exact replica. But by applying the rule of probability, generalisations concerning the population may be made, calculations made about the degree of confidence with which the results can be viewed.

Sample error arises from the variability of the sample and/or the size of that sample.

Simple random sampling: Individual units are assigned a number, a sample of these numbers then being selected either by using a 'lottery' system, or by the use of random number tables. The method is simple to use, and it obeys the laws of probability. However, it may produce samples which are highly unrepresentative of the population.

Stratified random sampling: This method accepts the variability of a population and by stratifying it before the sample is taken attempts to reduce its potential unrepresentativeness. Stratifiers, which may be geographical, demographic, etc., are imposed on the population like a grid, dividing it into groups whose members are alike as possible with respect to the stratifier. But it must ensure that all population units are included once and that none are excluded. Stratified random sampling adopts the position that each group/stratum is a population in its own right and then extracts a sample, by simple random means.

In *proportionate sampling*, the size of each sub-sample taken from a particular stratum is proportionate to the size of that stratum in the population. Thus if 25% of the population is aged between 30 and 40, then 25% of the sample should be composed of people in that age group. In *disproportionate sampling*, the proportion of a characteristic as possessed by the population is not reflected to the identical extent in the size of the sub-sample. Such a deliberate 'distortion' may improve the quality of the data if certain strata have an atypically large influence in the situation under investigation and need to be given a more significant role. In this case not every unit has an equal chance of selection, but the chance of selection is still known, thus the laws of probability still apply and appropriate weighting may be used when calculating the results. The method's major drawback is in finding stratifiers relevant to the research project.

Cluster sampling is similar to stratified sampling in that the total population is divided in strata, but it differs in that instead of sampling from each subgroup, a sample of the strata is taken, with a simple random sampling then taking place inside each of the selected groups. Thus while in stratified sampling each stratum represents a particular subset of the population (divided by age, sex, or car-ownership, for example) in cluster sampling each stratum should be a miniature of the full population. It is a method particularly useful in cases where the population is dispersed over wide geographical areas.

A particular form of cluster sampling is called *multistage sampling* and involves more than the single stage of the former system. If, after dividing a country into various areas (counties, states, etc.), they are found to have greatly varying sizes of populations, then they are sampled using a system called the probability proportionate to size method. Thus if a state has five times the population of the other states, then it should be allocated five times the chance of being selected. The first stage thus results in a number of states drawn from the population of states. Then, the research will select from these areas a number of, for example, cities, and again, they will be selected using the probability proportionate to size method. These stages may be repeated until the research arrives at the desired final sample. It has the advantages that the process delivers a sample, chosen at random, but concentrated in certain geographical areas; an advantage when the costs of travel and communication can be high. It also means that probability sampling may be used when, at the macro-level, there is no sampling frame. By the time several stages have been completed, and the research has arrived at the micro-level then sampling frames will be available – city maps, electoral rolls, etc.

Non-probability sampling techniques

Using non-probability sampling techniques mean that the researcher does not know the chances of a unit's selection. Therefore, the ability to generalise about a population, using the laws of probability, are much reduced, there can also be no calculable degree of confidence in the results. The sample is chosen at the convenience of the consultant or to fulfil the demands of some pre-determined purpose.

Convenience sampling: the sample is chosen for the convenience of the research worker. A street interviewer with the need to extract a sample of 50 people, for example, might survey the first 50 people who walk past a particular part of the city where the interviewer is sited. It is a quick and carries minimum cost. It is a method useful in exploratory research.

Judgement sampling makes an attempt to ensure a more representative sample than that gathered using convenience techniques. Research consultants use their expertise, or make use of experts in the appropriate fields, to assess populations and to make recommendations as to which particular units should be sampled.

With small populations and with accurate assessments and guidance as to a unit's selection, judgement sampling can render samples with less variable error than might arise with a sample chosen using a simple random technique, though this cannot be conclusively proved.

Purposive sampling does not usually aim for representativeness. Here the choice of the sample is made such that it should meet certain conditions deemed appropriate to the fulfil the objects of the research. Thus a project might stipulate that the top 50 thoracic surgeons be interviewed as part of the project; there would be no 'sampling' here, merely the need to contact those the research has already nominated.

Quota sampling attempts to reflect the characteristics of the population in the chosen sample, and in the same proportions. From national statistics, consultants gather the percentages for such 'stratifiers' as age groupings, income levels, sex, etc., and use them to construct 'cells', resulting in statements such as '23% of the population is female, aged between 30 and 40 and earning £12 000 to £15 000 per annum'. The sample would then be collected and 23% of it would have to fulfil those demands. Quota controls must be available, easy to use and up to date and

should, preferably, not result in too many 'cells'. These controls must also be relevant to the subject of the study. They shouldn't be used merely because they are available. This method may be cheaper to operate than a probability-based method, it is quick to use and relatively simple to administrate – it does not require a sampling frame. Disadvantages include the possibility of the interviewer showing bias in the way the individual units are selected and in the difficulty that may arise in uncovering relevant and available quota controls.

Probability v. non-probability sampling techniques

Tull and Hawkins (1990) provide the following list of factors to be considered when choosing between the two methods:

1. Are proportions and/or averages required or are projectable totals needed?
2. Are highly accurate estimations of population values necessary?
3. How large might non-sampling error be? What size of error due to frame choice, non-response, measurement and population specifications is likely?
4. Will the population be homogenous or heterogeneous with respect to the characteristic of interest?
5. What will be the cost, if the results are above/below the required error tolerance?

They say that 'the need for projectable totals, low allowable errors, high population heterogeneity, small non-sampling errors and high expected costs of error favour the use of probability sampling'.

☐ *Size of sample*

The size of a sample depends, primarily, upon the required degree of accuracy that the research objectives demand. This, in turn, will depend upon:

1. the degree of variability in the population, the more heterogeneous that population, the large the sample size required.
2. the presence of population sub-groups; the sample must be large enough to allow for a valid analysis of these.

Sample size estimation:

Judgement: this relies on the experience of the research consultant. But it may imply a quite arbitrary choice, ignoring such factors as cost, value and the required level of accuracy. The method of last resort.

What can be afforded: though commonly used, this method ignores the value of the information to be collected. E.g. a small sample may be more useful, though of a higher cost per unit, than a larger sample if the collected information is of high value.

Required size per cell: used in quota and stratified sampling techniques. It is usual to accept, as a minimum, 30 units per cell before any statistical analysis can proceed. Thus if there are 2 age groups and 5 geographical areas to be sampled, 10 cells will results. Resulting in a sample size of 10×30 or 300 units.

Statistical methods: Sample sizes may be calculated using the formula:

$$\frac{\sigma}{N} = \frac{\text{required level of accuracy}}{\text{level of confidence}}$$

Where σ = standard deviation and N = size of sample

■ Analysis of the results

The research will now, as a result of all the previous decisions and steps, be in possession of data from both primary and secondary sources. It must now be processed in the analysis such that it is possible to draw appropriate conclusions.

In commencing the analysis, two questions need to be answered:

1. with reference to the research objectives, what meanings should be obtained?

2. what statistical methods should be employed to obtain those meanings given the way in which the data was collected?

Luck and Rubin (1987) define statistical analysis as 'the refinement and manipulation of data that prepares them for the application of logical reference'.

After the statistical stage, comes that of interpretation – where data is transformed or refined into a state which will bring out its meaning; inductive and deductive processes are utilised.

Beveridge (1950) says that in inductive reasoning one starts from the position of the observed data and then proceeds to develop a generalisation that explains the observed interaction/situation. Deductive reasoning, on the other hand, moves from the general to the specific, by applying a theory to a particular case. Data interpretation should be concluded as objectively as possible. To ensure this the following points are important:

1. Honest/objective interpretations are helped by not exaggerating or distorting the findings.
2. Interpreters must remember that small samples limit the opportunity to generalise about a large population.
3. One should not try to reach a particular conclusion.
4. Validity and reliability of the data are ensured before interpreting the results and that there should be no confusion between facts and opinion.

Thus the steps in the analysis of data are as follows:

1. Put the data in order

The mass of raw data generated by field research is not in a suitable state for immediate interpretation; it needs to be transformed.

Editing involves, for example, checking the questionnaire to ensure that all the questions have been answered and that the respondent has given clear/unambiguous answers. If answers are missing or ambiguous, then steps should be taken to either fill them in, or respondents contacted to resolve areas of confusion. Interpreters should not try to guess at the incomplete answers.

Coding involves the assignation of a number, usually, to each particular response for each question. Most questionnaires are pre-coded, which saves a great deal of time at this stage. Open-ended questions also require coding, and this is usually carried out by expert analysts who review a representative sample of all the questionnaires and devise appropriate categories to which individual open answers can be assigned.

Tabulation involves arranging the data such that its significance may be appreciated. It requires that the data is placed into appropriate categories relevant to the research objectives. It can be done manually, mechanically or electronically. Such tables are very well suited to variables measured by ordinal or nominal scales because of their limited number of response categories. Cross-tabulation is a more developed form of the one-way tabulation described above and the system allows an investigation of the relationship between two or more key variables by counting the number of responses that occur in each of the categories.

2. Make a survey of the data

Unprocessed data needs to be transformed. The most common way to compress data is to calculate the data's central tendency: mean, median or mode. Other, more complicated measures of central tendency include such measures of dispersion or range, variance and standard deviation, and, if two or more distribution dispersions are being compared, the coefficient of variation. The results of the analysis so far need not be presented in purely mathematical forms; graphical display is very useful method of showing, for example, the frequency differences between different categories. Histograms, line and scatter graphs and pie-charts have all been found to be better at communicating results than bald tables of numbers.

3. Select an appropriate method of analysis

If the project's objectives cannot be reached by survey and cross-tabulation of the data and more sophisticated methods of analysis are required, then consideration should be given as to which particular analytical techniques will provide the appropriate information. But there are a vast array of available techniques, so some thought needs to be given to the way in which a research proceeds to the most appropriate method(s).

Luck and Rubin (1987) offer the following scheme:

a.   What is the technique required to show?

A commonly occurring request is to show whether the results are significant, i.e. are there significant differences between various groups or could the results have occurred by chance because only a sample of the population was under investigation.

b.   What scale was used to measure variables?

Only certain arithmetic manipulations are allowed on certain types of scale – it depends upon what level of measurement was reached. Non-metric scales, where the data was qualitative, rather than quantitative include nominal and ordinal scales. Metric scales work in real number systems and include ratio and interval scales

c.   Parametric and non-parametric data.

Parametric data is that which is distributed around a mean/central value in a symmetrical manner, as in a normal distribution, have been collected, at least, using an interval scale and may be analysed using probabilistic tests of statistical significance. Non-Parametric data has a distribution profile which does not conform to the normal curve of probability and appropriate tests assume that the variables have been measured using nominal or ordinal scales.

4. Number of variables to be analysed

Univariate analysis: where a single variable is analysed in isolation.

Bivariate analysis: occurs where some form of association is measured between two variables simultaneously.

Multivariate analysis: this investigates the simultaneous relationships between three or more variables.

5. Dependence and independence

Analysis may involve an investigation into the relationship between variables. By relationships is meant that changes in two or more variables are associated with each other. It may be important to be able to calculate by how much the independent variables are responsible for variations in the dependent variable.

6. How many samples are involved?

The choice of an appropriate statistical test depends upon whether the data is being tested to measure: (a) the significant differences between one sample and a nominated population; (b) the significant differences between two related or independent samples; (c) the significant differences amongst three related or independent groups; or (d) correlation and their significance tests.

■ Presentation of the final report

Research reports should communicate what they are supposed to communicate and do so in a manner appropriate to the intended readership. Those which are intended for a technically well-versed 'audience' may be written using specialist terms and may discuss, in detail, the complex issues of the research process. Those reports intended for a more general readership should not be used as an opportunity to 'dazzle' with a display of overt technical language and subject matter. Readers here are interested in the results, not in the way they were reached, though, of course, the appropriate amount of background to the project will need to be provided.

■ Conclusion

Marketing research should not be carried out merely for its own sake; it is a functional business technique to be used as a service, not as a means of providing employment for marketing research executives! But the technique does not need to be managed by senior management. It may be thought of as the equivalent of a taxi-cab service and its relationship with its passengers. The taxi-driver (marketing researcher) must be able to drive and know how to reach a certain intended destination. The passenger (client) must know where they wish to go and have the ability to pay the fare. Close co-operation between the parties will result in a mutually beneficial contract.

■ References

Aaker, D. A. and Day, G. S. (1990), *Marketing Research*, New York: John Wiley.

Allport, G. W. (1935), in *Handbook of Social Psychology*, ed. Murchison, C., Worcester, Mass.: Clary University Press.

Ajzen, I. and Fishbein, M. (1977), 'Attitude–behaviour Relations: A Theoretical Analysis and Review of Empirical Research', *Psychological Bulletin* 84, pp. 888–918.

American Marketing Association (1988), in *The Dictionary of Marketing Terms*, ed. Bennet, P. D.

Bagozzi, R. P. (1975), 'Marketing as Exchange', *Journal of Marketing* 39, pp. 32–39.

Baker, M. J. (1990), *Research for Marketing*, London: Macmillan.

Bellenger, D., Bernhardt, K. L. and Goldstucker, J. L. (1976), *Qualitative Research in Marketing*, Monograph Series, No. 3, Chicago: American Marketing Association.

Chase, D. A. (1973), *The Intensive Group Interviewing in Marketing*, MRA Viewpoints.

Cook, S. W. and Sellitz, C. (1964), 'A Multiple-indicator Approach to Attitude Measurement', *Psychological Bulletin*, 62, pp. 38.

Dickson, J. and Albaum, G. (1977), 'A Method for Developing Tailor-made Semantic Differentials for Specific Marketing Content Areas', *Journal of Marketing Research* (February), pp. 87–91.

Fishbein, M. and Azjen, I. (1975), *Belief, Intention and Behaviour*, Reading, Mass.: Addison-Wesley.

Kinnear, T. C. and Taylor, J. R. (1991), *Marketing Research: An Applied Approach*, 4th edition, New York: McGraw-Hill.

Gordon, W. and Langmaid, R. (1988), *Qualitative Marketing Research*, Aldershot: Gower.

Green, P. A., Tull, D. S. and Albaum, G. (1988), *Research for Marketing Decisions*, London: Prentice-Hall.

Luck, D. J. and Rubin, D. S. (1987), *Marketing Research*, 7th edition, Englewood Cliffs, NJ: Prentice-Hall.

Malhotra, N. K. (1993), *Marketing Research: An Applied Orientation,* Englewood Cliffs, NJ: Prentice-Hall.

Marketing Research Society (1979), Sub-committee of Qualitative Research: 'Qualitative Research – a Summary of the Concepts Involved'.

Newsom-Smith, N. (1988), in *Consumer Market Research Handbook*, 3rd edition, ed. Worcester, R. and Downham, J., London: McGraw-Hill.

Oppenheim, A. N. (1984), *Questionnaire Design and Attitude Measurement*, London: Heinemann.

Osgood, C. E., Suci, G. J. and Tannenbaum, P. H. (1957), *The Measurement of Marketing*, Urbana, Ill.: University of Illinois.

Parasuraman, A. (1986), *Marketing Research*, Reading, Mass.: Addison-Wesley.

Sellitz, C., Jahoda, M., Deutsch, M. and Cook, S. W. (1959), *Research Methods in Social Relations*, London: Methuen.

Southern, J. (1988), *Marketing Research*, M. Com., University of Strathclyde, Distance Learning Unit.

Suchman, E. A. (1950), 'The Scalogram Board Technique', in *Measurement and Prediction*, ed. Stouffer, E. A., Princeton: Princeton University Press.

Torgerson, W. S. (1958), *Theory and Methods of Scaling*, New York: John Wiley.

Tull, D. S. and Hawkins, D. I. (1993), *Marketing Research: Measurement and Method*, 6th edition, London: Macmillan.

Webb, J. R. (1992), *Understanding and Designing Marketing Research*, London: Dryden Press.

Weiers, R. M. (1988), *Marketing Research*, 2nd edition, Englewood Cliffs, NJ: Prentice-Hall.

■ *Chapter 8* ■

Modelling Markets

Peter Leeflang

■ Introduction[1]

Decision makers in marketing are often faced with rather complicated situations in which decisions have to be made. Let us consider the problem of determining the appropriate advertising budget. A brand manager is asked to determine the optimal budget. He knows that increases in advertising may lead to increased sales, but also lead to increased costs. The advertising expenditures in period t, say 1994, may not only lead to increases in sales in t, but also to increases in $t + 1$ (1995) and possibly may contribute to the value of the brand for a long time period.[2] Increases in sales will result in changes in profit. The decision maker is allowed to spend more advertising money if there is more profit and more sales, thus advertising spending depends on past sales and profit performance. In order to account for these and possibly other relationships it is necessary to formalise these relations. This means that the decision maker has to specify which variables influence which other variables and what the directions of causality between these variables are. To this end a model has to be formalised, data have to be collected and the formalised model has to be calibrated.

Let us consider another example.[3] The marketing director of a company has to determine the size of his sales force. He knows, of course, that a strong sales force is important, but that too large a force would be subjected to the law of diminishing returns. His intuition cannot tell him whether the optimal size of the sales force should be 5, 10 or 15 persons. A picture of the expected returns from sales forces of various sizes may assist him to choose the size that strucks the right balance between a demand for present return of investment and a desire for rapid growth. To this end he needs again, a formalised model, data and a model which is calibrated on these data. However, the marketing director is faced with the problem that the fluctuations in his sales force are rather limited over time. The size varies between 7 and 10 representatives. Past data only cannot be used to deduce what the relation will be between returns and size outside the range of values which are assumed in the past. This lack of variability of the data can be solved by collecting subjective judgements.

If the optimal budget is determined, the marketing manager has to formulate the directions in which the salesmen have to divide their time between large and small customers and/or between acquiring new customers and keeping old ones. Analytical treatment of an experiment may indicate how salesmen should optimally allocate their time. A distribution of customer sizes plus a measure of the effectiveness of the sales force may give answers:

- on how many customers the sales force should concentrate on;
- how much time should be spend on holding and on conversion of customers.

The director and the salesmen already know that it is harder to acquire a customer than to keep one. Their intuition fails to tell them *how much* harder. They also know that it is important to concentrate on large customers. However, their intuition could not tell them whether this should be the 500 largest, the 1,000 largest or the 5,000 largest.

From this example it is clear that the direction of a solution of a marketing problem can often be found by a non-quantitative analysis. A more quantitative treatment of the problem can be instrumental in finding the 'approximate length' of the solution. Models and data are necessary, although not always sufficient to determine this 'length'.

In this chapter we will first introduce the model concept and we will give a brief introduction to models which are used to generalise our knowledge of market phenomena and marketing decisions models which are actually used in practice. Then we will elaborate on the benefits of building marketing decision models. The last forty years, we have seen enormous productivity on the part of marketing model builders. A large number of the models resulting from their efforts are extensively reviewed and discussed in a variety of state-of-the-art textbooks.[4] We will then give some classifications of models. This is followed by an introduction to model building concepts and the model building process. This process consists of a number of steps and each of these steps is considered briefly. We then discuss well-known models which have been calibrated using objective data. As has been indicated in the second example of this Introduction models also can be calibrated using subjective judgements. This will be discussed in some detail.

Marketing is by its very nature concerned with the interaction between firms and the marketplace. Marketing models have been used primarily to quantify customer reactions to changes in marketing decision variables. The decline in many western economies in the 1980s and 1990s has shifted the attention from customers to customers *and* competitors. Thus the emphasis is on a marketplace that includes customers *and* competitors. In the past few years, models have been developed which can be used to estimate how competitors react to each other's marketing programmes. A number of those models are discussed.

■ The model concept

A model can be defined as: 'a representation of the most important elements of a perceived real world system'. Models are condensed representations, simplified pictures of reality. This definition is not very revealing. To be able to explain its significance we will discuss the various components.

1. First, there is the component 'system'. The manager's system can be defined as: 'everything that relates to his problem, i.e., the total environment of his problem'. Thus the system consists of all elements that have or might have a bearing on the problem being studied. In marketing problems the part of the real world system is considered which deals with the marketing environment. This in contrast to models pertaining to other activities of a firm such as production models, financial models, or more global models, for example, corporate models. Models as representations of the most important elements of a system are not restricted to the management sciences, but are found in all sciences. Thus one can distinguish physical, psychological, sociological, economic models. We should also observe that modeling is not a prerogative for scientists. As has been pointed out by, for example, Makridakis (1974, p. 18) modeling

is conducted on a large scale by all people. Because we are unable to deal with the complexity of its real form, we construct models of our environment, that is to say we use simplified pictures of reality.

2. What exactly is meant by 'most important elements'? The purpose of a model is to enable us to better understand the real world system it represents. If, however, the model is too complex, we will not be able to understand it. Thus simplification may be necessary. When studying complex marketing systems some elements can perhaps be aggregated, others might be thought of as having little or no effect, which brings us to the critical issue that only the most important elements will be represented or modelled. Whether an element is important or not, will depend both on the intended use of the model and on cost-benefit considerations.

3. In order to deal with a problem, we need a *representation* of the system being studied. This can be done in a number of ways. When we restrict ourselves to communicable forms of representation the simplest is the *verbal* one. It is often advisable to represent a model by explicitly formulating the relationship between the different variables it contains. Models without numerical specification of these relationships are defined as *formalised* models. Finally, models which contain numerically specified relationships are defined as *numerically specified* models. When mathematical symbols are used to represent the most important elements of a system, we talk about *mathematical* models or *symbolic* models. In this chapter we will concentrate on representations of marketing problems by way of *mathematical* models.

4. In the model definition it is said that a model is *a* representation. Several or even many alternative models can be employed to describe a situation. Model building is a highly subjective process the outcome of which is to a large extent a function of the factors considered most important, which in turn depend on both the user and the intended use. The notion that no unique or 'best possible' representation of a situation exists has been described by Lilien (1975, p. 12) as 'Model Relativism'.

In marketing, models are developed for different reasons.

□ *Generalisations*

Models may be helpful in *improving our knowledge and understanding* of marketing phenomena such as discovering lawlike *generalisations*. In this way new knowledge is acquired. This approach of modeling markets is long term oriented and transcends the specificity of a particular problem. The collection of outcomes of the study of marketing phenomena is also known as 'marketing science'. Some of the generalisations have been made very concrete through meta analyses. Meta-analysis is a formal approach to comparing the results from similar but non-replicative studies for consistency. This is how Farley, Lehmann and Oliva (1990) characterise it: 'to the degree that each properly done empirical study uncovers a piece of truth, meta-analysis attempts to integrate these pieces into a larger truth'.

We will give some examples of these generalisations.[5]

1. The diffusion of a new brand can be described by the so-called Bass-model (1969). This is originally a theoretical model that proceeded observation of the empirical generalisation. Hundreds of applications have shown that the observed patterns tend to be consistent with the theory. For practical applications the model has properties such that it is possible to guess the values of the model parameters before a new product is introduced. Sultan, Farley and Lehmann (1990) did a meta-analysis of 213 applications of diffusion models. The results from the meta-analysis can be used with new data which are specific for a new application to obtain the appropriate parameter estimates which are specific for that new application. The model and its generalisations has been especially

useful in forecasting the timing and magnitude of the peak in the adoption rate.

2. Meta-analyses in the area of so-called market response models focus on estimates of the elasticities of marketing instruments. So, for example, the elasticity of (selective) advertising on (own) brand sales is positive but low.[6] Another meta-analysis offers insight in the average value of price elasticities,[7] the effects of promotions[8] and shelf space[9] on sales.

3. Other generalisable phenomena in the area of buyer behaviour have been uncovered by Ehrenberg (1988). An example is: 'the average frequency of brand purchase per buyer in a given time period multiplied times the proportion of the population who did not buy the brand at least once in the period is approximately constant for all brands in a given product field'. This has come to be known as 'double jeopardy'. Brands with few buyers tend to be bought somewhat less frequently by them. These regularities have been found for many products and services.[10]

4. Marketing science has identified a number of factors that complicate the relationship of objective prices and consumer demand. Examples of these factors are:[11]

- the existence of imperfect price knowledge;
- the existence of internal reference prices to which perceived prices are compared;
- the complex form of the demand-price function;
- the existence of psychological price levels at which demand supposedly suddenly changes.

☐ *Marketing decision models*

These models focus on the manager's perception of the environment in which he operates. The management scientist models this world in such a way that he can give the decision-maker assistance. Thus, one starts from a particular problem in a particular firm, with a manager simply looking for help in making decisions. The resulting models do not necessarily provide final answers to the general problems of advertising budgeting, pricing, new product selection and shelf space allocation, etc. They will be helpful in specific situations, which of course, does not preclude that learning will take place, eventually resulting in knowledge of a more general nature. Decision models are based on what we know. Decision makers cannot afford to wait a decade or so for additional or new knowledge to be found on what is only known imperfectly. Thus, decision models must be directly applicable; they are more short-term oriented.

Many marketing decision models which have been developed by scientists have not been implemented yet. However, they may become operational a few years hence. Examples of models which are used in practice are given below.[12]

1. As has already been indicated by the example in the introduction, sales force management is often faced with strategy issues involving the structure and size of the sales force and deployment of the total sales effort by product and market segment. One integrated model-based approach for sales force structuring has been implemented in over 100 settings in more than 20 countries.[13]

2. The high historical failure rate of new packaged goods placed in test markets has encouraged firms to find ways to perform more thorough evaluations of new products before embarking on test marketing programs. One pre-test-market evaluation model is ASSESSOR.[14] This model has been used to evaluate more than 200 products in more than 50 organisations. ASSESSOR yields good accuracy in predicting test market shares.[15]

3. A. C. Nielsen's SCAN*PRO model is used to estimate the effects of promotional and other marketing activities such that more effective programs can be designed.[16] A conservative estimate is that SCAN*PRO has been used in 1000 different commercial applications. The service is available in the USA, Canada and several West European countries.

Marketing decision models are not only used in business. Many models have been developed for public purposes. Examples are models which calibrate the relation between advertising expenditures and the demand for 'harmful products' such as alcoholic beverages and cigarettes.[17] Other models have been developed to deduce whether there is competition between advertising expenditures in newspapers and/or magazines and the advertising expenditures in public and commercial broadcasting.[18] The benefits of models which improve our understanding and knowledge of marketing phenomena have been discussed implicitly above. Marketing decision models do have a number of benefits. In the following section we will discuss these benefits.

▌Benefits from marketing decision models[19]

We make a distinction between direct and side benefits. Although the line between these two types of benefits is not easy to draw, we could say that side benefits are those which are not related directly to the reasons for which the model was built in the first place. Most of the side benefits will only be realised in the course of time.

□ *Direct benefits*

Companies invest in model building presumably because it leads to better decisions. 'Better' is understood here as contributing to the fulfilment of the company's goals. For example, if the firm's single objective is to maximise profit, benefits of a model could be defined as the discounted differential profit generated by having the model as opposed to not having it. This implies knowledge of the amount of differential profit over time, or of some proxy measure.

Models may lead to better decisions because they explicate the ideas decision-makers have concerning real-world systems. In this way models are useful because:

1. they can be used as a forecasting tool;
2. they can *help* to determine which constructions are relevant to the decision maker and the nature of the causal relationships between them, because models are (condensed) representations of the most important elements of a real-world system;
3. they can *aid* by providing relatively objective evaluations of decision alternatives in an efficient manner.[20]

□ *Side benefits*

1. Without models decision makers need not be very explicit about their understanding of the environment in which they operate. They decide on a one million dollar advertising budget without detailed knowledge of the effectiveness of advertising in influencing sales. An advertising budgeting model would force them to be much more explicit in their description of how the market works. And, as such, model building will often lead (perhaps in time) to an *improved understanding* of their problem(s).
2. Models may even work as *problem finding* instruments which means that problems may emerge after a model has been developed.
3. Information is often available but is not used. Yet, there are many examples of decisions which would have been reversed if the information had been used. Managerial incompetence would be too easy an explanation. It might simply be a lack of knowledge that the data exist, or a lack of methods for handling the information. Models will be instrumental *in improving the process by which decision makers deal with existing information.*
4. Point 3 deals with the use of existing information. Another side benefit deals with the collection of information. Models help in deciding *what information should be collected.* Thus models will lead to improved data collection, and will avoid collecting and storing enormous amounts of data without any apparent purpose.[21]

5. Models can also *guide research* by identifying areas in which information is needed, as well as by pointing out the kinds of experiments which would provide useful information. By using models, managers have a more exact knowledge of what they would like to know and how experiments should be designed to obtain that information. To give an illustration: suppose that by parameterisation of a model it is found that the average effect of advertising on sales in a number of time periods differs from the average effect in other time periods. In order to explain these differences we need additional information about changes in advertising messages, the use of media classes, media vehicles, etc. We may also decide to perform some experiments in order to test different advertising messages using consumer panels.

6. Models provide a *framework for discussion at evaluation time*. When the model user's performance is going down, he can perhaps defend himself by pointing out the effect of various changes in the environment on his own performance such as new product introductions by competition. His superior might also use the model to point to poor decision or incompleteness in the user's understanding of his task.[22]

7. Finally, a model might result in a *beneficial reallocation of management time*, which means less time spent on programmable or structured activities, and more time on less structured ones. In this respect one might think of decisions which can be routinised such as inventory management, routing and planning of salesmen, media-allocation and salesforce allocation problems.

■ Classifications of models

Models are the ultimate outcome of a process which consists of a number of steps. In one of these steps a number of model development criteria has to be defined. Among these criteria are the intended use of the models, the level(s) of demand which have to be considered and the amount of behavioural detail the model should contain. Furthermore one has to determine to what degree the model should contain explicitly formulated variables. Here model builders have to make choices prior to the collection of data, the parameterisation, validation and use of the models. Before we discuss these and other steps in more detail it is necessary to know what kinds of models have been developed and what kinds of model development criteria have to be used.

Thus, in model building, the following dimensions are of particular relevance:

1. intended use;
2. level of demand;
3. amount of behavioural detail.

Furthermore it is useful to make a distinction between so-called time series and causal (econometric) models.

☐ Classification based on intended use

Models can be classified according to purpose or intended use, i.e. why does the firm engage in a model building project. Different purposes will lead to different models. We will make a distinction between: descriptive, predictive, and normative models.

Descriptive models, as the name indicates, are intended to describe decision or other processes. Let us first concentrate on descriptive models of decision processes. Such a model may be an end in itself, in the sense that decision making procedures are often quite complicated and not well understood. A decision maker may well wonder at some point in time *how particular decisions are arrived at* in his organisation. This reflection may induce him to want to trace the various steps leading to the decisions, and the various forces influencing the outcome(s) of the decision processes. As an example we refer to a recent study by Brand (1993) who described the purchasing process of an industrial buyer. The industrial buying process consists out of a number of steps. In each of these steps different criteria are used by different decision makers which decide whether the potential product which is bought should be considered in more detail in a following step or not.

Descriptive models are not necessarily restricted to decision problems. For example, one may describe a market by the structure of brand loyalty (the percentage of people buying product j in period $t + 1$, who bought the same brand on the last purchase occasion), and brand switching (percentage of people changing from brand i to brand j). Descriptive models also have been developed to describe and understand processes which occur on markets which are complicated and thus are difficult to study. As an example we mention the description of the heroin market's mechanism, i.e. the behaviour of participants on this market.[23]

Under the heading of *predictive models* we mean models aiming at forecasting or predicting future events. In the context of decision models, this will generally mean the prediction of the effect of alternative actions. For example, a firm may want to predict its market share for alternative prices, advertising spending levels, and package sizes.

Demand models make up a special class of predictive models. We refer to a demand model when we have a performance variable related to a level of demand. This performance variable depends among others on a number of instrument variables, such as, marketing decision variables of the firm being studied and of competition. A further break-down of this important class of prediction models is proposed below.

The final category consists of the *normative models*, or *prescriptive models*. The normative model has, as one of its outputs, a recommended course of action. This implies that an objective has been defined against which alternatives can be evaluated and compared. For example, the objective function in a media allocation model may be the maximisation of profit, or at a more operational level, the maximisation of exposure value.

A typology of models based on the level of demand

In a demand model, the performance variable is a measure of demand.
Demand may refer to:

1. the total number of units of a product category purchased by the population of all spending units. The corresponding demand model is called an *industry sales*, or *product class sales* model;
2. the total number of units of a particular brand bought by the population of all spending units. The demand model is then a *brand sales* model;
3. the relative number of units of a particular brand purchased by the total population, i.e. relative to the total number of units of the product class, in which case the demand model becomes a *market share* model.[24]

From these definitions it follows that market share of a brand j is equal to the ratio of brand sales of j and product class sales (i.e. brand sales summed over all brands). For example, we can refer to total sales of cigarettes in period t, to sales of, say, Lucky Strike in the same period, the ratio of the latter over the former being Lucky Strike's share in period t.

It is possible that two of those three types of demand models are part of one more complex model. For example, to describe, explain and predict sales of a brand, one will often develop a product class sales model in combination with a market share model. By multiplying the marketing performance measures, i.e. product class sales and market share, one obtaines brand sales. It is often preferable to arrive at brand sales in this way, rather than to relate brand sales to marketing instruments and environmental variables[25] directly. The core of the argument centres on the fact that different levels of demand are explained by different sets of variables. For example, variables used in explaining variation in market share of brand j, i.e. variation in a fraction, should themselves be fractional. To put it more specifically, if advertising is one of the variables determining market share, advertising share of brand *j* should be used rather than advertising expenditures in trying to explain fluctuations in *j*'s market share, with advertising share of brand *j* defined as advertising expenditures of brand *j*, divided by advertising expenditures of all brands.

The classification proposed here has been defined at the aggregate demand level. In an analogous manner, the demand for a product class, brand, or market share of a brand can be defined for segments.

☐ A classification based on the amount of behavioural detail

Another classification, which could be useful for our purposes, is the amount of behavioural detail a model contains. We will distinguish between three classes:

1. no behavioural detail;
2. some behavioural detail;
3. a substantial amount of behavioural detail.

Since the amount of behavioural detail is a continuous, not easily quantifiable variable, only the first class can be unambiguously defined.

In models with no *behavioural detail*, marketing instruments (instrument variables) and environmental variables are directly related to a performance measure, such as, sales or market share. That means that intervening variables such as awareness and attitudes are not considered. Or, stimuli (instrument and environmental variables) are directly related to response (performance measures or variables). Why stimuli cause a response is treated as a black box. These models are known as stimulus-response models.

The second category consists of models where *some behavioural detail* is explicitly built in. This can be done in different ways. Models where some behavioural detail is explicitly built in but in an aggregate way are called aggregate flow models. Many models of this type have been developed in the area of evaluating new product introductions. In these models, buyers move from one stage or state (for example, the potential triers class) to another (for example the potential repeaters class) after each purchase occasion. The

Figure 8.1. *Diagram of Urban III (version of SPRINTER Mod. III)*

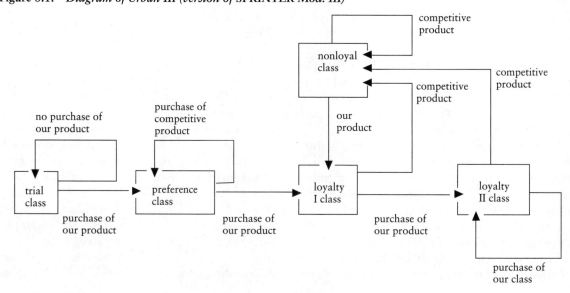

Source: Urban (1970), p. 811; see also Urban and Hauser (1980), p. 437.

models track the flow of the buyers through a network of possible states.[26] In Figure 8.1 an example of an aggregate flow model is given.

In Figure 8.1 five experience classes are considered. From each class we see two flows: the purchase of 'our' (new) product and the flow of purchases of a competitive brand. Behavioural detail may also be built in at the individual level. Examples of models which contain some behavioural detail at the individual level are the so-called partial models of consumer behaviour. These models represent a part of the consumer behaviour process, such as the hierarchy-of-effects caused by advertising, using mathematical equations. By the inclusion of more 'behavioural' variables, these models will soon belong to the category of models with a substantial amount of behavioural detail. These models generally consist of a large number of equations and parameters. As an example we mention the mathematical formulation of the Elaboration Likelihood Model developed by Petty and Cacioppo (1986). The mathematical model which represents this ELM-model is based on measured values of variables like involvement, knowledge, satisfaction and evaluation.[27] When going from models with no behavioural detail to models which contain a substantial amount, there is an increasing richness of representation of system phenomena, on the one hand. On the other hand data collection, estimation and validation become more and more difficult.[28]

□ Time series and causal models

Time series (models) model response behaviour over time with the emphasis on the lag structures of variables and disturbances. Its main concern is to explain the variability within one or more variables over time without using explicitly formulated (causal) variables.[29] The response variable's fluctuations are either explained by lagged independent variables and/or time as independent variable. As an example we show relation (1) in which the sales of brand j in period t (S_{jt}) are explained by some lagged variables ($S_{j,t-1}$, $S_{j,t-2}$):

$$S_{jt} = \alpha_j + \beta_{1j}S_{j,t-1} + \beta_{2j}S_{j,t-2} + u_{jt} \qquad (1)$$

where:

α_j	= a constant term,
β_{1j}, β_{2j}	= response parameters and
u_{jt}	= a random disturbance term.

Another example of a time series model is relation (2):

$$S_{jt} = \gamma_j + \delta_{1j}t + \delta_{2j}t^2 + v_{jt} \qquad (2)$$

where:

$\gamma_j, \delta_{1j}, \delta_{2j}$	= parameters,
t	= 1,2,3,...,T,
T	= the number of observations,
v_{jt}	= a random disturbance term.

Relation (2) can be estimated, for example, by monthly data covering a two-year period ($T=24$). If the estimated values of δ_{1j} and δ_{2j} are respectively positive and negative we obtain a bell-shaped curve which represents the well-known curve of the product life-cycle.

Time series can be *used* to yield useful forecasts for management but they are weak for producing knowledge about response behaviour. The approach does not reflect the belief of management that a performance measure like sales can be controlled by manipulating decision variables like price and advertising. Causal models assume that management control, environmental and other variables affect response in a direct way. The models focus on the relations between variables. As an example we show relation (3):

$$S_{jt} = \alpha_j + \beta_{1j}p_{jt} + \beta_{2j}a_{jt} + \beta_{3j}temp_t + \beta_{4j}p_{jt}^c + \beta_{5j}a_{jt}^c + u_{jt} \ (3)$$

where:

p_{jt}	= price per unit of brand j in period t (in dollars),
a_{jt}	= advertising expenditures (in dollars) of brand j in period t,
$temp_t$	= the average temperature in period t (degrees of Fahrenheit),
p_{jt}^c	= average price per unit of competitive brands in period t,
a_{jt}^c	= the advertising expenditures of competitive brands in period t,
u_{jt}	= a random disturbance term.

In relation (3) the fluctuations in the sales of brand *j* are explained by brand *j*'s own marketing instruments (price and advertising), an environmental variable (temperature) and marketing variables which refer to brand *j*'s competitors (p_{jt}^c, a_{jt}^c). The environmental variable temperature is an explanatory variable which cannot be controlled by neither brand *j*'s management nor by brand *j*'s competitors. This environmental variable may be a good candidate to explain the fluctuations of brand *j* in case we deal with products like beer, canned soup, winter clothes, etc. The sales fluctuations of these products depend on seasonal influences.

■ Model-building concepts

In the proceeding section we already introduced some model-building concepts like dependent and independent variables, parameters and disturbance terms.

Above, a model is defined as a representation of the most important elements of a perceived real world system. A mathematical model describes such a system by means of a number of mathematical relations between its elements or variables. In this section we will define some of the basic terminology with respect to:

1. the various components or elements of a model;
2. the kind of relations which may exist between these elements.

□ *Elements*

The various elements or components of a relation between variables can be introduced with the help of the following equation:

$$S_{jt} = \alpha_j + \beta_j a_{jt} + u_{jt} \quad t = 1,2,...,T \quad (4)$$

where:
- S_{jt} = sales (in units) of brand *j* in period *t*,
- α_j = a constant but unknown parameter,
- β_j = an unknown effect parameter,[30]

- a_{jt} = advertising expenditures (in dollars) of brand *j* in period *t*,
- u_{jt} = a random disturbance term, and
- T = the number of observations.

The object of the specification of relation (4) is to explain the variation in the unit sales of brand *j*. Thus, S_{jt} is the *variable to be explained or the dependent variable*. For this purpose one specifies:

1. the variable(s) with which one hopes to explain the variations in the dependent variable, referred to as *explanatory variable(s)* or *independent variables (a_{jt})*, and
2. the *mathematical form* between dependent variable and independent variable(s).

The mathematical form of (4) is relatively simple: it is a linear relation containing a constant term α_j. The effect parameter β_j indicates the variation in the number of units sold when a_{jt} changes by one unit (in the case, one dollar).

Because advertising spending does not fully determine sales, the relation:

$$S_{jt} = \alpha_j + \beta_j a_{jt} \quad (5)$$

is inadequate. To make the equation exact, a *disturbance term u_{jt}* has to be added to the right hand side. A disturbance term is a *random or stochastic variable*. The main characteristic of such a variable is that it assumes different values (or falls into different value intervals), with some probability other than one. It is obvious that because u_{jt} is stochastic, S_{jt} is stochastic as well. For statistical estimation and testing of the model, the probability distribution of the disturbance term is very important.

Given the above definition, the disturbance factor represents the part of sales which one is unable to predict, given knowledge of advertising spending. It is the unexplained part of the relation. In fact, the disturbance term will measure more than just random error:

1. the random disturbance term may represent *error of measurement* in the variables. One reason for such error is sampling;[31]

2. the disturbance term may also represent the effects of variables not included in the model;
3. not including relevant variables is one possible form of *misspecification or specification error*. Another relates to error in the functional relationship. For example, in (4) a linear relation between sales and advertising has been postulated. Given a general belief in decreasing returns to scale in advertising, a linear model (assuming constant returns) would appear to be inappropriate. Incorrect specification of the functional form will again contribute to the disturbance term.

All elements of equation (4) have now been defined. Other elements of mathematical models can be defined by considering the following set of *'structural relations'* (describing the structure of a market phenomenon):

$$m_{jt} = \beta_{0j} + \beta_{1j} \frac{a_{j,t-1}}{\sum_{r=1}^{n} a_{r,t-1}} + \beta_{2j} \frac{p_{jt}}{\frac{1}{n}\sum_{r=1}^{n} p_{rt}} + \beta_{3j} m_{j,t-1} + u_{jt} \quad (6)$$

$$Q_t = \gamma_0 + \gamma_1 \sum_{r=1}^{n} a_{r,t-1} + \gamma_2 y_t + v_t \quad (7)$$

$$S_{jt} = m_{jt} Q_t \quad (8)$$

$$R_{jt} = p_{jt} S_{jt} \quad (9)$$

$$TC_{jt} = c_j S_{jt} + FC_j + a_{jt} \quad (10)$$

$$\pi_{jt} = R_{jt} - TC_{jt} \quad (11)$$

$$\pi(AT)_{jt} = (1 - \tau)\pi_{jt} \quad (12)$$

where:

m_{jt} = market share of brand j in period t,
a_{jt} = advertising expenditures of brand j in period t,
p_{jt} = price per unit of brand j in period t,
u_{jt}, y_t = random disturbance terms,
Q_t = product class sales in period t,
y_t = disposable income in period t,
S_{jt} = sales (in units) of brand j in period t,
R_{jt} = revenue of brand j in period t,
TC_{jt} = total cost of brand j in period t,
c_j = variable cost per unit of brand j,[32]

FC_j = fixed costs of brand j,
π_{jt} = profit (before tax) from marketing brand j in period t,
$\pi(AT)_{jt}$ = after tax profit, and
τ = tax rate.

In relation (6) market share is a function of the price of j in period t, relative to the average price of the product class. It is also a function of advertising share in period $t-1$. This implies that price has a more immediate effect than advertising. Also in (6) market share in t is a function of its value in period $t-1$. This is a reflection of market inertia or of the fact that advertising share in periods prior to $t-1$, and relative price in periods prior to t are taken into account. When β_{3j} is smaller than one, the influence of market share in previous periods decreases as time goes by.

Relation (7) shows that variation in product class sales is explained by variation in total advertising expenditures of all brands, and by variation in disposable income.

From the definitions above, it follows that jt, is a dependent variable in relation (6). On the other hand m_{jt}, 'explains' the variable S_{jt} in (8), and is therefore an independent variable.[33] Thus in a model consisting of a set of structural relations, it is not always possible to classify variables as being dependent or independent. Instead, variables are placed in two distinct groups according to whether or not they are to be explained by the model. *Endogenous* variables are those which are to be determined by the phenomena expressed in the model. *Exogenous* variables, on the other hand, are determined outside the model. In a general way, we can say that a model represents the determination of endogenous variables on the basis of exogenous variables. In the model which is described in the relations (6)–(12), the following variables are endogenous: m_{jt}, Q_t, S_{jt}, R_{jt}, TC_{jt}, π_{jt} and $\pi(AT)_{jt}$. These variables are explained by the equations (6)–(12) respectively. Thus, in the model, the number of endogenous variables is equal to the number of equations.

The exogenous variables in the model being considered are:

$$a_{j,t-1}, \sum_{r=1}^{n} a_{r,t-1}, p_{jt}, 1/n\sum_{r=1}^{n} p_{rt}, y_t, c_j, \text{ and } FC_j.$$

The set of exogenous variables can be separated into instruments or decision variables or controlled variables and environmental variables or non-controllable variables. In our model, $a_{j,t-1}$ and p_{jt} are instrument variables for the decision makers of brand j. The variables y_t, p_{rt}, $r \neq j$, $r=1,...,n$, and $a_{r,t-1}$, $r \neq j$, $r=1,...,n$, are environmental variables for the decision maker of brand j.

In relation (6) market share of brand j in period t is an endogenous variable which depends, among others, on the market share of j in the preceding period $t-1$, i.e. a lagged endogenous variable. This means that we have to reformulate our statement with respect to the relation between endogenous and exogenous variables. The function of a system such as (6)–(12), is *to describe the current (i.e. non-lagged) values of the endogenous variables in terms of the current and lagged values of the exogenous variables and of the lagged values of the endogenous variables.* The current endogenous variables are called *jointly dependent*, and the set of all current and lagged exogenous variables plus the lagged endogenous variables *predetermined*. To summarize, we distinguish the following kinds of variables:

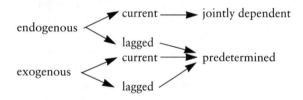

□ Relations

We can distinguish the following kinds of relations or equations:

1. behaviour or behavioural equations;
2. balance and definition equations;
3. institutional equations.[34]

Each of these is briefly described below.

□ Behavioural equations

As the name indicates, behaviour or behavioural relations refer to system behaviour. For example,

equation (6) relates to the behaviour of buyers of a brand, expressed in terms of market share, to price, advertising, and past buying behaviour. Similarly, equation (7) relates the behaviour of buyers of a product class, in terms of product class sales, to total advertising spending and to disposable income.

□ Balance and definition equations

Balance and definition relations feature parameters known *a priori*. One distinguishes:

Balance equations relating to points in time, i.e.:

$$Q_t = \sum_{t=1}^{n} q_{rt} \qquad (13)$$

where,
Q_t = product class sales in period t (say, April, 1994),
q_{rt} = sales of brand r in period t, and
n = total number of brands (at t).

Balance equations relating to intervals of time, i.e.:

$$Q_t - Q_{t-1} = \Delta Q_t = \sum_{r=1}^{n}(q_{rt} - q_{r,t-1}) = \sum_{r=1}^{n} \Delta q_{rt} \qquad (14)$$

or, on other words: The change in product class sales in a certain period t, say April, 1994, is equal to the sum of changes in sales of all brands $r=1,...,n$ on condition that the total number of brands in that particular period remains equal to n. Both (13) and (14) are identities, provided the definitions of the variables appearing in (13) and (14) are mutually consistent. Thus, all balance equations are also implicit definition equations. The reverse, however, is not true since not all definition equations are balance equations. An example is relation (9) a definition equation which is not a balance equation. Examples of definition relations are equations (8)–(11).

□ Institutional equations

In institutional equations, parameters result from decisions made by institutions such as governments (at various levels), or banks, to name just a few. An example is equation (12) relating before to after tax profit, the parameter τ being determined by the fiscal authorities. Another example is the relation between the interest rate on savings paid by banks, and the length of time during which these savings remain deposited.

■ The model-building process[35]

Model building is an activity which consists of a number of steps in a process. The steps of the process are (summarily) described below and are shown in Figure 8.2. The model-building process in Figure 8.2 is the process which is suggested to be followed when building models for decision makers.

□ Formulation of Priors

Model building starts with a *recognition* of the model-builders own *biases* and *prior* inclinations, by which favoured approaches and techniques of the model-builder are meant. Instead of forcing a particular problem to fit a certain approach, the

researcher should have a portfolio of approaches and a range of general models that could contribute to the real problem area. This step of the model-building process is taken before a confrontation with a problem in a real world situation has taken place.

□ Entry

In this step it has to be determined with whom the model-builder should communicate in the organisation and with whom he has a good first contact. In this view, the model-builder is seen as an outside organisational change mechanism. Because most models are developed by specialists outside a firm this is (still) a realistic view nowadays.

□ Problem finding

At this stage the problem should be defined unambiguously. This means, among other things, the determination of:

- existing model(s) or rules of thumb;
- characteristics of the decision process;

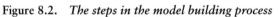

Figure 8.2. *The steps in the model building process*

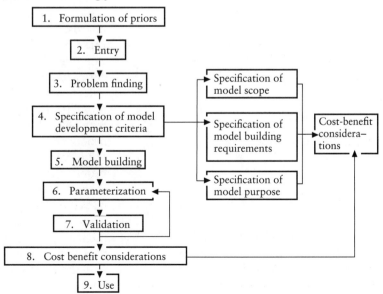

- existing flow, usage and availability of information.

This should lead to the specification of model-development criteria.

□ *Model-development criteria*

These criteria relate to the specification of:

a. *model scope.* Should one build company models or models of part of the company? Should one build models in which all elements of all relevant classes of instruments are considered or should one build models for each class of instruments, such as, for example, 'an advertising model' or 'a price model'.[36]
b. *criteria related to model-structure.* Models should satisfy a number of criteria in order to enhance the probability that they are being implemented. These criteria are discussed in more detail below.
c. *the model purpose.* The intended use of the model should be clearly established. This will be of relevance in determining the level(s) of demand which has (have) to be explained and the amount of behavioural detail the model should contain.

We will now elaborate on the criteria related to model-structure. Experience in model-building has led to the recognition of a set of criteria a model should satisfy to fit the label of a 'good model'.[37] More in particular Little (1970) has stated that a model should be:

1. simple;
2. complete on important issues;
3. adaptive;
4. robust.

These criteria are briefly discussed below. It should be clear that a large number of models exist which do not satisfy all four criteria. What we do want to say, however, is that the criteria are in themselves appealing and satisfying them should increase the likelihood of model acceptance. In that sense, criteria will not only mean requirements but also desired characteristics.

We should observe that some criteria may be conflicting. Being complete on important issues is a criterion that conflicts with simplicity,[38] and in some models completeness may conflict with robustness.

1. *Models should be simple* because managers tend to reject models they do not understand. If we want managers to use models a natural prerequisite would be for models to be simple enough so that managers can understand them.

   For the *model-builder* simplicity may mean something else than for the *model-user.* For the *model-builder* simplicity often implies keeping the number of variables down to a workable level. This can be achieved in one or more of the following ways:
   a. *Clustering of variables,* which is typical for many econometric studies. For example, various competing brands are often aggregated into 'the competition'. Or a number of marketing instruments are aggregated into a small number of classes, such as product, distribution, advertising, promotions and price. That means, for example, advertising expenditures are not split up into television, radio, newspapers, magazines and billboards, but are treated as a total.
   b. *Introducing relative variables.* For example, the variable disposable income per capita replaces two variables, disposable income, and number of people in the population. Similarly advertising share may be used instead of brand and product class advertising expenditures.
   c. *Dividing variables into segments* A problem is segmented into sub-problems, each of which is analysed separately, that is, considering only those variables related to each particular segment. When the sub-problems have been analysed they can be combined in order to represent the total problem. Examples would

be models of market segments, or models of individual products belonging to a wider assortment.

d *Phasing variables over different levels.* In demand models, for example, variables can be divided into classes according to the various levels of demand that can be distinguished. Fluctuations in product class sales can often explained by fluctuations in environmental variables (such as disposable income per capita, a weather index, etc.) and fluctuations in aggregate values of marketing instruments (average price, product class advertising expenditures, total number of outlets where the product is available, etc.). Variations in market share can largely explained by variations in relative or share values of the various classes of marketing instruments.

The model-builder-orientated notions of simplicity will not always be agreeable to the *user*. What does 'simple' mean for the user? The starting point is the observation that most models are not understood by managers and that they – as people in general do for that matter – tend to reject what they do not understand. It would be utopia to expect managers to be experts in mathematics, statistics, econometrics, operations research and computer science. They are not, neither do they pretend to be, nor do they want to be. The manager is not interested in the detailed intricacies of the model. What he wants is a basic understanding of the logic of the model and of what it can do for him. For the user, a model will be simple if this basic understanding is given to him. Communication and involvement are two means of achieving this.

Historically, communication between model-builder and user was almost nonexistent. Decision makers did not understand the jargon of the operations researcher and management scientist, and model building took place to a large extent in isolation. The situation has much improved in recent years. Models have become easier to communicate with as a result of the wide-spread availability of personal computers and on-line computer systems. Involvement means that the important factors bearing on the problem are described by the decision makers and not by the model builder. Also the model should represent their view of how the market works.

2. *Models should be complete on important issues* which means that they have to represent all relevant elements of the problem being studied. This means that a model should account for:
   - the effect of all marketing instruments and environmental variables;
   - the effect of competitive actions;
   - the effect of variables over time.

3. *Models should be adaptive* because model parameters and model structure are not fixed once and for all. Market behaviour is dynamic, and changing market conditions, such as the entry or exit of an important competitor will cause parameters to change. An increasing number of so-called varying parameter-models have been developed in the last decade which cope with this problem.[39]

4. *Models should be robust.* Little (1970, p.B-470) defines robustness as follows: 'here I mean that a user should find it difficult to make the model give bad answers. This can be done by a structure that inherently constrains answers to a meaningful range of values'. Robustness puts constraints on the mathematical form of the relations, such as:
   a. additivity or sum constraints, for example, market shares should sum to one;
   b. boundary or range constraints, for example, shares should be between zero and one.
The form of the relations should ensure that when variables are in reality subject to sum or range constraints, their model counterparts should satisfy these same constraints.

Such models are then called logically consistent.[40]

In a broader sense, robustness may also mean that a model should reflect:

a. correct marginal effects;
b. interdependencies which exist between different marketing instruments;
c. interdependencies between dependent variables (for example, response measures) and instrument variables.

While robustness is a desirable characteristic it is, just as completeness, a relative concept. *A priori* it is undesirable that a model should produce absurd results when controllable variables are given extreme values. The real importance, however, depends on the problem situation being modelled and on the use one intends to make of the model. If, for example, it is never the intention to implement extreme values, model behaviour at such values cannot be very relevant.

☐ *Model-building (specification)*

This step refers to the actual specification of the formalised relations on the basis of the model-development criteria decided upon the previous step. This involves two major steps:

a. specifying the variables to be included in the model, and making a distinction between those to be explained (the dependent variables), and those explaining (the explanatory or independent variables). For example, we want to explain market share of brand *j*. As variables which could be at the basis for the fluctuations in market share, one might think of price, advertising expenditures, promotions, distributions, quality, related to brand *j* and the same set of variables for competing brands;
b. the second aspect is the specification of a functional relationship between the variables. Here we have to define the mathematical form of the relation and the dynamics of the model. First we will elaborate on mathematical forms. Four types can be distinguished:

1. linear in both parameters and variables;
2. nonlinear in the variables, but linear in the parameters;
3. nonlinear in the parameters, but linearizable;
4. nonlinear in the parameters and not linearizable.

The distinction is important from the point of view of estimation. Forms 1, 2 and 3 are estimable by classic econometric methods, whereas 4 is not.

Models linear in the parameters and variables are also called linear additive models. Equation (15) is an example of a linear additive model.[41]

$$S_{jt} = \alpha_0 + \alpha_1 p_{jt} + \alpha_2 a_{jt} \tag{15}$$

where:

S_{jt} = sales of brand *j* in period *t*,
p_{jt} = price per unit of brand *j* in period *t*,
a_{jt} = advertising expenditures of brand *j* in period *t*.

While (15) is the simplest possible representation, it also has a number of serious drawbacks. The model assumes constant returns to scale with respect to each of the independent variables. This is easily seen by taking the first-order derivative of S_{jt} with respect to, for example, a_{jt}:

$$\frac{\delta S_{jt}}{\delta a_{jt}} = \alpha_2 \tag{16}$$

which means that increasing a_{jt} by one unit results in an increase of S_{jt} by α_2 units. In many cases, this assumption will only be reasonable within a relative small range of variation of a_{jt}.

An other important drawback of (15) is that it assumes no interactions between the variables: the first-order derivative (16) is independent of p_{jt}.

A second class of models are those which are nonlinear in the variables but linear in the parameters: *the nonlinear additive models*. Equation (17) is an example of such a model:

$$S_{jt} = \alpha_0 + \alpha_1 p_{jt} + \alpha_2 \sqrt{a_{jt}}. \qquad (17)$$

The first-order derivative of S_{jt} with respect to a_{jt} is:

$$\frac{\delta S_{jt}}{\delta a_{jt}} = \frac{\alpha_2}{2\sqrt{a_{jt}}} \qquad (18)$$

showing decreasing returns to scale, and tending to zero for a_{jt} very large. One of the most frequently encountered marketing response functions is the so-called *multiplication model*. This is an example of a model which is nonlinear in the parameters but linearisable. An example of such a model is equation (19):

$$S_{jt} = \alpha_0 p_{jt}^{\alpha_1} a_{jt}^{\alpha_2}. \qquad (19)$$

This model has the following desirable characteristics. First it accounts for interaction between the various instruments. This can easily be seen by looking at the first-order derivative with respect to say a_{jt}:

$$\frac{\delta S_{jt}}{\delta a_{jt}} = \alpha_0 . \alpha_2 . p_{jt}^{\alpha_1} a_{jt}^{\alpha_2 - 1} \qquad (20)$$

which also can be written as:

$$\frac{\delta S_{jt}}{\delta a_{jt}} = \frac{\alpha_2 S_{jt}}{a_{jt}}. \qquad (21)$$

The impact of a change in a_{jt} on S_{jt} is a function of S_{jt} itself, which means that it depends not only on a_{jt} but of p_{jt} as well.

Second, the exponents of a multiplicative response model are to be interpreted as constant elasticities. Letting η_a be the elasticity of S_{jt} with respect to a_{jt}:

$$\eta_a = \frac{\delta S_{jt}}{\delta a_{jt}} \frac{a_{jt}}{S_{jt}} \qquad (22)$$

and using (21) we find:

$$\eta_a = \alpha_2. \qquad (23)$$

A third advantage of the model is that, although it is nonlinear in the parameters, a simple transformation can make it linear. Taking the logarithm of (19) we obtain:

$$\ln S_{jt} = \ln\alpha_0 + \alpha_1 \ln p_{jt} + \alpha_2 \ln a_{jt}. \qquad (24)$$

This double-logarithmic relation is linear in the parameters. Models which are intrinsically nonlinear can be estimated using nonlinear estimation methods. In recent years, powerful nonlinear estimation methods have been developed which can be fruitfully applied in these cases.[42]

Marketing instruments generally have an effect which is spread over *time*, or builds up over time. This has already been discussed in the introduction section. This means, for example, that the effect of an advertising campaign does not end when the campaign is over, but will linger on into the future. That means that the effect is cumulated over time, and thus one refers to the cumulative effects of advertising. Looked at this phenomenon somewhat differently we may expect that in many cases the sales of brand j in t will be determined by advertising in t, but by spending in $t-1$, $t-2$ ... as well. This is known as distributed lag effects. The effects of advertising expenditures on t are distributed over time. This can be illustrated in the following *dynamic* model:

$$S_{jt} = \alpha_0 + \alpha_1 a_{jt} + \alpha_2 a_{j,t-1} + \alpha_3 a_{j,t-2} + ... + u_t \qquad (25)$$

where:

S_{jt} = sales of brand j in period t (say month t),
a_{jt} = advertising expenditures in period t,
u_t = a random disturbance term.

Dynamic models can be defined as models where at least two variables refer to different moments in time. They can be opposed to the *static models* where all variables refer to the same time period.

Another dynamic 'advertising' model is a model with a delayed response. Here the advertising expenditures in *t* may have an effect in the next period *t+1*, as is demonstrated in (26):

$$S_{jt} = \alpha_0 + \alpha_1 a_{j,t-1} + \alpha_2 p_{jt} + u_t. \tag{26}$$

□ *Parameterisation (estimation)*

The models which have been shown in the preceding subsection are all formalised models. Parameterisation of these models will lead to numerically specified models. Parameterisation is the determination of the parameters of a model. *First* in order to determine parameters, *data* are needed. Having good data is a prerequisite to meaningful decision making. 'Good data' refers to availability, quality, variability and quantity.

Availability[43]

Data from the internal accounting system (internal secondary data) and from standardised marketing information services (external secondary data) are important sources of information for the marketing researcher and the marketing executive. During the past decades the use of these secondary data for decision making purposes has become widespread. The introduction of mathematical marketing models has caused the demand for and production of these data to increase many fold. The data which are necessary to parameterise the models can be obtained, in principle, at different points in the marketing channel. Figure 8.3 shows three different opportunities.

Variables such as consumer sales and prices can be measured at the final consumer level by means of a consumer panel (1). They can also be measured at the retail level by means of a store audit (2). Finally, sales can be estimated using internal secondary data such as ex-factory sales and stocks at the retail and wholesale level (3).

Examples of Gfk in (a.c.) Germany consumer panels are MCRA in the United States and Attwood in Holland and in the United Kingdom. The *consumer panel* is comprised of families who use a preprinted diary to record their weekly

Figure 8.3. *Points in the marketing channel where measures are taken*

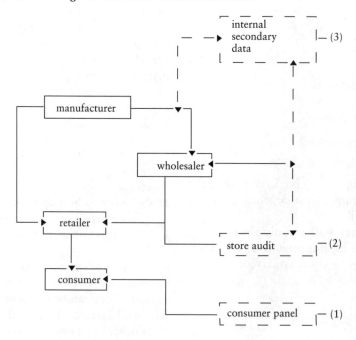

Source: Leeflang and Olivier (1985), p. 28.

purchases in many product categories. The type of product, brand, weight or quantity of unit, number of units, kind of package, price per unit, whether special promotion was in effect, and store name and data are reported for each product bought. The families are geographically dispersed while the panel is demographically balanced so it can be projected onto total purchasing in a certain country. Families are recruited so that the composition of the panel mirrors the population. Panel members are compensated for their participation with gifts and families are dropped from the panel at their request or if they fail to return their diaries. The diaries are returned weekly, the purchase histories are aggregated and reports prepared. Using these reports the subscribing company is able to assess among other things: the size of the market, the proportion of families buying over time, the amount purchased per buyer, brand share over time, frequency of purchase and amount purchased per transaction, average price paid, etc.

The most well-known *store audits* are managed by the A. C. Nielsen company in more then 50 countries. The store audit data are based on national samples of retail stores taken every two months. The data are obtained by sending field workers, called auditors, to a select group of retail stores at fixed intervals. On each visit each auditor takes a complete inventory of all products designated for each audit and notes the merchandise moving into the store by checking wholesale invoices, warehouse withdrawal records, and direct shipments from manufacturers. Inventory and merchandise movements are used to determine consumer's sales. Other information for each of the brands of each of the products audited are out-of-stock stores, prices, dealer support, etc.

The *internal accounting system* may be used to measure the 'shipped sales' or 'ex-factory sales'. The sales of the brands are 'corrected' for 'important changes' in the stocks at the wholesale and the retail level. Developments of inventory changes at the retail level are obtained by the store audit; the inventory changes at the wholesale level are estimates obtained from sales representatives who take on the role of intelligence gatherers. The 'corrections' of the 'ex-factory

sales' are performed twice a year. Pooling the ex-factory sales of the manufacturers' brands with the corresponding figures of competitive brands at an independent institute, estimates of the total industry sales, the industry sales per segment and the brands' market shares are obtained.

The availability of data which can be used to parameterise marketing models has been increased tremendously in the past decade by the introduction of scanners and the use of scanner data.[44] In the early 1970s laser technology in conjunction with small computers first enabled retailers in the US to record electronically or 'scan' the purchases made in their stores. Since then, after a period of slow growth, the adoption of scanning by retailers has been increasing rapidly and scanner data have more and more become available for decision support in marketing.

Although scanning was originally developed by the retail trade simply as a labour- and cost-saving device, its importance is by no means confined to the retail industry. The computerised accumulation of point-of-sale information puts a library of accurate and detailed purchase records at the disposal of marketeers and marketing researchers.

Several years after the first scanners were installed in the US, scanning was introduced in Europe. Since then organisations of industry and trade in many European countries developed and co-ordinated the encoding of products and the exchange of data. Clearing institutes have been established to amalgamate the data of the affiliated retailers and to provide basic reports. In addition systems for automated transmission of transaction data have been developed and the possibilities for natural electronic funds transfer systems (EFTS) have been studied. Table 8.1 illustrates this most significant development in the grocery marketing scene (Nielsen, 1988, p. 38).

In Table 8.1 the penetration of scanning devices (or scanners) among foodstores is represented, or measured, by the percentage of all commodity volume which is sold through the scanning stores. Clearly large differences exist between the US and Europe, and between European countries, In the US, Canada, and in most countries in Europe, scanning-based (store)

Table 8.1.   *Developments of scanning in food-stores*

Country	December 1987		January 1990		January 1994
	stores with scanners	% ACV turnover	stores with scanners	% ACV turnover	% ACV turnover
North America					
USA	14,660	55	18,530	62	71
Canada	1,011	38	1,390	45	50
Europe					
Finland	306	15	1,252	45	80
Sweden	697	22	1,158	44	85
France	1,529	28	3,200	43	74
Great Britain	495	17	1,497	39	76
Denmark	220	15	850	37	83
Belgium	410	15	686	31	83
Germany	985	10	2,730	29	39
Norway	311	15	537	26	58
Netherlands	385	13	638	25	56
Ireland	15	4	70	19	39
Italy	650	7	2,300	17	56
Spain	475	7	850	14	57
Austria	153	5	302	10	53
Switzerland	52	1	160	3	10

Source: Nielsen (1988), p. 39 and information from A. C. Nielsen (Nederland) BV.
ACV = All Commodity Volume.

audits are currently being developed. The figures in Table 8.1, however, point out that, at least in some European countries, the penetration of scanners is too low to rely solely on scanner data for decision making in marketing. For the time being, therefore, the use of these data will primarily be complementary to the use of the traditional consumer panel and retail store audit data in these countries.

Scanning has many advantages for consumers, retailers, whole salers and manufacturers.[45] In this chapter we will spend some attention to the advantages scanning offers to marketing research. Scanning-based samples have been constructed at the consumer level ('home scanning') and at the retail level ('scanning based store samples'). In order to get some ideas about the benefits of scanning we concentrate on the scanning-based store samples.[46] The following benefits of scanning-based store samples can be distinguished:

- Greater accuracy, in the sense that much of the human element in recording product movement is eliminated. Also, more accurate price estimates may be obtained as variations in prices are known and can be related to the relevant quantities. This does not mean, however, that no mistakes are made in recording data. Clerks may skip items and incorrectly load-in the data. Furthermore equipment problems do appear. Below we will elaborate these points in more detail.
- Relatively low costs of data collection.
- Shorter data intervals. Because at the retail level it is unlikely that changes in prices and promotions will be made within one week, scanner data are normally reported on a weekly basis. However, the data interval can be as short as a day, or even shorter. Compared with the traditional monthly or bi-

monthly interval, the shorter data interval provides more insight into the short-term fluctuations of the variables.

- Exact data intervals. In the traditional store audits the stores are audited on different days, resulting in a rolling sample. This approach greatly reduces the costs of collecting the data. As a consequence, however, the aggregated audit data may differ from exact bimonthly measures of marketing variables. These differences are referred to as 'instrument bias'. This bias does not occur with scanning.
- Speed of reporting. Instead of four to eight weeks after the period of observation, reports are available within five to ten days after the scanned period.
- More data, such as sales per purchase, per consumer, and per thousand consumers, become available.

Although there are many opportunities to obtain market data, we have to remark that this holds particularly for markets of (final) consumer products. It is much more difficult to collect data for industrial products and so it is much harder to develop numerically specified models for these markets.[47]

Quality

Some panels and surveys are subject to large response errors or even response biases (a lack of accuracy). In addition they are subject to sampling error (a lack of precision).[48] Even scanner data may be subject to biases.[49]

Variability

In behavioural relations the fluctuations in a dependent variable, which is quite often a response measure, are explained by fluctuations in the independent variables. If an independent variable shows no variation we cannot expect to be able to measure its impact on the variable we want to explain. Because scanner data, generally, refer to shorter intervals of time (weekly data instead of monthly or bi-monthly data) scanner data usually show sufficient variation. Still we may meet marketing variables which do not show any variation in a certain time period. Examples of these variables are packaging or the quality of a product. Mathematical marketing models which are parameterised using objective data cannot be used to determine the effects of these variables on a response measure.

Quantity

Other things being equal, the 'quality' of parameter estimates will improve with the number of observations. Having data in sufficient quantity is also important when models are to be properly validated. Validation indeed requires the availability of two independent, i.e. non-overlapping sets of data, a point we will return to below. Also in this respect scanner data offer much more opportunities than the 'classical' panel and store audit data.

The *second* aspect of *parameterisation* is the *choice of technique* to be applied for extracting estimates of the model parameters from the data collected. Here a distinction can be made between:

a. data-based parameterisation: parameter estimation from historical (time series) data and/or cross-sectional data;
b. subjective estimation: judgement-based parameter estimation.

We will return to the topic of subjective estimation below.

'The idea' of parameterisation can be elucidated by using equation (4):

$$S_{jt} = \alpha_j + \beta_j a_{jt} + u_{jt} \qquad t = 1,2,...,T \qquad (4)/(27)$$

where all variables have been defined before.

Parameterization of (4) leads to numerical specification of α_j and β_j. The estimated values of α_j and β_j are indicated by $\hat{\alpha}_j$ and $\hat{\beta}_j$. This is illustrated in Figure 8.4, where the values of monthly sales of brand j observed in 1994 are plotted against the corresponding monthly advertising expenditures.

Figure 8.4. *sales in units and advertising expenditures*

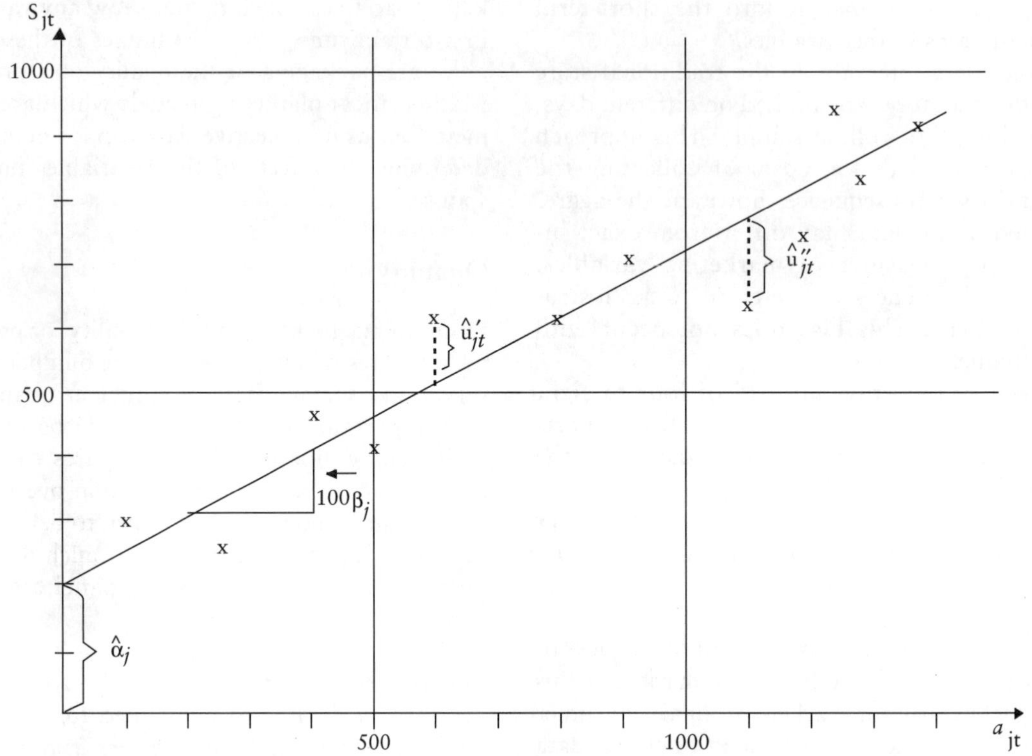

Source: Naert and Leeflang (1978), p. 58.

The figures clearly point to the existence of a relation between a_{jt} and S_{jt}. Low values of S_{jt} correspond to low values of a_{jt} and similarly for high values. Since the observations do not all fall on the same line, equation (4) will not explain all variation in sales by variation in advertising. But, one will try to determine $\hat{\alpha}_j$ and $\hat{\beta}_j$ in such a way that the estimated relation is the 'best' one can obtain. 'Best' implies that there exists a criterion by which different sets of estimates can be compared and evaluated against each other. In classical statistics and econometrics, the criterion usually is the minimisation of the sum of the squared deviations between observed values S_{jt} and estimated ones $\hat{S}_{jt}(= \hat{\alpha}_j + \hat{\beta}a_{jt})$, i.e., $\hat{\alpha}_j$ and $\hat{\beta}_j$

are the values which minimise, $\sum_{t=1}^{T} \hat{u}^2_{jt}$, where

$\hat{u}_{jt} = S_{jt} - \hat{S}_{jt}$. If this criterion is adopted, one refers to estimation by *the method of least squares*.[50]

The method assumes a *quadratic loss function*, which means that the degree to which deviations from observed values should be penalised is proportional to the squared deviations. In addition, the least squares criterion assumes that overestimation or underestimation are (ordinary) equally bad. For the data presented in Figure 8.41 the following estimates are obtained: $\hat{\alpha}_j = 200$, and $\hat{\beta}_j = 0.5$. Also indicated are two values of the estimated (random) disturbance terms (also called the *residuals*), $\hat{u}_{jt}$, and $\hat{u}''_{jt}$, corresponding to values $a_{jt} = 600$, and 1100 respectively.

The least squares criterion is just one of a myriad of possible criteria, on the basis of which best estimates can be found. Other estimation methods which are quite frequently used to parameterise marketing models are all kinds of modifications of the method of ordinary least squares which are known as 'generalised least squares methods'. Furthermore maximum likelihood methods are more and more frequently used.[51]

☐ *Validation (verification or evaluation)*

Validation of a model implies assessing the quality of the success of the model. Criteria of success might be considered in terms of:

a. the degree to which the results are in accordance with theoretical expectations or well-known empirical facts (face validity);

b. the degree to which the results pass a number of statistical criteria or tests;

c. the degree to which the result of a modeling effort corresponds to the original purpose:
   - is the model useful for clarifying and describing market phenomena?
   - is the model accurate in predicting the level of certain variables?
   - can the model be used as a basis for determining optimal marketing policies?

The criteria which are used to validate a model are related to its intended use. For example for a descriptive model face validity is very important. 'Normative validity' requires reliable parameter estimates. Validation with respect to the predictive ability of models is known as '*tracking*'.

Tracking starts with the comparison between forecasts of future events and observed values. A prerequisite for meaningful tracking is that either:

1. new data become available, or that
2. data already available at the parameterisation stage have been divided into two samples. The first one applies to the estimation or model fit, and is sometimes called the analysis sample. The second, called the validation sample, is needed for applying the model to a 'new' set of data. This is only possible if we have data of sufficient quantity.

Differences between forecasts and observed values may be due to:

1. errors in forecasting model inputs, such as differences between predicted price in period *t* and actual price;

2. inappropriate parameter estimates, which implies that they should be updated or re-estimated;
3. poor model structuring in terms of both the variables included and how they relate to each other;
4. changes in the environment being modelled, such as entry of a new (potentially) major competitor;
5. random variation, i.e. differences between forecasts and actual values which cannot be explained by any of the reasons given above.

Tracking involves more than just noticing differences between forecasts and realisations. It also means trying to determine the causes, an effort which will primarily be judgement-based, and doing something about it, such as updating parameters, changing inputs, thinking about expanding or contracting the model ...

☐ *Cost-benefit considerations*

The term 'cost-benefit considerations' occurs in Figure 8.1 at two different places. First costs and benefits should be evaluated before a model is built. Costs and benefits will determine the model scope and the amount of behavioral detail a model should contain. Costs and benefits, however, can only be determined more precisely after the model has been parameterised and validated. This means that in many cases, an investment should be made first (building a preliminary version of a model) in order to carry out a cost-benefit analysis. When a model is built, has been numerically specified and validated, a cost-benefit analysis can then be used to decide whether or not the model should be used. When it appears that the model should not be used, model development criteria can be modified and the sequence of steps started all over again.

☐ *Use*

Tracking and cost-benefit considerations lead to the final step of the model building process: the (continuing) use of the model. Through continuing use, there will be a gradual evolution in what the manger wants from his model, in his perception of the real world situation the model is supposed to represent. Thus the model becomes an integral part of his decision-making processes.

From the description above, it should be clear that the sequence is not undirectional. Model-building and continuing use may lead to a restructuring of the problem perception, which will in turn affect the specification. In other words, the process depicted in Figure 2 will normally contain a number of feedback loops.

■ Examples[52]

In this section we briefly discuss a number of numerically specified marketing models. We will give three examples of predictive models which differ in the level of demand which is explained. The first model is a predictive model, without behavioural detail.[53] In this model the fluctuations of industry sales (primary demand) are explained. The market which is modelled is the West German cigarette market. The data cover the period 1960–1975. The model has been estimated using annual, bimonthly and monthly data, and has the following structure:

$$S_t = e^{\alpha_0 + u_t} A_t^{\alpha_1} C_t^{\alpha_2} R_t^{\alpha_3} P_t^{\alpha_4} G_t^{\alpha_5} \qquad (28)$$

where:

S_t = the industry sales of cigarettes in period t,
A_t = industry advertising expenditure in t,
C_t = household consumption in t,
R_t = industry sales of 'hand rolled' tobacco in t,

P_t = industry sales of pipe tobacco in t,
G_t = industry sales of cigars in t,
u_t = a random disturbance in term in t,

and where all variables are defined per capita, the population being defined as those people who are over 15 years of age. All variables have been regressed with time and in this way the variables are free from trend influences. The estimated parameters and the regression statistics of equation (28) obtained from the annual, bi-monthly and monthly observations are given in Table 8.2.

With the exception of the variable G_t for the annual data, all coefficients have the expected sign. Independent of the level of temporal aggregation, the parameter estimates of the advertising variable are statistically significant at the 5% level. Relation (28) has been estimated for different time periods in order to test the variability of the parameter estimates. The analyses reveal that the influence of advertising on primary demand diminishes over time; the advertising elasticity did not even differ significantly from zero during the last sub-period of the period 1971–1975. In this study the long-term advertising elasticities have been determined for the different levels of aggregation (using a dynamic model).[54] These are .353 when annual data are used, .164 (bi-monthly data) and .142 (monthly data). These (and other) results provide support for the finding that the carryover effects of advertising tend to be over-estimated when annual data are used.

Another set of examples refers to models in which the response measure market share is used. We show three so-called market share models in which the fluctuations of the market shares of four brands on the German cigarette market are explained by using bi-monthly data.[55] First we give the specification of a linear additive model:

$$m_{jt} = \alpha_j + \beta_{1j} as_{jt} + \beta_{2j} m_{j,t-1} + u_{jt}, \quad j=1,...,4, \ t=1,...,T \qquad (29)$$

where:

m_{jt} = market share of brand j in period t,

as_{jt} = the advertising share of brand j in

$$t = \frac{a_{jt}}{\sum\limits_{r=1}^{n}}$$

a_{jt} = the advertising expenditures of brand j in t,
n = the total number of brands,
$m_{j,t-1}$ = lagged market share,
u_{jt} = a random disturbance term.

Table 8.2. *Parameter estimates and statistics of relation (28)*

	annual data	bimonthly data	monthly data
advertising	.110[c] (.028)[a]	.068[c] (.022)	.034[b] (.019)
household consumption	.497[b] (.196)	.585[c] (.088)	.601[c] (.088)
hand rolled tobacco	−.146[c] (.048)	−.097[c] (.034)	−.068[b] (.032)
pipe tobacco	−.053 (.030)	−.024 (.039)	−.007 (.035)
cigars	.191[b] (.088)	−.148[b] (.064)	−.077 (.052)
R^2	.961	.932	.848
DW[d]	2.399	1.591	1.952

[a] = the figures in parentheses are standard errors
[b] = significant at the .05 level
[c] = significant at the .01 level
[d] = value of the Durbin-Watson statistic
Source: Leeflang and Reuyl (1985), p. 96.

The multiplicative version of (29) is:

$$m_{jt} = e^{\alpha_j} as_{jt}^{\beta_{1j}} m_{j,t-1}^{\beta_{2j}} e^{u_{jt}}, \quad j = 1, \ldots, 4, \, t = 1, \ldots, T. \quad (30)$$

It can be easily shown that these are non-robust models. There is no guarantee that the estimated market shares sum to one ((29), (30)) and have a value between zero and one (29). A class of robust market share models are the so-called attraction models. An example of an attraction model is given in (31):[56]

$$m_{jt} = \frac{e^{\alpha_j + u_{jt}} as_{jt}^{\beta_{1j}} m_{j,t-1}^{\beta_2}}{\sum_{r=1}^{n} e^{\alpha_r + u_{rt}} as_{rt}^{\beta_{1r}} m_{r,t-1}^{\beta_2}}. \quad (31)$$

The estimated values of the response parameters of the models (29)–(30) are shown in Table 8.3.

From Table 8.3 we conclude that there are marked differences among the advertising parameters. For brands 1 and 3 these parameters have

the expected sign and are statistically significant. For other brands, however, results are less satisfactory. A number of parameters even have a negative sign. Fortunately, the latter are not significant. Generally, the parameter estimates of the lagged endogenous variable are highly significant.

Brand sales can either be modelled directly or indirectly. Directly means that sales of a brand j are explained by relating them to instrument variables of brand j, instrument variables of competing brands, and environmental variables. Indirectly means that brand sales (S_{jt}) is obtained as the product of product class sales (Q_t) and market share of the brand of interest (m_{jt}).

Modelling brand sales indirectly is preferably for a number of reasons:

1. It allows a distinction between changes in S_{jt} caused by changes in market size, Q_t, and by changes in the relative position of brand j in the market, expressed by market share, m_{jt}.

Table 8.3.   *Parameter estimates of market share models*

Specification		β_{11}	β_{12}	β_{13}	β_{14}	β_{21}	β_{22}	β_{23}	β_{24}
		Advertising Share				*Lagged Market Share*			
linear additive	(29)	0,036[a]	–0,005	0,040[a]	–0,017	0,498[b]	0,810[b]	0,669[b]	0,698[b]
multiplicative	(30)	0,13[a]	0,014	0,066[b]	–0,021	0,456[a]	0,839[b]	0,812[b]	0,691[b]
attraction	(31)	0,60[b]	–0,015	0,061[a]	–0,341	$\leftarrow$0,861[b]$\rightarrow$			

[a] significant of the .05 level
[b] significant of the .01 level
Source: Leeflang and Reuyl (1984), p. 214.

2. Using market share rather than sales quantity as the dependent variable has the following advantages: environmental variables, and seasonal or cyclical factors causing expansion or contraction of the entire market need not be included. As such, the model concentrates attention on the competitive interaction among all brands in the product class.
3. By phasing variables in this way over different levels we are able to reduce the number of potential independent variables per equation. So, more degrees of freedom are obtained in situations in which the number of observations is low relative to the number of independent variables.

The last reason has become less relevant for those cases in which scanner data are available. In the well-known SCAN*PRO-model[57] and the PROMOTIONSCAN-model[58] brand sales are used as dependent variable. The SCAN*PRO-model is a store-level model developed for the effects of promotional activities implemented by retailers on a brand's unit sales. The model accommodates temporary price cuts, displays, and feature advertising. In addition, it includes weekly indicator variables to account for the effects of seasonality and missing variables (such as manufacturer television advertising and coupon distributions) common to the stores in a metropolitan area. This model has been used in over 1000 different commercial applications in the United States, in Canada, in Europe, and elsewhere.

A slight modification of the original model is specified as follows, for brand k, $k=1,...,J$:

$$S_{ikt} = \left[\prod_{j=1}^{J} \left(\frac{P_{ijt}}{\bar{P}_{ij}} \right)^{\beta_{jk}} \prod_{l=1}^{3} \gamma_{ljk}^{D_{lijt}} \right] \left[\prod_{t=1}^{T} \delta_{kt}^{X_t} \right] \left[\prod_{i=1}^{N} \lambda_{ik}^{Z_{it}} \right] e^{u_{ikt}} \quad (32)$$

$$i=1,...,N, \; t=1,...,T$$

where:
S_{ikt} = unit sales (e.g., number of pounds) for brand k in store i, week t,
P_{ijt} = unit price for brand j in store i, week t,
$\bar{P}_{ij}$ = the median regular unit price (based on the non-promoted weeks) for brand j in store i,
D_{1ijt} = an indicator variable for feature advertising: 1 if brand j is featured (but *not* displayed) by store i, in week t; 0 otherwise,
D_{2ijt} = an indicator variable for display: 1 if brand j is displayed (but *not* featured) by store i, in week t; 0 otherwise,
D_{3ijt} = an indicator variable for the simultaneous use of feature and display: 1 if brand j is featured *and* displayed; 0 otherwise,
X_t = an indicator variable (proxy for missing variables and seasonal effects): 1 if the observation is in week t; 0 otherwise,
Z_{it} = an indicator variable for store i: 1 if the observation is from store i; 0 otherwise,
β_{jk} = the own price (deal) elasticity if $k=j$, or a cross price elasticity if $k\neq j$,
γ_{1jk} = the own feature ad multiplier if $k=j$, or a cross-feature ad multiplier if $k\neq j$,

Table 8.4. *Average values of parameter estimates of the SCAN*PRO-model*

own effects				cross effects			
feature	display	feature and display	price	feature	display	feature and display	price
1.69	2.27	3.07	−3.52	1.25	0.87	0.89	0.63

Source: Foekens, Leeflang and Wittink (1994).

γ_{2jk} = the own display multiplier if $k=j$, or a cross-display multiplier if $k \neq j$,

γ_{3jk} = the own display *and* feature multiplier if $k=j$, or a cross-display feature multiplier if $k \neq j$,

δ_{kt} = the (seasonal) multiplier for week t, when the criterion variable represents brand k,

λ_{ik} = store i's regular (base) unit sales for brand k when there are no temporary price cuts and no promotion activities for any of the brands j, $j=1,...,J$,

u_{ikt} = a disturbance term for brand k in store i, week t,

J = the number of brands used in the competitive set,

N = the number of stores in the sample for a major market,

T = the number of weeks.

Recently, this model has been numerically specified in a study in which the forecasting accuracy of this model at different levels of aggregation (store, chain, market-level) has been investigated. We will only consider the parameter estimates which are obtained if store level data are used. These estimates are obtained using UPC scanner data provided by A. C. Nielsen, for one large metropolitan area in the United States. Weekly data were available for three national brands competing in a frequently purchased food category. The average values of the parameter estimates based on significant estimates only are shown in Table 8.4. The averages are averages over the three brands and the 40 stores in the sample.[59]

The (promotion) multipliers with a value larger than 1 have a positive effect on unit sales.

Promotion multipliers with values smaller than 1 do have a negative effect on S_{ikt}. All cross effects, except feature, do have a negative impact on S_{ikt}.

The models which are shown in this section have been parameterised using objective data. Furthermore in all models *consumer* response is related to marketing instruments and environmental variables. In the following section we will discuss the parameterisation of models when no objective data are available. Finally, we show some examples in which *competitive* response is considered as the variable to be explained.

■ Subjective data

There are a large number of situations in which parameterisation on the basis of objective data is impossible or inappropriate. This may be caused by one or more of the following reasons:

1. Data are not available;
2. Data are available but at a cost and management is not prepared to incur this extra expense;
3. Data are available but there is no time to collect the data;
4. *Good* data are not available. This could mean that data are not available in sufficient quantity and/or variability and/or the quality of the data is not acceptable;
5. Objective and good data are available but the market conditions change dramatically. Suppliers may withdraw brands or the prevailing situation is changed completely by the introduction of a new entrant.

In all these cases the generation of subjective data may be very useful. In the literature and in practice there is a trend towards the use of these estimates and more specifically to the use of expert opinions and expert systems.[60]

We give an illustration of the use of subjective estimates. In this example, based on Little (1970) the following market share model is parameterised:

$$m_{jt} = \alpha_j + (\beta_j - \alpha_j)\frac{a_{jt}^{\delta_j}}{\gamma_j + a_{jt}^{\delta_j}} \qquad (33)$$

where:

m_{jt} = market share of brand j in period t,
a_{jt} = advertising expenditures of brand j in period t,
$\alpha_j\,\beta_j\,\gamma_j\,\delta_j$ = parameters to be estimated.

The estimated values of the parameters of (33) can be found by answering the following questions. What will be m_{jt} if:

1. $a_{jt} = 0$,
2. a_{jt} is at a maximum,
3. the advertising expenditures are at their present level (say $810 000),
4. the advertising budget is increased with 50 percent.

If $a_{jt} = 0$, $\hat{m}_{jt} = \hat{\alpha}$. This gives us an estimate of α. In a similar way the answer to the second question gives an estimate for β. Let us assume that $\hat{\alpha} = 0,10$ and $\hat{\beta} = 0,70$. Assuming that $\hat{m}_{jt}$ ($a_{jt} = 810\ 000$) $= 0.40$ and $\hat{m}_{jt}$ ($a_{jt} = 1\ 213\ 000$) $= 0.415$, the estimates for δ_j and γ_j are obtained by the following two equations:

$$0.40 = 0.10 + 0.60\frac{(810,000)^{\delta_j}}{\gamma_j + (810,000)^{\delta_j}} \qquad (34)$$

$$0.415 = 0.10 + 0.60\frac{(1,215,000)^{\delta_j}}{\gamma_j + (1,215,000)^{\delta_j}} \qquad (35)$$

The estimated values are approximately equal to $\gamma_j = 30$ and $\gamma g_j = 0.25$.

This procedure also can be executed if the model contains more explanatory variables.[61]

In consumer markets, predictions of the demand for a new product can be made using intention surveys. Intention surveys will result in subjective estimates. Intention surveys can also be applied to predict the effects of a new entrant into an industrial market as has been demonstrated by Alsem, Leeflang, Reuyl (1990, 1991) and Alsem, Leeflang (1994). In their studies predictions are made of the advertising expenditures in the Netherlands after the introduction of private broadcasting.

■ Competitive response

In modern marketing much attention is devoted to competition. Competition may be emphasised more now because the economic climate of the (early) 1980s and (early) 1990s is characterised by minimal growth in many markets and, as a consequence, by intense competition. Further, a more rapid rate of new-product introductions and reactions to new entries[62] may result from as well as contribute to a higher intensity of competition. Many methods and models have been developed to diagnose competition. Day and Wensley (1988) dichotomise them into competitor-centred methods and customer-focused approaches. Competitor-centred assessments are based on direct management comparisons between the firm and a few target *competitors*. Customer-focused assessments start with detailed analyses of customer benefits within end-use segments and work backward from the *customer* to the company to identify what actions are needed to improve performance.

Models can be used to diagnose competition. A competitor-centred approach using a mathematical marketing model is the use of reaction matrices. In these models the dependent variables are marketing instruments instead of response measures.

Lambin, Naert and Bultez (LNB) (1975) pioneered the use of reaction matrices to diagnose competitive reactions. In their model, they assume there is one market leader. They treat other competitors as followers. They define the market as consisting of the leader and the aggregate of the other firms. In the model, they estimate competitive reactions by parameterising the following relations, for $l = 1, \ldots k$:

$$U_{lt} = f([u_{ht}]_{h=1,\ldots,k}), t = 1, \ldots, T \tag{36}$$

where:

U_{lt} = the aggregate or average competitive value of the *l-th* marketing instrument of the followers in period t,

u_{ht} = the value of the *h-th* marketing instrument of the leader in period t.

To illustrate the LNB model, we assume, for simplicity, that all variables are related in the same period, although empirically reactions are allowed to occur after a time lag. For example, with two marketing variables let:

$$U_{lt} = P_t = \frac{\sum_{j=2}^{n} p_{jt}}{n-1}, u_{1t} = p_{1t}, U_{2t} = A_t = \sum_{j=2}^{n} a_{jt}, \text{and} u_{2t} = a_{1t} \tag{37}$$

where:

p_{jt} = the price per equivalent unit of brand j in period t,

a_{jt} = advertising expenditures for brand j in period t,

n = the total number of brands.

In their model, Lambin, Naert, and Bultez distinguish simple and multiple competitive reactions. A simple competitive reaction is one in which a competitor reacts using the same instrument used by the firm inducing the reaction (for example, if one firm changes the price for brand i, the competing firm changes the price of its brand j). A multiple competitive reaction is one in which the competitor reacts using instruments other than that used by the firm inducing the reaction. Competitor j may react to a change in the price for brand i not just by changing the price for j, but also by changing the advertising budget, the advertising message, product quality, promotions, or other factors.

In a number of extended-LNB models, researchers made no distinction between leaders and followers. They consider all brands separately in what amounts to a decomposition of competitive interactions.[63]

The customer-focused assessment to diagnose competition relies on estimating market response functions. We use an example to describe how we conduct customer-focused assessments by estimating market share response functions. We discuss this example in greater detail in Leeflang and Wittink (1993). We define the dependent variable as the natural logarithm of the ratio of market shares in successive periods for brand $j = 1, \ldots, n : \ln\left(\dfrac{m_{jt}}{m_{j,t-1}}\right)$. This variable is explained by the natural logarithm of the ratio of prices in two successive periods: $\ln\left(\dfrac{p_{jt}}{p_{j,t-1}}\right), i = 1, \ldots n$ and the first differences of all promotional variables (refunds (R), bonus activities (B), sampling (S) featuring (F)) of all brands $i = 1, \ldots, n$. Thus, the relations are nonlinear in the variables but linear in the parameters. The equations allow for asymmetry in effects. Asymmetries are reflected in differential cross-effects among brands. Brands are differentially effective with their ability to influence the shares and sales of other brands. Furthermore, firms differ in the degree for which they are influenced by other brands' actions.[64] This is illustrated in Table 8.5. Table 8.5 shows the independent (predictor) variables with statistically significant effects for each market share equation. The parameter estimates of the relations are obtained by parameterising market share relations for seven brands of a frequently purchased nondurable, non-food consumer product sold in the Netherlands. The competition among brands in the product category is dominated by price and promotional programs. Weekly scanner data pertaining to 76 weeks have been used to parameterise these market share models.

Table 8.5 shows that we obtain 13 own effects, that is, in 13 cases when $i = j$, *the marketing in-*

Table 8.5.   *Statistically significant effects*[a] in market share response functions

criterion variable	relevant predictors for each brand						
market share[b]	1	2	3	4	5	6	7
M_1	PF	F		S		S	
M_2		PBF	F	F	P	P*	
M_3			P		F		
M_4		F	F*	BF			S
M_5	P			B*	PF	SF	
M_6	P	PB	S			RS	
M_7	F	P				P*	P
maximum possible number of effects[c]	2	4	3	5	4	5	5

[a]   The letters indicate that this predictor variable has a statistically significant effect in the multiple regression; P = price, S = sampling, R = refund, B = bonus, F = feature. If the sign of the coefficient for the predictor in the multiple regression is counter to expectations, the letter has the symbol* next to it.

[b]   Market share: $ln(m_{it}/m_{i,t-1})$.

[c]   Own effects are in the cells on the diagonal; cross effects are in the off-diagonal cells.

Source: Leeflang and Wittink (1993).

struments of brand *i* have a statistically significant effect with the expected sign on the brand's own market share. Because each brand does not use all marketing instruments, the maximum possible number of own effects differs between brands (given in the last row). The 13 own effects can be compared with the maximum number of own effects which equals the sum of the maximum number of possible values: 28.

There are 18 cross-market share effects with the expected signs indicated as off-diagonal entries in Table 8.5. The maximum number of cross effects equals (the number of competitors minus one) times the maximum possible number of instruments or $6 \times 28 = 168$. Thus, the proportion of significant cross effects (18/168 or 11 percent) is much lower than the proportion of significant own effects (13/28 or 46 percent). From Table 8.5 we can draw several conclusions about the brands' competition based on con-

sumer response. For example, brand 3's market share is directly affected by few competitors, whereas brand 7 is hardly able to affect the market shares of other brands.

■ Concluding remarks

The models which have been discussed in the preceding section illustrate that markets can be modelled by explaining fluctuations in market response and competitive response. It also illustrates that developments in the marketing area such as, for example, the increased attention for competition and the value of a brand are guided by developments in mathematical model building. These developments do not only appear in theory but also in practice. At least to our opinion the managerial relevance of mathematical models or 'marketing science' is increasing. This is discussed in more detail in Parsons, Gijsbrechts, Leeflang and Wittink (1993).

In this chapter we discussed concepts which have to be used to model markets and some examples have been given. In this way, we have demonstrated that the modelling of markets is an integral part of marketing theory and marketing practise.

■ Notes

1. A part of this chapter is based on an earlier publication of the author, Naert and Leeflang (1978).
2. See Aaker (1991), Kapferer (1992).
3. This example is taken from Brown, Hulswit and Ketelle (1956).
4. Examples are Leeflang (1974); Naert and Leeflang (1978); Hanssens, Parsons and Schultz (1990); Lilien, Kotler and Moorthy (1992); Eliashberg and Lilien (1993).
5. See also Parsons, Gijsbrechts, Leeflang and Wittink (1993).
6. See Leone and Schultz (1980); Assmus, Farley and Lehmann (1984).
7. Tellis (1988).
8. Blattberg and Neslin (1989).
9. Leone and Schultz (1980).
10. See also Ehrenberg (1993).
11. See Leeflang and Wedel (1993).
12. For more examples we refer to, e.g., Parsons, Gijsbrechts, Leeflang and Wittink (1993) and Brand and Leeflang (1993). In the latter publication a survey is given of the models which have been developed in the area of industrial marketing.
13. See Rangaswamy, Sinha and Zoltners (1990).
14. Silk and Urban (1978).
15. See Urban and Katz (1983).
16. See Wittink, Addona, Hawkes and Porter (1988).
17. See, e.g., Leeflang and Reuyl (1985, 1995).
18. See, e.g., Alsem, Leeflang and Reuyl (1990); Alsem and Leeflang (1994).
19. This discussion partly follows Naert (1977).
20. See also Aaker and Weinberg (1975), p. 18.
21. For some illustrations of this collection process we refer to Leeflang (1977).
22. See for an example a model developed by Hulbert and Toy (1977).
23. This market has been studied and described by Hoekstra (1987), who developed a mathematical descriptive model to this end.
24. The terminology adopted here is not unique. Product class sales, brand sales, and market share models are also referred to as primary demand, secondary demand, and selective (or relative) demand models.
25. We define environmental variables as variables which are generated by the *environment* of the market being modelled, and not by the system itself or its decision makers.
26. For a recent, thorough, survey and evaluation of these models we refer to Nijkamp (1993).
27. See, for example, Nillesen (1992).
28. For a discussion of how much detail should be included in a model we refer to Naert and Leeflang (1978), Chapter 14.
29. Hanssens, Parsons and Schultz (1990), p. 11.
30. In the context of regression analysis, α_j and β_j may also be called the regression coefficients; β_j is also known as a response parameter.
31. See, for example, Leeflang and Olivier (1985).
32. Variable cost could also be time varying, in which case c_j becomes c_{jt}.
33. Perhaps this is not a very good example since (8) is a definition equation.
34. We refrain from discussing an other set of relations called technical equations. In these equations, variables are related on the basis of their technical connection. Examples are production functions.
35. This section is partly based on Leeflang and Naert (1978).
36. See, for example, Leeflang and Wedel (1993).
37. See also, for example, Leeflang (1974), Chapter 6.
38. This conflict can be resolved by building models in an evolutionary way. This means first a simple model is constructed. As the manager uses the model and builds up experience with the model, the model can be expanded to incorporate additional elements, etc. See Urban and Karash (1971).
39. See, for example, Parsons and Vanden Abeele (1981); Leeflang and Plat (1984).
40. See, Bultez and Naert (1975); Naert and Weverbergh (1981, 1985); Brodie and De Kluyver (1984); Ghosh, Neslin and Shoemaker (1984); Leeflang and Reuyl (1984).
41. In this section the disturbance term will be omitted for reasons of convenience.

42. See, for a recent example and application in marketing, Chintagunta (1992).
43. This part of the text is based on Leeflang and Olivier (1985).
44. See Leeflang and Plat (1988); Foekens and Leeflang (1992). The following text is based on Foekens and Leeflang (1992).
45. See Plat (1988), Chapter 5, Leeflang and Plat (1988).
46. See also Bloom (1980), Prasad, Casper and Schieffer (1984).
47. See for a survey of models for industrial markets, for example, Brand and Leeflang (1993).
48. See Leeflang and Olivier (1985).
49. See Leeflang and Plat (1988); Foekens and Leeflang (1992).
50. For a detailed description of this method we refer to econometric textbooks, such as, Judge, Griffiths, Hill, Lütkepohl and Lee (1984) and Wittink (1988).
51. See, for example, Kamakura and Russell (1989); Wedel (1990); Chintagunta (1993); De Sarbo and Wedel (1994).
52. The examples are biased, because they were taken from studies in which the author was engaged.
53. See Leeflang and Reuyl (1985).
54. The dynamic model has the following structures:
$$S_t = e^{\beta_0 + ut} A_t^{\beta_1} S_{t-1}^{\beta_2}$$
55. See Leeflang and Reuyl (1984).
56. Other examples of attraction models can be found in Cooper and Nakanishi (1988). See also Carpenter, Cooper, Hanssens and Midgley (1988).
57. Wittink, Addona, Hawkes and Porter (1988).
58. Abraham and Lodish (1992).
59. Foekens, Leeflang and Wittink (1994).
60. See for a recent survey Rangaswamy (1993). For some more specific examples see Rangaswamy, Eliashberg, Burke and Wind (1989); Burke and Rangaswamy, Wind and Eliashberg (1990). For a survey how subjective data and subjective estimates are generated see Naert and Leeflang (1978), Chapter 11.
61 See, for example, Naert and Leeflang (1978), Chapter 12.
62. Robinson (1988); Gatignon, Anderson and Helsen (1989).
63. See, for example, Hanssens (1980), Gatignon (1984), Leeflang and Wittink (1992). For a more thorough discussion of these and other models see Leeflang and Wittink (1993), and Moorthy (1993).
64. See Cooper and Nakanishi (1988), p. 57.

■ References

Aaker, D. A. and Weinberg, L. B. (1975), 'Interactive Marketing Models', *Journal of Marketing* 39 (October), pp. 16–23.

Aaker, D. A. (1991), *Managing Brand Equity: Capitalizing on the Value of a Brand Name*, New York: Free Press.

Abraham, M. M. and Lodish, L. M. (1992), 'An Implemented System for Improving Promotion Productivity Using Store Scanner Data', *Marketing Science* 12, pp. 248–269.

Alsem, K. J., Leeflang, P. S. H. and Reuyl, J. C. (1990), 'Diagnosing Competition in an Industrial Market', *Proceedings EMAC/ESOMAR Symposium on 'New Ways in Marketing and Marketing Research'*, pp. 161–178, 1991.

Alsem, K. J., Leeflang, P. S. H. and Reuyl, J. C. (1991), 'The Expansion of Broadcast Media in the Netherlands: Effects on the Advertising Expenditures', in *The Expansion of Broadcast Media: Does Research Meet the Challenges?*, Madrid: ESOMAR, pp. 65–79.

Alsem, K. J. and Leeflang, P. S. H. (1994), 'Predicting Advertising Expenditures Using Intention Surveys', *International Journal of Forecasting* 10, pp. 327–337.

Assmus, G., Farley, J. U. and Lehmann, D. R. (1984), 'How Advertising Affects Sales: Meta-analysis of Econometric Results', *Journal of Marketing Research* 24, pp. 65–74.

Bass, F. M. (1969), 'A New Product Growth Model for Consumer Durables', *Management Science* 15, pp. 215–227.

Blattberg, R. C. and Neslin, S. A. (1989), 'Sales Promotion: the Long and Short of it', *Marketing Letters* 1 (December), pp. 81–97.

Bloom, D. (1980), 'Point of Sale Scanners and their Implications for Market Research', *Journal of the Market Research Society* 22, pp. 221–238.

Brand, M. J. (1993), *Effectiveness of the Industrial Marketing Mix: An Assessment Through Simulation of the Organizational Buying Process*, Ph.D. thesis, RuG Groningen, the Netherlands.

Brand, M. J. and Leeflang, P. S. H. (1993), 'Research on Modeling Industrial Markets', in Laurent, G., Lilien, G. L. and Pras, B. (eds), *Research Traditions in Marketing*, Boston: Kluwer Academic Publishers.

Brodie, R. and de Kluyver, C. A. (1984), 'Attraction Versus Linear and Multiplicative Market Share Models: An Empirical Evaluation', *Journal of Marketing Research* 21, pp. 194–201.

Brown, A. A., Hulswit, F. L. and Ketelle, J. D. (1956), 'A Study of Sales Operations', *Operations Research* 4, pp. 296–308.

Bultez, A. V. and Naert, Ph.A. (1975), 'Consistent Sum-Constrained Models', *Journal of the American Statistical Association* 7, pp. 529–535.

Burke, R. R., Rangaswamy, A., Wind, J. and Eliashberg, J. (1990), 'A Knowledge-Based System for Advertising Design', *Marketing Science* 9, pp. 212–229.

Carpenter, G. S., Cooper, L. G., Hanssens, D. M. and Midgley, D. F. (1988), 'Modeling Asymmetric Competition', *Marketing Science* 7, pp. 393–412.

Chintagunta, P. K. (1992), 'Estimating a Multinomial Probit Model of Brand Choice Using the Method of Simulated Moments', *Marketing Science* 11, pp. 386–407.

Chintagunta, P. K. (1993), 'Investigating Purchase Incidence, Brand Choice and Purchase Quantity Decision of Households', *Marketing Science* 12, pp. 184–208.

Cooper, L. G. and Nakanishi, M. (1988), *Market-Share Analysis*, Boston: Kluwer Academic Publishers.

Day, G. S. and Wensley, R. (1988), 'Assessing Advantage: A Framework for Diagnosing Competitive Superiority', *Journal of Marketing* 52, pp. 1–20.

De Sarbo, W. S. and Wedel, M. (1994), 'A Review of Recent Developments in Latent Class Regression Methods', in Bagozzi, R. P. (ed.), *Handbook of Marketing Research*, pp. 352–388.

Ehrenberg, A. S. C. (1988), *Repeat-Buying: Facts, Theory and Applications*, London: Charles Griffin.

Ehrenberg, A. S. C. (1993), 'Theory or Well-Based Results: Which Comes First?', in Lilien, G. L., Laurent, G. and Pras, B., *Research Traditions in Marketing*, Boston: Kluwer Academic Publishers, pp. 79–108.

Eliashberg, J. and Lilien, G. L. (eds) (1993), *Handbook in Operations Research and Management Science*, vol. 5, *Marketing*, New York: Elsevier Publishing.

Farley, J. U., Lehmann, D. R. and Oliva, T. A. (1990), 'Are there Laws in Production? A Meta Analysis of Cobb-Douglas 1921–1980', working paper, no. 90-005, The Warton School, University of Pennsylvania.

Foekens, E. W. and Leeflang, P. S. H. (1992), 'Comparing Scanner Data with Traditional Store Audit Data', *Scandinavian Business Review* 1, pp. 71–85.

Foekens, E. W., Leeflang, P. S. H. and Wittink, D. R. (1994), 'A Comparison and an Exploration of the Forecasting Accuracy of Nonlinear Models at Different Levels of Aggregation', *International Journal of Forecasting* 10, pp. 245–261.

Gatignon, H. (1984), 'Competition as a Moderator of the Effect of Advertising on Sales, *Journal of Marketing Research* 21, pp. 389–398.

Gatignon, H., Anderson, E. and Helsen, K. (1989), 'Competitive Reactions to Market Entry: Explaining Interfirm Differences', *Journal of Marketing Research* 26, pp. 44–45.

Ghosh, A., Neslin, S. and Schoemaker, R. (1984), 'A Comparison of Market Share Models and Estimation Procedures', *Journal of Marketing Research* 21, pp. 202–210.

Hanssens, D. M. (1980), 'Marketing Response, Competitive Behaviour and Time Series Analysis', *Journal of Marketing Research* 17, pp. 470–485.

Hanssens, D. M., Parsons, L. J. and Schultz, R. L. (1990), *Market Response Models: Econometric and Time Series Analysis*, Boston: Kluwer Academic Publishers.

Hoekstra, J. C. (1987), *Handelen van Heroinegebruikers: Effecten van Beleidsmaat-regelen*, Ph.D. thesis, RuG Groningen, the Netherlands.

Hulbert, J. M. and Toy, M. E. (1977), 'A Strategic Framework for Marketing Control', *Journal of Marketing* 41 (April), pp. 12–20.

Judge, G. G., Griffiths, W. E., Hill, R. C., Lütkepohl, H. and Lee, T. C. (1984), *The Theory and Practice of Econometrics*, New York: John Wiley.

Kamakura, W. A. and Russell, G. J. (1989), 'A Probabilistic Choice Model for Market Segmentation and Elasticity Structure', *Journal of Marketing Research* 26, pp. 379–390.

Kapferer, J. N. (1992), *Strategic Brand Management*, London: Kogan Page.

Lambin, J. J., Naert, Ph.A. and Bultez, A. V. (1975), 'Optimal Marketing Behaviour in Oligopoly', *European Economic Review* 6, pp. 105–128.

Leeflang, P. S. H. (1974), *Mathematical Models in Marketing, a Survey, the Stage of Development, some Extensions and Applications*, Leiden: Stenfert Kroese BV.

Leeflang, P. S. H. (1977), 'Organizing Market Data for Decision Making through the Development of Mathematical Marketing Models', *Proceedings ESOMAR-SEMINAR on Marketing Management Information Systems: Organizing Market Data for Decision Making*, Brussels, pp. 29–54.

Leeflang, P. S. H. and Olivier, A. J. (1985), 'Bias in Consumer Panel and Store Audit Data', *International Journal of Research in Marketing* 2, pp. 27–41.

Leeflang, P. S. H. and Plat, F. W. (1984), 'Consumer Response in an Era of Stagflation: Preliminary Results', *Proceedings EMAC/ESOMAR Conference on Methodological Advances in Marketing Research in Theory and Practice*, Copenhagen, pp. 195–228.

Leeflang, P. S. H. and Plat, F. W. (1988), 'Scanning Scanning Opportunities', *Proceedings 41st ESOMAR Conference*, Lisbon, pp. 471–484.

Leeflang, P. S. H. and Reuyl, J. C. (1984), 'On the Predictive Power of Market Share Attraction Models', *Journal of Marketing Research 21*, pp. 211–215.

Leeflang, P. S. H. and Reuyl, J. C. (1985), 'Advertising and Industry Sales: An Empirical Study of the German Cigarette Industry', *Journal of Marketing 49*, pp. 92–98.

Leeflang, P. S. H. and Reuyl, J. C. (1995), 'On the Consequences of Banning Tobacco Advertising: A Critical Evaluation', *International Business Review*, forthcoming.

Leeflang, P. S. H. and Wedel, M. (1993), 'Information-Based Decision Making in Pricing', *Proceedings ESOMAR/EMAC/AFM Symposium on Information Based Decision Making in Marketing: Reconciling the Needs and Interests of Decision Makers, Data Collectors and Data Providers*, Paris, pp. 299–312.

Leeflang, P. S. H. and Wittink, D. R. (1992), 'Diagnosing Competitive Reactions Using (Aggregated) Scanner Data', *International Journal of Research in Marketing 9*, pp. 39–58.

Leeflang, P. S. H. and Wittink, D. R. (1993), 'Diagnosing Competition, Developments and Findings', in Laurent, G., Lilien, G. R. and Pras, B. (eds), *Research Traditions in Marketing*, Boston: Kluwer Academic Publishers, pp. 133–156.

Leone, R. P. and Schultz, R. L. (1980), 'A Study of Marketing Generalization', *Journal of Marketing 44* (1), pp. 10–18.

Lilien, G. L. (1975), 'Model Relativism: A Situational Approach to Model Building', *Interfaces, 5*, pp. 11–18.

Lilien, G. L., Kotler, Ph. and Moorthy, K. S. (1992), *Marketing Models*, Englewood Cliffs, NJ: Prentice-Hall.

Little, J. D. C. (1970), 'Models and Managers, the Concept of a Decision calculus', *Management Science 16*, pp. 466–485.

Makridakis, S. (1974), 'The Future of Models and Models of the Future', *European Research 2*, pp. 17–21.

Moorthy, K. S. (1993), 'Competitive Marketing Strategies: Game-Theoretic Models', in Eliashberg, J. and Lilien, G. L. (eds), *Handbooks in Operations Research and Management Science*, vol. 5, *Marketing*, New York: Elsevier Publishing, pp. 143–190.

Naert, Ph.A. (1977), 'Some Cost-Benefit Considerations in Marketing Model Building', in Topritzhofer, E. (ed) *Marketing – neue Ergebnisse aus Forschung und Praxis*, Wiesbaden: Gabler-Verlag.

Naert, Ph.A. and Leeflang, P. S. H. (1978), *Building Implementable Marketing Models*, Leiden: Martinus Nijhoff.

Naert, Ph.A. and Weverbergh, M. (1981), 'On the Predictive Power of Market Share Attraction Models', *Journal of Marketing Research 18*, pp. 146–153.

Naert, Ph.A. and Weverbergh, M. (1985), 'Market Share Specification, Estimation and Validation: Toward Reconciling Seemingly Divergent Views', *Journal of Marketing Research 22*, pp. 453–467.

Nillesen, J. P. H. (1992), *Services and Advertising Effectiveness: An Empirical Study of the Dutch Health Insurance Market*, Ph.D. thesis, RuG Groningen, the Netherlands.

Nijkamp, W. G. (1993), *New Product Macroflow Models – Specification and Analysis*, Ph.D. thesis, RuG Groningen, the Netherlands.

Parsons, L. J., Gijsbrechts, E., Leeflang, P. S. H. and Wittink, D. R. (1993), 'Marketing Science, Econometrics and Managerial Contributions', in Laurent, G., Lilien, G. L. and Pras, B. (eds), *Research Traditions in Marketing*, Boston: Kluwer Academic Publishers, pp. 52–78.

Parsons, L. J. and Vanden Abeele, P. (1981), 'Analysis of Sales Call Effectiveness', *Journal of Marketing Research 18*, pp. 107–113.

Petty, R. E. and Cacioppo, J. T. (1986), *Communication and Persuasion*, New York: Springer-Verlag.

Plat, F. W. (1988), 'Modeling for Markets: Applications of Advanced Models and Methods for Data Analyses', Ph.D. thesis, RuG Groningen, the Netherlands.

Prasad, V. K., Casper, W. R. and Shieffer, R. J. (1984), 'Alternatives to the Traditional Retail Store Audit: A Field Study', *Journal of Marketing 48*, pp. 54–61.

Rangaswamy, A. (1993), 'Marketing Decision Models: From Linear Programs to Knowledge-based Systems', in Eliashberg, J. and Lilien, G. J. (eds), *Handbooks in Operations Research and Management Science*, vol. 5, *Marketing*, New York: Elsevier Publishing, pp. 733–771.

Rangaswamy, A., Eliasberg, J., Burke, R. R. and Wind, J. (1989), 'Developing Marketing Expert Systems: An Application to International Negotiations', *Journal of Marketing 53* (October), pp. 24–39.

Rangaswamy, A., Sinha, P. and Zoltners, A. (1990), 'An Integrated Model-based Approach to Sales Force Structuring', *Marketing Science* 9, pp. 279–298.

Robinson, W. T. (1988), 'Marketing Mix Reactions to Entry', *Marketing Science* 7, pp. 368–385.

Silk, A. J. and Urban, G. L. (1978), 'Pre-test-market Evaluation of New Packaged Goods: A Model and Measurement Methodology', *Journal of Marketing Research* 15, pp. 171–191.

Sultan, F., Farley, J. U. and Lehmann, D. R. (1990), 'A Meta-analysis of Diffusion Models', *Journal of Marketing Research* 27, pp. 70–77.

Tellis, G. J. (1988), 'The Price Elasticity of Selective Demand: A Meta-analysis of Econometric Models of Sales', *Journal of Marketing Research* 25, pp. 391–404.

Urban, G. L. (1970), 'SPRINTER Mod. III: A Model for the Analysis of New Frequently Purchased Consumer Products', *Operations Research* 18 (5), pp. 805–855.

Urban, G. L. and Hauser, J. R. (1980), *Design and Marketing of New Products*, Englewood Cliffs, NJ: Prentice-Hall.

Urban, G. L. and Karash, R. (1971), 'Evolutionary Model Building', *Journal of Marketing Research* 8, pp. 62–66.

Urban, G. L. and Katz, M. (1983), 'Pre-test-markets Models: Validation and Managerial Implications', *Journal of Marketing Research* 20, pp. 221–234.

Wedel, M. (1990), *Clusterwise Regression and Market Segmentation: Developments and Application*, Ph.D. thesis, Landbouwuniversiteit Wageningen, the Netherlands.

Wittink, D. R. (1988), *The Application of Regression Analyses*, Boston: Allyn & Bacon.

Wittink D. R., Addonna, M., Hawkes, W. and Porter, J. (1988), 'SCAN*PRO: The Estimation, Validation, and Use of Promotional Effects Based on Scanner Data', Working Paper, Cornell University (February).

Chapter 9 ■

Diffusion Theory and Marketing

Michael J. Baker

■ Introduction

As we saw earlier, a natural consequence of the marketing concept, with its emphasis upon the determination of consumer wants and the deployment of resources to match these wants, is that the marketing function places particular stress upon new-product development. In this chapter we will attempt to demonstrate that the problems associated with introducing new products into the market-place appear to be remarkably similar to those experienced in gaining acceptance for innovations in other areas of activity. This being so, one might reasonably anticipate that there are considerable benefits to be gained by studying the process by which other innovations appear to secure acceptance as a basis for enhancing consumer reaction to new products.

The process by which innovations spread through a population of users or adopters is generally termed 'diffusion'. Accordingly, in this chapter we first consider the evolution of the diffusion research tradition as a preliminary to examining the marketing variant which is normally referred to as the 'product-life-cycle concept'. In turn, this examination leads us to enquire whether it is possible to operationalise the product-life-cycle concept and thereby make it a useful tool for marketing managers concerned with new-product development. To this end we describe briefly our own model of the adoption process which attempts to synthesise both economic and behavioural variables and so suggests how marketing may usefully borrow from other disciplines in developing valid theory of its own.

▋ The evolution of the diffusion research tradition[1]

The earliest research into the process of diffusion appears to have been triggered off by the interest of anthropologists in the spread of ideas between societies. This interest, which began to gather momentum at the beginning of this century, set out to determine whether particular ideas, activities and patterns of behaviour were transferred from society to society or were the result of parallel thought development. Essentially, the thrust of this work was historical and descriptive and laid greater emphasis upon the social consequences of the innovation. None the less certain important generalisations were advanced including one that has formed the foundation for much subsequent research – namely that acceptance of an innovation depends very much upon the prospective adopter's culture. Thus closed or traditional systems were found to hinder diffusion while open or modern social systems appear to stimulate it.

One of the earliest contributors to social theories of diffusion was Gabriel Tarde, whose *Laws of Imitations* was published in 1903.[2] In this work Tarde makes several novel proposals which have been very influential in shaping the development of diffusion theory, including the proposition that if adoptions of an innovation are plotted against time from introduction to complete diffusion they will assume the characteristics of a normal distribution, or if plotted cumulatively assume the familiar S-shaped curve which characterises the product-life-cycle. Tarde is also to be credited with identifying the relationship between cosmopoliteness and early adoption and of formulating the concept of the 'opinion leader' as a member of a social system to whom others look for advice.

During the 1920s a large number of studies were undertaken by empirically minded sociologists most of which were concerned with the tracing of a specific innovation through a population of adopters. With the benefit of hindsight one of the surprising features of this period of development of diffusion theory is that there was very little, if any, transfer of ideas from one branch of research to another. Thus only recently has any attempt been made to integrate the various findings into a single theory of diffusion.[3]

One of the major foundations of this newly emergent integrated theory are the findings of the rural sociologists. By the early 1960s contributions from this area numbered several hundred, many of which replicate the classic study of Ryan and Gross.[4] Among the many contributions of this study three have had a lasting impact:

1. the concept of adopter classification into categories;
2. the determination of the social characteristics which identified the earliest and latest adopters; and
3. recognition and statement of the deliberate nature of the decision to adopt an innovation.

A second major source of contributions to diffusion theory was provided by the area of medical sociology. Perhaps the most famous study in this area was that undertaken by Coleman, Katz and Menzel which is often identified as the Columbia University Drug Study or the 'Gammamyn' Study.[5] Perhaps the most significant contribution from this study was the establishment of a positive relationship between opinion leadership and innovativeness.

A survey of contributions from other areas such as that undertaken by Rogers[6] would seem to suggest that they have made very little original contribution to major concepts developed in rural and medical sociology. Thus, while educationists have been responsible for very large numbers of studies, these tend to have built upon, and confirmed, the findings of other researchers. Similarly in the marketing area the main thrust has been in the application of extant concepts in an attempt to reduce the high failure rate associated with the introduction of new products. More recently, however, there have been indications that this research is making an original contribution of its own in the field of what might be termed the 'characteristics of innovation area'.

As mentioned earlier, Everett Rogers made an invaluable contribution to diffusion research by summarising and pulling together contributions of the various and diverse research traditions. Certainly it is to Rogers that we owe a major debt for singling out the definitions and major concepts which now enjoy such wide currency among marketers. Particularly worthy of mention are his definition of diffusion, the stages in the adoption process, the five dimensions of an innovation and development of the concept of 'adoptive categories' in pursuit of an attempt to define an innovator profile. We review briefly these concepts below.

■ The diffusion process

The characteristics of the diffusion process may be summed up as: (i) acceptance (ii) over time (iii) of some specific item (iv) by adopting units – individuals or groups – (v) linked to communication channels (vi) to a social structure (vii) to a given system of values. In this context acceptance is probably best defined as 'continued use'. Thus, while purchase of a durable good would count as acceptance or adoption, first purchase of a low-price consumable item might only amount to a trial such that adoption would only be assumed given repeated purchase of the item.

Time of adoption is central to the whole concept of diffusion and underlies all attempts to describe the diffusion process in mathematical terms. In the case of most industrial and consumer-durable goods usually it is possible to establish the date of purchase and therefore the elapsed time since first introduction, and thereby identify the sequence in which organisations or individuals adopted the item. Unfortunately measurement of elapsed time from first introduction usually depends upon recall in the case of smaller consumable items and is a much less reliable guide to the sequence in which individuals actually adopted an innovation than is the case with industrial goods.

The specific item in our definition is the innovation under study while the unit of adoption has traditionally been conceived of as an individual. However, in recent years the role of joint-buying decisions in both the industrial- and household-buying situations has been increasingly recognised and may be expected to play a more important role in future studies. Clearly in the case of joint adoption decisions identification of the roles played by the respective parties to that decision should have a significant effect upon the promotional and selling tactics adopted by an innovator.

The role of channels of communication, social structure and its attendant value system have all been demonstrated to have a major influence upon the diffusion process. It follows, therefore, that in diffusion studies great importance is attached to identifying both the formal and informal channels of communication used by adopters. Similarly, from a marketing viewpoint the social structure defines the boundaries within which items diffuse and so constitute a statement of the total population of potential adopters. Finally, value systems have a major impact on the way in which a given innovation will be viewed by prospective adopters, and the need to achieve

consonance between an innovation and a value system in order to achieve adoption is obvious.

■ Stages in the adoption process

The assumption underlying the formulation of adoption-process schemes is that consumer acceptance of a product is not an instantaneous or random event, but a distinct mental and behavioural sequence through which the consumer must progress if adoption of a product is to occur.

Various representations of the adoption process have been suggested but all have a common aim of dividing up the adoption process into comprehensible parts in order to provide a conceptual framework for the analysis of how and why adopters move from first knowledge of a new idea, to its trial, to a decision as to whether to adopt or reject that idea. In 1955 a committee of rural sociologists defined a sequence of five stages through which an individual passes in coming to an adoption decision, namely: awareness, interest, evaluation, trial and adoption. In a marketing context Lavidge and Steiner[7] propose a six-stage sequence related to three basic psychological states:

Awareness Knowledge	the cognitive dimension
Liking Preference	the affective dimension
Conviction Purchase	the conative dimension

As noted earlier, the purpose of models of the adoption process is to provide an analytical framework, and it is not intended that one should consider the stages as necessarily being equidistant, as the importance attached to each will tend to vary in relation to both product and consumer characteristics. Similarly, while some researchers have suggested that individual stages in the sequence may be omitted in real life, our own preference is to accept the alternative hypothesis that stages cannot be omitted but that the individual adopter may move up several steps simultaneously, thereby collapsing the hierarchy of effects into a shorter time period. This latter explanation enables us to account for deviations such as impulse buying and also for the different weight attached to different stages dependent upon variations in product and consumer characteristics.

A number of other alternative models of the adoption process have been put forward of which perhaps the best known is the marketer's AIDA (Attention, Interest, Desire, Action) model which identifies four stages consisting of attention, interest, desire and action.

The basic adoption-process and hierarchy-of-effects models have been criticised on the grounds that the only certain indication from analysis of many diffusion studies is that awareness always precedes adoption.[8] As a consequence of these criticisms a number of more sophisticated models have been proposed, *inter alia*, by Robertson and Andreasen and Nicosia.[9] Space limitations preclude analysis of these alternative models and the reader should consult the original sources for a discussion of these.[10]

■ Dimensions of an innovation

Another important component of Rogers's model is identification and classification of the five dimensions of an innovation – relative advantage, compatibility, complexity, divisibility and communicability. These dimensions may be defined as follows:

(a) *relative advantage* is the degree to which an innovation is superior to the idea it supersedes;

(b) *compatibility* is the degree to which an innovation is consistent with existing values and past experiences of adopters;

(c) *complexity* is the degree to which an innovation is relatively difficult to understand and use;

(d) *divisibility* is the degree to which an innovation may be tried on a limited basis; and

(e) *communicability* is the degree to which the results of innovation may be diffused to others.

It is important to note that these characteristics must be defined in relative terms depending upon the potential adopter's status, knowledge and perception of the information concerning the innovation that is presented to him. With this proviso it is clear that the greater the relative advantage an innovation possesses, the more compatible it is with a potential adopter's status and beliefs; the less complex it is, the more readily it can be tried without risk to the trialist, and the easier it is to communicate information concerning the nature and effect of an innovation then the more readily it will be understood. At least two observations may be made about this statement. First, the more radical an innovation, the less will be its perceived compatibility, divisibility and communicability and the greater its perceived complexity, and therefore the more uncertain its relative advantage; and, second, any predictions concerning the reaction of a given potential adopter will depend very heavily upon our level of knowledge concerning the status of that adopter at the time that he becomes aware of the innovation.

■ Adopter categories

Earlier in this chapter it was noted that if one plots the number of adoptions against time from first introduction of an innovation, the resulting distribution is normal. The observed regularity of this distribution led to the use of the parameters of the normal distribution as a basis for classifying adopters into categories. Using standard deviation from the mean, adopters are divided into five groupings as indicated in Figure 9.1, namely innovators, early adopters, early majority, late majority and laggards.

By definition it is tautological that innovators should precede early adopters, that early adopters must precede the majority and so on. In consequence it follows that if we can pre-identify the characteristics of innovators for any given category of innovation, then we may concentrate our

Figure 9.1.   *Adopter categories*

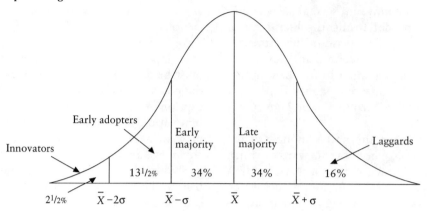

Innovators
Early adopters
Early majority
Late majority
Laggards

2½%   13½%   34%   34%   16%

$\bar{X} - 2\sigma$ $\bar{X} - \sigma$ $\bar{X}$ $\bar{X} + \sigma$

marketing efforts upon these individuals. Clearly the potential benefits of such an ability have not been lost upon either the marketing practitioner or his academic colleague. However, while a great deal of empirical work has been undertaken in trying to develop an innovator profile, the results to date of such studies have been both inconclusive and inconsistent. In large measure this inconsistency would seem to stem very largely from a failure to add marketing insights to borrowed concepts. Thus the product, for example, has become almost an adjunct to the researches undertaken rather than being recognised as a key variable *vis-à-vis* the individual consumer characteristics.

Despite some of the deficiencies noted, there can be no doubt that diffusion research has provided a fruitful source of ideas for marketers. Further, having recognised the deficiencies of existing ideas when translated into the marketing context, it becomes possible to see how modification may make such concepts even more useful to the marketing practitioner. In the remainder of this chapter we summarise briefly a modest attempt of our own to make use of diffusion concepts to improve performance when introducing new products into the market-place.

■ The product life-cycle

Earlier in this chapter we noted that the manner in which successful innovations diffuse through a population of adopters is sufficiently consistent to encourage the use of the parameters of the normal distribution to classify users into different adopter categories. If instead of plotting the number of adoptions against elapsed time from first introduction of an innovation we were to plot the cumulative adoptions, then our bell-shaped normal-distribution curve would be transformed into a symmetrical S-shaped curve. Such S-shape curves are particularly familiar to marketers for this is the shape assumed by the curve used to represent the life-cycle of a product. Such a life-cycle curve is reproduced in Figure 9.2 and is traditionally divided into the four phases indicated, namely introduction, growth, maturity and decay.

While most practitioners would readily agree that the product-life-cycle is an accurate reflection of the manner in which sales of a new product develop, many would question whether the concept has any practical or operational utility. Essentially, such doubts would seem to stem from the observation that in advance one very rarely can predefine the scales appropriate to the plotting of a diffusion curve. Thus if one does not know whether a population of adopters will be numbered in tens, hundreds, thousands or tens of thousands, or whether the appropriate unit of time is to be minutes, hours, weeks or even years, one hardly knows how to interpret the early performance of the new product as a basis for predicting the final sales volume and time to complete diffusion. For this reason many prac-

Figure 9.2. *The product life-cycle*

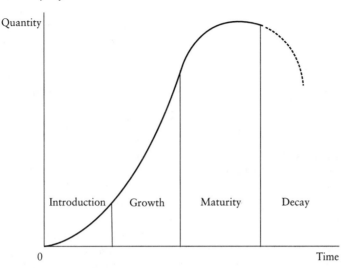

titioners tend to confine the product-life-cycle concept to the category reserved for many other theoretical constructs which can be labelled as academic, namely 'interesting but irrelevant'.

Our own view, which we develop at some length elsewhere,[11] is that while accepting the possible deficiencies of exponential curves as a forecasting device, the concept does provide one with an enormously useful strategic insight; namely, that the final shape of an exponential function is a direct consequence of its early shape. For example, if one assumes one of the more simple exponential functions, namely a geometric progression, then we would project a doubling of sales for each unit of elapsed time. This being so it follows that if the elapsed time to first purchase from introduction is six months, then we would forecast sales of two more units in the succeeding six-month period, four units in the six months after that, eight units in the following six months, and so on. If, however, the time to first adoption were halved to three months, then sales of fifteen units would be achieved in half the time, that is one year instead of two. Clearly the insight that underlines the search for a consumer innovator profile referred to earlier in this chapter is that the more quickly one pre-identifies potential adopters with a high receptivity to innovation,

then the more one can structure and concentrate one's marketing effort in order to secure early purchase. Thereafter, as the shape of the diffusion curve demonstrates, the very fact of first adoptions will influence and accelerate subsequent adoption giving rise to the so-called 'contagion' or 'bandwagon' effect.

Unfortunately, recognising the desirability of pre-identifying early adopters does not solve the problem of how to do this. Our own view is that prior deficiencies in this direction may very largely be attributed to over-reliance on borrowed concepts and failure to perform the synthetic and integrative function which we defined as essential to the formulation of true marketing theory in Chapter 2. Specifically, we feel it is essential to pull together economic and behavioural concepts of buying behaviour in order to approximate the real-world situation.

A composite model of buyer behaviour[12]

While recognising the dangers of overgeneralisation, the study of the literature of buyer behaviour would seem to warrant division into two distinct categories: a rational/economic model which is strongly associated with the marketing of industrial goods; and a behaviourist model commonly used to describe individual buying behaviour.

Notationally the economic model may be simply represented as:

$$A = f[EC, PC, (I - D)]$$

where A = adoption decision, EC = enabling conditions, PC = precipitating circumstances, I = economic incentives, D = economic disincentives.

The enabling conditions encompass all those factors that might conceivably be necessary to permit adoption. In both the industrial and the consumer context an obvious precondition is possession of, or access to, sufficient finance to cover purchase or lease of the new product. Other examples of EC in the industrial situation would be relevance to the prospective adopter's current or proposed area of activity, compatibility with the extant production system, and possession of the necessary technical and organisational ability to incorporate the innovation to the firm's operations. In a consumer context, sex, religion, age, physical condition, and so on, may all be highly specific determinants of an innovation's relevance to a potential adopter, and the absence of such an enabling condition would completely preclude any possibility of adoption. Operationally, therefore, we may regard EC as the first coarse screen in distinguishing between possible adopters and obvious non-adopters.

Having defined the population of potential adopters, logic dictates that among them some will be in a much more receptive state than others and so will perceive the stimulus (new product) as much stronger than other less receptive prospects. In our model, factors that predispose active consideration of an innovation are identified as precipitating circumstances. Given the existence of the necessary enabling conditions, PC may be thought of as encompassing all these factors which predispose the firm or individual to consider the adoption of an innovation. In terms of the hierarchy-of-effects model of the adoption process, PC coincides with the interest stage as it includes those instants or ele-

ments that move the prospective adopter from a possibly passive awareness to an active consideration. In an industrial context the breakdown of plant and equipment, a shortage of fabricated or raw materials, components or sub-assemblies, loss of market share due to price and/or quality differentials, or the opportunity to enter new markets, are but a few of the factors that might precipitate active consideration of an innovation.

Economic incentives and disincentives are specified separately in our model because it is believed that by doing so a better picture of the net economic benefit will emerge than by using a composite variable such as relative advantage. In a purely objective world economic logic would seem to demand that if one has a clearly identified need and is presented with a solution that offers a net improvement in one's economic status then one cannot refuse. In reality of course we all know of many instances where such apparently irresistible offers have been flatly rejected for subjective reasons; for example, the works manager who turns down a piece of labour-saving equipment of proven performance on the grounds that attempts to substitute capital equipment for labour would lead to trouble with unions.

Because of the role of such subjective factors one might be led to believe that the behaviourist explanation would be more satisfactory than that proposed by the economist. However, as we have already noted earlier in this chapter, a major deficiency of the behaviourist approach to buying decisions is an almost complete neglect of the product characteristics as an influence on the decision. In other words, the behaviourists ignore objective data that clearly are of importance in much the same way as economists neglect the importance of perception. Thus in order to operationalise our economic model of buyer behaviour we need to incorporate in it additional variables which represents the behavioural response of the potential adopter.

Over the past 20 years or so our original model of buyer behaviour first published in *Marketing New Industrial Products* (1975) has undergone a number of changes. In its original form the 'economic' model proposed above was qualified by the inclusion of a single summary variable designated BR for behavioural response. According to this model buyers (particularly of innovations) would undertake an economic evaluation of the proposed purchase but the final decision (behavioural response) would be conditioned by a whole host of subjective factors derived from their existing experience, beliefs and attitudes.

While the inclusion of this broadly defined variable considerably improved the conceptualisation of the model it failed to address the omission of the first element of the adoption process referred to earlier – *awareness*. While EC defines a potential state of receptiveness and PC the cue which would trigger interest our model omitted recognition of the fact that we are exposed daily to literally hundreds of selling cues and cheerfully ignore them all. To reflect reality it is clearly necessary to give explicit recognition to the phenomenon of selective perception (SP) whereby our sub-conscious decides which incoming cues or stimuli will receive conscious attention with the possibility that they will initiate the buying decision process.

The most recent version of the 'Baker Composite Model of Buyer Behaviour' is to be found in the 2nd edition of *Marketing Strategy & Management* (Macmillan, 1992) where it is described as follows:

P = f[SP(PC, EC, IS, PF, CB) BR]
P = Purchase
f = a function (unspecified) of
SP = selective perception
PC = precipitating circumstances
EC = enabling conditions
IS = information search
PF = performance factors
CB = cost-benefit
BR = behavioural response

The first point to be made is that this is a sequential process model very similar to the Buying Decision Process model developed by Robinson, Faris and Wind (1967). *PC* is equivalent to problem recognition, *EC* to *interest* (i.e. the problem is accepted as a real one deserving

further consideration), *IS*, a new variable corresponds to information search and recognises that if a review of the enabling conditions confirms a continuing interest then one will have to gather additional information on which to make a decision. *PF* and *CB* summarise the objective data concerning performance or 'fitness for purpose' and the economic benefits of acquisition and comprise the 'rational' elements of evaluation. *BR* is a surrogate for the subjective and judgemental factors which will invariably be taken into account when a prospective buyer has more than a Buy-Don't Buy choice, i.e. there are two or more objectively similar products or services which would solve the prospective buyer's consumption problem which initiated the process. Thus *BR* is a composite of one's prior experience and attitudes which may or may not include direct post-purchase experience of the object under consideration.

Second, the precise nature of the function is not specified for the simple reason that it is not known and that it is unlikely, to say the least, that any single functional form could capture the interaction between the other variables in the model.

SP or selective perception is a new variable in the model. In earlier versions the influence of this factor was subsumed within *BR*, which occurs at the end of the process. By placing *SP* at the beginning as a factor mediating the other variables it is possible to communicate that this is a process model and that selective perception will determine whether or not one will even become aware of a purchase opportunity *(EC)* besides conditioning the information selected for evaluation and the interpretation placed upon it.

Finally, the behavioural response may be almost automatic, as, for example, when the preceding evaluation indicates that one option is clearly to be preferred. Alternatively, it may be an extremely difficult and protracted stage when the preceding analysis has failed to suggest one choice before all others – a common occurence in many markets.

Having described the general model, some elaboration of the variables will indicate what sort of factors one would need to take into account to use it.

In the Pavlovian learning model of buyer behaviours reference is made to the need for some cue or stimulus to activate a drive and initiate action. In our model this factor is termed a 'precipitating circumstance' – what is it that would make a buyer consider a change in the status quo? Clearly, dissatisfaction with existing alternatives constitutes a marketing opportunity, and is one type of precipitating factor. The need to replace or renew a piece of capital equipment or consumer durable is another opportunity, whether the need is caused by breakdown, loss, destruction or a planned replacement policy. Knowing which customers might be in this state would enable the firm to focus its marketing effort to much greater effect, both in terms of the information to be conveyed and the means of conveying it. Similarly, being able to satisfy a known need – we have a faster computer, a more economical car and so forth – is a claim likely to precipitate active consideration of a new purchase.

'Enabling conditions' embraces all those factors which make it possible for a prospective purchaser to benefit from the new product. A television is no use if you have no electricity, nor a gas oven if you have no gas. In the same way, many manufacturers try to avoid mixing materials such as steel, aluminium and plastics, since each requires different skills and techniques in use and increases the investment necessary in both plant and labour. In other words, a new product must be compatible with the user's current status and, in many cases also with their self-image. In the absence of such enabling conditions, interest is likely to be short-lived and unlikely to proceed further to an evaluation.

Technology or performance and the economics or cost-benefit of a purchase are at the very heart of the Marshallian and 'rational' schools of buying behaviour models – *PF* and *CB* in our model. We have chosen to specify the advantages and disadvantages separately, partly because people do weigh up the pros and cons of courses of action, and partly because, if one is going to use the model, then one should specify as fully as possible what the merits and demerits are, weight these if necessary, and only then come up with an overall judgement as to how the new product measures up against the competition.

Some broad guidelines as to the relative importance of different features which go to make up an effective selling proposition in industrial markets generally are shown for machine tools in particular in Table 9.1 and more generally in Figure 9.3. But, while these offer an

Table 9.1.   *Features for effective selling in machine-tool markets*

Q. Reviewing the last five years, what factors or reasons appear to discriminate most between success and failure with new products?

	Total 62 (%)	F&D 34 (%)	Others 28 (%)
Product quality	53	65	39
Uniqueness of product	44	41	47
Level of trade acceptance	39	44	32
Level of advertising investment	36	35	36
Level of distribution achieved	32	35	29
Price	31	38	21
Company commitment	24	24	25
Sales force motivation	23	29	14

Source: R. Artingstall in *New Product Development*, Supplement to *Market Research Society Newsletter* 168 (March 1980).
Note: The sample comprises '62 major UK manufacturers'.

Figure 9.3. *Features of a machine-tool considered one of the three most important*

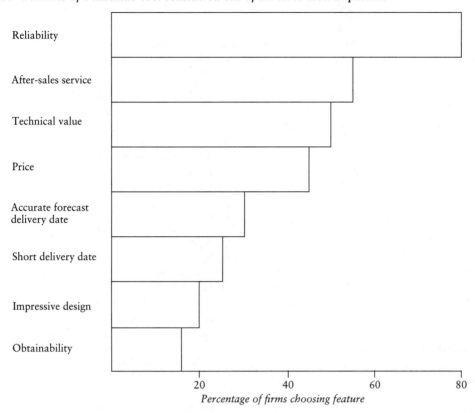

indication of the relative importance of groups of features, it must always be remembered that the majority of buying decisions turn on highly specific characteristics – another reason why a general model cannot possibly accommodate all conceivable sets of circumstances.

We have already stipulated that the importance of behavioural response will depend heavily upon the objective evaluation of the available facts (albeit that these are perceived subjectively), and build a better product at an equivalent price or an equivalent product at a lower price' is clearly the best advice to management. But, in most competitive markets, there is often little to choose objectively between alternative offerings, and the buyer will have to make deliberate recourse to subjective value judgements to assist in distinguishing between the various items available. Because housewives do this daily when preferring Daz to Omo, Sunblest to Mother's Pride and so

on and so forth, they are often characterised as choosing irrationally. Nothing could be further from the truth. The important objective decisions about a shopping basket relate to its overall mix and composition *vis-à-vis* the available budget – the choice decision is which detergent, which bread and so on. It would be a fatal mistake to imagine that the industrial buyer doesn't have just the same problems when deciding between Scania, Mercedes or Leyland for his lorries, or Cincinnati or Kearney & Trecker for his machine tools.

■ Summary

Over the years considerable research has been undertaken at Strathclyde University (and elsewhere) which tends to confirm that the model is indeed helpful in *conceptualising* the buyer decision process when faced with a modified or new-buy (innovation) situation. As with all the theoretical explanations contained in this book the critical question remains 'Does it help in practice?' On the basis that understanding is required to inform and improve practice the unequivocal answer must be 'Yes'. Operationalising the model is another matter however.

Clearly, all the 'variables' specified in the model are summary statements which embrace a multiplicity of separate factors in practice. It follows that an ability to operationalise the model will depend very much on situation specific factors and the practitioner's knowledge and experience to define, measure and explain their interaction. In other words, like so many other theoretical constructs in this book, the model is potentially a valuable contribution to successful practice but it depends upon the practitioner's skill to make it work effectively.

■ Notes and references

1. This description follows closely that contained in Baker, Michael J., Drayton, Jennifer L. and Parkinson, Stephen T., *The Adoption of New Products*, Paris: Marcel Dassault, Jours de France Foundation (1975).
2. *Laws of Imitations*, New York: Henry Holt, 1903.
3. See, for example, Rogers, E. M., *Diffusion of Innovations*, New York: Free Press, 1962.
4. Ryan, J. K. and Gross, N., 'The Diffusion of Hybrid Seed Corn in Two Iowa Committees', *Rural Sociology* 8 (1943).
5. Coleman, J. S., Katz, E. and Menzel, H., 'The Diffusion of an Innovation among Physicians', *Sociometry* 20 (1967).
6. Rogers, E. M., *Diffusion of Innovations*.
7. Lavidge, R. and Steiner, G. A., 'A Model for Predictive Measurements of Advertising Effectiveness', *Journal of Marketing* (1961).
8. See, for example, Mason, R., 'An Ordinal Scale for Measuring the Adoption Process', in *Studies of Innovation and of Communication to the Public*, ed. Wilbur Schramm, Stanford University Institute for Communication Research (1962); also Palda, K. S., 'The Hypothesis of a Hierarchy of Effects: A Partial Evaluation', *Journal of Marketing Research* 3 (1966).
9. Robertson, T. S., *Innovative Behavior and Communication*, New York: Holt, Rinehart & Winston, 1971; Andreasen, A. R., 'Attitudes and Consumer Behavior: A Decision Model', in *New Research in Marketing*, ed. Lee F. Preston, Institute of Business and Economic Research, University of California, 1965; and Nicosia, F. M., *Consumer Decision Processes*, Englewood Cliffs, N.J.: Prentice-Hall, 1966.
10. Or, alternatively, see Baker, Drayton and Parkinson, *The Adoption of New Products*.
11. Baker, M. J., *Marketing Strategy and Management*, 2nd edition, Basingstoke: Macmillan, 1992.

■ *Chapter 10* ■

New Product Development

Susan J. Hart

■ Introduction

The need for the constant development of new products which will enable a firm to gain and sustain competitive advantage is central to the practice of marketing. The opportunity to satisfy customer needs better, or more cheaply, than the competition is an important reason for the institution of some kind of facility for new product development within a company. Such a facility will have responsibility for monitoring technological and market change and for matching the company's products to take advantage of these changes, at a profit. Such a responsibility is onerous: a survey by the author suggested that an average figure for the number of R and D projects carried out by companies in a five year period was 22.6, resulting in an average of 13.4 new product launches (Hart, 1993). Clearly, a good deal of money invested in R & D is destined not to produce any direct market launches. Of the market launches, an average of 72% were successful, but with a very wide variation, evidenced by a standard deviation of 27%. In short, although fundamental to business survival, new product development is a risky undertaking. This being so, much research has been aimed at what factors differentiate successful and unsuccessful

new product programmes. The aim of this chapter is to review this research briefly and to draw out recommendations for more successful new product development. However, before embarking on this task, two issues of definition are discussed: new product development itself and the nature of success and failure in new product development.

■ Types of new product development

Product development comes in different degrees, which can be placed on a continuum from product modifications to the radically innovative or 'breakthrough' products. At either end of this continuum are new product strategies which may end in success, but for different reasons. The radical 'new-to-the-world' product is unique, may even carry a patent, which, in turn, allows it to achieve a highly differentiated status in the market, leading to success. On the other hand, a modification to an existing product, where a company is already expert in the technologies and markets and can fine-tune the product offering to those markets, possibly reducing costs through experience can lead to success by offering a competent product at a low price. Indeed, a recent survey by Kleinschmidt and Cooper (1991) showed that both highly innovative and least innovative development can be successful (in terms of ROI, market share, overall sales and other measures), but that problems occur with products that are 'middle of the road' in terms of innovativeness. The reason for these findings are thought to be that moderately innovative new products fall between two stools; they do not benefit from the advantages associated with uniqueness and market impact, nor do they gain from the experience and familiarity that fosters proficiency in marketing. This study, however, is one of very few which explicitly considers 'newness', the majority of studies into success and failure do not differentiate different types, and, consequently, their findings must be regarded as somewhat generalised. This is unfortunate, since it cannot be assumed that the factors that contribute to the successful launch of a radically new product will be the same for a minor modification to an existing product.

The nature of success and failure

The earlier studies of success factors in New Product Development (NPD) looked at new product failures, on the assumption that identifying the common factors would give clues to managers regarding what not to do (NICB, 1964; Cooper, 1975). The problem, however, is that companies often have difficulty in identifying and presenting failures to researchers, which may account for the relatively few studies which have taken this approach. Instead, several studies have focused on success stories of NPD, to identify common factors. Both approaches suffer from the possibility that the common factors they identify are also determinants of the *opposite* outcome. In other words, if a sample of successful product developments all exhibit a certain characteristic, how can one be sure that the characteristic is not also present in other, less successful product developments? A third approach is to compare successes to failures and this has remained the most

common research approach (Rothwell, 1972; Cooper, 1979; Cooper, 1984).

Measures of success are almost as numerous as research studies. A recent review by Hart and Craig (1993) identified five financially based and six non financially based measures, outlined in Table 10.1

Table 10.1. *Financial and non-financial measures of new product success*

Financial	Non financial
Profit	Design-based
Asset-based	Activity-based
Sales-based	Market-based
Capital-based	Technologically-based
Equity-based	Achievement of 'objectives'
	Strategically-based

Source: Hart, S. and Craig, A. (1993), 'Dimensions of Success in New Product Development', in *Perspectives on Marketing Management*, Baker, M. J. (ed.), Chichester: Wiley.

While a full discussion is beyond the scope of this chapter, it is salient to point out that:

(i) different types of success may be achieved by different means, although this has not been explored by research and
(ii) it cannot be assumed that success in one measure will mean success in another, a point confirmed by Hart (1993).

With these broad caveats in mind, attention is now turned to the factors, identified in research literature, that are said to determine the nature of NPD projects.

New product success factors

A previous review of the literature (Craig and Hart, 1992) has identified key themes in the NPD literature as being crucial to the success of NPD activities. These themes relate to two organisational levels: strategic and task. Strategic themes are those which exert an influence over each and every project in a company without being specific to any one project. Task themes are those which relate to the execution of a specific new product development. The important factors which differentiate success at a strategic level are: linking NPD to corporate strategy; directing a clear new product policy which specifies the level of innovativeness sought, the amount of acceptable risk, the amount of synergy with existing operations that is desired, and so on; supportive top management which sets goals and allocates resources, accepts risks and encourages flexibility and a multi disciplinary approach; and finally, an organisational structure which fosters an organic approach.

Those factors at the task level which differentiate success from failure include: completion of all the stages in the NPD process with particular proficiency in technological and marketing activities; attention to customer needs throughout the development cycles; eschewing a stage-by-department approach which reinforces functional distinction between phases of development and lengthens the process; inter-functional integration and direct lines of communication between those carrying out the project and top management. Two issues appear to underlie most of these themes, strategic or task, namely, the *process* of development and the *people* responsible for carrying out the process. Not only are they closely inter-related, they also bear directly on three of the most commonly cited critical success factors.

For example, they relate to **the need for inter-disciplinary inputs**. In order to combine technical and marketing expertise, a number of company functions have to be involved: R and D, manufacturing, engineering, marketing and sales. As the development of a new product may be the only purpose for which these people meet professionally, it is important that the NPD process adopted ensures that they work well and effectively together. However, the process cannot be re-organised without reference to the people involved.

Both are intrinsic to **the need for quality inputs**, as both technical and marketing information, which are the building blocks of NPD, have to be both accurate and timely and be constantly

reworked in the light of changing circumstances throughout the course of the development.

Finally, both have an impact on **the speed of the new product development**, since the process cannot unfold without the people. This implies that it has to be managed in such a way as to capitalise on a new product opportunity before competitors do so.

This, albeit brief, review of the success factors in NPD underlines the central importance of the decision-process and the tasks it encompasses. Further discussion of this process is the subject of the next section.

The new product development process

A useful starting point is the process expounded by Booz, Allen and Hamilton (BAH) (1982). It has been widely used in research, which has, to a large extent, validated its acceptability in practice (Cooper, 1983; Mahajan and Wind, 1992). The Booz, Allen and Hamilton model is used as a basis in Figure 10.1 and is linked to information inputs and decision outputs at each stage. This enables one to view the usefulness of the model in the light of success literature because the information needs and outputs are taken from the findings of this body of literature.

Distilling the lessons to be learned from the body of 'success' literature, it can be seen that the BAH model highlights the key tasks (inputs) which are needed for decisions (outputs) at each stage. These inputs have a variety of sources, implying the involvement of different functions The model, however, has been criticised on two counts:

1. In reality, the NPD process is idiosyncratic to each firm and to the project in question. It depends on the type of new product being developed (in terms of its innovativeness) and its relationship with the firm's current activities (Cooper, 1988; Johne and Snelson, 1988).
2. There is no clear beginning, middle and end to the NPD process. For example, from one

Figure 10.1.   *Analysis of the NPD process based on Booz, Allen and Hamilton (1982)*

Stage of development	Information needed for stage; nature of information	Source of information	Likely output of stage in light of information
1. Explicit statement of new product strategy, budget allocation	Preliminary market and technical analysis; company objectives	Generated as part of continuous MIS and corporate planning	Identification of *market* (NB not product) opportunities to be exploited by new products
2. Idea generation (or gathering)	Customer needs and technical developments in *previously* identified markets	Inside company: salesmen, technical functions Outside company: Customers, competitors, inventors, etc.	Body of initially acceptable ideas
3. Screening ideas: finding those with most potential	Assessment of whether there is a *market* for this type of product, and whether the company can make it. Assessment of financial implications: market potential and costs. Knowledge of company goals and assessment of fit	Main internal functions: – R&D – Sales – Marketing – Finance – Production	Ideas which are acceptable for further development
4. Concept development: turning an idea into a recognizable product concept, with attributes and market position identified	*Explicit* assessment of customer needs to appraise market potential. *Explicit* assessment of technical requirements	Initial research with customer(s). Input from marketing and technical functions	Identification of: key attributes that need to be incorporated in the product, major technical costs, target markets and potential
5. Business analysis: full analysis of the proposal in terms of its business potential	Fullest information thus far: – detailed market analysis – explicit technical feasibility and costs – production implications – corporate objective	Main internal functions Customers	Major go/no go decision: company needs to be sure the venture is worthwhile as expenditure dramatically increases after this stage. Initial marketing plan. Development plan and budget specification
6. Product development: crystallizing the product into semi-finalized shape	Customer research with product. Production information to check 'makeability'	Customers Production	Explicit marketing plan
7. Test marketing: small-scale tests with customers	Profile of new product performance in light of competition, promotion and marketing mix variables	Market research; production, sales, marketing, technical people	Final go/no go for launch
8. Commercialization	Test market results and reports	As for test market	Incremental changes to test launch. Full-scale launch

idea, several product concept variants may be developed, each of which might be pursued. Also, as an idea crystallises, the developers may assess the nature of the market need more easily and the technical and production costs become more readily identified and evaluated. The issue, problems and solutions become clearer as the process unfolds: it is easier to decide on which variants to pursue and how worthwhile the whole endeavour may be later in the process. This is important given that commentary attached to the process models stresses the importance of *early* assessment and evaluation, precisely at those stages when the credibility and accuracy of the information to be assessed are at their weakest.

The iterative nature of the NPD process results from the fact that each stage or phase of development can produce numerous outputs which implicate both previous development work and future development progress. Using the model provided by Booz, Allen and Hamilton, if a new product concept fails the concept test, then the development itself is terminated. In reality, a number of outcomes may result from a failed concept test, and these are described below.

It is possible that although the original concept is faulty, a better one is found through the concept tests; it would then re-enter the development process at the screening stage. Alternatively, a new customer may be identified through the concept testing stage, since the objective of

concept testing is to be alert to customer needs when formulating a new product. Any new customers would then feed into the idea generation and screening process. Figure 10.2 shows these and other possibilities and illustrates how, viewed as linear or sequential, the BAH model is inadequate, particularly regarding up-front activities.

A further point in relation to the sequencing of product development tasks is the existence of related strands of development. These complicate the picture further because they mean that product development activity is not only iterative *between* stages but also *within* stages. These related strands of development refer to marketing, technical (design) and production tasks or decisions that occur as the process unwinds. Each strand of development gives rise to problems and opportunities within the other two. For example, if, at the product development stage, production people have a problem which pushes production costs up, this could affect market potential. The marketing and technical assumptions need to be reworked in the light of this new information. A new design may be considered, or a new approach to the marketplace may be attempted. The crucial issue here is that the BAH model does not adequately communicate the horizontal dimensions of the NPD process.

This shortcoming has resulted in the advancement of the idea of 'parallel processing', which acknowledges the iterations between and within stages, categorising them along functional configurations. The idea of parallel processing is

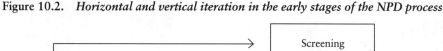

Figure 10.2. *Horizontal and vertical iteration in the early stages of the NPD process*

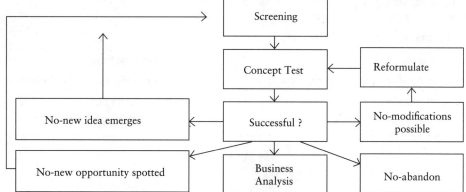

highly prescriptive: it advises that major functions should be involved from the early stages of the NPD process to its conclusion. This, it is claimed, allows problems to be detected and solved much earlier than in the classic task-by-task, function-by function models. In turn, the entire process is much speedier, which is now recognised to be an important element in new product success. It is said also to encourage a multi-disciplinary approach, which has also been proved important to the outcome of new products. Crawford (1991) depicts the parallel processes of technical, evaluative and planning tasks, and these are reproduced in Figure 10.3 below.

While this is clearly a step forward in that different functional tasks are shown, there are two conceptual problems embedded in the notion of parallel processing. Firstly, it ignores the important inputs to NPD that are provided by customers and suppliers. Secondly, if functions are to work *in parallel* then when do they *converge* to take decisions and move on to the next stage?

■ Multiple convergent processing: a proposed framework

A new analytical framework for the NPD process has been proposed by Hart and Baker (1992, 1994). Below is an explanation of the derivation of their 'Multiple Convergent Processing' (MCP) model.

Dictionary definitions of 'parallel' refer to 'separated by an equal distance at every point' or 'never touching or intersecting', and while there are references to simultaneity, particularly when related to computers, it is a somewhat trouble-

Figure 10.3. *Crawford's new product development process*

Strategic planning
for
new products
↓
Concept generation
and development
↓
Screening
↓

Development		
Technical	Evaluation	Marketing plan evolution
Original concept available technology	Concept testing	Concept preliminary strategy
Basic/applied research prototype	Screening prototype/concept testing	
Process planning	Preliminary financial evaluation	
Facilities planning		Final strategy
Pilot plant production	Product use tests	Preliminary technical planning
First run of production	Market testing	Control planning
Final physical product	Final evaluation	Final marketing plan

↓
Launch

some notion that suggests functional separation, when all the performance indicators in NPD point to the need for functional integration. On the other hand, 'to converge' is defined as 'to move or cause to move towards the same point' or to 'tend towards a common conclusion or result', and is therefore, a more precise indicator of what is required of NPD management.

Realising, however, that there are still functionally distinct tasks which must be carried out at specific points throughout the NPD process, it is clear that the tasks will be carried out simultaneously at some juncture and that the results must *converge*. Due to the iterations in the process, this convergence is likely to happen several times, culminating at the time of product launch. As previously mentioned, the process is a series of information gathering and evaluating activities, and as the new product develops from idea to concept to prototype and so on, the information gathered becomes more precise and reliable and the decisions are made with greater certainty. Therefore as the development project progresses, there are a number of natural points of evaluation and a number of types of evaluation (market, functional) which need to be carried out in an integrated fashion. Hence, there are multiple convergent points, which link this form of activity-stage model to the decision-stage models, as the convergent points can be set around decision outputs required to further the process. Figure 10.4 is an example of the early stages of the Multiple Convergent

Figure 10.4. *An example of the early stages of the multiple convergent process*

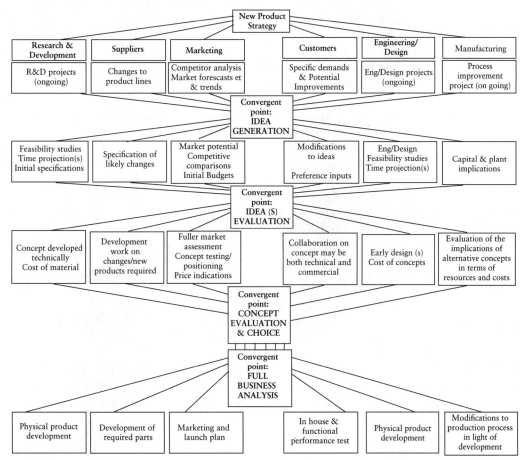

Process. It should be noted that whilst marketing is viewed as the spine of the process, it could be any function, or any person, which assumes this role within the organisation.

The advantages of viewing the process this way are as follows:

1. Iterations among participants within stages are allowed for;
2. The framework can easily accommodate third parties;
3. Mechanisms for integration throughout the process among different functions are set in the convergent points;
4. The model can fit into the most appropriate NPD structures for the company.

□ *Iterations within stages*

As the relevant functions are viewed in terms of their contribution to each stage in the process by their specialist contribution, the cross-functional linkages between stages are incorporated. The extent of involvement of different bodies or outside parties will be determined by the specific needs of each development in each firm. Thus, within stage iteration can benefit from both task-specialisation which will increase the quality of inputs and integration of functions via information sharing and decision-making.

□ *Accommodation of third parties*

Several studies have shown the importance of involving users in the NPD process to increase success rates (Von Hippel, 1988). Equally, there is growing interest in the need for supplier involvement, in order to benefit from the advantages of supplier innovation and JIT (Tzokas and Saren, 1991).

□ *Mechanisms for integration*

Although the success literature points to the need for integration, there is some evidence to suggest

that, in practice, this is not always easy to achieve. In Biemans' study (1992), most of the companies showed an understanding of the need to integrate R & D and marketing activities, although the desirability of this is not considered to be automatic, based on the evidence of the companies surveyed. In Gupta and Wilemon's work (1986, 1988, 1990), it is also stressed that the appropriate level of integration must be decided upon, and that this level is dependent upon organisational strategies, environmental uncertainty, organisational factors and individual factors. The key element in integration is the amount of information sharing, and the multiple convergent process provides the opportunity for information sharing, which is neglected by other models. Clearly, a host of other factors are likely to influence the amount of cross-functional information sharing, including organisational climate and structure. This said, the multiple convergent model carries within it the impetus for information sharing through the convergent points that can be located liberally throughout the process. Moreover, responsibility for the project can be located to suit each company. As Majahan and Wind (1992) have shown in their survey of 200 firms, the organizational locus of NPD may be in marketing departments, R & D departments or in some form of NPD department or team. The MCP can fit into any of these mechanisms since it is intended to promote the integration of market, technical and other forms of information with the purpose of moving the new product development from its inception to a successful market launch. The final section of this chapter deals with the subject of the organisation of new product development.

■ Organising for new product development

A number of different forms of new product management exist, which can be described according to whether they reside inside or outside the current line management structures within the firm. Those outside the existing line function include:

- venture teams
- new product departments or divisions

Those that are linked, albeit tentatively to existing line functions include:

- new product managers
- new product teams
- new product committees

We can see from the success literature, and from our discussion of the process, that new product development benefits from multi-disciplinary inputs. The major problem facing companies, then, is how to encourage multi-disciplinary integration – which emphasise a horizontal structure – within an organisation whose line functions (marketing, R & D, production, purchasing) are essentially vertical in structure. Simply put, how can companies get individuals to work together on projects when they are responsible to managers within functions? There is an inevitable tension between the need for integration and existing lines of authority and responsibility lines. Due to this tension, many firms will locate responsibility for NPD in one function, and bring others in as and when required.

This, of course, raises problems in that development work may be in conflict with the management of current business. This would be manifested in time pressures, whereby development work is squeezed by existing product management, stifled creativity, due to procedures in place for existing products and, finally, fresh business perspectives may be lacking in people who are expert in managing current business. It is these reasons that move managers to locate responsibility outside existing line functions to confront the basic tensions introduced earlier. Before going on to discuss these mechanisms in a little more detail, Table 10.2 shows the findings of a recent survey covering organisation of the new product process.

Venture teams tend to be a permanent 'maverick' group, with high status, separate budgets and report to the MD. Their responsibilities can vary, but include opportunity identification and feasibility studies, through to management of the new

Table 10.2. *Organisation of the new product process*

Organisation	% of companies (N=69)
Part of the planning department	3
Combination of marketing, planning, R & D	4
Task force venture team	9
Part of R & D department	14
Separate corporate or NPD group	17
New product department at SBU level	21
Marketing department	27

Source: Mahajan and Wind (1992) 'New Product Models: Practice, shortcomings and desired improvements', *Journal of Product Innovation Management* 9 (2), pp. 128–139.

product development. The advantages are that, freed from the 'hum-drum' of current business, creativity can be encouraged, and the development has high-level support. On the other side, they can turn into acquisition hunters, may be prone to get into unrelated areas and can be seen as a waste of time if they acquire much information from inside the company.

New product departments or divisions. These have the same status as functional divisions and are essentially outside the 'mainstream' of business. They are usually staffed by personnel from a combination of functions. They may be used in different ways: as idea hunters, where ideas are passed to the 'mainstream' for developers, or as developers, who manage the new product from idea through to the market launch. In the latter instance, the 'handover' of the product will take place at the launch, which may engender feelings of 'not invented here'.

Turning to mechanisms inside the existing line organisation, two major options apply; the marketing department, usually in consumer goods companies, or R & D departments, in industrial goods companies. The implementation can be effected in two ways, part or full time. The part time option involves individual managers who are responsible for current products being given 'part time' responsibility for NPD. Alternatively, a post of new products manager may be created in marketing or technical departments. The part time option can suffer from the time pressures raised earlier in the chapter, and, worse NPD can become something of a secondary goal. In addition, both teams tend not to be interdisciplinary which forces negotiation with other departments, as opposed to collaboration. As a result, there tends to be a 'pass-the-parcel' approach to the development project, which gets shunted around from one department to the next. Finally, both mechanisms tend to be low-level with little leverage for important resource decisions, leading to an incremental approach to NPD. A further mechanism inside a line function is a *new product committee*. This is made up of senior managers from salient functions, and has the purpose of encouraging cross-functional co-operation at the appropriate senior level. However, these mechanisms may suffer from a remote perspective, as the line managers are not really carrying out the task.

Finally, *new product teams* are put together out of separate functions for a specific project. This system capitalises on multi-functional inputs and existing skills and works well if it is given appropriate authority and sponsorship of top managers in the company.

To sum up, then, mechanisms used to organise the process must take cognisance of the need for integration across functions, must create space and time for creative new product development, and must have support from and access to top management. At the same time, the mechanisms should not be so cut off from current business experience that useful knowledge might be lost. Perhaps there is an argument for more 'isolated' mechanisms where new-to-the-world product development is concerned and more current business-related mechanisms where line extensions and product modification are concerned.

■ Concluding remarks

The area of new product development is heavily researched and documented, given its importance to continued business success. This chapter has given an overview of recent research in NPD, defining key terms and discussing the various models of the NPD process. In addition, it offers some thoughts on how best to manage product development, in the light of lessons that research into new product success and failure has provided.

■ References

Biemans, W. (1992), *Managing Innovations Within Networks*, London: Routledge.

Booz, Allen and Hamilton (1982), *New Products Management for the 1980s*, New York: Booz, Allen and Hamilton.

Cooper, R. G. (1975), 'Why New Industrial Products Fail', *Industrial Marketing Management* 4, pp. 315–326.

Cooper, R. G. (1979), 'The Dimensions of Industrial New Product Success and Failure', *Journal of Marketing* 43, pp. 93–103.

Cooper, R. G. (1983), 'The New Product Process: An Empirically Based Classification Scheme', *R & D Management* 13 (1), pp. 1–13.

Cooper, R. G. (1984), 'The Performance Impact of Product Innovation Strategies', *European Journal of Marketing* 18 (5), pp. 5–54.

Cooper, R. G. (1988), 'Predevelopment Activities Determine New Product Success', *Industrial Marketing Management* 17, pp. 237–47.

Craig, A. and Hart, S. J. (1992), 'Dimensions of New Product Success: A Literature Review', *Proceedings of the 23rd Annual Conference of the Maketing Education Group*, Cardiff (July).

Crawford M. C. (1991), *New Products Management*, Homewood, Ill.: Irwin.

Gupta, A., Raj, S. P. and Wilemon, D. (1986), 'A Model for Studying the R & D–Marketing Interface in the Product Innovation Process', *Journal of Marketing* 50, pp. 7–17.

Gupta, A. and Wilemon, D. (1988), 'The Credibility – Co-operation Connection at the R & D–Marketing interface', *Journal of Product Innovation Management* 5, pp. 20–31.

Gupta, A. and Wilemon, D. (1990), 'Improving R & D/Marketing relations: R & D's perspective', *R & D Management* 20 (4).

Hart, S. J. (1993), 'Dimensions of Success in New Product Development: An Exploratory Investigation', *Journal of Marketing Management* 9 (1), pp. 23-42.

Hart, S. J. and Craig, A. (1993), 'Dimensions of success in new product development', *Perspectives in Marketing Management*, ed. M. J. Baker, Chichester: Wiley.

Johne, F. A. and Snelson, P. A. (1989), 'Success Factors in Product Innovation: A Selective Look at the Literature', *Journal of Product Innovation Management* 5, pp. 114–128.

Kleinschmidt, E. and Cooper, R. G., 'The Impact of Product Innovativeness on Performance', *Journal of Product Innovation Management* 8 (4), pp. 240–251.

Majahan, V. and Wind, J. (1992), 'New Product Models: Practice, Shortcomings and Desired Improvements', *Journal of Product Innovation Management* 9 (2), pp. 128–139.

National Industrial Conference Board (1964), 'Why New Products Fail', *The Conference Board Record*, New York: NICB.

Rothwell, R. (1972), *Factors for success in industrial innovation: Project Sappho – A Comparative Study of Success and Failure in Industrial Innovation*, Science Policy Research Unit, University of Sussex.

Tzokas, N. and Saren, M. (1991), 'Innovation Diffusion: The Emerging Role of Suppliers Versus the Traditional Dominance of Buyers', *Journal of Marketing Management* 8 (1), pp. 69–80.

Von Hippel, E. (1988), *The Sources of Innovation* New York: Oxford University Press.

■ *Chapter 11* ■

Pricing

Adamantios Diamantopoulos

■ Introduction

Price is the *only* revenue-generating element in the marketing mix and, therefore, 'no matter how intelligently the product- distribution- and communication mixes are conceived, improper pricing of a product may nullify the effect of all other actions' (Staudt and Taylor, 1965, p. 450). Sound pricing decisions are essential for the long-run success of any company – whether a FMCG one, an industrial producer or a service provider. In this context, since the mid-1970s, 'the significance of price has been enhanced by the need to react to rising costs, sluggish domestic and world demand, intense home and foreign competition, fluctuating currency values and interest rates, product shortages, government regulations and widespread new product innovation' (Shipley, 1986, p. 1). The elevated importance of price is also reflected in numerous surveys of executives in which price has been identified as being the number one or number two success factor (Banting and Ross, 1973; Robicheaux, 1975; Said, 1983; Coe, 1983; Fleming Associates, 1984, 1986; Samiee, 1987; Simon, 1993).

In the sections that follow the literature relating to *some* key aspects relating to the pricing decision will be reviewed. Initially, attention will be drawn to those characteristics of price that make it so critical for the firm's prosperity but also quite difficult to manage properly. Next, the nature of the firm's pricing objectives will be discussed and followed by an examination of the 'three pillars' of price, namely cost, demand, and competition. Methods of price determination will be considered next and the chapter will be concluded with recommendations for further reading in the area. Suggestions for future research will be given at the end of each section.

In terms of orientation, the perspective taken reflects the price decision maker's (i.e. the firm's) point of view, rather than the buyer's. This is an attempt to redress the imbalance in the marketing literature between firm- and buyer-centred analyses of price, as 'the majority of pricing articles deal with consumers' reactions to, or perceptions of, pricing' (Jain and Laric, 1979, p. 75). Readers interested in such issues (including price awareness, sensitivity, deal-proneness, price as a quality indicator and price information processing) are referred to Lenzen (1983, Ch. 1–5), Nagle (1987, Ch. 10), Gabor (1988, Chs. 10–11), Simon (1989, Ch. 7), Monroe (1990, Chs. 3–4), Diller (1991, Ch. 4) and Simon (1993, Ch. 17) for comprehensive reviews.

■ Price as a decision variable

Price has a number of features that make it unique as a decision variable. First, as already noted, price is the only element in the marketing mix that generates revenue; the remaining elements – product, promotion and distribution – all involve cost-incurring activities (e.g. outlays for new product development, advertising and dealer support). Thus pricing has been described as the 'moment of truth' (Marshall, 1979) because it determines the reward to the company for all the investment in time, money and skill that has gone into its product offering. Second, price is the most flexible element in the marketing mix, in that price decisions can be implemented relatively quickly compared with decisions relating to the other marketing mix elements (Guiltinan and Paul, 1985). For example – assuming there are no legal controls – it is much easier for the firm to lower the price for a product for a given period than to offer a special package or alter an advertising campaign in an attempt to stimulate sales. The downside of this is that competition can also normally respond to price changes within a short time period, whereas competitive responses in the areas of new product development, promotion, or advertising require a longer time horizon due to the nature of the preparations involved (Simon, 1993). Third, and related to the previous point, competition is altogether much more likely to react to price changes in the first place than to changes in non-price variables (e.g. Lambin *et al.*, 1975). This is largely because the impact of price variations on demand is felt much quicker than the impact of, say, changes in advertising where lagged effects are common. Fourth, demand is typically more sensitive to price rather than non-price variables; empirical studies have shown that price elasticity can be as much as twenty times higher than advertising elasticity (e.g. Tellis, 1988). Fifth, price is a key factor affecting the likelihood of success in new product development (e.g. Cooper, 1979), a major buying decision variable in organisational markets (e.g. Shipley, 1985) and an aspect of company practice with wide-reaching public policy implications. In fact, 'in the final analysis it is an industry's pricing behaviour which determines whether or not it is competitive' (Reekie, 1981, p. 52), hence the proliferation of laws and regulations regarding monopoly and predatory pricing practices, price fixing and price discrimination (to name but a few). Finally, a major distinguishing characteristic of price is the multitude of roles it can play simultaneously; price can be used as a competitive signal for industry re-alignment (e.g. to limit potential entry), a positioning device (e.g. to offer 'value for money'), a promotional incentive (e.g. to stimulate new product trial), a segmentation variable (e.g. to delineate the deal-prone segments of the market), an image-building tool (e.g. to create an aura of exclusivity) and a strategic weapon (e.g. to capitalise on experience curve effects).

In the light of the above, it is not surprising that proper management of the price variable can provide a competitive edge to a company and 'a major reason for differences between the profit results of otherwise similar companies can be traced to their pricing methods and policy' (Marshall, 1979, p. 2). By the same token, *improper* management of price 'can cripple a business, no matter how otherwise efficient it may be' (Marshall, 1979, p. 1). However, despite the importance of price 'many companies fail to price effectively, even when they otherwise employ very effective marketing strategies' (Nagle, 1987, p. 1), a fact reflected in numerous empirical studies indicating reliance upon cost-based pricing methods, *ad hoc* rules of thumb and executive intuition (for a review, see Diamantopoulos, 1991). One reason for the lack of sophistication in price decision-making is the complex nature of the pricing variable itself, leading some authors to conclude that 'questions of pricing and pricing strategy are among the most difficult problems marketing executives face' (Morton and Rys, 1987, p. 12).

The complexity of price decisions can be illustrated in a number of ways. At a very basic level, even defining what one *means* by price can be very difficult because of other factors that are inextricably related with the 'true' price of a product. Things like order size, product quality, time of delivery, payment conditions, guarantee provisions, discounts and allowances, returnable policies, and 'free' services (e.g. maintenance and training) all influence the price charged and make straightforward comparisons among alternative offerings quite difficult (Monroe, 1990; Simon,

1993). Further complications arise because of the discrepancy between 'published', 'quoted', 'announced', or 'list' prices and the price actually paid by the buyer (e.g. Atkin and Skinner, 1975). Particularly in organisational markets, prices are subject to negotiation and can depend, to a large extent, upon the degree of delegation of pricing authority to the sales force (e.g. Kern, 1989). In addition, concealed price concessions to customers may further increase the discrepancy between list and transaction prices (Burck, 1972) and make it even more difficult for the firm to undertake valid price comparisons in the market. Price comparisons may be further hindered in inflationary periods when the distinction between actual and relative prices is confused by escalator clauses or 'price-at delivery' policies (e.g. Long and Varble, 1978), while the adoption of price bundling strategies (e.g. Paun, 1991) also make it difficult to identify the price of any one item in the bundle or to compare the total price of the bundle with the individual prices of its components. The complexity of the pricing decision is also due to the fact that 'price must be carefully meshed with the product, distribution and communication strategies of the firm' (Hutt and Speh, 1985, p. 360); this, of course, is easier said than done, not least because of the potential conflicts involved as to the 'right' price to charge (e.g. need for shelf-space calling for a low price vs desire to support a high-quality image calling for a premium price). Finally, the large number of company-specific and environment-specific variables that need to be considered (e.g. company objectives, demand and cost characteristics, competitive offerings, legislation) and inter-functional conflicts involved (e.g. production's concerns with capacity utilisation vs finance's preoccupation with cash-flow vs marketing's emphasis on long-run customer retention), have the effect that 'setting prices remains an inexact science' (Ross, 1984, p. 145).

■ Pricing objectives

Perhaps no other aspect in the pricing literature has attracted so much attention as the nature and specification of the firm's pricing objectives. Relevant literature can be traced back to the 1800s when the basic tenets of conventional price theory were developed and profit maximisation became *the* objective of the firm in microeconomic analysis; by the time of World War II, profit maximisation and the accompanying methodology of marginal analysis had become the standard features of price theory (a historical development of price theory is provided by Blaug (1985), while reviews of the relevant literature can be found in Brandt (1953), Ott (1962) and Krelle (1976)).

In 1939 Hall and Hitch challenged, on empirical grounds, the validity of the profit maximisation goal and the literature on pricing objectives began to mushroom. Theoretical developments took three directions (for a critical review, see Diamantopoulos, 1991). The first retained profit as the central objective of the firm, but either rejected maximisation in favour of a 'satisfactory' or 'conventional' profit level (e.g. Andrews, 1949a, 1949b) or replaced money profit with a different specification, such as return sales or return on investment (e.g. Hax, 1963). The second strand of contributions replaced the profit motive with another goal such as sales revenue (e.g. Baumol, 1959), output (e.g. Lynn, 1968) or growth (e.g. Marris, 1964) but still kept maximisation as the guiding principle. The third strand of the literature focused on *multiple* goals either encompassed in a utility function subsequently maximised (e.g. Williamson, 1964) or as a collection of partly complementary and partly conflicting demands (e.g. Cyert and March, 1963). Thus by the early 1970s a proliferation of conceptualisations of pricing objectives could be found in the literature. Having said that, the influence of the profit maximisation postulate is prevalent even today as evidenced by the orientation of many recent pricing texts (e.g. Dorward, 1987; Devinney 1988; Simon, 1989, 1993).

Concurrent with theoretical developments, a number of empirical studies of pricing objectives have been published following Hall and Hitch's (1939) seminal contribution. Some forty-five empirical investigations of pricing objectives in eight countries were identified in the recent review by

Diamantopoulos (1991) spanning the period 1924–1988, and more have appeared since (e.g. Shipley and Bourdon, 1990; Diamantopoulos and Mathews, 1994). The collective findings of these studies can be summarised as follows:

- Regarding the *number* of pricing objectives, the empirical evidence indicates that firms attempt to achieve multiple objectives through their pricing policies. The specific number of objectives varies from firm to firm and so does the particular combination of objectives that is pursued.
- Regarding the *types* of pricing objectives, these fall into six major categories, reflecting (a) profit objectives, (b) volume objectives, (c) financial objectives, (d) competition-oriented objectives, (e) customer-oriented objectives, and (f) miscellaneous goals. Table 11.1 presents a typology of pricing objectives based upon the empirical evidence. Note that while some sort of profit goal enters the objective function of virtually all firms, its exact formulation can vary substantially (see Table 11.1); regarding volume objectives, sales revenue and market share appear to predominate.

- Regarding the *desired level of attainment* and associated *time horizon*, little support can be found for short-run profit maximisation as postulated by conventional price theory; however, long-run profit maximisation has been observed in a number of studies. Nevertheless, the bulk of the evidence suggests that firms do not think in maximisation terms but rather seek to attain or maintain a 'satisfactory' profit position. The same orientation towards satisfactory levels rather than truly optimal positions also applies to real-life specifications of the other quantifiable goals (i.e. volume and financial objectives). It has also been shown that maximisation and satisficing can co-exist within the *same* firm, largely reflecting differences in the market conditions associated with the different product markets served.
- Regarding the *linkages* between pricing objectives, in addition to definitional relationships (e.g. by definition, money profit equals sales revenue minus costs), both complementarities and conflicts among pricing goals have been identified. These can relate to the same pricing goal across time horizons (e.g. a short-

Table 11.1. *A taxonomy of pricing objectives*

PRICING OBJECTIVES		
PROFIT	**VOLUME**	**FINANCIAL**
* Money Profit * Gross/Net Margin * Contribution Margin * Return on Sales * Return on Costs * Return on Capital Employed * Return on Net Worth * Profit Growth	* Market Share * Sales Volume * Sales Revenue * Sales Growth * Capacity Utilisation	* Cash Flow * Earnings per Share * Price Earnings Ratio * Dividends
COMPETITION-ORIENTED	**CUSTOMER-ORIENTED**	**MISCELLANEOUS**
* Matching/Undercutting Competition * Avoidance of Price Wars * Limit Entry * Price Stability * Money Profit	* Fair Price Levels * Goodwill * Value-for-Money * Full Price Range * Price Maintenance in the Channel	* Projection of High Quality Image * Avoidance of Government Intervention * Survival/Security

run profit emphasis may be detrimental for long-run profitability); to different pricing goals within the same time horizon (e.g. increasing market share in the short-run is likely to help with capacity utilisation); and to different pricing objectives across time horizons (e.g. emphasis on short-run profitability may, in the long run, attract new entry into the market). It should be noted that linkages between objectives is an area where little *rigorous* research has been conducted, as very few studies have explicitly addressed the issues involved.

- Regarding the *relative importance* of pricing objectives, profitability appears, on the whole to be the overriding (long run) goal, with volume objectives (particularly market share) holding second place. Financial, competition- and customer-oriented objectives seem to be moderating influences that affect the specific *targets* set with regards to profit, sales revenue, market share, etc. Note that the relative importance of objectives is not invariant over time; moreover the specific weights and priorities tend to vary from firm to firm as well as within firms producing different products and/or serving different product markets.
- Regarding the *influences* affecting the specification of and emphasis on different pricing objectives, both internal (i.e. company-specific) and external (i.e. environment-specific) factors have been found to play a role. For example, large firms are more likely to specify their profit goals in ROI terms, emphasise the long run and apply maximisation principles than small firms. Similarly, factors such as the stage of market evolution, the nature of competition and the degree of market concentration can explain a lot of the observed inter- and intra-firm variations in terms of pricing objectives. However, as was the case with the linkages among pricing objectives, little empirical research has been carried out in this area.

Given the volume and richness of the literature on pricing objectives, directions for future research have to be quite selective. What is certainly *not* needed is yet another descriptive study of pricing objectives based on survey or case study data. Instead, the key questions to be addressed include (a) what are the *factors* (internal and external) that affect the specification of pricing objectives, (b) what is the *process* by which pricing objectives are formulated and revised, (c) what kinds of *relationships* exist between different pricing objectives and how do these change over time, and (d) what *linkages*, exist between different pricing objectives and methods of price calculation (see also section on pricing methods). Many useful insights on all of the above can be gained by referring to the relevant German literature which contains a number of *generic* analyses of the notion of objectives from different perspectives (see, for example, Bidlingmeier, 1964, 1968; Heinen, 1976; Kupsch, 1979, and the extensive references therein).

▌ Costs, demand and competition: the three pillars of price

Forty years ago, reflecting on the state of pricing knowledge, Backman (1953, p. 119) stated that 'perhaps few ideas have wider currency than the mistaken impression that prices are or should be determined by costs of production'. This view was echoed twenty years later by Nimer (1971, p. 19) who warned that 'many businessmen deal with pricing as though it involved no more than a markup on costs, and remain quite unaware that with this attitude they may be doing serious damage to their and their companies interests'. These concerns, which partly reflect the proliferation of cost-oriented discussions of price in the pricing literature of the time (see also section on pricing methods), by no means imply that costs are *not* important for pricing. Rather they raise questions as to the relative *role* of cost in the pricing process and its relationship with the other two 'pillars of price', namely demand and competition.

The view taken here is that none of the three pillars is (in the long run) more important than the others and sound pricing decisions have to be based on *all three*. Focusing exclusively on the customer is not a sound strategy because price may be set at a level which does not allow the firm any profit; in the long run this is clearly an untenable position. Equally, focusing solely on costs ignores the fact that the latter depend on volume which, in turn, is a function of price; moreover, it ignores the fact that, in the final analysis, the customer does not *care* about the firm's costs but only about the *value* he/she is getting. In the extreme, a firm pricing on the basis of costs alone, may find itself *without* customers if the latter's reservation prices are lower than the firm's costs! Lastly, a preoccupation with competition at the expense of either customers or costs may also result in poor pricing decisions. Thus if the firm sets its own price at the competitor level without investigating customer perceptions of the value of alternative offerings, it may sacrifice profits by pricing lower than the market would actually accept. Similarly, by ignoring cost differences with competition the firm may forego opportunities for market share increases. In short, whichever way one looks at it, cost, demand and competition must all come into play in the development of pricing policy (Simon, 1993).

Focusing initially on costs, the latter have been studied from a number of angles in the pricing literature. One stream of contributions has concentrated on identifying *relevant* costs for pricing decisions. Thus distinctions have been drawn between total and per unit costs, fixed, semi-variable and variable costs, avoidable and sunk costs, forward-looking and historical costs, opportunity and sunk costs, etc. Each of these distinctions has implications for particular types of pricing decisions (e.g. Riebel, 1972; Corr, 1974; Oxenfeldt, 1977; Abel, 1978; Dorward, 1984, 1986; Kaplan, 1988; Cooper and Kaplan, 1988a, 1988b). A second stream of research has focused specifically on the relationship between costs and sales volume, addressing such issues as the shape of the firm's cost function (in particular the behaviour of average and marginal costs), the problems and techniques of cost/price forecasting, the establishment of price floors and the implications of economies of scale for pricing strategies (e.g. Reichman, 1973; Arnold, 1973; Stobaugh and Townsend, 1975; Wishart, 1978; Tayler,

1986). A third stream of contributions has approached costs from a dynamic perspective resulting in learning- and experience-curve explanations of cost behaviour; the concept of the experience curve, in particular, has come to play a major role in the formulation of long-run pricing policy as it can confer cost advantages to pioneer firms (e.g. Boston Consulting Group, 1972; Fogg and Kohnken, 1978; Day and Montgomery, 1983; Alberts, 1989). A final stream of papers has appeared on the impact of inflation on price decision-making and the options for pricing in inflationary times (e.g. Litaer, 1970; Dolan, 1981; Hatten, 1982).

The vast majority of the above literature tends to be conceptual or normative in nature and empirical studies are very much in the econometric tradition. Survey-type investigations of cost systems used in pricing, executive perceptions of cost curve shapes and descriptions of how experience-curve considerations are integrated in the development of pricing policy are much less frequent and the resulting evidence often conflicting (e.g. Eiteman and Guthrie, 1952; Ladd, 1965; Sizer, 1966; Lere, 1980; Wied-Nebbeling, 1975; Gordon *et al.*, 1980; Fremgen and Liao, 1981; Govindarajan and Anthony, 1983; Scapens *et al.*, 1983; Bruegelmann *et al.*, 1985; Outram, 1992). The collective picture based on the latter indicates that full-cost systems are more frequently used in practice than direct-cost systems (this is consistent with the findings on pricing methods discussed later); that more than one cost system may be in operation within the same firm; and that executive's descriptions of costs curves imply either constant or decreasing marginal costs (i.e. either a linear relationship between (variable) cost with output or continuous economies of scale). The typical cost function portrayed in microeconomic texts with first diminishing and then increasing marginal costs (reflecting initially economies and then *dis*economies of scale) is not widely reflected in practice.

Shifting attention to the demand side, again, there are a number of identifiable streams in the literature. The first, and probably the largest, has its origins in the traditional demand analysis of conventional price theory and its central concern is the form of the firm's demand curve (or price response function). A wide variety of functions with different elasticity properties have been used to theoretically model the link between price and customer response resulting in linear, multiplicative, logistic, kinked and doubly kinked demand functions (e.g. Sweezy, 1939; Brockoff, 1968; Culyer, 1971; Gabor, 1974; Reid, 1977; Gutenberg, 1965, 1984). While empirical studies have shown that Gutenberg's (1965, 1984) doubly kinked demand curve is the shape most often encountered in practice (Fog, 1960; Wied-Nebbeling, 1975, 1985; Tull *et al.*, 1986; Diamantopoulos and Mathews, 1993), it is also the case that within a relatively *narrow* range of price variation, there is little to distinguish empirically between different functional forms (Simon, 1993). A second stream of contributions has focused on methods for estimating price response functions, proposing such techniques as experimentation, customer surveys, expert judgment or econometric analysis of actual market data (e.g. Bennett and Wilkinson, 1974; Kass, 1977; Lawler-Wilson, 1979; van Helden, 1979; Blamires, 1981; Frappa and Marbeau, 1982; Mahajan *et al.*, 1982; Neslin and Shoemaker, 1983; Kucher, 1985; Coit, 1987; Morton and Rys, 1987; Morton and Devine, 1987; Hagerty *et al.*, 1988; Tellis, 1988; Jain and Rao, 1990; Simon, 1992); however, according to the (limited) empirical evidence, qualitative and intuitive methods still prevail, particularly among industrial firms (e.g. Morris and Joyce, 1988). A third stream of research has looked at dynamic aspects of demand focusing on such issues as (time-dependent) price level and price change responses, carryover and obsolescence effects, price expectation effects and the development of price elasticities over the product/brand/adoption cycle (e.g. Bass, 1969, 1980; Simon, 1979; Kucher, 1987; Mahajan and Muller, 1979; Mahajan and Peterson, 1985; Shoemaker, 1986; Narasimhan, 1989; Mahajan *et al.*, 1990; Parker, 1992); empirical findings on these issues are difficult to generalise because they depend very much on the particular type of product in question (e.g. repeat-purchase goods vs consumer-durables), the kind of market (i.e.

stable vs growing), and the stability of competition over time (for a review, see Simon, 1989, 1993). Finally, as already noted in the introduction, there is a well-developed body of behavioural literature on customer's perceptions of price; although outside the scope of the present review, price perception research is an important contribution of the marketing discipline to the study of pricing.

The third pillar of price, competition, has been very much in the forefront of discussions on price at least since Adam Smith's (1776) explanation of the 'invisible hand' mechanism of the price system. The relevant literature falls into three broad categories. The first is concerned with the development/description of competitive typologies and is very much embedded in microeconomic theory. Probably the best known one is the market structure (or morphological) scheme of perfect competition, monopoly, monopolistic competition and oligopoly, where the number of competitors is the key classification criterion (e.g. Bain, 1942). This has been extended (e.g. von Stackelberg, 1934) to include the market structure of the *buyer* side resulting in more narrowly defined categories (bilateral monopoly, polypoly, oligopsony, etc). Other typologies have been based on whether or not the firm is affected by competition (e.g Krelle, 1976), whether it considers competitive actions when it makes its price decisions (e.g. Frisch, 1933) or whether competition in the market is perfect or imperfect (e.g. Chamberlin, 1933; Robinson, 1933). In this context, the empirical evidence indicates that most firms consider themselves as operating in oligopolistic markets and tend to incorporate potential reactions by competition in their pricing decisions (Nowotny and Walther, 1978; Wied-Nebbeling 1975, 1985; Diamantopoulos and Mathews, 1993). Another part of the competition-related literature focuses on the issue of price positioning relative to competition (e.g. Hauser and Simmie, 1981; Bachem and Simon, 1981; Gavish *et al.*, 1983; Hauser and Shugan, 1983; Simon, 1988; Hauser, 1988; Horsky and Nelson, 1992). The empirical evidence is fragmented, however, it has been found that the success of price positioning strategies depends on the extent of the price differential from the market average and the degree of substitutability between competing products(Moran, 1978; Gardner, 1982; Ehrenberg *et al.*, 1989). A final set of contributions focuses on the relationship between competitors and their pricing conduct; most such analyses are undertaken assuming oligopolistic market structures and include questions of price leadership, price collusion, predatory pricing, price wars, parallel pricing, and limit-entry pricing. Most empirical studies in these areas have been undertaken in the industrial economics (industrial organisation) literature and consist of econometric analyses or industry case studies; for comprehensive reviews, the reader is referred to Scherer (1975, 1980).

Looking at future research, some questions that need empirical investigation include (a) how are *experience curve* concepts utilised by executives when setting/revising prices, (b) what *demand estimation methods* are actually used by firms and what benefits are they thought to confer, (c) what are the *demand and cost curve perceptions* of executives and how are these related to the market situation involved, (d) how are *dynamic* cost, demand and competitive considerations (e.g. carryover and obsolescence effects) incorporated in pricing practice and what time frames are considered, and (e) how is *pricing intelligence* managed within the firm and who is responsible for this.

■ Pricing methods

The development of the literature on pricing methods follows closely that relating to pricing objectives. Consistent with the emphasis on profit maximisation, up until 1940, the *only* method of price determination encountered in the academic literature was that of marginal analysis (i.e. the equation of marginal revenue with marginal cost, leading to the optimal price–output combination for maximising profits). It was, again, the Hall and Hitch (1939) study that cast doubt on the use of marginal analysis in practice that led to *other* methods of price determination starting to become part of the mainstream pricing literature.

Their findings that managers set their prices by first calculating costs and subsequently adding 'traditional', or 'conventional' allowances for profit, led to the establishment of the full-cost principle which was subsequently developed into a fully-fledged theory of pricing by Andrews (1949a, 1949b).

The issue of whether marginal analysis or full-cost pricing is *the* method of price determination that firms use became a point of major debate in the pricing literature for the next thirty years. Numerous theoretical analyses of full-cost pricing have been undertaken (for relevant reviews, see Oxenfeldt, 1951; Kuhlo, 1955; Heflebower, 1955; Haldi, 1958; Koutsoyiannis, 1979) and a number of empirical investigations have focused specifically on establishing the relative prevalence of full-cost pricing versus marginal analysis in practice (e.g. Wied-Nebbeling, 1975; Said, 1981). At the same time, developments in cost accounting, particularly in the direction of 'direct-', 'marginal-' or 'variable-costing' systems, lead to the contribution method of price determination being introduced in the pricing literature (for an early review, see Weber, 1966; for more recent discussions, see Kilger, 1981; Greenley, 1986; and Georges and McGee, 1987).

A parallel development was the explication (particularly by practitioners) of target pricing approaches (e.g. Beyer, 1949; Edson, 1959; Koch, 1961; Scheuble, 1964; Hapgood, 1965; ; Finerty, 1971; Deakin, 1975). By the mid-1960s yet another pricing method became known, namely the product analysis pricing approach developed by the Glacier Metal Company (Brown and Jacques, 1964; Simons, 1967). This method can be seen very much as an early application of the modern value pricing approach described in the marketing literature (e.g. Gross, 1978; Shapiro and Jackson, 1978; Forbis and Mehta, 1978, 1979, 1981; Christopher, 1982; Garda, 1984), which draws from the techniques of value analysis and value engineering (Kaufman and Becker, 1981).

On the empirical front, even more pricing studies have looked into pricing methods that into pricing objectives. Some sixty-five surveys and case studies were identified in the review by

Diamantopoulos (1991); this *excludes* econometric studies and material from governmental hearings! A brief summary of the collective evidence emerging from these studies as well as more recent ones follows.

- Regarding the *number* of pricing methods used by firms, while some firms may only apply a single method to their entire product range, in many (if not most) instances multiple methods are in use. A common pattern is that one method (e.g. cost-plus pricing) is applied to routine pricing decisions, while a different method (e.g. contribution pricing) for 'special' situations (e.g. to gain a large order).
- Regarding the *types* of pricing methods found in practice, these can be classified under three broad headings, namely cost-oriented approaches, demand-oriented approaches and competition-oriented approaches (Table 11.2). Cost-oriented approaches are characterised by an emphasis on covering some combination of cost elements. Demand-oriented approaches are characterised by a focus on the customer and the latter's likely reaction to price. Competition-oriented approaches are characterised by a concern with the firm's relationship with competition. A detailed description of the individual methods under each heading can be found in Diamantopoulos (1991).
- Regarding the relative *popularity* of different pricing methods, there is little doubt that cost-oriented methods predominate in industry, with cost-plus pricing being the most common form. From the demand-oriented approaches, pricing at the 'market' level (i.e. what the

market will bear) is the most frequently observed method (as well as holding second place in terms of overall popularity, i.e. after cost-plus pricing). Lastly, setting the price at about the same level as the market leader (or a combination of key competitors) appears to be the most frequent manifestation of competition-oriented pricing. The application of the remaining pricing methods under each heading in Table 11.2 seems, according to the evidence, to be more limited i.e. reflecting special circumstances (e.g. powerful buyers practically dictating prices, as in the case of monopsonistic pricing) or non-routine decisions (e.g. using trial-and-error methods in the pricing of new products). With regard to marginal analysis as espoused by conventional price theory, its application in industry appears to be very much the exception than the rule.

- Regarding the *implementation* of pricing methods, empirical research has shown that firms differ widely in terms of how they actually *use* a particular pricing method. For example, cost-plus formulae can vary in terms of the volume rates used to arrive at unit costs (e.g. historical vs forecast output), the cost items classified as overheads (e.g. inclusion vs exclusion of selling costs), the overhead allocation principle (e.g. proportion of direct unit cost vs direct allocation to output units) and the calculation of the profit mark-up (e.g. same for all products vs varying according to product type). Similar inter-firm variations have been observed with regard to the degree to which initial prices derived by a given pricing method are subsequently modified

Table 11.2. *Pricing methods*

PRICING METHODS		
COST-ORIENTED	**DEMAND-ORIENTED**	**COMPETITION-ORIENTED**
* Cost-plus Pricing	* Marginal Analysis	* Product Analysis Pricing
* Contribution Pricing	* Trial and Error Pricing	* Value Pricing
* Target (ROI) Pricing	* Intuitive Pricing	* Price Leadership/Followership
* Price-minus Pricing	* Market Pricing	* Competitive Parity Pricing
* Return on Costs	* Monopsonistic Pricing	

through the use of allowances, discounts, promotional deals or negotiation with individual customers.

- Regarding the *formalisation* of pricing methods within firms, the (admittedly limited) evidence indicates that the use of pricing guides or manuals describing the steps/components of the price-setting process is rather limited and that written-down pricing procedures are rare. Formal systems for monitoring the effectiveness of pricing decisions are also not widespread.

- Regarding the *influences* on pricing methods, the use of the latter has been shown to be linked to both organisational and environmental factors. For example, large firms are more likely to conduct return-on-investment analyses and tailor markups to different products and market conditions. The type of industry, the type of product, the production and distribution methods and the nature of competition has also been shown to impact on the adoption of different pricing methods. Lastly, tentative evidence exists that the choice of pricing method is partly dependent on the emphasis placed on particular pricing objectives; however, as was mentioned earlier (see section on pricing objectives), this is an area where more research is needed.

As was the case with much of the research on pricing objectives, the majority of empirical contributions on pricing methods are descriptive in nature (on this point, see also Diamantopoulos, 1991). Rather than solely focusing on *what* methods are employed in practice, the author feels that a more fruitful pursuit (both academically and managerially) would be to concentrate on *why* the various methods are used. Specific research questions include (a) what are the *facilitators* and *barriers* associated with the adoption (viz. non-adoption) of particular pricing methods, (b) under what *circumstances* is one method preferred over another, (c) what, if any, is the impact of *decision maker characteristics* on the choice of pricing method, (d) how is the use of different pricing methods integrated with the use of different types of *discounts/allowances*, and what

factors determine the extent of *formalisation* of price-making arrangements within the firm.

■ Conclusion

Twenty years ago, Alfred pointed out that 'company pricing policy is an area where the academic world has long since retreated in despair of ascribing consistency of principles or rationality of practice' (1972, p. 1). In responding to this criticism, some years later, Bonoma *et al.* state that 'it is not that academics cannot solve managerial pricing problems or that there is no interest in solving them. Rather it seems that academic researchers have not known, or do not focus on, the key pricing concerns of managers in order to conduct rigorous pricing research' (1988, p. 359). Partly responsible for this appear to be access and cooperation problems, since 'it has not been the tradition of management to be 'friendly' to the needs of academic researchers in the area of pricing' (Monroe and Mazudmar, 1988, p. 387); this, however, is an insufficient defense for 'the minimal contributions of models in the pricing area' (Jeuland and Dolan, 1982, p. 1). As should be evident from the discussion in the previous sections, there is often a gap between the focus of theoretical efforts and the findings of empirical research. There is plethora of elegant and mathematically sophisticated pricing models available, covering practically every conceivable aspect of pricing policy (for relevant reviews, see Monroe and Della Bitta, 1978; Nagle, 1984; Rao, 1984; Tellis, 1986; Monroe and Mazudmar, 1988; Lillien *et al.*, 1992); the trouble is, few firms seem to use them! Hopefully, addressing some of the areas for future research identified above will go at least some way towards closing the gap between the needs of the practitioner and the interests of the academic researcher. The use of process-oriented methodologies which were successfully applied to the pricing decision some years ago (e.g. Howard and Morgenroth, 1968; Capon *et al.*, 1975; Farley *et al.*, 1980) and resurrected recently (e.g. Bonoma *et al.*, 1988; Woodside, 1992) appear to be particularly promising in this respect as do the more quantitative efforts attempting to capture *intra*-firm variations in pricing practice (e.g. Diamantopoulos and Mathews 1993, 1994).

It goes without saying that the review of pricing undertaken in this chapter is neither exhaustive nor particularly detailed. Space limitations have meant that both the breadth and depth of coverage had to be restricted (as had the references), resulting in a *highly* selective treatment of pricing topics. Issues not addressed include pricing over the product life-cycle, product line pricing, price deals/discounts, channel pricing, non-linear pricing and bundling, new product pricing, price negotiation and the relationship of price to other marketing mix variables (particularly advertising). The same applies to more specialised areas such as the pricing of services and export/international pricing. Overviews of the above, as well as more extensive treatments of the issues covered in this review, can be found in the following sources:

- *General textbooks*: Nagle (1987), Gabor (1988), Monroe (1990). These offer good coverage of most issues and require little mathematical/statistical knowledge. They differ both in emphasis and in style, so they are rather complementary.
- *Model-oriented texts*: Schmalen (1982), Dorward (1987), Devinney *et al.* (1988), Diller (1991), Simon (1989), Simon (1993). These provide more rigorous and sophisticated treatments of pricing decisions but require at least a good grasp of calculus and regression analysis to benefit from them. In the author's opinion, Simon's (1993) book is by far the best, however, it is written in German; luckily, a condensed English version of the first edition of this book (Simon, 1982) is also available (Simon, 1989).
- *Managerial texts*: Winkler (1983), Montgomery (1988), Seymour (1989), Morris and Morris (1990). These are specifically written with the needs of the practitioner in mind so they are very readable, if not analytically rigorous. No mathematical/statistical background is generally assumed.

■ References

Abel, R. (1978), 'The Role of Costs and Cost Accounting in Price Determination', *Management Accounting* 60 (April), pp. 29–32.

Alberts, W. W. (1989), 'The Experience Curve Doctrine Reconsidered', *Journal of Marketing* 53 (July), pp. 36–49.

Alfred, A. M. (1972), 'Company Pricing Policy', *Journal of Industrial Economics* 21 (November), pp. 1–16.

Andrews, P. W. S. (1949a), 'A Reconsideration of the Theory of the Individual Business', *Oxford Economic Papers* 1 (January), pp. 54–89.

Andrews, P. W. S. (1949b), *Manufacturing Business*, London: Macmillan.

Atkin, B. and Skinner, R. (1975), *How British Industry Prices*, London: Industrial Market Research Ltd.

Bachem, A. and Simon, H. (1981), 'A Product Positioning Model with Costs and Prices', *European Journal of Operational Research* 7, pp. 362–370.

Backman, J. (1953), *Price Practices and Price Policies*, New York: The Ronald Press.

Bain, J. S. (1942), 'Market Classifications in Modern Price Theory', *Quarterly Journal of Economics* 56 (August), pp. 562–565.

Banting, P. M. and Ross, R. E. (1973), 'The Marketing Mix: A Canadian Perspective', *Journal of the Academy of Marketing Science* 1 (Spring), pp. 29–36.

Bass, F. M. (1980), 'The Relationship between Diffusion Rates, Experience Curves, and Demand Elasticities for Consumer Durable Technological Innovations', *Journal of Business* 53 (March), pp. 851–867.

Baumol, W. J. (1959), *Business Behaviour, Value and Growth*, New York: Macmillan.

Beyer, R. (1949), 'Pricing Products to Yield Planned Return on Plant and Working Capital Investments', *NACA Bulletin* 31 (October), pp. 143–152.

Bidlingmaier, J. (1964), *Unternehmerziele und Unternehmerstrategien*, Wiesbaden: Gabler.

Bidlingmaier, J. (1968), 'Zielkonflikte und Zielkompromisse im Unternehmerischen Entscheidungsprozeß, Wiesbaden: Gabler.

Blaug, M. (1985), *Economic Theory in Retrospect*, 4th edition, Cambridge: Cambridge University Press.

Blamires, C. (1981), 'Pricing Research Techniques: A Review and a New Approach', *Journal of the Market Research Society* 23 (July), pp. 103–127.

Bonoma, T. V., Crittenden, V. L. and Dolau, R. J. (1988), 'Can We Have Rigor and Relevance in Pricing Research?', in Devinney, T. M (ed.), *Issues in Pricing-Theory and Research*, Lexington, Mass.: Lexington Books, pp. 333–360.

Boston Consulting Group (1972), *Perspectives on Experience*, Boston: Boston Consulting Group.

Brandt, K. (1953), 'Die Problemstellung in der gegenwärtigen Preistheorie', *Zeitschrift für die gesamte Staatswissenschaft* 109, pp. 251–278.

Brockhoff, K. (1968), 'On Duopoly with a Doubly Kinked Demand Function', *Zeitschrift für die gesamte Staatswissenschaft* 124, pp. 451–466.

Brown, W. and Jacques, E. (1964), *Product Analysis Pricing*, London: Heinemann.

Bruegelman, T. M., Haessly, G., Wolfangel, C. P. and Schiff, M. (1985), 'How Variable Costing is Used in Pricing Decisions', *Management Accounting* 67 (April) pp. 58–65.

Burck, G. (1972), 'The Myths and Realities of Corporate Pricing', *Fortune* (April); reprinted in Vernon, I. R. and Lamb C. W. (eds) (1976), *The Pricing Function*, Lexington, Mass.: Lexington Books, pp. 5–17.

Capon, N., Farley, J. U. and Hulbert, J. (1975), 'Pricing and Forecasting in an Oligopoly Firm', *Journal of Management Studies* 12 (May), pp. 133–156.

Christopher, M. (1982), 'Value-in-Use-Pricing', *European Journal of Marketing* 16 (5), pp. 35–47.

Coe, B. (1983), 'Perceptions on the Role of Pricing in the 1980s among Industrial Marketers', *AMA Educators' Proceedings*, Chicago: American Marketing Association.

Coit, P. (1987), 'New Approach to Pricing Combines Speed, Market Data', *Marketing News* (8 May), p. 32.

Cooper, R. and Kaplan, R. S. (1988a), 'How Cost Accounting Distorts Product Costs', *Management Accounting* 70 (April), pp. 20–27.

Cooper, R. and Kaplan, R. S. (1988b), 'Measure Costs Right: Make the Right Decisions', *Harvard Business Review* 66 (September–October), pp. 96–103.

Cooper, R. G. (1979), 'The Dimensions of New Product Failure', *Journal of Marketing* 43 (Summer), pp. 93–103.

Corr, A. V. (1974), 'The Role of Cost in Pricing', *Management Accounting* 56 (November), pp. 15–18.

Culyer, A. J. (1971), 'A Taxonomy of Demand Curves', *Yorkshire Bulletin of Economic and Social Research* 23 (January), pp. 3–23.

Cyert, R. M. and March, J. G. (1963), *A Behavioral Theory of the Firm*, Englewood Cliffs, NJ: Prentice-Hall.

Day, G. S. and Montgomery, D. B. (1983), 'Diagnosing the Experience Curve', *Journal of Marketing* 47 (Spring), pp. 44–58.

Deakin, M. B. (1975), 'Pricing for Return on Investment', *Management Accounting* 57 (December), pp. 43–44, 50.

Dean, J. (1947), 'Research Approach to Pricing', in *Planning the Price Structure*, Marketing Series, No. 67, New York: American Management Association.

Devinney, T. M. (ed.) (1988), *Issues in Pricing – Theory and Research*, Lexington, Mass.: Lexington Books.

Diamantopoulos, A. (1991), 'Pricing: Theory and Evidence – A Literature Review', in Baker, M. J. (ed.), *Perspectives on Marketing Management*, vol. 1, pp. 63–192, London: Wiley.

Diamantopoulos, A. and Mathews, B. P. (1993), 'Managerial Perceptions of the Demand Curve: Evidence from a Multi-Product Firm', *European Journal of Marketing* 27 (9), pp. 3–16.

Diamantopoulos, A. and Mathews, B. P. (1994), 'The Specification of Pricing Objectives: Empirical Evidence from an Oligopoly Firm', *Managerial and Decision Economics* 15, pp. 73–85.

Diller, H. (1991), *Preispolitik*, 2nd edition, Stuttgart: Kohlhammer.

Dolan, R. J. (1981), 'Pricing Strategies That Adjust to Inflation', *Industrial Marketing Management* 10, pp. 151–156.

Dorward, N. (1984), 'Pricing: Formula to Tame those Wayward Costs', *Accountancy* 95 (November), pp. 101–106.

Dorward, N. (1986), 'Overhead Allocations and "Optimal" Pricing Rules of Thumb in Oligopolistic Markets', *Accounting and Business Research* 16 (Autumn), pp. 309–317.

Dorward, N. (1987), *The Pricing Decision: Economic Theory and Business Practice*, London: Harper & Row.

Edson, H. O. (1959), 'The Application of Return on Investment to Product-Pricing', *The Controller* (October), pp. 464–469.

Ehrenberg, A. S. C. *et al.* (1989), 'Price Parity for Very Close Substitutes: An Exploratory Result', *Marketing and Research Today* 17, pp. 84–88.

Eiteman, W. J. and Guthrie, G. E. (1952), 'The Shape of the Average Cost Curve', *American Economic Review* 42, pp. 832–838.

Farley, J. U., Hulbert, J. M. and Weinstein, D. (1980), 'Price Setting and Volume Planning by Two European Industrial Companies: A Study and Comparison of Decision Processes', *Journal of Marketing* 44 (Winter), pp. 46–54.

Finerty, J. J. (1971), 'Product Pricing and Investment Analysis', *Management Accounting* 53 (December), pp. 15–18.

Fleming Associates (1984), '1984 Key Pressure Points for Top Marketing Executives', *Fleming Associates*, Sarasota, Florida.

Fleming Associates (1986), '1986 Key Pressure Points for Top Marketing Executives', *Fleming Associates*, Sarasota, Florida.

Fog, B. (1960), *Industrial Pricing Policies*, Amsterdam: North-Holland.

Fogg, C. D. and Kohnken, K. H. (1978), 'Price-Cost Planning', *Journal of Marketing* 42 (April), pp. 97–107.

Forbis, J. L. and Mehta, N. T. (1978), 'Value-Based Strategies for Industrial Products', *Business Horizons* 21 (October), pp. 25–31.

Forbis, J. L. and Mehta, N. T. (1979), *Economic Value to the Customer*, McKinsey Staff Paper (February).

Forbis, J. L. and Mehta, N. T (1981), 'Value-Based Strategies for Industrial Products', *The McKinsey Quarterly* (Summer), pp. 35–52.

Frappa, J. P. and Marbeau, Y. (1982), 'Pricing New Products at Better Value for Money: The Ultimate Challenge for Market Researchers', in *Fitting Research to Turbulent Times, Proceedings of the 35th ESOMAR Congress*, Vol.2, Amsterdam, pp. 171–195.

Fremgen, J. M. and Liao, S. S. (1981), *The Allocation of Corporate Indirect Costs*, New York: National Association of Accountants.

Gabor, A. (1974), 'The Theory of Constant Arc Elasticity Functions', *Bulletin of Economic Research* 26 (2), pp. 114–127.

Gabor, A. (1988), *Pricing Principles and Practices*, 2nd edition, London: Heinemann.

Garda, R. A. (1984), 'Strategy vs Tactics in Industrial Pricing', *The McKinsey Quarterly* (Winter), pp. 49–64.

Gardner, S. R. (1982), 'Successful Market Positioning – One Company Example', in Bailey, E. L. (ed.), *Product-Line Strategies*, New York: The Conference Board, pp. 40–43.

Gavish, B., Horsky, D. and Srinkath, K. (1983), 'An Approach to Optimal Positioning of a New Product', *Management Science* 29, pp. 1277–1297.

Georges, W. and McGee, R.W. (1987), *Analytical Contribution Accounting: The Interface of Cost Accounting and Pricing Policy*, New York: Quorum Books.

Gordon, L. A., Cooper, R., Falk, H. and Miller, D. (1980), *The Pricing Decision*, Society of Management Accountants of Canada, Hamilton, Ontario and National Association of Accountants, New York.

Govindarajan, V. and Anthony, R. N. (1983), 'The Use of Cost Data in Pricing Decisions', *Management Accounting* 65 (July), pp. 30–36.

Greenley, G. E. (1986), 'The Contribution Method of Price Determination', *Quarterly Review of Marketing* 12 (Autumn), pp. 1–6.

Gross, I. (1978), 'Insights from Pricing Research', in Bailey, E. L. (ed.), *Pricing Practices and Strategies*, New York: The Conference Board.

Guiltinan, J. P. and Paul, G. W. (1985), *Marketing Management: Strategies and Programs*, 2nd edition, New York: McGraw-Hill.

Gutenberg, E. (1965), 'Zur Discussion der polypolistischen Absatzkurve', *Jahrbücher für Nationalökonomie und Statistik* 177 (4) (April), pp. 289–303.

Gutenberg, E. (1984), *Grundlagen der Betriebswirtschaftslehre*, 17th edition, Berlin: Springer-Verlag.

Hagerty, M. R., Carman, J. M. and Russell, G. J. (1988), 'Estimating Elasticities with PIMS Data: Methodological Issues and Substantive Implications', *Journal of Marketing Research* 25 (February), pp. 1–9.

Haldi, J (1958), 'Pricing Behaviour: Economic Theory and Business Practice', *Current Economic Comment* 20 (November), pp. 55–66.

Hall, R. L. and Hitch, C. J. (1939), 'Price Theory and Business Behaviour', *Oxford Economic Papers*, No.2 (May), pp. 12–45.

Hapgood, R. (1965), 'A New Approach to Profitable Pricing', *Financial Executive* 33 (December), pp. 14–21.

Hatten, M. L. (1982), 'Don't Get Caught with your Prices Down: Pricing in Inflationary Times', *Business Horizons* 25 (March/April), pp. 23–28.

Hauser, J. R. (1988), 'Competitive Pricing and Positioning Strategies', *Marketing Science* 7, pp. 76–91.

Hauser, J. R. and Simmie, P. (1981), 'Profit Maximizing Perceptual Positions: An Integrated Theory for the Selection of Product Features and Price', *Management Science* 27 (January), pp. 33–56.

Hauser, J. R. and Shugan, S. M. (1983), 'Defensive Marketing Strategies', *Marketing Science* 2 (Fall), pp. 319–360.

Hax, H. (1963), 'Rentabilitätmaximisierung als unternehmerische Zielsetzung', *Zeitschrift für handelswissenschaftliche Forschung* 15, pp. 337–342.

Heinen, E. (1976), *Das Zielsystem der Unternehmung: Grundlagen betriebswirtschaftlicher Entscheidungen*, 2nd edition, Wiesbaden: Gabler.

Horsky, D. and Nelson, P. (1992), 'New Brand Positioning and Pricing in an Oligopolistic Market', *Marketing Science* 11 (Spring), pp. 133–153.

Howard, J. A. and Morgenroth, W. M. (1968), 'Information Processing Model of Executive Decision', *Management Science* 14 (March), pp. 416–428.

Hutt, M. D. and Speh, T. W. (1985), *Industrial Marketing Management*, New York: Holt-Saunders.

Jain, D. C. and Rao, R. C. (1990), 'Effect of Price on the Demand for Durables: Modeling, Estimation and Findings', *Journal of Business and Economic Statistics* 8 (April), pp. 163–170.

Jain, S. C. and Laric, M. V. (1979), 'A Framework for Strategic Industrial Pricing', *Industrial Marketing Management* 8 (January), pp. 75–81.

Jeuland, A. and Dolan, R. (1982), 'An Aspect of New Product Planning: Dynamic Pricing', in Zoltners, A. (ed.), *TIMS Studies in the Management Sciences*, Special Issue on Marketing Models, Amsterdam: North-Holland.

Kaas, K. P. (1977), *Empirische Preisabsatzfunktionen bei Konsumgütern*, Berlin: Springer.

Kaplan, R. (1988), 'One Cost System isn't Enough', *Harvard Business Review* 66 (January–February), pp. 61–66.

Kaufman, J. J. and Becker, R. F. (1981), *Value Engineering: An Executive Overview*, Houston: Cooper Industries.

Kern, R. (1989), 'Letting your Salespeople Set Prices', *Sales and Marketing Management* 4 (August), pp. 44–49.

Kilger, W. (1981), *Flexible Grenzplankostenrechnung und Deckungsbeitragrechnung*, 8th edition, Wiesbaden: Gabler.

Koch, E. G. (1961), 'Make Return on Investment Work', *The Management Review* (February), pp. 20–24, 77–81.

Koutsoyiannis, A. (1979), *Modern Microeconomics*, 2nd edition, London: Macmillan.

Krelle, W. (1976), *Preistheorie, I Teil: Monopol- und Oligopoltheorie*, Tübingen and Zürich: Mohr Siebeck Verlag and Polygraphischer Verlag.

Kucher, E. (1987), 'Absatzdynamik nach Preisänderung', *Marketing ZFP*, Heft 3 (August), pp. 177–186.

Kuhlo, K. C. (1955), 'Eine Analyse des Vollkostenprinzips', *Weltwirtschaftliches Archiv* 75 (2), pp. 137–195.

Kupsch, P. (1979), *Unternehmungsziele*, Stuttgart: Gustav Fisher.

Ladd, D. R. (1965), *The Role of Costs in Pricing Decisions*, Hamilton, Ontario: Society of Management Accountants of Canada.

Lambin, J. J., Naert, P. A. and Bultez, A. (1975), 'Optimal Marketing Behaviour in Oligopoly', *European Economic Review* 6 (April), pp. 105–128.

Lawler-Wilson, C. (1979), 'Pricing New Products: The Application of a Multi-Attribute Model', *Management Decision* 17 (4), pp. 304–316.

Lenzen, W. (1983), *Die Beurteilung von Preisen durch Konsumenten*, Frankfurt am Main: Harri Deutsch Verlag.

Lere, John C. (1974), *Pricing Techniques for the Financial Executive*, New York: Wiley.

Lietaer, B. A. (1970), 'Prepare your Company for Inflation', *Harvard Business Review* 48 (September/October).

Lilien, G. L., Kotler, P. and Sridhar Moorthy, K. (1992), *Marketing Models*, Englewood Cliffs, NJ: Prentice-Hall.

Long, B. G. and Varble, D. L. (1978), 'Purchasing's Use of Flexible Price Contracts', *Journal of Purchasing and Materials Management* (Autumn), pp. 2–6.

Lynn, R. A. (1968), 'Unit Volume as a Goal for Pricing', *Journal of Marketing* 32 (October), pp. 34–39.

Mahajan, V., Green, P. E. and Goldberg, S. M. (1982), 'A Conjoint Model for Measuring Self- and Cross-Price/Demand Relationships', *Journal of Marketing Research* 19 (August), pp. 334–342.

Mahajan, V. and Müller, E. (1979), 'Innovation Diffusion and New Product Growth Models in Marketing', *Journal of Marketing* 43 (Fall), pp. 55–68.

Mahajan, V., Müller, E. and Bass, F. M. (1990), 'New Product Diffusion Models in Marketing: A Review and Directions for Research', *Journal of Marketing* 54 (January), pp. 1–26.

Mahajan, V. and Peterson, R. A. (1985), *Models for Innovation Diffusion*, London and Beverly Hills: Sage.

Marris, R. L. (1964), *The Economic Theory of Managerial Capitalism*, London: Macmillan.

Marshall, A. (1979), *More Profitable Pricing*, London: McGraw-Hill.

Monroe, K. B. (1990), *Pricing: Making Profitable Decisions*, 2nd edition, New York: McGraw-Hill.

Monroe, K. B. and Della Bitta, A. J. (1978), 'Models for Pricing Decisions', *Journal of Marketing Research* 15 (August), pp. 413–428.

Monroe, K. B. and Mazudmar, T. (1988), 'Pricing-Decision Models: Recent Developments and Research Opportunities', in Devinney, T. M (ed.), *Issues in Pricing-Theory and Research*, Lexington, Mass.: Lexington Books, pp. 361–388.

Montgomery, S. L. (1988), *Profitable Pricing Strategies*, New York: McGraw-Hill.

Moran, W. T. (1978), 'Insights from Pricing Research', in Bailey, E. L. (ed.), *Pricing Practices and Strategies*, New York: The Conference Board, pp. 7–13.

Morris, M. H. and Joyce, M. L. (1988), 'How Marketers Evaluate Price Sensitivity', *Industrial Marketing Management* 17, pp. 169–176.

Morris, M. H. and Morris, G. (1990), Market-Oriented Pricing – Strategies for Management, New York: Quorum.

Morton, J. and Devine, H. J. (1987), 'How Prices Really Affect Sales', *Sales and Marketing Management* 72 (May), pp. 90–101.

Morton, J. and Rys, M. E. (1987), 'Price Elasticity Prediction: New Research Tool for the Competitive "80s"', *Marketing News* 2 (January), p. 12.

Nagle, T. (1984), 'Economic Foundations for Pricing', *Journal of Business* 57 (January), pp. 3–26.

Nagle, T. (1987), *The Strategy and Tactics of Pricing*, Englewood Cliffs, NJ: Prentice-Hall.

Narasimhan, C. (1989), 'Incorporating Consumer Price Expectations in Diffusion Models', *Marketing Science* 8 (Fall), pp. 343–357.

Neslin, S. A. and Shoemaker, R. W. (1983), 'A Model for Evaluating the Profitability of Coupon Promotions', *Marketing Science* 2 (Fall), pp. 361–388.

Nimer, D. A. (1971), 'There's More to Pricing Than Most Companies Think', *Innovation* (August); reprinted in Vernon, I. R. and Lamb, C. W. (eds) (1976): *The Pricing Function*, Lexington, Mass.: Lexington Books, pp. 19–33.

Nowotny, E. and Walther, H. (1978), 'The Kinked Demand Curve – Some Empirical Observations', *Kyklos* 31 (1), pp. 53–67.

Ott, A. E. (1962), 'Preistheorie', *Jahrbuch für Sozialwissenschaft* 13, pp. 1–60.

Outram, R. (1992), 'In Search of More Reliable Cost Control', *Management Consultancy* (September), pp. 35–36.

Oxenfeldt, A. R. (1951), *Industrial Pricing and Marketing Practices*, New York: Prentice-Hall.

Oxenfeldt, A. R. (1977), 'The Computation of Costs for Pricing Decisions', *Industrial Marketing Management* 6, pp. 83–90.

Parker, P. M. (1992), 'Price Elasticity Dynamics over the Adoption Life-Cycle', *Journal of Marketing Research* 29 (August), pp. 358–367.

Paun, D. (1993), 'When to Bundle or Unbundle Products', *Industrial Marketing Management* 22, pp. 29–34.

Rao, V. R. (1984), 'Pricing Research in Marketing: The State of the Art', *Journal of Business* 57 (January), pp. 39–60.

Reekie, W. D. (1981), 'Innovation and Pricing in the Dutch Drug Industry', *Managerial and Decision Economics* 2.(1), pp. 49–56.

Reichmann, T. (1973), *Kosten und Preisgrenzen. Die Bestimmung von Preisuntergrenzen und Preisobergrenzen im Industriebetrieb*, Wiesbaden: Gabler.

Reid, G. C. (1977), 'Discontinuity Problems in a Generalized Price Leadership Model', *Journal of Economic Studies* 4 (May), pp. 38–44.

Riebel, P. (1972), *Kosten und Preise*, 2nd edition, Opladen: Westdeutscher Verlag.

Robicheaux, R. A. (1975), 'How Important is Pricing in Competitive Strategy?', in Nash, H. W. and Robin, D.P. (eds), Proceedings Southern Marketing Association (January).

Ross, E. (1984), 'Making Money with Proactive Pricing', *Harvard Business Review* 62 (November/December), pp. 145–155.

Said, H. A. (1981), *The Relevance of Price Theory to Pricing Practice: An Investigation of Pricing Policies and Practices in UK Industry*, Ph.D. Dissertation, Department of Marketing, University of Strathclyde.

Samiee, S. (1987), 'Pricing in Marketing Strategies of US and Foreign-Based Companies', *Journal of Business Research* 15 (February), pp. 17–30.

Scapens, R. W., Cameil, M. Y. and Cooper, D. J. (1983), 'Accounting Information for Pricing Decisions: An Empirical Study', in Cooper, D., Scapens, R. W. and Arnold J. (eds), *Management Accounting Research and Practice*, London: Institute of Cost and Management Accountants.

Scherer, F. M. (1970), *Industrial Pricing*, Chicago: Rand McNally & Co.

Scherer, F. M. (1980), *Industrial Market Structure and Economic Performance*, Chicago: Rand McNally & Co.

Scheuble, P. A. (1964), 'ROI for New-Product Policy', *Harvard Business Review* 42 (November/December); reprinted in *Pricing for Profit* (HBR Reprints), pp. 92–102.

Schmalen, H. (1982), *Preispolitik*, Stuttgart: Gustav Fischer Verlag.

Sethuraman, R. and Tellis, G. J.(1991), 'An Analysis of the Tradeoff Between Advertising and Price Discounting', *Journal of Marketing Research* 28 (May), pp. 160–174.

Seymour, D. T. (ed.) (1989), *The Pricing Decision – A Strategic Planner for Marketing Professionals*, Chicago: Probus.

Shapiro, B. P. and Jackson, B. B. (1978), 'Industrial Pricing to Meet Consumer Needs', *Harvard Business Review* 56 (November/December), pp. 119–128.

Shipley, D. D. (1985), 'Resellers' Supplier Selection Criteria for Different Consumer Products', *European Journal of Marketing* 19 (7), pp. 26–36.

Shipley, D. D. (1986), 'Dimension of Flexible Price Management', *Quarterly Review of Marketing* 11 (Spring), pp. 1–7.

Shipley, D. and Bourdon, E. (1990), 'Distributor Pricing in Very Competitive Markets', *Industrial Marketing Management* 19, pp. 215–224.

Shoemaker, R. W. (1986), Comment on 'Dynamics of Price Elasticity and Brand Life-Cycles: An Empirical Study', *Journal of Marketing Research* 23 (February), pp. 78–82.

Simon, H. (1979), 'Dynamics of Price Elasticity and Brand Life-Cycles: An Empirical Study', *Journal of Marketing Research* 16 (November), pp. 439–452.

Simon, H. (1988), 'Management strategischer Wettbewerbsvorteile', *Zeitschrift für Betriebswirtschaft* 58 (April), pp. 461–480.

Simon, H. (1989), *Price Management*, Amsterdam: North-Holland.

Simon, H. (1992), 'Pricing Opportunities – And How to Exploit Them', *Sloan Management Review* (Winter), pp. 55–65.

Simon, H. (1993), *Preismanagement*, 2nd edition, Wiesbaden: Gabler.

Simons, L. (1967), 'Product Analysis Pricing', in Taylor, B. and Wills, G. (eds) (1969), *Pricing Strategy*, London: Staples Press.

Sizer, J. (1966), 'The Accountant's Contribution to the Pricing Decision', *Journal of Management Studies* 3 (May), pp. 129–149.

Smith, A. (1776), *An Inquiry into the Nature and Causes of the Wealth of Nations*, ed. Conman, E. (1961), London: Methuen.

Staudt, T. A. and Taylor, D. A. (1965), *A Managerial Introduction to Marketing*, Englewood Cliffs, NJ: Prentice-Hall.

Stigum, B. P. (1969), 'Entrepreneurial Choice over Time under Conditions of Uncertainty', *International Economic Review* 10 (October), pp. 426–442.

Stobaugh, R. B. and Townsend, P. L. (1975), 'Price Forecasting and Strategic Planning: The Case of Petrochemicals', *Journal of Marketing Research* 12 (February), pp. 19–29.

Sweezy, P. (1939), 'Demand under Conditions of Oligopoly', *Journal of Political Economy* 47 (August), pp. 568–573.

Tayler, P. (1986), 'The Development of the Theory of Economies of Scale', *Warwick Papers in Management*, No.2, Institute for Management Research and Development, University of Warwick.

Tellis, G. J. (1986), 'Beyond the Many Faces of Price: An Integration of Pricing Strategies', *Journal of Marketing* 50 (October), pp. 146–160.

Tellis, G. J. (1988), 'The Price Elasticity of Selective Demand: A Meta-Analysis of Econometric Models of Sales', *Journal of Marketing Research* 25 (November), pp. 331–341.

Tull, D. S., Köhler, R. and Silver, M. S. (1986), 'Nachfrageerwartungen und Preisverhalten deutscher Unternehmen: Eine empirische Studie', *Marketing* 7 (November), pp. 225–232.

Van Helden (1979), 'Measuring the Price Sensitivity of Household Electricity Consumption by Means of Interview Data', *European Journal of Marketing* 13 (4), pp. 183–193.

Weber, C. (1966), *The Evolution of Direct Costing*, Center for International Education and Research in Accounting, Urbana: University of Illinois.

Wied-Nebbeling, S. (1975), *Industrielle Preissetzung*, Tübingen: Mohr Siebeck Verlag.

Wied-Nebbeling, S. (1985), *Das Preisverhalten in der Industrie*, Tübingen: Mohr Siebeck Verlag.

Williamson, O. E. (1964), *The Economics of Discretionary Behaviour: Managerial Objectives in the Theory of the Firm*, Englewood Cliffs, NJ: Prentice-Hall.

Winkler, J. (1983), *Pricing for Results*, London: Heinemann.

Wishart, R. S. (1978), 'Price Forecasting', in Bailey, E. L. (ed.), *Pricing Practices and Strategies*, New York: The Conference Board, pp. 62–68.

Woodside, A. G. (1992), 'Ecological Research on Pricing Decisions in Manufacturer–Distributor Channels', *Proceedings of the American Marketing Association Conference* (Summer), pp. 474–480.

■ *Chapter 12* ■

Channel Management

Sean Ennis

■ Introduction

The question of gaining access to and penetration of markets has increasingly occupied the minds of senior management in many companies in recent years. Except in very rare circumstances, it is impossible to reach the ultimate consumer without utilising various middlemen who take responsibility for numerous tasks which the manufacturer would find impossible to perform, either from an economic or practical perspective.

The market place has become more complex in recent decades. This has been caused in no small measure by a more sophisticated, demanding consumer with greater levels of disposable income. This has led to increasing product proliferation, with resultant fragmentation of markets as companies seek to satisfy the ever changing needs of the market place. It has also forced them to seek improvements in areas such as customer service in order to distinguish themselves from the competition and thus hopefully gain a competitive advantage. As geographic boundaries disappear and manufacturing and information technology allow companies to develop a global perspective of their business operations, the potential opportunities for exploiting new markets have to be tempered by the threats which may come from foreign competition as they in turn seek new business.

Given these changes in the business environment, it is now becoming a strategic imperative for companies to address the management of the distribution function in general and in particular to devise a channel strategy which gains them *access, penetration, coverage, visibility and aggressive representation* in the market place.

The purpose of this chapter is to provide the reader with a clear understanding of those issues and considerations which impact on the management of the intermediaries which lie between the manufacturer and the final customer. The early section places channel management in the context of its contribution to overall business strategy in general and in particular, its role as part of the supply chain. The influencing factors which have forced management to consider distribution as a strategic weapon as opposed to an isolated activity to be performed when production, marketing and sales decisions have been made, are examined.

The second part considers the process involved in designing a channel strategy and in so doing, evaluates the managerial tasks which need to be undertaken in order to effect its implementation. Specifically channel objectives, the selection, motivation and evaluation of intermediaries and strategies for utilising power and offsetting conflict are examined.

The latter part of this chapter considers the steps which need to be taken when a company is contemplating a change in its existing channel strategy.

■ Channel management defined

Bowersox and Cooper[1] define a channel as 'a system of relationships existing among businesses that participate in the process of buying and selling products and services'. In this respect, a number of tasks and functions have to be performed by the various parties in such a system. These activities along with their associated costs, are described in Figure 12.1.

A number of observations can be made at this point. Clearly some of the activites are more onerous and involve greater risk and levels of responsibility than others. Channel members who take on ownership of the product automatically incur risk as there is always the possibility that they may not be able to seel the product subsequently. Other activities, while highly important to the process, do not encounter the same levels of risk and are more specialised in nature – an example of this would be where a channel member passes on market information to another participant.

In the ideal situation, a manufacturer would wish to perform all of the various functions. This would allow for complete control to be retained from the time the product leaves the factory gate to the time it gets to the final customer. Inevitably as various tasks are passed on to intermediaries there is a reduction in the control and power which a company has on its products and services. This occurs in a situation where the middlemen used bythe manufacturer operate in an autonomous fashion and indeed may also be carrying competitive products as well. This can pose problems as conflict can arise between the channel participants who may be pursuing individual business objectives which may be incompatible with each other. This reinforces the view

Figure 12.1. *The channel as a system of relationships*

MARKETING FLOW	COSTS REPRESENTED
PHYSICAL OWNERSHIP	*STORAGE AND INVENTORY*
OWNERSHIP	*INVENTORY CARRYING COSTS*
PROMOTION	*PERSONAL SELLING, ADVERTISING, SALES PROMOTION, PUBLICITY PUBLIC RELATIONS COSTS*
NEGOTIATION	*TIME AND LEGAL COSTS*
RISKING	*PRICE GUARANTEES, WARRANTIES, INSURANCE, INSTALLATION, REPAIR, AFTER-SALES SERVICE COSTS*
FINANCING	*CREDIT TERMS, TERMS AND CONDITIONS OF SALE*
ORDERING	*ORDER PROCESSING COSTS*
PAYMENT	*COLLECTIONS, BAD DEBT COSTS*

Source: L. I. Stern and A. I. El-Ansary, *Marketing Channels*, 4th edition, Englewood Cliffs, NJ: Prentice-Hall (1992).

that channel decisions can have a major impact on the overall success or failure of a company's performance in the market place.

In the design of a channel strategy therefore, the company must decide who is going to perform the various functions. The point needs to be made that responsibility for such functions can shift from one party to another, depending on the nature and complexity of the product-market being addressed. In other words, certain functions which have been traditionally performed by the producer may shift downstream to the wholesaler or retailer. For example Michman[2] notes that in the motor industry, companies such as Ford are increasingly seeking advice from their suppliers on everything from car design to vehicle mechanics. This *functional shiftability* has significant implications for channel design because it highlights the dynamic and constantly changing nature of the channel structure. While such functions can be moved around the various participants, it is a maxim of channel management that you can eliminate the middlemen – but not the functions which they perform.

The precise nature of the relationship between the various participants is more difficult to define. At face value, it would appear that intermediaries and suppliers operate on a level of independence, given that in most cases there are no ties of ownership involved. Yet beneath this layer of superficial autonomy lies a need for mutual dependence. This type of relationship has been referred to as *symbiotic* (Adler[3]) and has been defined by Varadarajan and Rajaratnam[4] as 'the living together in intimate association of two dissimilar organisms for mutual benefit'. This of course has major ramifications for channel strategy and will be examined later in this chapter.

Channel management in the corporate context

A number of factors have conspired to force senior management to consider more carefully the way in which they approach their relationships with external intermediaries. Christopher[5] pinpoints four main developments which affect the way in which companies need to manage the supply chain i.e. the management of the flows of materials, finished product and information, from the sources of supply right through the point of ultimate consumption.

- The customer service explosion
- Time compression
- Globalisation of industry
- Organisational integration.

1. Customer service: As companies increasingly try to find a means by which to differentiate themselves from the competition, many have latched onto customer service as a conduit for achieving such a position. In truth, improving customer service can no longer be considered a competitive luxury. Rather it needs to be viewed as a competitive necessity. This is because in many markets it is becoming easier for companies to match the competition in such areas as product quality and product 'add-ons' due to the advent of advanced manufacturing technologies and the adoption of world-class manufacturing techniques. Fuller *et al.*[6] argue that because customer needs vary, as does their perception of service levels provided, companies can in effect tailor their logistics systems to suit the individual requirements; providing a customised level of service more profitably as a consequence. The net result is that the basic product is augmented through an adding of value thus providing a platform for achieving a competitive advantage. Clearly the intermediaries which are involved in performing certain tasks will play a major influencing role in determining the initial perception which potential customers will form of the customer service package and in the subsequent maintenance of that image.

2. Time compression: Time to market is fast becoming an important consideration in the formulation of business strategies. This phenomenon is reflected in the reduction on product life-cycles and in the length of time spent on new product development, the advent of just-in-time and its impact on order cycles and the access of com-

panies to information technologies such as electronic data interchange (EDI). Truly speed is becoming the essense if companies wish to exploit opportunities in the market-place. The critical question therefore in Christopher's view is how they can 'handle the myriad of complex activities which must be managed'[7] spanning the spectrum from the sourcing and procurement of resources through to the final distribution and after-market support provided to the ultimate customer. Viewed in this context the influencing role of the intermediaries cannot be underestimated.

3. Globalisation of industry: Ohmae[8] has observed that the increasing globalisation of business has resulted in the expansion of the size of a firm's activities, heightened the expertise needed to compete effectively and at the same time demanding an increase in capital requirements. These thoughts can be coupled with the views of Bovet[9] who notes the trend to global sourcing which can provide companies with greater flexibility in addition to potential cost savings and quality advantages. In a European context the move towards a single market is resulting in companies having to reconsider the logistics issues in terms of location of key functions such as warehousing, materials handing and local market support activities. Christopher considers that the difference between profit and loss on an individual product can ultimately 'hinge on the extent to which the global pipeline can be optimised, because the flow of goods and materials is so great'.[10] This raises questions as to whether such companies should invest in setting up local operations which are wholly owned by them or contract out certain activities such as warehousing to third party operators. This can be complicated further by the fact that although there is a move to remove national boundaries, considerable local preferences still exist. Christopher states that the dilemma facing a company is 'how to achieve the standardisation while still catering for the local demand for variety'.[11]

4. Organisational integration: The preceding discussion in a sense preempts this section. In order for companies to achieve the necessary improvements in their logistics and channel strategies, it is clear that much greater levels of inter-departmental integration will have to occur. The 'fiefdoms' created by production, marketing and technical departments in many Western companies need to be broken down in order to facilitate smoother co-operation and co-ordination of activities such as information sharing. This may be difficult to achieve in practice as it requires a shift in the 'mindset' of senior management – not an easy exercise, given the tendency in Western society to produce praduates who specialise in a certain discipline and as a consequence adopting a narrow perspective of how a business operates.

In addition to these trends, the move to *mass customisation* needs to be examined. Davis[12] suggests that this is more than just an intriguing oxymoron, having major implications for how the companies of the future will organise and plan their activities. In short, such a concept; making products tailor-made for each individual buyer, in which even the base components are varied, is already a reality in Japan and clearly represents a new source for obtaining a competitive advantage. Westbrook and Williamson[13] present a number of case studies highlighting how Japanese companies have utilised this concept. Figure 12.2 indicates how National Panasonic Bicycle (NPB) tailor design and provide a bicycle to suit individual requirements.

When embarking on this strategy in 1987, NPB set itself the following strategic objectives:

* to create demand for high value-added products which meet diverse individual needs
* to clearly distinguish themselves from the competition
* to avoid producing any unsold stock or obsolete products
* to prevent retail price cutting

In 1992 NPB produced 15 000 customised bicycles in its pilot plant. Given the development in the areas of new technologies, CAD and CAM, and the adoption of production cells, the

Figure 12.2.   *Custom choices at National Panasonic Bicycle: 11, 231, 862 total variations*

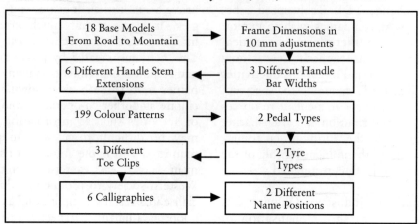

company argues that further improvements in output can be achieved.

Westbrook and Williamson[14] postulate that it will not be long before every car, camera and personal organiser will also be produced in such a manner. Apart from the obvious implications for manufacturing and sales, mass customisation will also drive major changes as to how the channels are handled. In the case of NPB they had to select, train and provide 1500 dealers with the kind of facilities and staff necessary to handle such a situation. The necessary expertise and commitment required on the part of such intermediaries arguably has to increase one hundred fold. Any slackness or flaws which show up on their part will affect the perception of the product offering and do damage to the manufacturer as a consequence.

The combined influence of the customer service explosion, time compression, the globalisation of business, the need for organisational integration and the move towards mass customisation has implications for the way in which companies develop their business strategies and the resulting role which channel intermediaries will play.

Porter[15] has argued that companies can pursue either one of three generic strategies: based on overall cost leadership, differentiation or a focused approach, to develop a strategic advantage. He is strong in his view that it is dangerous for a firm to pursue more than one generic strat-

egy. Given the trends identified in the proceding discussion it would appear that a strong argument can be put foward to suggest that it is no longer possible for a company to concentrate on one aspect of value such as quality, customer service or low cost operator and expect to sustain a competitive advantage in that area for a protracted period of time. Such an approach is one dimensional in nature when the reality (if the trends are accepted) is that it companies will need to achieve excellence in a combination of areas. Westbrook and Williamson[16] argue that many Japanese firms have already demonstrated that low cost leadership and differentiation are not mutually exclusive.

If the management of the channels is considered in the corporate context, it is clear that many companies will have to reconsider the approach which they will need to adopt. They will have to utilise channels in the future which will give them a unique route to the customer, aggresively promote and represent the product range while at the same time performing more cost effectively than the competition.

■ Channel structure

Before examining the issues involved in channel strategy design, it is necessary to give some consideration to what actually constitutes the channel structure within which participants operate. The nature of the working relatioinships between the various participants forms the basis for the type of *channel structure* which exists in a particular industry sector. The simplest channel structure is one where there is *direct distribution* between the manufacturer and the end user. This can exist in very specialised and focused markets, where there is a very small potential customer base and it is viable for companies to handle the distribution issues themselves, without recourse to utilising various intermediaries. The business-to-business sector provides the best example of where this structure can be found.

However when products and services which are geared for the mass market are considered, then clearly direct distribution is simply not a practical option for companies. As economies grow in size, sophistication and affluence, the need for intermediaries to perform various activities increases. This in turn leads to a situation where participants develop an expertise and a specialisation in certain tasks, which in turn means that other parties rely on them to perform those tasks. Thus, over time a form of mutual dependence tends to occur between the participants.

Before a company can consider specific elements of channel strategy, it must decide on the most appropriate channel structure. Bowersox and Cooper[17] identify three channel classifications based on a continuum ranging from least to most open acknowledgement of dependence:

Single transaction channels: This type of activity occurs with the expectation that the business relationship between the two parties will not be repetitive. Once all the requirements associated with the fulfilment of the transaction are completed, then mutual obligation ceases. A good example of this type of arrangement can be found in the case of certain categories of durable industrial equipment which have a very long life span and where the opportunity for repeat business does not really exist. They can also be found in international trading where an import agent may participate in a large scale, one-off purchase. The likelihood is however that in many such cases the possibility does exist for further business relationships to occur.

Conventional channels: Participants in this type of structure do not perceive a situation where there is extensive dependence on any one party. They will tend to specialise in the performance of certain tasks which ensures that there will be a demand for their services, whilst at the same time retaining their relative independence. The main motive of each channel member is profit and individual goals are pursued with no common objectives laid down by any one party. As a consequence, decision-making takes place at the level of the individual channel member. This can result in a distinct lack of loyalty to any one member of the channel. Because such a loose arrangement exists, it is relatively easy to enter or exit the channel. this can lead to instability over time and certainly does not offer a positive picture for companies who wish to impose an element of control or systemisation to the structure.

Vertical marketing systems: In this form of channel structure, the main characteristics indicates that they 'are professionally managed and centrally controlled networks... designed to achieve technological, managerial and promotional economies through the integration, co-ordination and synchronisation of the marketing flows from the points of production to points of ultimate use' (McCammon[18]). Implicit in this definition is the realisation that participants are actively aware of the need for mutual dependence on other parties and that their long term survival may occur precisely because of such an involvement. In addition to any potential economies which may accrue, it is expected that participants would also benefit from a synergistic effect due to the pooling together and sharing of resources and information. Bowersox and Cooper[19] note that for such a channel to operate effectively one of the members must emerge as a leader – usually because of the dominant position which it holds in the market. Clearly that member will be in a position to wield the greatest amount of power in the channel as a consequence. A number of variations can be found within Vertical Marketing Systems:

- Corporate vertical marketing system: These exist when the various channel members participating within the chain are owned by one organisation. This can occur through forward integration – where a manufacturer acquires or sets up its own wholesaling or retailing structure; or through backward integration – where a retailer or wholesaler owns its own supplier base.

- Contractual vertical marketing systems: The main distinguishing feature of this form of arrangement is that the relationships are formalised through a contractual agreement. This specifies the precise functions and responsibilities of each member. Typical examples of this type of structure are franchises, exclusive dealerships, and joint ventures. There is a marked absence of ownership in this situation (as compared to corporate arrangements).

- Alliances: Bowersow and Cooper[20] suggest that this structure is characterised by a voluntary form of extended organisations – where two or more firms agree to develop to close working relationship. At a basic level this can be described as a partnership – without necessarily producing changes or modifications in the individual way in which the parties conduct their operations. Clearly this may change over time, where parties are willing to alter their practices as they perceive individual and mutual benefits accruing. This type of structure can be described as a *strategic alliance*.

- Administered vertical marketing systems: Marketing institutions in such systems 'generally pursue their individual goals and have no formal organisational structure to bind them together. The marketing programme, on the other hand, allows these organisations to collaborate informally on the goals they do share' (Stern *et al.*[21]). While an attempt is made to inculcate a systematic approach to the planning and co-ordination of certain marketing activities, on the part of the channel participants, is to the individual rather than to the overall channel.

Clearly a company wishing to develop an effective and efficient channel strategy must first consider the most appropriate channel structure. This is critical because the type of channel structure determines the nature of the working relationships which will exists in that market and will also influence the amount of control and power which it can utilise.

■ Designing channel strategy

Every company needs to periodically review its existing channel strategy to take account of changes in the environment. The reality however is that very few companies undertake this exercise with any regularity. This is surprising given the increasing competition for customers. Such an exercise is not easy. On the contrary, the ability of companies to drive changes in their existing channel is often restricted by the unwillingness of senior management to move away from the status quo.

Stern *et al.*[22] present an eight-step process for channel design. This approach focuses from the outset on designing a strategy which is based on the needs and demands of the customer in areas such as order size, location, convenience, delivery time, product variety and so on. Such a schema also takes cognisance of the fact that there are likely to be differing requirements from the customer base. Given that a low level of homogeneity exists in most markets, it is necessary therefore for customers to be segmented on the basis of their distribution needs and requirements.

This end-user analysis will result in the company creating an 'ideal' channel system, based on the perceptions of the customer base. Such an 'ideal' system would include a multichannel format given that each segment would exhibit a wide range of preferences for different customer service levels. Of course this service along, while providing an almost perfect channel design in theory, is unduly simplistic. The existing channel system must also be examined. This incorporates a detailed evaluation of the sales and distribution functions currently in operation, their cost-effectiveness in relation to the competition and whether they presently meet the

Figure 12.3. *Channel design*

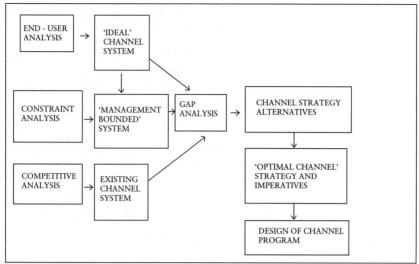

requirements of the customer base. The analysis of the existing system must also relate to the company's overall strategic objectives in terms of its technological position, its product positioning strategy and its utilisation of price and quality relative to the competition.

The analysis thus far provides the company with an 'ideal' channel system, as perceived by the customer base, concurrent with a detailed assessment of the existing system. However a further examination is needed – namely a 'constraints analysis'. This forces the company to recognise any limits or 'bounded areas' which have to be built into any revised channel structure. This might be reflected in specific rates of return or sales target which prospective channel participants must meet, company loyalties to a number of existing intermediaries and so on. This phase of analysis in essence, recognises potential managerial biases which currently exist and may be very difficult to overcome if a radical shift is required to move to the ideal system identified in the earlier phase. While these biases may ultimately weaken the potential for implementing the revised channel strategy, failure to adequately examine and understand them would in all probability lead to an unrealistic, unachievable position.

Having carried out an analysis of the ideal and existing systems and pinpointed the potential constraints associated with implementing change, the company is now in a position to identify the *gaps* which exist. This exercise will identify the areas which have to be addressed in order to move closer to the ideal from the existing strategy. Typically the gaps will be large as very few companies carry out a regular and systematic review of their distribution activities. The confronting of such gaps can be a painful experience for companies as many traditionally held views and perceptions may need to be challenged. Stern *et al*.[23] note that 'it is much more difficult getting companies to implement specific marketing channel suggestions that it is getting them to participate in and verbally endorse the results of the eight-step procedure'

The channel alternatives clearly need to be considered in the context of both the gaps identified and the willingness of senior management in the company to move towards the optimal channel strategy. The term 'optimal' is used because this position reflects the most efficient and effective channel configuration given the constraints and prejudices which remain in the company. It may not be the 'ideal' position identified at the start of the design process. However it represents the most viable and achievable position for the company.

■ Implementing channel strategy

Once the company has examined it present distribution strategy and decided on the specific changes (if any) which need to be made, the fundamental question as to how these alterations can be effected, needs to be addressed. The success of the strategy will be largely determined by the nature of the relationship between the company and the intermediaries. This can be influenced by a number of factors:

- the level of commitment required from intermediaries
- the level of support which needs to be provided to the intermediaries
- the potential conflict which may arise between the various channel participants
- the bases for acquiring and utilising power in the channel
- changes in competitive channel strategy
- the kind of leadership and motivation provided by the channel captain

The formulation of objectives is a necessary prerequisite for implementing channel stragegy.

This exercise helps the company to provide a focus or direction for the channel participants and a set of guidelines by which their performance can be evaluated over time. From a managerial point of view it is also essential as no strategy can be successful unless it is capable of being measured. Table 12.1 presents a range of typical objectives.

Bowersox *et al.*[24] observe that 'while channel objectives must be specified concerning traditional financial performance measures such as volume, market share, profitability and return on investment, operational channel objectives should also be developed in terms of market coverage and distribution intensity, channel control and flexibility'.

Market coverage and distribution intensity

Whether a company pursues an intensive, selective or exclusive distribution strategy depends on its overall strategic corporate objectives. For example if a cost leadership strategy is adopted, an intensive approach will reflect the emphasis on lower prices and convenience. A selective strategy on the other hand may be more appropriate if a company adopts a differentiation strategy, where a selective range of intermediaries can enhance

Table 12.1. *Channel objectives*

- Gaining access to the market
- Gaining appropriate and adequate distribution
- Building market share
- Achieving cost-effectiveness in gaining access
- Determining the level and type of effort required from the intermediaries
- Maximising revenue returns from the intermediaries
- Developing programmes which will *motivate* resellers
- Achieving the most cost-effective physical distribution of products
- To present a cost-effective level of customer service which will at the same time maximise potential for competitive advantage
- Achieving consistency with other elements of the marketing mix

Source: Adapted from A. R. Morden *Elements of Marketing*, DPP Publications (1987), p. 329.

issues such as quality and image. Exclusive distribution can help to augment a focused or niche strategy and can be very relevant to a product which requires major input from intermediaries in terms of selling and promotional effort.

□ *Channel control*

This refers to the need for companies to retain as much control as possible over all of the activities which have to be performed inthe distribution process. Clearly the more intermediaries that appear in the chain of distribution then the less likelihood that the manufacturer can maintain maximum control. This will be particularly the case in areas such as pricing, determination of margins, the type of selling effort required and the maintenance of a consistent product image and quality. It is important that companies achieve a consistency between market coverage and control objectives. In this respect, 'blanket' coverage of the market-place would be inconsistent with a strong desire on the part of the company to retain as much control as possible.

□ *Flexibility*

Given that most markets are dynamic in nature and that changes occur in the technological, competitive, legal and economic environments, it can be dangerous for companies to lock into a rigid approach in their relationiships with intermediaries. It may very well be the case that existing channel structures may need to be changed in order to counteract changes in customer preferences for example. Crucially by being in a position to alter distribution channels, companies may be in a position to gain a competitive advantage. In this respect, Dell Computers succeeded by moving to a form of direct marketing (selling through direct mail and telephone), thereby cutting out much of the expense associated with the more traditional channels such as the distributors and dealers. Established companies such as IBM are now engaged in a major review of their channel systems as a consequence.

■ Choosing channel partners

The ultimate success of the channel strategy employed is of course dependent on the performance of the intermediaries. In this respect, the way in which the partners are selected can have a major bearing on what happens afterwards. Many potentially successful products have failed to make an impact because the intermediaries have been unable, unwilling or uninterested to providing the required level of support or 'push' to ensure access and penetration to the market-place. A number of important issues can be identified which can help a company to arrive at an accurate assessment of the relative merits of potential partners. These can be summarised as follows:

Table 12.2. *Criteria for assessing prospective partners*

- The financial positions?
- Depth and width of product lines carried?
- Are competitive lines carried?
- Evidence of marketing, sales and promotional ability?
- Approach to order processing and order fulfilment?
- Evidence of investment in information technology?
- Reputation within the industry?
- Willingness to share data?

This list is by no means exhaustive and the relative importance of each criterion will need to be considered in relation to the specific industry sector. The exercise of rating potential members is not easy. While it may be possible to obtain an accurate picture of a company's financial position, it becomes more complex and subjective when trying to judge enthusiasm, managerial capabilities or willingness to upgrade existing facilities.

Companies can adopt a *weighted average* rating system. This approach is demonstrated in Table 12.3.

Table 12.3.   *The weighted average method*

Criterion	Weight	Intermediary Score (1–10)		
Evaluation of potential intermediaries				
		A	B	C
Managerial expertise	.40	5	5	5
Approach to order processing	.25	4	7	5
Level of investment in facilities	.15	6	2	7
Financial strength	.20	7	4	7
Total		5.3	4.85	6.75

■ Managing the channel system

Once the intermediaries have been chosen and put in place, the next task facing the company is that of providing the correct balance of leadership and motivation to ensure that the channel system functions effectively. This is not made easy by the fact that in most situations, the intermediaries are independent operators with no direct ties or commitments to any individual channel member. In addition, intermediaries and suppliers tend to have different perceptions about their roles and functions. Hanmer-Lloyd[25] in summarising the literature in this area, observes that the typical intermediary's perception of himself can be outlined as follows:

- he is first and foremost an independent businessman
- he emphasises his ability to provide a broad range of products and full customer service
- customers for a supplier's product are *his* customers, not the suppliers'
- he sees himself as a large and desirable customer of the supplier
- he is more customer-oriented (his customer) than supplier oriented.

By contrast the supplier's view of the distributor evokes a different set of views and tend to reveal that:

- the distributor is part of his (the supplier's) channel structure

- the distributor is unwilling to carry sufficient stock to ensure the best customer service
- the end-users of the product are the supplier's customers, not the distributors
- the distributor is there to handle small accounts, and physically distribute the goods
- the distributor's sales force are only order-takers, unable to develop new accounts or markets, nor to provide technical service
- the distributors has a poor level of management experience and competence. There is no provision for management succession when the principal of the company retires, and financial control is poor.

These findings reveal a potentially wide discrepancy in the respective levels of expectations from both parties. Of greater concern, from a managerial perspective, is the fact that such differences can create a pattern of adversarial behaviour which can result in an unhealthy atmosphere in channel relationships.

Before examining the specific causes of conflict and methods for resolving them it is important to consider how *power* can be utilised in an effort to achieve a level of co-operation and co-ordination in the channel.

▌ Utilising power in channel management

The concept of power is crucial in gaining an understanding of how the various activities and responsibilities are negotiated and subsequently allocated among channel members. Utilising power refers to the ability of one party to influence and ultimately get other channel members to do something which they otherwise might not have done. The ability to use power is influenced by the level of dependency which exists between channel members. In this respect it is fair to say that all members of the channel are inter-dependent – so that to some extent at least, some potential for using power resides with everyone in the channel. However as channels develop and become established, a channel leader emerges and that company (or group of companies) can wield considerable influence on other parties in the channel structure. There are a number of sources from which power can be derived. Much of the research in this area has come from the area of sociology (see French and Raven[26]) and can be summarised as follows:

Reward: This is based on the notion that if a channel member performs a specific function successfully, something of value will be given to them as a positive form of reward. Likewise the promise of a reward can also lead to a change in behaviour on the part of a channel member. In essence, the is the 'carrot' approach. Examples would include discounts, co-operative advertising programmes, preferential shelf space or extended payment terms.

Coercive: This is the 'stick' approach – where a channel member can threaten or cajole another member into performing certain roles or tasks by withdrawing certain privileges or terminating an agreement if they do not deliver to expectations. Clearly this source of power can only be utilised if one channel member is in a very strong position of dominance in the channel system as other members will tend to resist such a negative force, if they can.

Legitimate: This is based on an understanding that one channel member 'has a right' to exert influence on other channel members. This may stem from the fact that patent and trademark laws may give a channel member the right to

exercise power in terms of supervising how middlemen handle their products. It may also be based on a traditional acceptance by other members that because one member has been well established in the industry then power in certain areas has traditionally resided there. Clearly as a channel structure develops, there is ample opportunity for members to challenge such authority.

Referent: This source of power may stem from the attraction of one channel member to another. This is particularly evident in situations where one channel member has a brand franchise and where intermediaries take a certain pride in stocking such brands or where manufacturers delight in having their products stocked in exclusive retail establishments. This can allow for example, certain brands to gain preferential treatment in terms of shelf display. In cases where there is a long-term relationship established between two parties a much higher level of *trust* exists. This means that leverage can be placed by one party on another to effect a change in distribution arrangements, because there may be a greater willingness on the part of that party to take risks due to favourable past experiences in the relationship.

Expert: If a channel member has access to a more cost-effective supply base or retains more detailed and accurate industry information than other channel members, then this can lead to that member wielding considerable influence within that sector. Clearly there can be a reluctance on the part of the holder of such sources of information to *share* with other members, and once shared, that basis of power disappears.

While the sources of power have been examined separately in the preceding discussion, the reality is that in practice a combination of sources is often used by channel members. The utilisation of power can help greatly to influence the level of control and co-operation that can be achieved in the channel structure. If used correctly and in the right balance, a company can drive more efficiency and effectiveness among channel members. However if the focus of power is based on unduly harsh or negative measures, then it creates a potential recipe for dissatisfaction and ultimately, conflict.

■ Managing conflict

Periodically, manufacturers/suppliers in reviewing existing channel policy, may wish to instigate changes, in an attempt to improve their performance in the market-place. This may need to happen quickly if it is a response to competitive moves or where changes in the environment mean that the company may lose a competitive advantage or fall behind the competition. This task can be made difficult, from a managerial point of view, if discontent or open conflict exists among the channel members.

Magrath and Hardy[27] identify a number of strategies employed by companies which can create conflict:

1. Bypassing channels: skipping established channels and selling direct to the customer.
2. Over-saturation: appointing too many resellers in a designated geographic area.
3. Too many links in the chain: requiring small dealers to buy from bigger dealers who may not be perceived as being any better than themselves.
4. New channels: developing innovative channels that pose a threat (not to mention a loss of potential business) to the established channels.
5. Cost-cutters: utilising dealers that are viewed as 'discounters' by established dealers and as a consequence could damage the image of the product lines.
6. Inconsistency: treating some intermediaries more favourably than others and generally behaving in an arbitrary manner, thus provoking confusion and ill-feeling among channel members.

These procedures, if employed consistently over time, only succeed in perpetuating an adversarial relationship between the manufacturer/supplier and the intermediaries. This is not a happy situation for either party, and while the onus is on the manufacturer to foster a climate of co-operation, there is also a responsibility on the part of the intermediary to play a more proactive role in establishing greater levels of stability in the relationship. In this respect Wilson[28] argues that there is a need to move away from such an adversarial position to one where the concept of a partnership between both parties is fostered.

Narus and Anderson[29] suggest that in order to improve the quality of the working relationship, distributors need to:

1. Reach consensus with their manufacturers on the role of distributors in the marketing channel. This requires both parties accepting that the overall objective of the distribution channel should be to minimise the total cost and/or to maximise the total value associated with moving goods from the point of production to the point of consumption. Thus in some circumstances the preferred channel for achieving these objectives may differ. Likewise there needs to be a mutual acceptance that traditional channels may need to alter in the future, in order to accommodate developments in the market-place.

   This involves both parties engaging in market research, establishing distributor councils where views and ideas can be discussed. Open lines of communications need to be established and documents of understanding drawn up in order to clarify the position.

2. Appreciating manufacturing requirements. By visiting the manufacturing plant and closely observing such areas as ordering procedures and quality control procedures, the distributors can gain a clearer appreciation of the potential difficulties which can occur in terms of getting orders delivered on time. Likewise by jointly attending trade fairs and making visits to customers with the manufacturer's sales representatives, distributors can work more harmoniously with the manufacturer. A sharing of information on future sales patterns and so on can also help the manufacturer plan his production schedule more accurately.

3. Fulfilling commitments. Given that most manufacturers will look for evidence that distributors should be proficient in a combination of the following areas: marketing penetration ability, prompt payment of bills, financial stability and knowledge, the onus is on the distributor to examine performance levels in these areas and to seek improvements where possible. This will require a proactive, aggressive approach instead of thepassive, reactive stance which many distributors traditionally exhibit.

Wilson[30] cites the concept of the marketing support system (MSS) as another approach to developing distributor partnerships. He suggests that under this philosophy 'the function of the of institutions in the marketing channel is to support the marketing effort of those involved in the channel...based on the fact that those institutions collectively serve one another as key off-balance-sheet resources and that integration of strategies affecting inter-organisational marketing relationships among those resources enhances the effectivenss of the channel process' (p. 99). This approach calls for much closer levels of communications between manufacturers and intermediaries. If such a proposal is to work, it will require much greater levels of trust and understanding from both parties and as we have said earlier this is easier to put forward in theory than it is in practice. The devisors of MSS suggest a ten-point plan for intermediaries which can help to achieve a closer, more harmonious working relationship. The actual intricacies of driving this philosophy into the minds of intermediaries will undoubtedly take time and will not be without its 'teething problems'. This plan is summarised in Table 12.4.

The MSS concept has a number of positive outcomes for participants who pursue it with enthusiasm. Greater levels of co-operation and

Table 12.4. *MSS ten-point plan for intermediaries*

What we are
- We are in business to support your marketing effort; our resources are dedicated to that end
- We are more than just another company to process your goods through the marketing channel; we are a marketing support system
- We are an off-balance-sheet marketing resource of your company, and we consider you to be one of our resources

Why we are here
- To discover opportunities. We are here to help you discover potential customer-service problems – before they erode your profits. Tell us your customer-service objectives; we will use our resources to help you attain them.
- To solve problems. We are here to help you solve existing customer-service problems that are hurting your profits. Tell us about your marketing process; we will try to design our operations around it.
- For strategic reasons. We are here to help you design and implement your strategy for getting your goods to the target market. Tell us about your marketing opportunities; we will help you exploit them.
- For operational reasons. We are here to help you design and implement your tactics for getting your goods to the target market. Tell us about your operating process; we will help you manage your costs.
- To improve your profit. We are here to help you manage your costs associated with getting your goods to your target market. Tell us about your operating process; we will help you manage your costs.
- To serve wants and needs. In short, because we are a marketing supporting system, we see ourselves as your resource (and you as ours), working as an extension of the arms of your company in channel matters and serving the wants and needs of you, your customers and your customers' customers. Tell us about these wants and needs; we will help you to meet them.

Source: A. Wilson, *New Directions in Marketing: Business-to-Business Strategies for the 1990s*, London: Kogan Page (1991), pp. 100–101.

co-ordination within the channel system should ensure. However the benefits may take some time to emerge as the adoption of the concept requires a major shift in behaviour from all parties, particularly from the traditional adversarial, independent 'mind-set' which prevails in many cases.

▌ Training and motivating intermediaries

Implicit in the foregoing discussion is the need for the manufacturer/supplier to provide adequate training and motivation for the intermediaries. A proactive approach in these areas, if nothing else, will create a more favourable environment for harmonious working relationships. A recent study (Shipley *et al.*[31]) presents some evidence as to the type of training provided by companies to their distributor base:

Table 12.5.   *Training of distributors*

	Never	Occasionally	Usually
Product knowledge	23%	3%	73%
Company knowledge	23%	23%	53%
Feedback skills	53%	30%	17%
Selling skills	67%	27%	7%
Market research skills	67%	27%	7%
Marketing skills	67%	30%	3%
Administration skills	67%	30%	3%
Financial mgmt. skills	87%	13%	0%
Personnel mgmt. skills	87%	13%	0%

This study would appear to support the view that many companies adopt a 'minimalist' approach in terms of providing training to their distributors. Apart from the obvious areas such as product and company knowledge, quite a larger percentage of companies ignore the need to provide guidance in areas such as selling, promotion and general marketing. If companies wish to cultivate closer working relationships then clearly a more comprehensive approach to training is required.

The same study also examined the main motivators used by companies. They are summarised in Table 12.6.

Table 12.6.   *Main motivators used by companies*

	Not used	Used as a minor motivator	Used as a major motivator
Provided with exclusivity	10%	–	90%
Keep him up to date	–	13%	87%
Regular personal contact	7%	13%	80%
Focus on problems	10%	37%	53%
Provide financial incentives	30%	20%	50%
Provide salespeople	47%	3%	50%
Frequent interchange of views	23%	30%	47%
Joint Planning	23%	33%	44%
Assurance of long-term commitment	27%	33%	40%
Threaten to terminate	27%	40%	33%
Advertising/promotion	30%	37%	33%
Marketing research	53%	27%	20%
Sales training	67%	13%	20%
Financial assistance	40%	47%	13%
Distributor conferences	57%	33%	10%
Provide management training	87%	13%	–

These figures also suggest that companies are reluctant to engage in specific marketing motivators such as sales training and organising annual distributor conferences. Indeed if companies aspire to the view that the concept of partnership is the correct procedure to follow, then the sharing of marketing and sales related information and support services need to be viewed as necessities rather than potential motivators.

Improvements in the management of information flows allied to the adoption by companies of information technologies such as electronic data interchange (EDI) mean that the foundations are in place for the facilitation of transfer of data and speedier communications between the various channel participants.

Performance criteria for channel members

In order to effectively implement channel strategy it is critical that the company has some mechanism in place which it can use to monitor the performance of its middlemen. No plan can hope to succeed without a control procedure. Typically the following issues need to be considered in such an exercise:

SALES PERFORMANCE MEASURES
Sales achieved versus budget
Market coverage versus planned levels
Inventory levels against planned stock holding levels
Selling skills and expertise against planned levels

CURRENT CHANNEL MEMBER/SUPPLIER INTERACTION
Attitudes and co-operation of the channel member over the past planning period
Competitive lines: changes in stocking procedure (if any and if desired)

MEASURING CHANNEL MEMBERS'
PERFORMANCE-CUSTOMER SATISFACTION
Product availability
System capability
Information support
Pre and post-sales support systems

MEASURING CHANNEL MEMBER'S
PERFORMANCE-SERVICE QUALITY
Reliability
Responsiveness
Credibility
Competence
Courtesy
Communication

FUTURE CHANNEL PERFORMANCE
Growth prospects – by geographic region, segment, account size, etc.

The evaluation exercise allows the company to make a number of judgements (based on quantitative and qualitative analysis) about the individual performance of each channel member. Such information can help to determine the allocation of resources and the level of commitment which the company needs to provide to its middlemen for the next planning period. Likewise comparisons can be made between the relative productivity of each intermediary, pinpointing above average, average and below average performers. This detailed assessment of performance means that any subsequent allocation of resources is based on an objective analysis and protects the company from accusations of favouritism to certain channel members. More critically, from a marketing perspective, it presents an opportunity to see whether the needs and requirements of the ultimate customer are being met; and what cost to the company.

From a strategic planning point of view, areas of weakness and competitive vulnerability can also be recognised. This in turn can identify the necessary changes in direction which need to be brought about.

Concluding remarks

Managing the channels has been described as requiring 'the wisdom of Solomon and the guile of Machiavelli'.[32] This neatly encapsulates the skills required to get the best results from intermediaries. Unless the supplier owns the channel network, the dilemma of how to motivate middlemen who ultimately owe little allegiance to any one supplier in the chain must be addressed. Let there be no doubt that this challenge must be considered in a managerial context, i.e. the basic functions of planning, leading organising and controlling need to be exercise. Effective channel management calls for a systematic approach which examines existing channel policy on a regular basis and remains flexible in order to take advantage of new developments in the marketplace. This latter point requires management to have an open mind about such changes that may need to be made from time to time.

The channel management function can be viewed as simply an economic exercise which divides up the basic tasks and duties among the intermediaries and a subsequent monitoring of performance. However this is an unduly simplistic approach. Channel systems are social networks as well. As suppliers and middlemen establish relationships, attachments and bonds are formed and because the frequency of interaction is high, the precise nature and shape of these commitments needs to be understood by both parties. This chapter has examined the concepts of conflict and power and how they can be respectively resolved and utilised. A review of the relevant literature in these areas reveals a high level of suspicion and ignorance on the part of suppliers and middlemen. There is still a reluctance on the part of many suppliers to regard intermediaries as a strategic asset which needs to be managed on the basis of mutual dependence and trust, with a strong focus on *relationship management*. By contrast, many distributors and dealers place an over-emphasis on the margins which they can attain from individual suppliers, resulting in little loyalty being shown to any one supplier.

■ Future research directions

The Industrial Marketing and Purchasing Group[33] generated ground-breaking research during the 1980s on the issues of interaction, relationships and networks between manufacturers and their supplier base. This volume of work has helped to clarify and improve the level of understanding about such relationships. The vast bulk of the research concentrated on the purchasing–marketing interface. However the same concepts and principles also emerge when one moves downstream to the distribution activities. Thus there is a need to consider and apply the theories generated from the research carried out by the IMP group to the specific challenge of getting a closer insight into the nature of the interactions, networks and relationships between manufacturers/suppliers and intermediaries. The same level of understanding does not exist at this part of the supply chain. Indeed one of the main conclusions from this chapter is that a high level of distrust, misunderstanding and misuse of tactics exists within and between both parties. A lot can be learned from the IMP groups' research output which can subsequently be utilised to provide greater clarity of thinking. This in turn can improve the level of quality of channel management in an environment where companies are globalising their businesses and where fragmentation of markets means that companies have to reconsider their approach to distribution.

■ References

1. Bowersox, D. J. and Cooper, M. B. (1992) *Strategic Marketing Channel Management*, New York: McGraw-Hill.
2. Michman, R. D. (1990), 'Managing Structural Changes in Marketing Channels', *The Journal of Business and Industrial Marketing* 5(2) (Summer/Autumn), pp. 5–14.
3. Adler. L. (1966), 'Symbiotic Marketing', *Harvard Business Review* 44 (November–December), pp. 59–71.
4. Varadarajan, P. 'Rajan', and Rajaratnam, D. (1986), 'Symbiotic Marketing Revisited', *Journal of Marketing* 50 (January), pp. 7–17.
5. Christopher, M. (1992) *Logistics and Supply Chain Management: Strategies for Reducing Costs and Improving Services,* London: Pitman Publishing.
6. Fuller, J. B. *et al.* (1993), 'Tailored Logistics: The Next Advantage' *Harvard Business Review* (May–June), pp. 87–98.
7. Christopher, M. (1992), p. 18.
8. Ohmae, K. (1980), 'The Global Logic of Strategic Alliances', *Harvard Business Review* (March–April), pp. 143–154.
9. Bovet, D. (1991), 'Logistics Strategies for Europe in the Nineties', *Planning Review* (July–August).
10. Christopher, M. (1992), p. 18.
11. *Ibid.*, p. 20.
12. Davis, S. M. (1989), 'From Future Perfect Mass Customisation', *Planning Review* (March–April), pp. 16–21.
13. Westbrook, R. and Williamson, P. (1993), 'Mass Customisation: Japan's New Future', *European Management Journal* 11 (1) (March), pp. 38–45.

14. *Ibid.*, p. 45.
15. Porter, M. *Competitive Advantage* (1980), New York: The Free Press.
16. Westbrook, R. and Williamson, P. (1993), p. 45.
17. Bowersox, D. J. and Copper, M. B. (1992), pp. 102–108.
18. McCommon, B. C. Jr. (1970), 'Perspectives for Distribution Programming', in Bucklin, Louis P. (ed.), *Vertical Marketing Systems*, Glenview Ill.: Scott, Foreman, pp. 48–49.
19. Bowersox, D. J. and Cooper, M. B. (1992), p. 106.
20. *Ibid.*, p. 106.
21. Stern, L. I. *et al.* (1989), *Management of the Marketing Channel*, Engelwood-Cliffs, NJ: Prentice-Hall, p. 274.
22. Stern, L. W., Sturdivant, F. D. and Getz, G. A. (1993), 'Accomplishing Marketing Channel Change: Paths and Pitfalls', *European Management Journal* 11 (1)(March), pp. 1–8.
23. *Ibid.*, p. 8.
24. Bowersox, D. J. and Cooper, M. B. (1992), p. 165.
25. Hanmer-Lloyd, S. (1993), 'Relationship Appraisal: A Route to Improved Reseller Channel Performance', *9th IMP Conference Proceedings* (Bath) (September).
26. French, R. P. and Raven, B. (1959), 'Bases of Social Power' in *Studies in Social Power*, ed. Durwin Cartwright, Ann Arbor: University of Michigan.
27. Magrath, A. J. and Hardy, K. G. (1987), 'Avoiding the Pitfalls in Managing Distribution Channels', *Business Horizons* (September–October), pp. 29–33.
28. Wilson, A. (1991), *New Directions in Marketing: Business-to-Business Strategies for the 1990s*, London: Kogan Page, p. 98.
29. Narus, J. A. and Anderson, J. C. (1987), 'Distribution Contributions to Partnerships with Manufacturers', *Business Horizons* (September–October), pp. 34–42.
30. Wilson, A. (1991), p. 99.
31. Shipley, D. *et al.* (1989), 'Recruitment, Motivation, Training and Evaluation of Overseas Distributors', *European Journal of Marketing* (2), pp. 45–58.
32. Hardy, K. G. and Magrath, A. J. (1988), 'Ten Ways for Manufacturers to Improve Distributions Management', *Business Horizons* (November–December), pp. 65–69.
33. Ford, D. (ed.) (1990), *Understanding Business Markets: Interaction, Relationships and Networks*, London: Academic Press.

■ *Chapter 13* ■

Marketing Communications

Keith Crosier

■ Introduction: what is 'marketing communications'?

The term 'marketing communications' was chosen deliberately and carefully as the title of this chapter, despite its being less widely used in practice than other descriptions, because it defines the subject matter as precisely as possible.

First, 'marketing' limits the scope of the topic by telling us what kinds are *not* under consideration. Marketing communication is quite different from *mass communication*, in which an organisation addresses a largely undifferentiated mass audience (hence the term) for a non-commercial purpose by such means as press editorials, radio news, television documentaries, drama or political propaganda. The organisation would instead be aiming at a deliberately differentiated audience for a commercial purpose, and would employ such vehicles as advertising, sales presentations or pack design. This distinction may seem almost too obvious to need making, but is not always clearly enough observed in the specialist theoretical literature, as we shall see later.

Corporate communications also decribes the use of such vehicles to address a differentiated audience for a commercial purpose, but that audience does not exclusively consist of potential consumers. Many authors have observed that business firms, especially larger corporations, have a considerable number of recognisable separate 'publics' and may need to address all of them at one time or another. However, the impetus for communicating with the financial community, the workforce, the local community or suppliers (only four out of seventeen first identified by Britt more than twenty years ago[1]) is unlikely to be a specific *marketing* imperative, but rather a corporate one. This particular distinction firmly categorises *public relations*, a familiar communication activity practised by many commercial firms, as corporate and not marketing communication because its aim is generally to foster relationships with the public at large, not specifically to promote products or services to markets. PR may play an important role in creating favourable conditions for subsequent marketing initiatives, but that is beyond the scope of this chapter.

Having established that the simple criterion of a *marketing purpose* establishes the boundaries of the 'marketing communications' concept, it is next necessary to define more precisely the communication practices within those boundaries. Let us start with the fundamental notion of a *marketing mix* – those variables in the marketing equation that are capable of manipulation by executive action – conveniently summarised by McCarthy's 'four Ps':[2]

P1 = product
P2 = place
P3 = price
P4 = promotion

The most communicative element in this mix is clearly 'promotion'. (The other three are certainly capable of communicating something about a firm and its offerings in particular circumstances, as I have observed elsewhere[3], but the constraints of space dictate that we focus here on typical rather than special practices.)

This element itself comprises a mix of at least seven major strategic-tactical actions:

P4.1 advertising
P4.2 publicity
P4.3 packaging
P4.4 direct marketing
P4.5 sponsorship
P4.6 personal selling
P4.7 sales promotion

To all intents and purposes, these are the ingredients of 'marketing communications'.

Since the prime purpose of this chapter is to explain the theoretical underpinnings of practice, it would be inappropriate to dwell unduly on the relationships among these elements of the marketing communications mix, though they do have important implications for the formulation of marketing communications strategy. Readers interested in clarification can refer to Chapter 21 of *The Marketing Book*[3], which provides a full set of original definitions constructed so as to form a proper taxonomy and discusses the planning issues arising.[4]

'Communications' in the chapter title is an explicit clue to the nature of the effects following a *marketing communications* initiative, such as an advertising campaign or sales call. In everyday usage, according to the *Oxford Dictionary*, 'communication' describes the act of *imparting* or *transmitting*. For thirty years now, however, theorists have been stressing that communication is not simply transmission of a message or sign from one party to another, but rather an *exchange* between them. Schramm, a highly influential academic writer on mass communications whose basic theoretical propositions have been accepted and re-used by succeeding generations of marketing authors, defined it as 'the process of establishing a commonness or oneness of thought between a sender and a receiver'.[5] While few would dispute the transactional nature of person-to-person communication, there is a definite tendency among textbook authors and practitioners to take a far more unilateral view of marketing communication. It is a central tenet of this chapter, in contrast, that firms equally communicate *with* potential customers and not *at* them.

The dictionary furthermore defines communication as the transmission of *information*. In the marketing context, this is not always so. An advertisement, for instance, may provide its audience with entertainment or a feeling about the advertiser and the offering as well as objective facts. Indeed, some well-known current advertising campaigns, particularly for cigarettes and spirits, offer virtually no hard information at all but rather a set of much softer clues and cues for the audience to detect and follow. To imply that the strictly informative function of advertising is the only valid one, as some textbooks and most commentators typically do, is to take too unilateral a view again – this time by undervaluing the audience's discretion in how it chooses to *use* the advertisement. As used in this chapter title, 'communications' is intended to remind us that individuals in a marketing communicator's audience are not passive recipients but *active participants*.

While it is quite true that the firm makes the first move by taking a marketing communications initiative, the audience's co-operation in responding to it is required, and their response may even so not be what the initiator intended. Indeed, the *impetus* may come from the audience, in the sense that they deliberately expose themselves to marketing communications relevant to their present needs. The communicator's 'initiative' is thus the audience's 'message', a point that re-emphasises our central tenet that marketing communication is a *transaction*.

The consequences of this important proposition appear not to have been fully assimilated by marketing practitioners, by social commentators or the authors of current textbooks, with the notable exception of McDonald.[6] One receives a very strong impression that they believe all forms of marketing communications to be what powerful firms do to powerless, though sometimes stubborn, audiences and not something that the latter can choose to consume and use, or not to. It is not enough to build a 'feedback loop' into diagrams of the process or to stress the need to monitor public reaction to marketing communications initiatives; this is a *post-hoc* concession and not at all the same as treating the whole process as a *mutually beneficial exchange* from the outset. The balance of power in this transaction is thus a crucial issue which we will be considering in detail later.

For all the reasons implicit in the term 'communications' in its title, the remainder of this chapter will therefore approach the process of marketing communication as both a planned initiative by the communicator and a purposeful act of consumption behaviour by the audience. Before doing so, however, it may be useful to establish an agreed vocabulary.

■ Working definitions

1. *Marketing communication*, in the singular, is shorthand for 'communication for a marketing purpose'.
2. *Marketing communications*, in the plural, concerns the transactional processes by which such communication is or is not achieved.
3. *Marketing communications mix* describes the full range of actions by means of which a firm (or other type of organisation) can initiate the exchange.
4. *Marketing communications initiative* describes either (a) a single corresponding tactical action on the part of a firm, or (b) the purposeful act of consuming the resulting message or sign on the part of a individual.

Some writers on this subject have made significant use of the term 'persuasive communications'. The phrase does not occur here because it would not be correct to assume that marketing communications initiatives – in sense (1) above – must necessarily always have persuasion as their prime short-term objective, or that – in sense (2) above – they will always be used for self-persuasion. 'Marketing communications' strongly suggests persuasive intent, while permitting us to acknowledge the possibility of other motivations.

■ Marketing communications as a consumption transaction

Figure 13.1 presents a simplified interpretation of the classic flowchart models of consumer behaviour, explained in very much more detail in Chapter 4. The cycle of behaviour is initiated by conscious or subconscious awareness of a need which seems capable of eventual satisfaction by the acquisition of a consumer product or service. (For the sake of convenience, we will continue to speak of consumers and consumer products, but there is in fact no reason to believe that the model is inapplicable to industrial purchasing officers or the target audiences for public service advertising, for instance; the respective behaviour presumably varies in degree rather than in kind).

The felt need is next modified by a set of internal and external influences. The former comprise such modifiers as the consumer's own values, attitudes, beliefs and priorities; the latter consist of such factors as the consumer's perception of his or her social position, subcultural norms or family consensus. In its thus revised form, the original need now becomes a *drive* to find a satis-

Figure 13.1. *A simplification of the classic models of consumer behaviour*

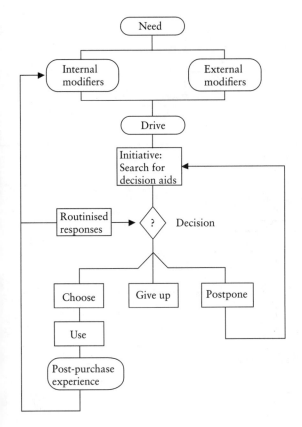

could be to postpone the choice, for lack of a clear solution, in which case the sequence of actions can be expected to loop back to the search stage and continue to cycle until a solution is found. Theory predicts that the third depicted possibility, to give up with the need unsatisfied, is an extremely unlikely outcome. The process does not end with a choice among alternatives, however. *Use* of the product or service is the basis of *post-purchase experience*, which in turn becomes one of the internal modifying influences when an identical or comparable need arises. Thus, the model is now 'closed', suggesting the possibility of indefinite repetition of the process, with a concomitant steady accumulation of consumption experience.

Consider, however, satisfaction of a very simple need – for example, to be able to light domestic gas appliances. The obvious solution is a box of matches – available brands are relatively little differentiated, the cost is low, the consequences of a poor choice are unlikely to be damaging, and the need is probably urgent. In circumstances such as these, consumers are likely to employ *'routinised response behaviour'*[6] rather than the more deliberate problem-solving described so far. The basis for routinising is again post-purchase experience, as depicted by the shorter return loop in Figure 13.1.

Advertising and publicity departments, sales forces, sales promotion agencies, direct marketing consultancies, design studios and so on are all organisations of people, of course. It is therefore entirely possible to fit their corporate behaviour into a similar framework, as Figure 13.2 does. In this case, the need is to satisfy established advertising, publicity or sales objectives. It is modified by such internal and external influences as collective experience of similar situations and collective perceptions of the 'atmosphere' appropriate to output on behalf of the firm in question, and then becomes the drive to devise a communication solution. After a formal search for decision aids, via strategy planning and creative development sessions, for instance, the decision is duly made. If it is not to postpone or abandon the project, the result will be a *marketing communications initiative*. While the initiative is in progress,

faction, which in turn stimulates a deliberate – perhaps mostly subconscious – *search* for aids to decision-making. Two central tenets of orthodox consumer behaviour theory are (i) that a need demands satisfaction and cannot simply be ignored, and (ii) that consumers are not helpless or haphazard in their consumption behaviour, but actively search for aids to systematic decision-making.

In due course, the search operation will be terminated by one or more of three circumstances arising: a decision deadline has arrived; the effort demanded to pursue the search further does not seem to match the probable benefits of doing so; the mass of data already acquired threatens to overload the capacity to handle it. The *decision* must now be made. Generally, it will be to make a choice among available products or services which deliver acceptable satisfactions. Instead, it

Figure 13.2. *Marketing communications practitioners' behaviour*

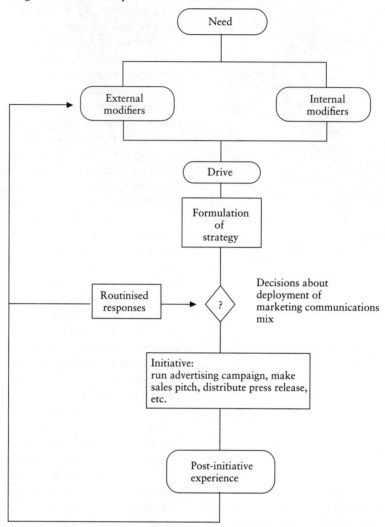

reaction is monitored to provide *post-initiative experience*, which in turn modifies comparable needs arising in future. As before, we can surmise that relatively undemanding needs will probably be met by *routinised responses*.

■ A 'synapse'

The crucial step in building a model of marketing communication as a *transaction* is to join the two flowcharts together. Figure 13.3 introduces the notion of a *synapse*. Borrowed from zoology, this term defines a place in the central nervous system where impulses pass from one nerve ending to another despite the fact that the two cells are not actually in physical contact. At the marketing communications synapse, user and originator of marketing communications initiatives come in contact while remaining in their own distinct domains. This analogy reminds us that consumers are not passive recipients, as so many marketing communications practitioners give the appearance of believing, but participants. They initiate the transaction by choosing to expose themselves to marketing communications initiatives – and

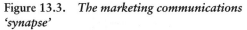

Figure 13.3. *The marketing communications 'synapse'*

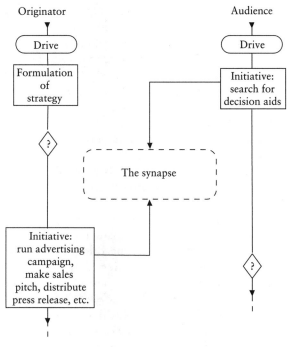

other inputs: that is their 'marketing communications initiative'. Among the models of consumer behaviour from which Figures 13.1 and 13.2 ultimately derive, the Engel-Blackwell-Miniard variant[7] is most obviously consistent with this theoretical proposition.

The decision aids commonly available to the searching consumer can be broadly categorised as solicited or unsolicited. Driven to search for aids to decision-making by the need to cover our floors, for example, we will become more aware than before of manufacturers' marketing communications activity, in the form of *advertisements, publicity* in editorial pages of magazines, so-called *junk mail*, and so on; this is unsolicited information. In a department store, with our sensitivity to floorcoverings heightened, our attention is perhaps attracted by other marketing communications initiatives, such as special *display* stands and the associated colourful *packaging*: more unsolicited information. Finally visiting a carpet showroom, we expect a marketing communications initiative in response: the offer of *sales promotion* material, a *sales pitch*, or

both. Indeed, we are liable to be put out if we do not promptly receive this attention, having solicited it by loitering in the sales area. All of these inputs are accepted and used, actively and voluntarily, because of the circumstances. At the synapse, a transaction takes place in which *both* parties are willing participants.

Furthermore, we will typically ask friends whose advice we value about their experiences with flooring materials; this is solicited opinion. If we simultaneously happen to mention our preoccupation to neighbours, there is a very good change that we will receive much unsolicited opinion. Although opinion is thus as important an input to consumption decisions as information, we are more likely to solicit it from lay people than from the manufacturers' representatives; presumably, we feel we can already guess the opinion of the latter. Furthermore, the typical structure of modern retailing, discussed in detail in Chapter 9, means that suppliers and potential customers seldom come very close together. As a chairman of Beecham Products once remarked in a television interview, 'advertising has replaced the shop assistant'. Checkout and cash-and-wrap personnel are not trained to dispense opinion about the relative suitability of the options offered on the shelves.

The specialist literature of persuasive communication suggests that the distinction between opinion and information (in the broad sense) has significant implications for marketing communications strategy by reporting evidence for a change in emphasis between the two as the search initiatives progress. Sociologists studying the uptake of agricultural innovations in America in the 1940s[8] found that while farmers were simply thinking about a new practice or device in the early stages of the decision process, they sought mainly *information* from formal sources such as government advisers (salespeople) and publications (sales promotion), whereas when the eventual decision became imminent, they turned to the *opinions* of neighbouring farmers and other influential personal contacts. It was not until the 1960s that marketing theorists took up this observation and put it to the test in more conventional marketing settings. A study of convenience-food buying in 1971, for instance, confirmed that brand information culled from advertising created the 'preconditions of success' but that the eventual choice decision rested on 'word-of-mouth communications' – in other words, the opinions of personal contacts who already used the brands under consideration.

Other theorists have further speculated that the likelihood of recourse to peer-group opinion varies with the degree of risk perceived to be inherent in the decision. These findings suggest that the role of marketing communications initiatives could be seen as to prompt the solicitation of opinion from peers, while conveying basic information, rather than to precipitate choice directly. This possibility has obvious strategic implications, which observation suggests are not widely recognised.

■ The balance of power

To postulate that audiences are willing participants with marketing communicators in a transaction poses an important question: how is the balance of power distributed between the two parties? We have already remarked on the apparently widespread belief that advertising (the most commonly discussed form of marketing communication) is something which relatively powerful advertisers do to relatively powerless audiences.

This is not to say they believe that advertisers can sell anything to anybody. On the contrary, whenever charged by critics with 'making people buy things they don't need and shouldn't want', advertising people are quick to point out the very numerous, well-documented cases of heavily advertised new-product failures. Nevertheless, observation of advertisers at work leads to the inescapable conclusion that, to be blunt, they believe they are practising a form of *sorcery*: given auspicious circumstances, copywriters and art directors can weave spells that will bewitch a significant proportion of the audience. This is sorcery rather than science because the sorcerers do not actually know how the effect is achieved. Indeed this very fact explains why researchers

have not yet found a dependable way to test the effectiveness of advertising campaigns, as we shall see later. Thoughtful advertising practitioners acknowledge the lack of a sound theoretical base to practice, while the less scrupulous hide behind the trappings of sorcery: bizarre uniforms, arcane jargon and a closed brotherhood. But even those who do not believe their power over the consumer to be absolute, likewise do not really believe that the balance of power is equal. Fundamentally, they expect to do something *to* the audience, not *with* it. To return to the previous analogy, if the spell fails to work, that is because it was cast wrongly, not because the magic is in doubt.

If this deliberately provocative statement of the case seems too extreme, consider the evidence that interested parties on the other side of the fence also subscribe to the view that the advertiser has the whip hand. The Independent Television Commission's *Code of Advertising Standards and Practice* forbids the advertising on television of products and services which may be openly sold and promoted in other ways: for instance, 'betting and gaming', 'fortune tellers and the like', 'all tobacco products', 'guns and gun clubs'. These prohibitions rest on the assumption that television advertising, to a captive audience with its defences down in the security of its own home, could induce normal people to make rash buying decisions with potentially serious consequences. The Advertising Standards Authority cannot similarly prevent non-broadcasting advertisements from appearing, but subjects them to scrutiny against the *British Code of Advertising Practice*, a document very similar to the ITC's *Code*, after the event. Consumer activists lobby for the strengthening of direct legislative control over advertising in all media. Their case rests on the assumption, often explicitly stated, that advertising can 'manipulate' ordinary shoppers. Furthermore, political opinion leaders on the broad left have been arguing for the last twenty years that advertising has a 'tendency to over-encourage gross materialism and dissatisfaction',[9] going on to call for tighter controls on the grounds that it causes, rather than encourages, antisocial attitudes. Other forms of marketing communications initiative are regulated by the Radio Authority *Code of Advertising Standards & Practice and Sponsorship*, the ITC *Code of Programme Sponsorship*, the *British Code of Sales Promotion Practice* and the Direct Marketing Association's *Code of Practice*, as well as by some eighty Acts of Parliament and statutory Regulations.

Thus, a fundamental assumption about the mechanism of marketing communication can be seen to be widely held, though seldom made explicit. Its prevalence among both practitioners and marketing academics was remarked upon fully thirty years ago by Cox, who dubbed it the 'egotistical view' and forcefully stated his own view that to think of the audience as an inert mass that can be persuaded at will 'exaggerates the power of advertisers and underrates the power and initiative of audiences'.[10] Today, it is apparent that the implicit assumption of a straightforward stimulus–response learning relationship between marketing communicators and their audiences can be severely challenged by a growing body of experimental evidence.

■ Learning the rules of the game

'Socialisation' is the process by which individuals learn to cope effectively with the challenges of everyday life and thus become competent participants in their own culture, society and community. Ward has coined the term 'consumer socialisation' to express the idea that, throughout life, people steadily 'acquire skills, knowledge and attitudes relevant to their functioning as consumers in the market place',[11] and thereby become effective participants in contemporary consumer society. One of the challenges of everyday consumer life is, of course, to cope with marketing communications initiatives. Ward's thesis is that we all learn – from our parents, our peers, our teachers, the media and many other influences – how to handle advertisements, salespeople, and so on. One might add to his analysis the observation that all such manifestations of marketing communications at work have been part of our collective cultural experience for so

long that society has had ample opportunity to learn to cope with them confidently. Posters were advertising book-sellers' latest offers to the literate on the temple columns of ancient Greece; medieval town criers habitually inserted paid-for commercial announcements into their 'programme', as radio and television presenters do in the United States today; and commercial television, the advertising medium that most regularly arouses fears of manipulation, will celebrate its fortieth birthday the year this volume is published.

Consumer socialisation is *not* a long process that leaves us vulnerable to marketing communications initiatives throughout childhood and adolescence. Both Ward[12] in the United States and Smith[13] in Britain found in field investigations that children begin to discriminate between advertisements and editorial in television programming, evaluate the intent and reliability of the commercials, and resist persuasion at a much earlier age than is generally assumed. The consensus is that discrimination begins at seven or eight years old and the ability to cope with advertising reaches the individual's own adult level by the age of fourteen or fifteen. These findings were repeatedly supported and confirmed in an extensive review of the literature conducted more than ten years ago by ten American researchers on behalf of the National Science Foundation.[14]

One of the skills that young consumers thus acquire is to 'use' marketing communicators and their initiatives, rather than be used by them. As Figure 13.3 depicted, the communicator is one source of information that can help in decision-making. The skill consists of both recognising that fact and learning to cope with the partisan nature of the communicated information.

One such technique must presumably be to allocate *credibility weightings* to each of the sources of opinion and information exploited at the 'search' stage. Advertising, being perceived as wholly partisan and persuasive in intent, is obviously discounted heavily; sales pitches perhaps even more so. But the unsolicited opinions of friends and neighbours cannot necessarily be taken at face value either. By the process of consumer socialisation, consumers learn not only to use marketing communications but also to erect the barriers of *selective attention and perception* against them when the information is irrelevant or unwelcome. These defence mechanisms are explained more fully in Chapter 4.

Consumers use marketing communications initiatives as more than just decision aids, however. Advertisements, in particular, are used for a variety of other purposes. Crosier and May[15] proposed, in addition to information: entertainment, involvement, vicarious experience, identification (a sense of belonging to a shared culture), internalisation (the taking of a behavioural lead from the lifestyles portrayed in advertisements), value-addition and implied warranty.

Though social commentators often assert that people resent the intrusion of advertisements into editorial and programme material, casual enquiry soon reveals that British viewers are just as likely to welcome commercial breaks as cleverly conceived and well executed relief from the tedium of predictable programmes and that cinema audiences positively enjoy advertising films that deploy all the technology of the main features themselves, compressed into mini-epics which do not demand an extended attention span. Formal surveys in Britain over the last three decades[16] have found that three quarters of all respondents say they 'approve' of advertising and that 'interesting' or 'entertaining' consistently figures prominently among their reasons for saying so. The same surveys show that the concrete manifestations of the abstract concept are 'disliked' only by a small minority: fewer than one in ten in the case of press advertisements, just over that proportion in the case of posters and fewer than one in five in the case of television commercials. A prolific and respected practitioner-author recently identified a 'new generation' of consumers who have 'grown up with television ... learned to decode sophisticated advertising messages ... neither wanted nor needed to be hectored by hard-sell propositions ... indeed demanded to be entertained and amused while being sold to'.

Simple social observation provides ample evidence of the extent to which this and other audiences are willing to take their behavioral lead from advertisements and thereby express membership in a shared culture. Scrutiny of typical consumer advertising confirms the potential for straightforward pleasure from vicarious experience of otherwise inaccessible lifestyles, which seems neither to strike an incongruous chord nor to boil over into social envy. The ability of advertising to deliver added value with products and services can be readily detected in typical patterns of ownership; intuition suggests that drivers of certain car brands wish to be associated with the aura projected to user and non-user alike in the advertising.

As for the reassurance of an 'implied warranty', economists have long recognised that, far from invariably choosing stores' own brands or unbranded goods because they cost less, consumers may prefer the 'tremendous spiritual satisfaction in buying a trusted brand of cocoa – not a shovelful of brown powder of uncertain origin'.[17]

Thus, ordinary people can cope satisfactorily if not perfectly with marketing communications, and initiate the transaction themselves. Advertisers or salespeople do not enjoy the persuasive advantage so often imputed to them by practitioners and commentators. The spectre of manipulation, so frequently raised by critics, is difficult to accept in the light of theory and experimental evidence (except in the important special cases of audiences disadvantaged by lack of education, culture or old age).

We might summarise the argument developed in this section by picturing marketing communications as a form of *game* for two players: tennis, for instance. There are well-established *rules*, which we learn at an early age. To win the game, a server must first achieve a valid service that clears the net and falls within the confines of a fairly narrowly defined part of the court, then outwit the receiver by superior skills while keeping the ball firmly in play, and finally maintain that advantage for long enough to outscore the receiver by the required margin. Otherwise, the server loses the point and possibly the whole game. Service faults, out-of-play returns, gamesmanship and outright cheating are detected and punished by a variety of arbiters. Thus, the marketing communicator needs to fashion an initiative which does not fall foul of the many regulatory codes of practice, to gain the upper hand in a battle of wits against an audience that is itself a sophisticated player of the game, without transgressing any other rules in the process, and to maintain the upper hand until the audience submits. Furthermore, receivers in this particular game have the unusual advantage of being able to ignore the server's deliveries without losing the point, though it is in general not to their advantage to do so.

They also enjoy the benefit of a *team trainer*, in the shape of the Consumers' Association, and have the option of joining a *club* – their local consumer group. As a last resort, they have recourse to the *law*, via the local government consumer protection service and the Office of Fair Trading. As in all games, *practice* improves performance. In all, then, the two parties in the marketing communications transaction are in fact more evenly matched than is generally implied in the literature. As Hedges[18] put it more than twenty years ago, 'it isn't so important to know what advertising does to people as what people do with advertising'.

Models of marketing communication

Our finished model of the marketing communication process, reduced to its simplest form in Figure 13.4, is essentially descriptive; it explains *what* is thought to happen, but not *how*. To be complete, it should attempt verbal and mathematical representation of the mechanisms by which internal and external modifiers operate, the audience processes information and opinion received at the synapse, and the decision is made once the search process is terminated. The first of those considerations is somewhat beyond the scope of this chapter; the basis for answers to that particular question 'how?' will be found in Chapter 4. This section now turns from a *sociological* analysis of the initiator-audience transaction to a *psychological* account of audience behaviour in order to investigate the second and third.

Figure 13.4. *The marketing communications transaction*

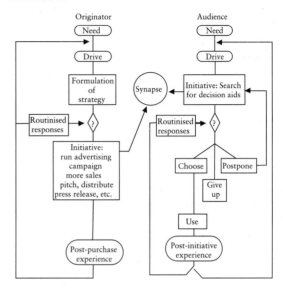

□ *A hierarchy of effects*

Textbooks of advertising almost invariably explain what happens at the synapse by describing one or more members of a family of seven *hierarchical models of advertising effect*. These can be thought of as a micro-model located within the macro-model, at the synapse. Table 13.1 presents them in chronological order.[19] Strong's AIDA appeared in his *The Psychology of Selling* and DeLozier's model in his *The Marketing Communications Process*, reminding us that all seven can be seen as general models of marketing communication effect, not specific to advertising. Collectively, they represent an attempt to extend the *stimulus-response model* of advertising effect, by postulating a series of intermediate states between awareness (stimulus) and action (response).

In the original versions, the models were not arranged horizontally, as in Table 13.1, but vertically, to emphasise the concept of a hierarchical series of events. McGuire's took the especially step-wise form of a staircase. Some ran from awareness upwards to action, which others were in exactly the opposite sequence. Table 13.2 rearranges them all into the first of these two

Table 13.1. *Hierarchical models of advertising effect*

STARCH, 1923: *to be effective, an advertisement must be...*
seen → read → believed → remembered → acted upon

STRONG, 1925: *AIDA* (a) (b)
attention → interest → desire → action

SANDAGE and FRYBURGER, 1935: *Interaction Model*
exposure → perception → integration → action

LAVIDGE and STEINER, 1961: *Hierarchy of Effects*
awareness → knowledge → liking → preference → conviction → purchase

COLLEY, 1961: *DAGMAR* (c)
unawareness → awareness → comprehension → conviction → action

McGUIRE, 1969: *Information Processing Model*
presentation → attention → comprehension → yielding → retention → behaviour

DeLOZIER, 1976: *Psychological Responses to Advertising*
attention → perception → retention → conviction → action (d)

PRESTON and THORSON, 1984: *Expanded Association Model* (e)
Exposure → awareness → perception → evaluation → stimulation → search → trial → adoption

Notes:
(a) The initials of the four steps.
(b) It is an interesting comment upon the intellectual condition of marketing communications practice that this model was found to be the most widely quoted of the seven in a range of current British, American and French textbooks, despite being today well past normal retirement age.
(c) Colley's model is always called 'Dagmar', actually the initials of the monograph in which it was first proposed: Defining Advertising Goals for Measured Advertising Results.
(d) DeLozier's model includes a final step, 'post-purchase behaviour', which is omitted here – partly for purposes of comparison and partly because it is not actually a response to advertising but a consequence of action.
(e) The Preston and Thorson model appears very different from the rest because of its many incorporated ramifications – for example, separating awareness of the advertisement from awareness of its elements from awareness of the advertised product.

vertical models and manipulates the spaces between the steps in the individual hierarchies, to demonstrate unequivocally that they do belong to a single family. It also incorporates the notion, explicitly stated by some of the originators but not the others, that such hierarchies can be related to the three principal categories of mental activity recognised by general psychological theory: *cognitive*, to do with knowledge; *affective*, to do with attitudes; *conative*, to do with motives (alternatively labelled 'behavioural' or 'instrumental'). These levels are sometimes described more colloquially, but also more descriptively, as 'think, feel, do'.

In this rearrangement, McGuire's and DeLozier's retention steps have been placed at different levels because they do not mean the same thing. In describing one task of advertising as 'to facilitate consumer retention of the advertised brand', DeLozier implies the view that retention of the message must precede formation of the intention to purchase. McGuire's model was proposed in a symposium paper which is difficult to trace, but Robertson[20] reports that the term refers in his case to retention of impetus towards action; this is quite distinct usage.

Critical inspection of Table 13.2 will reveal that terminology, while compatible except for the case just noted, is inconsistent across and within the schemes: labels assigned to steps describe two different sorts of phenomena, which may be

Table 13.2. The hierarchies as a family of models

Starch	Strong	Sandage and Fryburger	Lavidge and Steiner	Colley	McGuire	DeLozier	Preston and Thorson	
Acted upon Remembered	Action	Action	Purchase	Action	Behaviour Retention	Action	Adoption Trial Search	*Conative level:* doing
Believed	Desire	Integration	Conviction Preference Liking	Conviction	Yielding	Conviction	Stimulation Evaluation Perception	*Affective level:* feeling
Read Seen	Interest Perception Attention	Perception Exposure	Knowledge Awareness	Comprehension Awareness Unawareness	Comprehension Attention Presentation	Retention Perception Attention	Awareness Exposure	*Cognitive level:* thinking

indiscriminately mixed within one hierarchy. Therefore, Table 13.3 proposes a distinction between *performance characteristics*, relating to marketing communications initiatives, on the one hand, and *target responses*, relating to the audience on the other. Simultaneously, it synthesises the twenty-three separate terminological labels into two sets of six and attaches to those the level numbers I to VI. It is our working model of the models.

Table 13.3.   *A consolidated hierarchical model of advertising effect*

Level	Performance Characteristic: This advertisement should achieve...	Target Response: The audience is expected to exhibit...
VI	Motivation	Action
V	Persuasion	Conviction
IV	Empathy	Sympathy
III	Communication	Comprehension
II	Involvement	Interest
I	Impact	Attention

□ *Conceptual criticisms*

Since the 1960s, hierarchical models of advertising effect have been subject to more or less continuous criticism. Most influential among the critics is Palda,[21] who published a widely reported evaluation of the Lavidge and Steiner model five years after its promulgation. The first of his three most fundamental objections, all based on *a priori* reasoning, is that the progression from one step in a hierarchy to the next does not necessarily mean a greater probability of eventual action. His second is that, in particular circumstances such as impulse-buying, the deliberate step-by-step progression implied by the model may actually be 'telescoped'. The third objection is that he could find no conclusive evidence in the literature for the proposition that affective changes (Level IV responses) necessarily preceded change in behaviour, rather than resulting from it. By thus exposing an untested assumption, he calls into

question the very sequence of the hierarchical progression, and hence the stimulus-response basis of the models; his third criticism is certainly the most important of the three.

Over the last quarter-century, Ehrenberg has published empirical findings and theoretical analyses that support Palda's doubts about sequence;[22] Murray[23] provides a useful summary of the work up to the end of the 1970s. The field research has been careful and extensive, although it involves a limited range of product categories – commodities such as bread and petrol, and fast-moving consumer goods – and no services. Ehrenberg's view is that, once the decision to try a new product has been arrived at, probably somewhat arbitrarily, and provided the first trial is not an unsatisfactory experience, a stable pattern of reselection develops. The user then deliberately pays attention to advertising for the product (and presumably other marketing communications initiatives), which in turn reinforces the choice. Thus, action (Level VI) determines attention (Level I), which reinforces conviction (Level V). The hierarchy is violated. Ehrenberg and his co-workers have derived a series of mathematical models from their empirical data to express this view more rigorously, and summarised them in a simple verbal model: attention → trial → reinforcement.

Ray[24] takes the argument further by proposing that three variations in hierarchical sequence are possible, according to circumstances:

'Learning'	: cognitive → affective → conative
'Dissonance-attribution'	: conative → affective → cognitive
'Low involvement'	: cognitive → conative → affective

The learning version corresponds to the conventional think-feel-do hierarchical models. He argues that it holds true when the advertising is salient for the audience and there are clear differences among the options available. The dissonance-attribution version, do-feel-think and therefore exactly the reverse of the learning version, will apply when the advertising is salient and the differences are small. In such circumstances, choice has to be based on some factor other than advertising; thereafter, attitudes modify in order to reduce dissonance if satisfaction is not delivered in use; finally, cognitive responses to the advertising are rearranged. This is close to Ehrenberg's view. Ray believes the low involvement version, think-do-feel, applies if salience is low and the differences are small. Low involvement implies lowered perceptual defences, permitting advertising to rearrange cognitions (awareness, recall); when a choice is due, the best remembered option is selected; thereafter, attitudes steadily modify to reinforce the choice. In laboratory experiments, Ray could find evidence for only the first and third variants; the conventional hierarchies thus received some support and the Ehrenbergian version was rejected. A decade earlier, Krugman[25] had argued that what was in fact a 'low involvement' sequence best explained responses to television advertising in particular, though in the context of distinctively American styles of execution and patterns of viewing.

As a final criticism of the seven prevalent hierarchical models (and, indeed, the variants proposed), we might object that they tend to contradict the hypothesis that marketing communication is a transaction, formulated and defended earlier in this chapter. Even with the refinements suggested in Table 13.3, there remains a strong implication that marketing communications initiatives propel passive targets inexorably up a hierarchy of responses and through a sequence of altered behaviour states.

Despite the many objections and variations reported, the conventional 'learning' hierarchies – in particular AIDA, Dagmar and Lavidge and Steiner's – still dominate the frame of reference of typical practitioners and the conceptual frameworks of those textbooks which make any effort at all to explain how market communications initiatives are thought to work. It was reported to the 1991 Annual Conference of the Market Research Society that 38 per cent of practitioners in a field survey sample had endorsed the simple hierarchical view.

Such adherence to a model at best simplistic and at worst defective is a fact of *practice* which

has to be accepted as such until a better alternative explanation, sufficiently straightforward and robust to hold the promise of applicability, can be offered to practitioners. For the meantime, the hierarchy of effects at least provides a common, codified and consistent conceptual framework for practitioners. But its ultimate value is determined by the degree to which performance characteristics derived from it can be made operational: what do impact, involvement, communication, empathy, persuasion and motivation consist of? The answer must for the present remain, as Palda first recognised, that followers of hierarchical principle do not really know. On balance, then, the consolidated version presented in Table 13.3 may be considered a *useful* conceptual aid but not necessarily a *valid* model.

People as information processors

The preamble to this section stated the intention to investigate how audiences 'process' information and opinion received at the synapse. As we have just seen, the conceptual framework prevailing in the marketing communications business does not actually do that. However, the term itself is a signpost to another direction in social psychology which holds the promise of explaining what the hierarchy only describes: *information processing theory*, in which 'purchase and consumption decisions are viewed in terms of how individuals acquire, organise, and use information'.[26] It is inherent in this approach that consumers – who consume marketing communications as well as products – are not passive 'target audiences' but active seekers and users of information. This reinforces the position already emphatically adopted by this chapter.

Figure 13.5 is a simplified representation of information-processing behaviour, synthesised from several sources. Like Table 13.3, it is a micro-model within the macro-model, located at the synapse. The sequence of information-

Figure 13.5.   *Information-processing behaviour*

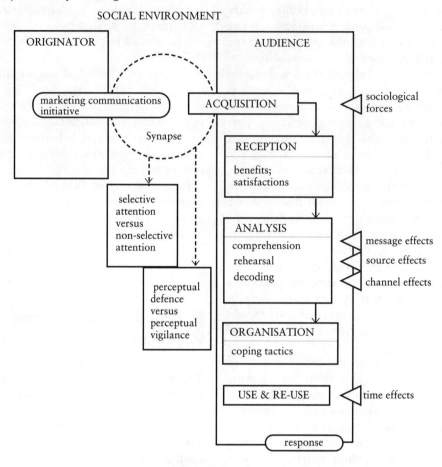

processing operations is triggered by the stimulus of a marketing commmunication initiative.

We have already noted that the 'information' it provides is not likely to consist only of hard facts but also of softer clues and cues for the audience to detect and follow. This alternative to the hierarchy-of-effects model will nevertheless be described hereafter as the 'information-processing model', partly because the terminology is well established in the social psychology literature from which it has been borrowed but, more practically, because no workable substitute for 'information' comes readily to mind in this context.

■ Acquisition and reception

'Acquisition' of a stimulus available at the synapse will not occur unless it is noticed, of course, the point made in five of the eight models in Figure 13.2. Starch observed that an advertisement had to be seen if any progress was to be made further up the hierarchy of effects; Colley specified that a state of 'unawareness' typically preceded awareness; McGuire made 'presentation' (by the advertiser) a necessary precondition of 'attention' (by the audience); Sandage & Fryburger and Preston & Thorson included 'exposure' as the lowest level of their hierarchies. The other three and the consolidated model in Table 13.3 assume that the stimulus has at least been noticed, by starting the sequence of events at 'attention', 'awareness' or 'impact'. A vital ingredient of marketing communications planning is to formulate strategies for achieving that initial impetus, so that the initiative does impinge upon the audience's consciousness and has the chance to progress to the later stages of information processing. This is the concern of advertising media planners and creative directors, of the writers of press releases, of the designers of direct-mail shots, of sales-pitch scriptwriters and so on.

Provided bad strategy does not render an initiative invisible, the probability that it will pass into the audience's consciousness is high. The sociological analysis of the originator-audience transaction undertaken earlier in this chapter came to the conclusion that the audience for marketing communications is a sophisticated one (in Britain and other similar societies, at least), which is unconcerned about advertising, professes to approve of it if asked, likes advertisements on the whole, and is an active partner in an intellectual transaction with advertisers rather than a passive recipient of messages. In short, it subconsciously feels able to cope with the consequences of 'acquiring' advertisers' initiatives and therefore does not engage in deliberate avoidance behaviour.

It would not be unreasonable to argue that people are less sanguine about other kinds of marketing communication and therefore less likely to acquire the corresponding initiatives quite so automatically. Their reaction to editorial publicity, advertising posters, sales promotions, sponsorship, direct mail shots, second-hand car salesmen, telesales callers and unsolicited fax messages may perhaps be ranged on a spectrum from attention by default (taking in the gist of a television commercial while talking on the telephone, for instance) to non-attention by design. To put this another way, as Figure 13.5 does in summary, circumstances will determine whether the audience is perceptually defensive or positively vigilant and whether their attention is selective or virtually random. The process of consumer socialisation can be expected to result in a steady shift over time from defence to acceptance with respect to each technical innovation with which marketing communications strategists hope to regain the upper hand.

Once a marketing communications initiative has passed from the synapse into the audience's consciousness, the next event in the information-processing system, 'reception', will take place if the content is perceived to be salient in the context of current consumer-behaviour pre-occupations and if it promises to have some practical utility. If not, the initiative will have been acquired willingly enough but no more than that. Reception is the stage at which audiences 'receive' the 'information' in the stimulus, potentially including not only the soft cues as well as the hard facts but also non-informative benefits and satisfactions such as entertainment, vicarious experience and a behavioural lead.

Marketing communications strategists would do well to pay careful attention to the distinction between acquisition and reception, rather than concentrating as narrow-mindedly as they appear to on 'impact' and 'grabbing attention'. The information-processing model of audience response suggests that attention is easily gained but interest and involvement need to be won.

An analogy may help to clarify the concepts of acquisition and reception. It would be seen as an act of eccentricity to block up one's letterbox. Yet we know that the mail can deliver unwelcome and even unpleasant experiences. Familiarity with the system has bred the sophistication to weigh that outcome against the possibility that it will contain expected communications and pleasant surprises. We therefore permit the post to enter our private space uninvited, in the expectation that we will later be able to ignore or reject the contents if they prove to be neither salient nor useful. In short, people normally 'acquire' post as a matter of course but do not necessarily 'receive' the contents.

■ Analysis: comprehension

If a marketing communications initiative achieves both acquisition and reception, 'analysis' can follow. The first operation within this process is 'comprehension' of the 'message' contained in the initiative, corresponding to the third level of the hierarchy of effects. This description can be taken to relate mainly to the strictly informative elements of the content. Where more abstract cues are concerned, analysis will involve the more complex operation of 'decoding', which we shall return to in due course. Comprehension is not in itself entirely straightforward, however. In practice, post-testing of a campaign can reveal not only non-comprehension but also miscomprehension: a gap between the 'message' the originator intended to convey by apparently hard facts and the 'meaning' constructed by the audience. Far from acting as the passive recipients implied by the hierarchy-of-effects model, they are, as one industry commentator put it, prone to perverse and wilful misinterpretation. Tone-of-voice, mood, ambience, the very 'creativity' of the execution, and a host of other variables explain the incongruence rather than simple misunderstanding, of course, and pose a strategic challenge not even hinted at by the hierarchy-of-effects model.

■ Analysis: rehearsal

Analysis of comprehended material proceeds by means of an operation described as 'rehearsal', which entails association of the comprehended information with previously processed information held in the memory, in order to frame 'support arguments' and 'counterarguments' with respect to the proposition contained in the communication. In other words, the individual is now prepared to self-persuade – or not, as the case may be. The arguments deployed are not developed wholly objectively, but are modulated by 'predispositions' stored in the memory, which are in turn formed by combinations of attitudes, beliefs, personal values and socially conditioned norms of behaviour, and by previous experience relevant to the current communication.

Relevant predispositions may not in fact be available to perform this modulation, for lack of related prior experience or for some other reason. In that case, according to Sternthal and Craig,[27] the information-processing consumer may decide to try the advocated product or service without passing through the remaining stages of the ideal

sequence, in order to acquire the necessary experience. This recognition of exceptional situations recalls the variations on the hierarchy-of-effects sequence proposed by Palda and by Ray and Ehrenberg, discussed in the previous section. Presumably, the full cycle of information-processing behaviour will be short-circuited in this way only in conditions of comparatively low risk and price.

The rehearsal process is mediated not only by the 'endogenous variables' which form an audience's cognitive predispositions but also by 'exogenous variables' related to the stimulus itself. These can be classified as *source effects*, *channel effects* and *message effects*.

Message formulation is the only part of the marketing communications process that is more or less wholly under the originator's control and is consequently dealt with in considerable detail by a variety of managerially orientated textbooks published in the 1970s and 1980s.[28] This is all to the good, for practitioners' ignorance of the theoretical principles too often encourages the creative process to develop a logic of its own and miscomprehension or non-comprehension to result. Message effects are normally discussed in terms of 'codes', 'appeals' and 'structure'.

Drawing upon the abundant literature of social communication, the various authors describe the principles of verbal and 'nonverbal' or 'paralinguistic' coding. The former entails study of denotative and connotative meanings of words and phrases; the latter concerns modulation of verbal meaning by such agencies as tone of voice, cadence, personal appearance and 'body language'. Manifestly absent from text treatments are three non-human coding elements: typography, colour and sound-effects (including music). The omission is almost certainly accounted for by the fact that the source literature concerns itself exclusively with social persuasion, in which those elements are either absent altogether or relatively insignificant. A field experiment reported in the marketing literature compares recall and intention-to-purchase in test subjects exposed to respectively black-and-white and colour-monochrome press advertisements for a canned food, and a paper on advertisements directed at children theorises that jingles work by enhancing participation. Otherwise, empirical evidence is not easily found.

There is a serious need for examination of the literature of graphic design and musical composition, to suggest preliminary hypotheses about the *modus operandi* of these codes, and marketing-specific experiments to test them. The lack of a theoretical basis for this aspect of message formulation has two unsatisfactory practical consequences: first, strikingly arbitrary use of typography and music in many advertisements and television commercials (less obvious in the case of radio); second, a marked bias towards copy at the expense of design in many advertising and sales promotion agencies' creative departments.

The texts deal with the topic of message appeals in terms of the very familiar dichotomy between 'rational' and 'emotional', with its roots in the Aristotelian concepts of pathos and logos. Evidence for the relative effectiveness of the two turns out to be equivocal, to say the least. Only four empirical investigations are cited by the three texts collectively. These were conducted between 1935 and 1960, all in a non-marketing context. Two contradict one another and the other two come to no firm conclusion. It is observable that advertisers and salespeople can seldom resist the temptation to deploy an emotional appeal, even within an ostensibly rational argument. Yet there is a general problem with this strategy, explained by Percy and Rossiter[29] with particular respect to the fear that the relationship between the strength of an emotional appeal and its effectiveness is non-linear; both weaker and stronger expressions of the appeal are less effective, for different reasons.

Only two categories of emotional appeal are discussed in the texts: fear and humour. Sex-appeal and snob-appeal, both easily observable in advertisements and sales promotion material, are not acknowledged. Where fear appeals are concerned, a study by Janis and Feshbach[30] seems to have found a permanent place in advertising folklore, despite a much later investigation by Ray and Wilkie[31] that contradicted it. The former concluded, on the basis of experiments involving messages about dental hygiene delivered by 'live' presenters to a student audience, that effectiveness had an inverse linear relationship to the strength of the appeal. Advertising-specific experiments by the latter led them to conclude that 'moderate' fear appeals would be most effective. A conceptual weakness of any such studies, not generally mentioned in the authors' reviews, is the difficulty of grading the strength of a fear appeal objectively. There is certainly room for doubt that Janis and Feshbach's 'strong' appeals were in fact any stronger than Ray and Wilkie's 'moderate' appeals.

Many case examples that have been widely disseminated verbally demonstrate remarkably convoluted efforts to avoid any hint of an appeal to fear in advertisements for toothpaste, air travel and life assurance. In contrast, an unarguably strong fear appeal was used in a 1979 anti-smoking advertisement: the headline 'ashes to ashes', with reinforcing graphics. Pre-testing showed that the appeal evoked correspondingly strong perceptual defences of selective misperception or, if that was countered by changing some elements of the design, wilful rationalisation. The researchers noted that the negative nature of the action demanded – 'stop smoking' instead of, for example, 'brush your teeth' – complicated the conclusions to be drawn.[32]

In the case of humour as an appeal, the texts report a careful review of the literature by Sternthal and Craig,[33] which led them to mainly negative conclusions: that humorous treatments are no more persuasive than serious versions of the same message and may detrimentally affect comprehension. Their only definitely positive finding was some evidence that humour could 'distract' the audience from rehearsing counterarguments. Despite this, humour remains a very popular ingredient of marketing communications in practice – including sales pitches, if in moderation.

The Scottish Health Education Group adopted a humorous approach for its first 'general life style' advertising campaign in 1978. This was a deliberate decision, based not on the notion of distraction but on the accepted psychological explanation of laughter as a means of releasing tension. Their researchers conceded that conceptualisation of the mechanism is again rendered more complicated by the fact that the message is negative: don't behave this way if you value your health.[34]

Although sex-appeal is not treated by the texts under review, some relevant studies have been conducted. Most researchers set out to relate sex-appeals of graded intensity in advertisements to audience responses such as awareness, recall, perceived quality of the product and perceived reputability of the advertiser; a few tried to identify the components of sex-appeal, none successfully addressed the question of how the appeal achieved its effect. This lack of applicable knowledge notwithstanding, it can easily be observed that sex-appeals are at least as usual in practice as fear or humour appeal. They are especially common in advertising and sales promotion for industrial products and services, where relevance to their nature and use is not part of the rationale.

Discussing message structure, the texts under review examine 'polarity', 'order' and 'completion'. *Polarity* is treated in terms of the relative persuasiveness of one-sided versus two-sided arguments. Research studies conducted more than forty years ago by Hovland and his colleagues[35] are cited in support of the proposition that persuasiveness is mediated by audience characteristics such as general intellectual capacity and initial stance on the issue in question. What is seldom made clear enough is that the original experiments involved arguments about military tactics and an audience of soldiers. A marginally more recent study, reported by one text only, did involve advertisements for cars, cookers and floor polishes.[36] But the test audience was students, who would not normally be experienced users of such products. In any case, observation of current advertising suggests that the two-sided variant is almost never used in practice; presumably the fear of being seen to own up to weaknesses outweighs any knowledge of the possible benefits of two-sided argumentation. This objection can be expected to apply equally to sales pitches.

Order concerns 'recency' versus 'primacy', or the relative persuasiveness of 'climax' and 'anti-climax' order: respectively saving the best argument to the end or putting it at the beginning. The authors report that 'Lund's Law of Primacy in Persuasion' ruled unchallenged from 1925 until the 1950s, when a burst of experimentation identified such intervening variables as interest, familiarity, salience and the nature of the topic. Rosnow and Robinson[37] finally concluded, on the basis of all available evidence, that climax order is indicated if the intervening variables are positive, anticlimax order if not. In practice, one suspects that advertising and sales promotion copy is conceived by copywriters as a 'story' rather than an 'argument'. Stories conventionally build to a climax or denouement; copy does likewise in imitation and not because of Rosnow and Robinson. Sales pitches, on the other hand, probably can be thought of as arguments, and the classic experiments will have more relevance.

It is noticeable that the texts devote no attention at all to visual order – that is, disposition of the graphic elements of an advertisement or sales promotion piece. This unfortunately reinforces the verbal bias of practitioners, already noted. As in the case of visual coding, exploitation of source literature in the graphic design field is urgently needed.

Completion concerns the relative persuasive merits of leaving an argument open-ended and drawing an explicit conclusion. Several experimental studies conducted between the 1950s and the 1970s are cited, including a second series by Hovland and colleagues;[38] again, none took place in a marketing context. The general conclusion is, as before, that intervening variables mediate the response. A 'rule' is offered, that arguments should be closed when intellectual capacity is low, complexity high and salience low.

One is obliged to be sceptical about the applicability of the reported empirical evidence to marketing communications practice, because almost all the experiments involved neither marketing communications initiatives as stimuli nor typical consumers as audiences. Two further objections relate especially to advertisements and may not invalidate transfer of the general findings to the formulation of sales pitches, publicity releases or sales promotion pieces. First, they do not typically deploy arguments of the sort presented on such topics as military tactics or dental hygiene; the concepts of polarity, order and completion prove difficult to apply in practice. Second, a high proportion of all advertisements contain relatively little 'copy'. Posters generally rely on headlines only, and one famous campaign of considerable duration has used no words at all (Benson & Hedges Special Filter). In these cases, the concepts are wholly inapplicable. Even in real examples with more wording, practical exercises with our own students have shown that message structures defy analysis according to theoretical principles. The practical relevance to advertising copywriting of the texts under consideration must therefore be severely limited. For the present, there is no body of theoretical knowledge that might permit scientific evaluation of such prevalent structural fashions as: ultra-short sentences, artifically punctuated; 'clever' headlines; boastful straplines; introverted style; arbitrary line-breaks.

Turning to the issue of *source effect*, the texts under review introduce the intuitively reasonable proposition that an audience's response is determined not only by its own characteristics and those of the message but also by its perception of the source of the message. Most of the empirical evidence cited in support of generalisations about source effect consists of experiments in persuasive *social* communication. In these cases, the source of the message is always clearly either a person or an organisation represented by a speaker. In marketing communication, the source can be ambiguous, even compound. It may perhaps be seen as a firm, a presenter (or sales representative), an actor playing a part, the brand itself, or some combination of these. Counterproductive interaction is a distinct possibility in practice. Social-communication experimenters furthermore assume that a target audience will rate a source either credible or not. In the marketing context, the audience can be expected to rate the source neither wholly credible nor wholly non-credible, and a sliding scale of credibility must be visualised. The literature does not recognise this shortcoming of its source material.

There is general agreement that source effect has three components, though terminological confusion can make it seem that more are postulated. These are 'credibility', 'attractiveness' and 'power'. It is argued that source *credibility* operates by evoking a response of 'internalisation' on the audience's part: the source's perceived values and behaviour are accepted and in part adopted. This process has already been suggested as one of the benefits to be derived by audiences from marketing communications initiatives. The consensus of an extensive literature, in which Hovland and various fellow-researchers again figure prominently, is that credibility is determined by perceived 'expertise' and perceived 'objectivity' (often called 'trustworthiness').

Expertise must be relevant, of course. When a company or salesperson is seen to be the source, this will not generally pose a problem; when a presenter intervenes, as in much television advertising, there is a strong chance that it will. Thus, this credibility dimension is by no means as straightforward in practice as it appears in social communication theory.

Where objectivity is concerned, the reported finding of empirical studies (not conducted in a marketing setting) is that sometimes 'blatant attempts to persuade' are more effective in producing change in attitude or behaviour than the more 'commonsense' notion of minimising persuasive intent.[39] This is just as well for the formulators of sales pitches, of course, and good news for advertisers. Three experiments from the 1960s are further reported to have surprisingly found that generally low-credibility sources were more effective persuaders than high-credibility sources. They were not conducted in a marketing context either, however, and it would be a rash marketing communicator who adopted a deliberate low-credibility strategy.

Source *attractiveness* is thought to operate by evoking a response of 'identification' on the audience's part. Reported empirical investigations concern the attractiveness of persons, not organisations. It is a moot question whether or not people in fact assess companies as attractive or unattractive and will identify with them or not, but there is evidence that advertisers do think so:

'friendly' building societies and 'caring' stores. The use of presenters may also be interpreted as a tactic to provide audience with a human surrogate with which to identify. The consensus of an extensive literature, again exclusively non-marketing, is that source attractiveness is determined by perceived 'similarity' and 'familiarity'. Observation suggests that presenters and endorsers are seldom similar to the target audience. We may therefore extend the original argument by postulating that they represent an ideal self or fantasy self. As for familiarity, the evidence contradicts the old adage that it breeds contempt; this is an encouraging rationale for recall as an advertising objective, repetition as a scheduling strategy and persistence in a salesperson. A study by Zimbardo and others[40] which unexpectedly showed that an unattractive source is more persuasive is widely quoted. Before this is taken as vindication of the Procter & Gamble school of television advertising, it should be noted that the experiment actually involved 'persuasion' to eat fried grasshoppers by strong authority figures.

Source *power* evokes the response of compliance. At first sight, it seems unlikely that advertisers or salespeople could wield power over an audience, but the instruments of power are punishment and reward, and it is the latter that can be relevant in the marketing context. Furthermore, the almost universal use of male presenters to female advertising audiences may be a subconsciously executed power ploy, given the power accorded to men by the social conditioning of women in many sections of society.

There is an evident possibility of conflict among the components of source effect in practice; high credibility might coincide with low attractiveness, for instance. If so, there is non-marketing empirical evidence that attractiveness prevails.[41] On the other hand, it seems equally reasonable to expect synergy if the combinations are right.

Before finally leaving the topic of source effect, it will be as well to re-emphasise a caveat introduced into the discussion at several stages: virtually every one of the empirical studies on which the authors under review have based their theoretical explanations of marketing communication and their consequent strategic frameworks was concerned with *social* persuasion. Percy and Rossiter's 363-item bibliography contains only thirty-six references specific to *marketing* persuasion, for instance. The texts thus rest extremely heavily on an assumption of the transferability of findings from the one context to the other.

If it can be shown that an audience's response to a marketing communications initiative is affected by perceptions of the credibility, attractiveness and power of the source, it is reasonable to propose that it will similarly be mediated by perceptions of the channel through which it is transmitted – for example, the media vehicle or the sales representative. Indeed some authors regard these channels as one of several sources recognised by the audience, or alternate between treating them as channels and as sources.[42] *Channel effect* is also one main theme of McLuhan's essay, 'The Medium is the Message',[43] a cult success of the 1960s that has been surprisingly neglected by marketing academics. A contemporary survey of American practitioners demonstrated strong majority agreement with the statement that 'the attitudes of readers toward a magazine can greatly influence their reaction to advertisements in it'.[44] In practice, British media planners certainly accept the message-modifying potential of vehicles in the channel, implicitly, when they use such adjectives as 'relaxed', 'urgent' or 'chatty' to describe types of newspaper, or discuss 'media values' and 'rub-off effects' in their professional journals.[45] Nevertheless, the virtual absence of an organised body of formalised knowledge, such as does exist in the case of source effect, obliges practitioners to make media selections 'on the basis of intuition and folklore'.[46]

Authors who do discuss the components of media effect generally deduce them by analogy with source effect. Aaker and Myers suggest 'unbiasedness', 'expertise', 'prestige' and 'mood created',[47] while Percy and Rossiter offer 'identification', which is the response corresponding to 'attractiveness' as a dimension of source credibility.[48] McLuhan's celebrated 'hot/cool' categorisation refers to the degree to which media involve their audience, from which a 'power' component might be deduced. Consolidating, we find a familiar trio: credibility (unbiasedness, expertise, prestige), attractiveness and power. There is empirical evidence only for the first of these. It has been found that: doctors were more influenced by editorial in technical journals than by the same material in general magazines, a finding relevant to publicity initiatives; media planners rated medical journals very differently on sixteen attributes related to media effect; high-prestige magazines had a more positive effect on consumers' evaluations of promotional messages than low-prestige magazines; housewives' perceptions of the expertise and prestige of general magazines affected their perceptions of the expected price, quality and reliability of advertised products. Another study found that response to television or radio commercials could be similarly mediated by perceptions of surrounding programmes.

The dearth of experimental support for the reviewed explanations of channel effect is explained by the fact, becoming a tiresome truism in this chapter, that the authors have drawn mostly upon the literature of *social* persuasion. In that context, no channel vehicles intervene – or, at least, none with obvious mediating potential. It is not entirely clear whether no marketing-specific research has in fact been carried out, or whether it has but is not yet reported.

Interactions between audience and source and audience and channel do not take place in isolation, of course, but in turn interact with one another. The outcome may be synergy, but could equally be counter-synergy. The textbooks do not deal with this complication well, if at all. The key to understanding the resolution of the many forces involved lies in 'cognitive consistency theory'. A single chapter does not permit an adequate explanation here, but Lowe Watson[49] provides a complete and conveniently accessible one, specifically relating to advertising.

■ Analysis: decoding

The literature of message effects, reviewed earlier, makes the tacit assumption that the audience simply decodes an encoded message, that the end product assembled from the kit supplied by the originator takes exactly the intended form. In practice, matters are seldom so straightforward and miscomprehension is as likely an outcome as comprehension. This is especially so when marketing communications strategists fall victim to genre conformity and the self-indulgent cult of 'creativity', consequently encoding the message in their own visual and verbal language, not the audience's. They would benefit greatly from study of an established sociological discipline that is for the present familiar only to the intellectual wing of the advertising business, consisting of advertising agency 'planners' and the readership of *Admap*.

Semiotics (or 'semiology') is concerned in effect with the grammar and syntax of signs and symbols, rather than words. Its main objective is to 'deconstruct' assemblages of signs and symbols so as to arrive at their intrinsic meaning. Advertisements are a popular subject for deconstruction. As one exponent puts it, 'by deconstructing an ad we learn how it was constructed and discover the underlying message, and can thus determine how ads work'.[50] It will always be a moot point in practice whether a given advertisement has been constructed purposefully, with some theoretical framework or conventional genre in mind, however vaguely, or whether its structure has been arrived at haphazardly, by intuition and inspiration. The potential relevance to the strategic planning and execution of advertising campaigns and other forms of marketing communications initiative is nevertheless clear enough, especially if the stimulus contains as little conventional narrative verbal material as many a poster or magazine advertisement, a pack design or the identification of a sponsor.

It is therefore surprising that the general principles of semiotics are not more widely familiar in the business, even though they are admittedly rendered somewhat inaccessible to interested ousiders by the difficulty of the semioticians' working vocabulary. Umiker-Sebeok's American textbook[51] provides an invaluable framework for the application of the discipline to marketing communications, but in language as disconcertingly unfamiliar as the author's own name is unconventional. The British writer most closely associated with the deconstruction of advertisements is Williamson.[52] She was the first accessible author to acknowledge, in the nineteen-seventies, that the typical audience was conversant with advertising, at ease with the jargon of the business, appreciative of advertisements as a popular art form, and quick to spot accidental mistakes. In her view, the deconstructive capability of acedemic semioticians differed from the performance of ordinary consumers of advertising only in the degree of sophistication of explanation and not in kind. The most readable introduction to semiotics in relation to marketing communications is a 22-page chapter in Dyer's paperback, *Advertising as Communication*.[53] Because the constraints of a single chapter unfortunately preclude the analysis of case examples necessary for further explanation of semiotic deconstruction, scanning of the second two texts is strongly recommended.

■ Organisation

Provided that the analysis of an acquired and received input has not been frustrated by circumstances, it will be followed by 'organisation' of the comprehended, rehearsed and decoded content. This operation is essentially a device for coping with the volume of material which demands to be transferred from the short-term working memory to the long-term storage memory, along with the mass of information of quite different kinds being processed more or less simultaneously.

It consists of the subconscious deployment of a set of four 'decision rules', which are an innate constituent of human intellectual ability. The 'linear compensatory' rule is an optimising procedure, which consists of scoring all options on every collective attribute judged relevant to the choice. Though easy enough to represent algebraically, this would presumably be an extremely taxing mental task in practice, bearing in mind that it could only be allocated a limited period of mental real-time. The remaining three rules are all satisficing routines and therefore perhaps more realistic. In the 'conjunctive' variant, the total range of attributes is reduced to a manageable number and all options rated on each remaining dimension. The 'disjunctive' rule reduces the number of options to be considered by fixing a threshold level on each dimension and summarily rejecting any which fails to reach that level on any one of them. The most simplified variant, the 'lexicographic' rule, selects one attribute as a more salient criterion than all others and then scores the options on that single dimension only.

When the foundations of present-day marketing communications practice were being laid, mass consumption had not yet reached modern levels and the second information explosion (Gutenberg having started the first) had not yet happened. Today, product choice is greatly increased and marketing communications initiatives proliferate relentlessly. Despite all advances in education, the capacity of the human mind has not expanded commensurately; we are intellectually scarcely any better equipped than our grandparents. About twenty years ago, Miller[54] was struck by the fact that human ability to discriminate among related stimuli or memorise inventories was highly consistent across a range of experiments reported by other psychologists: the ceiling on performance was always close to seven separate 'pieces' of information. He was further intrigued by the amount of circumstantial evidence to suggest a general rule and one can easily produce instances from one's own experience. We can distinguish seven colours in the visible spectrum and seven tones in the musical scale; we have fixed the week at seven days; we sort objects into dozens and half-dozens; market researchers' rating scales seldom have more than seven positions; telephone numbers do not exceed seven digits without the STD code and car registration plates typically contain three numbers and four letters, in Britain; there are seven examples in this list, which would seem to be too long if it were continued any further. Thus, Miller proposed that the upper limit to the amount of information the mind can handle in any one context is fixed by 'the magical number of seven, plus or minus two'. Despite his excellent academic reputation, we may feel intuitively that the figure is too pessimistic to apply in the marketing situation, when the audience voluntarily seeks out information for decision-making purposes rather than being asked to memorise irrelevant inventories. However, Wright points out that present-day consumers have to operate under considerable general pressure and amid unprecedented communicative hubbub: they are 'harassed decision makers.[55] Consequently, they must either go mad or devise some ploy to enable themselves to *cope*. It is an observable fact that the great majority do cope, and information-processing theory provides the framework for explaining how.

The audience's coping strategy is, first, to ignore information that cannot satisfy the criterion of utility, already explained, to reject and forget any 'acquired' information that does not meet the salience criterion, and then to reject any 'received' information that cannot be comprehended. To phrase this in hierarchy-of-effects terms, only a proportion of all marketing communications initiatives will produce the responses of attention, interest and comprehension; to use another familiar teminology, selective attention and preception are at work. These tactics reduce sensory overload to an amount of material that can be stored in the permanent memory and periodically retrieved for the purposes of further analysis. When the time comes for its use as a decision-making input, however, the implication of Miller's and Wright's hypotheses is that the amount of part-processed and stored information will exceed the capacity of the 'current file', and further coping tactics will be needed. The key to their nature lies in how decision rules decided earlier are deployed: the more complex the decision and the more harassed the decision-maker, the more simple the operation. Indeed, Wright seems to suggest that the marketing situation will almost invariably invoke the brutally simplified *lexicographic* rule, in which choice hinges on how options rate with respect to one attribute only among all those retailed by the competing marketing communications.

Two American advertising practitioners have coined the vivid and highly descriptive phrase 'a ladder in the mind' to describe the outcome.[56]

Figure 13.6 applies their concept to a choice among models of car. Each ladder is labelled with the single product attribute subconsciously rated most important, the competing options are placed on the rungs on the basis of received and organised information, and the one on the top rung is chosen. If it happens not to be available locally or in the preferred colour, the second-rung occupant will simply be promoted. This explanation is perhaps too draconian for most real situations, however. There is ample evidence that consumers view brands not as unidimensional entities, but as multidimensional. It seems more likely, in that case, that the *conjunctive* aggregation rule will be employed first: the mind will create a limited number of separate ladders, each labelled with one of the attributes common to the brands under consideration, and the options will be independently ranked on all of them.

The 'ladders' configuration may be held in the permanent memory store and revised periodically as salient information is newly received, or it may be used immediately. In either event, the final choice seems likely to be made by employing either the *disjunctive* rule, which reduces the complexity by removing from contention the contenders on the lower rungs of the existing ladders, or the *lexicographic*. We can intuitively agree wih Wright that, given the surfeit of informtion available to prospective car purchasers, *linear compensatory* aggregation is out of the question. This analysis has thus added to the previous description of information-processing theory the notion that decision rules may be deployed in combination and episodically.

However, the general principles of information processing are not straightforwardly applicable to marketing communications practice. General cognitive theory predicts that rank order of preference, once established, will be highly resistant to reordering by outside agencies such as marketing communications initiatives. This being so, head-on competition as a marketing communications tactic is unlikely to persuade individual prospects to rearrange the ladders in their minds. Lateral thinking on the part of the originators of the concept has suggested a radical alternative to the

Figure 13.6.   *Coping with information overload: 'ladders in the mind'*

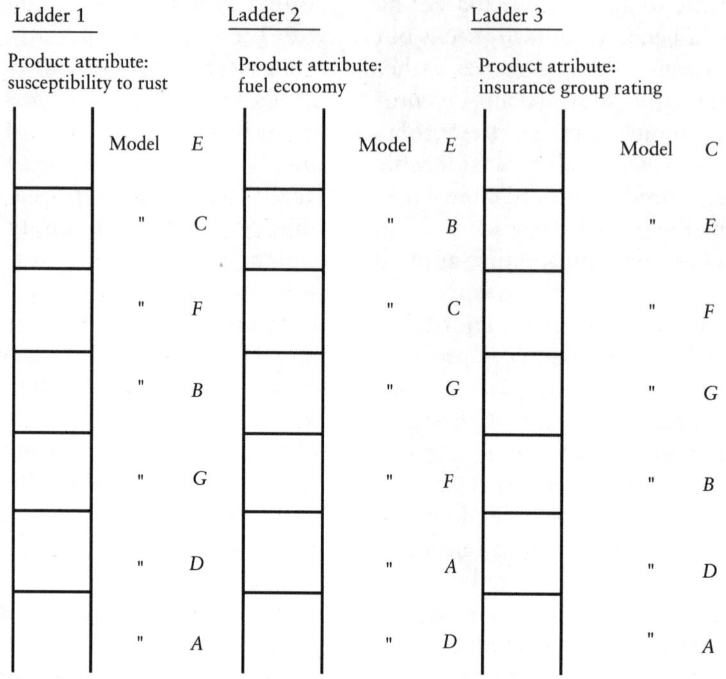

Ladder 1	Ladder 2	Ladder 3
Product attribute: susceptibility to rust	Product attribute: fuel economy	Product atribute: insurance group rating
Model E	Model E	Model C
" C	" B	" E
" F	" C	" F
" B	" G	" G
" G	" F	" B
" D	" A	" D
" A	" D	" A

locked-horns school of advertising strategy (which can readily be confirmed as very prevalent by simple observation). They advocate the introduction of an entirely *new* ladder into the prospect's mind: an attribute that has not previously been thought of as a way of evaluating products in the class. By being the first to propose it, the advertiser stands a very good chance of capturing the top rung immediately. The success of the initiative then depends on which decision rule or rules the individual prospects use to manipulate the new ladder and the existing ones, but the high probability of failure that accompanies occupation of a lower rung on any ladder has at least been totally avoided.

The new ladder must be salient, of course, otherwise, the advertising message will not pass beyond acquisition to reception. Intuition may be enough to ensure this in a handful of cases, but it will generally be necessary to derive it from formative research procedures such as group discussion or perceptual mapping. Furthermore, the transition from concept to execution can too

easily be spoiled by the reintroduction of overburdening information which obscures the basic proposition. It is a fundamental lesson of information-processing theory that any marketing communications initiative should be used like a rapier, not as a blunt intrument with which to batter the audience senseless. This conclusion clearly contradicts the conventional wisdom of the advertising business with respect to our working example, cars.

The Avis Rent-a-Car advertising campaign of the 1970s provides an instructive case example of an implemented new ladders strategy.[57]

■ Use and re-use

With the organisation of acquired, received and analysed inputs complete, we reach the final stage in the information-processing model, the 'use' of the organised material for decision-making purposes (if a given input is in fact ever used for that particular purpose).

In the information-processing literature, 'utilisation' is closely linked to 'behaviour', implying that the act of consumption inevitably and immediately concludes a single cycle of informtion processing. But let us now remind ourselves that this chapter is concerned with the consumption of marketing communications initiatives, not of products or services. The former is a prelude to the latter, certainly; but equally the latter is not an immediate consequence of the former. Marketing communications initiatives may be processed and used in their own right several times before they are finally involved in choice among a range of products or services available. Practitioners acknowledge this fact implicitly; for instance, advertisements do not normally appear once only, but in *campaigns*; this is even true of most recruitment advertising and 'small ads'. The object may be to maximise numbers in the audience who have a chance to see the advertisement at least once, to expose at least some of them to it more than once, or to present a series of different treatments of the message in sequence. In all typical situations, then, part of the audience will be exposed more than once during a given period. Furthermore, although retail sales assistants may expect to close the sale or lose it in a single transaction, field sales representatives normally expect to make more than one call on each prospect. Consider two more facts: that sales promotion initiatives, such as calendars or bookmarks, may well be referred to repeatedly over a period, and that editorial resulting from a publicity initiative is very often kept for future reference if the topic is especially salient. For all these reasons, a single marketing communications initiative must be conceptualised as one episode in a series of events, and it is reasonable to postulate that audience response will therefore be subject to 'time effects', as well as being mediated by message, source and channel characteristics. The mechanics of learning, remembering and forgetting thus assume theoretical importance.

One way to describe the objective of a marketing communications initiative is that the audience should *learn* new behaviour as a result.

A factor worth singling out from the mass of details in the literature of learning theory is the principle that rewards reinforce learning. In the advertising context, this may provide a straightforward rationale for two particular creative strategies which always precipitate prolonged and usually inconclusive discussion. The rewards offered by 'teaser' campaigns and 'puzzle' advertisements[58] are participation and, upon successful decoding, self-esteem. Similarly, humorous advertisements may offer the reward of entertainment, an alternative to the explanation put forward in the discussion of message appeals. It is a moot point whether or not purchase is the change of behaviour learned as a result of being rewarded, however.

The literature explains that learned responses are not permanent, because of simple forgetting ('decay', in advertising terminology) and the retroactive inhibiting effect of intervening events. Marketing communication strategies for gaining repeat exposure can thus be seen as having the fundamental purpose of reinforcing learning by counteracting the effect of both phenomena.

The first attempt to relate the *scheduling* of advertisements to learning theory was made as long ago as 1912 by Strong,[59] later to originate the AIDA hierarchy-of-effects model. The principal finding of his laboratory experiments was that an optimum scheduling interval could be identified, beyond which forgetting would occur between exposures but below which no improvement in recall (his measure of learning) could be detected. This pioneering work was eventually taken up forty-seven years later by Zielske,[60] whose carefully controlled field experiment initiated a whole series of related studies and led ultimately to formulation of the concepts of *threshold* and *wearout*. It is postulated that no learning takes place until a threshold level of 'advertising pressure' – number of repetitions within a given period. Thereafter, learning is progressive and new behaviour patterns – such as search, trial and purchase – may result, until a saturation level is reached beyond which each repeat exposure produces fewer new learned responses than the previous one. This is the wearout phenomenon. It is easily confused with simple forgetting, but the latter is a function of the passage of time alone, while the former is related to advertising pressure.

The twin concepts are clarified diagrammatically in a thorough literature review by Corkindale and Newall,[61] who also undertook a field survey to investigate their applicability to media scheduling practice in Britain in the mid-1970s. They found that both concepts were seen as salient by more than 80 per cent of respondents, most of whom nevertheless seemed to use informed guesses to fix advertising pressure in terms of *OTS* or *TVRs* (measures of potential exposure), or cost. The majority did not think they would ever enjoy a budget large enough to run the risk of wearout; the researchers disagree, believing that the onset of wearout is earlier than their respondents' guesses, and suggest that many advertisers actually waste a significant fraction of their budgets on counterproductive repetition.

Sixty-two years after E. K. Strong's initial impetus, E. C. Strong[62] combined Zielske's data with his own, devised a set of regression equations, ran a computer simulation of various scheduling patterns and concluded that recall was highest when repetitions were spaced in 'flights' rather than in a continuous series. These two patterns correspond to media planners' alternative strategies, 'burst' and 'drip'.

Since the early 1970s, several computer programs have been developed for scheduling media campaigns, the best known probably being the earliest: MEDIAC.[63] It is important to be clear that the scheduling decision should in practice take account of several variables, among which are competitors' past and future schedules, seasonality, media owners' discount terms, creative treatment and conventional practice. Since none of the software packages in fact incorporates all of these, they should be used only as an aid to decision-making and not as decision-makers. With that caveat, and supposing that computer assistance is a feasible option, it certainly enhances the traditional practices: drawing on past experience, imitating or adapting conventional practice, buying media

owners' off-the-peg solutions, or making symmetrical patterns on a scheduling grid.

Use and re-use of processed inputs provide experience, which is in turn stored in the memory and updates the *predispositions* that will influence the process of 'rehearsal' when comparable information is next 'acquired' from a marketing communications initiative. This feedback loop closes and completes the model information processing, but is omitted from Figure 13.5 for the sake of clarity.

■ The two models compared

The information-processing model enhances the explanatory power of the hierarchy-of-effects, by suggesting *how* and *why* individuals move through a sequence of altered mental states in response to marketing communication, initiatives, but remains entirely compatible with it in so doing. Table 13.4 proposes direct correspondence between four of the five stages in the information-processing model and all six levels of the consolidated hierarchy of effects introduced in Table 13.3. *Acquisition* and *attention* can both be seen as the result of a stimulus satisfying the information-processing criterion of 'utility'; similarly, *reception* and *interest* both imply satisfaction of the criterion of 'salience'. (Sternthal and Craig actually define the reception stage as comprising both 'arousal' and 'attention',[64] the former being a familiar alternative to 'interest' in discussions of the hierarchical principle). At the *analysis* stage of information processing, the message must first satisfy a 'comprehensibility' criterion, unequivocally relating this stage to the *comprehension* level of the hierarchy. If this test is passed, the process of 'rehearsal' can follow, in which the individual marshals arguments and counterarguments, stimulated by the message, in order to self-persuade (or not); this operation seems clearly enough to correspond to both *sympathy* and *conviction* in the hierarchical scheme. *Organisation* has no direct equivalent in the hierarchy of effects. Finally, 'use' corresponds exactly to *action* – provided we recall that the act in question is the consumption and use of marketing

Table 13.4. *Relationship between information-processing theory and the hierarchy of effects*

Stage in information-processing sequence (Figure 13.5)	Level and target response: hierarchy of effects (Table 13.3)
Acquire stimulus	Pay attention
Receive it	Be interested
Comprehend it	Comprehend
Analyse input — Rehearse	
counter-arguments	Feel sympathetic
	Be convinced
Organise data	
Use processed input	Act

communications messages rather than of the product or service to which they refer.

It is now clear that even the most sophisticated available representation of the transaction occurring at the synapse is still firmly rooted in the stimulus-response explanation of human behaviour. What the information-processing model does offer is a more complete conceptual framework, more prospect of rendering the constituent concepts operational, a better chance of valid prediction and measurement, and hence more effective strategic planning of marketing communications initiative.

In this section we have seen that the hierarchy of effects is the almost universal conceptual model, among practitioners, of what happens at the communicator-audience synapse. On its own, it encourages the 'egotistical' view of marketing communications and does not adequately explain how consumers use the practitioners' initiatives. The information-processing model elaborates the hierarchical concept and renders much of it potentially operational. It is thus a promising underpinning for marketing comnmunications strategy and deserves to be more widely studied by practitioners.

■ Measuring effectiveness

To conclude a long chapter on a complex subject, we turn to a final important issue: the measurement of effectiveness. The discussion that follows relates mainly to the considerable inventory of techniques used to evaluate advertising; by comparison, other classes of marketing communications initiative are hardly tested for effectiveness at all.

As in any field of activity, this should be a matter of comparing actual results with *criteria* derived from pre-determined *objectives*. Advertising effectiveness is seldom measured so scientifically, however, despite Colley's famous 'DAGMAR' statement more than thirty years ago.[65] This is quite simply the consequence of a very widespread failure among practitioners to state relevant and measurable objectives in the first place, which is often reported in the literature[66] and can be readily verified by informal survey. Without objectives, there are no criteria. In their absence, practitioners use a limited number of off-the-peg, standardised procedures.

Inspection of the inventories of advertisement testing procedures listed in a typical text reveals to the quizzical reader that they can all be related to an implicit *hierarchical model* of advertising effect. Neither authors of texts nor research practitioners make explicit that quite fundamental conceptual underpinning, but this section will shortly demonstrate that advertisement testing procedures in common use do indeed correspond to one of the hierarchical *performance characteristics* or *target responses* set out in Table 13.3. The advertisements in question are thus required to 'pass a test' quite literally, rather than to satisfy specific criteria of effectiveness derived from specific objectives. (The celebrated American advertising agency chief, Bill Bernbach, is reputed to have said: 'The client wants some research, so cut him a yard of it.') If this proposition is valid and advertisement testing is in fact presented as being much more precise and scientific than it actually is, that is a highly critical shortcoming of advertising practice – which the great majority of practitioners either do not or will not recognise. It is barely hinted at in the only recent British textbook to deal intellectually with advertising effect and the measurement of advertising effectiveness.[67]

At the lowest level of the hierarchy of effects, we find the performance characteristic *impact*, with the accompanying target response of *attention*. Much advertising research effort is directed in practice at measuring these qualities. In advertising parlance, 'pre-testing' measures the reaction of a sample of the target audience to almost-finished treatments of the proposed advertisements before the campaign is due to start. Pre-testing for impact consists of assessing by questionnaire the amount and quality of attention paid to such treatments presented in folders with other existing advertisements ('folder test'), in dummy magazines, as 'storyboards' (cartoon trip summaries of television commercials) or 'animatics' (videotaped storyboards, electronically edited to simulate continuity, with integral sound-track), even as semi-finished artwork for poster designs optically superimposed on a photograph of a real poster site and film-projected. Such pre-tests are often conducted on a paired comparison basis. This is ingenious and valid assessment of a useful performance characteristic, *provided that* those who make decisions on the basis of the results understand that 'effectiveness' has been measured only at the lowest level of the hierarchy of effects.

This may well be so in the cases so far described, but the 'post-testing' of impact (that is, measuring attention paid to the actual advertising in real conditions) is a quite different matter. The criterion chosen for this purpose is almost invariably recall, as typified by 'reading-and-noting' tests in the case of press advertisements and 'day-after recall' testing of television commercials. As before, one cannot disagree that the simple fact of recall does demonstrate impact. However, recall figures are customarily presented in practice as far more general indicators of effectiveness. Researchers imply, and advertisers seem willing to believe, that a respondent who can remember particular ingredients of an advertising message or treatment is significantly more likely to follow the advocated course of action than otherwise. But this is in reality a highly debatable proposition. It is equally possible to argue that recall represents nothing more than 'repeat attention' (voluntarily recalling the original to mind), in which case it simply measures impact

or, perhaps, a certain amount of *involvement*. If so, the procedure is being invested with a diagnostic power out of all proportion to reality by the implication that it can test motivational effectiveness, a sixth-level performance characteristic. Furthermore, recall testing is typically used as a criterion of effectiveness quite regardless of the nature of the advertising objective in question, which might in fact have been related to comprehension, for example.

Effectiveness is said to be measured in practice at the next level of the hierarchy-of-effects, involvement or *interest*, by a battery of laboratory tests. Most record physiological measures of arousal when sample members of the target audience are exposed to the advertisement: psychogalvanometer, EEG, pupillometer, blink-rate meter, polygraph (the 'lie detector'). While there is no doubt that the arousal level of the subjects can be measured, since these techniques are long established in experimental psychology, their value as indicators of involvement with the advertisement is severely limited by the fact that they do not show what form the arousal takes. Does a sweating palm mean fear or pleasure? Despite this, they are regularly offered and accepted as valid measures of 'effectiveness'. Four laboratory tests were developed specifically for the evaluation of advertising, and measure respondent-indicated interest: ASL interest dial, Alpha quiz chair, CONPAAD and Sync. While these are unquestionably valid indicators of a specific performance characteristic, the fact remains that they measure only at a very low hierarchical level and may therefore fail to demonstrate that an advertisement has in fact met other intended objectives.

Typical texts describe no test procedures specifically directed at measuring performance at the middle-order levels of the hierarchy:- *communication*, *empathy* and *persuasion* (or comprehension, sympathy and conviction). In the case of the latter two, one can perhaps guess why not, but comprehension is a criterion that figures with great regularity in statements of advertising objectives, either explicitly or implicitly. It is therefore surprising that the non-expert but inquisitive reader is obliged to deduce from the literature, in the absence of direct explanation, that middle-order performance characteristics are measured by means of ad hoc depth interviews and group discussions, and that such measurement seems to be infrequently attempted. (A notable exception to this rule is the case of public-service advertising on themes such as smoking and drinking; because these are sensitive and complex issues, comprehension is an especially important criterion of effectiveness which is carefully measured by such procedures).

The remainder of the commonly reported pre- and post-testing procedures all correspond to the performance characteristic at the highest hierarchical level: *motivation* or *action*. Into this category fit such 'intention-to-purchase' measures as the Sherman Group's 'Buy Test', controlled experiments such as ASL theatre tests, attitude measurement and sales monitoring. These are presented as complete tests of advertising effectiveness, understandably, because they measure probable or actual action on the audience's part. The latter two require special comment, however.

Readers may be surprised to find *attitude* measurement included in this list. Indeed, it is normal for texts to treat attitude scaling as though it were quite unrelated to the hierarchy of effects. It is here placed at the top of the hierarchy because psychologists define an attitude as (among other things) a 'predisposition to act'. It is therefore reasonable to suppose that advertising researchers believe they are testing motivation by measuring attitudes, even though they do not say so explicitly. Unfortunately, the cause-and-effect relationship between attitude and action has never been conclusively proved, however reasonable it may seem intuitively; attitudes are predispositions, not precipitators. Practitioners seem unaware of this complication, or reluctant to recognise it. Because attitude-measurement techniques are easily available for borrowing from social psychology, they are widely and regularly used as criteria in practice – but without due regard to their surrogate nature.

The *sales* criterion has the appeal that it is easily measured, either by in-house monitoring or by subscribing to syndicated services such as the Nielsen Indexes, TCA or TGI. But serious methodological problems are concealed in the apparently straightforward procedure. For instance, the criterion is invalid if some other dimension of effectiveness was in fact called for by the campaign objectives. It is tempting to insist that sales are what advertising is all about, as the 'hard school' often does, but the fact is that it would be foolish to condemn a corporate image campaign, for instance, because increased sales did not result within the time of horizon of the post-test. This example also raises the question of response-lag. Advertising takes time to make its effect felt, especially in the case of less frequently repeat-purchased products. If the sales criterion is applied too soon after the event, it may produce excessively pessimistic results. Moreover, there is a problem of seasonality: sales are not always constant throughout a period. If the timing of the test happens to coincide with either a peak or a trough, misleading conclusions may again be drawn. Sales monitoring needs to be repeated at intervals over a suitable period if this problem is to be avoided. Finally, there is the quite fundamental methodological drawback that, unless all intervening variables (other marketing mix elements or environmental factors such as weather, for example) can be controlled, a cause-effect relationship between advertising and sales change cannot be assumed, let alone proved. However tempting it may be to credit advertising or blame it, according to circumstances, the fact remains that any one of several other factors could have outweighed its effect.

This necessarily incomplete survey of common advertisement testing procedures (or rather, those claimed by textbooks to be in regular use) confirms the proposition that they are indeed implicitly founded on a hierarchical model of advertising effect. Furthermore, the techniques most usually reported in the literature are confined to the bottom and top ends of the hierarchy-of-effects, capable of measuring only either impact and involvement or motivation. Valid performance criteria, such as communication, cannot therefore be tested unless advertisers are alert enough to insist that the criteria implicit in the proposed test procedures bear some relationship to the objectives the advertising is intended to meet, and researchers are willing to construct purpose-designed measuring instruments accordingly. Otherwise, it will continue to be counterproductively typical that advertising budgets are slashed or swollen on such test criteria as sales movements, attitude shifts or recall scores, which are not only off-the-peg surrogates but also too often conceptually dubious in themselves.

■ Summary

'Marketing communications' is a transaction between firms and people. While marketing communications initiatives originate with firms, the fact is that people often initiate the transaction in the process of a deliberate search for information which can help with their consumption decisions. At other times, they consume and use such marketing communications as advertisements for several other purposes, including entertainment. People are active participants in the transaction, not passive recipients.

The balance of power is less weighted in favour of the firms than is generally believed – both outside and inside the marketing communications business. The transaction can be likened to a game for two players. People learn the rules at an early age, by the process of 'socialisation', and social institutions of various kinds exist to be arbiters of fair play.

The heart of the marketing communication transaction is typically described in terms of a 'hierarchy of effects'. Although this model is distinctly elderly, does not explain how people 'use' marketing communications and has been subject to continuous conceptual criticism from influential quarters, it still forms a day-to-day frame of reference for the majority of practitioners. A key to better understanding of what happens in the transaction is offered by information-processing theory, not yet integrated into the familiar texts and still unfamiliar to most practitioners. This theory has the further potential to explain how people manage to cope with the information overload that characterises the contemporary market-place. Familiarity with the basic principles of semiotics can enhance understanding of the analysis operation at the heart of the information processing model.

Measurement of effectiveness continues to be dominated by the hierarchy-of-effects framework, seldom made explicit. Instead of being required to satisfy criteria derived specifically from marketing communication objectives, initiatives have only to pass a set of ready-made tests relating to levels in the hierarchy. Three particular surrogate criteria, popular in practice – recall, attitudes and sales – do not in fact measure what they purport to.

A great deal has been written about marketing communications. Much of it can unquestionably be helpful in practice, if cautiously interpreted, but much more remains to be verified or is yet to be discussed.

■ Notes and References

1. Britt, S. H., 'The Right Marketing Mix for the Corporate Imagery Mix', *Business Horizons* 14 (February 1971), pp. 87–88.
2. McCarthy, E. J., *Basic Marketing: A Managerial Approach*, 7th edition, Homewood, Ill.: Irwin, 1981, pp. 431–433.
3. Crosier, Keith, 'Promotion' in *The Marketing Book*, (ed.) Michael J. Baker, London: Butterworth-Heinemann, 1994, pp. 492–493.
4. *Ibid*, pp. 485–490.
5. Schramm, Wilbur, *The Process and Effects of Mass Communications*, Urbana, Ill.: University of Illinois Press, 1955, p. 3.
6. McDonald, Colin, *How Advertising Works: A Review of Current Thinking*, London: The Advertising Association in association with NTC Publications, 1992, p. 94.
7. Engel John F., Blackwell, Roger D. and Miniard, Paul W., *Consumer Behavior*, 5th edition, Hinsdale, Ill.: Dryden Press, 1986, p. 35.
8. Ryan, B. and Gross, N., 'The Diffusion of Hybrid Seed Corn in Two Iowa Communities', *Rural Sociology* 8 (March 1943), pp. 15–24.
9. Labour Party, *Opposition Green Paper: Advertising*, London: The Labour Party, 1972, p. 55.
10. Cox, Donald F., 'Clues for Advertising Strategists', *Harvard Business Review* 39 (November–December 1961), p. 160.
11. Ward, Scott, 'Consumer Socialization', *Journal of Consumer Behavior* 1 (September 1974), p. 2.

12. Ward, Scott, 'Children's Reactions to Commercials', *Journal of Advertising Research* 12 (April 1972), pp. 37–45.
13. Smith, Glen, 'Children as the Target for Advertising', *Advertising* 67 (Spring 1981), pp. 40–2; *Research into the Effects of Advertising on Children*, London: Oyez Publishing, 1980, pp. 54–62.
14. Adler, R. P. *et al.*, *The Effects of Television Advertising on Children: Review and Recommendations*, Lexington, Mass: Lexington Books, 1980.
15. Crosier, Keith, 'Using Advertisements: How Audiences Actively Participate with Advertisers in a Consumption Transaction', *Proceedings of the Annual Conference of the Marketing Education Group*, Cranfield School of Management, 1983, pp. 357–372: May, John P., 'Promotion: Do We Understand the Customer?', *ibid.*, pp. 373–381.
16. Advertising Association, *Public Attitudes to Advertising 1992*, London: The Advertising Association, 1993. This report contains data relating to all surveys since the first in 1961.
17. D. H. Robertson, *Lectures on Economic Principles* London: Staples, 1958, p. 169.
18. Hedges, Alan, *Testing to Destruction: A Critical Look at the uses of Research in Advertising*, London: The Institute of Practitioners in Advertising, 1974 and 1982, p. 29.
19. The original sources are: Starch, Daniel, *Principles of Advertising*, Chicago A. W. Shaw, 1923; Strong, E. K., *The Psychology of Selling*, New York: McGraw-Hill, 1925; Sandage, C. H. and Fryburger, Vernon, *Advertising Theory and Practice*, Homewood, Ill: Irwin, 1935; 9th edn 1975, esp. pp. 79–86; Lavidge, Robert C. and Steiner, Gary A., 'A Model for Predictive Measurements of Advertising Effectiveness', *Journal of Marketing* 25 (October 1961), pp. 59–62; Colley, Russell H., *Defining Advertising Goals for Measured Advertising Results*, New York: Association of National Advertisers, 1961 reprinted in *Modern Marketing Management*, (eds) R. J. Lawrence and M. J. Thomas, Harmondsworth: Penguin, 1971, pp. 282–92, McGuire, William J., 'An Infomation Processing Model of Advertising Effectiveness', *Symposium on Behavioral and Management Science in Marketing*, Chicago: University of Chicago, 1969; DeLozier, M. Wayne, *The Marketing Communications Process*, New York: McGraw-Hill, 1976, esp. pp. 219–220.
20. Robertson, Thomas S., *Consumer Behavior*, Chicago: Scott, Foresman, 1970, p. 46.
21. Palda, K. S., 'The Hypothesis of a Hierarchy of Effects: A Partial Evaluation', *Journal of Marketing Research* 3 (February 1966), pp. 13–24.
22. Ehrenberg, A. S. C., *Repeat-buying: Facts, Theory and Applications*, 2nd edition, London: Charles Griffin, 1988.
23. Murray, Hugh, 'So You Know How Advertising Works?', *Management Decision* 17 (5) (1979), pp. 369–390.
24. Ray, Michael L., 'Marketing Communication and the Hierarchy of Effects', in *New Models for Mass Communication Research: Sage Annual Review of Communication Research, Volume II*, (ed.) Peter Clarke, Beverly Hills: Sage Publications, 1973, pp. 147–176.
25. Krugman, H. E., 'The Impact of Television Advertising: Learning without Involvement', *Public Opinion Quarterly* 29 (Fall 1965), pp. 349–356.
26. Sternthal, Brian and Craig, C. Samuel, *Consumer Behavior: An Information Processing Perspective*, Englewood Cliffs, NJ: Prentice-Hall, 1982, p. 313.
27. *Ibid.*, p. 67.
28. DeLozier, M. Wayne, *The Marketing Communications Process*, New York: McGraw-Hill, 1976, esp. pp. 1–4, 16–21, 170–173; Percy, Larry and Rossiter, John R., *Advertising Strategy: A Communication Theory Approach*, New York: Praeger, 1980, esp. pp. 13–17; Aaker, David A. and Myers, John G., *Advertising Management*, 2nd edition, Englewood Cliffs, NJ: Prentice-Hall, 1982, esp. pp. 233–235.
29. Percy and Rossiter, *Advertising Strategy: A Communication Theory Approach*, p. 106
30. Janis, Irving L. and Feshbach, Seymour, 'Effects of Fear Arousing Communications', *Journal of Abnormal Social Psychology* 48 (1) (1953), pp. 78–92.
31. Ray, Michael L. and Wilkie, William L., 'Fear: The Potential of an Appeal Neglected by Marketing', *Journal of Marketing* 34 (January 1970), pp. 54–62.
32. For instance, see Leathar, D. S., 'Fear-inducing Advertising', *Journal of the Institute of Health Education* 19 (2) (1981), pp. 42.
33. Sternthal, Brian and Craig, C. Samuel, 'Humor in Advertising', *Journal of Marketing* 37 (October 1973), pp. 12–18.
34. Leathar, 'Fear-Inducing Advertising', pp. 50–55.

35. Hovland, Carl I., Lumsdaine, Arthur A. and Sheffield, Fred D., *Experiments in Mass Communication*, vol. III, Princeton: Princeton University Press, 1949, pp. 201–227.

36. Faison, E. W. J., 'Effectiveness of One-Sided Versus Two-Sided Mass Communications in Advertising', *Public Opinion Quarterly* 25 (Fall 1961), pp. 468–469.

37. Rosnow, R. L. and Robinson, E. J. (eds), *Experiments in Persuasion*, New York: Academic Press, 1967, pp. 101–102.

38. Hovland, Carl I., Janis, Irving L. and Kelley, H. H., *Communication and Persuasion*, New Haven: Yale University Press, 1953, pp. 103–105.

39. DeLozier, *The Marketing Communications Process*, pp. 76–77.

40. Zimbardo, Philip G., Weisenberg, Matisyo, Firestone, Ira and Levy, Burton, 'Communicator Effectiveness in Producing Public Conformity and Private Attitude Change', *Journal of Personality* 33 (March 1965), pp. 233–255.

41. Mehrabian, Albert and Weiner, Morton, 'Decoding of Inconsistent Communications', *Journal of Personality and Social Psychology* 6 (1) (1967), pp. 109–114.

42. Aaker and Myers, *Advertising Management*, p. 459; DeLozier, *The Marketing Communications Process*, pp. 22, 73, 85, 87.

43. McLuhan, Marshall, *Understanding Media: The Extensions of Man*, New York: McGraw-Hill, 1964, Chapter 1.

44. Blair, William S., 'Attitude Research and the Qualitative Value of Magazines', *Attitude Research at Sea*, (ed.) Adler, Lee and Crespi, Irving, Chicago: American Marketing Association, 1966, pp. 153–162.

45. Joyce, Timothy, 'Attitude Research as a Measure of Media Values', *Admap* 17 (December 1981), pp. 609–614.

46. Percy and Rossiter, *Advertising Strategy: A Communication Theory Approach*, p. 173.

47. Aaker and Myers, *Advertising Management*, pp. 459–461.

48. Percy and Rossiter, *Advertising Strategy: A Communication Theory Approach*, p. 180.

49. Lowe Watson, D., 'Advertising and the Buyer–Seller Relationship', *Journal of the Market Research Society* 11 (April 1969), pp. 125–146; reprinted in *Modern Marketing Management*, (ed.) Lawrence, R. J. and Thomas, M. J., Harmondsworth: Penguin, 1971, pp. 332–347, esp. pp. 331–342.

50. Zakia, R. D. and Naam, M., 'Semiotics, Advertising and Marketing', *Journal of Consumer Studies* 4 (2) (Spring 1987), p. 6.

51. J. Umiker-Sebeok, *Marketing and Semiotics*, Berlin: Newton DeGruyter, 1987.

52. Williamson, Judith, *Decoding Advertisements: Ideology and Meaning in Advertising*, London: Marion Boyars, 1978.

53. Dyer, Gillian, *Advertising as Communication*, London: Methuen, 1982, Chapter 6.

54. Miller, George A., *The Psychology of Communication*, Harmondsworth: Penguin, 1970, pp. 21–49.

55. Wright, Peter L., 'The Harassed Decision Maker', *Journal of Applied Psychology* 59 (5) (1974), pp. 555–561.

56. Ries, Al and Trout, Jack, *Positioning: The Battle for Your Mind*, New York: McGraw-Hill, 1980, esp. pp. 33–42.

57. Crosier, Keith, 'A New Strategy for Advertising to Over-Communicated Target Audiences', *Quarterly Review of Marketing* 7 (July 1982).

58. Crosier, Keith, 'Puzzle Advertising', *Proceedings of the Fourteenth Annual Conference*, Dublin: Marketing Education Group (July 1981), pp. 311–329.

59. Strong, E. K., 'The Effect of Length of Series upon Recognition', *Psychological Review* 19 (January 1912), pp. 44–47.

60. Zielske, Hubert A., 'The Remembering and Forgetting of Advertising', *Journal of Marketing* 23 (March 1959), pp. 239–243.

61. Corkindale, David and Newall, John, 'Advertising Thresholds and Wearout', *European Journal of Marketing* 12 (5) (1978), pp. 329–378.

62. Strong, E. C., 'The Use of Field Experimental Observations in Estimating Advertising Recall', *Journal of Marketing Research* 11 (November 1974), pp. 369–378; Space and Timing of Advertising', *Journal of Advertising Research* 17 (December 1977), pp. 25–31.

63. Little, John D. C. and Lodish, Leonard M., 'A Media Selection Mode and its Optimization by Dynamic Programming', *Industrial Management Review* 8 (Fall 1966), pp. 15–23; 'A Media Planning Calculus', *Operations Research* 17 (January–February 1969), pp. 1–35.

64. Sternthal and Craig, *Consumer Behavior: An Information Processing Perspective*, p. 81.

65. Colley, *Defining Advertising Goals for Measured Advertising Results*.

66. For instance, Lovell, Mark and Potter, Jack, *Assessing the Effectiveness of Advertising*, London: Business Books, 1975.

67. McDonald, *How Advertising Works, passim.*

■ *Chapter 14* ■

Analytical Frameworks for Strategic Marketing Planning

Douglas Brownlie

■ Introduction

The process of strategic marketing planning is essentially an information driven process, at the heart of which lies an intensive need to gather data on a continuing basis about the firm's external and internal marketing environment. Marketing technology offers various analytical frameworks to help *organise* such data: that is, to place it in a context where *interpretation* becomes possible. Through the use of those frameworks marketing managers are able to ascribe *meaning* to marketing data, thence to diagnose and define strategic marketing problems. And in theory those steps are followed *prior* to taking resource allocation decisions.

This chapter describes the analytical frameworks that have been developed to help process such data, and specifically to reduce and recast it in a form of some value to the marketing strategist. It introduces analytical frameworks such as the Product Life-Cycle, the Growth-Share Matrix, the Business Assessment Array and the Directional Policy Matrix. It also considers the benefit and pitfalls associated with the use of those frameworks in a marketing management context. Finally, it considers the role of managerial judgement in the process of imposing structure on the complex analytical problems that confront strategic marketers.

Although the tenor of the chapter is descriptive, it also adopts an analytical theme in an attempt to establish the theoretical foundations of business strategy. In this way it sets out to help readers evaluate for themselves the validity of the general propositions the area advances. The chapter also hopes to help readers take an informed view of the value of the analytical frameworks it describes, and to do so bearing in mind that the *analytical context* for which those frameworks were originally conceived is very different to the *organisational context* in which they find application.

■ The context of strategic marketing

Strategic marketing embraces activities and decisions that draw on some view of the future. There is no logical or empirical way in which anyone can know the future. Yet, the management of marketing strategies is driven by a sense of direction and purpose that must take a view of the future on some basis. So, strategic marketing requires the marketing manager to deal with issues that involve a higher degree of uncertainty than many of the day to day operational marketing activities: time horizons are longer; previous experience of handling similar situations will be limited; the need is greater to re-frame perceptions of the business in its context; and the resource implications of decisions will be greater and irreversible in the medium term. Broadly speaking, this chapter is about how marketing managers respond to this uncertainty.

The conventional wisdom has it that marketing managers cope with this uncertainty by means of the strategic marketing planning process (Doyle, 1994; Kotler, 1988; McDonald, 1984; Greenley, 1986). Kotler (1988) goes so far as to say that the marketing plan is the central instrument for directing and coordinating marketing effort. Marketing managers should then carefully gather all the relevant marketing information and process it to reveal the optimum course of action. Clear objectives are established. Alternative routes should then be mapped out with both risk and return considered. The most efficient route is chosen. Clear and detailed plans are drawn up, operationalising the chosen route and objective. Measurable yardsticks are established against which performance can be evaluated. And so marketing planning becomes a central activity to the management of marketing (Piercy and Giles, 19889; Greenley 1989). Indeed, Kotler (1988) sees the marketing planning process as driving the organisation's overall strategic planning. And Doyle (1994) states that 'strategic marketing planning *facilitates* the company's ability to adapt to a changing and increasingly competitive world.'

The frameworks that are about to be described have much in common. They are essentially aids to managerial decision-making, often taking a supply-side perspective. They provide analytical engines which help to clarify the nature of strengths, weaknesses, opportunities and threats facing an organisation. Their constructions share a number of conceptual underpinnings, largely derived from observations about the character of competition in certain market environments and the putative relationship between market growth, market share and performance. They typically find application in the context of organisational processes by means of which strategic marketing plans are developed. They are of *particular* value in driving the analytical elements of the process, especially the SWOT analysis and the marketing audit. They can also help to generate a set of benchmarks against which to judge internal practices, procedures and performance. But, probably their most important contribution is that the act of employing the frameworks as analytical engines provides managers with a means of facilitating strategy discussions. It can give them ownership of those discussions through appropriating the set of concepts and the vocabulary by means of which ideas and opinions are expressed.

At one level this does help managers to have a meaningfully focused dialogue about the complex issues of organisational marketing strategy. At another level, the appropriation of language does provide a way of exercising power over the strategy discourse. And so these frameworks can be seen to be influential at two levels. First, as analytical devices which take a set of data, and through organising it in particular ways, lead interpretation by virtue of the associations implicit to their structure. This also sets limits on the sort of discussion made possible. And this leads to the second level, where the frameworks *produce* and thus *control* the strategy discourse. The frameworks can then be seen as organisational artefacts, or instruments of power.

The reader is referred to the works cited above for a detailed treatment of the strategic marketing planning process.

■ Theoretical perspectives

The analytical frameworks considered in this chapter have been widely discussed, typically in the context of *diagnosing* how a firm should **position** itself among rivals in order to achieve specific strategic goals. Indeed, the conventional wisdom of only a few years ago would have said that those frameworks not only provide a data transformation mechanism, but can also *specify* the content of strategy in given situations. Contemporary writers are less sanguine in the views they express about the diagnostic powers of these frameworks. They are also less likely to 'rubbish' them completely and more likely to take a balanced tone, as does Baker (1992) when he characterises them as 'currently *useful* generalisations' – where a very broad view is taken of the nature of *usefulness* to managers in organisations.

The validity of this diagnostic role has been the subject of considerable debate. Much criticism addresses the dangerous epistemological leap which appears to have been made between the two very different tasks of description (data capture and transformation) and prescription (strategy specification).

Critics, such as Wensley (1981) challenge the general propositions which underpin the prescriptions of these frameworks, arguing that they are not *universal* in nature, but highly *situation specific*. It is also argued that there is little evidence to support the view that *recurring* patterns of strategic competitive activity are to be found in response to given environmental conditions, or in pursuit of the attainment of specific performance goals. Of course, were this to be so, business strategy theory would be the first in the area of management studies to offer a counsel of perfection. Business leaders could then sleep peacefully in the knowledge that the strategy *problem* had been solved. Unfortunately, or perhaps fortunately, the real world complexities of organisational strategy are not easily captured by formulaic approaches.

Care should be taken not to underestimate the power of the frameworks (in their data reducing role) to direct analysts to particular areas, thus to draw their attention towards some questions and away from others; and in so doing to superimpose a view which alters their perception of the range of strategy options available in any set of circumstances. Morrison and Wensley (1991) recently referred to this effect, in the context of discussing the Growth-Share matrix, as the 'boxing-in' of strategy discussions to a limited set of options and prescriptions. The notion is not new that the application of the frameworks involves a process of selective perception and

attention. Indeed, it is a cornerstone of the view that the indiscriminant application of the tools leads to an over-reliance on assumption and dogma and ultimately to myopia (Mckiernan, 1992).

The reader will find that the literature on business strategy currently reflects an ambivalence towards concepts and models that claim to *specify* strategy content. The current vogue is with the task of describing the strategy formation *process* at the expense of the *content* of strategies. Contemporary thought is moving *back to the future*, in the sense that it is taking a more sociologically informed view of management processes, including that of strategy formation – which is in any case where the subject has its origins.

Clearly, in a subject that owes some allegiance to practising managers, there is a need for a reasonably secure organising framework that fulfils the dual obligations of data transformation and strategy specification. One could speculate that such a framework would provide the following broad facilities:

(i) A universally applicable means for identifying the underlying factors which are critical for long term success at the individual business level and which are sufficiently fundamental that their effects can be expected to persist indefinitely in the face of general environmental change.

(ii) A way of establishing the implication of these factors for the allocation of limited resources – especially cash – within a firm which is comprised of a number of business areas/units.

Most empirical and conceptual work on the determinants and performance of business strategy draws on the *Strategy, Conduct and Performance* model which has its origins in the field of industrial economics. At the level of the firm, this model proposes that the conduct, or behaviour of any organisation is the outcome of strategies that are put in place by decision-makers in response to the competitive environment they perceive themselves to be part of. The model then proposes that the performance of an organisation is a function of the *match* it achieves between its capabilities and resources and the opportunities and risks perceived to be present in its environment (Doyle, 1994).

It is possible to draw an analogy between this model and Skinner's view of the determinants of human behaviour. He contended that human behaviour is a form of response to environmental stimuli. Thus, if one could specify the environment completely enough, it would be possible to predict exactly the behaviour of individuals. Unfortunately, because of the multitude of factors that influence human behaviour, we have only partial classifications of environmental stimuli and thus are only able to make, at best, probabilistic predictions of behaviour.

Some readers may detect in this model the influence of Darwin's ideas on the evolution of species and natural selection, i.e. that survival is a question of adaptation to the imperatives of changing surroundings and the competition to secure scarce resources. The theory of natural selection predicts that the species best fitted to the contingencies of the environment will survive and prosper, whilst less fit rivals will fail and become extinct because of their inability to secure adequate resources. And since, in the context of organisational species, this environment is constituted by suppliers, competitors, customers, distributors, economic institutions, stakeholders and other social agents, all of which are in a constant state of flux, the potential for turbulence in the environment is enormous.

In the area of business strategy the dominant research paradigm is still struggling with the classification of environments, organisational responses to them (strategies) and outcomes (performance). Of course, an incomplete specification of organisational environments will mean that behaviour propositions (strategies) for the attainment of particular outcomes (performance goals) will be heavily qualified.

Progress with the development of a robust universal theory of business strategy is hampered by the partial classifications of environments and strategies and the highly situation-specific nature of existing propositions. Although Porter's (1980)

typology of business strategy is currently popular, several others are available, e.g. Buzzel *et al.* (1975); Utterback and Abernathy (1975); Kotler (1965); Hofer and Schendel (1978); Miles and Snow (1978); and Wissema *et al.* (1980). But, as Speed (1994) argues, empirically derived taxonomies can help to improve the quality of marketing strategy research, especially if they are subject to continuous testing and re-examination.

That a contingency approach was appropriate to the development of a theory of business strategy was realised as early as 1923 by researchers in the area of marketing. Copeland (1923), Aspinwall (1962), Miracle (1965) and Udell (1968) were early proponents of the development of typologies of marketing strategies based on the classification of exhibited patterns of customer purchasing behaviour. Copeland and Aspinwall offered 3-way classification schemes, namely (respectively): *convenience* goods, *shopping* goods and *speciality* goods; and pure *red* goods, pure *yellow* goods, and *orange* goods. A more elaborate 5-way classification scheme was developed by Miracle on the basis of the following characteristics:

- Unit value of product.
- Significance of the purchase to the customer.
- Time and effort spent on the purchase by the customer.
- Rate of technological and fashion change.
- Technical complexity.
- Customer service needs.
- Frequency of purchase.
- Rapidity of consumption.
- Extent of usage or variety of ways in which the product provides utility.

After several lean years, the area of strategic marketing and its high degree of overlap with business strategy is once again gaining momentum. Given the continuing need for business strategy to have a marketing perspective if it is to take into account customer needs, perceptions and preferences, this emerging interest holds promise to enrich, expand and increase the relevance of marketing processes. Although in some ways the promise, recognised over a decade ago by Anderson (1982), Wind and Robertson (1983) and Day and Wensley (1983) has yet to be fulfilled. Perhaps the research agendas mapped out by those authors were themselves contextually specific.

■ PIMS

One of the most influential programmes of research in the area of Business Strategy is the Profit Impact of Market Strategy (PIMS) project (Schoeffler *et al.*, 1974; Buzzell and Gale, 1974, 1987; Buzzell and Wiersema, 1981). Although the project has its origins in General Electric (G.E.) in the 1960s, it has been managed by the Strategic Planning Institute since 1975. When it was an internal G.E. project, Schoeffler (1974) used data from the firm's various business units to establish the relationship between business strategy and performance. His early work provided the foundation for the development of a cross-sectional model founded on the ideas of industrial economics. It consisted of computer-based multivariate regression equations which used pre-tax ROI and Cash Flow as the dependent variables and various characteristics of the businesses being studied as independent variables.

The scope of the PIMS work was greatly expanded by Schoeffler when, having left G.E. in 1969, he was able to secure data from other firms in a variety of industries and business environments. He established a databank which recorded empirical evidence of the strategic experience of 57 firms, collectively participating in over 600 businesses.

Firms which now contribute to the PIMS database are described in terms of 37 characteristics which explain around 80% of the observable variance in performance (Abell and Hammond, 1979). Of these 37 characteristics, the following are among the most powerful explanatory variables: market growth rate; market share; product quality; capacity utilisation; R & D spending; degree of vertical integration; productivity. Around 200 firms representing about 2000 business operations currently participate in the PIMS database. By means of the six PIMS data forms,

participants submit over 150 items of data, covering a period of at least 5 years, on the performance, operations, financial structure and market environment of each business. Over 500 variables are constructed from this data. The computer model uses these variables to diagnose strategic position and identify the options to be considered in strategic planning.

Specific ROI and cash flow models are available, not only to evaluate performance, but also to establish what ROI and cash flow would normally be expected to be achieved (the Par ROI and Par Cash Flow) by a comparable firm in a similar strategic position. Moreover, these models can also then be used to determine what changes would occur in ROI and cash flows given specific strategic changes or hypothesised positions. Several other reports are available on businesses for which the members submit data, including the Strategy Sensitivity Reports, which predict what would happen if certain strategic changes were made.

Several research studies have used the PIMS database to examine various aspects of the relationship between business strategy, environment and performance. It has proved to be a rich source of hypotheses on the *content* of effective business strategies. However, one very contentious area is the PIMS finding that ROI is closely related to market share, specifically *that high market share leads to high profitability*. On the basis of this proposition there is apparent empirical support for the view that firms must seek to dominate their served market, irrespective of its rate of growth. Several researchers take exception to this view. Of this sort is the work of Kijewski (1978) and Jacobsen and Aaker (1985). Those authors use the PIMS database to establish the nature of the relationships between investment in market share and different market conditions.

Using the PIMS database, Jacobsen and Aaker(1985) found that a large proportion of the association between market share and ROI is spurious in the sense that both market share and ROI are the joint outcome of some other factors. They also found that the direct impact of market share on ROI is much smaller than previous studies have indicated.

That it is easier to gain market share in high growth markets is disputed by Kijewski (1978) and Aaker and Day (1986). Kijewski found that 'the cash costs of gaining share vary substantially between moderate and rapid growth markets. When the cash costs are approximately adjusted for average point change in market share in each environment, the cost of a point in share is only slightly lower in the more rapidly growing markets (and, indeed, lowest in low growth markets).'

Over the years the contention that greater market share leads to greater profitability has also been disputed by a number of other writers such as Fruhan (1972), Bloom and Kotler (1975), Hamermesh *et al.* (1978) and Woo and Cooper (1982). Debate has often been stoked-up by a tendency in some quarters to generalise heroically from the basic PIMS findings. More thoughtful marketing scholars and industry commentators have drawn attention to the limitations of the greater market share doctrine.

Industry commentators have found a readily accessible plethora of exceptions to the market-share rule. In the academic world the major weaknesses of the PIMS work have been summarised by Weitz and Wensley (1984) as the specification of the model and the interpretation of its results. The limitations imposed by the specification question concern, firstly, the structure of the model, i.e. the choice of independent (investment intensity) and dependent (ROI) variables; and secondly, its validity across a diverse array of businesses for which the choice of priority factors from the given 337 may vary. The latter question raised by Weitz and Wesley concerns the validity of the assumption of causality which is implicit to the PIMS model – or at least the way in which causality has been imputed to the model by various commentators.

As Weitz and Wensley note 'owing to the cross-sectional nature of the analysis, one cannot infer that changes in the independent variables will cause changes in the dependent variable'. Because of these weaknesses one cannot assume the PIMS findings to be equally valid across industries and firms. So the perennial problem of the *situational*, not *universal* nature of strategy propositions once again emerges to confound the

search for robust generalisations. And although PIMS does provide a large and accessible database for researchers to plunder in their quest for a set of testable propositions, nowadays few would subscribe to the notion that this work will lead to a robust diagnostic framework relating environment and strategy to performance. This is especially so in the context of research which uses the PIMS database to test the adequacy of the strategy prescriptions inherent to the framework that is discussed below.

■ The product life-cycle

The concept of an organisation's strategy in central to the study of strategic marketing. As the previous section tried to explain, much of the research of recent years has followed a well-trodden route which relates the behaviour of organisations to the effectiveness with which they attain performance goals. In so doing it has aimed to generate a series of contigent propositions that guide the strategist toward a course of action that is thought likely to lead to improved performance. Such propositions are made on the basis of a classification of business environments, firms' reactions to them (strategies and plans), and achieved outcomes (performance).

Among the many methodological problems besetting the attainment of that aim is the extensive list of variables which need to be considered in the formulation of secure classification schemes. Indeed, Hofer (1975) has calculated that with 54 strategically significant variables 254 different circumstances would need to be examined. Clearly, of much value to the researcher, and the manager, are tools which help to reduce the number of such variables and to specify values which are of strategic importance.

The grandfather of these tools is the Product Life-Cycle (PLC), introduced as a concept by Joel Dean (1950) some 45 years ago. It has long been promoted as a concept to help marketing decision makers adapt their strategies to changing market conditions. So, underlying the guidance it provides managers is a classification of business environments and appropriate strategies.

Few marketing concepts have been written about so widely and yet so widely criticised as the PLC. Over the years opinions have polarised around two camps: those supporters who believe the PLC provides the basis, not only of a comprehensive understanding of market development, but also of the marketing strategies that should be followed based on the pattern of competitive activity thought to characterise its various stages. At the other extreme reside those critics, such as Lambkin and Day (1989) who assert, often as a mantra sung in monotonous unison, that 'the generalised descriptions and prescriptions of the PLC literature would be unlikely to find empirical support because key assumptions are flawed and important dimensions of evolutionary processes are overlooked'.

Irrespective of the serious questions which other critics have raised concerning the *shape* of the curve, or the *length* of its phases, a more moderate middle ground is taken by authors such as Baker (1992) who strive to bridge the gap between esoteric academic flatulence and the profane world of the hard-headed manager. Baker argues that the value of the PLC is 'as an important tool for planning at the strategic level, always recognising that it is not of itself deterministic and may be influenced significantly by environmental changes and/or marketing action'. However, not all writers have been as circumspect as Baker in their advocacy of the concept and many who write normatively, from a supply-side, or managerial perspective, assert faithfully that it provides the foundations for marketing propositions such as those that follow (Hofer 1975):

(i)   In the *Introductory* stage of the life-cycle, the major determinants of business strategy, are the newness of the product, the rate of technological change in product design, the needs of the buyer, and the frequency with which the product is purchased.

(ii) In the *Maturity* stage of the life-cycle, the major determinants of business strategy are the nature of buyer needs, the degree of product differentiation, the rate of technological change in process design, the degree of market segmentation, the ratio of distribution costs to manufacturing value added, and the frequency with which the product is purchased.

(iii) In the *Decline* stage of the life-cycle, the major determinants of business strategy are buyer loyalty, the degree of product differentiation, the price elasticity of demand, the firm's share of the market, product quality and marginal plant size.

At its simplest, the PLC literature *hypothesises* that the evolution of products passes through the stages of Introduction, Growth, Maturity and Decline, and that these stages are defined by inflection points in the rate of change of product sales. The growth of product sales is then said to follow the S-shaped pattern depicted in Figure 14.1. As it shows, during the introductory phase unit sales grow slowly. This is said to occur because of the need to create awareness, overcome buyer inertia and stimulate trial at the level of the user and the intermediary. Rapid growth then occurs as customer recognition and acceptance follows the development of awareness, availability and successful trials – the entry of competitors to the market precipitates these developments. The rate of growth subsides as penetration of the potential buyer group reaches saturation. Demand growth is determined by the underlying rate of growth of the buyer group, the average usage rate and the level of repeat purchases attained. Growth declines as substitute products emerge, customers are persuaded to switch and the level of repeat buying declines.

Figure 14.1. *The idealised product life-cycle curve*

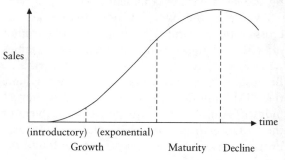

A more elaborate description of the stages would also take a supply-side view. Accordingly, the rate of sales development is said to be influenced by the number of suppliers that enter the market; the speed and timing of their entry; and the level of resources they invest in their entry strategies. Furthermore, the marketing strategies of pioneering entrants regarding price, promotion and distribution significantly affects the rate of growth of primary demand for the product class through either impeding, or facilitating the entry of competitors with substitute products. The normative literature typically characterises the introductory phase, from a supply-side perspective, as exhibiting a high degree of supplier concentration and low economies of scale and experience effects.

Writing from a supply-side perspective, Levitt (1965), Doyle (1976) and Wasson (1974) have *prescribed* in some detail the different patterns of management action that they believe each stage of the the product life-cycle calls for. Each author pays specific attention to how strategic objectives and the mix of marketing variables should be modified as the nature of competition changes. That sales development has those characteristic stages seems to highlight the commercial prudence of having a variety of products and markets with different present and anticipated growth rates. In the long term, because people get bored, or as Baker (1992) puts it more prosaically, because *the act of consumption changes the consumer*, the firm's survival depends on having a balanced mix of products, some of which are mature, are generally accepted by consumers, widely available and generate cash; and others which are promising new products, not widely accepted or available and that need cash to support growth during market development.

The idealised product life-cycle curve is a portayal of the underlying pattern of sales development. But, as critics remind us, it largely ignores the complex variations which occur in practice. The basic characteristics of each stage are said to be determined independently of the absolute length of the product's life. However, product life-cycles are also known to assume multifarious forms (Wasson 1974), not necessar-ily conforming to the stages of development outlined in the ideal life-cycle curve which is only one of 12 broad archetypal PLC patterns that have been identified by Rink and Swan (1979). Even for those cycles that follow the classical pattern of growth, the initial rates of sales development varies greatly, especially where the product is a basic technological innovation. For example, the electric typewriter took 20 years to achieve an exponential growth rate, but sales of black and white TV sets rose to a peak very rapidly, with no perceptible period of market development.

It would be misleading to suggest that it is possible to determine accurately the *shape* of a PLC curve and the *length* of each of its phases. To do so would be to try to impose one general pattern of evolution where many are appropriate. That growth and decline will invariably occur is as deterministic a view as should be counselled, although as Mercer (1994) recently argued, as have others before him, its use as a deterministic tool is criticised on the grounds of insufficient empirical validation of its general pattern at the level of the brand.

In practice, market share and market growth rate are two of the most fundamental factors to determine product-market strategy, measures of each being commonly used to establish strategic objectives. The influence of both these factors has been shown by several authors to vary according to the different stages of the product life-cycle (Wind and Claycamp,1976; Cravens, 1975; Catry and Chevalier, 1974; Enis, 1980). Indeed, stage in the life-cycle is generally understood to be a proxy for management decisions (Enis *et al.*, 1977) as well as for market growth. This quality has been exploited by some authors (Wind and Claycamp, 1976; Cravens, 1975; Catry and Chevalier, 1974; Enis, 1980), who have developed analytical frameworks which offer strategic guidelines based on what they consider to be two broad components of strategic performance: stage in the product life-cycle, or rate of market growth; and in competitive market position, expressed in terms of market share. The *Product Evaluation Matrix* of Wind and Claycamp (1976), the *Product/Market Matching Matrix* of

Enis (1980), and the *Product Market Evolution Matrix* of Hofer (1977), typify the methods of analysis that have thus emerged. Hofer's matrix is discussed later as an adjunct to the Growth-Share and Attractiveness-Capabilities matrices.

The early work of Chevalier (1972) was concerned with the impact of market share on performance in the US cement, automobile and biscuit manufacturing industries. It provided empirical evidence to support what was part of the mythology of the marketer, namely the cherished belief that market share has a strong positive impact on profitability. However, having studied industries that were in the saturation and maturity stage of the PLC, Chevalier's findings must be seen to be situational in nature and not universal. The general validity of the proposition that firms should seek to dominate the market segments in which they operate must be demonstrated for the various stages of the PLC.

Fruhan's work (1972) presented an early challenge to the conventional wisdom regarding the value of seeking to gain a large market share. He found that market share could be increased only at great expense in his study of the US mainframe computer, retail grocery and domestic air-transport businesses.

He argues that the cost of gaining market share varies at different stages in the product life-cycle. Market share can be increased at relatively low cost during the growth stage, when capacity utilisation is high and customer purchasing habits relatively fluid – and this has led to work on the nature of first-mover advantages. However, during the maturity stage, dominant competitors seek to defend their strategic position and, consequently, as Fruhan (1972) observes, market share is increased only at great cost. The PLC counsels against investment at the maturity stage on the grounds that the intensity of competition drives down the rate of return on capital invested to what Porter (1980) calls the 'competitive floor rate of return'. But timely investments at the early stages of the life-cycle will yield attractive returns during later stages when the rate of growth declines and market shares stabilise. In the case of high added-value products, where the firm has a patent protecting some aspect of its product or process technology, or otherwise has a significant technical advantage, there are significant barriers to entry which will assist in the pursuit of market leadership and a position of competitive strength. Nevertheless, as EMI found to its cost with the Body Scanner, competitors can enter the market and erode the dominant market share of the innovating firm where they attend, in great detail, to the particular needs of evolving market segments (i.e. focus strategy).

Writing in an evangelical mode, Hofer (1975) contends that the stage of the PLC is 'the most fundamental variable in determining an appropriate business strategy'. This view is also shared by Levitt (1965) when he argues for the use of the stage of the PLC as the basis for proposing marketing strategy guidelines. These include specific recommendations on variables of the marketing mix, such as the type and level of promotion, product differentiation, pricing, distribution, etc. On the basis of this he offers broad strategic guidelines such as those that follow:

1. In the growth stage, instead of seeking ways of getting customers to try the product, the originator should try to get them to prefer his brand.
2. Typically, the market maturity stage forces the producer to concentrate on holding his distribution outlets. In the case of branded products in particular, the originator must communicate directly with the consumer.

The application of the PLC as a strategic planning tool has also been discussed in the context of the functional areas of purchasing (Berenson, 1967), finance (Fox, 1973), logistics (Davis and Brown, 1974), and sales management (Dodge and Rink, 1978).

The use of the PLC as a prescriptive strategic marketing planning tool is widely criticised not only on the basis of the lack of empirical validation for its general shape and the length of its phases (Wind and Claycamp, 1976; Dhalla and Yuspeh, 1976, Rink and Swan, 1979; Lambkin and Day, 1989), but also for its imprecision in the context of forecasting the transition from one phase to another and when establishing which stage of its life-cycle a product form or brand is at. It is also argued that the strategic guidelines based on the product life-cycle concept, and endorsed by authors such as Levitt (1965), can often lead to inappropriate strategic marketing decisions (Wind and Claycamp, 1976; Dhalla and Yuspeh, 1976).

Other work has produced similarly conflicting viewpoints on the value and efficacy of the product life-cycle as a strategic planning tool (Enis, La Garce and Prell, 1977; Dhalla and Yuspeh, 1976; Smallwood, 1973). The main points of contention concern, first, the definition of products and markets for which the product life-cycle concept could be valid; and second, the extent to which the characteristic stages of the concept occur as a result of management decisions taken in response to changing market conditions.

With respect to the definition of *units of analyses*, much debate concerns the level of aggregation which is thought to be appropriate to the formulation of business strategy. At the level of the individual brand, changes in demand in the short to medium term are largely determined by the marketing activities of the firm and its rivals competing with substitute brands. The incisive criticisms of Dhalla and Yuspeh (1976) are based on an examination of the validity and efficacy of the life-cycle concept at the brand level (Weitz and Wensley, 1984). At the level of the product class or form, longer term changes in demand are more likely to be a function of broad environmental forces outside the firm;s control. They key question is, as Weitz and Wensley (1984) note: 'Which level of aggregation best captures the changing nature of the environment to which marketing strategy must respond?'

In one of the few recent empirical studies of product life-cycle theory, Mercer (1994) critically examined its applicability using UK data on the sales of 929 FMCG brands over a 20 year period. Specifically, Mercer's study compared the results of the 1989 Target Group Index Survey conducted by the British Marketing Research Bureau with those of the comparable survey of 1969. Among other interesting findings, he noted that the leading brands in a wide range of market

sectors in 1969 were still very much alive and kicking as leaders in 1989 – even though their features and specifications had changed. He concluded, as have others before him who looked at a set of sales data for trends that conformed to the broad shape of the PLC, that since the time horizon of most marketing managers is about two years, at the level of the brand, the PLC has little value as a prescriptive marketing management tool.

A major criticism of the product life-cycle as a basis for taking strategy decisions is, therefore, the aggregation of product-market segments which must occur for the concept to be meaningful (Dhalla and Yuspeh, 1976). This 'aggregation' will be misleading where market boundaries cannot be delineated accurately, leading in turn to the inappropriate positioning of a product with respect to the life-cycle curve, leading to an inappropriate choice of strategic guidelines.

The definition of the market is therefore important to the validity of the product life-cycle concept (Enis, La Garce and Prell, 1977). It not only prescribes the competitive arena in which a product is marketed, it also has a direct effect on how market share and hence, market growth will be assessed. Ideally, markets should be defined on the basis of all products catering for the same consumer need (Sissors, 1966). Alternatively, they should group together customers who have in common *situational or behavioural* characteristics that are significant in a strategic sense (Wasson, 1974). However, in practice it is more common for markets to be defined in terms of strategic groups of competing brands within a specific product category, perhaps perceived as substitutes by the consumer.

A relative, rather than absolute, measure of market share is used in the Boston Consulting Group's Business Portfolio. By measuring market share relative to the leading competitor, a pragmatic approach is taken to the problems of market delineation. It remains the responsibility of management to decide what market definition is most appropriate to what product market situation.

As a prescriptive strategic planning tool the product life-cycle has also been widely criticised on the grounds of the generality of the analysis it enables. Rarely is it possible to predict for a given product or brand, with any confidence, when the turning points of the curve are likely to occur, and therefore, to decide which of the strategy guidelines will be appropriate in what specific circumstances. However, as a descriptive tool, middle-ground advocates such as Doyle (1976) and Baker (1989) argue that it does offer an organising framework of some value to the strategist in thinking about strategic problems. In the course of diagnosing the strategy requirements of a given situation a rich variety of signs and symptoms may have to be evaluated and synthesised. In this context the product life-cycle may be of some managerial value. But it is also considered to be deficient (Dhalla and Yuspeh, 1976) in that it overlooks the influence of uncontrollable environmental elements and controllable marketing instruments on the shape of the curve and the length of each stage. As Lambkin and Day (1989) note, market development is also influenced by circumstances, trends and events in the surrounding resource environment, including:

- developments in product and process technology
- the availability and cost of input materials and systems;
- the presence or absence of supporting industry infrastructure;
- the presence or absence of a favourable regulatory environment.

Dhalla and Yuspeh (1976) argue that 'the PLC is a dependent variable which is determined by marketing actions it is not an independent variable to which firms adapt their marketing programme'. Thus, the management of a firm can affect the length and shape of the PLC by the decisions it takes, or does not take. Clearly, if the PLC is taken as being deterministic and given, it can become a damaging and misleading self-fulfilling prophecy. Porter (1980) argues that the strategic guidelines associated with the PLC must be questioned because the nature of competition at each stage is different for different industries. Furthermore, as Wind and Claycamp (1976) argue,

'[PLC] recommendations have usually been vague, non-operational, not empirically supported, and conceptually questionable, since they imply that strategies can be developed with little concern for the product's profitability and market share position'.

Therefore, as this section reminds us, a number of conceptual gaps in the PLC have been identified and written about at length over 45 years of claim and counter-claim. Its status as a deterministic, and thus prescriptive decision-making algorithm is no longer tenable, as numerous authors have asserted. But, like most management ideas, as they become sacrilised on entering the everyday parlance of management thought, their effects become self-fulfilling. The concepts and language they provide become no longer representative of a marketing or management problem, but rather constitutive of it. It is possible to speculate that the PLC is now part of everyday management and marketing consciousness. Ideas of it figure in the strategy discourse within firms and if this knowledge is used in the exercise of power in organisations, it will then have self-fulfilling effects. Marketing has yet to come to terms with this possibility in its research agenda.

■ Market life-cycles

Several attempts have been made to develop 'recycled' versions of the product life-cycle which are sufficiently comprehensive to yield a unifying concept for developing product-market strategy (Wind and Claycamp, 1976; Cravens, 1975; Catry and Chevalier, 1974; Enis, 1980; Enis, La Garce and Prell, 1977). But, it would seem that it is the fundamental notion of *evolution* itself which is of most value to strategic planning frameworks. The work of Hofer (1977), Buzzell (1979), Abell (1980), Day (1980), Biggadike (1983) and Lambkin and Day (1989) did signal the emergence of research which was moving toward the development of a general theory of market evolution. This work attempted to address the reported weaknesses of the particular theory of product life-cycles by de-emphasising product evolution, and introducing the concept of the evolution of the 'Market for a particular generic need' (Biggadike, 1983).

This research envisages a shift in perspective so that the market for a particular generic need becomes the unit of analysis. Time (being a proxy for marketing action) is not used as an independent variable so that the theoretical framework offers a classification of the stages of market evolution which de-emphasises the temporal pattern of market development, thus avoiding the trap of merely substituting market for product life-cycles. Kotler (1979) has argued that the PLC concept needed to be developed in the form of a product-market life-cycle model since the joint effects of product and market life-cycles are important.

The notion of an evolving market is based on the study of two major constructs (see Figure 14.2). Firstly, on the *demand* side, the heterogeneity of customer demand as measured along the notional continuum of *low differentiation* (i.e. homogeneous customer needs and mass markets) to *high differentiation* (i.e., heterogeneous customer needs and market segments); and secondly, on the *supply* side, the extent to which scale and

experience effects occur, measured along the continuum of concentration of supply, from a position of *low concentration*, or fragmented supply (i.e., a mass market and industry wide scale and experience effects are not available) to one of *high concentration* (where these effects are available).

By summarising the effect of a number of factors which tend to drive market evolution, the constructs discussed above each offer a unidimensional image of what is really a multi-dimensional process. As Table 14.1 shows, several broad indicators of stages of market evolution are available, partly reflecting the multi-dimensional nature of the evolutionary process. However, to be able to predict the way in which a market is likely to evolve, the forces which drive evolution must be examined and, as Biggadike (1983) notes, answers provided to questions such as those that follow:

DEMAND
(*i.e. extent of differentiation*)
- How are market boundaries changing?
- What is the nature and extent of segmentation?
- The degree to which the nature of customer needs (problems) and the pattern of buying behaviour (decision-making) are changing.
- What is the rate of growth?

SUPPLY
(*i.e. level of concentration*)
- How many competitors will there be?
- What pattern of entry and exit will persist?
- What will the relative sizes and market shares of competitors be?
- How will the value-added structure (cost and price characteristics) change?
- What substitute products will become available?
- How will market boundaries change?
- Price sensitivity/volume sensitivity of profits.

Figure 14.2.   *Taxonomy of market evolution*

		Extent of Concentration	
D	S	L	H
Extent of Differentiation	H	Fragmented + Differentiated	Concentrated + Differentiated
	L	Fragmented + Undifferentiated	Concentrated + Undifferentiated

Source: D. Brownlie, 'Strategic Marketing Concepts and Models', *Journal of Marketing Management* 1 (2) (1985), pp. 157–194.

Sociological explanations of the processes that operate to give rise to the life-cycle pattern of evolution are to be found in the area of the diffusion and adoption of innovation (Baker, 1992;

Table 14.1.   *Indicators of PLC Stage*

Indicator	Early Stages	Late Stage
Market growth rate	High	Low
Mass producer's sales (%)	Low	High
Competitor entry	High	Low
Competitor exit	Low	High
New feature introductions	Low	High
Age of products/services	Young	Old
Rate of technological change	High	Low
R & D/sales revenue (%)	High	Low
Marketing sales revenue (%)	High	Low
Real price behaviour	Decline	Stable
Replacement sales as percent of total sales	Low	High
Customer education emphasis of promotional mix	High	Low
Customer emphasis on price (pressure on margins)	Low	High
Elasticity of advertising and SP spend	High	Low
First time buyers as percent of total sales	High	Low

Source: Adapted by the author from Biggadike (1983).

King, 1973; Rogers and Shoemaker, 1971). This body of ideas is derived deductively from a set of sociological postulates regarding the behaviour of individuals. By seeking to explain why consumers react with varying speeds to a marketing proposition, it sheds light on the social forces which may underpin the PLC. Similarly, in the area of business strategy, a number of dynamic processes (see Table 14.2) have been observed to operate with varying degrees of intensity in many industries, thereby driving the evolutionary cycle itself.

The changing nature of customer demand is a familiar and fundamental marketing concept usefully summarised by Baker's maxim: 'the act of consumption changes the consumer' (Baker, 1992). Indeed several authors consider the notion implicit to this maxim to describe one of the driving forces of the product life-cycle (Porter, 1980; Smallwood, 1973; Weitz and Wensley, 1984; Baker 1983). Underlying the product life-cycle is the diffusion process and the associated concept of adopter categories (innovators, early adopters, early majority, late majority, laggards)

Table 14.2.   *Processes driving evolution*

– long-run changes in growth;
– changes in buyer segments served;
– buyers' learning;
– reduction of uncertainty;
– diffusion of proprietary knowledge;
– accumulation of experience;
– expansion (or contraction) in scale;
– changes in input and currency costs;
– product innovation;
– marketing innovation;
– process innovation;
– structural change in adjacent industries;
– government policy change;
– entries and exits.

Source: Porter (1980).

(Rogers and Shoemaker, 1971) which classifies the buying behaviour of individuals according to its reactivity, or rate of acceptance. Potential buyers pass through, or drop out of an adoption process that culminates in observable trial and first-purchase adopter behaviour. The rate of acceptance is influenced by factors such as these:

- the perceived comparative advantage of the new product in relation to the best available alternative.
- the perceived risk, jointly determined by financial exposure in the event of failure and uncertainty about the outcome.
- barriers to adoption that impede acceptance.
- information about the product and its availability.

Diffusion theory tells us that the attitudes, values, needs, expectations, motivations, etc., of the buyers who are likely to adopt at various stages, will differ. Consequently, during the maturity phase of the life-cycle, where repeat purchasing accounts for a large proportion of expressed demand, any first time buyers will exhibit the characteristics of laggards – previous first time buyers taking more of a 'system' view of their needs during the second and third purchase as opposed to their initial problem-solving approach (Abell, 1980).

The emerging theory of market evolution argues that the extent of likely convergence or divergence of customer needs fulfilled by the product, is of strategic importance to the supplier. A major strategic marketing planning *assumption* will then concern the way in which the nature of demand is thought likely to change. Where the evolving pattern of customer demand tends to be divergent, so that the generic need that constitutes the market is able to be differentiated, secure competitive positioning and a targetted marketing effort will dictate the strategy requirements to be fulfilled by the firm. The theory prescribes that where the assumption is made that a fragmented market will emerge and persist, the marketing mix decisions are taken in pursuit of selective distribution and promotional effort; product features and capabilities consistent with the user's needs for quality and the freedom to exercise a premium pricing strategy that reflects the perceived value of the product offering. If this is so, strategies are of dubious value if they pursue the accumulation of industry-wide

market share, particularly where localised pockets of demand persist and distribution channels are incapable of affording a wide coverage of the overall market (i.e. where the market could be described as having attained a fragmented and differentiated stage of evolution). Such market conditions traditionally prevail in the distributive trades and service industries (e.g. tourism, hotels, restaurants, specialist retailers, furniture, jewellery) where the local flavour is to be guarded jealously.

Where a few substantial market segments are expected to prevail and wide distribution coverage is available, the market could be described as concentrated and differentiated. In this case it may be a viable strategy to use a differentiated product and a specialised marketing mix to pursue a large share of one of the market segments and within it a low cost position via scale and experience effects.

Where customer needs are thought likely to exhibit the tendency to converge over time, becoming more homogeneous and giving rise to mass markets of the concentrated and undifferentiated variety, for firms with access to the capital resources it is a viable strategy to pursue the accumulation of industry-wide market share and, as a result of scale and experience effects, an appropriate position of cost leadership based on the standardisation of goods and services. However, capacity planning decisions taken in a buoyant business environment frequently lead to poor capacity utilisation rates when market conditions deteriorate. The core marketing problem would then seem to be the *reconciliation of manufacturers' past investment decisions with the current mood of the market*. Thus the cycle of market evolution must be seen as being dynamic so that the core strategic marketing problem is not merely to 'predict' if and when one particular stage of evolution will occur, but what sequence of evolutionary stages the market is likely to pass through in the long term. Only in this way is the firm likely to be able to develop and maintain a sustainable comparative advantage.

Having opted for the assumption of convergence, the strategic marketing choices available to the firm are then all guided by the goals of market share growth and per unit cost reductions with accumulated experience.

In many ways this body of ideas still fails to provide an adequate account of the processes that drive market evolution. The unit of analysis has changed and a broader perspective is afforded, but, the underlying ideas are still normative and heavily informed by the ghosts and habits of thought that haunt and taunt the PLC.

However, in more recent years marketing scholars have visited, or re-visited, the ideas of the population ecology school of thought in an attempt to provide a more robust account of competition in dynamic product-markets. In an agenda setting piece, Lambkin and Day (1989) map out the terrain of the ecological paradigm as a basis for identifying its potential for contributing to our understanding of the evolution of competition in product-markets. In their view the ecology model provides the basis for a robust supply-side theory of market evolution which embraces the following elements:

- A *population growth process* that accounts for differences in the competitive environment over time, particularly in the intensity of competition.
- A *typology of strategies* for competing in new markets that recognises the diversity of resources and skills among the business population, as well as differences in their order of entry.
- An *integrative model* that provides predictions about the likely success of different generic strategies as the product-market evolves through different stages.

At the heart of their representation of the ecology model is the proposition that competitive conditions change over time as the *density* of the supplier population increases. The cornerstone of the model is provided by the concept of *population growth* which specifies, in mathematical terms, the exponential process by which the population of suppliers grows to some ultimate equilibrium level. The rate of change in the population is a function of some natural rate of increase and the upper limit sustainable, given the carrying capacity of the resources available in the environment.

The following conceptual building blocks are introduced by Lambkin and Day (1989) in an attempt to derive an elaborate theory of market evolution which draws on the principles of population ecology:

- *Density dependence*

This concept encompasses the way in which competitive conditions in any population are a function of the number of organisations competing for the finite level of resources available to that population. As the density of the population increases, demands on limited resources increase and it becomes increasingly difficult to avoid direct competition, so that the gains of one competitor are made at the expense of another. The population density increases until the resource space is filled and a shake-out occurs. In a new population, where the population density is low, competition is likely to be indirect and diffuse because the abundance of resources means that the gains of one competitor are not made at the expense of another. Given that the density of a developing population is constantly changing with the coming and going of competitors, the level of resources available and the nature of the prevailing competitive conditions are continually changing.

- *Niches*

This concept embraces the way in which each unique combination of resources and competitive conditions is thought to be sufficient to support one type of organisation. But, because a market typically contains several overlapping niches, competition is likely to alter the extent to which an individual organisation can proliferate in its chosen niche. Taking the premise that organisations are fashioned from the resources available to them at their time of founding, those founded at the same time tend to have similar a form. Hence the development of a new population occurs in *waves of organising*, with different types of organisations appearing in each stage. And once a particular type of organisation emerges, it tends to be preserved in its original form because of *structural inertia*, in the form of commitments to past technologies, vested interests and ways of thinking. This produces a resistance to change that impedes the ability of established competitors to adapt their structure to meet changing circumstances, but provide the opportunity for new entrants to emerge.

● *Niche width*

This concept embraces the idea that an organisation can choose to spread its resources across a broad, or narrow spectrum of the environment, i.e. to generalise, or specialise, through the width of its product line, the size and diversity of its customer base and the extent of its geographic coverage.

On the basis of the descriptive framework provided by those concepts, Lambkin and Day (1989) go on to develop a typology of market entry and stages of market evolution. It is well worth consulting. The level of *population density* is in some ways substituted for the rate of growth of product sales in the PLC. Thus, in an embryonic market, the population density is low; in a developing market it is increasing; and in a mature market it is high.

At this stage of their discussion it becomes clear to this author, that the set of concepts and categorical descriptions they are proffering are as open to the criticism of tautology as those of the PLC. One significant difference lies in the provenance of the underlying ideas of population ecology and their novelty in the marketing domain. Yet, at its core is the idea of efficent markets, not managers, as resource allocation mechanisms. Moreover, the population ecology school of thought does promote the idea that organisations are selected for survival by the market, and that managers have, at the end of the day, very little influence on which organisations the market chooses for survival and which for decline and demise.

■ The growth-share matrix

This chapter now progresses from a discussion of one highly influential, yet contentious marketing framework to further discussion of yet another.

The Boston Consulting Group's (BCG's) Growth-Share matrix (Henderson, 1970), otherwise known as the Business Portfolio (Henderson, 1973) or Boston Box has stimulated a great deal of interest and heated debate in the hallowed halls of the marketing academy, much of which has close parallels in the debate surrounding its auld stablemate the PLC. Like the PLC, the ideas of the Growth Share Matrix (GSM) are simple to grasp and have intuitive appeal.

The history of the Growth-Share Matrix (GSM) makes an interesting story in itself, as Morrison and Wensley (1991) and McKiernan (1992) relate. In its early years, during the late 1960s and early 1970s, it was described and discussed as if its menagerie bulged heroically with analytical power sufficient to solve the problems of the most tormented strategist. And many novice lecturers were seduced by this imputed analytical muscle and its apparent elegance, the present author included. But, if you revisit the literature of those heady days you will discover a degree of reverence, seldom seen in journals these days, which borders on the partisan blind faith of the convert. The youthful ebullience of the 1970s led, inevitably it seems, to the lean years of the 1980s, as academic interest in the GSM took a nose dive, and it fell into obscurity and contempt.

The exodus began around the late 1970s when a number of critics of the GSM began to creep out of the woodwork. These heretics soon gained force over the faithful and it was not long before their heresy became a new orthodoxy. The main bone of contention had to do with the severe conceptual weaknesses of its underlying principles which ultimately emasculated its power as a diagnostic. However, thoughtful critics were also motivated to expose what they saw as the uncritical and uncreative way in which the technique was being taught, particularly to MBA students, as a robust prescriptive device. Yet, the criticisms of the GSM were often repeated like a debunking-doctrine mantra in some quarters and the original set of ideas were strip-mined, leaving a carcass of little interest to anyone but the most emaciated vulture. Like the PLC before it, the GSM was accused of being built on dangerously reductive generalisations awaiting the homage of facts; its classificatory scheme was arbitrary and lacked a sound metrology; and its rhetoric had more in common with the evangelism of the soap box than the tightly defined and qualified prose of the scientific journal.

Yet, with the benefit of some distance from the heat of the debate, and 20-20 hindsight, one wonders what all the fuss was about. For, just as with the PLC, much of the criticism focused on the technique as if its utilisation was self-contained and inevitable, adhering closely in all cases to the conditions laid down by BCG. Indeed, the BCG frequently counselled caution concerning the importance of the GSM as a management tool, where less astute commentators seemed to throw caution to the wind. Perhaps it was just a little vainglorious and self-deluding to believe that organisations actually formed strategies on the basis of the GSM prescriptions alone. Indeed, in some ways the belief that they did, or might have done, which was often claimed to be one reason for criticising the GMS, says as much about how little was understanood about how organisations work, than the dangers inherent to adhering blindly to simple prescriptions.

Very little systematic study has been conducted into the ways in which the GSM has opened up the possibilities of strategy discourse, or indeed closed them down as many critics assert. In spite of this, many contemporary commentators, including Morrison and Wensley (1991) and McKiernan (1992), have enumerated the *restrictive* effects of the GSM terminology. Its simple and vivid language is said to be both powerful and picturesque. And doomsayers often warn of the disastrous consequences that will inevitably follow from the unquestionning acceptance of this language by naive managers. Seeger (1984) provides an interesting, if typical, reaction to the imputed power of the GSM language, warning of the dangers of substituting its over-simplifying language for analysis and common-sense. Yet, much of this commentary is anecdotal, often drawing on the accounts given by senior executives as they attempt to communicate, sometimes to an academic audience, the bases of their

organisations' strategies. That there may be a vast difference between what those executives *choose to say* to a particular audience and what they *do* within their organisational context, often seems to have been overlooked in the heat of debate. After all, senior executives are always under pressure to manage impressions and reputations, or to *talk a good story*, that is to present a face of the organisation which is acceptable to the audience at hand. So, one wonders who is really wet behind the ears when those accounts are accepted as uncritically as it is often claimed the GSM dogma is.

The author is tempted to speculate that, like the PLC, the GSM has provided a language which has facilitated and empowered the strategy discourse. And he suspects that this is inevitably the case for all intuitively appealing management concepts, such as Parkinson's Law and the Peter Principle, that provide a simple and powerful imagery by means of which managers can make sense of the world they inhabit. Today the language of cash cows and dogs is very much part of the collective consciousness of marketing and strategy, both in the sacred world of academia, as well as the profane world of practitioners. So, as with the PLC, you could then argue that the GSM is no longer simply representative of marketing strategy knowledge, but constitutive of it.

What follows below is an attempt to recount the tale of the GSM.

At its simplest the message of the GSM was a diagnostic one. It was said to be capable of assigning broad product-market strategies to products on the basis of the market growth rate and its market share relative to competitors' products. By relating cash flow to market share and market growth, it could then determine those products that represent opportunities for investment, those that should generate investment funds, and those that drain funds and which should be liquidated or divested.

The logic of the GSM draws on the fundamental ideas underpinning the *Product Life-Cycle*, and the *Experience Curve* and it is partly as a result of this that the tool was imputed with such analytical power.

☐ *On the experience curve*

Study of the experience curve effect was first advanced by the Boston Consulting Group (BCG) as a result of its work with firms in industries, such as electronics and motor cycles (Hedley, 1977; Henderson, 1968; BCG, 1975). Essentially the experience curve as it was then formulated generalised the 'learning-effects' (Hirschmann, 1964) that had earlier been found to occur in aircraft manufacture (Wright, 1936), where a significant inverse relationship was observe between labour costs and cumulative production: i.e. *the rate of change of direct labour costs with respect to cumulative output (the first differential) was seen to be negative.*

Although the terms *learning curve* and *experience curve* are often used interchangeably, they can and should be distinguished. Learning effects typically refer in a narrow way to labour costs alone, as they reflect short term cost reductions achieved through *learning by doing*. On the other hand, experience effects refer to the reduction in total costs achieved over the total life of a product. Both are measured by total accumulated output to date. But, as Hall and Howell (1989) observe, learning and experience curves differ with respect to the range of costs covered; the range of output during which the reduction in costs supposedly takes place; and the causes of cost reduction. Learning by doing is then seen to be something that not only affects assembly operators, but everyone involved in an organisation, from the chairperson to the first-year apprentice – all whom should improve the performance of their role through experience.

The experience curve is based on the postulate that the length of time required to complete a task is inversely related to the number of times the task is performed – or, more specifically, that *the total unit costs, in real terms (inflation adjusted) of producing, distributing and marketing a particular item (value added costs) decline by a fixed percentage (usually 10 to 30%) each time the cumulative number of units produced (experience) is doubled.* This is just a fancy way of saying that *practice makes perfect.*

Henderson (1968) expresses the general form of the experience curve in this way:

$$y_n = a_m \cdot x^{-b}$$

where :

- y_n is the cost of producing, distributing, selling, etc., the nth item;
- n is the current level of cumulative production (i.e., experience);
- a_m is the cost of the mth item;
- m is the cumulative production at some earlier date;
- x is the ratio of experience at one point in time to that at another, given in this case by n/m;
- the exponent b is a parameter representing the learning rate, which for a 95% experience curve has a value of 0.074, and for a 60% experience curve, 0.738.
- So, where a learning rate of 0.738 apples, and the ratio of experience is 2, the value of the experience effect is given by $2^{-0.738}$. Where this ratio is 3, the value of the experience effect is given by $3^{-.0738}$.
- Thus, where a 60% experience curve is observed, the cost of producing the 200th unit will be about 60% that of the 100th unit, or per unit, costs decrease by 40% for every doubling of cumulative production. On linear axes the rate of cost decline is seen to be logarithmic; on logarithmic axes the decline is linear as Figure 3 illustrates.
- The historical cost-volume curve plotted in Figure 14.3 involves the marriage of two time series: one tracks the historical behaviour of inflation-adjusted average total costs; and the other tracks the historical behavior of cumulative output.

This formulaic expression of the experience curve and its diagrammatic representation in Figure 14.3, may give the impression that its effects are immutable and that some natural economic law has been captured and reduced to the interplay of five variables. However, this not so, as the BCG did warn by way of a caveat in their

Figure 14.3. *Industry experience curve using log/log scales*

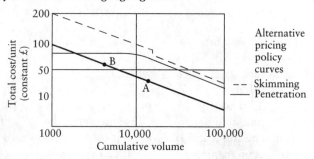

seminal report *Perspectives on Experience* (1972) . Experience effects and the associated reductions in per unit total costs do not occur automatically (Hedley, 1976). A precondition of the realisation of these effects is that an explicit aim of competent management in all areas of the firm, including manufacturing, sales, purchasing, distribution and marketing, is the aggressive pursuit of a downward trend in costs and the attainment of economies of scale. And as Alberts (1989) reminds us too, as did Abell and Hammond (1979) and Hayes and Wheelwright (1984) before him, driving costs downwards is not merely an automatic function of repetition or growth. They are very important keys, but managers must be able to turn them. So, forcing down costs also involves management imagination, innovation and commitment.

Other forces are known to contribute to the experience effect. These are: investment in cost saving equipment as volume increases; the development of specialised knowledge and skills so that managerial decision taking and labour efficiency is improved; the substitution of cheaper or more efficient raw materials and technology; tight operations control so that the build-up of non-productive overheads is managed downwards. Table 14.3 summarises the likely sources of the experience effect.

Generally speaking, the effects of scale and experience are thought to occur together, even if they are conceptually very difficult to separate (Abell and Hammond, 1979). For instance, the benefits of work specialisation and standardisation become possible, not only because of the size of an operation, but also because of the

Table 14.3. *Sources of the experience effect*

– Labour efficiency
– Work specialisation and methods improvements
– New production processes
– Changes in the resource mix
– Standardisation
– Product redesign
– Performance improvements

ingenuity, skill and dexterity of the labour force. However, in very high fixed cost, capital intensive industries, such as petrochemicals, the scale effect can be achieved alone. Thus, new entrants can use this feature to gain a cost advantage over high experience competitors where new process technology is utilised – such a situation is has evolved where the high priced and cost competitive products of the Saudi Arabian petrochemicals industry have become a threat to the market shares and capacity utilisation rates of the well established (experienced) West European producers.

As Figure 14.3 suggests, the experience curve for an industry can be used to forecast changes in costs over long-term accumulated production. In this regard the experience curve is then thought to be a valuable conceptual framework for long-term strategy development (Day and Montgomery, 1983, 1984). Although as Henderson (1984) warns, the application of the experience curve 'requires careful analysis of the definitions of cost components and the definitions of products and markets. It can be misleading when applied to policy decisions if it is used without reference to the effects that will be common to the competitors.'

Where its doctrine is adhered to, the experience curve may then have implications for the strategic pricing policy of firms operating within an industry. Ideally, if the firm could predict the pattern of growth in a product market and the sensitivity of demand to changes in prices, the experience curve could then be used to predict costs and the cash flow positions arising from different pricing strategies. Under a 'skimming' policy the firm with a new and unique product would earn monopoly profits by charging a high initial price and limiting the costs of launching the product. In this way it is possible to avoid the initial losses normally associated with the introduction of new products. But, if imitative innovators are attracted by the margins available, growth in market share could be stifled with a subsequent loss of competitive leverage unless price reductions are made to widen the products appeal. Under a 'penetration' policy the firm with a new and unique product would sacrifice short-term profitability expedients. Instead it would pursue the longer term growth in market share and cash flow which could occur if the firm consolidated its costs advantage by descending the experience curve ahead of the imitative innovators. For any firm, the question of which policy to pursue depends on its growth and profit objectives, and its assessment of the impact on environmental trends on competition within the industry.

In its study of the strategy alternatives for the British Motorcycle Industry (BCG, 1975), the BCG argue that 'experience-based price reductions went a long way toward explaining the historical competitive effectiveness of the Japanese in the market place in small and medium motorcycles'. For machines in the range 126–250 cc they found Japanese manufacturers to have an experience curve of 76%; slopes of 81% and 88%, respectively, were found for their machines in the ranges 51–125 cc, and under 50 cc. The strong and consistent downward trend in real price levels was found to reflect experience-based cost reductions and not diminishing margins.

The principal implication of the experience effect is thought to be that the firm with the greatest accumulated experience will have the lowest per unit costs, the highest margins and the highest profits. Hedley (1977) supports this view when he argues that since the profitability of the firm with respect to its competitors is a function of its relative market share, then high share businesses are more profitable than low share businesses. The research of the PIMS study provides notional empirical support for the experience curve explanation of the profitability-market share relationship, and as Weitz and Wensley (1984) note, it 'supplants any explanation that claims that market power had permitted monopolistic pricing'.

An important conclusion drawn by the BCG from the Experience Curve is that market share is a surrogate measure of a firm's position on this curve (Henderson, 1968). A firm (or SBU) with the largest share of a market, it suggests, will be the most profitable at the prevailing price level because it will have the lowest unit costs and highest margins (indicated by the point A in Figure 14.3); less experienced competitors (indicated by the point B in Figure 14.3) will have lower market shares and, therefore, higher unit costs and lower margins. Consequently, the maxim in this instance is that margins, and generated cash flow, increase with relative market share (Sissors, 1966).

So, on the basis of the above paragraphs, you may already be able to guess the nature of the *strategic imperative* which underpins the experience curve doctrine. Because costs decrease with repetition and growth, the key to any organisation's cost position in relation to the position of its rivals is its relative growth. So, as Aaker (1984) notes, competitive cost advantage flows from increasing volume faster than your rivals. Clearly, this view mirrors the greater market share argument outlined previously, whereby greater market share leads to lower costs and, therefore, higher profits. The strategic imperative is then that for firms to be a market leader they must build market share by some combination of aggressive pricing and promotion and pre-emptive capacity expansion (Day and Montgomery, 1983).

The argument that building market share will work to create competitive cost advantage presumes that increasing the level of cumulative volume *causes* lower costs. As Alberts (1989) observes, where this presumption is not tenable, the strategic imperative is inappropriate; and without the strategic imperative, there is no experience curve doctrine.

As previous sections have discussed, there is opposition to the view that holds that the most profitable long term strategy is the pursuit of a dominant market share (Wensley, 1981; Baden-Fuller, 1981; Wensley, 1983). Researchers have raised several questions regarding the universality of the high market-share doctrine in general, and the BCG's experience-curve conclusions in particular. As a result of their study of the US automobile, commercial airframe, mainframe computer and TV picture tube industries, Abernathy and Wayne(1974) question the applicability of the experience curve in situations where product differentiation opportunities are high, or buying motives are principally non-economic in character. They argue that the market's demand for product innovation, the rate of technological change in the industry, and competitor's ability to use product performance as a basis for competing, all place practical limits on the degree to which a firm can continue to pursue volume/cost reductions. They also argue that the process of market development often creates market segments with differential needs which cannot be satisfactorily met by an undifferentiated approach.

More recently writers such as Alberts (1989) and Hall and Howell (1985) have provided very comprehensive and elaborate reviews of the conceptual underpinnings of the experience curve, as well the empirical validity of its claims. Both are strongly recommended to you.

In a penetrating analysis of the experience curve from the economist's perspective, Hall and Howell (1985) do not dispute that its effects are widely observable across products. However, they suggest that costs may be equally as closely correlated with current output as with accumulated output, implying the impact of economies of scale rather than long-term learning effects. They also point to various statistical and accounting reasons which they say can generate wholly or partly spurious experience curves. That experience trends can only be derived ex-post leads them to argue that the curves have very little pre-

dictive value. And on the basis of their detailed review of empririca studies, they conclude, as does Alberts (1989), that the experience curve largely fails the tests of empirical validity.

Alberts (1989) rebuts the experience curve doctrine on various counts. His main point of contention is that it mis-states the causes and processes of innovation within organisations that precipitate opportunities for cost reduction, especially where complex activities are involved. He states that it also over-states the role of economies of scale in reducing costs.

So, it is not surprising that writers such as Hall and Howell (1989) and Alberts (1989) dispute the operational usefulness of the experience curve. But, let's pause for a note of caution here. As with the PLC and the GSM, the basic ideas of the experience curve – i.e., of managing costs downwards, of costs reducing with volume gains, of learning by doing, of practice makes perfect – are all very popular with the business community and have become very much a part of its collective consciousness often as taken-for-granted notions. And if these ideas inform and empower the strategy discourse in ways that are not yet understood, it is perhaps a little bit imprudent to dismiss them out of hand. This author firmly believes that it is no longer enough to bracket those sort of issue off to the realm of *organizational behaviour*, as do Hall and Howell, as if *rationality* existed independently of social agents and the interactive processes through which meaning is negotiated.

☐ *Back to the GSM*

In addition to the ideas of the PLC and the experience curve, one other important concept informs the approach of the GSM – that of *sustainable growth*. The underlying principle is that the *net free cash flow* of a company must be kept *positive* for a company's growth to be financed through internal funds and its debt capacity. A company's *sustainable growth rate* is then determined by the relative cash positions of its portfolio of businesses. And since some businesses can be *cash* deficient, whilst others are *growth* deficient, it is possible that the latter can provide the cash to support the growth of the former. It then follows that there is a need to strike a balance between cash-generating businesses and cash-using businesses if growth is to be funded by the company.

From the principle of sustainable growth, which has its origins in financial portfolio theory, a number of propositions follow: growth needs to be financed and requires significant cash investments over time before a positive net cash flow is achieved; the cash needed to support businesses operating in rapidly growing markets exceeds that needed for those operating in slower-growth markets, this being a consequence of the greater fixed and working capital requirements associated with expanding productive capacity and developing marketing leverage; and it is theoretically possible for companies with the highest returns to also be the fastest growers.

The latter proposition provides, as McKiernan (1992) observes, the bridging mechanism between the building blocks of *experience* and *sustainable growth* which underpin the GSM. He expresses the link as follows: 'If the company with the highest returns can grow the fastest (the sustainable growth principle) and the company with the highest market share has the highest profit margin (the experience effect), then the latter should be able to finance the highest growth rate'. As McKiernan (1992) notes, the GSM is essentially a presentational device which seeks to 'encapsulate in four variables a strategic profile of a multi-business organisation'. In this way it can be used to generate a first cut analysis of the dynamics of the competitive environment. And if used in this way, as the BCG originally intended, it has no peers. McKiernan argues that 'it is arguable, even now, whether there is a simpler, more concise and more powerful means by which managers can begin to think in strategic terms about their spread of businesses'.

The GSM provides a means of classifying businesses or products according to the criteria of *competitive position* (measured by market share relative to that of the firm's largest competitor) and *market growth rate*, adjusted for inflation (see Figure 14.4). This presentational model can

Figure 14.4. *The business portfolio and associated cash flow*

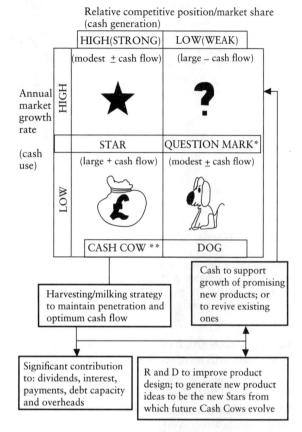

*Also known as Wildcat or Problem Child.
**Examples of Cash Cows include Nestlé's Yorkie Bar, Cadbury's Dairy Milk, Dreft, Carnation Evaporated Milk and the VW Golf.

Source: Day (1977).

be further developed by dilating the point representing a business's or product's position in terms of the given dimensions, to form a circle, the area (or diameter) of which is proportional to sales (see Figure 14.5).

The lines which determine the high and low divisions of each dimension are located so that businesses or products in the upper left and lower right quadrants experience a roughly balanced cash flow, whilst those in the upper right quadrant use cash. Those in the lower left quadrant generate cash. Those positioned to the left of the competitive position (or market share) dividing

Figure 14.5. *Sequences of product-market strategies*

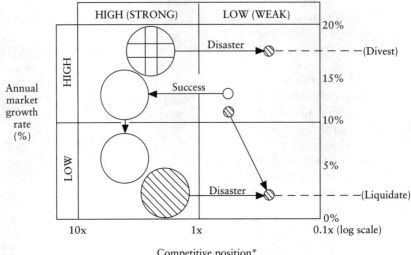

Competitive position

*Competitive position is largely measured by relative market share. This is plotted on a logarithmic scale to be consistent with experience curve effects. Relative market share is defined as the ratio of the firm's size to that of its largest competitors. Prior to 1976 this axis of the matrix was labelled 'relative market share'. The definition of 'the market' clearly influences the validity of this measure of competitive position.

line will, therefore, have strong cash flows, those to the right will have weak cash flows.

Products or businesses below the market growth dividing line need relatively little investment to maintain market share. Those above it need significant investment to keep astride of market growth.

According to the GSM a firm has four basis alternative product-market strategies that it can adopt in pursuit of its objectives: investment (Question Mark); maintenance (Star); harvesting (Cash Cow); withdrawal (Dog). Table 14.4 briefly indicates the important characteristic of each of these strategies. It also shows that there is a clear relationship between the stage of evolution of a product-market segment and its GSM classification: *Question Marks* being the uncertain new products at the introductory stage of their evolution; *Stars* being those products experiencing rapidly growing demand, and rapid growth in the firm's capacity to manufacture and distribute them; *Cash Cows* being those products with a large share of a mature market; and *Dogs* being those products with a low share of a declining market.

Figure 14.5 illustrates some of the possible sequences of product-market development that can occur. The path to 'fame and fortune' is shown on this diagram as the 'success' sequence. It represents the ideal case where considerable investment is made in a promising new product (Question Mark) to support it during phases of market development and growth, in order to obtain a strong competitive position. It is then managed as a source of cash (harvested) when market growth decelerates and the product enters the mature stage of its life-cycle.

In discussing the product life-cycle it was stated that the long-term survival of a firm depends on there being a *balanced mix* of products that generate cash (Cash Cows/Stars) – the 'bread and butter' products – and other promising new products (Stars/Question Marks) that need cash to support growth during periods of market development. An imbalanced portfolio can take several forms (see Table 14.5). However, the eventual effect of it, given no corrective action, is likely to be at best a cash crisis, and at worst bankruptcy. Indeed a common cause of bankruptcy occurs where firms invest heavily in promoting and dis-

Table 14.4. *Growth-share matrix guidelines*

	Strategic management guidelines
STAR	Market growth is rapid. Shake-outs will occur as firms jostle for competitive position. Large cash balances are generated but heavy investment is required to maintain market share growth and consolidate competitive position. Low margins may be essential to deter competition, but longer-term prospects improve as growth slows, when large cash returns should be obtained. If investment is cut back during growth to gain cash returns in the short/medium term the DISASTER sequence occurs, a STAR becoming a DOG.
CASH COW COW	A STAR becomes a CASH COW as market growth slows during maturity. Investment requirements are low and limited to those needed to reduce costs and maintain marketing leverage. Large cash surpluses are generated. Market positions become entrenched as the '3 or 4' dominant competitors consolidate their positions of strength. CASH COWS are managed for cash.
QUESTION MARK	QUESTION MARKS are managed to gain market share and strengthen their competitive position. To do so considerable investment is needed since rapid market growth occurs and cash generation is low as a result of low market share. The initial step of the SUCCESS sequence occurs when a QUESTION MARK becomes a STAR because of market share gains. However, if growth slows and competitive position is still weak, a QUESTION MARK becomes a DOG. Where STAR potential is not evident divestment is recommended. As a market contracts during decline because of, e.g., product substitution, a CASH COW becomes a DOG.
DOGS	DOGS have relatively weak competitive positions in low-growth and mature markets. In most cases they have little potential for gaining market share and are not very profitable. However where it is possible to obtain a relatively strong competitive position in a market segment, a modest cash return may be generated (CASH DOG). Liquidation of DOG products (SBUs) is usually recommended.

tributing a new product in anticipation of sales growth, without possessing the profitable and well established products from which it can fund the endeavour internally. Similarly, as Figure 14.6 suggests, a portfolio dominated by cash cows also suggests a shortage of ideas for the product innovations which will be the stars and cash cows of the future. Clearly, determining the nature of this balance, and achieving it, is of strategic concern to top management.

In the present era of low economic growth, pursuing the 'success sequence' is, for many firms, becoming an increasingly forlorn mission. Not only are potential Cash Cows and Stars difficult to find, but the life blood of many firms is being supplied by products that the GSM rationale

Table 14.5. *The imbalanced portfolio*

Cause	*Effect*
Too many Dogs	Inadequate cash flow, profits and growth
Too many Question Marks	Inadequate cash flow and profits
Too many Cash Cows	Inadequate growth
	Excessive cash flow
Too many Stars	Excessive demands on cash and managerial resources. Unstable growth and profits

Figure 14.6. *A portfolio of Caterpillar's construction equipment products*

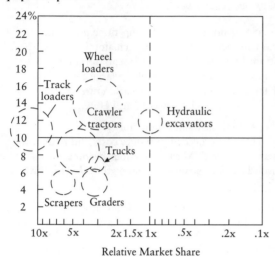

Relative Market Share

Source: Luck and Ferrel (1985).

classes as Dogs. Indeed, McNamee (1988) estimated that these days 80% of businesses lie in the Dog category. So, what strategic options do managers of such businesses face, when the stark GSM prescription is to divest? McKiernan (1992) explores this issue in some depth in his recent book on the topic of what he calls the 'forgotten cell'. He identifies three alternative strategies for managing Dog businesses focussing on recovery and rejuvenation through managing organisational change and transformation.

Considerable criticism has been made for some time of the BCG's belief that 'Dogs are essentially worthless' and that they should be liquidated or divested if possible. Research indicates that there are considerable managerial problems associated with eliminating the Dogs (Avlonitis, 1985). It has also been shown that in a wide range of stagnant industries, firms can compete successfully with Dog products (Hammermesh and Silk, 1979). In some industries Dogs provide a platform for the development of future Stars, act as loss leaders or otherwise help to complete a product range. US Manufacturers of EPROM semiconductors have argued that they need to be involved in the low profitability, high volume production of commodity memory chips if they

wish to operate in the more specialist and profitable sectors of the market: it is the former activity that is the proving ground for new semiconductor production technology.

The apparent response of the BCG to criticism of its guidelines concerning Dogs has been the emergence of the Cash Dog. On the subject Michael Goold, then of the BCG, stated that 'in a business where competition is mature and direct, that is where there is little opportunity for product differentiation, or for competition based on serving the specific needs of particular customer groups through distinctive marketing approaches, it will be necessary to consider liquidation'. However, where firms operate with moderate success in segments less exposed to the competitive dominance of the market leader, 'maintenance of position and competitive stability' are recommended for what must then be Cash Dogs. As Goold noted 'the common factor in successful strategies of segment focus is that they permit the Dog to build some sort of competitive advantage in the segment that he lacks more generally... Consequently it is essential to analyse precisely how the economics of competition in the segment differ from those in the more broadly defined business and whether they can offer any real protection from the strengths of the industry leader' (Goold, 1981).

Additional criticisms of the GSM approach tend to focus on its over-simplified, and somewhat misleading representation of possible strategy positions and its use of the dimensions Growth Rate and Market Share, which are themselves considered to be inadequate descriptions of, respectively, industry attractiveness and competitive position. As Wensley (1981a) concludes, this approach to strategy development 'encourages the use of general rather than specific criteria as well as implying assumptions about mechanisms of corporate financing and market behaviour which are either unnecessary or false'. Indeed, it has been observed that market leadership does not always offer the benefit of lower costs, more positive cash flow and higher profits. On the contrary: 'the number of highly viable companies occupying market 'niches' is legion, and growing by the day' (Lorenz, 1981).

Recent trends which have favoured the development of greater specialisation in some markets include the growth of private label consumer products and the emergence of differential preferences in some industrial markets, e.g. computers, as customers become familiar with products, or develop relevant expertise.

The GSM also tends to overlook other important strategic factors which are more a function of the external competitive environment (Day, 1977). For example, technological change, barriers to entry, social, legal, political and environmental pressures, union and related human factors, elasticity of demand and the cyclical nature of sales. The application of the GSM to strategic decision taking is in the manner of a diagnostic rather than a prescriptive aid in instances where observed cash flow patterns do not conform with those on which the four product-market categories are based. This commonly occurs where changes in product-market strategies have short-term transient effects on cash flow. Further limitations occur in three specific situations:

1. Where barriers to entry are great, so that margins are wide enough in rapid growth to finance further growth and generate cash simultaneously.
2. In a mature market, where price competition reduces margins, so that despite declining financing needs, cash flow deteriorates.
3. If experience or scale effects are small or not proprietary, for example: where differences in experience are negated by innovations in production technology which are quickly adopted by existing competitors or offer potential new entrants the opportunity to subvert the value of current experience; where capacity utilisation rates differ, or where a competitor has established a low-cost source of raw materials, irrespective of his relative market share.

McKiernan (1992) organises the criticisms of the GSM into three groups: first, those concerning its construction and operation; second those concerning the dangers of naive and careless use; and third those calling for a re-focussing on other variables which some claim the GSM overlooks. Mckiernan provides a comprehensive review of these criticisms and his book is recommended to you.

In its 1981 Annual Perspective, the BCG discussed the development of its then new tool for guiding strategy development – the Strategic Environments Matrix (Figure 14.7). This two-dimensional matrix is based on the assumption that 'the strategy requirements of any business are ruled by the competitive environment and the potential for change in that environment'. Thus, the BCG argue (as does Porter, 1980, 1985) that the competitive environment, and therefore the strategy choices the firm faces, is determined by whether the firm has few or many sources of competitive advantage, and whether they are large or small. The matrix is designed to focus attention on the overriding importance of developing and sustaining comparative advantage.

As Table 14.6 shows, the two attributes of the competitive environment of relevance to the new-improved matrix are firstly, the size of the advantage that can be achieve over competitors, and secondly, the number of unique ways it can be achieved. The matrix combines these attributes to give four possible competitive environments and associated strategy requirements. Porter (1980) has identified five 'generic industry environments' which 'differ most strongly in their fundamental strategic implications' along the key dimensions

Figure 14.7.   *Strategic environments matrix*

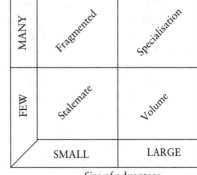

Size of advantage

Source: Boston Consulting Group (1981).

Table 14.6.   *Strategy requirements dictated by the competitive environment*

Size of advantage over competitors
(Concentration)

●━━━●

Low   High

'Fundamental difference between businesses where it is high and where it is low. The reward potential of a successful strategy is only large where the size of the advantage that can be created is also large. Only when real advantage exists can real returns accrue.'

Number of unique ways to create the advantage
(Differentiation)

●━━━●

Few   Many

'Fundamental difference between businesses that offer only one or a few ways to achieve advantage and those that present several. When differentiation is costly and not valued by customers, low price and relative cost position determine success. Firms can also succeed by tuning their offering and costs exactly to meet a specific segment's demand'.

Source: Adapted by the author from Boston Consulting Group (1981).

of industry concentrations; state of industry maturity; and exposure to international competition. Indeed, the current predilection of 'leading edge' writers for the typification of business environments shows a renewed concern for what is a fundamental characteristic of all scientific endeavour – the classification of phenomena (Wind and Robertson, 1983). Until the central organising themes are secure, the generalisations and propositions of business and marketing strategy will be unable to guide the behaviour of firms in specific situations towards the goal of comparative advantage.

To a great extent the variables of the strategic environments matrix resemble those by which the stages of market evolution are classified in Figure 14.2. Indeed the four cells of the taxonomy of market evolution more or less replicate the four competitive environments of the strategic environments matrix. For example, the Concentrated and Differentiated (Fragmented and Undifferentiated) cell of the former is the Specialisation (Stalemate) cell of the latter. Both matrices use measures of the nature of the competitive business environment and the potential for change in it which helps evaluate the long term value of a business (SBU). Of course, for this to be of predictive value, major planning assumptions have to be made with respect to the way in which the

competitive environment is likely to evolve – which involves an evaluation of the way in which customer demand (the number of approaches to achieve advantages) is likely to change and the way in which the availability of experience effects (size of advantage) is likely to change.

Although the BCG argues that the strategic environments matrix is not a substitute for the GSM, but an additional tool, the relationship between the two is readily apparent. The stalemate situation, for instance, where achieving profitability is difficult, has the ring of the Dog position about it, as the world's Aluminium Smelting Industry has discovered. Similarly, the Volume position is akin to that of the Cash Cow, where a low cost, high volume strategy is pursued. The Specialisation position embraces the specialist or selective approach to developing a business by means of market segmentation and product positioning. The growth of many a Question Mark has been managed in this way.

Attractiveness-capabilities matrices

Although the business portfolio is widely discussed in the literature, there is very little published empirical evidence, apart from the PIMS work, to demonstrate that the assumptions it makes are indeed valid. For instance, the subject of some debate is the contention that preferential investment should be made in businesses operating in high growth markets, as opposed to those in low growth markets. Underlying the debate is concern for the validity of the assumption that it is easier to gain market share in high growth markets and that there exists any quantifiable relationship between the ease with which market share can be gained and the rate of market growth. Wensley (1981b) argues that 'to justify a general bias towards the high growth markets there must [therefore] be significant evidence that the longrun incremental benefits of market share gains in such markets are greater'.

In practice, the four-cell growth-share matrix is known to have widespread appeal, despite its limitations. It was reported in 1972 ('Mead's Technique to Sort Out the Losers', 1972) that more than 100 companies worldwide incorporated the ideas of the growth-share matrix into their analyses of strategic issues – the compelling logic, apparent simplicity and intuitive appeal of the technique being in no small way responsible for this. Less interest has apparently been shown in the nine-cell matrices such as the Business Assessment Array (BAA) and the Directional Policy Matrix (DPM), both of which offer a more detailed two-dimentional framework by which

possible competitive environments and their strategy requirements can be classified.

Current thinking recognises that despite the insights provided by the GSM it frequently offers an inadequate analysis of strategic problems, especially in situations where experience curve effects are not known to occur. As Day (1980) comments 'when there are complex usage patterns and many alternative products/technologies which can satisfy customer needs, then the balance should shift toward a demand perspective', i.e. away from the cost-reduction strategies associated with periods of growth, to strategies based on segmenting customer needs. The inadequacy of the growth-share approach, becomes apparent where factors other than relative market share, or market growth, need to be used to assess the relative attractiveness of one investment opportunity compared with another.

General Electric, in consultation with McKinsey & Co., pioneered the development of the nine-cell Attractiveness-Capabilities matrix. In the context of taking resource allocation decisions among and between a wide portfolio of disparate SBUs, these matrices, although two-dimensional. offer a more elaborate strategic planning tool – largely because they make use of multivariate dimensions and are able to cope with the businesses that occupy the twilight zones between *High* and *Low* positions. The Business Assessment Array (see Figure 14.8) substitutes for

Figure 14.8. *The business assessment array and 'business postures'*

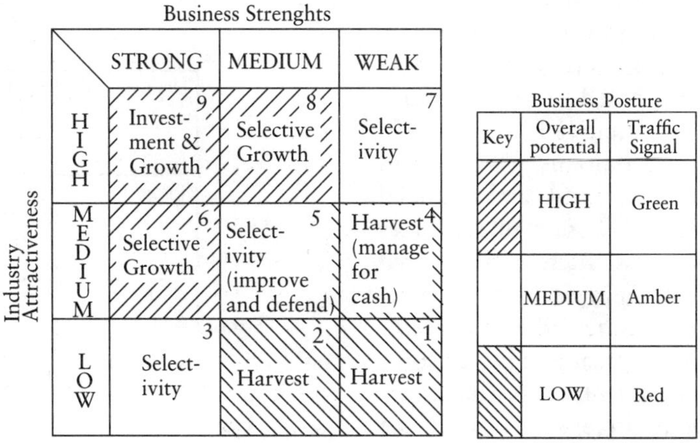

Table 14.7.   *Measures used in the BAA by General Electric*

Industry Attractiveness (Business sector prospects)	Business Strengths (Capabilities)
Market size	Domestic market share
Market growth	World (export) market share
Profitability	Market share growth
Cyclicality/seasonality	Relative market share
Ability to recover from inflation	Product quality (substitution threats)
World scope	Technological skills (product, process, R&D)
	Costs (scale and experience)
	Marketing capability
	Relative profitability

the univariate dimensions of the GSM, multivariate dimensions which combine six factors in measuring '*Industry Attractiveness*' and nine in measuring '*Business Strengths*' (Lorange, 1975) (see Table 14.7). In so doing it counters some of the early criticisms that were raised about the use of the GSM, namely that:

(i) A four-cell matrix overlooks the predominance and value of middle positions.

(ii) And that Growth Rate and Market Share are inadequate descriptors of, respectively, Industry Attractiveness and Company Competitive Position.

The development of the BAA by General Electric was primarily motivated by the immense planning problems it was encountering as a multiproduct, multi-market firm. Similarly, the world events that precipitated the 1973/74 OPEC oil crisis also gave a platform to a host of newly emerging ideas that questioned the validity of strategic decision making based on extrapolative corporate forecasts of quantitative factors.

The Shell Chemical Company (Wind and Mahajan, 1981) found that traditional financial measures for guiding the allocation of resources within a diversified business, such as forecasted rate of return on capital employed were, in some respects, becoming inadequate aids to strategic decision making. To take consideration of some of the important qualitative factors that were seen to influence competitive strategy in the

petroleum based sector of the chemical industry the two-dimension Directional Policy Matrix was conceived.

Like the BAA, the DPM also uses multivariate dimensions to measure attractiveness and capabilities. Therefore, the application of the DPM involves identifying, first, the main criteria with which to judge the prospects for a business sector (SBU); second, those criteria by which a company's position in a sector may be judges to be strong, average or weak. These criteria are then used to establish the separate ratings of the two principal dimensions, as shown in Figure 14.9. The main criteria which Shell applies in the context of the petroleum-based chemical business are shown in Table 14.8.

Figure 14.9.   *The directional policy matrix*

Prospects for sector profitability

Company's competitive capabilities	Unattractive	Average	Attractive
Weak	Disinvest 1	Phased withdrawal 4	Double or quit 7
Average	Phased withdrawal 2	Custodial (proceed with care) 5 Growth	Try harder 8
Strong	Cash generation 3	Growth 6	Leader 9

Source: Shell (1975).

Table 14.8.   *Shell's DPM criteria*

Business Sector Prospects	Company's Competitive Capabilities
Market growth rate	Market position
Market quality	Production capability
Industry feedback situation	Product research and development
Environmental (regulatory) aspects	

The dimensions of the BAA and the DPM are thought to be generally representative of the more significant elements of a firm's internal and external environment, from which strengths and weaknesses and strategic threats and opportunities arise (Dhalla and Yuspeh, 1976). However, the relative importance of these dimensions will vary from one firm (SBU) or industry to another. For example, where technical sophistication is a source of comparative advantage, technical skills and product R&D will influence business strengths and competitive capabilities; patent protection and technological substitution trends will influence industry attractiveness and business prospect. Schemes have been devised whereby the various factors contributing to the broad measures of attractiveness and capabilities can be scored and weighted according to their relative importance in specific circumstances. It is also possible to rate the sub-factors according to their attractiveness or importance as business strengths. A weighted score is thus achieved by multiplying the sub-factors' weight by its rating.

Shell's experience in applying the DPM has shown some criteria to be easier to express in quantitative terms then others. For instance, the impact of regulatory restrictions on the manufacture, transportation and marketing of petroleum products has been found to be largely quantifiable. But, it has been very difficult to quantify the importance of the factors product range, product quality and technical competence which in combination represent the criterion 'product R&D'.

The inherent ambiguity of the DPM criteria can be partially overcome by posing a number of pertinent questions. Some combination of the answers to these questions is judged and assigned

a rating score. Some of the important questions posed by Shell to establish the rating of a business's market position are listed below:

1. Has the sector a record of high, stable profitability?
2. Can margins be maintained when manufacturing capacity exceeds demand?
3. Is the product resistant to commodity pricing behaviour?
4. Is the technology of production freely available or is it restricted to those who developed it?
5. Is the market supplied by relatively few producers?
6. Is the market free from domination by a small group of powerful customers?
7. Has the product high added value when converted by the customer?
8. In the case of a new product, is the market destined to remain small enough not to attract too many producers?
9. Is the product one where the customer has to change his formulation or even his machinery if the changes suppliers?
10. Is the product free the risk of substitution by an alternative synthetic or natural product?

Since there is no universal means of weighting the importance of strategic variables independently of the specific business context, not only will assigned weightings by arbitrary in nature, but the operation of the schemes will clearly require a considerable qualitative input in the form of specialist management judgement and foresight. A team of specialists will be used to assign ratings.

The BAA and DPM diagnose strategic position and possible strategy alternatives according to the firm's (SBU's) location with respect to the two composite dimensions. As Figures 14.8 and 14.9 show, the dimensions of both matrices are conveniently divided to give a 3 × 3 matrix with nine zones (although the zones and dimensions are arranged differently in each case). Each zone represents, as with the growth-share matrix, a unique combination of industry attractions, or prospects, and company strengths. The type of strategy associated with each zone is indicated by a key word, for example, 'try harder' (DPM) or 'selective growth' (BAA). In practice the zones are frequently found to assume an irregular shape and often shade into each other or overlap. As Robinson remarks in the case of the DPM' the most appropriate boundaries can only be determined after (further) practical experience of comparing business characteristics with positions plotted in the matrix' (Robinson, Hichens and Wade, 1978).

Figure 14.8 displays the three business postures which circumscribe the nine possible classifications of the BAA. As Table 14.9 reveals, each business posture is associated with a different set of product-market objectives, management styles, important strategic variables and organisational structures. To convey the overall potential of each business posture, General Electric have drawn on the analogy of traffic signals. Strategies which locate the firm (SBU) in one of the positions 6, 8 and 9 have high potential (i.e. growth and a good competitive position prevail) and should be proceeded with – i.e. the green light shows; in positions 3, 5 or 7, the firm should proceed with caution (i.e. low growth and selective investment to defend competitive position) – i.e. the amber light shows; in position 1, 2 or 4, where the signal is red, the firm should minimise investment and ultimately consider divestment or liquidation. There is no denying that much of what the 'Attractiveness-Capabilities' matrices have to offer in the way of strategy guidelines largely replicates what the GSM prescribes. Indeed, positions 1, 3, 7 and 9 of the former broadly correspond to the Dog, Cash Cow, question Mark and Star positions, respectively of the latter. Furthermore, the imaginary point which represents the SBU's position can be dilated, as

with the growth-share matrix, to form a circle, the area (or diameter) of which is proportional to sales.

Variations on the rich theme of Industry Attractiveness-Company Capabilities provide the basis for A.D. Little's Strategic Condition Matrix; Ansoff's (1965 and 1984) Life-Cycle Balance Matrix; and Hofer's (1977) Product/Market Evolution Matrix (Figure 14.10). These matrices take the composite dimension of *Company Capabilities* and relate it to the *stage of product/market evolution*. In effect they adopt only one of the sub-factors otherwise used in the composite measure of *Industry Attractiveness*. They can also be thought of as substituting the stage of product-market evolution for the market growth dimension of the BP. In the case of Figure 14.10, the high growth position of the BP subsumes the development and growth stages of evolution; the low growth position subsumes the remaining phases.

Proponents (Hofer and Schendel, 1978) of these hybrid matrices argue for their application in circumstances where the stage of product-market evolution is weighted heavily on assessing the attractiveness of a business area; i.e. where it will be a major determinant of the magnitude and type of opportunities and threats facing the firm. Hofer (1975) considers this to be so during the emerging, maturing and declining stages of the product life-cycle, when, he proposes, major changes in business strategy are most likely to be needed. Support for this view is to be found within Porter's (1980) paradigmatic work on the theme of descriptive generic industry environments – three of which take the stage of industry evolution (stage of industry maturity) as a dimension of major consequence for competitive strategy. Clearly Porter's and Hofer's conceptualisation of the relationship between the stage of product-market evolution and competitive strategy options differ with regard to the degree of aggregation they apply. Hofer's work focuses on SBU-level strategy, where the life-cycle of a particular product, or even a technological feature, may be an appropriate unit of analysis. Porter deals with the broad issue of the evolution of industries which would subsume a number of PLCs.

Table 14.9. *Some characteristics of the three main business postures of the BAA*

Strategy	Invest/Grow (6, 8, 9)	Selectivity/Earnings (3, 5, 7)	Harvest/Divest (1, 2, 4)
Objective	Growth	Earnings	Cash Flow
Strategy characteristics	– Intensive pursuit of market share – Earnings generation subordinate to building dominant position – Focus predominantly on long-term results and payout – Emphasis on technical innovation and market development	– Intensive pursuit of maximum earnings – Focus balanced between long and short term – Emphasis on complex analysis and clear plans – Emphasis on increased productivity, cost improvement, strategic pricing	– Intensive pursuit of maximum positives cash flow – Sell market share to maximise profitability – Intensive pruning of less profitable products/segments – Emphasis only on short term
Organisation characteristics	– Must enable future growth – Product or venture operations – Separate 'futures' from operations – Build technical competence – Strong international focus – Highly competent staff functions	– Must provide flexibility at moderate cost – Matrix organisation (balance cost and people development) – Centralised product planning – Overseas sourcing operations – Pooled sales and distribution utilisation – Centralised finance	– Must be low cost/no frills – Functional structure (lowest cost) – Collapse product departments into functionally organised division – Reduce/eliminate R&D labs. and forward engineering – Maximum pooling where cost effective – Combine manufacturing/engineering operations
Management characteristics	– Emphasis on entrepreneurs – Young, ambitious, aggressive – Strong development and growth potential – High risk tolerance – Highly competitive by nature	– Emphasis on 'solid businessman' – Tolerates risk, but does not seek it – Comfortable with variety and flexibility – Careful, but not conservative – Trades-off short term, long term risk/reward	– Emphasis on 'hard nosed' operators – Seasoned and experienced – Seeks high efficiency – Low change tolerance – Wants instant results, does not look ahead

Source: Channon (1979).

As Figure 14.10 shows, the diameter of the circle is proportional to the size of the product-market; the pie wedges indicating the proportion of total sales in the product market taken by the firm in question (pie wedges can also be used in the BAA to indicate the proportion of total business area or industry sales taken by the firm).

Consequently, they are more likely to be of value in formulating short to medium term marketing plans and strategies, where attention will focus on the analysis of individual, or small groups of related product-market segments. But, in formulating long term, corporate marketing strategy, analysis will demand the aggregation of product-market segments, and of SBUs in some cases, so that the broader multivariate approach of the BAA is more appropriate. The matrices can both be used to provide insights of value to the formulation of marketing strategy. But, the user has to be clear and consistent in his choice of the degree of aggregation and data reduction that is appropriate to his analysis, whether at the level of an Industry. Business Area or product-market.

The multivariate approaches of the DPM and BAA encourage a detailed analysis of a range of environmental factors which determine the strategic position of a firm (or SBU). In this respect and in the two others that follow, those tools may have more general validity as diagnostic tools than the growth-share matrix. Firstly growth rate and market share alone are inadequate measures of a firm's long term potential and secondly, the key success factors in each situation will vary, as will the firm's objectives, markets, and the synergies it achieves. However, it is inevitable that a trade-off will occur between the comprehensiveness of the dimensions of the matrix and the time wasted on considering factors of secondary importance (i.e. the paralysis of analysis trap, Hunsicker, 1980).

Consequently, although the GSM approach is criticised for placing too great an emphasis on cost economics and shifting attention away from the inherent ambiguity and risk of strategic decision making, the application of the BAA and the DPM, although they are very comprehensive diagnostic aids, is no less free of the twin burdens of ambiguity and uncertainty. Each of the matrices has a role to play in facilitating strategic thinking, but you will delude yourself if you take their simple prescriptions at face value.

Figure 14.10. *A product-market evolution portfolio matrix*

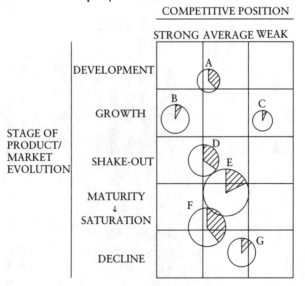

Source: Hofer (1977).

■ Concluding remarks

Words of caution and encouragement are perhaps appropriate at this point. It would be naive and misleading to argue that the matrices can be applied to all situations without modification. The prudent view is that they provide a way of organising the firm's thinking about its marketing strategy, and of visualising its options and possible outcomes. They are also of some practical value in reducing the masses of data generated by an analysis of customers, competitors, environmental trends, etc., and of recasting it in a form that is of meaning and value to the marketing strategist. However, the user must take care to ensure that the assumptions and dimensions of a preferred matrix are indeed valid and appropriate to the competitive circumstances the firm confronts. What is important is the *quality* of the analysis and the internal consistency of the end strategy.

A chronic problem that besets the user is that of broadly defined units of analysis, which tends to delegate to the user the decision as to which level of aggregation is appropriate when applying the matrices. It is difficult to offer general advice on this issue except to counsel internal consistency in the planner's choice of the key dimensions to be used in analysing strategic issues; and a healthy scepticism of the validity of the general propositions and assumptions on which the matrices base their dogma.

Key definitional difficulties will primarily concern the delineation of product-market boundaries – next to the individual customer, probably the most important unit of analysis in strategic marketing planning. Clear-cut product-market situations are possible in theory, but rarely occur in practice. For multi-product, multi-market firms they are inextricably related, making it a difficult task to disaggregate an industry or business area into product-market segments. Clearly the user must then seize the initiative by imposing definitions of product-markets and levels of aggregation that are meaningful to his specific situation.

One final concluding remark is worth making about the way in which management ideas, such as the PLC and the GSM, have entered the common consciousness of marketing and management and empowered the strategy discourse. The author holds that much of the criticism of the frameworks discussed in this chapter is premised on a view of the construction of management knowledge, and thus its utilisation, which overlooks issues of *power* and *socially negotiated meaning* in organising activities.

The heat has largely gone out of the PLC and GSM debate. But, new concepts and language are continually being developed and refined to help *represent* issues of current concern to management. Yet, there is a danger in not appreciating the way in which concepts and language, on entering the common consciousness, however this happens, then become constitutive of this consciousness rather than representative of it. Much marketing decision-making research assumes that what marketing managers say in response to its questions is representative of the marketing world, not constitutive of it.

In recent years Porter's ideas have very much become an institution and, just like the PLC and GSM before them, are now very much part of the strategy discourse that managers have. As Knights (1993) observes, this has important implications for those engaged in researching Porter's ideas, or any management or marketing idea. Researchers should be aware of how their representations of the strategy pratices of organisations actually constitute the subjectivity of management, as practitioners draw upon Porter's ideas and others like them in their attempts to define their strategic practices. Like those of the GSM, Porter's ideas seem to figure prominently in the strategy discourse within firms and managers secure their sense of reality and exercise power through being committed to those ideas. When Porter's ideas, or those of the GSM are employed by management, they will then have the effect of transforming individual managers and employees into subjects who secure meaning, purpose and identity through engaging in practices that reflect and support the strategies perceived to improve competitive advantage. Those ideas then become a totem around which to rally the troops, i.e. they become organisational artefacts.

▌Postscript on managerial judgement

This chapter opens by setting the scene for its discussion of analytical frameworks in the context of the strategic marketing planning process. It portrays this as an information driven process in which the sophisticated marketing technology of the PLC and GSM finds application as a means of facilitating the decision-making of top marketing managers. And whilst this view broadly represents the normative school of thought which tends to prevail in the marketing textbooks, in practice the process of strategic marketing does not conform to this model very well, even when behavioural and contextual issues are factored in as suggested by Piercy and Morgan (1990). One possible reason might be that sophisticated marketing technology is not able to reduce or accommodate much of the uncertainty endemic to strategic thinking.

But what does this mean for top marketing managers? Should they abandon analytical frameworks and depend on intuition? The final section of this chapter briefly considers this issue.

As marketing staff move into the upper strata of their organisations the nature of their work changes (Piercy, 1986). Typically, they leave behind much of their involvement in the detail of day-to-day marketing operations and take a greater part in the process of formulating the longer view and in developing the organisation through new ventures. They will retain ultimate responsibility for the actions of the marketing group, where such exists, despite being involved in a broader operating arena.

Forming a longer-term view means getting to grips with the ambiguities and uncertainties of the organisation's situation and the frameworks presented in this chapter have a role here. These uncertainties may be attributable to actions taken by external agents, typically governments, customers, distributors or competitors; or they may be attributable to the action, or inaction, of internal agents. Each situation has its own pattern of ambiguity and uncertainty. This makes analysis and decision difficult, sometimes impossible.

Uncertainty and ambiguity are all around us, in the unexpected, the unrecognised, the accidental and the serendipitous. It is axiomatic that the broader a marketing manager's responsibilities are, the greater will be his exposure to ambiguity and uncertainty. As individuals we can judge uncertainty and ambiguity in the way they prevent us being coolly rational, or being able to exercise complete control over our lives and the circumstances that surround them. As marketing managers we can judge them in the way that unforeseen changes in economic climate, or in the behaviour of a client, or supplier, can suddenly emasculate even the most careful and rigorous market analysis and planning.

Being devil's advocate for just a moment, you could speculate that were it not for the attempts of marketing managers to be rational and analytical, those uncertainties would not exist. For, if managers did not try to gather relevant information and process it in a meaningful way, they would not become aware of their inability to plan, to find best courses of action, to think through, for instance, the consequences of introducing a new product or altering the positioning of a key brand. Uncertainty then does not exist apart from managers' attempts to be rational. And perhaps some of the behavioural problems widely associated with attempts to operationalise normative marketing planning models (Piercy and Morgan, 1990) have their roots in experienced managers' realisation of the essential incompatibility between the uncertainty marketing planning models can cope with, and the uncertainty they experience as decision makers.

The author argues that uncertainty is resolved by an act of managerial judgement. Judgement is what the decision maker adds to cope with the uncertainty which exists in the situation he or she confronts.

Judgement differs from analysis. Analysis means finding the answer that lies hidden in the data. Business schools are good at teaching various techniques such as the GSM for analysing the many different kinds of market-related data which marketing managers must consider: market share and growth; sales trends; volume, cost and revenue; price sensitivity and stabilty; contribution and profitability; seasonality effects; inflation vulnerability; capacity utilisation; investment intensity; competitive position; experience effects; market penetration; repeat buying rates; TV ratings; sales coverage; etc.

The conventional view (Kotler, 1988) is that judgement is what the marketing manager brings to a problem when there is not enough data, or good enough data, for there to be a clear answer through the application of analytical marketing techniques. This marketing technology then represents the careful systematisation of judgement. It reduces marketing judgement to sets of algorithms which have built-in associations, yardsticks, data processing rules and rules of correspondence and evidence.

So marketing managers have access to a formidable analytical armoury to help take decisions and reduce the reliance on judgement. The application of judgement should then become a last resort when a technique is unable to point towards an appropriate course of action.

However, this presupposes only one type of uncertainty, i.e. incompleteness, where data is missing, so that the judgement that is called for is to make the data complete, perhaps through some extrapolation. It also betrays the implicit notion that uncertainty is an exceptional circumstance for the marketing manager. The authors dispute those views on two counts. First, incompleteness is not the only type of uncertainty that managers face. Building on Shubik's (1954) work, Spender (1986) defines four different types of uncertainty in most managers' information, where information is not simply data, but interpreted data:

- incompleteness
- indeterminacy
- irrelevance
- incommensurability

Incompleteness is partial ignorance of any type. *Indeterminacy* means recognising and respecting the presence of some other actor whose interests and world view may be quite discontinuous with our own and whose responses cannot therefore be forecast. *Irrelevance* is when we assume some

correspondence rules between our theoretical model and the world which are completely inappropriate and thus make our model irrelevant to the problem at hand. *Incommensurability* is when our knowledge is not intergrated so that we cannot process what we know in a wholly rational manner.

Spender (1989) articulates the general principle of this typology in terms of uncertainty being resolved by a corresponding act of judgement. If uncertainty is incompleteness, the judgement makes the data complete; if it is indeterminacy, the judgement is to decide how other people will react; if it is incommensurability, the judgement makes the data coherent.

Despite the popularity of the rational model of marketing management, there are marketing decisions that cannot easily be taken through analysis, no matter how rigorous and careful, where uncertainty is not merely a matter of incomplete data, eg. should we proceed with the introduction of this new product in this particular way? And decisions such as those are usually ascribed to the domain of strategic marketing, where top marketing managers deal with uncertainty in the broader context of the organisation's strategy. Implicit to the strategic and operational categorisation of marketing decisions is the notion that strategic decisions are less amenable to analysis than operational decisions because of incomplete data, so that judgement is typically thought of as being more widely exercised in the upper ranks of marketing management.

The author argues that the type of uncertainty that top marketing managers face in taking strategic marketing decisions, or in contributing in some way to other strategic decisions, is not merely a function of incomplete data, but indeterminacy, irrelevance, and particularly incommensurability. The judgements that operational and strategic marketing managers have to make differ to the extent that they have to cope with different types of uncertainty. Strategic marketing decisions expose the top marketing manager to all four types of uncertainty simultaneously perhaps, whilst the uncertainty of operating decisions may be resolved by a judgement that makes data less incomplete.

Whatever the marketing decision to be taken, and irrespective of the rank of the person who has to take it, where uncertainty exists some judgement will be exercised. The nature of managerial judgement may vary in different decision making settings as does the uncertainty. But, the author holds that the fact that it is exercised brings us back to the importance of the experience and skills of individual marketing managers, not merely sophisticated analytical technology.

The second point at dispute is the position of uncertainty in the marketing manager's job. The author takes the view that far from being the exceptional circumstance, uncertainty is the marketing manager's constant companion. The marketing management literature inherits the positivist view of the world which underpins Simon's (1957) work and that defines uncertainty as a transient condition of our appreciation of the world, so that it is not an essential feature of the human condition. Spender (1989) argues that this positivist position leads us to overlook the fragmentary nature of our knowledge and its internal inconsistencies. So, when marketing managers have to act in partial ignorance it is their judgement that is tested, not their data gathering or analytical skills. Marketing managers are forced to use judgement when they are ignorant of facts, outcomes and relationships in the world around them, a condition the authors believe to be normal, not exceptional.

Judgement comes from the person making a decision, not the data. To exercise judgement is to invest data with meaning through an interpretative process (Pfeffer and Salacik, 1978; Weick and Daft, 1983) which operates at group and individual levels in organisations and also involves scanning, or data collection; and management learning through reflection on actions taken (Daft and Weick, 1984). Organisations do not have mechanisms separate from the individuals that set goals, process information, or perceive the business environment. Yet they do interpret as a system where managers are able to achieve some convergence in their perceptions (Weick, 1979). The conventional marketing view ascribes this convergence to the planning apparatus and adopts, by default, classical management theory's imputation of a unique 'rationality'.

Rationality is often portrayed as some grand transcendental thought process to which we should aspire as a basis for our actions. To be sure, rationality is an instrument which, if correctly employed, helps us draw inferences from given premises, without inconsistency, and about which other people would agree. Perhaps in the material world of objects and statistics, there is room for one way of seeing things, but not in the social world where there is discourse, interaction and negotiated meaning. If there was, would we ever need arbitration courts and anti-discrimination laws to govern so much of our lives?

The authors agree that the planning apparatus, including its analytical frameworks, can facilitate the convergence of ideas through wider involvement, improved communication and even *diktat*. But, the planning process itself is driven by an 'analytical knife', or *a priori* template that has its origins in the interpretive frameworks of individual top managers. Spender (1989) believes that the 'rationality' of classical management theory is simply one of a whole universe of possible rationalities. As individuals, top managers may not agree fully about their perceptions (Starbuck, 1976), but a thread of coherence among them is what characterises organisational interpretations (Daft and Weick, 1984). So, in the context of strategic decision making, the exercising of judgement is a collective activity that is informed by, and derives legitimacy from the judgements of individuals and groups.

Many managers may play some part in environmental scanning or data processing, but the organisation's interpretations are formulated by a relatively small group of top managers who bring together and interpret information for the organisation as a whole (Daft and Weick, 1984). His or her proximity to customers and competitors may put the top marketing manager in the driving seat of the process by means of which market-related events and circumstances are given meaning. But, the other members of the top management coalition will also have roles to play in developing the shared understandings and conceptual schemes that facilitate interpretation.

The concept of 'bounded rationality' (Simon, 1957) tells us that top decision makers construct simplified mental models to help them deal with complex strategic problems. Strategic decision making is thus influenced by the cognitive frames and decision processes of individual top managers (Hambrick and Mason, 1984). Researchers have identified a number of cognitive heuristics, or 'rules of thumb', which top managers use to simplify complex strategic problems and a number of decisional biases which may also influence strategic decisions (Schwenk, 1988). The authors believe that by means of applying such heuristics to strategic marketing problems the judgement of top marketing managers is factored into the strategic thinking of the organisation and so becomes part of its cultural web. The defining characteristic of such heuristics is that they enable the top marketing manager to come to a conclusion without being able to assess the quality of that conclusion.

Spender (1980) coined the term 'Industry Recipe' to denote the core set of beliefs and assumptions that he argues are shared by the top managers of organisations within the same industry. An industry's recipe then comprises a set of axioms which establishes what the industry generally regards as the questions that management must address if they are to have a viable company. It also melds into a comprehensive meaning system with which managers can make sense of their experiences and interpret the actions of others.

The resolution of uncertainty is to create a rationality, a recipe, or interpretive scheme within which an organisation's problems can be couched and analysed. Top managers socially construct this rationality and will do so in ways that create the information differentials that underpin competitive advantage. They must also revise or re-invent this rationality as events and circumstances dictate. It is unlikely that the top marketing manager will possess outstanding judgement in all areas of the organisation and so the creation of this rationality is an extended managerial task that involves the top management coalition. But, by dint of his proximity to the changing market place, the top marketing manager may find himself policing elements of the organisation's 'recipe' as a way of detecting emerging inconsistencies between it and market trends.

King (1985) writes that judgement will always be more important than technique in marketing. In his view marketing is different from finance and production, where operations research and econometrics seem to have been applied forcefully and effectively. The data on which marketing decisions are based are always unreliable; consumers are irrational; competitors confound cause-effect models; rules are broken. To focus on marketing techniques is in King's view to sacrifice relevancy.

It may be argued then that marketing managers succeed when they are recognised by someone to have exercised good judgement. Few senior marketing managers use very complex methods of analysis, as numerous surveys have discovered, for such tasks are easily delegated. Marketing managers succeed when they have made good judgements about which organisational capabilities to define as a strength and which a weakness; which marketing opportunities to take up; which people to hire; which customers, competitors or suppliers to stay away from; which price to set; which distributors to deal with; which new product idea to develop – and the nature of all those judgements is sensitive to the setting in which they are made. What someone sees as a threat, someone else may see as an opportunity. The process of arriving at a view of an organisation's SWOTs, or a definition of its business and markets may then be less an analytical task than a political one, involving the exercise of power and conflict resolution. It is not merely a matter of plugging data into an technique to decide how to define something in your SWOT analysis. Luck and serendipity have parts to play, but so do judgement, negotiation and conflict resolution.

Many analytical marketing techniques, including the GSM, the PLC and the stalwart SWOT analysis, break down in their perspective role under close scrutiny, often because they are used out of context to deal with uncertainties they have no capacity to reduce. We cannot escape the consequence that such techniques may then have a limited role to play as ready reckoners for strategic marketing decision taking. And if this is so, it demands no mean stretch of the imagination to argue that judgement and uncertainty are not the exceptions to the marketing decision making rule, but the norm.

■ References

Aaker, D. and Day, G. (1986), 'The Perils of High Growth Markets', *Strategic Management Journal 7*, pp. 409–421.

Asker, D. (1984), *Developing Business Strategies*, New York: John Wiley.

Abell, D. F. (1980), *Defining the Business: The Starting Point for Strategic Planning*, Englewood Cliffs, NJ: Prentice-Hall.

Abell, D. F. and Hammond, J. S. (1979), *Strategic Marketing Planning*, Englewood Cliffs, NJ: Prentice-Hall.

Abernathy, W. J. and Wayne, K. (1974), 'Limits of the Learning Curve', *Harvard Business Review* (October), pp. 109–119.

Alberts, W. (1989), 'The Experience Curve Doctrine Reconsidered', *Journal of Marketing*, 53 (July), pp. 36–49.

Anderson, P. (1982), 'Marketing, Strategic Planning and the Theory of the Firm', *Journal of Marketing* 46 (Spring), pp. 15–26.

Ansoff, I. (1965), *Corporate Strategy*, New York: McGraw-Hill .

Ansoff, I. (1984), *Implanting Strategic Management*, Englewood Cliffs, NJ: Prentice-Hall.

Aspinwall, K. (1962), 'The Characteristics of Goods and Parallel Systems Theories', in *Managerial Marketing: Perspectives and Viewpoints*, (eds) Lazer, W. and Kelly, E. Homewood, Ill.: Irwin, pp. 633–643.

Avlonitis, G. J. (1985), 'Product Elimination Decision Making: Does Formality Matter', *Journal of Marketing* 49 (Winter), pp. 41–52.

Baden-Fuller, C. (1981), *The Implications of the Learning Curve for Firm Strategy and Public Policy*, London Business School.

Baker, M. J. (1983), *Market Development: A Comprehensive Survey*, Harmondsworth: Penguin, p. 18.

Baker, M. J. (1992), *Marketing Management and Strategy*, 2nd edition, London: Macmillan.

✓ Berenson, C. (1967), 'The Purchasing Executives' Adaptation to the Product Life-Cycle', *Journal of Purchasing* 3 (May), pp. 52–68.

Biggadike, R. E. (1983), 'The Contributions of Marketing to Strategic Management', in *Perspectives on Strategic Marketing Management*, (eds) Kerin, R. and Peterson, R., Boston: Allyn & Bacon.

Bloom, P. and Kotler, P. (1975), 'Strategies for High Market Share Companies', *Harvard Business Review* (November/December), pp. 62–72.

Boston Consulting Group (1972), *Perspectives on Experience*, Boston: Boston Consulting Group.

Boston Consulting Group (1975), *Strategy Alternatives for the British Motorcycle Industry*, London: HMSO.

Boston Consulting Group (1981), *Annual Perspective*, Boston: Boston Consulting Group.

Buzzell, R. D. (1979), 'Are There "Natural" Market Structures?', *Working Paper*, 73–79, Harvard Business School.

Buzzell, R. and Gale, B. (1974), 'Market Share – A Key to Profitability', *Harvard Business Review* (January/February), pp. 97–106.

Buzzell, R. and Wiersema, F. (1981), 'Successful Share Building Strategies', *Harvard Business Review* (January/February), pp. 135–144.

Buzzell, R. and Gale, B. (1987), *The PIMS Principles: Linking Strategy to Performance*, New York: Free Press.

✓ Catry, B. and Chevalier, M. (1974), 'Market Share Strategy and the Product Life-Cycle', *Journal of Marketing* 38 (4), pp. 29–34.

Channon, D. F. (1979), 'Commentary on Strategy Formulation', in *Strategic Management*, (eds) Schendel, D. E. and Hofer, C. W., Boston: Little, Brown.

Chevalier, M. (1972), 'The Strategy Spectre Behind Your Market Share'. *European Business* 34 (Summer), pp. 63–72.

Copeland, M. T. (1923), 'Relation of Consumer Buying Habits to Marketing Methods', *Harvard Business Review* (April), pp. 282–289.

Cravens, D. (1975), 'Marketing Strategy Positioning', *Business Horizons* (December), pp. 53–68.

Daft, R. and Weick, K. (1984), 'Toward a Model of Organizations as Interpretation Systems', *Academy of Management Review* 9 (2), pp. 284–295.

Davis, G. and Brown, S. (1974), *Logistics Management*, Lexington, Mass.: D. C. Heath.

Day, G. (1977), 'Diagnosing the Product Portfolio', *Journal of Marketing* 42 (April), pp. 27–38.

Day, G. (1980), 'Strategic Market Analysis: Top-down and Bottom-up Approaches', Marketing Science Institute Working Paper, 80/105 (August).

Day, G. (1983), 'Diagnosing the Experience Curve', *Journal of Marketing* 47 (Spring), pp. 44–58.

Day, G. and Wensley, R. (1983), 'Marketing Theory with a Strategic Orientation', *Journal of Marketing* 47 (Fall), pp. 78–89.

Dean, J. (1950), 'Pricing Policies for New Products', *Harvard Business Review* 28 (November/December), pp. 45–53.

✓ Dhalla, N. and Yuspeh, S. (1976), 'Forget the Product Life-Cycle Concept!', *Harvard Business Review* (January/February), pp. 102–112.

Directional Policy Matrix – A New Aid to Corporate Planning (1975), Shell International Chemical Co.

✓ Dodge, R. H. and Rink, D. (1978), 'Phasing Sales Strategies and Tactics in Accordance with the Product Life-Cycle Dimension Rather Than Calendar Periods', in *Research Frontiers Marketing: Dialogues and Directions*, (ed.) Jain, S., Chicago: American Marketing Association.

✓ Doyle, P. (1976), 'The Realities of the Product Life-Cycle', *Quarterly Review of Marketing* (Summer), pp. 1–6.

Doyle, P. (1994), 'Marketing Management and Strategy', Hemel Hempstead: Prentice-Hall.

✓ Enis, B. (1980), 'Strategic Planning and the Product Life-Cycle', *Business* (May/June), pp. 10–18.

✓ Enis, B., La Garce, R. and Prell, A. (1977), 'Extending the Product Life-Cycle', *Business Horizons* (June), pp. 40–56.

✓ Fox, H. (1983), 'Product Life-Cycle – An Aid to Financial Adminstration', *Financial Executive* 41 (April) 28–34.

Fruhan, W. (1972), 'Pyrrhic Victories in Fights for market Share', *Harvard Business Review* 50 (September/October), pp. 100–107.

Goold, M. (1981), 'Why Dicey Definitions are so Dangerous', *Financial Times*, management page (16 November) and 'How Dogs can be Given More Bite', *Financial Times*, management page (13 November).

Greenley, G. (1986), *The Strategic and Operational Planning of Marketing*, Maidenhead: McGraw-Hill.

Greenley, G. (1989), 'Managerial Perceptions of Marketing Planning', *Journal of Management Studies* 25, pp. 575–601.

Hall, G. and Howell, S. (1985), 'The Experience Curve from the Economist's Perspective', *Strategic Management Journal* 6, pp. 197–212.

Hambrick, D. and Mason, P. (1984), 'Upper Echelons: The Organisation as a Reflection of its Top Managers', *Academy of Management Review* 9, pp. 193–206.

Hamermesh, R. Anderson, M. and Harris, J. (1978), 'Strategies for Low Market Share Businesses', *Harvard Business Review* (May/June), pp. 95–102.

Hamermesh, R. and Silk, S. (1979), 'How to Compete in Stagnant Industries', *Harvard Business Review* (September/October), pp. 161–168.

Hayes, R. and Wheelwright, S. (1984), *Restoring our Competitive Edge, Competing Through Manufacturing*, New York: John Wiley.

Hedley, B. (1976), 'A Fundamental Approach to Strategy Development', *Long Range Planning* 9 (December), pp. 2–11.

Hedley, B. (1977), 'Strategy and the Business Portfolio', *Long Range Planning* 10 (February), pp. 9–15.

Henderson, B. (1968), 'The Experience Curve', *Perspective Series*, Reviews I–V, Boston: Boston Consulting Group.

Henderson, B. (1970), 'The Product Portfolio', *Perspectives* 66, Boston: Boston Consulting Group.

Henderson, B. (1973), 'The Growth Share Matrix of the Product Portfolio', *Perspectives* 135, Boston: Boston Consulting Group.

Henderson, B. (1984), 'The Application and Misapplication of the Experience Curve', *Journal of Business Strategy* 4 (Winter), pp. 3–9.

Hirschmann W. (1964), 'Profit from the Learning Curve', *Harvard Business Review* 42 (January/February), pp. 125–139.

Hofer, C. (1977), 'Conceptual Constructs for Formulating Corporate and Business Strategy', no. 9, pp. 378–754, Boston: Intercollegiate Case Clearing House.

Hofer, C. W. (1975), 'Toward a Contingency Theory of Business Strategy', *Academy of Management Journal* 18 (4), pp. 784–809.

Hofer, C. W. and Schendel, D. E. (1978), *Strategy Formulation: Analytical Concepts*, St Paul, Minnesota: West Publishing Co.

Hunsicker, J. Q. (1980), 'The Malaise of Strategic Planning', *The McKinsey Quarterly* (Spring), pp. 42–12.

Jacobson, R. and Aaker, D. (1985), 'Is Market Share All That It's Cracked Up To Be?', *Journal of Marketing* 49 (Fall), pp. 11–22.

Kijewski, V. (1978), 'Marketing Share Stragegy: Beliefs vs. Actions,' *PIMS Letter* 9/2, Cambridge, Mass.: Strategic Planning Institute.

King, S. (1973), *Developing New Brands*, London: Pitman.

King, S. (1985), 'Has Marketing Failed or Was It Never Really Tried?', *Journal of Marketing Management* 1 (1), pp. 1–20.

Knights, D. (1992), 'Changing Spaces: The Disruptive Impact of a New Epistemological Location for the Study of Management', *Academy of Management Review*, pp. 514–536.

Kotler, P. (1979), *Marketing Management – Analysis, Planning and Control*, 4th edition, Englewood Cliffs, NJ: Prentice-Hall.

Kotler, P. (1988), *Marketing Management – Analysis, Planning and Control*, 6th edition, Englewood Cliffs, NJ: Prentice-Hall.

Kotler, P. (1965), 'Competitive Strategies for New Product Marketing Over the Life-Cycle', *Management Science* 17 (December), pp. 104–119.

Lambkin, M. and Day, G. (1989), 'Evolutionary Processes in Competitive Markets: Beyond the Product Life-Cycle', *Journal of Marketing* 53 (July), pp. 4–20.

✓ Levitt, T. (1965), 'Exploit the Product Life-Cycle', *Harvard Business Review* (November/December), pp. 81–94.

Lorange, P. (1975), 'Divisional Planning: Setting Effective Direction', *Sloan Management Review* (Autumn), pp. 77–91.

Lorenz, C. (1981), 'Why the Boston Theory is On Trial', *Financial Times*, management page (11 November).

McDonald, M. (1984), *Marketing Plans*, London: Heinemann.

McKiernan, P. (1992), *Strategies of Growth: Maturity, Recovery and Internationalisation*, London: Routledge.

McNamee, P. (1988), *Management Accounting: Strategic Planning and Marketing*, Oxford: Heinemann.

'Mead's Technique to Sort Out the Losers' (1972), *Business Week* (11 March), pp. 124–130.

∨ Mercer, D. (1993), 'A Two-Decade Test of Product Life-Cycle Theory', *British Journal of Management* 4, pp. 269–274.

Miles, R. and Snow, C. (1978), *Organizational Strategy, Structure and Process*, New York: McGraw-Hill.

Miracle, G. E. (1965), 'Product Characteristics and Marketing Strategy', *Journal of Marketing* (January), pp. 18–24.

Montgomery, D. and Day, G. (1984), 'Experience Curves: Evidence, Empirical Issues and Applications', in *Strategic Management and Marketing*, D. Gardner and H. Thormas (eds), New York: John Wiley.

Morrison, A. and Wensley, R. (1991), 'Boxing-up or Boxed-in? A Short History of the Boston Consulting Group Growth/Share Matrix', *Journal of Marketing Management* (April).

Pfeffer, J. and Salancik, G. (1978), *The External Control of Organizations: A Resource Dependent Perspective*, New York: Harper & Row.

Piercy, N. (1986), 'The Role and Function of the Chief Marketing Executive and the Marketing Department', *Journal of Marketing Management* 5 (1), pp. 19–31.

Piercy, N. and Morgan, N. (1990), 'Organization Context and Behavioural Problems as Determinants of the Effectiveness of the Strategic Marketing Planning Process', *Journal of Marketing Management* 6 (2), pp. 127–143.

Porter, M. E. (1985), *Competitive Advantage: Creating and Sustaining Superior Performance*, New York: The Free Press.

Porter, M. E. (1980), *Competitive Strategy: Techniques for Analysing Industries and Competitors*, Chapter 2, New York: The Free Press.

✓ Rink, D. R. and Swan, J. G. (1979), 'Product Life-Cycle Research: A Literature Review', *Journal of Business Research*, pp. 219–242.

Robinson, S. J. Q., Hitchens, R. E. and Wade, D. P. (1978), 'The Directional Policy Matrix – Tool For Strategic Planning', *Long Range Planning* 11 (June), pp. 8–15.

Rodgers, E. M. and Shoemaker, F. F. (1971), *Communication of Innovations*, 2nd edition, New York: Free Press.

Schoeffler, S., Buzzell, R. S. and Heany, D. F. (1974), 'Impact of Strategic Planning on Profit Performance', *Harvard Business Review*, 52 (March/April). pp. 137–145.

Schwenk, C. (1988), 'The Cognitive Perspective on Strategic Decision Making', *Journal of Management Studies* 25 (1), pp. 41–55.

Seeger, J. (1984), 'Reversing the Images of BCG's Growth/Share Matrix', *Strategic Management Journal* 5, pp. 93–97.

Shubik, M. (1954), 'Information, Risk, Ignorance and indeterminacy', *Quarterly Journal of Economics* 4, pp. 624–629.

Simon, H. (1957), *Administrative Behaviour*, New York: Macmillan.

Sissors, J. (1966), 'What is a Market?', *Journal of Marketing* 30 (July), pp. 17–21.

Smallwood, J. E. (1973), 'The Product Life-Cycle: A Key to Strategic Market Planning', *MSU Business Topics* (Winter), pp. 29–35.

Speed, R. (1994), 'Maximizing the Potential of Typologies for Marketing Strategy Research', *Journal of Strategic Marketing* 1(3), pp. 171–188.

Spender, J. C. (1980), *Strategy-Making in Business*, Ph.D. Thesis, Manchester Business School.

Spender, J. C. (1989), *Industry Recipes: An Enquiry into the Nature and Sources of Management Judgement*, Oxford: Basil Blackwell.

Starbuck, W. (1976), 'Organisations and their Environments', in Dunnette, M. (ed.), *Handbook of Industrial and Organizational Psychology*, New York: Rand McNally, pp. 1069–1123.

Udell, J. G. (1968), 'Toward a Theory of Marketing Strategy', *British Journal of Marketing* (Winter), pp. 298–303.

Utterback, J. M. and Abernathy, W. J. (1975), 'A Dynamic Model of Process and Product Innovation', OMEGA 3, pp. 639–656.

Wasson, C. (1974), *Dynamic Competitive Strategy and Product Life-Cycles*, St Charles Ill.: Challenge Books.

Weick, K. (1979), *The Social Psychology of Organizing*, Reading, Mass.: Addison-Wesley.

Weick, K. and Daft, R. (1983), 'The Effectiveness of Interpretation Systems', in Cameron, K. and Whetten, D. (eds), *Organizational Effectiveness: A Comparison of Multiple Models*, New York: Academic Press, pp. 71–93.

Weitz, B. A. and Wensley, R. (1984), *Strategic Marketing, Implementation and Control*, Boston, Kent Publishing, pp. 132–139.

Wensley, R. (1981a), 'Strategic Marketing; Betas, Boxes or Basics', *Journal of Marketing* (Summer), pp. 173–183.

Wensley, R. (1981b), 'PIMS and BCG: New Horizons or False Dawn in Strategic Marketing', *Strategic Management Journal*, pp. 147–158.

Wind, Y. and Claycamp, H. (1976), 'Planning Product Line Strategy: A Matrix Approach', *Journal of Marketing* 40 (January), pp. 2–9.

Wind, Y. and Mahajan, V. (1981), 'Designing Product and Business Portfolios', *Harvard Business Review* (January/February), pp. 155–165.

Wind, Y. and Robertson, T. S. (1983), 'Marketing Strategy: New Directions for Theory and Research', *Journal of Marketing* 47 (Spring), pp. 12–25.

Wissema, J. G., Van der Pole, J. and Messer, H. M. (1980), 'Strategic Management Archetypes, *Strategic Management Journal* 1, pp. 37–47.

Woo, C. and Cooper, A (1982), 'The Surprising Case for Low Market Share', *Harvard Business Review* (November/December), pp. 106–113.

Wright, T. P. (1936), 'Factors Affecting the Cost of Airplanes', *Journal of Aeronautical Sciences* 3, pp. 12–18.

■ *Chapter 15* ■

Business to Business Marketing

Ken Bernard

■ Introduction

Until perhaps the mid 1980s there was a general tendency to treat the subject of marketing as if it had several more or less discrete, subordinate areas of study; bodies of literature therefore emerged dealing with, for example, international marketing, services marketing, societal marketing, and industrial marketing. It was apparently taken as axiomatic by many authors that the differences in product type or of physical environment brought about or justified significant differences in the concepts as well as in the managerial practices involved. More recently, fallacies have been exposed in such a line of thought, to the extent that it is now more generally recognised that where differences do exist they are matters of practice necessitated or facilitated by the environment surrounding the *activity*, rather than differences in the concept or philosophy of marketing itself.

One of the major areas where this change in outlook has manifested itself most clearly, and caused a reassessment of thought and terminology, is that previously conventionally entitled 'industrial marketing'. The term has been identified by many – perhaps erroneously – as being associated with industrial products, with factory-produced goods and perceived as having little, if anything, to do with consumer goods and consumption. More recently however, there has emerged a recognition that this perspective is over-narrow, and furthermore that it diverts attention away from the fact that the world of business operates as a broad, flexible, interlocking and more or less continuous system rather than comprising a series of independent transactions. The concept of 'supply chains' thus embraces consideration of both upstream and downstream, direct and indirect influences on any given individual transaction. Furthermore, whilst it remains true that the sole long term justification for the production of any product or service is the ultimate facilitation of consumption, the focus of marketing activity must embrace satisfactions of different types for different chain members, and do so irrespective of the specific type of product or service involved.

As opposed to the former segmentation of marketing on the basis of supposed product or output types, what is emerging is a more market orientated perception of the subject, being treated along customer-type lines, or according to types of buying decision. Whilst consumers are imagined to buy for reasons of individual satisfaction, business organisations are generally accepted as purchasing for more objective (usually economic) motives. This is seen to be the case with respect to more or less all types of business organisation – manufacturers and distributors, profit orientated and non- profit orientated – irrespective of the type of product handled. Conceptually, the well established principles of Organisational Buying Behaviour can accommodate business purchasers of chocolate bars just as easily as purchasers of steel bars. It is therefore not illogical to envisage a classification of 'organisational marketing' based upon the need to respond to or interact with the participants in the organisational buying process (Bernard, 1988).

As far back as 1969 Kotler and Levy used the phrase 'Organisational Marketing' but it did not gain significant currency until the mid-1980s, when textbooks by several authors sought to break free from the product orientated mould by which the discipline had become constrained, with a switch from titles embracing the word 'industrial' to adoption of terms such as 'Industrial and Organisational' and 'Business to Business' (see for example Morris, 1988, 1991; Hutt and Speh, 1985, 1989; Mahin, 1991; Powers, 1992). The change in terminology and implicit focus is not yet universal, but the general trend in treatment of the subject appears to have undergone a major psychological shift such that far from being a minor subset of the overall marketing discipline, the 'business' segment is now perceived as being of crucial significance – both theoretically and managerially.

One further and far reaching consequence of the change in perspective has been a recognition that, for a number of years, the dichotomy of views of marketing between academics and managerial practitioners has hindered the understanding of its strategic and tactical significance (Thomas, 1993). This has taken many forms, for example

a)   among the general public and in many organisations, marketers are perceived as being preoccupied with matters of promotion and/or market research, and with the manipulation of the marketing mix;

b)   within many business schools, emphasis is laid upon the strategic, integrative roles of marketing, whereas in corporate contexts, these functions are perceived as the responsibilities of general management.

Only recently has there begun to emerge an appreciation of the mutual interdependence between marketing and the other generic business disciplines, although in some environments – notably the distributive trades – this has been practised *de facto* for many years. In manufacturing industry the essential complementarity of marketing, procurement, logistics and production management is gaining recognition, especially perhaps where drives for competitiveness and efficiency are leading to the re-examination of working practices and organisational structures as necessitated, for example, by consideration of Just-In-Time programmes. Conversely, academics have come to recognise the importance of study across the traditional disciplinary divides of marketing, production and finance management. At the same time, the awareness of the significance of upstream and downstream coordination among supply chain members has gained currency: the need to facilitate delivery of satisfactions beyond the context of the immediate transaction is seen as an essential of competitive activity. This in turn has

i)   given rise to some rapprochement between academe and the practitioner world, and

ii) in particular, led to a greater understanding of the significance of both internal and external relationship management (McKenna, 1991, Christopher *et al.*, 1991, Bernard and Rajagopal, 1991).

In this chapter, the principal objective is to provide an overview of the significance of marketing in a business-to-business context, with particular attention being paid to changes in the perceived role of marketing management in recent years. Much of the discussion is therefore focused on the specific features of the business environment, the interactions between marketers and other corporate functionaries and upon the broader environments of business marketers. Since it is maintained that conceptually business-to-business marketing is no different from any other 'branch' of the discipline, some aspects of theory and practice are touched on but lightly. Conversely issues such as interfaces with logistics, production and procurement receive rather more attention, together with consideration of those 'conventional' marketing functions, such as research, segmentation and communications, where the business environment imposes particular conditions, constraints or modifications on general theory.

The extended awareness of the significance of supply chain issues and of relationship management is of the essence of current managerial practice and logically falls within the scope of discussion of business marketing – in theory and in practice. However their significance is also such that, along with Customer Care, Organisational Buying Behaviour and New Product Development, the subject of Relationship Marketing is accorded a separate chapter in the present book. These topics are all perforce relevant in this chapter, but they will be treated in the context of other considerations of the business marketing environment.

Marketing orientation in a business environment

The broadening of the perceived scope of business marketing has a major consequence in that it increases the importance of understanding the significance of market – and marketing – orientation. Crosier (1975) noted that this could be taken to comprise one of three generic groups of definitions of marketing but observed also that there appeared to be very few formal statements within this group. That however should not be taken to indicate any diminished degree of relevance.

Rather, the opposite is the case. If one accepts the general proposition that marketing is concerned with the provision of benefit and the achievement of mutual satisfaction for supplier and customer, it follows that, to reach and maintain that state in conditions of market dynamism and turbulence, a supplier must seek actively and continually to satisfy direct and indirect customers more effectively than can competitors. Only thus can the supplier achieve an advantage which can yield market share and a level of profitability sufficient to permit reinvestment and development. That is the central conclusion of studies of competitiveness from the PIMS project onwards (Buzzell *et al.*, 1975), which appear both logical and incontrovertible. Kotler (1994) succinctly defined market orientation (and by implication, successful corporate strategic planning) as being based on high levels of attention being given to *both* the needs of customer *and* the activities of competitors (Figure 15.1)

Figure 15.1. ***An orientation matrix***

Attention to Competitors Activities ↓ / *Attention to Customers Needs* →	LOW	HIGH
LOW	Product Orientation	Customer Orientation
HIGH	Competitor Orientation	Market Orientation

Source: Based on P. Kotler, *Marketing Management: Analysis Planning Implementation and Control*, 8th edition, Englewood Cliffs, NJ: Prentice-Hall (1994).

The achievement of such a dual objective, however clearly it may be defined or quantified, is, however, likely to be beyond the sole capability of the marketer – or indeed beyond any one other corporate function. The delivery of any benefit must, in practical terms, involve at least the production and logistics functions of the firm, and in all probability the procurement, accounting and human resources functions as well.

The business marketing environment is therefore very broad in its scope. At the philosophical level it encompasses all the conventional aspects of need identification, customer analysis and strategic planning. At the managerial level, implementation of marketing strategies entails establishment and maintenance of close relationship – externally with customers and suppliers, and internally with all functions in the organisation, in order to add the value appropriate to the needs of the company and its customers – bearing in mind that the point of ultimate consumption may be at several stages remove from the company's direct transaction. Fletcher (1990) offers a value provision model, conceptually similar to Porter's (1986) illustration of the upstream and downstream processes which shape a company's productive, satisfaction producing potential (Figures 15.2 and 15.3).

Figure 15.2. *Upstream and downstream activities*

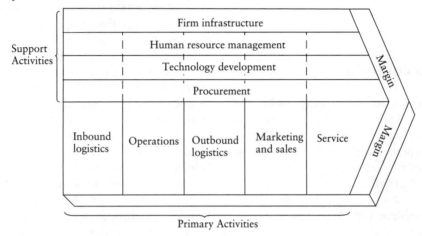

Source: M. E. Porter 'Changing Patterns of International Competition', *California Management Review* 28 (2) (Winter) (1986), pp. 9–40.

Figure 15.3. *The value cycle*

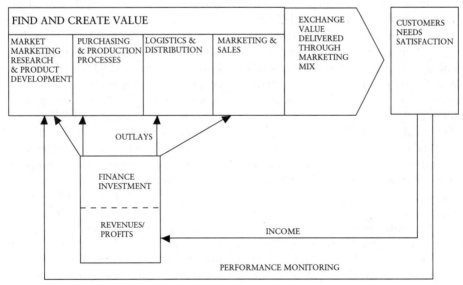

Source: Based on K. P. Fletcher, *Marketing Management and Information Technology*, Englewood Cliffs, NJ: Prentice-Hall (1990), p. 28.

The orientation of the firm towards the satisfaction of its markets must therefore not only embrace all corporate functions, but also entail management of the relationships among them. This necessitates not only communication but also acceptance and common understanding of the overall objectives, whilst at the same time involving an appreciation by everyone concerned of the motivations, constraints and limitations operative in and on each individual discipline or department.

■ Risks and conflicts

It is of the essence of decision making and entrepreneurship – and hence of marketing – that an element of risk exists. Given the very nature of the business environment, it is, in practical terms, inconceivable that marketers can have *total* foreknowledge of external conditions or of customers' preferences and actions, no matter how sophisticated the research methods which may be employed. The 'scientific' approach to marketing seems to address this issue by quantification of options and probabilities, but ultimately the outcomes remain only probabilities until they are tested empirically in action: elements of skill, belief and judgement are therefore implicit and essential in the management function (Borden, 1964). Despite advances in the tools and techniques available to the marketer, this situation is largely unchanged, and risk management remains a central element of the strategic marketing planning function.

However fully this proposition is accepted, and however clearly the company defines its overall mission or its specific objectives, it does remain apparent that conflicts of interpretation, interest and action continue to arise. The development of organisational structures, beyond the nuclear proprietor/manager stage, of necessity demands an element of specialisation and separation of responsibilities. This in turn fosters sectional perceptions of loyalty, skill and motivation which require to be coordinated and harnessed if they are not to lead to frag-

mentation of effort and to ineffectiveness. Such differences are evident between shareholders (proprietors) and managers just as much as between operational departments. They have their origins in different perspectives on the company's *raison d'êre*, just as much as they do in the different operational environments, measurement constraints and the social/educational background or aspirations of the people concerned (Wildsmith, 1973; Hutt and Speh, 1995). Numerous attempts have been made to devise structural palliatives for this situation – such as the abolition of hierarchies, the development of lean structures and processes and conduct of interfunctional training courses, but the common ingredient remains the simple one of communication. In terms of management this has been formulated into the principle of 'internal marketing' which is seen as the foundation necessary to ensure the two-way flow of essential information between the customer and the producer – using the marketer as a two way intermediary. This can be applied within any business organisation, rather than solely in the 'services' context envisaged by Gronroos (1984), and is a critical step in ensuring a market – and a marketing – orientation for the firm. It has particular relevance in business to business contexts in that the sales representative: buyer interface merely facilitates the development of wider and deeper long term contacts between other 'specialists' in both organisations (Kotler, 1994; Hutt and Speh, 1995), and thus permits total corporate awareness of, and involvement in, the process of supply chain development.

Lean management and 'shallow' hierarchical structures facilitate but do not of themselves cause improved communications. The essential elements are, firstly, an awareness of the need to communicate continuously, which permits the development of a consensus interpretation of corporate strategy; and secondly the operation of mechanisms to ensure a disciplined adherence to company policy, without stifling individual initiative and creativity. Relationship development and management are thus of the essence of both risk management and conflict minimisation.

■ The features of business markets

As noted earlier, the key determinant of any marketing related environment must be the customer: in the context of the business marketing environment, the key factors must therefore be the nature and motivations of the organisational customer (Webster and Wind, 1972; Hutt and Speh, 1995). Whilst each generic type of customer has its own characteristics, and offers its own challenges to the marketer, there has emerged a remarkable degree of consensus amongst analysts who have attempted to codify the supervening characteristics of organisational customers and markets.

The main features are worthy of enumeration since they have significant impact upon the ways in which companies or firms seek to interact with their organisational customers and their suppliers in the business chain (Kotler, 1994; Hutt and Speh, 1995; Chisnall, 1995; Morris 1992, among others).

- *Smaller numbers* of customers usually exist than in most consumer circumstances. This normally results in customers placing *smaller numbers of orders*, albeit of individually *larger scale and higher aggregate value*. It also renders customers *more easily identifiable*, and has a direct bearing upon research methods which may be used to explore their needs, as well as upon the significance of research findings.
- *Heterogeneity of customer size* is evident in most markets, since corporate growth is rarely uniform: this renders some customers more important than others, again with significant implications for researchers and for subsequent processes of segmentation.
- *Concentration* of business is evident not just in numbers of customers or of personnel within the firm, but also in geographical terms. Economic factors generally stimulate the establishment of business clusters, centred on raw materials sources, manpower sources, major markets or groups of suppliers, or a combination of some or all of these elements. Once again there are implications for research techniques as well as for marketing operations.

- Demand from business customers is considered to be *derived* from customers further downstream, and thus ultimately (however indirectly) from individual consumers. Absence of real and economically sustainable demand ultimately has fatal repercussions for the entire upstream supply function, as has been demonstrated in cases as diverse as European shipbuilding and the production driven economics of the erstwhile centrally planned economies. For marketers, the operational and research problems are both complex and chronic, made more so by the fact that many industrial items have *multiple applications* and are therefore affected by diverse demand trends.
- *Reciprocity* of demand and supply exists in several respects, and this frequently clouds comprehension of its real significance. Broadly it can be described in two ways:
  a) as a practice of *reciprocal buying* between two companies. As is implicit in the 'system' view of business this is more or less inevitable at some point, although legislation exists in many places (especially in the USA and the EU) to regulate the practice and to eliminate anything which may be perceived as a restriction of free competition.
     Conversely reciprocal trading is sometimes legitimised in the form of 'offset deals' in order to minimise balance of payments consequences of major international investment programmes and/or to ensure maximum benefit of technological diffusion;
  b) in the true marketing sense of *mutuality of benefit*, not solely in a direct monetary sense, but also including the potential for development of the experience base.

The significance for marketing management is self evident since the achievement of ongoing benefit and the potential for repeat business is a key corporate objective for most firms. This in turn emphasises the practical importance of maintaining secure customer:supplier relationships.

- *Buyer: seller inertia* is not entirely an expression of negative impetus – on the contrary it may represent a positive desire to avoid the multiplicity of real costs and risks involved in changing suppliers. Marketers may seek to exploit the potential offered by the prospect of repeat business by relationship building to exclude competition from other suppliers or products, and to provide collaborative benefits in new product development and introduction. Such relationships also have implications for the conduct of marketing research in that buyers may also perceive the practical benefit of in-depth discussion.

- *Technical complexity* of the 'products' being offered, of the purchasing environment and of the ultimate destination/use of the resultant product has many consequences, in several respects related to the issues of *demand derivation*. From the marketing researcher's standpoint, this adds further to the difficulties of establishing realistic estimates of true demand potential.

  Familiarity with *performance specifications* and awareness of problems associated with their translation into *production specifications* becomes a desirable attribute for both marketers and purchasing agents involved in negotiation of mutually satisfactory outcomes.

- *Technological and economic trends* are likely to bear upon business customers and marketers more directly and more acutely than on consumers, in the contexts of both products and production processes. Noticeable effects include

  a) magnification of impact on upstream suppliers in response to sharp changes in the trend of consumer demand (as in the case of orders for civilian aircraft in the wake of the Gulf War) or the availability of new solutions to chronic problems with pent-up unsatisfied demand (as in the case of new drugs to combat long running health conditions);

  b) imperfect ability of downstream producers to take immediate advantage of advances in production technology or new sources of supply due to existing materials commitments and capital investment/ammortisation limitations.

  Researchers thus rely heavily on in-depth techniques so that operational managers may attempt to gauge not only product appropriateness, but also timing of launch date and production output.

- *Buying processes* tend both to be *rational* and to involve *numbers of individuals/functions* in business contexts. To some extent the cause is to be found in the preceding factors, but the effects are considerable for marketing researchers and strategist who must uncover a multiplicity of needs and motives, and match them with a coordinated package of techniques and strategies.

Whilst the features outlined may be considered typical of inter-firm environments, the reader may well be able to expand upon them. Collectively these features exert influences on the conduct of business which differentiate the commercial supply environment from the retailer: consumer environment.

Typically, business transactions – as well as being economically motivated – are perceived to be:

- recurrent or repetitive
- based on mutual evaluation and solution of common 'problems' and handling of perceived 'risks' to both/all parties
- part of a business environment broader than the specific transaction
- dominated to an increasing extent by professional functionaries – purchasers as well as marketers
- of high profile and significance in corporate contexts.

As is suggested by Figure 15.4 the critical features of business markets in terms of supplier impact are perhaps customer size/number; order size/frequency; buying rationality and supplier: customer relationships. These factors determine research capabilities and methods, strategic marketing approaches to mix management, as

Figure 15.4.   *A summary of effects of business manner characteristics*

Factor	Principal Consequences for:		
	Marketing Research	Marketing Management	Other Functions
1. SMALL/FINITE CUSTOMER NUMBERS	• Identifiable targets • Focused research • Qualitative as well as Quantitative approaches	• Personal contact • Relationship cultivation • Potential to react to individual customers' needs.	• Need for close liaison with customers for Product/Innovation requirements.
2. FEWER BUT LARGER ORDERS	• Need for comprehensive and continual information and intelligence about customers and competitors.	• Necessity for competitiveness • Use of relationships/knowledge to get and remain 'in'. • Customer closeness. • Predictability of demand.	• Irregular demand for specific products • Complexities of plant scheduling and/or inventory carrying • Time a critical variable.
3. HETEROGENEITY OF SIZE	• Inappropriateness of small percentage and random samples • Focus on stratified/census techniques • Need to secure deep knowledge of major players.	• Segmentation by size/importance • Focus of effort on major players/opinion leaders • Customisation of products for major users. • Risk of ignoring requirements of other segments.	• Request for priority for major customers affecting – production schedules – terms of business • Dependence on oligopolistic customer demand. • Potential proliferation of product varieties.
4. CONCENTRATION OF BUSINESS	• Accessibility of populations.	• Ease of communication • Structure of sales function • Structure of distribution channels.	• Choice of transportation • Use/location of warehouses.
5. DERIVED DEMAND	• Complexity of downstream research • Need to research end markets • Familiarity with/use of consumer research techniques.	• Need to identify end markets • Multiple product users • Contact with customer; derivation of demand pull as well as supply push strategies • Establishment of *consumer* preferences/loyalties.	• NPD/R&D focus on end use applications • Delays in implementing new products due to customer redesign requirements • Need for sustainable demand for end product.

Figure 15.4. *(continued)*

Factor	Principal Consequences for:		
	Marketing Research	Marketing Management	Other Functions
6. RECIPROCITY OF BUYER/ SELLER	• 'Captive' research environment	(a) • Stable customer relationships • Risk of unwanted inertia/'Buyer pressure'. (b) • Mutuality of benefit • Repeat business • Loyalty/Relationship development	(a) • Risk sharing • Inertia/brake on corporate R&D development • Potential 'offset' deals (b) • Experience sharing → improved cost effectiveness • Relationship development with corresponding customer functions
7. BUYER/SELLER INERTIA	• Accessibility/regularity of contact	• Relationship building opportunities • Supply chain development • Market stability • Risk of competitor outflanking.	• High switching costs • Collaboration in NPD • Risk of lack of innovation.
8. TECHNICAL COMPLEXITY	• Multiplicity of uses confuses research environment • Need for access to user markets.	• Need for familiarity with specification processes • Involvement in negotiations pre/during/ post transaction • Tendency towards technically qualified sales personnel • Need for detailed comprehension of user environments.	• Delays in introducing new products (see Derived Demand) • Multifunctional 'sales' teams • Enhanced importance of process innovation
9. TECHNOLOGICAL/ ECONOMIC TRENDS	• Need for continual monitoring of end markets.	• Understanding of end markets and close relationships with end users and intermediaries • Development of more than one operational market • Technology forecasting.	• Operational flexibility • Ability to reassess forward orders • Minimise lead times • Maintenance of technological updatedness.

well as conditioning the management of the production, logistics and R&D functions of the organisation. The one outcome of perhaps most pervasive significance is that of relationships: intra-company as well as inter-company. The enduring nature of customer: supplier associations both encourages and necessitates the development and exploitation of personal and func-

Figure 15.4. *(continued)*

Factor	Principal Consequences for:		
	Marketing Research	Marketing Management	Other Functions
10.RATIONAL/ GROUP BUYING	• Need to gain access to several elements of DMU. • Need to employ indirect as well as direct instruments • Increased importance of 'intelligence' • Increased emphasis on intentions/attitude research.	• Multi level communications strategies • Need to identify users and deciders • Need to focus on real motivation of each DMU element • Relationship building at all levels • Development of corporate image of 'customer friendliness'/ 'customer closeness'.	• Need for total corporate market orientation • Involvement in major promotional activities, exhibitions etc. • Development of TQM/ Total Customer Service • Integration of Production strategies with Marketing.

tional relationships both for the benefit of the parties to a specific transaction, and for the well being of the economic environment or system as a whole.

■ Research and forecasting issues

Given the basic company/marketing orientation desired for the firm, the fundamental prerequisite is the accumulation and interpretation of an adequate body of information about customers, their needs, competitors, opportunities and threats. Conventional approaches to strategic planning – for example SWOT or Porter's '5 Forces' model – all subsume the existence of an adequate information base. It is however important to bear in mind that such a presumption is less than universally fully understood, in that successive researchers have found that deficiencies in this regard remain a major cause of product failure (Cochran and Thompson, 1964; Hopkins, 1981; Cooper, 1982; Hart and Snelson, 1989).

□ Outputs

Key areas where research output may be of major importance include

- *investment decision making* – where long term trends in demand, customer preferences and motivations, technological changes and end user requirements are critical
- *new product developments* – where demand for existing products requires to be evaluated against new opportunities and (perhaps latent) competitive threats, taking account also of suppliers and their forward plans and limitations
- *pricing and distribution strategy formulation* – where medium and shorter term data is required regarding demand patterns, elasticity and the activities of competitors
- *communications strategy formulation* – where intimate knowledge of structures and workings of the Decision Making Units or buying centres is vital to optimise the use of media and to ensure correct message selection

- *target market selection* – where effective segmentation strategies depend upon the ability to identify viable groups of customers in terms of both quantifiable attributes and behavioural characteristics.

These various activities will be discussed in detail later in this chapter as appropriate. At this juncture however it is relevant to note that the provision of adequate *sales forecasts* and quantitative comment thereon is at the heart of planning activity for the company as a whole as illustrated schematically in Figure 15.5. Clearly the terms in which the forecast is expressed will tend to vary according to functional requirements, whilst the degree of statistical accuracy required will be dictated or constrained by the time horizon envisaged, the extent of research funding

Figure 15.5　*The central role of sales forecasts in corporate planning and operations*

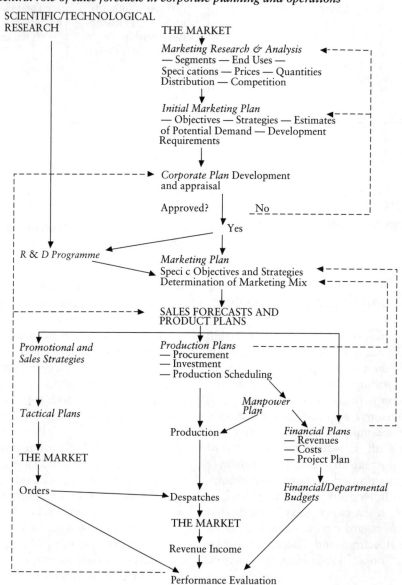

available and the level of risk perceived in the associated decision process.

The outputs required from marketing research go beyond the 'simple' provision of quantitative forecasts, although ultimately all information acquired is related to the ability of the company to develop its business. The significance of individual customers, the long term nature of the buying process and its consequences, the complexity of the buying centre all emphasise the need for understanding and knowledge about the customer, and the personalities, preferences and prejudices that contribute to the eventual decisions. 'Customer closeness' (Peters and Waterman, 1982) is not something which is acquired osmotically: it has to be sought and created, which places considerable emphasis on qualitative research rather than purely quantitative analysis.

□ *Methodologies*

At a conceptual level, there is little, if any, difference between conducting research in business markets from doing so in a consumer context. The fundamental questions to be answered are the same:

● Who are our actual or potential customers?
● What are their real or perceived needs?
● What are their preferences and intentions?
● Why?
● Who else has the ability to satisfy them?

– and hence

● What can/should/must the company do in order to provide a superior benefit package to the customer?

The answers to these questions permit the formulation of product policies, marketing and communications strategies, and provide a measuring point for performance evaluation.

The instruments theoretically available are the same for any business research environment: the essential factors governing usability are dictated by the structures of the market and its compo-

nent customers and by matters of access and co-operation. As far back as 1979, Katz identified seven characteristic elements which distinguish business marketing research from any other context:

i) the finite size of the research *population*
ii) problems and opportunities in *accessibility*
iii) possibilities of acquiring respondent *cooperation*
iv) limitations of *sample* size and hence on research techniques
v) the ability to *identify* and define ideal *respondents*
vi) the need for and scarcity of knowledgeable *interviewers*
vii) the level of *costs* (financial and temporal) needed to conduct effective research.

As already noted earlier in discussion of Figure 15.4, these factors have impacts on the selection of data sources and research instruments.

□ *Data sources*

The general principle of examining secondary data before embarking on primary investigations not only holds good in business markets; frequently it may obviate the need for potentially complex primary research altogether. In developed industrialised countries, the volume and quality of secondary information in the public domain is very considerable, whilst most companies are also able to draw upon comprehensive internal records of customers, sales, product output and costs to produce a reasonably complete picture. Secondary data does, of course, have well acknowledged limitations – most particularly in respect of consistency between sources, and of age – but nevertheless it can frequently be used to gain an overall perspective of an individual major company's policies or development, of a general market situation, given careful evaluation and interpretation. Such a facility is much more likely to apply in the context of business markets than in consumer environments, but even so, if more detailed or more recent information is needed, recourse to primary research becomes unavoidable.

One particular form of secondary information which is of value in business markets is that of marketing intelligence. Most, if not all, companies acquire a great deal of incidental information about customers, suppliers, competitors and markets both systematically and serendipitously, via routine reporting systems, chance observations and deliberate communications. Such intelligence can well be of vital significance. It requires systematic recording, retrieval and analysis: in that respect it demands great care and attention if it is not to be consigned to a dead file. It also requires careful segregation of data which is 'nice to know' from that which one 'needs to know'.

As far as primary data collection is concerned, Hart (1987) among others has reported on detailed studies which have been carried out on research methods in industrial markets. The essence of the findings was that

a)   limitations of access normally prevent or constrain the use of observational or experimental techniques in business markets; hence
b)   surveys are the most commonly used instruments;
c)   considerations of market size and individual customer significance frequently demand sample stratification, if not indeed a complete census approach;
d)   the importance of key customers frequently renders it advantageous to conduct interviews on a personal in-depth, semi-structured or unstructured basis.

As always, the costs involved in conducting the research must be weighed against the benefits derivable. However given the characteristic of many business markets to be dominated by small numbers of players with oligopolistic power, the need for detailed appreciation not only of objective factors, but also of intentions, preferences and attitudes of – and within – the respondent organisation frequently militates in favour of the personal approaches to data collection (Figures 15.6 and 15.7).

Whatever the desirability or theoretical attractions of particular methodologies, the practical constraints imposed by the imperative needs to obtain specific items of information or of contacting specific respondents frequently introduces an element of opportunism into the process (Buchanan et al., 1988), and gives added point to the observation by Hutt and Speh (1995) that an effective research process and information system is governed by four essential criteria:

- Managerial capability
- Analysability
- Flexibility
- Usability

Throughout, however, managers and researchers need to keep in mind that whilst possession of information is a fundamental prerequisite of dependable decision making, it is the interpretation and use of that information rather than its simple possession or existence which is the real key to advantage. Recognition of this apparent truism lies behind drives for 'customer closeness' and 'customer understanding' – and hence has stimulated awareness of the importance of qualitative, management orientated research as an essential complement to quantitative 'number-crunching' (Peters and Waterman, 1982; Easterby-Smith et al., 1991).

□ *Segmentation issues*

Marketing research outputs are crucial to virtually every strategic decision process in the company: in the business environment, perhaps more critically than in a consumer context, the definable nature of customers renders target selection and approach matters of vital importance. 'Small numbers' and 'large size' as customer characteristics are potentially double edged weapons: they offer procedural advantages and strategic risks

On the beneficial side, these characteristics imply or facilitate

- greater depth of potential understanding of the needs of individual customers – and hence

Figure 15.6 *Advantages and disadvantages of different types of interviews*

	Advantages	Disadvantages
Standardised or structured interviews	Interviewer briefing and training simplified Less scope for interviewer bias Less interviewer variation Classifying, coding and analysis simpler Results comparable Higher reliability Greater opportunity for measurement	Questions must be simple and (usually) closed Data lack depth Lower validity Cannot probe Cannot obtain clarification of ambiguities
Depth, focused or unstructured interviewers	Questions can be deep, searching Data rich and full High degree of validity Probing possible Can obtain clarification of ambiguities	Interviewers need skill and training Interviewer bias may increase Greater interviewer variability Result often not comparable Reliability questionable Less scope for measurement

Source: S. J. Hart, 'The Use of the Survey in Industrial Marketing Research', *Journal of Marketing Management* 3 (1) (Summer 1987), p. 32.

potentially can cause major customers to become the focus of individually tailored strategies: virtually single-member segments;
- depth of market analysis which can assist in the formulation of generic strategies of differentiation or focus (Porter 1980);
- segmentation of customers on the basis of known behavioural/attitudinal characteristics as well as or instead of 'simple' demographic or observable attributes (Wind and Cardozo, 1974).

On the other hand, small customer numbers, large size and relative heterogeneity increase the risks from an inappropriate appraisal and potentially increase the costs (financially and otherwise) of needing to tailor-make product and marketing strategies.

Much of the conventional business marketing literature leans heavily upon Wind and Cardozo's so called 'two stage' approach to business market segmentation. Perhaps because it is distinctively applicable to the business environment, it is often assumed to be automatically 'right', and always used. However, there is a risk of potential misinterpretation of the precepts of the model in that the 'two stage' descriptor is not infrequently taken to refer to the *application* of the segmentation criteria rather than as a means of differentiating between macro and micro variables themselves. As Corey (1975) pointed out, not only was such a perception not intended by the original analysts, it is inappropriate: there is no logical reason why at both macro and micro 'level' of differentiation, several criteria cannot be used in sequence ... geography, customer size, end use, SIC code, DMU structure, and so on. What

Figure 15.7. *Preferred data collection methods under different survey conditions*

	Conditions of survey			Possible data collection method(s)		
Funds	Time	Type of Data	Personal Interview	Mail	Telephone	
Restricted	Restricted	Few items			x	Assuming telephone population representative
Restricted	Restricted	Much Information	x			If funds permit
Restricted	Ample	Few items		x	x	Assuming telephone population representative
Restricted	Ample	Much information	x	x		Non-respondent follow-up needed
Restricted	Ample	Few items		x	x	
Restricted	Ample	Much information		x		
Ample	Restricted	Few items	x		x	Assuming telephone population representative
Ample	Restricted	Much information	x			
Ample	Ample	Few items	x		x	Assuming telephone population representative
Ample	Ample	Much information	x			
Ample	Ample	Few items	x	x	x	
Ample	Ample	Much information	x	x		Either joint or one method alone

Source: S. J. Hart, 'The Use of the Survey in Industrial Marketing Research', *Journal of Marketing Management* 3 (1) (Summer 1989), p. 36; based on R. Ferber and P. Verdoorn, *Research Methods in Economics and Business,* London: Macmillan (1962).

matters is that suppliers should be able to isolate groupings of customers to the point where each group is cost effectively manageable.

By contrast with the Wind and Cardozo model, alternative representations of the process exist, although in academic texts they attract less attention. For example, Bonoma and Shapiro (1983) utilise much the same variables, but portray the process of segmentation as a continuous process of refinement, without emphasis on the macro/micro variable split. By visualising the process in terms of their 'nested' approach, there is significantly less risk of misperception of the concept, and (arguably) greater ease of appreciation that the analyst can terminate the process once a segment has been defined in terms consistent with segment viability (Kotler, 1991), and

matching the capabilities and objectives of the supplier (Figure 15.8).

Irrespective of one's choice of representational approach, the central tenets of business market segmentation are constant:

i) Because of the numbers, identifiability and significance of business customers; because of their inherent rationality, and because of the general tendency for long-term relationships to exist between customer and supplier, more information about needs, preferences and intentions is generally both required and available;

ii) Because of the complex structure of buying centres, their own inherent interest in sourcing ideal suppliers, together with the limited

Figure 15.8.   *Bonoma and Shapiro's nested approach to segmentation*

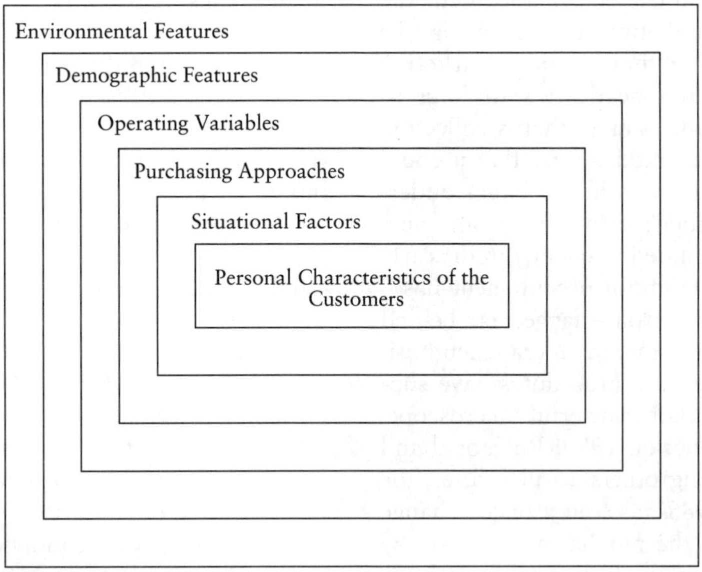

Source: T. V. Bonoma and B. P. Shapiro, *Segmenting the Industrial Market*, Lexington, Mass.: Lexington Books (1983).

numbers involved, it is generally essential to rely heavily on in-depth research techniques to establish the nature and applicability of micro variables. Usually this cannot be determined from existing secondary material: care must therefore be exercised to determine whether the benefit derivable from microsegmentation will justify the costs of acquiring the necessary data.

Furthermore, in a very practical respect, for many business market suppliers, the processes of segmentation are complicated by the existence of multiple distribution channels, especially in circumstances where some customers are Original Equipment Manufacturers themselves, whilst others are more conventional distributors. Customer selection and target market strategic planning must not only take account of multiplicities of customer types, but also of potential multiple product users even within customer types, and multiple levels of relationship with the company itself and other members of the supply chain. The process of segmentation thus becomes potentially very complex – but at the same time more strategically important.

Procurement: the obverse of marketing?

Virtually since the outset of academic study of 'industrial' marketing, the precepts of Organisational Buying Behaviour (OBB) have been used pragmatically and conceptually to differentiate the business environment from the consumer context. However, until perhaps the mid 1980s, apart from academic journals, the overwhelming emphasis in textual material was focused on one or two organisational models such as that of the Decision Making Unit (Webster and Wind, 1972), and the Buy Grid (Robinson, Faris and Wind, 1967). Without questioning the validity of these as concepts, they scarcely explain the organisational decision making process itself in any *behavioural* sense, neither do they account for, nor accommodate, the major changes in managerial emphasis and practice which have emerged more recently.

The organisational buyer (the customer), the buying and decision making processes and the influences thereon are at the heart of the philosophical and managerial study of business to business marketing.

Despite the fundamental logicality of such an approach, and its complete consonance with the foundations of the marketing concept, it may be considered remarkable that it took marketing managers, analysts and academics so long to realise the OBB was and is more than a collection of structural/procedural models, and that it could not be studied adequately without equal understanding of the procurement function. Furthermore, as has been noted frequently in the early 1990s, the academic study of procurement has – for some inexplicable reason – lagged far behind managerial practice, and that in an era when business theories, practices and procedures have supposedly been under a more powerful 'microscope' than ever before (Monczka, 1989; Rajagopal and Bernard, 1993a, among others). Still further, the period since about 1985 has seen a major change in the perceptions of the purchasing function by managers and academics alike. The underlying change has been to depart from traditional perceptions of 'buying' as a purely reactive 'service' function within a firm, towards a broader view of 'procurement' or 'sourcing' as being a creative, proactive function which can be regarded as a profit centre not as a cost centre for the organisation (Baily and Farmer, 1990, among others).

Whilst it is difficult – and of doubtful real benefit – to try to reconstruct or deduce causal links in this series of changes of viewpoint, the most notable turning points in the shift away from simple structural approaches are perhaps

i)   Sheth's (1973) integrative model which introduced *behavioural* issues in the study of organisational buying, subsequently summarised by Morris (1988) into four heads of evaluation in arriving at a product, brand or supplier selection decision:
   ● Analysis of *Expectations*
   ● Determination of the *Buying Centre* and its priorities
   ● *Conflict Management*
   ● Identification and Rationalisation of *Situational Factors*.
ii) Bonoma and Johnston's (1978) model of *exchange elements* in the buying and marketing process, showing links between the

   ● buyer and sales representative
   ● sales representative and the supplying firm
   ● buyer and the purchasing firm
   ● sales representative and the purchasing firm
   ● buyer and the supplying firm
and ● corporate perceptions between the respective firms themselves;

– and perhaps the most widely recognised of all,

iii) Hakansson's (1983) postulation of an *interaction* which identifies four key sets of decision influencing variables
   ● an *iterative process of interaction* between the buying centre and the marketing organisation
   ● the roles of the individual *participants*
   ● the corporate or business *atmosphere* of the interaction
   ● the overall business and macroeconomic *environment* in which the interactions take place.

Subsequently, as discussed further in Chapters 5 and 21 of this book, Hakansson's model has frequently been regarded as having been a stimulus for the development of studies of relationship marketing and relationship management, as well as reflecting the inherent dynamism of the purchase decision making process.

The changes which have arisen in both managerial practice and academic thinking have considerable significance, especially at a strategic level, in that they highlight once again the significance of detailed customer knowledge, the need for two way information exchanges, and the essential commonality of interest for all transaction parties in arriving at solutions which produce benefits for all (Figure 15.9).

More recently still, as argued by Arnold and Bernard (1994) the achievement of mutually acceptable transactions and the development of interactive and substantial relationships depends upon mutually competent and acceptable negotiation processes and outcomes, and in turn upon a perceived balance in information possession.

Figure 15.9. *Exchange processes in business-to-business marketing*

Element of Linkage	Direction of Flow
Information/Intelligence	Two-way
Problem Solving	Seller to Buyer
Negotiation	Two-way
Friendship/Trust	Two-way
Products/Services	Seller to Buyer
Payment	Buyer to Seller
Reciprocity of Benefit	Two-way

Source: Adapted from M. D. Hutt, W. J. Johnston and J. R. Ronchetto, 'Selling Centres and Buying Centres: Formulating Strategic Exchange Patterns', *Journal of Personal Selling and Sales Management* 5 (May 1985).

Without such a balance, one or both parties may well perceive an undue element of risk which will stimulate further searches for its resolution – quite possibly with alternative business partners.

Marketers, purchasers and logistics management

The changes discussed above represent more than a progression from concern with *buying procedures* to a focus on *procurement processes*, and more than a recognition of the change from reactive buying to proactive procurement. Current practice and analysis indicates realisation of the potential for internal integration of management of the marketing and procurement functions to enhance corporate efficiency, and development of inter company supply chain linkages to enhance competitive effectiveness. In some respects this is not a new discovery: it has, for example, long been recognised that intra-company cooperation is an essential ingredient of successful product innovation and introduction (Booz, Allen and Hamilton, 1982; Cooper, 1978, Freeman *et al.*, 1972, for example). More recently however, the development of Just-In-Time practices, the evolution of technology alliances and the trend towards disintegration of previously vertically integrated corporations have stimulated formation of supply chain based, vertical al-

liances. The key ingredient – beyond expediency or simple commonality of interest – is recognition of the benefits of synergy in developing secure but flexible niches in increasingly turbulent markets (Nueno and Oosterveld, 1988; Thackray, 1986, for example).

Numerous particular factors may have contributed to or precipitated this change in orientation, but the most commonly advanced are perhaps

- actual or potential threats to *security of supplies* causing competition among customers for available sources;
- technologically stimulated *excesses of long term supply* capability over aggregate demand potential leading to endemic competition among suppliers for customers;
- *shortening product life cycles* accentuated or caused by increased emphasis on innovation as a competitive necessity, but resulting in difficulties of investment recovery and product obsolescence;
- increasing *product and production complexities*, demanding increases in technical competence, investment and risk;
- internal and external demands for *cost effectiveness and cost efficiency* to safeguard survival, profitability, satisfaction and advantage;
- continual *emergence of new sources of supply* for products, components and technologies resulting in both opportunities and threats.

Drives for leanness, cost efficiency and competitiveness do not just place the business marketing function at the interface between the customer market and the supply function, they critically entail the integration of marketing, procurement and supply functions. Whilst a conventionally purist interpreter of the marketing concept might argue that such a perception is neither new nor exceptional, the outcomes in managerial terms imply or produce structural interpretations rather more radical than might be inferred from most extant marketing text books.

Research by Rajagopal *et al.* (1994) builds on the previous observations by Womack *et al.*,

(1990) among others that leanness entails functional collaboration and integration – and in turn perhaps leads to the elimination of certain functional activities – at least on a regular basis. The development of close functional and corporate relationships necessary to operate JIT to its ultimate advantage eliminates the necessity for frequent meetings between 'buyers' and 'marketers' for the negotiation and placement of routine orders. Functionally as well as conceptually the routine acquisition or transfer negotiating function between the organisations becomes a matter of partnership, consolidation and structural integration.

Such an eventuality has long been foreshadowed. In the context of logistics management, Stern and El-Ansary (1992) identify interfaces and conjoint activities linking logistics with production and marketing functions, seeing purchasing and inventory management as key elements in that process. Business marketers thus find themselves in situations where, in order to deliver the required satisfactions to their customer and to their own company, they need to be able to

- identify and understand the culture and functioning of their customer's organisation as well as the customer's objective needs;
- comprehend and negotiate effectively on all aspects of the procurement process, including logistics, inventory levels, JIT and associated concepts and practices;
- take part in detailed analyses of costs, pricing strategies, value analysis and discussions of the 'make or buy' option with *all* parties potentially involved;
- take a holistic view of the supply process and to devise and integrate marketing into that system, such that the customer achieves the optimal level of benefit and value for money, and that the marketer's own organisation is enabled to provide that benefit competitively and efficiently.

(Bernard and Rajagopal, 1992)

Arguably, the acid test of a supplying firm's marketing orientation is the extent to which the management of supply side activities is function-

ally integrated. The achievement of optimal benefits from a JIT operation is less than likely if the negotiations do not include detailed consideration of downstream marketing issues as well as upstream procurement opportunities (Rajagopal *et al.*, 1994).

Business marketers and the marketing mix

It is customary for marketing textbooks to devote considerable amounts of time and space to discussion of the functional issues of mix management. Certainly these are vital issues for the manager, but in practice the treatments tend to revolve around well-rehearsed generalised principles, or to focus on situations perceived as 'exceptions to the general rule'. Whilst tending towards to second of these approaches, the present author suggests that the 'business' environment *per se*, far from being the exception, is in fact the norm, as more marketing activities take place between businesses than between businesses and consumers.

What is, however, important in the present context, is to draw distinctions between the two environments, where these have germane bearing on the formulation of models or strategies. Still more so, it is necessary to engender awareness that despite the underpinning of principles and generalities, practitioners face realities where each situation requires a different blend of emphases on mix elements from preceding or following decision scenarios. As has been discussed above, this means that marketers are unable to act effectively, in isolation, from customers, suppliers or 'internal' colleagues. It also means that especially in environments where complex, often technical, negotiations must be carried out (internally with producing departments or procurement colleagues, or externally with customers), it is a matter of practical benefit, if not a formal necessity, for marketing personnel to possess sufficient technical knowledge for themselves to be both competent and credible.

Whilst therefore it is possible to temporise and to postulate 'differences' in respect of all of the mix elements, to do so is somewhat misleading. Issues of channel selection and management are, for practical purposes, always in the 'business' domain, as are many aspects of pricing strategy and tactics, no matter whether or not the impact of the business marketer's decisions can be detected in the marketability of the eventual end product to the consumer.

Similarly, as has already been outlined, logistics management is both an interface between marketing and other corporate functions, and a potential source of competitive advantage. Acknowledgement of the legitimate interest of marketers in logistical issues has emerged somewhat erratically. As a legacy from traditions of 'sales orientation' in business, the marketing function has conventionally been expected to accept responsibility for the liquidation of inventories of finished goods, whether or not any excesses arose from erroneous forecasting! Similarly, as noted by Hutt and Speh (1995), marketing executives

i)   are frequently perceived as pushing for the company to hold inventory as a means of capitalising on, as yet unknown, opportunities;

ii) are increasingly seen as being influential in the determination of inventory levels for materials and work-in-progress, as a result of forecasts of demand.

As noted earlier, research and forecasting are, at best, inexact sciences. Nevertheless, elimination or prevention of excess inventories is in the interest of all corporate functions: whether or not any inventory at all is required depends as much upon market volatility and profitability as it does upon the security of supplies and suppliers.

◼ Product management

It is a matter of simple extension from the above discussion to argue that logistics management ultimately falls within the purview of the Product Manager, rather than being the sole preserve of the production function or of a narrowly focused purchasing department. Such a line of thought is not inconsistent with the conventional definitions of marketing, neither is it in conflict with managerial practice, especially in respect of distribution channels for consumer goods.

Where differences of perception arise is more in academic than in managerial contexts, due in part at least to terminological confusions and debates about the similarity or distinction between 'Brand' and 'Product' management. Examination of the objectives of job holders (irrespective of precise title) suggests that conceptually there are few, if any, real differences, although in practical terms industrial goods product managers have rather different working parameters from their fast moving consumer goods counterparts. Given, however, that irrespective of title, the function of product/brand management has more or less agreed scope:

● customer identification, needs analysis, demand quantification, target selection;
● product range specification;
● competitor analysis and product positioning strategy determination;
● product performance monitoring;
● identification of threats/opportunities for the product line and devising of appropriate marketing strategies

(Bureau, 1983)

one must look elsewhere for any functional differences between the two environments and traditions.

Superficially the origin of the perceived distinctions of emphasis between product and brand management may appear to lie in the technical expertise required of the manager. However, it can be argued that, at a more basic level still, it stems from the power of the customer to 'unbundle' the total product offering and to negotiate separately, on a more or less zero base, in respect of all aspects of the offering – core utility, differentiating features and augmented benefits (Kotler, 1994). Hutt and Speh (1995) observe that the greater the level of customer input to the product specification process, the more the function of the product manager moves away from macro level demand prediction towards generic forecasting of the level of production facilities required to meet a range of possible demand scenarios. Customisation policies and negotiations require not merely technical levels of product – and production – knowledge; they also necessitate the ability to communicate directly with technical staff in both the supplying *and* the customer company, as well as having command of procedural concepts such as inventory, logistics and distribution.

In a very real sense therefore the role of the product manager in business markets may be seen as a cameo of the marketing management function. As such, it is normally seen as a senior function, and not infrequently, in industrial goods companies, is filled by 'promotion' from the ranks of production managerial staff. Clearly, in such a situation there is great potential for interfunctional conflict, or at least for the non appreciation of the concepts of marketing by someone apparently filling one of the key marketing posts in the organisation. Aside from glib answers to the problem in the shape of 'education' or 'communication', it seems reasonable to propose that the long term direction to ensure avoidance of the problem is to aim for a degree of integration of the functional management tasks of product management, procurement and logistics management, reporting at the highest level in the company. This indeed appears to be one of the characterising features in the success of British Airways, for example, by comparison with other airlines who have adopted high profile communications strategies but without apparently paying sufficient attention to the organisation and coordination of supply side functions (Rajagopal and Bernard, 1993b).

The one key area of product management in business markets which has been singled out for attention in the literature for many years is that of product development, and to a lesser extent, product deletion (Von Hippell, 1978; Hart, 1988; Foxall, 1989, among others).

The general proposition has been that finite customer numbers and relatively large customer size not only means that supplier: customer relationships can become close enough to give advance warning to suppliers in respect of customers' emerging new needs, but also that customers will possess enough internal knowledge to formulate performance specifications for products which they will then actively encourage suppliers to develop. This is at the heart of von Hippel's (1978) postulation of a Customer Active Paradigm for new industrial product development. Such a concept has many attractions:

- it can be applied to all manner of organisational buying circumstances, not simply industrial products;
- it will reduce 'go error' in the development process and reduce the time and cost absorbed in scanning the market for unmet needs (Kotler 1994);
- it will speed up the adoption and diffusion processes by guaranteeing at least some level of initial orders.

Indeed if the supplier selects the right customer and the right product to develop, the supplier can benefit from the opinion leadership characteristics of the customer, and at the same time steal a time-to-market advantage over competitors. Similarly, if the customer picks the right supplier, then the customer also will secure time benefits in competition. For large, complex and expensive products, development risks have become such that suppliers are reluctant to enter the development phase without reasonable certainty of actual orders. Boeing, for instance, even with the proven success of the generic 747 product behind them, were unwilling to develop the 747–400 without the security of advance orders, and probably would not have gone ahead with designs without impetus from specific customers.

Not all product developments involve such clear cut relationships. More recent research has uncovered two new strands of practice. Foxall (1989), in discussing User Initiated Innovations identified four classes of such new products distinguished by their perceived relevance to the customer/innovator's core business; by the willingness and ability of the customer both to take the idea through the 'tangible' development programme and/or to market the outcome directly or via some form of franchising or licensing deal. By contrast, the concepts of partnership and 'comakership' have emerged from proactive, strategically orientated, procurement departments who actively seek suppliers to help them to develop their own new products (Deans and Rajagopal, 1991).

The function of product management and the role of the product manager are therefore very difficult to define in explicit terms. Whilst different organisations will arrive at situation specific, and perhaps *ad hoc*, interpretations, the constant feature is that the role of the manager is to act as an interface between customers, the company and suppliers; to monitor, shape and position the product line – in short to ensure that the company can deliver not just 'products' but also the benefit package which the customer requires, and at a rate of return which is acceptable to the firm.

■ Communications

Although conventionally regarded as the fourth 'P' (Promotion) of the marketing mix, marketing communications is in fact a mix of techniques and variables, which individually and collectively have the objectives of conveying information, establishing preference, leading to a decision and promoting post-purchase satisfaction on the part of the customer. The general structure of the communications mix is not a matter of controversy, and has been discussed in detail elsewhere. However the balance of use among the variables is liable to considerable variation depending primarily upon:

the numbers, identifiability and accessibility of the intended audience members, and in particular the 'internal' members of business Decision Making Units;
the nature of the purchase – repeat or infrequent purchase – and its perceived buy class;
the amount of risk perceived by buyer and marketer, and hence the scale of information exchange required;
the length of the distribution channel involved, the position in the channel of the immediate target customer, the perceived balance of power in the channel, and thus the

extent to which pull or push strategies can be adopted;
● the present position of the supplier – 'in' or 'out';
● the speed with which diffusion of information and market reaction is required;
● the resources of the supplier;
● competitive activities and the relative profile and standing of the supplier in the marketplace.

As a broad generalisation, as observed by Kotler (1994) and others, indirect mix elements such as advertising and editorial publicity are of greatest benefit in

a) reaching relatively large, undifferentiated audiences in concentrated time periods;
b) conveying factual information and generating awareness;
c) gaining access to 'behind the scenes', unidentified customers and/or DMU members;
d) reinforcing or preceding more direct or focused approaches by other means such as sales calls (Morrill, 1970).

On the other hand, despite much higher levels of cost per effective contact, more direct approaches such as direct mail, telemarketing and personal selling have distinct advantages in business markets, especially in that

● they permit the development of personal contact and relationships, encourage information exchanges and a joint approach to solving customers real needs
● the sales representative is able to represent the *whole* company to the customer
● personal contact is considered to be more effective than impersonal contact in developing preference and in precipitating decisions
● personal contact is capable of interacting with indirect communications for greater effectiveness
● personal contact is more certain of securing an actual response (positive or negative) than indirect approaches.

The generalised consequences of these factors cumulatively is that the great majority of business marketing companies, find it beneficial to employ sales forces of one type or another to maintain regular contacts with actual customers, as well as to develop new leads and opportunities. In this context therefore, there exists a somewhat different balance in the utilisation of mix elements than is perceived to be the case in 'consumer' contexts. It has to be borne in mind however that this different skew risks being misinterpreted unless one remembers that business markets handle all types of merchandise, and not simply industrial products (Kotler, 1991).

□ *Exhibitions and trade shows*

One mix element which is vastly more significant in the business environment than in a consumer context is the trade show or exhibition. In both environments, an exhibition has the benefits of providing a shop window for the company's products – as well as of providing an extra opportunity for the placing/securing of actual orders.

Research publications suggest a variety of motives form and benefits which may be derived from, attendance at exhibitions, which require evaluation against the generally high total costs of such operations. These costs extend beyond the primary elements of stand rent and display building, encompassing in addition

- costs of staffing the display
- opportunity costs incurred by staff absence from normal routine functions
- accommodation and entertainment
- preparation and transportation of display samples, equipment and so on.

It is clearly essential therefore that any intending exhibitor should select the most appropriate forum to display the company's wares, and to ensure that the target audience both visit the show, and come to the stand. In this context it is somewhat surprising to note that about one exhibitor in six apparently does little if anything to encourage prospective target customers to attend, beyond perhaps relying entirely on word of mouth communication from sales representatives (Hart, 1988).

The basic problem which exists for many exhibitors is that of evaluation of exhibition effectiveness, and hence of justification of the cost involved. In business markets this in rendered particularly difficult because

i) negotiations and discussions take place which do not bear fruit for some considerable time after the event, and the outcomes may not be solely attributable to the exhibition

ii) orders placed at exhibitions may well have been 'in the pipeline' already, and it may thus be difficult, if not impossible, to identify the extent of truly additional business.

By comparison with commonly held belief that the value of business transacted is the most usual yardstick used to evaluate exhibition effectiveness, research cited by Gopalakrishna and Williams (1992) suggests that the generation of new leads and opportunities is the most frequently quoted reason for attendance. The authors quote from research by the American Trade Show Bureau, conducted in 1988, which indicated that from a sample of 472 firms, no less than 86 per cent identified lead generation as being their primary objective. This is consistent with earlier studies by Cavanaugh (1976) and Calginaitis (1980) which suggested that the five most important objectives of exhibitors were:

- lead generation
- prospect evaluation
- reaching inaccessible influencers
- introduction of new products
- acquisition of orders

Hart's (1988) researches suggested that to this list might be added:

- research into competitors' activities
- evaluation of new products' potential
- exposure of senior management/non marketing personnel to the marketing environment

This last point is of benefit to both marketer and customer in that the customer may have an opportunity to meet senior members of staff of the supplying company otherwise inaccessible, in exactly the same way that the suppliers may well have the opportunity to meet members of the DMU who would not normally come into contact with visiting sales representatives.

A well attended exhibition may therefore present exhibitors with many opportunities, of establishing contacts, obtaining feedback, conducting research, concluding orders or contracts and developing relationships. Psychologically however, the exhibition stand represents something of a reversal of roles which may be seen as a threat or deterrent by the exhibitor. Under normal conditions, the sales representative may consider that he or she has a degree of initiative and control, in that although most sales interviews take place 'on the customer's territory', the representative can to a large extent determine the date and timing of the call – and whether it will take place at all. At an exhibition, the marketer is totally at the mercy of the customer, who will have the discretion to call only on those suppliers whom the customer wishes to contact. Relationship building *before* the event is thus no less critical than exercises carried out during the show itself. To the *buyer*, there are benefits which tend to reciprocate those of the supplier, most important among which are:

- an opportunity to conduct purchasing research and to seek new sources of supply
- a chance to see a number of actual and potential suppliers in a concentrated period of time
- a chance to 'get away from the office' and into a more objective environment

Growth in awareness of the tactical, pragmatic benefits of trade shows is reflected in that fact that such activities occupy a very prominent position in the promotional expenditure hierarchy:

- Various surveys suggest that exhibitions rank about third in order of financial spend in the business to business communications environment (Hart, 1988).

- Expenditure on exhibitions accounts for about 20 per cent of business communications costs (excluding personal selling/sales force costs) (Hart, 1988).
- In the USA in 1988 the exhibition business itself had an estimated turnover of US$9 billion, drawing 35 million visitors (i.e. equivalent to about one eighth of the US population) to some 11000 trade exhibitions (Gopalakrishna and Williams, 1992).

Budgeting and performance evaluation

The foregoing section has raised an issue which is of ongoing concern in all sections of the communications business: how best to determine the size of the promotional expenditure budget and how to evaluate the effectiveness of its use. There is a great deal of debate in the literature as regards the pros and cons of the various generic techniques; what is noteworthy however is that despite the alleged rationality of organisational buyers, when it comes to the purchase of communications media or space, the decision is characterised by a large element of irrationality! Hart (1988) reports figures from two industrial market surveys in the UK indicating that a very large, albeit not conclusively dominant, proportion of companies rely heavily on arbitrary targets or figures derived from the sales turnover or sales budget. By comparison Mahin (1991) cites American research which although claiming 74 per cent adherence to the objective/task method, also shows heavy dependence on other techniques – affordable levels (33 per cent); percentage of past or anticipated sales (39 per cent); follow the competition (21 per cent) – among others. Overall, in the sample surveyed business marketers on average used 1.85 methods of budget determination, suggesting clearly that they had less than complete faith in any method to produce a budget which was likely to be appropriate, in line with perceived normality of practice and affordability.

Similar problems afflict the measurability of promotional effectiveness. As in consumer markets, it is difficult to disaggregate the impacts created by the various promotional mix elements: however in business markets, the problems tend to be further complicated by market characteristics.

a) There frequently exist long delays between promotional activity and order placement – especially in producer goods industries.

b) As Morrill (1970) has shown, personal selling and advertising often operate synergistically.

c) It is difficult to track media reach in the 'inaccessible' parts of the DMU, or to evaluate the impact there.

d) Business press media is highly fragmented with considerable risk of overlap in readership of journals, coupled with variability in journal 'life'.

e) Aside from issues related to awareness, measurement techniques for other communications objectives, such as preference development, are extremely imprecise and difficult to implement.

In consequence, emphasis tends to be focused on sales volume, on the implicit assumption that, over time, aggregate business achieved will be influenced by aggregate promotional expenditure, albeit lagged by a period of time, which may or may not be constant. Such an uncertain scenario scarcely engenders confidence in scientific approaches to communications strategy or evaluation, representing yet another reason why the easy to measure, but illogical, budgeting basis of relationship to turnover persists and flourishes in practice.

▌ Concluding comments – future trends in business marketing

As has been demonstrated, the subject of business to business marketing is in a state of flux.

From a managerial standpoint, practices have developed and evolved over a considerable period of time whereby high levels of integration between the marketing function and other corporate disciplines have been achieved. This evolution has not taken place suddenly, neither has it been precipitated by any single stimulus,

nor has it affected all segments of business activity equally in terms of extent or timescale. Studies in the fast-moving consumer goods industries – especially in the food/confectionery sectors – suggest that integration of activities within companies, and establishment of strategic supply chains as well as the formation of horizontal alliances among non-competing organisations, is at a stage considerably further developed than in most producer goods industries (Dawson and Shaw, 1992). However certain manufacturing industries, notably automotive and electronics, have also undertaken fundamental reappraisals of their management structures and strategies stimulated by the need to enhance international competitiveness.

It has to be said that academic studies and management education have lagged significantly behind functional practice in terms of both research and teaching (Thomas, 1993; ESRC, 1994). Only since the mid-1980s have there been significant numbers of research studies of the impacts of such subjects as Just In Time (JIT) and Total Quality Management (TQM) on business as opposed to production management functions.

Nevertheless, the changes in research focus do appear to have taken root, and it is likely that the change in direction will prove to be both irreversible and of positive benefit to both academic and functional management branches of business disciplines. In retrospect, the change in academic approach may be seen as having been precipitated by three separate but interrelated stimuli

i) the broadening of the base of marketing research and education from a narrow 'consumer' and 'industrial' dichotomy to a 'business' foundation, focusing on customer types and motivations rather than on product types;

ii) a recognition that the distributive trades – for long the 'Cinderella' of academic studies of marketing and business/management research – not only occupy a crucial position in the business environment, but also have developed integrated functional management practices to a sophisticated level and at a much earlier date than much of manufacturing industry;

iii) the fundamental change in orientation of the supply side of industry from narrow preoccupations of 'buying' and 'production' to a wider and deeper understanding of the strategic significance of sourcing and procurement.

As evidence of the magnitude of the changes in direction in both the academic and practitioner worlds one needs only to consider two recent and ongoing developments. Firstly, there is a continuing focus on functional integration and interaction within and between companies, typified by the establishment of supply chain alliances, partnering, and comakership and by attention to logistics management as a source of cost effective advantage. Secondly, one can cite the introduction of formal academic studies of Procurement Management as a corollary to studies of Marketing, which are receiving enthusiastic support from practitioner markets worldwide.

For the foreseeable future, the study of business marketing appears likely to be characterised not so much by new knowledge as by the development of new paradigms founded on assimilation of existing knowledge, principles and practices from a variety of disciplines. This will involve the exploitation of concepts already in existence and the exploration of new frontiers in their recognition and application.

Taking as the focal point the need for whole companies – not just marketing functionaries – to concentrate on delivering *total customer care* as a competitive necessity, increased attention to benefit augmentation in the form of TQM is likely to emphasise still further the role of internal marketing. JIT will come to be seen still more clearly not merely as a financial or production orientated, cost saving strategy but as a dynamic philosophy which integrates the whole focus of the organisation on delivering exactly what the customer requires, when it is needed and at the most attractive all-in cost. The first steps in this direction have already been taken: the realisation of the real benefits will come from the recognition that such a philosophy demands managerial and academic integration of the disciplines of marketing, procurement and production operations.

This is entirely consistent with the long established concept of market orientation and represents a total justification for business to business marketing activity being seen as the crucial ingredient of long term competitiveness and success.

■ References

Arnold U. and Bernard, K. N. (1994), 'Relationship Management as a Marketing Task', *Journal of Business Research* (forthcoming).

Baily, P. J. H. and Farmer, D. H. (1990), *Purchasing Principles and Management*, 6th edition, London: Pitman.

Baker, M. J. (1983), *Marketing Theory and Practice*, 2nd edition, London: Macmillan.

Bernard, K. N. (1988), 'Consumer Demand or Customer Satisfaction?', *European Journal of Marketing* 22 (3), pp. 61–72.

Bernard, K. N. and Rajagopal, S. (1991), 'Relationship Management in Marketing and Purchasing: Internal and External Perspectives', *Vezetéstudomány* (Management Science) (Hungary), pp. 11–20.

Bernard, K. N. and Rajagopal, S. (1992), 'The Role of Costs Containment in Integrating Strategic Marketing and Procurement to Develop Competitive Advantage', *Department of Marketing Working Paper Series*, MWP 92/11, University of Strathclyde.

Bonoma, T. V. and Johnston, W. J. (1978), 'The Social Psychology of Industrial Buying and Selling', *Industrial Marketing Management* 7 (October), p. 216.

Bonoma, T. V. and Shapiro, B. P. (1983), *Segmenting the Industrial Market*, Lexington, Mass.: Lexington Books.

Booz, Allen and Hamilton (1982), *New Product Management for the 1980s*. New York: Booz, Allen and Hamilton.

Borden, N. H. (1964), 'The Concept of the Marketing Mix', *Journal of Advertising Research* (June), pp. 2–7.

Buchanan, D., Boddy, D. and McCalman, J. (1988), 'Getting In, Getting On, Getting Out and Getting Back', in Bryman, A. (ed.), *Doing Research in Organisations*, London: Routledge, pp. 53–67.

Bureau, J. R. (1983), *Brand Management*, London: Macmillan.

Buzzell, R. D., Gale, B. T. and Sultan, R. G. M. (1975), 'Market Share – A Key to Profitability', *Harvard Business Review* 53 (January–February), pp. 97–106.

Calginaitis, C. (1980), 'Trade Shows Exhibit Some Promise', *Advertising Age* (9 June), p. 14–15.

Cavanaugh, S. (1976), 'Setting Objectives and Evaluating the Effectiveness of Trade Show Exhibits', *Journal of Marketing* 40 (October), pp. 100–103.

Cochran, B. and Thompson, G. (1964), 'Why New Products Fail', *National Industrial Conference Board Record* 1 (October), pp. 11–18.

Chisnall, P. M. (1995), *Strategic Business Marketing*, 3rd edition, Hemel Hempstead: Prentice-Hall.

Christopher, M., Payne, A. and Ballantyne, D. (1991), *Relationship Marketing*, Oxford: Butterworth-Heinemann.

Cooper, R. G. (1979), 'Dimensions of Industrial New Product Success and Failure', *Journal of Marketing* 43 (Summer), pp. 93–103.

Cooper, R. G. (1982), 'New Product Success in Industrial Firms', *Industrial Marketing Management* 11 (July), pp. 215–223.

Corey, E. R. (1976), *Industrial Marketing: Cases and Concepts*, 2nd edition, Englewood Cliffs, NJ: Prentice-Hall.

Crosier, K. C. (1975), 'What Exactly is Marketing?', *Quarterly Review of Marketing* (Winter), pp. 21–25.

Dawson, J. A. and Shaw, S. A. (1992), Inter-Firm Alliances in the Retail Sector: Evolutionary, Strategic and Tactical Issues in their Creation and Management', *Department of Business Studies Working Paper Series*, 92/7, University of Edinburgh.

Deans, K. R. and Rajagopal, S. (1991), 'Comakership: A Worthwhile Word', *Purchasing and Supply Management Journal* (March), pp. 15–17.

Easterby-Smith, M., Thorpe, R. and Lowe, A. (1991), *Management Research: An Introduction*, London: Sage.

ESRC (1994), 'Building Partnerships: Enhancing the Quality of Management Research', *Report of the Commission on Management Research*, Economic and Social Research Council.

Fletcher, K. P. (1990), *Marketing Management and Information Technology*, Englewood Cliffs, NJ: Prentice-Hall (2nd edn, 1995).

Foxall, G. R. (1989), 'Marketing New Technology: Markets, Hierarchies and User-Initiated Innovation', *Managerial and Decision Economics* 9, pp. 237–250.

Freeman, C. (ed.) (1972), *Success and Failure in Industrial Innovation*, Centre for the Study of Industrial Innovation, SPRU, University of Sussex.

Gopalakrishna, S. and Williams, J. D. (1992), 'Planning and Performance Assessment of Industrial Trade shows: An Exploratory Study', *International Journal of Research in Marketing* (3), pp. 207–224.

Gronroos, C. (1984), 'A Service Quality Model and its Marketing Implications', *European Journal of Marketing* 18 (4), pp. 36–44.

Hakansson, H. (ed.) (1983), *International Marketing and Purchasing of Industrial Goods: An Interaction Approach*, Chichester: Wiley.

Hart, N. A. (1988), *Practical Advertising and Publicity*, 4th edition, New York: McGraw-Hill.

Hart, S. J. (1988), 'The Causes of Product Deletion in British Manufacturing Companies', *Journal of Marketing Management* 3 (3), pp. 328–343.

Hart, S. J. (1987), 'The Use of the Survey in Industrial Marketing Research', *Journal of Marketing Management* 3 (1), pp. 25–38.

Hart, S. J. and Snelson, P. A. (1989), 'The New Product Development Process: Areas for Research', *Department of Marketing Working Paper Series MWP 89/4*, University of Strathclyde.

Von Hippell, E. (1978), 'Successful Industrial Products from Customer Ideas', *Journal of Marketing* 42 (January), pp. 39–49.

Hopkins, D. S. (1981), 'New Product Winners and Losers', *Research Management* (May), pp. 12–17.

Hutt, M. D. and Speh, T. W. (1985, 1989, 1995), *Business Marketing Management*, 5th edition: Dryden Press (3rd edition 1989; 2nd edition published as *Industrial Marketing Management*, 1985).

Katz, M. (1979), 'Use Same Theory, Skills for Consumer, Industrial Marketing Research', *The Marketing News* (12 January).

Kotler, P. (1994), *Marketing Management: Analysis, Planning, Implementation and Control*, 8th edition, Englewood Cliffs, NJ: Prentice-Hall.

Kotler, P. and Levy, S. J. (1969), 'Broadening the Concept of Marketing', *Journal of Marketing* 33 (January), pp. 10–15.

McKenna, R. (1991), *Relationship Marketing: Successful Strategies for the Age of the Consumer*, London: Addison Wesley.

Mahin, P. W. (1991), *Business to Business Marketing*, Boston: Allyn & Bacon.

Monczka, R. (1989), 'Are You Aggressive Enough for the 1990s?', *Purchasing* (6 April), pp. 50–56.

Morrill, J. E. (1970), 'Industrial Advertising Pays Off', *Harvard Business Review* (March/April), pp. 4–14.

Morris, M. H. (1986, 1991), *Industrial and Organisational Marketing*, Columbus, Ohio: Merrill.

Nueno, P. and Oosterveld, J. (1988), 'Managing Technological Alliances', *Long Range Planning* 21/3 (109), pp. 11–17.

Peters, T. J. and Waterman, R. H. (1982), *In Search of Excellence*, New York: Harper & Row.

Porter, M. E. (1980), *Competitive Strategy*, New York: The Free Press.

Porter, M. E. (1986), 'Changing Patterns of International Competition', *California Management Review* 28 (2) (Winter), pp. 9–40.

Power, T. L. (1991), *Modern Business Marketing*, St Paul, Minnesota: West Publishing.

Rajagopal, S. and Bernard, K. N. (1993a), 'Strategic Procurement and Competitive Advantage', *International Journal of Purchasing and Materials Management* 29 (4) (Fall), pp. 13–20.

Rajagopal, S. and Bernard, K. N. (1993b), 'Strategic Procurement in the Airlines Industry: An Examination of the Impact of Purchasing Effectiveness on Marketing Competitiveness', *Proceedings of the 22nd Conference of the European Marketing Academy*, Barcelona, pp. 1301–1322.

Rajagopal, S., Bernard, K. N. and Tritschler, P. (1994), 'Functional Integration of Just in Time: A Path for Competitiveness', *23rd Annual Conference of the European Marketing Academy*, Maastricht, Netherlands, pp. 777–794.

Robinson, P. J., Faris, C. W. and Wind, Y. (1967), *Industrial Buying and Creative Marketing*, Boston: Allyn & Bacon.

Sheth, J. N. (1973), 'A Model of Industrial Buyer Behaviour', *Journal of Marketing* 37 (4) (October), pp. 50–56.

Stern, L. W. and El-Ansary, A. I. (1992), *Marketing Channels*, 4th edition, Englewood Cliffs, N. J.: Prentice-Hall.

Thackray, J. (1986), 'America's Vertical Cut-Back', *Management Today* (June), pp. 74–77.

Thomas, M. J. (1993), 'Marketing – In Chaos or Transition?', *Department of Marketing Working Paper Series*, MWP 93/8, University of Strathclyde.

Webster, F. E. and Wind, Y. (1972), *Organisational Buying Behaviour*, Englewood Cliffs, NJ: Prentice-Hall.

Wildsmith, J. R. (1973), *Managerial Theories of the Firm*, London: Martin Robertson.

Wind, Y. and Cardozo, R. N. (1974), 'Industrial Market Segmentation', *Industrial Marketing Management* 3 (March), pp. 153–166.

Womack, J. P., Jones, D. T. and Roos, D. (1990), *The Machine that Changed the World*, New York: Rawson Associates.

■ *Chapter 16* ■

Retailing

Sara Carter

■ Introduction

This chapter considers the role of retailing in the wider economy and the importance of the sector in terms of employment and wealth generation, before moving on to consider recent developments within the trade and their effect on the marketing mix. Throughout the 1980s and 1990s, there has been a growing polarisation in the structure of the trade between the small independent shop usually run as a family owned enterprise (Dawson and Kirby, 1979) and the large retail multiples, responsible for over half of all employment within the sector. After outlining the structure of the trade, the chapter considers how changes in the pattern of consumption have brought about new developments in retail sales which have both increased the influence of the large multiples and brought about the increased specialisation of smaller stores. The chapter concludes with a brief analysis of how elements of the marketing mix are utilised within the retail sector.

■ Retailing in the wider economy

The importance of retailing in the UK economy can be illustrated by a number of factors. There are approximately 250 000 retail businesses in the UK which account for the direct employment for over two million people (McGoldrick, 1990).

In addition, retail sales volume, estimated to be in excess of £131 000 million in 1990 represents a large proportion of total consumer expenditure (Institute of Retail Studies, 1990). Nevertheless, the turbulence inherent in the sector can be seen by looking more closely at the complex patterns of growth and decline experienced throughout the 1980s. Between 1981 and 1989 there were fluctuations in the number of retail businesses in the UK, but an overall increase from 247 000 in 1981 to 252 000 in 1989 (Institute of Retail Studies, 1990). Although retail businesses as a percentage of the total business stock showed a modest decline throughout the 1980s, from 22 per cent in 1981 to 17.5 per cent in 1989, this is largely due to the more rapid growth in other businesses over the same period. Nevertheless, an analysis of VAT registrations and deregistrations, the main economic indicator of business start-ups and cessations, showed an overall decline in retail businesses of 2.2 per cent between 1980 and 1989.

Over 2.3 million people are directly employed in retailing, the greatest number within the food sector which employs over 800 000 (Institute of Retail Studies, 1990). Between 1980 and 1987 there was a decline of 3.7 per cent in total direct retail employment, although this masks patterns of growth and decline which were not evenly spread across retail sectors. Sectors which experienced growth in employment were 'drink, confectionary and tobacco', 'household goods' and the

Table 16.1. *Number of UK retail businesses, (000s), 1981–1989*

Year	Retailing No.	Retail as % Total	All UK businesses
1981	247.5	22.0	2125.8
1983	240.1	21.1	1136.6
1985	249.6	19.6	1272.2
1987	248.2	18.8	1319.8
1989	252.2	17.5	1441.7

Source: Institute of Retail Studies.

miscellaneous category of 'other non-foods' which saw increases of 9.2 per cent, 5.1 per cent and 1.7 per cent respectively. Employment decline was seen most notably in the 'hire and repair' and 'mixed retail' sectors which experienced losses of 28.9 per cent and 15.7 per cent respectively. The largest retail employment sector, 'food', experienced above average losses of 4.3 per cent between 1980 and 1987 (Institute of Retail Studies, 1990).

■ The structure of the trade

Throughout the 1980s there was a net loss of 6.2 per cent in the number of retail outlets in the UK. Decline was most apparent in the retail food sector which experienced a decline of 19.4 per cent in the number of outlets between 1980 and 1987. More modest decline of 6.6 per cent and 5.0 per cent respectively was seen in the 'household goods' and 'clothing, footwear and leather goods' sectors. Sectors which experienced an increase in the number of outlets during the same period were 'other non-food', 'drink, confectionary and tobacco' and 'mixed retail' (Institute of Retail Studies, 1990). The domination of the large retail businesses can be seen in an analysis of the structure of the retail sector. Although 98 per cent of all retail businesses have a turnover of less than £1 million, these small retail businesses account for only 79 per cent of all retail outlets, only 39 per cent of employment (including self-employment) and only 29 per cent of total retail turnover. Large retail businesses with a turnover in excess of £100 million account for less than 1 per cent of the total number of businesses, yet are responsible for 9 per cent of all outlets, 43 per cent of employment and 54 per cent of total turnover (Institute of Retail studies, 1990).

Large multiple retailers are most visible within the food sector and the disproportionately high levels of capital expenditure in this sector are mostly accounted for by new superstore openings by the large multiples. While there was a decline of 1528 mostly small independent grocery outlets between 1990 and 1991, large supermarkets

Table 16.2. *Total retail trade by broad kind of business, 1987*

Retail sector	No. of businesses	No. of outlets	Total turnover (incl. VAT) (£m)	Capital expend. (£m net)
Food	73,681	98,016	37,146	1,676
Drink, confectionary & tobacco	47,296	59,801	10,538	149
Clothing/footwear/leather	31,162	58,380	10,255	305
Household goods	42,760	60,406	17,353	529
Other non-foods	38,973	52,473	8,983	229
Mixed retail	4,937	11,363	19,060	548
Hire & repair	2,045	5,020	1,293	146
Total retail trade	240,853	345,467	104,627	3,581

Source: Institute of Retail Studies.

Table 16.3. *Market share by sector, 1981–1991*

Year	Multiple %	Co-op %	Independent %
1981	62.7	13.7	23.6
1983	66.7	12.6	20.7
1985	70.1	11.6	18.3
1987	72.9	10.9	16.1
1989	74.2	10.8	15.0
1991	78.2	9.6	12.2

Source: Institute of Grocery Distribution.

(defined as having a sales area between 10 000 and 24 999 sq. ft) increased to nearly 1200 and superstores (defined as having a sales area in excess of 25 000 sq. ft.) increased in number to approximately 800. It is estimated that superstores now account for about 38.6 per cent of all grocery sector sales (IGD, 1992). In addition, the market share of multiple food retailers increased from 62.7 per cent in 1981 to 78.2 per cent in 1991. This was largely at the expense of independent food retailers (defined as having between one and nine outlets) whose market share fell from 23.6 per cent in 1981 to 12.2 per cent in 1991 and co-operatives whose market share fell from 13.7 per cent to 9.6 per cent in the same period (IGD, 1992).

Throughout the 1980s it became increasingly apparent that there was a polarisation between the large and the small retail business with large stores increasingly locating in edge of town sites and multi-store retail parks and small stores competing either on the basis of convenience or specialisation (Key Note, 1990). In part, the move to edge of town locations for large multiples was to allow new build superstores where volume sales could be achieved but the move also followed the population which was increasingly drifting to the suburbs of major towns (Guy, 1984).

Changing patterns of retail buying

The trend towards larger retail chains has affected the way retail buying is undertaken. Retail buying differs from industrial buying in that products are usually bought for a straightforward resale rather than as a component part of a different product as is often seen in industrial sectors. Nevertheless, retail buying is complicated by the fact that a retailer attempts to create a product from the resale. Davies (1993) describes the retailer's product as 'a distinctive service offer to the shopper, something that can be described as the retailer's position in the market... The position the retailer holds in the marketplace is but one of the factors that will influence the retail buyer, and the buying process itself' (p. 64–65).

Traditionally retail buying has often been seen as an exchange process between two individuals, the retail buyer and the supplier, who form the main or only linkage between the two firms. Research concentrated on the role and personal characteristics of the retail buyer. Retail buyers, however, particularly those who work in larger organisations, generally work as part of a buying team or Decision Making Unit. A Decision Making Unit will vary in size according to the type of products being bought and the complexity of the buying decision. The difficulty with this type of approach is that it tends to concentrate on the buying organisation. Increasingly, evolving models of retail buying take into account the complex relationships between different elements of both supplier and retailer organisations (Davies, 1993). This type of approach is of growing relevance for larger retail concerns where the scale and importance of the buying decision ensures that the development of long term relationships between retailers and suppliers is worthwhile. As Davies (1993, p. 74) states 'the size and importance of the transaction will have an important effect on the predisposition of the retailer to become more closely involved with any one supplier and the size of the retailer will determine whether the manufacturer deems it economic to invest the necessary time and effort'.

While this approach has its obvious attractions for large multiple retailers, it is of less relevance to the smaller chains and independent retailers, who lack the financial and human resources necessary to invest in developing relationships with a potentially vast number of suppliers.

Nevertheless, there have been developments in buying which allow many smaller retailers to exploit buying economies and developing supplier relationships through the use of buying groups. Examples of buying groups have long existed in retail sectors such as pharmacy, which are characterised both by fragmentation of suppliers and a tendency towards small-scale retail outlets. Buying groups often mirror the roles of wholesalers in that volume purchases enable price discounts and save time in dealing directly with suppliers. Buying groups operating in some sectors, such as pharmacy, also offer the attraction of daily or even twice daily delivery services. New developments in buying groups have seen the emergence of 'own-label' supplies and the spread of buying groups into other sectors, such as food retailing, enabling the smaller chains to benefit from the same economies as the large multiples.

Retail sales and patterns of consumption

Retail sales volume and consumer expenditure data provides an insight into the strength of the sector and trends within markets. However, patterns of retail expenditure and consumption also reflect the strength of the wider economy. While the recessionary period of the late 1980s which was characterised by business failures, unemployment and stagnation undoubtedly affected consumer spending, long term economic growth has ensured that at least some retail sectors have flourished (Davies, 1993). Between 1985 and 1992 retail sales volume increased year on year although consumer expenditure fell in real terms by 1.7 per cent in 1991, the first time this had happened in five years (IGD, 1992). Retail sales volume accounts for approximately 40 per cent of total consumer expenditure and this proportion is relatively constant (Institute of Retail Studies, 1990; IGD, 1992).

Growth in retail sales volume has increased at disproportionate rates within different retail sectors. Retail sales volume for food showed the largest increase in 1990 over the previous year's

Table 16.4. *Retail sales volume, 1990*

Sector	Retailers sales (£ mill)	% Change on year earlier
Food	49,479	10.3
DIY Stores	4,973	7.6
Clothing & footwear	13,363	6.2
Household goods	22,517	3.4
Retail chemists	2,355	5.8
Booksellers/stationers/ specialist newsagents	1,945	8.8
General mail order	3,715	0.8
Total retail sales	131,001	6.4

Source: Institute of Retail Studies.

figures, closely followed by 'booksellers, stationers and speciality newsagents' and the DIY retail sector (Institute of Retail Studies, 1990). However, it is forecast that as personal disposable income grows, the proportion of expenditure on basic necessities such as food will fall and increases in consumer expenditure will be seen in other sectors such as consumer durables and, in particular, electrical goods (Shaw, Dawson and Blair, 1992; Davies, 1993).

An analysis of weekly household expenditure reveals that the largest single proportion of total household income is spent on housing (19.4 per cent) and food (17.8 per cent). Motoring and travel, leisure and household purchases also make up an important element of weekly expenditure of 15.3 per cent, 13.2 per cent and 12.8 per cent respectively. Purchases of alcohol and tobacco at 6.2 per cent, clothing and footwear at 6.1 per cent, and fuel and light at 4.7 per cent account for more modest expenditure. The relative proportions spent on each varies by income level and the socio-economic groups C2 and DE spend a slightly higher proportion of their income on food and the better off groups AB and C1 spend proportionately more on clothing and footwear, household items and leisure (Key Note, 1993).

Many commentators have noted that changes in the demographic structure of the market place influence consumer needs and desires and ultimately effect retail change (Cook and Walters, 1991; Shaw, Burt and Dawson, 1989;

Table 16.5.   *Weekly household expenditure by socio-economic group, (%), 1991*

Item	AB	C1	C2	DE	All
Housing	18.6	18.4	17.1	20.0	19.4
Fuel and light	3.7	3.9	4.3	6.0	4.7
Food	16.4	16.2	19.3	19.7	17.8
Alcohol and tobacco	5.3	5.7	8.2	7.0	6.2
Clothing and footwear	6.2	6.8	6.5	5.6	6.1
Household	13.1	13.5	11.6	12.7	12.8
Motoring and travel	16.0	17.9	17.9	13.7	15.3
Leisure	16.2	13.0	10.7	10.8	13.2
Miscellaneous	4.4	4.6	4.3	4.5	4.5
Total (£ per week)	382	307	282	198	259

Source: Key Note.

McGoldrick, 1990; Davies, 1993). Social and economic changes which were reflected in the shopping behaviour of consumers were first noted in the 1960s (Baker, 1976). Contemporary analysts have suggested that the main demographic elements which will bring about future change in consumption and shopping patterns include: declining rates of population increase, declining family sizes, increases in divorce rates, increases in the number of smaller households, increases in the proportion of older people, increases in the number of working women, increases in educational levels, greater personal mobility and a polarisation of income levels with a growth in real income for those in employment and a residual pool of unemployed low income groups (Shaw, Burt and Dawson, 1989; McGoldrick, 1990; Davies, 1993). In addition, it has been noted that earlier purchases of consumer durables have in themselves influenced patterns of shopping behaviour. Davies (1993) states that increased purchases of cars over the past thirty years not only affected retail car sales and associated purchases, but the mobility given to consumers through possession of a car had an even greater impact on retailing. Car ownership was a factor in the decline of local shops and the growth of large edge-of-town stores which enabled bulk purchases. Possession of freezers and microwave ovens similarly have a greater impact on retailing than simply the initial purchase. Possession of these durables affects shopping behaviour as they allow

shopping for food products to become less frequent (Davies, 1993).

The effect of these trends on patterns of consumption can be illustrated by the rise of discount food stores, believed to be the fastest growing sector in retailing. Throughout the 1980s consumers became more discerning about where they shopped and more sophisticated in their choice of goods. As affluence and leisure time increased consumers became more accustomed and willing to travel to find the right shopping experience and more prepared to spend leisure time shopping (Key Note, 1990). However, large segments of the population, in particular the elderly, the immobile and the less affluent, were effectively excluded from this trend. For these groups, price consciousness and convenient locations were more important, in addition these groups often had the time to spend seeking cheaper products. As the effects of the late 1980s recession spread, consumers became more price conscious. At the beginning of the 1990s there were only two discount food chains operating in the UK, this number has now reached fourteen. Typical operating margins of discount chains are 2 per cent or less and profits are made by selling large volumes of goods with low overheads from cheap sites and few staff and little investment in technology or fittings. An efficient discount store can turn around its entire stock in less than twenty days, often selling stock before suppliers have been paid (Key Note, 1993). It appears that UK trends towards increased use of discount stores are following those in mainland Europe where discount retailers now hold market shares of up to 23 per cent (Germany) and 20 per cant (Belgium). The market share of discount stores in the UK is currently estimated to be 8 per cent but it is predicted that this will grow to 15 per cent by 1996 (Key Note, 1993).

A survey commissioned by Key Note from Social Surveys (Gallup Poll) Ltd. investigating popular perceptions of the attributes possessed by a good shop supports the changing consumer preference towards the 'no frills' approach to food retailing. The survey used a national sample of 943 adults asking respondents to identify important attributes from a prepared list of twelve. The four preferred attributes identified in 1990 were 'friendly staff', 'speedy check-out service', 'wide product range' and a 'well laid out store'. By 1992, 'lower prices' replaced a 'well laid out store' in the top four attributes. Importantly, in the two year period there appeared to be a major swing in consumer preference towards 'assistants who leave you alone', 'good special offers' and 'lower prices', all attributes of discount retail chains. Perhaps as expected, the survey also found that lower prices were more important to the lower socio-economic groups and in the under 45 age groups and those over 65. Lower prices were also more popular in the northern than in the southern regions of the UK. 'Good special offers' were identified by more women than men and again appealed to the under 45 and over 65 age groups. The use of credit and store cards were found to be twice as important to socio-economic groups A and B than to others and to people aged between 25 and 44 and those in the South (Key Note, 1993).

■ Marketing mix elements and retailing

The retail trade is characterised by high fixed costs, both in terms of premises and staffing levels, and as a result profits are generally volume driven. Large profits can accrue from increases in volume sales and conversely, poor volume sales have the effect of cutting profits dramatically. A fundamental tenet of the trade, therefore, is to sell goods even if prices are so low that extra sales have only a marginal impact on profits (Key Note, 1993). This point was seen clearly in food retailing in the early 1990s. A negligible growth in the UK population meant that consumption of food rose in real terms by only 3 per cent between 1985 and 1990, reflecting a largely static market within which retailers sought to improve profitability. As a result, opportunities to improve profitability have to be sought internally if retailers are to gain the competitive edge and win market share from competitors (IGD, 1992). This is largely achieved by the efficient utilisation of the marketing mix elements. Three elements, location, merchandising and promotion, are considered below.

Table 16.6. *Attributes of a good shop, (%), April 1990 and April 1992*

Attribute	1990	1992	% Change
Friendly staff	63	78	24
Speedy checkout service	52	59	13
Lower prices	34	57	68
Wide product range	44	52	18
Good special offers	23	48	109
Well laid out	43	40	−7
Sells high quality goods	31	38	23
Assistants deal personally with you	28	35	25
Assistants leave you alone	5	35	600
Very spacious	22	22	0
Accept credit/ store cards	14	20	43
Attractive decor	14	16	14
Don't know	3	1	n/a

Source: Key Note.

□ *Store location*

The tendency for the large retail businesses to dominate and move to edge-of-town locations has occurred in many retail sectors. This trend was apparent from the early 1960s when economies of scale and new patterns of location emerged as important features of food and grocery retailing (Guy, 1984). Throughout the 1970s and 1980s this trend continued with food multiples, DIY multiples, furniture and carpet stores and builders merchants all moving to out-of-town sites. While early retail parks were often characterised as being suitable for selling goods purchased relatively infrequently, in recent years it is more typical for frequent purchases to be made at edge-of-town sites. In part this is because new types of multiple superstores have increasingly located at this type of site. Towards the end of the 1980s toy retailers such as Toys R Us and Children's World joined the retail parks and in the early 1990s pet store multiples such as Pet World also started locating in these developments (Key Note, 1990).

The impact of superstore and hypermarket development on shopping behaviour has been the subject of many studies since the 1970s (cf. Unit for Retail Planning Information, 1976, 1978; Guy, 1980; 1984; Davies and Rogers, 1984). The focus of attention has generally been on the, largely negative, effect of edge-of-town superstore location strategy on traditional town-centre re-

tailers. As pointed out in Baker (1983, p. 233) the issue of store location has received more attention 'from geographers than from planners who create the problem and retailers who discover it'. Guy (1984) points out that the edge-of-town superstore has a larger catchment area than older district centres with shoppers prepared to travel further than necessary in order to visit their favourite store. Inner urban superstores, however, tend to attract more bus and walk trips and as a consequence, customers visit the store more frequently for shopping visits with lower spend. Guy (1984) also provides an analysis of locational categories for hypermarkets, superstores and retail warehouses.

A potentially important development for food retailers in the 1990s has been the introduction of the American food warehouse club Costco which opened its first UK site in the Lakeside shopping complex at Thurrock, Essex in January 1994. The opening of the 140 000 sq. ft. warehouse was the subject of a High Court appeal by Sainsburys, Tesco and Safeway. The case centred on the fact that as a warehouse club Costco did not have to meet the same retail planning criteria as a new-build supermarket. The decision by

Figure 16.1. *Locational categories for hypermarkets, superstores and retail warehouses*

Location	Site characteristics	Catchment population	Planners' attitudes
Edge of town	Open land, usually agricultural, close to major roads	Car shoppers from wide area	Unfavourable
New district centre	Open land, but coordinated with residential development	Walk in shoppers from local area, plus car shoppers from wider area	Favourable
Established town or district centre	Vacant site or building on edge of shopping area	As above	Favourable if traffic problems can be overcome
Industrial estate	Vacant site or building, well away from shopping area	Walk in shoppers if close to residential area plus car shoppers	Unfavourable, except for DIY warehouses in some areas
Other urban location	Vacant site or building, usually close to major road	Walk in shoppers if close to residential area plus car and bus shoppers	Unfavourable

Source: Guy (1984), p. 80.

Thurrock Council to grant Costco *sui generis* – a general class of planning consent which is neither retail nor wholesale – was upheld and further food warehouse clubs are planned both by Costco and by Nurdin and Peacock under the Cargo Club fascia (Super Marketing, 1993).

□ *Merchandising*

Merchandising has become the subject of much research by the retail trade as retailers are put under increasing pressure to improve their operational efficiencies. The high costs associated with developing new retail outlets has ensured that retailer attention is now firmly fixed on maximising the efficiency of their retail space. Merchandising policy centres both on ensuring stock availability and reducing out-of-stocks which may lead to loss of sales and on exploring the efficient use of in-store space. Both elements have become increasingly important as retail competition increases and consumer satisfaction becomes a vital part of improving sales and spend. The importance of merchandising in the purchase decision process can be seen in the fact that more than 50 per cent of purchase decisions are made in-store and it is the responsibility of the retail merchandiser to ensure that product layout, display standards, pricing policy and frequency of promotion make the buying decision as easy as possible (IGD, 1992). It has been noted that merchandising offers considerable benefits to retailers. In their 1992 report, the Institute of Grocery Distribution (1992) defined eight 'hard' and 'soft' benefits.

While traditionally merchandising has been seen as maximising sales through effective store and shelf lay-out, the use of technology in recent years has transformed merchandising into a highly complex process. EPOS and bar coding technology has allowed retailers to know precisely what is sold in a given trading period and under what conditions. As a consequence, EPOS data enabled greater knowledge in assessing the return on shelf space. In turn, this scan data enabled retailers to use computerised space management systems in store lay-out and was the key to integrating management information systems with marketing and merchandising applications (IGD, 1992). An interesting development has been the sharing of electronic retail sales data with suppliers. In the past this information was withheld from manufacturers on the basis that they may mistreat the confidentiality of this information. Increasingly, however, particularly within the grocery sector, the sharing of scan data has been an important element in the commitment by retailers to establish long term and mutually beneficial trading partnerships with their suppliers.

□ *Promotion*

Competition between retailers has increased throughout the 1990s. While for large multiple retailers in many sectors the 1980s was characterised by market growth and development through new-build superstores in new locations, a continuing theme of the 1990s has been market saturation and competition for customers

Figure 16.2. *Benefits of effective retail merchandising policy*

Informed decision making; product mix and range rationalisation
Identification and promotion of profitable lines
Control of inventory investment
Accurate response to demand
Higher basket value
Reduction in costs, labour, shrinkage etc.
Enhancement of trading image
Fulfilment of customer expectations

Source: Institute of Grocery Distribution (1992).

between retailers. As a consequence, many retailers have had to consider their promotional and advertising strategies both to maintain market growth and also as a defence against other similar organisations. More than any other retail sector, the retail food multiples have faced the threat of market saturation. Asda Chief Executive Archie Norman was the first to raise the issue publicly in November 1993 and since then Argyll have reduced their 1994 capital expenditure programme by £100 million and have cut the number of store openings from 125 to between 105 and 110 over the next five years (Super Marketing, 1994). The response to the threat of market saturation has been twofold. First, retailers are exploring other areas for long term expansion, notably Europe, and into new product ranges, with food retailers becoming increasingly interested in new product ranges such as DIY and clothes. Secondly, retailers are looking to promotion as a short term mechanism to improve sales. Partly as a reaction to market saturation and partly in response to the growing consumer interest in discount food stores, promotion within the retail food sector in the 1990s has concentrated on prices to the extent that a common theme of the trade press has been the threat of a retail food 'price war'.

The increased promotional effort of retailers throughout the 1980s can be seen in Table 16.7, which documents annual press and television advertising expenditure from 1982 to 1989. Retailers' attitudes to spending money on promotion varies according to their competitive situation. Those in competition with similar stores need to remind customers of their own offerings, so grocery sector advertising spend is usually high. Stores also need to advertise when they have relevant information – such as a change in policy – to communicate to customers. As Baker (1983) points out, retailing is like any other sector of industry where the marketing mix is likely to vary from one firm to another and retailers competing for the same or similar markets must find ways of differentiating their appeal.

Increasingly retailers are becoming aware of the need to co-ordinate promotional activities

Table 16.7. *Annual press and television retail advertising expenditure*

Year	Expenditure £ million
1982	2346
1983	2779
1984	2886
1985	3060
1986	3419
1987	3650
1988	3920
1989	4198

Source: Institute of Retail Studies.

with other elements, such as their merchandising programme and availability of supplies. The trend is towards fully integrated and highly complex management systems.

■ Concluding remarks

This chapter has considered the role and growing importance of the retail sector within the UK. It was noted at the beginning of the chapter that retailing as a sector is characterised by turbulence with a large number of business start-ups and cessations annually. The turbulence is most apparent among smaller retail concerns who attempt to compete directly on price, convenience or specialisation at a time when larger concerns are able to exploit the long term trend towards suburban residence within the population by locating in edge of town sites. Increasingly, the trend in the structure of the trade is towards large, multiple retailers operating huge and complex businesses which are responsible for employing state of the art management systems. The management and use of marketing elements by the larger retail concerns ensures that their position as leading organisations within the sector will continue well into the future.

■ References

Baker, M. J. (1976), *Marketing Theory and Practice* London: Macmillan.

Bellinger, D. N. and Goldstucker, J. L. (1983), *Retailing Basics*, Homewood, Ill.: Irwin.

Cook, D. and Walters, D. (1991), *Retail Marketing: Theory and Practice*, Hemel Hempstead: Prentice-Hall.

Davies, G. (1993), *Trade Marketing Strategy*, London: Paul Chapman.

Davies, R. L. and Rogers, D. S. (1984), *Store Location and Store Assessment Research*, New York: John Wiley.

Dawson, J. A. and Kirby, D. A. (1979), *Small Scale Retailing in the UK*, Farnborough: Saxon House.

Gist, R. R. (1971), *Management Perspectives in Retailing*, 2nd edition, New York: John Wiley.

Guy, C. M. (1984), 'The Urban Pattern of Retailing', in Davies, R. L. and Rogers, D. S. (1984).

Institute of Grocery Distribution (1991), *Retail Product Merchandising*, Watford: IGD.

Institute of Grocery Distribution (1992), *Food Retailing 1992*, Watford: IGD.

Institute of Retail Studies (1990), *Distributive Trades Profile 1990: A Statistical Digest*, Stirling: IRS.

Key Note (1989), *Mixed Retail Businesses*, London: Key Note Publications.

Key Note (1990), *New Trends in Retailing*, London: Key Note Publications.

Key Note (1993), *Convenience Retailing*, 6th edition, London: Key Note Publications.

Kirby, D. (1986), 'The Small Retailer', in J. Curran, Stanworth, J. and Watkins, D. (eds), *The Survival of the Small Firm: The Economics of Survival and Entrepreneurship*, Aldershot: Gower.

Livesey, F. (1979), *The Distributive Trades*, London: Heinemann.

McGoldrick, P. (1990), *Retail Marketing*, London: McGraw-Hill.

Rosenbloom, B. (1981), *Retail Marketing*, New York: Random House.

Shaw, S. A., Burt, S. L. and Dawson, J. A. (1989), 'Structural Change in the European Food Chain', in Traill, B. (ed.), *Prospects for the European Food System*, Barking: Elsevier.

Shaw, S. A., Dawson, J. A. and Blair, L. M. A. (1992), 'Imported Foods in a British Supermarket Chain: Buyer Decisions in Safeway', in *Retail, Distribution and Consumer Research* 2 (1), pp. 35–54.

Stampfl, R. W. and Hirschman, E. C. (1981), *Theory in Retailing: Traditional and Nontraditional Sources*, Chicago: American Marketing Association, Proceedings Series.

Super Marketing (1993), 'Editorial' (10 December), p. 5.

Super Marketing (1994), 'Counting the Days?' (7 January).

Unit for Retail Planning Information (1976), *Hypermarkets and Superstores: Report of a House of Commons Seminar*, Reading: Unit for Retail Planning Information.

Unit for Retail Planning Information (1978), *Discount Retail Warehouses: Report of an URPI Workshop*, Reading: Unit for Retail Planning Information.

Chapter 17

Customer Care

Bill Donaldson

■ Introduction

Customer care is perceived in the commercial and industrial world as an important and relevant topic in managing the successful competitive enterprise. While some would argue customer care is a passing fad or flavour of the month topic in marketing (Coyne, 1989), it is, and should be, much more than this. In many companies, customer care is strongly emphasised in their corporate mission or vision statement, in their organisations by specific personnel or departments and by increased resources allocated to service support areas of the business. This importance is confirmed by the number of courses, practice based texts, articles and citations which have appeared in the last decade on the importance of being customers driven and how to implement customer care programmes. By contrast, treatment of the subject in marketing curricula and mainstream marketing textbooks appears to have been neglected. If we take customer care and customer service as a topic, an analysis of 10 U.K. and 10 U.S.A. popular marketing textbooks, published since 1990, showed that only 4 U.K. and 6 U.S. books mentioned the term. If reference to the marketing of services is excluded only 5 of these books devote more than 50 words to customer service or customer care as a strategic or tactical element in marketing strategy or marketing management. The remainder made no mention of the

term in a specific way and the aim of this chapter is an attempt to correct this imbalance by:

- explaining what is meant by customer care
- identifying if, and why, customer issues are increasing in importance
- offering an explanation as to the management of customer care from a seller perspective as a prescription for more effective and efficient management of marketing exchange
- identifying the characteristics of the customer driven organisation.

■ Definition and meaning

The primary aim of a competitive enterprise should be the delivery of customer satisfaction. Satisfied customers place repeat business and tell others of their experience which contributes to long run profitability. There are different ways this can be achieved. For example, sales growth. A business may improve profitability by winning new business through price, product or distribution advantage, by sales generation activities using promotional and salesmanship techniques or, by a combination of all of these. Alternatively reducing costs may increase competitiveness or improve the profitability of existing business. Another approach may be to attempt to create a monopoly position based on technical or marke-

power. Whatever approach a company pursues, its effect can be enhanced by improved customer care. Customer care is not an alternative but a complement to the effectiveness of a business in delivering customer satisfaction.

A firm must identify whether the product or service is a one-off transaction, a repeat transaction or a relationship type of exchange as shown in Figure 17.1. The essence of Figure 17.1 is that a firm pursuing new business will have to prove superior in some competitive dimension. Suppliers, operating in a relationship mode where interaction between buyer and seller is of major importance, can only lose business. The supplier's objective, in this context, is to service and consolidate existing customers by preserving and expanding the volume of business these customers do. This means maintaining and reinforcing inertia, increasing co-operation and participation with customers and ensuring a favoured supplier relationship.

Customer loyalty, customer satisfaction and customer care are not the same. A customer may be loyal because of an absence of alternatives. Therefore, a village with only one pub may have loyal customers who are not satisfied with the service, the decor or the beer, but the absence of competing alternatives may still encourage repeat business, although presumably at a level much lower than could be achieved if customers were also satisfied. Likewise, in the U.K., public utilities such as electricity, gas and postal services, in the absence of alternatives, have traditionally had a high degree of customer loyalty. This loyalty will remain only if customers are satisfied as real competitive alternatives emerge. This is the difference between customer satisfaction and customer loyalty. Most firms, in a competitive environment, have long realised that to achieve customer loyalty then they must deliver customer satisfaction. Customer loyalty can be measured but it is earned and cannot be delivered.

Customer satisfaction is also a problem for a supplier. It can also be measure (e.g. very satisfied, satisfied, not very satisfied, not at all satisfied) but, as a concept, it is not unidimensional and consists of various elements which may be different across customers. Therefore, customer satisfaction can be delivered but it is not a management activity rather a measure of customer responsiveness to marketing stimuli in a given competitive environment.

Customer service/customer care are different from customer satisfaction and customer loyalty in that they represent the approach adopted by the supplier and are management tasks. Are they the same?

To operationalise a concept, the meaning must be clear and unambiguous. The literal definition of a customer as a person who buys and service as an act of help or assistance, is useful in terms of accuracy and simplicity but it is necessary, for research and for management purposes, to be able to scale and measure the variable. If the term is too general it will fail to provide insight on reality and the aim is therefore to be as specific as possible. In a thoughtful review of the area, one author identifies the rationale for customer care development as having emanated from different schools but driven primarily by competition and the quest for customer satisfaction (Stewart, 1992). She concluded that customer care is more

Figure 17.1. *Type of exchange*

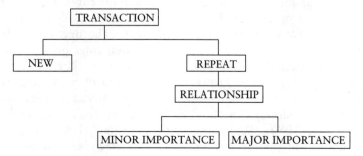

than customer service while acknowledging that service activities have themselves developed and expanded. As Stewart observed 'The literature is unanimous on the requirement for customer care to be fundamental rather than peripheral' (Stewart, 1992). In practice, the very opposite seems to apply. A number of firms have embarked on so-called customer care programmes which entail a new slogan stressing the importance of customers, a directive from the chief executive, some 'smile training' or 'charm school ethics' for front line staff and a few add-ons to reduce customer dissatisfaction or match a good idea from competitors. In this respect, customer care seems not be fundamental at all but to be one element in an effort to remain competitive by improving customer service.

Although sympathetic to Stewart's argument, it must be concluded that customer service and customer care mean the same and can be defined *as all those activities provided by the seller which have value for the buyer thus increasing customer satisfaction and encouraging patronage and loyalty between the parties.* Customer care is part of a management process to develop greater customer orientation. This process identifies the current philosophy and orientation of management and staff, measures different aspects of company performance via a managerial audit and implements improved customer care programmes via personnel training, improved customer friendly systems and innovative customer support activities.

The increasing importance of customer care

The impetus for the increasing importance of customer care in the management of a business has occurred for a number of reasons, the most important of which appear to be:

a) *The growth of services.* In developed economies the importance of services has grown relative to agriculture, extracting or manufacturing industries. 'The bill of final demand' is shifting towards services (Uno, 1989). While the definition of service is not unambiguous, (e.g. the chemical engineer, designer and business lawyer working for I.C.I would be considered to be in manufacturing) both in terms of inputs (research and development, pollution control, safety, software, information databases, transport, communications, insurance, etc.) and outputs (leisure activities, travel, health, education, television, etc.), services are the most important and fastest growing part of the economy. Services contribute to both technological change and the growth in final demand. Several factors suggest this trend will continue. First, highly developed industrialisation calls for increased inputs of ancillary services. Secondly, increased income levels and greater leisure time leads to the diversification and sophistication of personal consumption, resulting in a more discriminating customer. Thirdly, high technology leads to greater inter-relationships in the various branches of the economy as service specialists are needed to operate as inter-organisational boundary spanners. Finally, social changes such as smaller family size and changing age distribution in the population require more service support in areas such as transport, communications and leisure with greater division and specialisation of labour. These trends have been observed and confirmed by economists, socialists, information scientists and marketing commentators (Galbraith, 1992; Machlup, 1982; Porat, 1976; Levitt, 1976).

b) *The wider concept of product.* Relatively few products are sold as commodities in perfectly competitive markets. 'Products consist broadly of anything that can be marketed, including physical objects, services, persons, places, organisations, and ideas' (Kotler, 1988). It is useful with this definition to consider a product on three levels – the core benefit or service, the tangible product, and the augmented product. 'The new competition is not between what companies produce in their factories, but between what they add to their factory output in the form of packaging, services, advertising, customer advice, financing, delivery arrangements, warehousing, and other things that people value' (Levitt, 1983). The implication of this statement is that the convenient fiction of homogeneous markets is changing from one of viewing an entire nation of consumer wants to a fracturing of mass markets. To cope with this diversity, managers must drastically alter how they design, manufacture, market, sell and service their products. In other words, how they care for their customers.

c) *Customer orientation.* There is still some controversy as to whether companies are market and customer driven, how this can be measured and the extent to which marketing contributes to competitive success (Baker and Hart, 1989; Wong and Saunders, 1993). Nevertheless, greater awareness of the marketing concept has led to increased resources being allocated to market identification and understanding of customer needs. This has the effect of motivating entrepreneurs to seek new ways to satisfy potential customers and by implication, putting more emphasis on customer care dimensions to match the needs of a variegated market. 'If you're not serving the customer you better be serving somebody who is!' (Peters and Austin, 1988). Adding value in a customer focused way is the essence of customer care.

d) *Competitive advantage.* With the advance of technology, a reduction in international trade barriers and a more discerning customer, firms must seek new ways to obtain and sustain a competitive advantage. One of the means of achieving this is to increase the scale of customer support. By varying the type of service offered, the supplier can match their offer more closely to the needs of individual customers or specialised market segments.

e) *Relationship marketing.* In most markets, business to business markets in particular, firms are aware of the need to improve efficiency in their exchange relationships. Many firms are limiting the number of suppliers with which they do business while working more closely with those they retain. In other cases, firms are seeking to develop markets in collaboration with suppliers and customers rather than in conflict which existed hitherto. Such arrangements, whether formalised in joint ventures or operating informally are characterised by increased levels of customer support and closer collaboration. The role of cus-

tomer care in the establishment, maintenance and adaptation of relationships between seller and buyer is therefore important.

f) *The pursuit of quality.* The ideas of Deeming, Juran and others to encourage the adoption of total quality management have been significant in improving the tangible product and the service support which add value to the total offering the customer receives (Deeming, 1982; Juran, 1979; Crosby, 1979). Quality commands higher prices by increasing customer satisfaction, data supported by P.I.M.S. findings (Buzzell and Gale, 1987). Quality can also reduce costs through less wastage and more productive work (Deeming, 1982). The British Standard 5750 requires that: 'Within the organisation, consideration should be given to the verification tasks required to deliver the product or service in accordance with the quality objectives.' These objectives are either those prescribed by the supplier which are perceived as satisfying a market need or, requirements prescribed by the purchaser. The standard also states that: 'An organisation providing a product or service needs to meet the customers' needs and expectations fully but in the most economical way' (B.S. 5750 Pt. 4, 1990). Theses requirements, currently being enhanced by the Baldridge awards in the U.S.A. and by the new European awards for excellence, give additional and formal recognition to the importance of customer care programmes and the delivery of total customer satisfaction.

The management of customer care – vision, implementation and quality

Customer care must not be regarded as empty rhetoric or a passing fad. It is an activity that is to be managed by, for example, a mission statement reflecting a customer orientation, written plans specifying customer support activities and organisational commitment to the customer. Analysis of this management activity is divided into three parts relating to business vision, implementation and quality.

☐ *Business vision*

Many companies express commitment to customers but do not truly believe it. The problem is that they are committed to their shareholders, or paymasters, or possibly motivated by greed. The result is that true customer commitment is sacrificed for short term profits yet the real measure of the worth of an organisation must be its ability to retain its customers profitably. A second problem is that true innovation in serving customers is sacrificed by 'me-too' competitive reactions. The threat of losing business forces companies to improve customer care but this is reactive. The first priority should be for everyone in the organisation, especially the chief executive, to believe the best way to run the company is for the benefit of its customers. This does not mean profits and employees are not important but it does mean the order of priority is customers →profits→employees. The equation cannot work in any other combination, at least not for long, except by acquisition or take-over. To turn this belief into reality requires strategic vision.

Customers should be the strategic core of a business and the management task is the origination of the strategy, the maintenance of strategy and the continual development and renewal of strategy in response to environmental change (Reve, 1990). In this sense, customer care must be embodied in the prevailing management philosophy of an organisation, in the corporate culture and in the practices of the corporate leadership. This view has received increased support in the literature (Webster, 1988; Christopher, Payne and Ballantyne, 1991). Evidence to support this position has also come from a 4 nation study which found that 'Those companies demonstrating superior marketing effectiveness will also be those companies which can be characterised as close to their customers, which show an identifiable set of corporate values, and have an external focus' (Norburn, Birley, Dunn and Payne, 1988).

Problems can occur in translating the corporate vision into reality. In evaluating strategy, the interest should focus on measurement of the distinctive competencies of the firm and indicators of positional advantage which result in the firm achieving its objectives (Day and Wensley, 1988). The extent to which customer care and its service dimensions contribute to goal attainment is difficult to measure in a dynamic and evolving environment. Indeed, the customer service mix, although strategic, must adjust to the emerging patterns in the environment and in particular to the level of competition (Marr, 1987; Kyj and Kyj, 1987). So it is also reactive and adaptable but part of a process. Customer care should be variable, dependent on whether the purchase is a routine order product, a procedural problem product (learning to be used), a performance problem product (reliability), or a political problem product (organisational buying) (Lehmann and O'Shaughnessy, 1974). In the strategic sense, there is a need for a wider view of customer care which is 'able to predict the reactions of actual and prospective customers to changes in the levels of certain service factors to be predicted' (Marr, 1984). Pre-purchase customer service which helps qualify an organisation in the customer's mind is part of corporate positioning strategy. Firms which fail to design such a strategy will acquire one by default.

This future role of customer care as a strategic weapon is endorsed by a recent survey among 300 managers of European companies when asked: 'Do you think that in future service will be a major part of the philosophy of the successful company?' 76% replied yes, to a great extent and 24% yes, to a certain extent. Despite the obvious bias in the question there is an undeniable trend in the increasing and strategic importance of service to the firm (Lillebo, 1983). This trend has created a new word in the marketing literature referred to as the 'servitisation' of business which implies that a business is driven by customers establishing and maintaining relationships with their suppliers. 'More and more corporations throughout the world are adding value to their core corporate offerings through services. This trend is pervasive in many industries and is customer, demand driven. This movement is termed the servitisation of business and is clearly a powerful new feature of total marketing strategy being adopted by the best companies'

(Vandermerwe and Rada, 1988). A similar idea of combining the production and the service systems within an organisation in a customer oriented way, called 'servuction', has also been suggested (Stone and Young, 1992). While agreeing with this more enlightened service approach the addition of two new words to the vocabulary is an unnecessary gimmick.

☐ *Implementation*

Belief, expressed in the corporate vision and mission of the business is important but the true challenge for management is to make care for the customer a reality. For this to happen the offering provided must meet customer needs. This can be achieved by product and service in combination, the augmented product, rather than by considering them as alternatives. Rarely is a product supplied without some form of service support or a service supplied without some form of tangible dimension. This point is made most forcibly when product and service quality are combined to provide customer satisfaction (Gummesson, 1988). The factors which affect the service level should be related to the nature of the transaction (risk, time), the nature and role of the material elements, and the impact of affective and interpersonal elements (Flipo, 1988). Some conclude that customer care should be evaluated by relating to specific strategic objectives, by measuring intangible as well as tangible dimensions and should combine operational efficiency with strict financial controls (Fitzgerald, 1988). Customer service is often seen with two goals in mind which are not always mutually compatible. These goals are operational efficiency and customer satisfaction (Lovelock, 1991).

'The most important issue in marketing is to establish, strengthen and develop customer relationships where this can be done at a profit and where individual and organisational objectives are met' (Gronroos, 1990). While not new, this perspective, by advocating close contact with customers and relationship building, seems particularly appropriate to the ideal of marketing as a mutually satisfying exchange. It is incumbent upon the supplier to add services which sustain and enhance customer relationships. Likewise, buyers who are better informed, more discerning and faced with alternative options will have increased expectations of what their suppliers should be providing in terms of customer support.

In exchange, where service and inter-organisational relationships are important, the role of marketing cannot be considered as merely a separate function. With many points of contact within and between organisations, a functional solution (marketing department) or individual response (salesperson) will be inadequate. The marketing department or marketing manager's role, in addition to assessing customer requirements, becomes one of 'orchestrating the interaction of the various functional groups in an organisation that are central to serving the customer and achieving competitive advantage' (Spekman and Johnston, 1986). This is similar to the idea of a marketing services unit advocated by Turnbull for buyer-seller relationships in industrial marketing (Turnbull, 1979).

The service literature offers much advice on managing customer service, some of which can be adapted or applied directly to other forms of marketing exchange. 'When examining the customer contacts of many firms marketing industrial goods and systems one may notice that many of the characteristics of service firms can be found. Hence, concepts and models developed for service firms may also be useful for industrial firms. Research projects that explore the commonalties between service marketing and industrial marketing ... seem to be able to achieve very fruitful results' (Gronroos and Gummesson, 1985). This distinction between services and other goods 'rests upon arbitrary definitions which have little or no ultimate significance for the understanding of customer behaviour, competitive analysis or managerial action' (Foxall, 1985). Notwithstanding, the services literature has provided significant theoretical and empirical work which can be and is of relevance to other areas of marketing, particularly in the understanding of customer care as a component in building and sustaining relationships. Many service businesses now have a leadership role in the economy and can provide guidance and insight into ways of boosting productivity, competitive positioning and increased customer satisfaction. For example, following a tour of 23 American companies renowned for the outstanding levels of customer service, it was reported that while there is no single common reason for success there were characteristics or themes for success (Moores, 1990). These characteristics included a customer imperative which drives the business and forms the corporate ethos and culture, an acknowledgement of the link between service and profit, employee initiatives and rewards for service excellence, constant performance evaluation, commitment to quality and the equivalent of a product champion whose aim is not merely satisfaction but customer delight (Moores, 1990).

One book reporting on an extensive survey conducted under the Technical Assistance Research Programs (T.A.R.P) for the White House Office of Consumer Affairs reported that 96% of unhappy customers don't let the company know; 1 complaint = 26 customers with a problem, 6 of which are serious; complainers are more likely to stick with you; 54–70% of custom is repeat business; 95% of complaints raised are dealt with adequately; of complainers, the average customer tells 9–10 people about it and 13% tell more than 20 people; customers who complain and are well treated tell on average 5 people (Albrecht and Zemke, 1985). These authors take a comprehensive view of service which focuses on the customer but as a managed endeavour by the enterprise. The core elements include involvement, measurement, information, reward and follow-through. Their thesis is that service is a top management concern and must encompass a service audit, strategy development, education, implementation and maintenance. The advice given is empirically based and confirms that customer based activity should be proactively managed by the supplier (Albrecht and Zemke, 1985).

One approach to implementing a successful customer care programme is to adopt the idea of the service delivery process and the service man-

agement system (Normann, 1991). Normann suggests that the need for innovation is pervasive and it is not confined to product or technology but extends to social innovation (client participation, role sets, new linkages, new sources of human energy). Profits come from customer relationships. Normann, plausibly if not unequivocally, suggests that if an existing customer can be given an equivalent cost index of 100, then a new customer is 130 and the cost of regaining a lost customer is 150 (Normann, 1991, p. 22). He further suggests that the nature of transactions is changing via the augmented product with service loading, the development of relationship marketing, broadening the customer contact (e.g. 24 hours a day), unbundling and rebundling of services to suit different requirements and increased enabling activity by customers taking an active part in the process, e.g. ATMs in bank delivery systems. The conclusion is that there are more intangibles, closer and increased complexity in interaction and an interactive logic between providers and customers. Normann's prognosis is that it is increasingly difficult to separate the service, the process of delivery of the service and the service delivery system. He advocates the service management system whose core ideas include:

- The market segment relates to the characteristics of the customers who comprise the target market for the supplier.
- The service concept constitutes the benefit offered which have tangible and intangible characteristics, consist of core and peripheral activities and possess features some of which can be measured and specific (explicit) while others may be equally or more important but are imprecise (implicit).
- The service delivery system can be adapted to incorporate the idea of a logistics system including production, distribution and service support. It therefore embraces the personnel of both provider and customer, the support activities employed in transaction and relationships and the management of the system as well as the interface between systems and people.

- The image. Many factors influence a company's reputation including its image influencing activities, its culture, organisation and people. In the long run, the products or services provided and the customers served are the main influences on a company's image.
- The culture and philosophy embraces the total package that the customer perceives when entering into a relationship. It embraces the prevailing orientation towards quality and excellence, customer orientation, investment in people and managerial commitment.

Normann's book therefore contains many aspects which are difficult to ignore in understanding customer service and is helpful in explaining what being 'close to the customer' really means. Customer care is a concept that is not confined to services marketing but one which should be at the heart of any competitive enterprise.

The strategic management of customers embraces the idea of service as a total business philosophy. Without doubt customer service is now a competitive tool and a versatile concept that has important strategic consequences and opportunities. With advanced economies requiring sophisticated service and technology support, with more complex industrial products and increasingly demanding and discerning buyers, there is a need for a total customer care approach and greater relationship building between buyer and seller. While this can be observed, it now requires to be measured. 'We can invest in relationships and we can borrow from them. We all do both, but we seldom account for our actions and almost never manage them. Yet a company's most precious asset is its relationships with its customers. What matters is not whom you know but how you are known' (Levitt, 1983).

To implement a customer care programme requires trained and committed people in the organisation. One analysis of this employee/customer involvement is based on a format for 'managing people power', with each group requiring different skills and training to meet their customers' requirements (Judd, 1987). Such an analysis mirrors what many successful companies are already aware of, that employee training and empowerment are crucial to successful buyer-seller relationships. This empowerment needs to be formalised and managed if a company is to be effective in its relationships with its customers. This can be achieved at three levels. The lowest and simplest level is consistency, or the absence of inconsistency. This would mean, for example, that staff handling low price, no frills, products with minimum service support, operate efficiently and accurately. Level two is integration, where the service is compatible with customer requirements and the relative price and competitive position. At this level, staff must be adaptable and responsive to customers' needs. The third level is where the service exerts leverage on the purchase decision and the buying group. Staff operating here need higher-level interactive skills which requires not only the right people, but investment in training, staff participation and an appropriate reward system. Firms, some of whom may claim to be customer led, who reward staff on traditional output measures such as number of orders of sales value, are unlikely to be operating satisfactorily at this level. What is required is a reward system based, for example, on the number of customers retained and how satisfied these customers are with the service provided. Achievement at level three will place most firms way ahead of the competition. A fourth level, which few firms attain, is the 'wow' factor when staff far exceed expectations and delight the customer with exceptional service performance.

□ *Quality*

Quality in customer care can be conceptualised as an alignment of customer's perceptions of actual service experienced with their service expectations. Gronroos identifies the two constituents of customer service quality as technical and functional dimensions of quality (Gronroos, 1984). Technical aspects of service relate to physical aspects capable of objective measurement by the customer whereas functional aspects relate to the manner in which service is delivered, including such areas as personal contact between buyer and seller personnel. Although Gronroos's conceptualisation was intended for service industries, the concept can apply in other areas, particularly industrial marketing. In industrial marketing, a fundamental question concerns whether, and to what extent, a buyer-seller relationship depends on technical performance, what is delivered, vis-a-vis functional performance, and how it is delivered, although the answer may well depend on the distinction between transactions and relationships as much as technical versus functional quality.

Significant among the contributions to this topic has been the work of Parasuraman, Berry and Zeithaml. They advocate a measurement instrument called SERVQUAL (Parasuraman *et al.*, 1988) based on 22 statements culled from five dimensions of service quality – tangibility, reliability, responsiveness, assurance and empathy. These five dimensions were derived from an initial list of ten (tangibility, reliability, responsiveness, communication, credibility, security, competence, courtesy, understanding/knowing the customer, access) by factor analysis and testing. As a result of evaluating these dimensions they advocate measuring a customer's perception of service quality and perceived value, to develop their service quality model (Zeithaml, 1988). This model identifies five gaps between customer and supplier which, they suggest, affects the quality of the service delivery (Zeithmal, Berry, and Parasuraman, 1989). These gaps are expressed as the differences between

- customer expectations and management perceptions of customer expectations
- management perception of customer expectations and service quality specifications
- service quality specifications and the service actually delivered
- service delivery and what is communicated about the service to customers
- customer expectations and perceptions of actual service.

It is clear that customers who have low expectations and receive average service have a greater degree of satisfaction than do those customers with high expectations who receive average service. 'The quality perceived in a service is a function of the gap between consumers' expectations of the service and their perceptions of the service actually delivered by the organisation' (Parasuraman *et al.*, 1988). The idea of a gap analysis has been explained as the evaluation of service encounters, i.e. the difference between experiences and expectations (Brown and Swartz, 1989). Elsewhere, the expectation theory of service quality has been referred to as the 'expectancy disconfirmation paradigm' (Schnaars, 1991). He suggests that the paradigm consists of four constructs – prior expectations, service or product performance, confirmation or disconfirmation and customer satisfaction or dissatisfaction. Prior expectations are pre-purchase anticipation about a product's performance based on previous experience, word-of-mouth communications and marketing efforts. Confirmation of expectations is a result of product performance meeting expectations. Positive disconfirmation is experienced when service performance exceeds expectations while negative disconfirmation occurs when service performance falls short of expectations. The first two of these possible outcomes will lead to customer satisfaction but the last will lead to dissatisfaction. It is not only product satisfaction that is of concern but also the customer's satisfaction with the organisation. This may be the core product, the quality of added services and the enterprise satisfaction (Nagel and Cilliers, 1990). This more holistic view of service as customer satisfaction can mean that even a well performing core product is not sufficient for a customer to rate service quality as satisfactory. SERVQUAL is an admirable effort to measure service quality but customers may interpret expectations and importance on the same scale and the gap analysis becomes invalid. Measures should attempt to measure perceptions and/or importance but not the difference between the two constructs.

An alternative method of measuring service quality is to view service as a journey which begins with the customer searching for a suitable organisation and ending with follow-up after the transaction or customer contact has been made (Whittle and Foster, 1989). Their 'customer profiling' technique is claimed to view service from the customer's perspective rather than that of the organisation. Unlike SERVQUAL, customer profiling focuses on the total service journey instead of the individual components. On this journey there are many different 'moments of truth' (Normann, 1991, p. 16) which contribute to the customer's experience in dealing with the organisation and the customer may judge by the weakest point of that journey (Horovitz, 1990). The advantage claimed for the customer profiling approach is that the service journey can be profiled for different types of customer and for different organisational communication. This approach is more qualitative and does not directly involve the opinions and perceptions of actual customers. The model can identify weak links in the customer chain and implement necessary changes, but it does not account for changes in marketplace dynamics, customer perceptions or competitive offerings.

This last point is of particular significance and outlines a need to analyse the total spectrum of customer satisfaction in relation to competitors. To overcome this 'competitive bench marking' is advocated (Christopher and Yallop, 1990). This involves researching customer needs to identify which service elements are most important to customers. These are then traded off against one another to develop an importance ranking of the various elements. Customers are then surveyed to see how they perceive key competitors' performances on each element. A profile of customer service performance vis-à-vis competitors on key value attributes can then be established with any shortcomings providing a clear guide for managerial action (Christopher and Yallop, 1990). As such, the method can highlight interest considerations for the firm's customer service positioning strategy. Measurement of customer service in terms of customer retention rates, is crucial in terms of profitability. It has been suggested that a 5% swing in an organisation's customer retention rate levers profits by between 25% and 85% across a broad spectrum of industries (Dawkins and Reichheld, 1990). Zero defection by cus-

tomers, i.e. retaining every profitable customer, is therefore a performance measure and profit indicator of the utmost importance. In the authors' own words: 'Top management directly monitors its competitive advantage when it focuses on achieving and maintaining a customer retention rate better than any of its competitors' (Dawkins and Reichheld, 1990). The measure of customer satisfaction and customer retention is the key to long run profitability. These measures help management to evaluate whether their strategy is working or not. Some evidence exists that leading companies such as Xerox are implementing these measures (Christopher *et al.*, 1991). As a rule of thumb, one source suggests that it is five to eight times less expensive to retain loyal customers than to attract new ones (Muller, 1991). The pursuit of customer loyalty and measures to evaluate such loyalty is therefore deemed to be profitable marketing practice.

The characteristics of a customer driven company

Several factors consistent with a service oriented, customer driven company emerge from the literature and are considered below.

Customer based mission statements

The customer driven organisation will have identified customer requirements, decided how best to satisfy these requirements, and consequently translated these actions into a meaningful policy or plan. Part of this process will be a mission statement which reflects customer commitment. A mission statement is not a vapid platitude but 'an enduring statement of purpose that distinguishes one organisation from similar enterprises... [and is] a declaration of an organisation's reason for being' (David, 1989). The mission statement is but one indicator of the importance of corporate leadership and top management commitment to, and involvement in, superior customer service. Such a statement should encourage management debate to allow effective articulation of the organisation's purpose. It also serves as a device for ensuring that strategy formulation remains within the objectives of the firm and acts as an integrating philosophy to guide planning, objective setting and performance evaluation. When such a statement embodies commitment to customers then standards of service and measures to evaluate them will follow. Firms with a service mission statement are more likely to conduct customer surveys and to measure customer service (Germain and Cooper, 1990). These findings applied to manufacturers, industrial and consumer service firms although each group monitored different dimensions of customer service performance. Firms with a written customer service statement attach more importance to customer service and were more likely to use customer service as a weapon against competition (Kyj, 1987).

☐ *Service as part of a strategic positioning*

Probably the most important benefit to be gained from pursuing an intensive customer based strategy is a sustainable competitive advantage. Despite the popularity of Porter's strategic model (Porter, 1980), there is only one source of competitive advantage, that of differentiation. Cost leadership and focus are forms of differentiation 'all successful strategies are differentiation; cost is just one of the factors in which a firm can be different from the competition' (Fulmer and Goodwin, 1988). In an effort to establish differentiation, customer service can be a distinguishing feature and a source of leverage. Several authors have proposed that customer service is emerging as the best tool to use in planning for a sustainable competitive advantage (Lewis and Mitchell, 1990; Muller, 1991; Singh, 1988). In crowded and competitive markets cost and technology improvements may fail to make a lasting or significant impact on an organisation's cost leadership or differentiated competitive position (Singh, 1990). Recent advances in quality management and cost savings achieved as a result of

effective strategic materials management will not continue to allow differentiation of products along a price/quality axis (Muller, 1991). As customer expectations continue to increase, demands for service-related activities must also grow. Customers often perceive only marginal differences in products or services in term of price and quality while appeals via marketing communications are less attractive because of escalating costs, uncertain returns and a frequent lack of distinction. The customer driven organisation characterised by top management commitment, a service culture and customer oriented activity can be a source of uniqueness not easily imitated. Further, such an organisation faced with oversupply in end markets and softening demand can prove more resilient to low price competition (Allan, 1988).

☐ *Commitment to quality*

Service also gains in strategic importance as a result of the link with total quality management and in the U.K. this is expressed directly in meeting or exceeding the requirements of B.S.5750 (B.S.I., 1990). The outcome is that product quality and service quality should be combined to establish and maintain a strategic position whether pursuing market penetration, development or diversification strategies (Gummesson, 1988; Wagner, 1987). In industrial exchange processes, strategy is formulated by considering the behaviour of individual accounts over time rather than customers being members of markets or market segments. The emphasis is on service support to establish and enhance the relationship rather than merely concluding the transaction (Jackson, 1985). Increasingly, firms accept that a co-operative approach to trading is preferred to an adversarial one and service ought to be defined and measured in expressions of adaptability and flexibility (Cecil-Wright, 1988). This has a direct effect on customer satisfaction which drives customer loyalty (Muller, 1991). There are finite limits to the service dimension since 'eventually, customer and competitive forces combine to drive a market-place into a highly price-sensitive mode. If the vendor is to protect its market position, strategies that emphasise account management, product augmentation, and customer service must give way to a strategy based at least partly on price' (De Bruiler and Summe, 1985). The idea of diminishing returns from customer service was a problem highlighted by several authors (Levy, 1981; Sabath, 1978).

Organisational integration and people

A mission statement embracing customer service, top management involvement and commitment to quality are all important but implementation can only come from the people in the organisation understanding the objectives set and meeting the standards required. Many people within an organisation can affect customer relationships and members of staff must be aware of expected standards and customer needs. In the service industries it has been suggested that all employees are part-time marketers, capable of influencing the customer relationships which ultimately determine how successful the organisation is in the long term (Gronroos, 1990). In other firms, e.g. shipbuilding, relatively few employees are in contact with customers, or need to be. Nevertheless, there is still a need for integrated organisation which share the common commitment to quality and ultimately customer satisfaction. This has ben referred to as internal marketing which focuses on treating fellow employees as internal customers and their jobs as internal products. Internal marketing has four main objectives:

a) To help employees understand and accept the importance of interactions with customers and their responsibility for the total quality and for the interactive performance of the firm.
b) To help employees understand and accept the mission, strategies, goods, services, systems, and external campaigns of the firm.
c) To continuously motivate employees and inform them about new concepts, goods, ser-

vices and external campaigns as well as economic results.
d) To attract and keep good employees. This extends the idea of the value chain backwards to the employee carrying out a task for an internal buyer prior to supplying your customer (Ishikawa, 1985). Internal marketing, by striving to gain the commitment of employees, is a means of developing a corporate culture which places the customer first. Management's task, internally, is to identify the service role played by different groups of employees and to signal to these employees managerial commitment to a service philosophy. Keeping employees informed, trained and rewarded for service excellence can achieve management objectives and competitive advantage.

Investment in customer research and feedback

Customer service, like any other activity, should reflect customer requirements and be research based. Some authors suggest that with more discerning customers and market segments becoming smaller, this need for research to customise the offer is all the more acute (Clutterbuck, 1989; Brown, 1989). Resources will not be optimally allocated if service is under- or over-provided. If an organisation does not fine-tune its service to specific customer requirements then an under- or over-emphasis may be placed on individual service components out of line with customer expectations (Christopher and Yallop, 1990). Market research can elicit the importance customers place on service dimensions in comparison with other attributes, e.g. price or product quality, and the relative importance of different service components. While formal market research techniques can provide great insight on customer needs using trade-off analysis (Christopher and Yallop, 1990), informal research and a variety of customer feedback sources should also be used. This reflects the organisation as one which is obsessive about knowing customer requirements. Research into service dimensions has been critised for reflecting what an organisation thinks it wants to know about its customers rather than giving customers the scope to express themselves individually (Boggis, 1990). Panels, focus groups and more innovative research methods are advocated. The use of cost-free information, telephone hotlines, 'Management by walking about' and so on are also advocated. This reflects staying close to the customer, being responsive and customer driven.

Investment in information technology for service

Information technology (I.T.) is playing an increasingly important role in the achievement and maintenance of customer service (Domegan and Donaldson, 1992). First, at the strategic level by gathering information on competitors and analysing competitors' service performance. This is different from market research in that I.T. is a method of continuous environmental scanning and intelligence gathering whereas market research involves studies directed at specific, recognised informational deficiencies that hinder objective decision making with respect to customers or markets. Secondly I.T. can be used to enhance organisational efficiency at the tactical and operation level. Instant hard data on customer order status, stock availability and accounts provides improved speed and personalisation of service. This new area, database marketing, adds a new dimension to customer service and facilitates closer links with customers. State-of-the-art I.T. may replace people in transactions with customers and this may not always be desirable. Improved accuracy, immediate response and cost reduction needs to be weighed against the importance of personal relationships (Singh, 1990). If I.T. allows employees to be more efficient and effective in serving their customers then I.T. objectives can be satisfied in service terms.

Communication with customers

After determining a customer service mission from research findings and developing an inte-

grated organisation capable of delivering the appropriate level and quality of service, it is necessary to communicate what that level is to customers. An organisation that is confident about its service delivery capability can influence customers' expectations of its performance. It is imperative that only a level of service that can be consistently performed should be communicated (Horovitz and Cudennec-Poon, 1990). By influencing expectations, organisations can minimise the differences between what customers expect and what they actually get. Communication messages are not always easily controlled since messages to the customer concerning service quality arise from diverse sources such as telephone answering, literature, surroundings and so on, some of which result in signal confusion for the customer. Communications can shape expectations but all aspects of an organisations' communication output should collectively deliver a consistent and coherent message.

Innovating in service

If customer service does provide a competitive edge this will only be achieved by constant renewal and improvement which requires the introduction of innovative service dimensions to support the product, as well as innovative products. The results of continuous improvement in service is a pre-emptive advantage and superior profit potential. Such innovations concentrate on simplifying the customer purchase process, increasing the usefulness and availability of the product or reducing buyer's uncertainty (Cunningham and Roberts, 1974; Muller, 1991). Innovation in service may be either at one stage of the purchase decision process or designed to secure advantage at several stages, e.g. improve stock control at one stage or, complete automatic order entry and despatch processes across a number of stages. Ways of achieving this can be from employees themselves, service circles similar to the idea of quality circles and, from more enlightened management involving employees and customers to participate and be involved in service innovative processes.

Measuring and monitoring service delivery

An organisation's service performance cannot be determined without measuring it. Only by comparing organisational opinions with those internal employees and especially customers themselves can confirmation or refutation of service effect and delivered performance be made. Deciding on the basis of appropriate measures is no easy task. Are specific measures of activity to be made or is it the overall effect which is to be measured? Can quantitative measures represent performance or, are qualitative dimensions more important?

The characteristics which drive increased service are part of the trend by buyers to be more explicit in their needs, the increasing trend to relationship building and the pursuit of quality and excellence by suppliers. Higher service is found in the better-performing companies and is a continuing process whereby organisations strive for competitive advantage and customer loyalty and satisfaction. There are complex organisational issues involved which necessitate marketing effectiveness be viewed as concomitant with organisational theory (compare Piercy, 1992).

The conclusion must be that there are visible signs which characterise the customer driven company. These signs include a commitment to high service as part of marketing strategy, service levels set higher than competitors, and employees who are customer oriented, trained and promoted on the basis of service. Such companies measure and obtain feedback on service performance, pursue super quality and service and have meetings to discuss quality and service issues. These firms are doing most things and doing them well. These 'things' are customer based.

■ References

Albrecht, K. and Zemke, R. (1985), *Service America, Doing Business in the New Economy*, Homewood Ill.: Dow Jones-Irwin.

Allan, M. (1988), 'Turn Up Your Marketing Candlepower', *Strategic Marketing* (March/April), pp. 28–35.

Baker, M. J. and Hart, S. J. (1989), *Marketing and Competitive Success*, Hemel Hempstead: Philip Allan.

Boggis, F. (1990) 'Customer Care: A "bottom–up" view of a "top–down" policy', *European Journal of Marketing* 24 (12), pp. 22–34.

British Standards Institute, BS 5750 PT. 4 (1990).

Brown, A. (1989), *Customer Care Management*, Oxford: Heinemann.

Brown, S. B. and Swartz, T. A. (1989), 'A Gap Analysis of Professional Service Quality', *Journal of Marketing* 53, (April), pp. 92–98.

Buzzell, R. D. and Gale, B. T. (1987), *The PIMS Principles*, New York: Free Press.

Cecil-Wright, J. (1988), 'Flexibility is the Key to Service', *Management Services* (April), pp. 18–20.

Christopher, M. and Yallop, R. (1990), 'Audit Your Customer Service Quality', *Journal of Physical Distribution and Materials Management* 9 (5), pp. 4–12.

Christopher, M., Payne, A. and Ballantyne, D. (1991), *Relationship Marketing: Bringing Quality, Customer Service and Marketing Together*, Oxford: Butterworth-Heinemann.

Clutterbuck, D. (1989), 'Developing Customer Care Training Programmes', *Marketing Intelligence and Planning* 7 (19), pp. 34–37.

Coyne, K. (1989), 'Beyond Service Fads – Meaningful Strategies for the Real World', *Sloan Management Review* 30 (Summer), pp. 69–76.

Crosby, P. B. (1979), *Quality is Free*, New York: McGraw-Hill.

Cunningham, M. T. and Roberts, D. A. (1974), 'The Role of Customer Service in Industrial Marketing', *European Journal of Marketing* 8 (1) (Spring), pp. 15–28.

David, F. R. (1989), 'How Companies Define Their Mission', *Long Range Planning* 22 (1), pp. 90–97.

Dawkins, P. M. and Reichheld, F. F. (1990), 'Customer Retention as a Competitive Weapon', *Directors & Boards* (Summer), pp. 42–47.

Day, G. S. and Wensley, R. (1988), 'Assessing Advantage: A Framework for Diagnosing Competitive Superiority', *Journal of Marketing*, 52 (April), pp. 1–20.

De Bruiler, F. A. and Summe, G. L. (1985), 'Make Sure Your Customers Keep Coming Back', *Harvard Business Review* (January/February), pp. 97–98.

Deeming, W. E. (1982) *Out of Crisis*, Chicago: MIT.

Domegan, C. and Donaldson, B. (1992) 'Customer Service and Information Technology', *Journal of Information Technology* 7, pp. 203–212.

Fitzgerald, L. (1988), 'Management Performance Measurement in Service Industries', *International Journal of Purchasing Management* 8 (3), pp. 109–111.

Flipo, J. P. (1988), 'On the Intangibility of Services', *Services Industries Journal* 8 (3) (July), pp. 286–298.

Foxall, G. (1985), 'Marketing is Service Marketing', *Marketing in the Service Industries*, ed. Foxall, F., London: F. Cass, pp. 1–6.

Fulmer, W. E. and Goodwin, J. (1988), 'Differentiation: Begin with the Consumer', *Business Horizons* (September–October), pp. 55–63.

Galbraith, J. K. (1992), *The Culture of Contentment*, London: Sinclair-Stevenson.

Germain, R. and Cooper, M. B. (1990), 'How a Customer Mission Statement Affects Company Performance', *Industrial Marketing Management* 19, pp. 47–54.

Gronroos, C. (1984), 'A Service Quality Model and its Marketing Implications', *European Journal of Marketing* 18 (4), pp. 36–44.

Gronroos, C. and Gummesson, E. (1985), *Service Marketing – Nordic School Perspectives*, University of Stockholm.

Gronroos, C. (1990), 'Marketing Redefined', *Management Decision* 28 (8), pp. 5–9.

Guirdham, M. (1979), 'Boundary-Spanning and Inter-organisational Relations. Theory and Marketing Implications', *MEG Proceedings*, Bristol.

Gummesson, E. (1988), 'Service Quality and Product Quality Combined', *Review of Business* 9 (3), pp. 14–19.

Horovitz, J. (1990), *How to Win Customers Using C. S. for a Competitive Edge*, London: Pitman.

Horovitz, J. and Cudennec-Poon, C. (1990), 'Putting Service Quality Into Gear', *Service Industries Journal* 10 (2), pp. 249–265.

Ishikawa, K. (1985), *What is Total Quality Control? The Japanese Way*, Englewood Clifts, NJ: Prentice-Hall.

Jackson, B. B. (1985), *Winning and Keeping Industrial Customers: the Dynamics of Customer Relations*, Lexington, Mass.: Lexington Books.

Johnston, W. J. and Spekman, R. E. (1982), 'Industrial Buying Behaviour: a Need for an Integrative Approach', *Journal of Business Research* 10 (June), pp. 135–146.

Judd, V. C. (1987), 'Differentiate With the 5th P: People', *Industrial Marketing Management* 16, pp. 241–247.

Juran, J. M. (1979), *Quality Control Handbook,* 3rd edition, New York: McGraw-Hill.

Kotler, P. (1988), *Marketing Management: Analysis, Planning and Control*, 6th edition, Englewood Cliffs, NJ: Prentice-Hall.

Kyj, M. J. and Kyj, L. S. (1987), 'Customer Service Competition in Business-to-Business and Industrial Markets: Myths and Realities', *The Journal of Business and Industrial Marketing* 2 (4), pp. 45–52.

Kyj, M. J. (1987), 'Customer Service as a Competitive Tool', *Industrial Marketing Management* 16, pp. 225–230.

Lehman, D. R. and O'Shaughnessy, J. (1974), 'Difference in Attribute Importance for Different Industrial Products', *Journal of Marketing* 38 (April), pp. 36–42.

Levitt, T. (1976) 'The Industrialisation of Service', *Harvard Business Review* (September–October), pp. 63–74.

Levitt, T. (1983), 'After the Sale is Over' *Harvard Business Review* (September–October), pp. 87–93.

Levy, M. (1981), 'Diminishing Returns for Customer Service', *International Journal of Physical Distribution and Materials Management* 11 (1), pp. 14–24.

Lewis, B. R. and Mitchell, V. W. (1990) 'Defining and Measuring the Quality of Customer Service', *Marketing Intelligence and Planning* (6), pp. 11–17.

Lillebo, A. (1983), 'Serving Tomorrow's Needs', *Profile* (Autumn), ITT Europe Magazine.

Lovelock, C. H. (1991) *Services Marketing: Texts, cases and readings*, 2nd edition, Englewood Cliffs, NJ: Prentice-Hall.

Machlup, F. (1982) *Knowledge: Its Creation, Distribution and Economic Significance*, Princeton: Princeton University Press.

Marr, N. E. (1984), 'The Impact of Customer Services in International Markets', *International Journal of Physical Distribution and Materials Management* (Autumn), pp. 45–53.

Moores, S. B. (1990), 'The Service Excellence Experience', *Marketing Intelligence and Planning* 8 (6), pp. 18–24.

Muller, W. (1991), 'Gaining Competitive Advantage Through Customer Satisfaction', *European Management Journal* 9 (2) (June), pp. 201–211.

Nagel, P. G. A. and Cilliers, W. W. (1990), 'Customer Satisfaction: A Comprehensive Approach', *International Journal of Physical Distribution & Logistics Management* 20 (6), pp. 1–46.

Norburn, D. Birley, S. Dunn, M. and Payne, A (1988), 'A Four-Nation Study of the Relationship Between Marketing Effectiveness, Corporate Culture, Corporate Values and Market Orientation', *Marketing Education Group Conference Proceedings*, Huddersfield.

Normann, R. (1991), *Service Management Strategy and Leadership in Service Businesses*, 2nd edition, Chichester: John Wiley.

Parasuraman, A., Zeithaml, V. A. and Berry, L. L. (1988), 'SERVQUAL: A Multiple Item Scale for Measuring Consumer Perceptions of Service Quality', *Journal of Retailing* 64 (1) (Spring), pp. 12–44.

Peters, T. and Austin, N. (1988), *A Passion for Excellence: The Leadership Difference*, Glasgow: Collins.

Piercy, N. (1992), *Market Led Strategic Change*, London: Thornsons.

Porat, M. U. (1976), *The Information Economy*, Washington.

Porter. M. E. (1980), *Competitive Strategy*, New York: Harper & Row.

Reve, T. (1990). 'The Firm as a Nexus of Internal and External Contracts', in *The Firm as a Nexus of Treaties*, (eds) Aoki, M., Gustafsson, B. and Williamson, O. E., London: Sage, pp. 133–161.

Sabath, R. E. (1978), 'How Much Service Do Customers Really Want?' *Business Horizons* 21 (2) (April), pp. 26–32.

Schnaars, S. P. (1991), *Marketing Strategy: A Customer Driven Approach*, New York: Free Press.

Singh, J. (1988), 'Consumer Complaint Inventions and Behaviour: Definitional and Taxanomical Issues', *Journal of Marketing* 52 (January), pp. 93–107.

Singh, M. P. (1990), 'Service as a Marketing Strategy: A Case-Study at Reliance Electric', *Industrial Marketing Management* 19, pp. 193–200.

Spekman, R. E. and Johnstone, W. J. (1986), 'Relationship Management: Managing the Selling and the Buying Interface', *Journal of Business Research* 14, pp. 519–531.

Stewart, K. (1992), 'A Review of Customer Care and Customer Service', in *Perspectives on Marketing Management, vol. II*, (ed.) Baker, M. J., London: John Wiley.

Stone, M. and Young, L. (1992), *Competitive Customer Care: A Guide to Keeping Customers*, Kingston upon Thames: Croner.

Turnbull, (1979), 'Roles of Personal Contacts in Industrial Export Marketing', *Organisation, Marknad och Samhalle*, 16 (5), pp. 325–328.

Uno, K. (1989), *Measurement of Services in an Input–Output Framework*, Amsterdam: Elsevier.

Vandermerwe, G. and Rada, J. (1988), 'Servitization of Business: Adding Value by Adding Services', *European Management Journal* 6 (4), pp. 314–324.

Wagner, W. B. (1987), 'Customer Service in Industrial Marketing: Hedge Against Competition', *European Journal Marketing* 21 (7), pp. 7–17.

Webster, F. E. (1988), 'The Rediscovery of the Marketing Concept', *Business Horizons* (May–June), pp. 29–39.

Whittle, S. and Foster, M. (1989), 'Customer Profiling: Getting into Your Customer's Shoes', *Management Decision* 27 (6), pp. 27–31.

Wong, V. and Saunders, J. (1993), 'Business Orientations and Corporate Success', *Journal of Strategic Management* 1 (1) (March), pp. 20–40.

Zeithaml, V. A. (1988), 'Consumer Perceptions of Price, Quality and Value: A Means–End Model and Synthesis of Evidence, *Journal of Marketing* 52 (July), pp. 2–22.

Zeithaml, V. A., Berry, L. L. and Parasuraman, A. (1989), 'Communications and Control Processes in the Delivery of Service Quality', *Journal of Marketing* 52 (April), pp. 35–48.

■ *Chapter 18* ■

Consumerism

Daniel Tixier

Consumerism, based on the word 'consumer', refers to a social protest movement expressing dissatisfaction or angry reactions on the part of consumers faced with the abuses or excesses of the production or distribution systems. All developed countries have experienced consumerism to some degree, and it is evident in many other nations as well. Although in some cases it has been a major factor which marketers have had to take into consideration during the 1970s or even the early 80s, it has not been discussed as much since the latter part of the decade, and it has even met with a new kind of criticism during the years of continuing economic crises which have become a part of life in most Western countries.

However, great progress has been made in the treatment of consumers over the past twenty years, much of it as a result of their pressure, whether they were an organised force or not. Progress has been made in product or service design and quality, as well as in better treatment of consumer dissatisfaction. So it can also be said that the clear decline which is visible in consumer activism today is not proof of declining interest, but rather of diminishing necessity. To a large extent, consumerism may have served its purpose, and real improvements in the total quality of products and service which today's consumers are enjoying may just be a tribute to the work achieved by those pioneers who dared question the economic, social and legal responsibilities of organisations in the past. It

is a lesson which today's marketers had better not forget, for consumer activism could revive very rapidly if it proved necessary. The legacy of the great years of consumerism is better quality achieved through protest, and this has in turn led to a kind of armed peace.

Although legislation protecting consumers had continued to progress over time, the advent of a society of mass consumption, with the rationalisation of production and distribution, has created new imbalances between producers and consumers. The development of consumerism with the advent of mass consumption in the 60s and 70s has covered three major phases or historical periods which can be seen in most modern countries. Its roots have always been in the repression of theft, a matter for the policy and justice systems and which, under different forms, has long existed within organised human communities.

It seems that early on fraud was assimilated to theft and repressed as such. For instance, in many European countries, specific and infamous public punishment already existed in the Middle Ages for people watering milk. In Paris, by royal order, convicted merchants were chained at the pillory with a block of butter on their heads and left under the midday sun until it fully melted. To go even further back in history, it is legendary that Archimedes developed his principle because he was asked by the king of Syracuse to invent a non destructive technique for checking fraud in the use of gold and other metals. But it took considerably longer to consider deceit, and, even more so, the intention to deceive, as serious offences. The famous Roman saying 'caveat emptor' (let the buyer beware) is a reminder of the responsibility of the buyer in an age when buyer and seller were relatively equal in size and power. The structural inadequacy of 'caveat emptor' is a child of the industrial revolution which, generally speaking, destroyed that balance.

▌ Three historic phases of active consumerism

The first phase of active consumerism can be traced to the dawn of the 20th century in both America and Europe. Social writers, such as Upton Sinclair with his famous book, *The Jungle*, succeeded at the turn of the century in bringing to light public scandals in which both workers and consumers were victims of big industry, a situation which politicians could not ignore. The result has been a series of laws enforcing product purity and repression of fraud. The Great War, and the Roaring Twenties in its aftermath, left little time for consumer activism. It took the Great Depression to bring about a second phase to protect the buying power of the poorer and the weaker.

From these two periods, the consumer movement developed an image of social justice and protection of the little guy against ruthless giants prone to easy rip-offs, which climaxed with the third phase in the 70s. Heralded by Ralph Nader in the United States, crusades against abuses by Big Business succeeded in attracting smart young professionals plying the legal trade. It generated massive legislative advances in the field of consumer rights in many countries. Legal action ran alongside enough successful consumer boycotts to convince business that it made good sense to be more responsive to consumer demands.

▪ And now maturity

By the 1980s, consumerism had roots in social activism, in housewives' and family movements, in legal activism, in the 'green' movement, and even in advanced marketing. Big scandals were history. Nader's Groups had turned into Public Citizens' and Watch movements. The words Consumer Society no longer had a negative connotation in the mouths of people considering themselves as socially advanced, but had become a re-emerging dream for many victims of a new and structural economic crisis generating a two-speed society. By the early 90s, one heard or read more often than not that consumerism had been overtaken and was behind us, or at least it had fallen to a low priority level. The current question had become 'Is consumerism dying as a social movement?', with its variation 'Is consumerism dead as a management constraint?' Some advertising gurus have recently answered 'yes' to these questions, adding that consumers were victims of consumerism fatigue. On the other hand, researchers in management tend to say and write that, in its fourth type, consumerism has become the natural watchdog of marketing.

As long as the quality of the consumer *quid pro quo* remains acceptable, and above all true, marketers no longer run into social head winds. Let marketers believe that they have won some kind of victory against activists and feel free to 'optimise' in the name of costs and production constraints, and the backlash could be brutal. Most managers know this and have learned to deal better with occasional crises, including offering excuses to consumers as well as recalling products, that is, salving wounds in addition to correcting economic short-changes.

One of the most famous examples of this new attitude on the part of business is Lee Iacocca's public apology through advertising, in the summer of 1987. Chrysler cars at the time were randomly taken off the production line and thoroughly tested before being sold as new after careful checks and reconditioning. The headlines of the paid advertisements ran the chairman of the company's words, 'Testing cars is a good idea. Disconnecting odometers is a lousy idea. That's a mistake we won't make again at Chrysler', and he gave his personal guarantee to that. As usually happens in consumer affairs, the press somehow leaked the news that questionable practices were carried out by one of the top manufacturers, and it denounced the fact that, while no particular action was illegal, information was withheld from prospective customers which would have decreased the value of the cars they were buying and influenced their choice if they had known in advance.

What is interesting is that, perhaps for the first time, a major corporation had not tried to defend itself technically on the ground that the cars were just as good, if not better, than non-thoroughly tested new ones and were guaranteed as such, or that it was legal, but had offered total apologies from its chairman, although the ads carried these reassuring explanations as well. Chrysler had come a long way on the road to recovery, its major repositioning being on quality. Engineers had done a better job and locked it up with better quality checks done at random. They could prove that thoroughly tested cars returned to the selling line were statistically at least as good as the others. If anything, they expected congratulations. But following the attacks in the press by consumer activists accusing Chrysler of tampering with odometers after some cars had been torture tested, reconditioned, and then sold as new, the chairman was quick to recognise that today's sophisticated consumers not only demand quality of products, but also total quality of information. At a fairly high cost, a system for tracing car numbers was set up, and compensation was offered in the form of product exchange or extended warranty.

Just a few years earlier, business would probably have denied any wrongdoing, such as in the famous Firestone 500 case, when, at the end of the 70s, the tyre manufacture attacked consumerists who were denouncing that model as unsafe and tried to stop a product recall by the National Highway Transportation Safety Administration. The offering of public apologies to consumers indicates a new attitude towards them. It may also be just smart management. Consumers have obviously pardoned Chrysler for the incident, as they have believed in its chairman's word. Firestone ended up so badly shaken that it became prey to raiders. As to the demand for quality of information on top of quality of product or service, it is a legacy of the first three phases of consumerism, and the basis of the fourth one.

The rapid progress of advertising and marketing which have accompanied, or perhaps caused, the mass consumption revolution have sometimes led to commercial practices exceeding the bounds of legal protection and deemed by some to be disloyal and abusive. Some have even gone so far as to say that these practices were a natural byproduct of wild capitalism. But it is also very clear that non capitalist countries do not offer a better deal to consumers. The obvious fact is that free-market operations require checks and balances. Organised consumer pressure is a major force capable of achieving this.

Countries are not equal in the probability that these consumer forces will exist, since this depends on culture and tradition, as well as on the amount of freedom enjoyed by the population. But the existence of an arsenal of legal protection for consumer rights is a major factor. An excellent example of this is so-called Chinese pragmatism. During the legislative session ending in October 1993, the National People's Congress voted a law dealing with the protection of consumers' rights and interests as scientific application of Deng Xiaoping's theory of building socialism with Chinese characteristics, a theory which is the guide to China's reform and open policy as well as to its modernisation. A report 'Lawmakers Set to Protect Consumers', *China Daily*, 23 October 1993, by Ma Chenguang runs: Dishonest and careless businesses faced a new crackdown as legislators yesterday began the final review of China's first consumer law. The Law on Protection of the Rights and Interests of Consumers is due to be approved at the current session of the Standing Committee of the National People's Congress (NPC). It will protect the public from dishonest businessmen and guarantee their right to refunds for shoddy goods and services. Victims will be able to take their complaints to people's courts or administrators and they will be due refunds double the price of their substandard goods, said a top lawmaker yesterday. Legislators also warned businessmen across the country that they will receive severe penalties for cheating customers.

Hence, and even beyond free market economies, in order to counteract deleterious effects of the economic and social organisation inherent to the system in which we live – whether it be on the economic, health or, more recently, ecological levels – consumers have formed or will form organisations to put pressure on public bodies, retailers and manufacturers. The concept of defending the consumer existed long before consumerist movements arose, but the new development of the 60s and 70s was the transition from individual defence to organised and institutionalised collective action.

What were the form and objectives of the movement? Was it a matter, through denouncing excesses of the capitalist system, of improving its efficiency or of revoking it altogether? What were the reactions of manufacturers and public officials? Last, what conclusions can now be drawn from the years of struggle and their implications for the coming decade?

■ Root of the problem: abuse

Insufficient accounting of real consumer needs by manufacturers and dubious practices have always existed. It is with the advent of large industries and economic liberalism, starting in the 18th century, that the buyer (not yet considered a consumer) seemed most vulnerable vis-à-vis the manufacturer. Production rather than consumption was then seen as the aim of a liberal economic system. The elimination, in the name of free trade and industry, of medieval corporations, and with them of the numerous regulations they had helped establish, placed the buyer in a vulnerable position. It was a paradox of the Age of Enlightenment that it destroyed corporations and associations in the name of equality or of that of the myth of the social contract and the primacy of man as an individual over the group.

In the 20th century dubious practices have not disappeared, and new means have continually been found to push the consumer to purchase or to manipulate him. Several types of abuse have been denounced: threats to the consumers' health, pitches aimed at selling at any cost with complete disregard for the consumer's interest, and more recently a general denunciation of the waste of natural resources and damage to the environment.

The American Ford Pinto is one of the most famous examples of products of questionable safety arbitrated on the rationale that it made good management sense. Following a collision in 1972, the poorly protected gas tank of a vehicle of this type exploded, badly burning the driver, a nineteen-year old youth. Ford was fined $125 million in punitive damages in 1978. The most serious aspect of the case was that Ford knew of the Pinto's defect when rear-end collisions were involved, because this had been revealed by in-house laboratory tests, but the company had not wanted to invest in corrections. Because of the sums reimbursed to victims of road accidents by courts at the time ($200 000 for death, $67 000 in case of burns and $700 for the vehicle on an average), Ford had decided, upon launching the Pinto, that it was less expensive not to change the design of the tank (cost estimated at $137 million). In 1977, under pressure from Ralph Nader and following many public complaints, Ford decided to recall the Pinto and correct the problem.

Other dramatic examples exist, such as that of Sulphanilamide Elixir, registered in the United States in 1937. The medication was marketed without previous toxicity studies and caused the death of nearly 1000 people due to the extremely toxic nature of the solvent used.

An unfortunate event which took place in France involved the Mohrange talcum power for babies, containing hexacholorophene, a component toxic at a high level of concentration, a situation which accidentally happened due to lack of control in subcontracted packaging. The affair received wide press coverage throughout the country in the 70s since many babies died or were gravely injured with mental handicap as a result. The first symptom of intoxication was a redness on the baby's bottom. Certain parents were not unduly worried at first or assumed it was simply a skin irritation and increased the dose of the talcum power to sooth the skin. This case was one of the first in which health authorities launched a systematic hunt for a killer product as soon as statistics started showing abnormalities. Most countries now have alert bureaux of some type.

Many other abuses were denounced, bringing forth a sense of consumer impotence vis-à-vis practices and relations unfavourable to them: false advertising, products not in line with what was promised, non-adherence to delivery dates, shoddy workmanship, abuses in door-to-door selling, lack of guarantees...

In general consumers questioned the adequacy of products in terms of their real needs.Indeed, product characteristics are defined unilaterally by manufacturers or the deliverers of services, but do they really meet the expectations of the buyer in terms of quality, durability or adaptation to the expected usage? With mass production, products are conceived and manufactured in advance. Thus needs must, to some extent, adapt to the product.

This last point is probably one of the paradoxes of the society of abundance created after World War II and the high growth of demand. To meet the needs of the greatest number of people, mass production and distribution requirements have resulted in a standardisation of products not allowing for the satisfaction of the precise needs of each person.

The techniques of modern marketing used by manufacturers (market studies and surveys, advertising, packaging, direct marketing...) and distributors were also singled out by consumer movements. They denounced the reign of the gadget and the futile object, of consumer fads and the manipulation of the consumer, of encouraging him to buy without justification.

▌Organised reaction by consumers

☐ *Origins*

The abuses of manufacturers and distributors mentioned above at first brought about sporadic and badly organised consumer reactions which progressively focused on common claims. Based initially on the desire to inform and defend the individual, consumer associations later sought a more general perspective, using a more offensive strategy, aimed at modifying the economic functioning of society at times picking up themes close to those later advanced by the ecologists.

The United States was the obvious birthplace of consumer defence organisations. The first dates back to 1936. Called the Consumer's Union, it remains today among the largest, with a membership of 150 000, and there are nearly a million subscribers to its magazine. However, modern consumerism truly came into its own in the 60s with the arrival of Ralph Nader. A lawyer by training, he created the Public Interest Research Groups in 1970, defended consumers wronged by the American industrial giants and won many trials. A year later he founded another organisation, the Public Citizen, with action in mind. The word 'crusader' provides a fairly accurate description of the character of this man, with his reputation of asceticism, incorruptibility and hard work. These qualities were such that personal attacks by General Motors at the outset (efforts to discredit him with consumers) in no way diminished him and indeed strengthened his reputation. His first action was against General Motors, which was forced to recall and abandon a car named the Corvair for safety reasons.

Ralph Nader's main objectives were:

- to defend consumers, particularly through legal action, against the abuses of a consumer society. Damages and interests paid by industry after litigation were a source of financing for other action.
- to reinforce anti-trust legislation and fight on behalf of small and middle-sized firms, which are deemed to be closer to the needs of the consumer.
- to redefine growth objectives and the priorities given to the use of resources.

Obviously this last aim, involved as it is with unbridled consumption and wasting resources, is close to those of the ecologists. However, his action was not to be interpreted as questioning the capitalist system but rather was aimed at developing free enterprise and encouraging competition.

Three methods of public intervention

- A standardisation effort aimed at influencing the physical and economic protection of consumers provided by laws and standards. The main areas covered are product safety, advertising, sales (consumer credit, sales contracts, false advertising, door-to-door selling ...). Other legislation concerns services, product durability, after-sales service, but these areas are not completely covered.
- Institutional action by the State through specialised services in ministries, ministerial groups and organisations and, last, coordination bodies including consumer associations. At the beginning of the 80s seven countries set up a Ministry of Consumer Affairs: Australia, Austria, Canada, Spain, France, Norway and Great Britain. The Office of Consumer Affairs in the United States can be considered a kind of junior Ministry of Consumer Affairs, although the fight to establish a new federal agency for consumer protection ended in defeat in 1978 and was one of the first strong signals that the public acceptance of the theory that consumerism needed to be active and in defence of consumers against big business had peaked. Other nations, such as the Scandinavian countries, have set up independent mediation boards. The other aspect of institutionalisation consists of measures allowing consumers to be consulted and represented in the elaboration of government polices on consultative committees.
- Action on behalf of consumer organisations to further their development (financial subsidies, access to television, increased possibility of taking legal action against manufacturers, free legal counsel, technical means...).

Some aspects of consumer protection in specific countries

United States

The United States is considered the cradle of consumerism, which arose in its present form during the 60s. Kennedy was among the first to promote the idea of protecting the consumer. In 1962, during a message to Congress, he proclaimed the four fundamental rights of the consumer: safety, information, choice, and representativeness. The road chosen by the United States was essentially legislative with the passing by Congress of many laws over the years and establishment of new federal agencies and the widening of the field of others. Among federal agencies dealing with consumer matters, one can find:

Consumer goods	Federal Trade Commission
	Consumer Product Safety Commission
	National Highway Safety Administration
	Food and Drug Administration
Environment	Environmental Protection Agency
Safety in the workplace	Occupational Safety and Health Administration
Energy	Department of Energy

Great Britain

The British consumer movement is basically pragmatic. The weight of general legislation is lighter than in countries such as France, and, in contrast, greater importance is given to decentralisation and consultation, rather than to repression. Institutional relations link the Confederation of British Industry to the National Consumer Council, the Office of Fair Trading and consumer associations. In this approach can be seen the influence of Common Law, a legal system based on jurisprudence rather than general and abstract law. In cases of constantly changing societal attitudes the system gains in efficiency over that of written law. The various public organisations that exist have a flexible structure, which is decentralised and can react quickly. Last, we should mention the access to justice of the individual consumer which is facilitated by the small claims procedure.

It is therefore not surprising, under such conditions, to note that employer organisations are hostile to reinforced legislation, notably from the European Parliament.

It is the Ministry of Commerce which is directly concerned with consumer questions. Three organisations comprise the Ministry: the National Consumer Council, the Office of Fair Trading and the Consumer Council of Nationalised Industries.

- The NCC was set up in 1975 with the aim of watching over consumer interests and being their standard- bearer with government, nationalised industries, public and private services and industry. It is financed by the government but remains completely independent. Its function is to propose legislation. Its credibility rests on its impartiality and competence. It is not an arbitration council to solve disputes.
- The Office of Fair Trading encourages commercial ventures to establish 'good conduct codes' to improve quality or resolve conflict. This body does not directly handle individual consumer complaints either. For such action, it informs the Consumer Protection Advisory Committee, which emanates from the Secretary of State for Consumer Affairs.
- Consumer Councils of Nationalised Industries (NICC) are official bodies whose members are appointed by government. Their main task is to examine requests for information and consumer claims.

Other non-public bodies taking into account consumer interests exist in the United Kingdom. These are professional organisations. Under the impetus of the OFT, many professional associations have drawn up codes of conduct to which members of the profession adhere. This is an example of self-discipline. With *Which?* the U.K.

also enjoys what is probably the strongest consumer magazine in Europe.

France

In France more than a dozen organisations operate on the national level. Some of them were created shortly after World War II and others during the 70s. They emanate from the cooperative, family or feminist movements or from trade unions. Closely linked to the Christian or socialist currents, their primary activity has been to challenge and encourage families to consume better in order to live better.

The oldest of these organisations are those which have come from the cooperative movement, such as the Co-op group, a industrial and commercial association of members who put their interests in common, more or less in line with the famous model of the Cooperative Wholesale Societies established in England by the Rochdale Pioneers in the 19th century. These were inspired by the humanitarian socialism of Robert Owen in reaction to the social brutality of conservative manufacturers and merchants. Their presence on both sides of the barrier has left such groups open to reproach by other organisations.

Not before the 1960s did the various organisations mentioned above turn to defending the consumer *per se*. At the time apathy by the public at large towards consumerist ideas mixed with reticence and even hostility from manufacturers. Legislation setting up the Institut National de la Consommation in 1968 was adopted with some difficulty.

A characteristic of most associations in France is their small number of militant members, their limited financial means (public subsidies are very small and are sometimes seen as a threat to independence), their great dispersal and, last, their relative weakness compared with their Anglo-Saxon counterparts.

The Co-op group, which was the only consumerist group operating in the market place against capitalist competition, is now dismantled, as other and more efficient retailers operating for money are generally offering equal or better terms. It is symbolic that FNAC, the famous

French retailer of 'cultural' goods, which had been set up as a white collar cooperative by people with strong socialist views, turned to the Co-op Group in the 70s to guarantee its philosophical independence, and it is ironic that it is now a 'regular' retailer fighting Virgin Megastores as its major competitor and facing problems with its employees, who would not have considered themselves as working for a capitalist trust. This is another sign of the evolution of consumerism towards roles less basic than the search for a lower cost of living and the defence of the economic interests of the working class.

However the historical link between the defence of consumer interests and that of working class as such has been strong enough for the major trade unions to set up their own consumer organisations in the mid-seventies, arguing that the best consumer policy was better salaries, and ignoring the fact that consumers' interests could be in conflict with workers' rights, particularly as regards public services, and the right to strike for better salaries or working conditions against the right to have transportation when it has been prepaid, or even the right to go to work. As they have automatically made union members into members of their consumer organisations, they suddenly appeared as major actors sharing in public subsidies granted to consumer organisations on the basis of the number of members. That fact has not been very well accepted by the other organisations, and particularly by those considering themselves as purely consumerist, or without political objectives.

Notwithstanding their tradition of disagreements for very many reasons, essentially those relating to their origins or purposes, consumer unions in France have been obliged to come to agreements regarding certain objectives in order to optimise resources and manage the Insitut National de la Consommation (National Institute for Consumption). This public body was set up in 1968, largely through the will of the government. Defence of the consumer was then perceived as one means of bearing down on prices. The government had become conscious of the imbalance that existed between manufacturers and consumers. The INC was a government initiative which did not come about through public expectations or pressure.

The government of the early 70s saw the INC, a public body, as a tool of economic policy which could be put into the hands of consumer unions. The socialists, who were then in the opposition, would have preferred it to be seen as a technical institute belonging to the unions and solely at their disposal. An early difficulty arose from the fact that INC was financed to operate comparative testing and publish the results, and given by law access to prime time televisions. This ran into conflict with the activities of the Union Fédérale des Consommateurs (Federal Union of Consumers) founded in 1951, the only purely consumerist association in France. Its publication, *Que Choisir?*, is based on the British and American magazines *Which?* and *Consumer Report*. For years, it has accused INC as a government body of using its public charter giving it access to free T.V. to advertise its own publication, *50 Millions de consommateurs*, and to depend so much on it for financing that it has become a self justified body. The situation deteriorated to such a degree that in 1993 the Union Fédérale des Consommateurs sued the Institut National de la Consommation for unfair practices and disloyal competition.

In France the role of public bodies dealing with consumer affairs can be divided into four periods:

- from 1945 to 1960, slowly awareness grew of the consumer as an economic partner. In 1945 the Ministry of Economic Affairs set up an Office of Consumer Affairs. At the start of the 50s the CREDOC (Centre for Research and Documentation on Consumption) and the AFIEF (French Association for Information on Family Economics) were established.

- from 1960 to 1970 a more deliberate political will emerged with the setting up of the Comité National de la Consommation (National Committee for Consumption) in 1960, and the INC in 1968. The latter, much more than the CNC, was the true starting point of public action. Its triple role was as a testing centre, information office and consumer protection organisation. In 1976 a Secretariat of State for Consumer Affairs was set up, but as a unit of the Ministry of Economic Affairs with few means at its disposal. It disappeared in 1978 after having succeeded in passing major laws, in particular concerning the repression of consumer fraud in door to door selling, the creation of a cooling-off period when major purchases requiring credit were concerned and, as regards product safety, the establishment of a legal right for public authorities to organise compulsory product recalls in times of emergency. These were the years when products banned as unsafe in the United States, such as children's night-wear treated with the chemical code-named 'tris' that had been found to be a cause of skin cancer, were legally shipped to Europe, which then lacked adequate laws. Sadly enough, as soon as those products could be banned and recalled in Europe, in this case in France, they emerged in the third world at bargain prices...

- from 1970 to 1981 the government implemented legislation to protect consumers and to accelerate its movement into an economic partnership (a law passed in 1973 recognised that consumer associations had the right to defend members' rights in court and also improved the truth in advertising legislation by adding 'advertising misleading by nature' to the offence of 'false advertising').
- since 1981 France has become the sixth country to set up a Ministry of Consumer Affairs after Great Britain, Australia, Austria, Canada and Norway.

Sweden

The Swedish example, as a model of Northern European consumerism, rests mainly on two institutions having wide powers of injunction, somewhat similar to American models:

- a consumer Ombudsman, set up in 1971, whose role it is to be an intermediary between manufacturers and consumers and to arbitrate litigation. His intervention procedures are

very flexible, creating maximum efficiency. The implementation procedure is very simple. His intervention with manufacturers is often sufficient to resolve the dispute. For more complex affairs the Ombudsman sends the file to a Market Tribunal.
- the Market Tribunal has parity jurisdiction and often hands down a judgement of dissuasive economic penalties.

To that can be added a complete legislative arsenal. Stress is placed on prevention rather than repression. Sweden is thus probably the one country where consumer protection is best assured and where the constraints weighing on manufacturers and distributors are the greatest. Consumer associations have a relatively reduced role because of the efficient structures which have been implemented.

Japan

In Japan consumer action was more virulent than in the United States in that it used the legal weapon rather than economic pressure, which resulted in the voting in of legislation. This action was largely directed by women's associations, which are very active groups with high membership rates. Their main action concerned prices, in the hopes of forcing them down considerably. They therefore produced and distributed cosmetic products which were one tenth the price of the others. An action to boycott the purchase of television sets, lasting eight months, also encouraged manufacturers to lower their prices.

Europe and the European Union

Within the EU three organisations comprise the various national groups: the European Office of Consumer Unions, Euro-Co-op and the Committee of Family Organisations within the European Community. Since 1973 there also has been a Consultative Committee of Consumers, made up of representatives of trade unions and consumers. On the legislative level, there is legislation protecting consumers, which can serve as a basis for the various legal texts in force in member countries. A resolution of the Council of the Community in 1975 determines the real programme of consumer protection and information(safety rights, protection of economic interests, reparation of damages, the right to information and education). Another means of action involves standardisation, which is often an extension to all members of the standards of one country on which the others agree. Actually this is another difficult point in creating consumer protection at the European level, as some member states consider that to agree on the norms of another state is to give firms operating in that country an unfair economic advantage in the open competition within the Community.

Beyond the strict framework of the Community, the Council of Europe (which includes the Western European nations, whether nor not they are members of the Community) has established a Charter for Consumer Protection.

■ Reaction of the manufacturers

The rise in power of consumer defence groups and the change of legislation towards better protection have naturally led manufacturers to take account of the new situation in their environment.

This was not an immediate result however, and the first reactions were often disdain or aggression (as was the case during Ralph Nader's effort against General Motors). Manufacturers who are challenged as to the quality, price or distribution methods of their products or services generally adopt a defensive attitude. Some feel persecuted, victims of both government and consumer groups. They have come to realise that a purely defensive attitude is futile or harmful (in case of a lively campaign or a boycott) and that consumers are expecting solutions.

Four distinct attitudes can be discerned:

- A wait-and-see attitude, reflecting either scorn or a certain anxiety vis-à-vis the consumerist movement or the anti-company campaign. The firm doesn't know the effects of the campaign targeted against it and doesn't know how to deal with it.

- An attitude of individual defence by the manufacturer incriminated who will counter the attack either through a disclaimer or on a blow-by-blow basis, with perhaps an attempt at discreditation. At this stage, there is not yet solidarity on the part of other members of the profession, who are sometimes only too happy at the misfortunes of a competitor. It should be noted that *many legal actions on misleading advertising have historically been introduced by competitors rather than by consumer organisations.*

- An attitude of collective defence by the profession. Other manufacturers have understood that they too can be attacked and decide to act rapidly as a group to develop synergy and greater weight. This phase does not always occur.

- An attitude of adaptation, corresponding to acceptance of the idea that it is better to go along and take into account consumer interests as expressed in the protest.

Whether done on their own initiative or through constraint, manufacturers today have by and large accepted consumer demands, as attested by the implementation of consumer services. The pattern was developed in the United States in the 1960s and has slowly spread to Europe, more or less successfully. To recognise the validity of consumer demands presupposes deep reflection on the part of a company, and perhaps calling into question and reorienting the commercial function.

The two principal positive answers on the part of firms are therefore self-discipline and consultation. Self-discipline is not limited to the strict observation of legal regulations but rather presupposes a voluntary decision to improve the quality of goods and services as well as to provide information. Thus were established professional unions or bodies entrusted with defining objectives and supervising internal activities. With regard to information, an example of private initiative is that of the Bureau de Vérification de la Publicité (Office of Advertising Verification) in

France, which includes advertising media, advertisers and advertising agencies. Labelling standards have also been devised. Consumer consultation has led to collective agreements and new structures (private structures such as the above-mentioned consumers services or semi-public bodies such as the Swedish Ombudsman).

However, even today the complaints of manufacturers and retailers vis à vis consumer groups are many and the realistic approach taken by several firms does not eliminate all claims or complaints.

■ A new deal for the consumer?

Undeniable progress has been made in thirty years of struggle and the preoccupations of consumers have been integrated by firms into their quality programmes. We can ask ourselves today whether consumerism still needs to exist. Indeed, as mentioned previously, public thinking has progressed through legislation and encouragement and companies have made a considerable effort to understand the consumer better and to develop consumer services. An extra step has been taken with the search for quality, particularly under the prodding of the Japanese. It is obvious that the cost of quality control is not as high as has been said, and that, on the contrary, the cost of the absence of quality has continued to rise (after-sales service, replacement of defective parts, loss of image ...). Quality objectives have gone from a small, but set, percentage of accepted defects in parts to total quality. Action is taken directly on the industrial process and, in certain cases, it is the entire organisation and the company culture which have had to be modified. The move is from less control to a conception of quality from the outset as regards designs and production procedures.

Through the search for quality, we can see how marketing has integrated consumer preoccupations. It can also be seen that the great liberal trend of the 80s, which saw the privatisation of many public services, was accompanied by an improvement in service and a move into commercial law of that which was administrative until now.

During the decade certain company executives have criticised the perverse effects of consumer protection, particularly excessive legislation. Legislation has accumulated, and the yoke of an excessively rigid legal framework can have an opposite effect to that intended. There is an obvious criticism of the excessive cost and inefficiency sometimes ascribed to public bodies in charge of supervising consumer interests. A certain deregulation has been seen as the way to make progress. Direct consultation between the private sector and consumer movements has become a way of resolving conflict. The effect of deregulating monopolies is to reintroduce competition and to make the constraints weighing on the commercial and technical processes more flexible.

Nevertheless that must be put into context because we have seen certain negative effects of deregulation, and this is still an area of conflicting views which are often based on quasi doctrinal beliefs. The idea of collective consumer agreements now seems obsolete since they are of limited use and can present a risk of rigidity. Last, there is a debate on the appearance of neo-corporatism linked to deregulation. The adoption of class action, as it exists in the United States, would make it possible to encounter these negative effects in many countries where such action is not yet legally possible.

It can be estimated that today few areas of confrontation remain for consumers. As soon as consumers had the impression of being taken into account and better treated by companies, violent collective action, such as previously existed, lost its legitimacy. It is also perhaps due to the multiplication and therefore the fragmentation of organisations, which sometimes became mutually competitive.

That does not mean consumer struggles have ceased but simply that they have found new ground with other preoccupations. The appearance of green products is an example. Today expectations centre on the idea of environment, public service, opening hours... It seems that the non-competitive sectors are those where progress is still to be made. Paradoxically, the government which makes it possible to improve consumer protection through legislation and standards is itself badly served. We are perhaps seeing the birth of a more responsible consumerism. The distinction between worker, consumer and citizen is gradually disappearing. The individual is considered as a whole and preoccupations of general interest have become of utmost importance: the environment, urban and rural development, transportation....

In previous decades better protection was achieved by cutting across the many dimensions of human life and targeting abuses one by one. This approach has been so successful that it now appears out of date. The current trend is toward reglobalisation. It is also the consequence of the shift of the economy from products to services. Consumerism in services has long existed and has resulted in improvements when clear promises were involved, such as in banking or utilities. Things will be more difficult when we talk about being consumers of a better life.

This potentially leads to new fights for global rights. Is a right to a job a right of a citizen or that of a consumer of the economic side of political services? When there is failure to provide decent housing in a country, is it economic hardship or the failure of government to deliver on socially prepaid basic rights due to their natural consumers? What about the evolution of the Welfare state across Europe? What about pensions? It seems that everywhere it is the idea of consumers' rights that prevails. We are leaning towards the consumption side rather than towards the pride of contributing to progress for all. We could see this in the 'cocooning' and later in the 'burrowing' attitudes which have recently become fashionable, indicating a return to 'me and mine' as opposed to a larger social role. And in dealing with civil hardships we will not easily switch our attitudes from those of wronged consumers who can demand compensations and redress. We will increasingly be calling upon the services of lawyers for this.

The current scandal of blood contaminated with the AIDS virus spreading over several European countries will probably become the symbol of complex and modern consumerist cases. There is a reminder that products and services will not always be naturally safe without controls and adequate sanctions. The idea is growing that not-for-profit and sacrosanct services are consumed just like anything else and have to be held accountable as such, since they are bought directly or indirectly. There is the obvious reality that government regulators have failed in their mission, sometimes because the standards of responsibility applying to free enterprise do not always apply to civil servants. In the future, consumerism will extend much beyond truth in buying and selling goods or services, and into the quality of the protection provided to the individual by the society in which he or she lives. Perhaps as much resistance can be expected from those who feel that they are unfairly held accountable for accidental failures of regulation as was felt by many company executives twenty to thirty years ago. That may turn out to be the consumerist challenge of the turn of the century.

Daniel Tixier is Professor of Marketing at E.S.S.E.C. where he holds the Chair of Consumer Products

Thanks are expressed to Manuel Samakh, Research Assistant, and Jane Triaureau for translation, editing and typing.

■ References

Baker, M. and Tixier, D. (1980), 'Consumerism, Public Policy and Consumer Protection', University of Strathclyde and Social Science Research Council.

Belkin, L. (1985), Consumerism and Business Learn Together', *The New York Times* (13 April).

Bihl, L. (1989), *Le Droit penal de la consommation*, Paris: Nathan.

Bloom, P. N. and Greyser, S. A., (1981), 'The Maturing of Consumerism', *Harvard Business Review*, (November–December).

Bon, J. (ed.) (1980), *L' Etat et la publicité*, Paris: Ceressec / Fnege.

Feldman, L. P. (1980), *Consumer Protection: Problems and Prospects*, 2nd edition, St Paul, Minnesota: West Publishing Co.

Garbett, T. F. (1988), 'What to Do When Disaster Strikes', in *How to Build a Corporation's Identity and Project its Image*, Lexington, Mass.: Lexington Books.

Tixier, D. (1979), *Le Consumérisme en action*, Paris: Ceressec / Fnege.

Tixier, D. (1986), 'Consumérisme: la paix armée', *Revue Française de Gestion* (March–May).

Tixier, D. (1983/84), 'Perspectives du développement du consumérisme et de son impact sur la communication marketing', *Revue Française de Marketing 95*.

■ Chapter 19 ■

International Marketing: It's a Mad, Mad, Mad, Mad World

Michael C. McDermott and K. C. Chan

▌ Introduction – *Back to the future*

This is the third edition of *Marketing: Theory and Practice* and yet this edition is the first to feature a chapter on International Marketing. When the second edition was published (1983), research in international marketing was fragmentary and exploratory without a strong theoretical framework (Boddewyn, 1981; Cavusgil and Nevin, 1981; and, Albaum and Peterson, 1984). However, Aulakh and Kotaabe (1993) in their article 'An Assessment of Theoretical and Methodological Development in International Marketing: 1980–1990' concluded that there had been 'substantial progress both in the development of conceptual frameworks for the studies conducted and in the empirical testing of concepts and theories'. Their detailed review of 893 published international marketing articles showed that researchers had focused on the following issues:

- the marketing environment (155 articles)
- Marketing management (452 articles)
- the internationalisation process (87 articles)
- consumer behaviour (84 articles)
- collaborative business arrangements (49 articles), and
- globalisation (66 articles).

Accompanying this trend has been a large increase in the number of international marketing textbooks on the market. The purpose of this chapter is not to attempt to condense textbooks of more than 900 pages (e.g. Czinkota and Ronkainen, 1993) to one chapter, but rather to present the authors' own views of the major issues that international marketers may need to address in a future which is increasingly difficult to predict. Moreover, as will be seen later, the international marketing environment (IME) is complex and subject to rapid change. The international marketing manager needs to be future-oriented. If the applauded practices of today may well be the derided ones of tomorrow, then theoretical developments to explain yesterday's behaviour are already obsolete. This has major implications for the academic and business communities. Each is represented in the writing partnership of this article. Moreover, one is Occidental, the other is Oriental. Nevertheless, despite such differences, the authors share a common vision of global business in the future. Their views, presented below, may prove to be woefully misguided, but this chapter is not yet another contribution to prescription learning. This chapter aims to achieve action-learning – where the readers' horizons are extended and they formulate their *own* vision of the challenges facing international marketers in the future.

The literature on international marketing management discusses at great length the adaptation versus standardisation issue. In doing so, there is the danger of losing sight of the fact that the international marketing manager needs to ensure that each element of the marketing mix is consistent with the company's objectives.

The International Marketing manager is essentially concerned with ensuring that the company analyses the IME in order to select the most appropriate country market(s) and having done so, for each market determine:

- the market entry mode which produces the desired combination of control, cost and risk;
- the product(s) to sell in the preferred market and what modification(s) if any is required and how it should be positioned;

- the means of promoting the product to reach and appeal to the desired target;
- the channels of distribution required to make the product available on a basis compatible with customer demand;
- the price necessary to meet the goals of the organisation.

The International Marketing Manager must therefore concern himself with three broad areas:

- the international marketing environment
- the international market entry mode
- international marketing management

The international marketing environment – *Alien*

International marketing as a form of human endeavour is a highly complex and high-risk undertaking. The uncontrollable environmental factors far exceed the controllables. The international firm has to operate and develop its strategies whilst embedded in the environmental forces of the global economy and of its constituent parts at the regional, national, firm and intra-firm levels. It has to contend with these environmental forces.

Consideration of the IME is of vital importance for all firms, whether large or small, engaged in international marketing. Firms screen the international marketing environment in order to identify current and future marketing opportunities and threats so that they can prioritise markets and allocate resources appropriately. The IME consists of the following elements:

- the demographic environment
- the economic environment
- the socio-cultural environment
- the legal environment
- the political environment
- the technological environment
- the financial environment
- the ecological environment, and
- the competitive environment

The techniques for market screening can vary from the complex to the most straightforward. Obviously, the larger firm with more resources can afford to devote much more time and resources to this exercise than the small owner-managed enterprise. Figure 19.1 summarises a complex market screening process. However, for the SME a much more straightforward screening approach may be appropriate. One author was advising a small Scottish company which manufactured environmentally friendly personal soaps. The company had very low production capacity

Figure 19.1. *A formal approach to country/market screening*

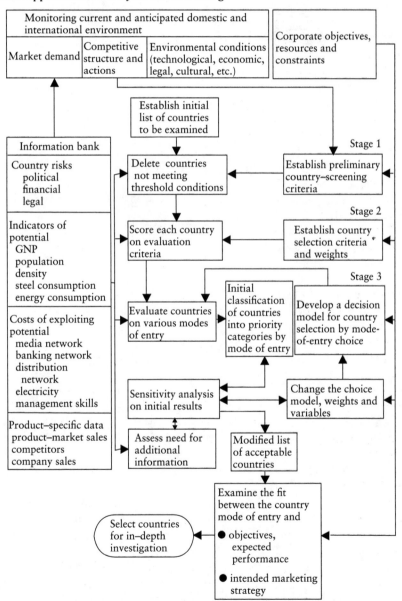

Source: S. P. Douglas and C. S. Craig, *International Marketing Research*, Englewood Cliffs, NJ: Prentice-Hall (1983), Figure 4.2.

Table 19.1. A review of the innovation-related internationalisation models

Bilkey and Tesar [1977]	Cavusgil [1980]	Czinkota [1982]	Reid [1981]
Stage 1 Management is not interested in exporting	Stage 1 Domestic marketing: The firm sells only to the home market	Stage 1 The completely uninterested firm	Stage 1 Export awareness: Problem of opportunity recognition arousal of need
Stage 2 Management is willing to fill unsolicited orders, but makes no effort to explore the feasibility of active exporting	Stage 2 Pre-export stage: The firm searches for information and evaluates the feasibility of undertaking exporting	Stage 2 The partially interested firm	Stage 2 Export intention: Motivation, attitude, beliefs, and expectancy about export
Stage 3 Management actively explores the feasibility of active exporting	Stage 3 Experimental involvement: The firm starts exporting on a limited basis to some psychologically close country	Stage 3 The exploring firm Stage 4 The experimental firm	Stage 3 Export trial: Personal experience from limited exporting
Stage 4 The firm exports on an experimental basis to some psychologically close country	Stage 4 Active involvement: Exporting to more new countries – direct exporting – increase in sales volume	Stage 5 The experienced small exporter	Stage 4 Export evaluation: Results from engaging in exporting
Stage 5 The firm is an experienced exporter	Stage 5 Committed involvement: Management constantly makes choices in allocating limited resources between domestic and foreign markets	Stage 6 The experienced large exporter	Stage 5 Export acceptance: Adoption of exporting/rejection of exporting
Stage 6 Management explores the feasibility of exporting to other more psychologically distant countries			

Source: O. Anderson, 'On the Internationalisation Process of Firms: A Critical Analysis', *Journal of International Business Studies* (Second Quarter) (1993), pp. 209–231.

and it was debatable as to whether it was ready to internationalise. Nevertheless, it was a reactive exporter (see Table 19.1 for a review of internationalisation models), exporting small amounts to a large number of countries. Having spoken to the owner and established a screening criterion, four screening variables were selected which very quickly reduced the number of target markets to a manageable proportion (see Table 19.2).

In order to appreciate the challenge of environmental analysis facing the firm engaged in international marketing simply consider the world of ten years ago when the second edition of *Marketing: Theory and Practice* was published:

- the EC consisted of just nine countries and there was a clear ideological divide between western and Eastern Europe with the Berlin Wall a potent symbol of that divide
- Mrs Thatcher and President Reagan brought Britain and America's 'special relationship' to a new peak, with both strongly united in their condemnation of 'the evil empire' – the Soviet Union

Table 19.2. *Simple country screening process for Scottish manufacturer of environmentally friendly personal soaps*

Stage	Criterion	Retain
1	Countries with low-risk financial environment	All EC countries All EFTA countries North America Japan Asia's four 'tigers' Australia, New Zealand
2	Countries where English language is an acceptable business language legally acceptable	Benelux, Eire, Germany Denmark, Italy Scandinavia Japan Asia's four tigers Australia, New Zealand
3	Countries with: population of at least 10m with high population density levels; or, those with at least three cities with combined population in excess of ten million	Netherlands, Germany, Italy, USA, Canada Japan South Korea and Taiwan Australia
4	Countries where 'Green' movement is developed, or environment is a major political issue	Netherlands, Germany, USA Australia, Japan, South Korea, Taiwan

Source: Authors' data.

- Neil Kinnock replaced Michael Foot as leader of Britain's Labour Party, and 31-year-old Tony Blair became a Member of Parliament
- IBM was about to transform the computer industry with its PC and gain a dominant market position. Compaq had just been founded and Michael Dell was still at high school.
- Apartheid was still government policy in South Africa and Nelson Mandela was still in prison
- in Latin America and other developing nations many countries continued to be led by dictators and the economies were experiencing negative growth and rampant inflation as the international debt crisis took its toll
- doctors warned of the dangers posed by a recently discovered illness, anti-immune deficiency syndrome (AIDS)
- Michael Jackson's latest album *Thriller* had broken all sales records and international companies (e.g. PepsiCo) paid him vast sums to endorse their products
- chewing gum was available in Singapore

How times have changed! Of course, uncertainty is an inherent part of the marketing environment, whether domestic or international, and companies need to confront this turbulence. Some of the key ones which we expect to come to the fore are discussed below.

The superpowers and interdependence – *Sleeping with the enemy*

There is some concern that Asia will become an arena of intense economic and political rivalry between Japan and the US. Both also depend on the Middle East for vital supplies and Japan's and the US's mutually supporting roles as financier and warrior respectively in the Gulf War confirmed their status in the 'new order'. Should such rivalry intensify in the scramble for Asia, then the current win-win relationship may deteriorate with dreadful consequences to a zero-sum

game, in which each party seizes every opportunity to gain at the expense of the other. Fukuyama's (1992) thesis that with the end of the Cold War 'history is dead' thus missed the point; the Cold War was the equivalent of the card-game 'Snap' involving two parties – a tedious affair requiring no skill. Poker is the new game – there are a number of players, the stakes are high, and brain power will triumph over 'brawn'. International marketers thus face an international environment of unprecedented complexity.

During the Cold War the nations of Western and Eastern Europe and their allies were united by their mutual terror of the other side. The removal of this ideological barrier and its accompanying military threat has already resulted in the re-emergence of more traditional divisions (e.g. cultural, ethnic, religious, racial and territorial). This manifests itself not simply in international conflict but internal strife (e.g. Rwanda, Yemen) and perhaps separatism. For the first time in centuries, economic and military hegemony are not enjoyed by the one nation, but instead are vested for the time being in Japan and the US respectively, with Europe struggling to compete and China emerging as a potential rival in both areas.

Regionalism and separatism – *Someone to watch over me*

Economic theory still assumes that the sovereign national state is the sole, or at least the predominant unit, and the only one capable of effective economic policy. But increasingly decision-making power is shifting to regional political centres (e.g. the European Parliament). The 1990s witnessed the speed with which the world's trading nations grouped themselves into trade blocs – and generated a mountain of acronyms – which will have an enormous impact on the multilateral trading system hitherto guided by GATT. The European Community (EC) led the way, establishing a Single European Market among its then twelve members to form the European Union (EU), and also an even mightier European

Economic Accord (EEA) that took in the seven members of the EFTA. In January 1992 the ASEAN Free Trade Association (AFTA) was formed. The US, Canada and Mexico agreed in the August to form the North American Free Trade Association (NAFTA). Countries in both AFTA and NAFTA belong to the same larger grouping in the Asia Pacific Economic Community (APEC). A key focus of the 1990s and beyond will be how these groupings deal with one another. In the long run, regionalism may well be a positive development for the world. Unrestricted trade within regions and managed trade between regions may well be the long run route to freer world trade.

One interpretation of these events is that it is simply too big a leap to move from national economies to a world economy and that it is necessary to take smaller intermediate steps first, and quasi-trading blocs combined with managed trade, may be just such a necessary intermediate step (Thurow, 1992). However, an alternative perspective is that countries may break up as particular areas (e.g. the Basque region and Catalonia in Spain; Brittany in France; Scotland and Wales in the UK) become increasingly disenchanted with their current 'national' identity and a political system which precludes effective representation of their views. Thus, it is the authors' view that at least in Europe the nation state is facing a scissors-cut effect, whereby on the one hand it is being pulled towards a much larger regional centre, whilst simultaneously moving towards fragmentation (e.g. Andorra, population 47,000, nestling in the Pyrenees became the 184th member of the United Nations). Already Freddie Heineken, owner of the Dutch brewer, has proposed a Europe of over 75 countries each with a population of five to ten million based upon ethnic and linguistic history (Naisbitt, 1994).

In the past, large size was seen as an advantage at the macro (e.g. national) and micro (e.g. corporate) level. Reality challenges this conventional view. Tiny Singapore is the role model of national efficiency. Its critics tend to denigrate its achievements by arguing that it has the advantage of small size. Precisely! And as more and more

global consumers witness the possibilities that can be achieved through national 'downsizing' or 'rightsizing', then they will not settle for the inefficient 'status quo', which has a relatively short history.

The large nation state is thus likely to prove a temporary aberration. This can be seen in the growing number of UN member countries: 51 in 1945, 100 in 1960, 159 in 1984, 184 in 1993. This trend is likely to accelerate as democracy spreads and the opportunity for self-rule arises. As Naisbitt (1994) contends: 'The bigger the world economy, the more powerful its smallest players.'

The overwhelming feature of international marketing is the ever changing IME driven by internationalisation, deregulation, consumer awareness and technicalisation (see Table 19.3). International companies need to be better and faster at analysing, comprehending, and responding to the IME. This places great demands upon the international organisation. 'Think global, act local' is only one tension to be mastered. The world class company is characterised by its use of yin and yang forces or dualities (i.e. properties that seem contradictory or paradoxical, but which in fact are complementary) to obtain competitive advantage (see Table 19.4).

International market entry modes

International acquisitions – Fatal attraction or Lethal weapon?

The need to master dualities has manifested itself in a radical departure from corporate strategy of the 1960s and 1970s. In the 1960s and 1970s, the order of the day was *business diversification, geographical consolidation*. This saw the creation of conglomerates in the USA and Europe, especially in the former as firms such as ITT and United Technologies expanded rapidly through domestic acquisitions. Expansion overseas took the form of exporting and/or

Table 19.3.   *Four strong market forces that create change*

Market	→	Change Dynamic	→	Resulting Environment
• Internationalisation		• Global Factory and Global Markets		• Greater Turbulence
				• Greater Uncertainty
				• Greater Complexity
• Deregulation		• Reduction of Barriers to Entry		• Greater Rates of Change
				• Greater Ambiguity
• Consumer Awareness		• Sophisticated and Discerning Buyers		• Decreased Stability in Structures, Markets, and the Workforce
• Technicalisation		• Access to Specialised Technologies		• Decreased Utility of Rules and Procedures
				• Decreased Utility of History to Predict Future Events

Source: S. A. Stumpf and T. P. Mullen, *Taking Charge: Strategic Leadership in the Middle Game,*
Englewood Cliffs, NJ: Prentice-Hall (1992), pp. 22.

greenfield investments. The latter was often necessary in developing countries which remained inward-oriented and had an import-substitution policy (e.g. Indonesia).

Each international market entry mode is characterised by different degrees of commitment, control and risk. Exporting scores low on each count, but foreign direct investment scores highly. However, perhaps the most costly and risky type of investment is the international acquisition and despite this drawback it was of paramount importance in the late 1980s to virtually every large international western firm – and the more adventurous Japanese (e.g. Bridgestone, Fujitsu, Matsushita, and Sony). MNEs based in Asia's NIEs (e.g. Acer, Hong Kong and Shanghai Bank) have also resorted to this approach.

In short, during the second half of the 1980s the corporate fad was for *business consolidation, geographical diversification*, where firms aimed to become global leaders in relatively narrowly defined areas. Hence international marketing assumed an unprecedented importance, especially when firms believed that their position in any part of the Triad (i.e. North America, Europe, Japan) was influenced by their performance in the other two.

Positions of global leadership could be and were achieved by undertaking large international acquisitions and the formation of strategic alliances. Attaining this status required ownership of a stable of successful brands. The structures of entire industries – from advertising to agro-chemicals, cars to confectionery, telecommunications to tyres – were transformed by this process and often it resulted in higher concentration levels. For example in 1985 the USA was the home country to five of the world's top ten tyre companies and Goodyear was the industry leader. By the end of the decade, four were owned by non-US multinationals and France's Michelin had overtaken Goodyear.

During the latter part of the 1980s a number of features were dominant among MNEs from developed countries:

- the strategy was international expansion into other developed country markets
- the means was international acquisitions

- the driver was best-selling brands that were already or had the potential to become global brands

Thus by the 1990s a number of industries were essentially dominated by four or five global giants.

Retrenchment in developed country economies – *Honey I shrunk the business!*

However, as firms bought market share they also acquired duplication of functions. Therefore in

Table 19.4. *Some common dualities in today's complex organisations*

Competition	Partnership
Differentiation	Integration
Loose	Tight
Control	Entrepreneurship
Planned	Opportunistic
Formal	Informal
Vision	Reality
Decentralization	Centralization
Business Logic	Technical Logic
Analysis	Intuition
Delegation	Control
Individuality	Teamwork
Action	Reflection
Change	Continuity
Formal	Informal
Top-down	Bottom-up
Tolerance	Forthrightness
Flexibility	Focus

Source: P. A. L. Evans and Y. Doz, 'Dualities: A Paradigm for Human Resource and Organizational Development in Complex Multinationals', in V. Pucik, N. M. Tichy and C. K. Barnett (eds), *Globalizing Management: Creating and Leading the Competitive Organization*, New York: John Wiley (1992), p. 86.

pursuing the strategy outlined above, firms were progressing in that they expanded their brand portfolios and/or entered new markets, but they were at the same time adversely affecting their cost base by creating unnecessary duplication of activities. Moreover, they bought extra capacity just as the developed world was entering a period of severe economic recession brought about by the transition from an industrial (second wave) to an information society (third wave) where knowledge replaced capital as the strategic resource (Naisbitt and Aburdene, 1992).

Now these firms need to cut away such duplication, and position themselves to take advantage of the international marketing realities of the 1990s. The latter entails a quite different approach from just a few years ago:

- the strategy is retrenchment
- the means is divestment
- the driver is scale efficiencies

In developed country markets, the priority is to maximise economies of scale by plant specialisation. Leading companies in some industries are doing this on a regional basis (e.g. CPC, Nestlé, Unilever's restructuring programme announced in 1993/1994). In others (e.g. Ford in automobiles) regional specialisation dates to the late 1960s and it announced in the spring of 1994 a radical global specialisation programme.

These developments obviously have implications for international product policy, and for many firms it means unprecedented levels of product standardisation. In the past, MNEs such as Nestlé and Unilever had hundreds of plants world-wide and massive labour forces. In future they will require far fewer, but more capital-intensive plants. The technological advances in the machine-tool industry plus the availability of quality tools from low-cost sources (e.g. China, Taiwan) threaten to compound further the expected problem of massive unemployment. At the same time, these MNEs have just spent billions of dollars in the belief that the key to profitability was brand power. That may well prove a costly error, for consumers are now increasingly buying the own-label brands of retailers.

As the authors argue in a later chapter (see Chapter 21), a world-class firm must be world-class in manufacturing *and* marketing. Some global firms assume that their strength in the latter precludes the need to achieve the former. In pharmaceuticals, for example, the global giants have been those which were first-to-market with quality products. This is no longer enough to guarantee success. Cost considerations and appropriate distribution channels are now vital. Firms like Glaxo ignore the new reality at their peril. The world-class companies of the early 21st century will probably have a work force of just half the current level, produce twice as much, three times more profitably.

The authors' view is therefore that these developments could well result in unprecedented levels of unemployment in developed countries before the end of the 1990s. Ironically, the main source of new jobs in Europe is likely to be inward investment by the new generation of multinationals based in Asia's 'four tigers' and other economies such as Malaysia, Indonesia and even China. By the end of the decade, as many as five South Korean car producers could have a manufacturing presence in the EU, including electronics giant Samsung which only entered the industry in 1995. Moreover, by the year 2010, China – if it still exists as a single entity – could rank as the world's single largest foreign investor as its companies, currently state-owned, emulate the internationalisation strategy of Japanese, South Korean and Taiwanese multinationals.

▌ Boom time from the Amazon to the Ganges to the Yangtse – *La Belle équipe*

Developing countries have begun to attract significantly higher levels of investment due to the introduction of economic reforms and lower levels of political risk. After decades in the doldrums, the economies of China, India, and Latin America can be expected to prosper as never before. With an expected GDP growth rate of 6 per cent in 1995 they are growing twice as fast as

rich OECD countries. If this forecast is correct, Asia's GDP will have increased by 44 per cent on 1990. Latin America and Africa also have an impressive record, 16 and 11 per cent respectively.

Labour costs have increased rapidly in Asia's NIEs and so the 'tigers' have long since ceased to be cost-competitive for labour-intensive operations. These economies now represent the largest investors in the next generation of 'tigers' (i.e. south-east coast of China, Vietnam) that are now receptive to international marketing. Indeed the 'tigers' are forming partnerships with particular Provinces in China (e.g. Hong Kong with Guangdong, Taiwan with Fujien, Singapore with Suzhou, and South Korea with Shandong). Singapore has formed a 'Golden Triangle' with Johor in Malaysia and the Riau Islands in Indonesia. The formation of the these National Economic Territories (NETs), entities cutting across political boundaries to pool capital, manpower and natural resources (e.g. energy, water) is likely to spread from East Asia to other regions. As provinces develop partnerships with others in different countries, their commitment to, and membership of, a large nation state and remote central authority becomes increasingly meaningless. Moreover wide economic disparities within the nation state threaten its very fabric, as China may soon discover.

In 1993 China attracted more foreign direct investment than any other single country. As the coastal regions develop and the gap widens between urban and rural dwellers, and Provincial governments gain more power at the expense of central government, it is easy for a westerner to envisage the break up of China, where already the population of leading Provinces exceeds that of large western European nations.

In contrast to their strategy for developed country markets, the international firm has a quite different approach for successful developing country markets:

● the strategy is expansion
● the means is joint ventures with local partners and greenfield investments
● the driver is accessing markets which are open for the first time due to the introduction of

economic reforms that are characterised by liberalisation and privatisation

Collapse in the former Soviet Union – *Apocalypse now*

In contrast to the success of China (and more recently Vietnam), the former command economies of Eastern Europe (excluding Poland, the Czech Republic and Hungary) and the former Soviet Union have suffered a massive fall in output. Russia, for example, is locked in a vicious circle which could result in a 'social explosion' according to the country's Ministry of Economy (*Financial Times*, 9 May 1994). Since declaring independence in 1991, neighbouring Ukraine has been a model of mismanaging economic reform. This country, which has the world'st third-biggest nuclear arsenal and Europe's second largest conventional army, could so easily be the Bosnia of tomorrow. The West may come to rue gloating over the break-up of the former Soviet Union.

Conducting international marketing research on Eastern European economies is very frustrating due to the absence of reliable data. In the case of the former Soviet Union, the consolation is that these countries probably represent the world's least attractive national markets. Those with a more optimistic perspective would do well to heed the opening, though hardly uplifting line of the Ukranian national anthem: 'Ukraine is not dead – yet' (*The Economist*, 6 May 1994)

International product policy – *In the line of fire*

The first decision is whether or not to develop and invest in a brand name. The selected option tends to reflect the firm's stage of development and experience in international markets. Initially firms may chose to be a contract manufacturer to either another manufacturing concern, a major distributor, or both. This reliance on international sub-contracting is normally referred to as OEM sales (i.e. sales to original equipment manufacturers) and the emphasis is on maximising sales rather than profits. As economies of scale become more important, distributors more powerful, and customers less brand loyal, leading MNEs may have to overcome their traditional disdain for this type of international marketing. IBM in recent years, for example, which once refused to enter the OEM market, has revised its policy.

The second option is for the international marketer to rely instead on sales of its own branded products (i.e. these are referred to as own brand manufactured [OBM] sales). It entails though a number of other options which the international marketer has. In terms of international branding strategy the company has to decide whether to have:

- national brands for national markets;
- regional brands for regional markets; and,
- global brands for global markets.

For example, Europe's leading manufacturer of white goods is Electrolux and the company is renowned for having transformed the European domestic appliance industry from one which operated on a country-centred basis to a pan-European market. Nevertheless, Electrolux's branding strategy is such that it uses Electrolux as a global band, Zanussi as a regional brand in the European Union market, but it then has an array of more than 20 other brand names which may be best described as national brands in European countries.

Apart from deciding on the geographical coverage of individual brand names, the international marketer also has to decide upon the product coverage. Increasingly companies are recognising the opportunities of transferring highly successful brand names associated with one particular type of product to another related product. This approach is referred to as umbrella branding and it can be seen in the personal products industry for example. Unilever enjoyed great success in the 1980s with its Timotei brand of shampoo. This success has led the Anglo Dutch multi-national to utilise this brand name across a range of related products.

An umbrella branding strategy obviously has advantages in terms of the transferral of positive attributes and associations from one product to another. On the other hand, should one product being sold under an umbrella brand name find its reputation for quality being tarnished, then the great danger is that these negative associations then impact upon all other products being sold under the same umbrella brand name.

Undoubtedly brand policy is a major challenge facing the global consumer marketer. When companies have a massive array of products which are sold in virtually every country in the world, then international branding becomes a major challenge. In the past, many companies had a fairly standardised product which was sold under different brand names in different countries. However, the creation of the single European Market has encouraged many companies to adopt a pan-European approach in their marketing activities. One conspicuous example involved Mars Corporation, the large US confectionery company, which has implemented a pan-European branding policy. Thus in the UK for example, the Marathon brand has been replaced by a new brand name, 'Snickers'.

Given the value of brand names and trademarks, etc., it is vitally important that companies ensure that these powerful marketing tools enjoy the appropriate levels of legal protection in their international markets. In countries which have a legal system based on Common Law, ownership of a brand name or trademark is created and maintained through use with the registration providing additional protection. However, in those countries where the law is based on the Roman Civil Code (i.e. Continental Europe), trademarks are generally awarded to whoever first registers such brand names or trademarks.

In some developing country markets, the legal protection afforded to brand names and trademarks, etc., leaves much to be desired. In the absence of effective legal protection, many multinationals were deterred from entering such markets. In recent years, the USA and the EU have placed more and more pressure on governments to clamp down on offenders. In some cases, this has been justified, but one could be forgiven for concluding that penalties imposed on certain nations, ostensibly for their failure to enforce intellectual property rights, has been motivated partly by protectionism. In the 1990s developed countries are likely to find other disingenuous reasons for imposing trade restrictions on particular economies (e.g. those which have a poor human rights record; those which supply hard drugs; those which insist on flogging foreign citizens vandalising cars).

In the future though, distributors' copy-cat own-label products rather than counterfeiting represent the biggest threat to branded products. On 18 April 1994 Sainsbury, the huge UK retailer, launched 'Classic Cola' much to the consternation of Coca-Cola, which claims the name and packaging infringe its trademarks. The fears of the US soft drinks company appear justified. Prior to the launch it held 62 per cent of the retailer's cola market, while Sainsbury's own-label brand had a mere 24 per cent. After two weeks the relative positions in terms of Sainsbury's sales had been reversed. Coca-Cola's sales slumped to 27 per cent, while Classic-Cola held 70 per cent of the market. Should this trend endure and spread, then the traditional brand leaders face catastrophe (*The Sunday Times*, 1994).

▌International promotion policy – *Live and let die!*

☐ *Global advertising expenditure*

In 1994 it was expected that global advertising expenditure would increase by 5.5 per cent. This figure however, disguises enormous variations from country to country. For example between 1993 and 1996 it is expected that advertising expenditure in China will increase by 71.2 per cent. This huge increase is attributable to media owners cashing in on overseas advertisers seeking to reach the country's 1.2 billion consumers. Furthermore the rates for foreign advertisers are significantly higher in China than for Chinese companies. At the moment demand far outstrips supply in advertising space and air time. After China the next major growth market will be Greece with an increase of 71.3 per cent expected

Table 19.5. *Advertising growth: top ten countries, 1993–1996*

Country	Forecast % Growth
China	71.8
Greece	71.3
Thailand	59.0
Venezuela	58.2
Philippines	57.4
South Korea	43.4
Chile	31.1
Colombia	31.0
Singapore	26.5
Taiwan	26.3

Source: 'Bright Spots in a Cloudy Forecast', *Financial Times* (9 December 1993).

in the period 1993–1996. This is the only European country included in the top ten growth countries, and this is due to the fact that the Greek government has issued new licences to six national operators (see Table 19.5).

□ *Pan-regional advertising*

Europe is setting the pattern for the world's other regions. In the early 1990s the advertising industry like many others experienced the ravages of economic recession. However, one bright spot was the growth in pan-European advertising campaigns. According to *Euro-marketing* (Advertising Agency's weekly newsletter), the top 100 pan-European brands in the main EC markets increased their TV advertising spending by 28 per cent in 1992. US$5.3bn was spent promoting the top 100 pan-European brands and this amounted to 42 per cent of all TV advertising in Britain, France, Germany, Italy, The Netherlands and Spain. This confirms the tendency for many multinationals to treat Europe as a single market in order to achieve cost savings and in recognition of the convergence of consumers' tastes. Eleven of the top 50 European brands are American, including Kelloggs at No. 1.

Regional promotion campaigns are attractive and necessary because they achieve large cost reductions and because short product life-cycles demand regional product launches with the appropriate promotional support. Obviously it's much cheaper to shoot just one commercial and then use it across Europe, rather than have individual campaigns for each national market. DBH makes pan-European adverts for Levi's Jeans. A one minute television commercial costs about £300 000 to shoot. Therefore by shooting a single TV ad to span six European markets, Levi's Jeans can save itself £1.5m. However, this would not be possible for many products (e.g children's toys) because the rules governing toy advertising vary so much from country to country.

In terms of the sectoral distribution of the top 100 pan-European brands, the automobile industry dominates with a total of 16 brands which had $1.3bn spent on their promotion in 1992. Cars are followed by toiletries and cosmetics (16 brands with expenditure of $720m), foods (9 brands with $630m advertising expenditure) and confectionery (11 brands with expenditure of $558m). In the 1990s the xowners of these brands will need to revise radically their promotion strategy. Direct marketing will become much more important and by the end of the decade; we predict that expenditure on direct marketing will exceed that on TV advertising. The information revolution makes this possible, while distributors' own label products provide the incentive for FMCG companies to establish a more direct relationship with their customers.

The most successful pan-European campaigns are those which have got their central proposition clearly defined. It is of much less importance how that central proposition is interpreted in the local market. In other regions (e.g. Asia), individual countries have populations much larger than the whole of Europe, and in some the advertising industry is just developing, so pan-regional in such a diverse cultural and legal environment appears problematic. As of 1993 China had around 1700 daily newspapers, mostly provincial, and about 7000 periodicals. Thus even implementing a national advertising campaign is not without its difficulties.

In 1993 Mr Rupert Murdoch's News Corporation bought a majority stake in Star TV, the Hong Kong based Asian satellite venture. Potentially Star can reach three billion people or half the world's population. However, governments of countries such as China, Singapore, Malaysia and Indonesia have with some justification been suspicious of western media and concerned that they may lead to the importation of unacceptable influences. In China direct satellite link-up is illegal for individuals. Despite this an estimated 500 000 dishes were sold in China in 1992 and there is now evidence of moves to enforce the law. However, as technology advances and dishes get smaller it is increasingly difficult for government officials to enforce the law and to restrict Star's reach. China is expected to follow the Singapore model and develop its own cable network, thereby enabling it to control what appears on the screens. Already there are more than 1000 licenced cable television networks operating in China.

□ *Cultural sensitivity*

International Marketing textbooks are replete with *faux pas* by sophisticated multinationals which failed to consider fully the cultural environment. A favourite involves a US FMCG company launching some time ago a detergent in a poor Arabic country where TV ownership was low and illiteracy high. The solution was to mount a bill-board champaign which comprised three pictures. The one on the left showed the housewife disapproving of a dirty shirt, the middle her washing it, and the right, a contented lady admiring a brilliant white shirt. The promotion campaign started about four weeks after the product launch. Sales slumped. Arabs 'read' from right to left!

On the other hand, some international companies enjoy great success in certain markets because their promotion strategy touches the right nerve amongst consumers. Philips encourages consumers in some Asian countries, which place a premium on education, to buy its light bulbs because the soft tone enables children to

study longer, and thus get better grades. Needless to say what works well in one market, may prove disastrous in another. Humour (e.g. Foster's lager) and sex (e.g. Haagen-Dazs ice-cream) are often used to great effect in advertising in the West. In some countries, use of the former would be ineffective due to cultural factors, and the use of the latter would be prohibited.

The IME influences not only the content of the promotion campaign but the actual choice of communication tool. Given that personal selling is a labour intensive activity, one finds that personal selling in developed countries or in Asia's NIEs is strongly focused on selling expensive products. However, in countries where there is an abundant pool of cheap labour then personal selling represents a low cost promotional strategy and can be used even for selling low cost consumer products. For example, in China Avon Products has an army of sales people to sell their cosmetics and other personal products to the increasingly affluent Chinese population.

▌ International distribution policy: *Dangerous liaisons* or *Cry freedom*

For many multinational companies, control of distribution is considered vital – and rightly so. However, in the rapidly growing markets of today, control will have to be sacrificed to the local partner, otherwise the company will make little or no impression in the market-place. This will place a severe strain on the organisational culture of those MNEs which in market after market have insisted on a majority stake with their local partners in overseas markets. If control could not be gained, they were reluctant to enter the market. Surely though it's better to have 49 per cent of a successful business than 51 per cent of an unsuccessful business? Indeed in many developing country markets, the pendulum has swung very much to the advantage of the local partner. In some cases, the multinational seeks to redress the situation by buying its local partner, and then dispatching a few expatriates to run the business. So much for relationship marketing! A few cases are presented below to stress the importance of (a) establishing a partnership in certain international markets, and (b) the need to choose wisely.

□ *Warner Lambert in Japan*

In February 1994 trade talks were held in Washington as trade relations between the USA and Japan deteriorated further. At these discussions a complex number of factors were identified to explain the failure of US companies in the Japanese market. However, some US and other western companies have done exceptionally well in the Japanese market.

Warner Lambert's Schick brand of razor blades holds 70 per cent of the Japanese market for wet shave products, despite competition from two Japanese brands. It has been much more successful in Japan than Gillette, which lags in the US market and many international markets.

One reason Warner Lambert has been so successful with the Schick brand name has been due to its tie up with Hattori Seiko, its Japanese distributor, which began selling Schick razor blades in Japan in 1960, Hattori Seiko handles all importation, warehousing and distribution. Until 1993 it also handled selling, but Warner Lambert has since set up its own sales force.

The Japanese distribution system is exceptionally complex with layers of wholesales. Western companies must therefore be patient in their efforts to understand and penetrate the system. It is exceptionally difficult to get products onto retail shelves by directly approaching the retailer. The system has a considerable number of disadvantages. The number of wholesalers inflates the retail price beyond that in the US and often a listing fee must be paid to ensure retailers make a profit. The lengthy distribution channel complicates communication between manufacturer and retailer. As far as the retailers are concerned, it was almost as if Hattori Seiko made Schick. Nevertheless, without the tie-up with Hattori Seiko, it is unlikely that Warner Lambert would have succeeded in getting Schick onto the shelves of retail outlets ('Use the System, Win Shelf Space', The *Financial Times*, 16 February 1994).

□ *Carlsberg in Thailand*

In some industries, distribution channels within particular national markets are controlled by leading local players. This is a problem which many western companies have discovered when they have tried to penetrate some of Asia's markets. Recently, Carlsberg, the Danish brewer, has entered the Thai beer market in the only way possible, namely with the help of a powerful local partner that produces and distributes Mekong, the most popular Thai whisky and therefore has a ready made distribution network across Thailand. Other brewers entering the Thai market in the past have failed because they did not ensure that their product was widely available.

The local partner has exacted a high price, namely 90 per cent ownership of the joint venture with Carlsberg in the $80m plant north of Bangkok. In order to make the product more acceptable in the Thai market, Carlsberg has upped the alcohol content of its beer to 6 per cent and is spending between 30 and 40 per cent of the $10m spent on promotion by all Thai brewers in 1993 on television and other main media. Moreover, Carlsberg has been obliged to take the unusual step of producing own brands of bottled soda water and still water. It has been forced to do so because these are essential mixers for Mekong whisky and Carlsberg's local partner was concerned that Boon Rawd whose Singha brands accounted for 90 per cent of the beer sold in Thailand, and also the country's main soda water manufacturer, would threaten to withhold supplies from retailers who accepted Carlsberg beer.

□ *PepsiCo in France*

In 1992 the US soft drinks group secured victory in its three-year-long battle to reclaim control over the marketing and distribution of its brand in France from Perrier. The legal battle had begun in 1989 when Pepsi had attempted to rescind the contract struck in 1962 which gave the mineral-water company full control over the production, bottling and sales of Pepsi Cola in the French market. Perrier entered into a legal fight in order to prevent the US company from terminating the contract.

Pepsi on the other hand claimed it needed to regain control of its brand in France precisely because Perrier was not managing it properly. Pepsi said its volume share of the French market had fallen from 17 per cent to 7 per cent during the 1980s. The companies reached a compromise whereby they agreed that Pepsi would regain the rights over marketing and distribution, but that Perrier would continue to produce and bottle Pepsi Cola in France. It had struck similar deals in Spain and Germany but it stressed that it would not necessarily pursue the same strategy in every country and that marketing and distribution would continue to be organised according to the different requirements of individual markets ('Pepsi Cola Wins Perrier Battle', *Financial Times*, 18 December 1993).

■ International pricing – *Beguiled*

The price floor is determined by production costs, whereas the price ceiling in international markets is determined by competitors' prices (i.e. the competitive environment), the ability (i.e the economic environment) and willingness (i.e. the cultural environment) of customers to pay, and in some cases governmental action (i.e. the legal environment).

In some industries (e.g. construction, defence, pharmaceuticals, telecommunications equipment) the main customers are in the public sector. This can pose a number of difficulties in a complex relationship involving the seller and its government, and the buyer and government officials. In some countries, pricing policy may have to include 'commissions' to those involved in the buying process. Western businesses wishing to succeed in other large regional markets may thus face a moral dilemma: do they include the 10 per cent

'commission' in their pricing policy or do they perhaps endanger domestic employment?

Political considerations also impact upon pricing in international markets, and again ethical considerations come to the fore. Developed country governments are forcing down the price of drugs, leading to lower profit margins for the leading drug firms. Their budgetary constraints provide the incentive. In order to gain re-election, governments need to improve the people's standard of living. In the future, governments are likely to monitor the pricing policy of international firms to ensure that their voters are not paying artificially high prices. National governments in the EU have compared prices in the EU (e.g. the UK looked at car prices) and are now doing so on a trans-atlantic basis (e.g. the UK for CDs). How long will it be before Hong Kong is the benchmark for electronics, the USA for jeans, etc. Traditionally, the MNE was the main force behind global pricing and the aim was to maximise the price. In future, political pressure is going to be the key driver behind global pricing and the aim will be to minimise the price. The sole consolation for the international marketer is that parallel imports will cease to be a major problem.

In setting prices for international markets, careful attention has to be paid to the rate of inflation (i.e. the economic environment) and the exchange rate (i.e. the financial environment). On top of this, the company has additional costs to bear which do not arise in purely domestic marketing (e.g. shipping, letters of credit, etc.). Many SMEs enter all international markets simply on a cost-plus basis, failing to recognise the need to consider differences in national environments.

In Europe there are many supporters of a single currency. In seeking to achieve this goal, countries entered the Exchange Rate Mechanism (ERM) but this proved a disaster for many economies, resulting in huge losses in money markets and when these forays failed, substantial devaluation. Even government ministers in some countries are threatening to challenge their Prime Minister over this issue. All this economic, financial and political instability could be justified if the creation of a single currency led to a huge improvement in the international marketing environment. However, the turmoil is so unnecessary. Technology (i.e. electronics) acts as a single currency.

Switch to profit maximisation from sales maximisation

The penetration pricing strategy of Japanese and other Asian firms has led to a spate of anti-dumping investigations in the USA and the EU. Not surprisingly the Asian companies and their governments view such measures as protectionism, a view upheld by GATT which has criticised the EU's use of its anti-dumping policy. In future, fewer cases are likely to be levelled at Japanese companies in particular. Their priority is now profits not market share. On the other hand, developing countries are already resorting to anti-dumping measure to safeguard their industries.

In recent years, the tougher competitive environment has led to chaotic pricing where price changes are unpredictable and frequent. This has already happened in the computer industry where firms like Compaq engineered their own recovery by audacious price cuts, and spectacularly by Philip Morris in 'Marlboro Friday'. These price cuts though are necessary paradoxically in order to ensure future profits.

Sometimes the country-of-origin effect proves more influential than brand power. For example, the sophisticated customers of Singapore differentiate between products made by the same company in different locations. Thus they are prepared to pay more for a Sony product made in Japan than a Sony equivalent made in lower-cost Malaysia. Thus companies need to consider the impact of their plant location upon their pricing policy. On the other hand, Nike uses a subcontractor in Fuzou (China) to produce its shoes. Yet it can command as high a price in China as in developed country markets despite enormous differences in per capita income.

In other cases, companies are handicapped by their origins. Despite offering a considerable price advantage and models which have won critical acclaim, Hyundai with a mere 0.5 per cent of the UK market has had to accept the painful reality that 55 per cent of UK consumers continue to associate South Korean products with poor quality. Its TV advertising campaign therefore does not plug a particular car, but challenges the British stereotype of South Korea.

In early 1994 Bozell-Gallup announced the results of their *Worldwide Quality Poll*. A total of 20 000 people in 20 countries were asked how they rated the quality of manufactured goods produced by the world's 12 leading exporting nations. Ratings were given on a 5 point scale rating from poor to excellent. Some 38.5 per cent of interviewees considered products made in Japan to be either very good or excellent. Germany was second with 36 per cent and was followed by the US with 34.3 per cent in third place. Some way down, came Britain, France, Canada, Italy, Spain, China, Taiwan, Mexico and Russia ('Japan Tops Consumer List for Best Quality Goods', *Financial Times*, 11 February 1994).

International marketing managers – *Top gun*

There are many global businesses, but few global organisations. This will change, but currently the demand for global managers exceeds supply. The domain of the global manager pulsates with the rhythm of economies, markets and nations. The business sphere of global manager is made up of the controllable and non-controllable variables. Changes are rapid and radical. The world class global manager must acquire the ability to learn faster than change itself. In short s/he must become a 'Master of Change'. This requires a *Top gun* approach:

- **Think** – learn to think independently and logically
- **Organise** – time management to alleviate stress
- **Prioritise** – separate the trivia from the urgent
- **Gumption** – discern and decide, avoid paralysis by analysis
- **Unique** ability to experiment and learn from one's own mistakes arising from creativity

Table 19.6.   *Elements of an international manager*

GLOBAL MINDSETS	PERSONAL CHARACTERISTICS	COMPETENCIES	ACTIONS
Bigger, broader picture	Knowledge	Managing competition	Manage competitiveness through knowledge by driving for the broader picture
Balance of contradictions	Conceptualization	Managing complexity	Manage complexity through conceptualization by accepting the balance of contradictions
Trust process (i.e. systems, policies, norms of behaviour to respond rapidly to change)	Flexibility	Managing adaptability	Manage adaptability through flexibility by trusting process over structure
Teamwork and diversity	Sensitivity	Managing multicultural teams	Manage teams through sensitivity by valuing diversity
Change as opportunity	Judgement	Managing uncertainty	Manage uncertainty through judgement by flowing with change
Openness to surprises	Reflection	Managing learning	Manage learning through reflection by seeking to be open

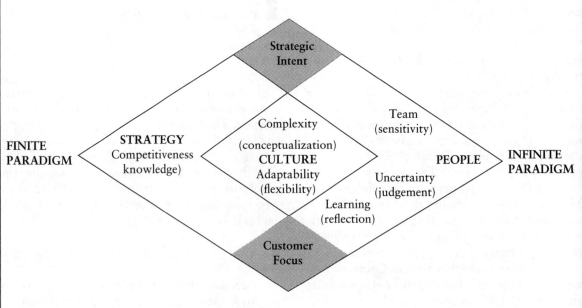

Source: Adapted from S. H. Rhinesmith, *A Manager's Guide to Globalization: Six Keys to Success in a Changing World*, Homewood, Ill.: Business One, Irwin (1993), pp. 27–34.

Figure 19.2.   *Current issues in international marketing*

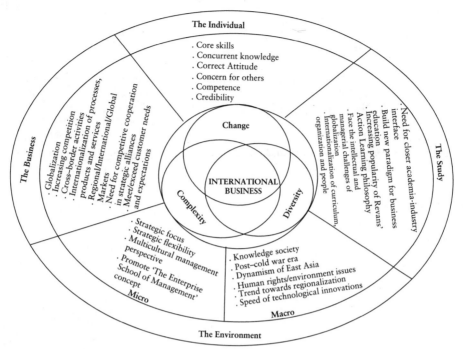

Source: Authors's data.

and innovativeness – the heart of an entrepreneur's skills

● Nimbleness to adjust and adapt to changes and new trends

Table 19.6 considers the essential elements of an international marketing manager. Given such requirements the interface between academia and industry is of vital importance to ensure the availability of suitable managers for an international business environment dominated by change, complexity and diversity (See Figure 19.2).

◀ References

Albaum, G. and Paterson, R. A. (1984), 'Empirical Research in International Marketing: 1976–1982', *Journal of International Business* (Spring/Summer), pp. 161–173.

Aulakh and Kotaabe (1993), 'An Assessment of Theoretical and Methodological Development in International Marketing: 1980–1990', *Journal of International Marketing* 1 (2), pp. 5–28.

Baker, M. J. (1983), *Marketing: Theory and Practice*, 2nd edition, London: Macmillan.

Boddewyn, J. J. (1981), 'Comparative Marketing: The First 25 Years', *Journal of International Business Studies* 12 (Spring/Summer), pp. 61–79.

Cavusgil, S. T. and Nevin, J. R. (1981) 'State-of-the Art in International Marketing: An Assessment', in *Review of Marketing*, Enis B. M., and Roering, K. J. (eds), Chicago: American Marketing Association, pp. 195–216.

Czinkota, M. R. and Ronkainen, I. A. (1993), *International Marketing*, 3rd edition, Fort Worth: The Dryden Press.

Douglas, S. P. and Craig, C. S. (1983), *International Marketing Research*, Englewood Cliffs, NJ: Prentice-Hall.

The Economist (1994), 'Survey on Ukraine' (6 May).

Evans, P. A. L. and Doz, Y. (1992), 'Dualities: A Paradigm for Human Resource and Organisational Development in Complex Multinationals', in Pucik, V., Tichy, N. M., and Barnet, C. K. (eds), *Globalizing Management: Creating and Leading the Competitive Organization*, New York: John Wiley.

Financial Times (1993), 'Bright Spots in a Cloudy Forecast' (9 December).

Financial Times (1993), 'Pepsi Cola Wins Perrier Battle' (18 December).

Financial Times (1994), 'Japan Tops Consumer List for Best Quality Products' (11 February).

Financial Times (1994), 'Use the System, Win Shelf Space' (16 February).

Financial Times (1994) (9 May).

Fukuyama, F. (1992), *The End of History and the Last Man*, London: Hamish Hamilton,

Naisbitt, J. and Aburdene, P. (1992), *Megatrends 2000: Ten New Directions for the 1990s*, New York: Avon Books.

Naisbitt, J. (1994), *Global Paradox*, London: Nicholas Brealey Publishing.

Stumpf, S. A. and Mullen, T. P. (1992), *Taking Charge: Strategic Leadership in the Middle Game*, Englewood Cliffs, NJ: Prentice-Hall.

The Sunday Times (1994), 'Sainsbury Wins First Round in Cola Battle' (8 May).

Thurow, L. (1992), *Head To Head: The Coming Battle among Japan, Europe and America*, New York: William Morrow.

■ *Chapter 20* ■

Marketing to Eastern Europe

Pervez Ghauri

■ Introduction

The end of the cold war and liberalisation of East and Central Europe are perhaps the most dynamic and exciting events of recent years. The introduction of *perestroika* in 1985 and the fall of the Berlin Wall in 1989 have created enormous opportunities for the world economy and for western firms. The importance of East and Central Europe, with a population of 429 million people, cannot be questioned. Its population is 30 per cent more than the European Community (EC) and almost double that of the United States. The new situation has enhanced the importance of Europe as a whole with a population of 720 million people. Moreover, Eastern and Western Europe have complementary resources. Eastern Europe has huge raw material production and reserves including metal ores, coal, oil, gas and agricultural products, while Western Europe has the technology (Buckley and Ghauri, 1994). The countries that are referred to as Eastern Europe are listed in Table 20.1.

As shown in the Table, different countries have different commitments in regard to reforms and transforming the economy to a purely market economy. The German Democratic Republic (GDR) became a part of the Federal Republic of Germany in 1990, but shares many of the characteristics of Eastern European countries. The former Soviet Union countries have strong regional differences in commitments to reforms.

Table 20.1. *The countries of Eastern Europe*

Country	Population (million)	Commitment to change
Albania	3.00	UN
Bulgaria	9.00	R
Czech & Slovak Federal Republics	16.00	T
Former German Democratic Republic (GDR)	17.00	T
Hungary	11.00	T
Poland	38.00	T
Romania	23.00	R
Former USSR	288.00	T
Former Yugoslavia	24.00	UN
Eastern Europe (Total)	429.00	

Key: Commitment to transform
T = in transition to or now primarily a market economy
R = committed to reforms while largely maintaining central planning
UN = unsure of making reforms

Source: Based on Daniels and Radebaugh (1992), and Lindsay (1992).

The Commonwealth of Russian States (CIS) is still struggling with political instability and the Asian Republics have different levels of ambitions and goals depending upon their location, resources and political leaders.

Today in most East European countries there are democratically elected governments which are committed to establishing market economies based on free competition. Most of the countries are desperately trying to attract foreign companies in order to establish technology transfer and trading links. However, the situation in many of the countries is uncertain, complex and difficult to predict and is considered an enormous challenge for companies planning to invest in these markets. There are some apparent leaders; Poland, Hungary and the Czech Republic now have free pricing, convertible currencies and a considerable amount of foreign investments. These countries have clear goals and objectives to achieve western style market economies and have taken rigorous measures to achieve that (Havlik, 1991; Kase, 1992; and Buckley and Ghauri, 1994).

The comparative progress in Czechoslovakia, Hungary and Poland is illustrated in Table 20.2.

▍ Progress in privatisation and investment opportunities

Although most countries of Eastern Europe are committed to improving their economies, there are still too many inter-related obstacles in the path of growth to be dealt with. Issues such as trade barriers, development of banking and loan

Table 20.2. *Comparative progress in Poland, Hungary and the Czech Republic*

	Poland	*Hungary*	*Czech Republic*
Economy	GDP rose by 5% in 1994. Inflation rate around 30%. Unemployment rate 15% (1993). Growth in industrial production 7%.	GDP rose by 2% in 1994. Inflation rate around 20%. Unemployment 30% (1993). Growth in Industrial production 4%	GDP rose by 1% in 1994. Inflation 19%. Unemployment 33% (1993).
Finance	Huge foreign investments over $ 10 billion of foreign aid pledged by Western countries since 1989. Foreign banks agreed to write off 45% of their $ 12 billion debt claim in 1994. Western governments agreed in 1991 to write off 35% of their $ 35 billion debt claim.	Huge foreign investments, biggest recipient. OECD pledged $ 9 billion assistance.	Former Czechoslovakia was a aid donor country. Czech republic has received enormous foreign investments. Some major investments by private firms e.g. VW. Most developed industrial and financial institutions.
Privatization	Major sector of the economy is now privatised, 80% of the previously state run companies are privatised.	Biggest number of privately owned companies. Due to tax incentives, most private companies have foreign partners. Most major foreign companies present in the market.	More than 100,000 companies auctioned to private investors. Some companies given back to original owners. A number of major foreign private companies are operating in the country.

Table 20.3. Western retailers in Eastern Europe by country of origin.

Country of operation	Bulgaria	Czechoslovakia	Hungary	Poland	Romania	USSR	Yugoslavia	Total
					Host country			
Austria	–	3	5	1	–	1	3	13
Belgium	–	–	2	–	–	1	–	3
Denmark	–	–	–	1	–	–	–	1
Finland	–	–	–	–	–	1	–	1
France	3	–	–	3	–	3	–	6
Germany	3	2	8	4	–	6	2	25
Italy	1	2	2	2	2	3	2	14
Netherlands	–	2	–	–	–	–	–	2
Spain	–	–	–	–	–	–	1	1
Sweden	–	1	1	1	–	1	1	5
Switzerland	–	–	1	–	–	–	–	1
UK	–	–	1	1	–	1	1	4
USA	–	1	–	–	–	–	–	1
Total	4	11	20	13	2	17	10	77

Source: 'Cross-Border Retailing in Europe', the Corporate Intelligence Group

systems, pricing mechanisms, property- and contract-law all need immediate attention. Privatisation is considered a solution to achieve market economies and growth, but there is no easy way to achieve privatisation in Eastern Europe. Over-optimistic estimates are now being revised and people have started realising that it might take a decade or two before a privatised market economy is achieved (Edwards, 1991; Lindsay, 1992).

For the above reasons, reactions from Western companies have been rather cautious. however, in spite of this reluctance, most multinationals have entered these markets. Companies such as McDonalds, Pepsi Cola, Coca Cola, Statoil, Ericsson, IKEA, Fiat, Nokia, Volkswagen, Estée Lauder, Philip Morris, almost all pharmaceutical firms and several small and medium-sized companies have already established operations in these markets. The governments are providing a number of incentives to foreign companies to invest in their countries. For example by the end of 1991, there were 77 Western retailers active in Eastern Europe as illustrated by Table 20.3.

In spite of the reluctance of Western Companies to invest, there has been a considerable increase in registered joint ventures. By March 1992, there were 34 121 registered joint ventures between Western Companies and organisations from Eastern Europe. The joint ventures registered and in what countries are illustrated by Table 20.4.

Table 20.4. *Registered joint ventures in selected countries, March 1992*

Country	Registered JV's
Bulgaria	239
Czech & Slovak Republics	3,000
Hungary	11,000
Poland	5,286
Romania	9,327
Russia	2,600
Former Yugoslavia	2,669
Total	34,121

Source: Based on Van Berendonk, Oosterveer and Associates (1992).

A major part of these Joint ventures are, however still non-operative, as the Western companies are sitting and waiting for these economies to stabilise. Other than the three market leaders, Hungary, Poland and the Czech Republic, there are a number of problems that need to be solved before a proper marketing involvement can be expected from Western companies.

These problems are listed as follows:

- Difficult to dismantle existing power structure from earlier years;
- No clear priorities;
- Black markets;
- Political instability;
- Obscure legislative system;
- Unlimited demand;
- Extremely high inflation;
- Lack of infrastructure;
- Ineffective banking and monetary system.

All these problems are critical, but cannot be solved simultaneously and immediately. The companies that want to enter these markets have thus to handle these problems. In any case, there are great opportunities in these markets and a number of western companies are already very active, especially in the three leading economies. Some major foreign companies have already established considerable interests and investments in the three leading countries. This development is illustrated by Table 20.5.

The problem of excessive demand

In Eastern Europe consumption and demand for products and technology is enormous. There is a shortage of almost everything; at the top of the list are communication products such as consumer electronics, modern photographic equipment, books, records, CDs, followed by consumer products from garments to automobiles. In 1986 an international study revealed the following number of cars per 1000 head of the population.

Table 20.5.   *Large international business investments in Czechoslovakia, Hungary and Poland, 1989–91*

Home country	Investor	Partner	Industry	Commitment[a] ($m)
Germany	Volkswagen	Skoda, Baz (C)	Cars	6,630
US	Dow Europe	Sokolov (C)	Chemicals	200
France	CBS	Tourinvest (C)	Hotels	175
US	Gen. Electric	Tungsram (H)	Lighting	150
US	Gen. Motors	Raba (H)	Engines, Cars	150
		BAZ (C)	Engines, Cars	150
UK	Pilkington	HSO Sandomierz (P)	Glass	140
US	Guardian	Hungarian Glass (H)	Glass	120
Japan	Suzuki	Autokonzem (H)	Cars	110
Germany	Linde	Technoplyn (C)	Gases	106
Sweden	Electrolux	Lehel (H)	Appliances	83
Austria	Hamburger	Dunapack (H)	Packaging	82
US	Ford	New plant (H)	Car components	80
France	Sanofi	Chinoin (H)	Pharmaceuticals	80
US	US West	Czech govt. (C)	Telephones, Switches	80

Note:
[a] The figures here should be interpreted with considerable caution as declarations of intended investment at the time the deal was stuck. The final outcome will be dependent on many variables which can only be more closely specified as the project develops. For this reason commitment figures have not been declared in many projects.

Table 20.6.   *Number of cars per 1000 people*

USA	570	Hungary	145
W. Germany	446	Yougoslavia	125
France	388	Bulgaria	120
Japan	235	Poland	105
East Germany	204	USSR	42
Czechoslovakia	177	Romania	11

Source: CIA (1988); Tietz (1994), p. 71.

The above table illustrates the demand potential in Eastern Europe. In the case of consumer goods, there is already a demand awareness. Western brand products, despite their scarcity and high cost, are well known and in high demand. There is an unlimited demand for products such as Coca Cola, Levis Jeans, Canon Cameras, branded cigarettes, Bata shoes and McDonalds. It is also clear that there is a demand for high quality products. McDonalds inaugurated its restaurant in Moscow in 1990 and on the first day an estimated 30 000 customers were served, beating the previous record of 9100 for one day in 1988 in Budapest. McDonalds had 700 seats (indoor) available and opened in January, a very cold month. Although McDonalds did not use advertising for the opening, people stood in lines for hours. In order to avoid black-marketing of hamburgers outside the restaurants McDonald's had to limit the number of Big Macs per customer (Daniels and Radebaugh, 1992).

So far, Eastern Europe has not been involved in international trade, outside COMECON. Considering the population and demand opportunities, until 1992, they accounted for less than 10 percent of world imports and exports including the trade they conduct with each other. This reveals the potential of international marketing and business opportunities in these countries (Franklin and Moreton, 1985).

Differences in marketing to Western and Eastern Europe

In terms of area, Eastern Europe is the largest group of countries in the world. The large area and population lead to an optimistic perception of commercial opportunities, but it is also in some ways a hindrance to the marketing activities of western firms. The communication, distribution channels and infrastructure are not there. Moreover, due to the fact that there is no stable price mechanism in these markets, it is very difficult to use the same marketing planning and strategies as used in the West. One of the biggest problems in marketing products to these markets is that there are no retailers, wholesalers or any other effective distribution channel.

In Eastern Europe the retail sector is divided in three major groups (Tietz, 1994):

1. Food retailers;
2. Retailers of industrial goods;
3. General retailers.

However, the number of retailers in Eastern Europe is increasing rapidly, mainly as a result of privatisation and free-trade regulations within each country. Most of the new firms registered in these countries are sales outlets. Earlier, most of these retailers were under state ownership or co-operative ownership and there were very few privately owned retail outlets. After 1990 the ratio of privately owned retail outlets has increased considerably. However, the proportion of total retail sales handled by state-owned outlets is still much higher than in terms of actual proportion of outlets. The retail sales space per head of population is 20–30 percent of that of Western Europe. The average size of retail stores is also very small by comparison with that found in Western Europe. Due to the limited infrastructure and transport facilities available to most people, households have to do their shopping in nearby stores or in city centres.

The profit margins are very low and the inflation rate is very high, which leads to decline in total turnover. In most Eastern Europe countries the consumption rate has dropped by 40–60 percent. Another difference is that in almost all Eastern European countries there is an increasing grey and black market sector. It is, however, hoped that once the problems of excessive demand and scarcity of goods are solved and the

infrastructure is improved, the grey and black sector will automatically disappear.

Now that it has been established that there exist vast opportunities for Western firms to market their products and technologies in Eastern Europe, we must realise that the marketing situation is quite different from that in Western countries. It is not as simple as selecting a market and one of the existing market entry strategies. There exists a new set of problems and situations to be handled in these markets. Kraljic (1990) and Jain and Tucker (1994) characterise these problems as 'gaps' that exist between Western and Eastern economies:

1. *Marketing gap*: goods are normally distributed, not marketed. The marketing concepts and the importance of consumers are unknown as demand has always been greater than supply.
2. *Technology gap*: there exists a huge gap between Western and Eastern technologies, in machinery, equipment and in know-how. The concepts of technical standards, plant efficiency and operating efficiency are missing. In this respect the mentality is different and will take some time to change.
3. *Capital gap*: the investment and profitability capabilities are much lower than in the West. This is widely experienced by Western firms seeking local partners in these markets. In many cases, there are several interested parties, but they have nothing more to contribute other than the claim that they understand the local market.
4. *Management gap*: there is practically no management know-how at middle and upper levels. It is therefore very difficult for foreign firms to organise effective agents, distributors or partnerships with local staff. Moreover, it is even more difficult to have expatriates manage the local staff. Some companies bring middle-level managers and supervisors to the West to provide them with some training.
5. *Motivation gap*: the motivation of the work force was seriously damaged due to years of 'equalisation' of the work force. There is hardly any willingness to take responsibility and the work of morale and ethic is very

weak (taking initiative in your work and having drive are relatively new concepts).

In addition to these gaps, there are some fundamental differences between marketing to the West and the East. In Eastern Europe, despite the fact that most countries have democratically elected governments and that there is a high degree of privatisation, government still plays a major role in the business sector.

This role is even greater when a foreign company is involved. The most important difference between Western and Eastern Europe is the fact that there exist at least two or three generations gaps in terms of productivity and infrastructure, and progress is far behind that of Western Europe. Even in the most advanced countries; Hungary, Poland and the Czech Republic, there is some progress in maintaining property rights and removing some market imperfections (but this remains far behind Western Europe).

There are three important factors that would influence whether Eastern European economies would integrate with Western Europe. First, the ability of governments to promote and influence the restructuring and to convince their people that they have to suffer through a transitional period before they can see some real benefits of market economy. Secondly, the development of the Commonwealth of Independent States (CIS) and the course it will take. If the transition is smooth in CIS, it would have linkage effects to other East European countries and would encourage foreign investment to the entire region. Thirdly, the investments and capital-flow coming into this region are important factors. These factors will be realised if the global economy is prepared to allocate some finances to the long-term development of this region (Cantwell, 1990; Dunning, 1994).

■ Implications for companies

It has been established by now that there are great opportunities available in Eastern Europe. Furthermore, although these countries have numerous problems in achieving economic growth comparable to Western Europe, it is in the interest of the international community and especially the European Community (EC) to encourage and support the development in Eastern Europe. The establishment of European Bank for Reconstruction and Development (EBRD) and commitments by various other international agencies, such as the World Bank, are some positive signs that the international community is willing to assist Eastern Europe. According to one estimate by Michael Palmer, former Director General of the European Parliament (Palmer, 1991), an aid package of $16.7 billion a year is needed from the advanced industrial nations if economic reconstruction of Eastern Europe is to be completed within the next two decades.

Therefore, it is in the interest of the companies to *enter these markets as soon as possible*. The problem is that before 1990–1991, the economies of Eastern Europe were overestimated, partly because there were no statistics available and partly for political reasons. According to the CIA (Central Intelligence Agency), the GNP of the Soviet union was about half of that of the U.S. This gave Western companies an exaggerated and overly optimistic picture. After 1990, due to recent devaluations of the rouble, the estimated GNP of former Soviet Unions is about one tenth of that of the U.S., with a *per capita* income that is only 14 per cent of that of the United States. This is apparently an underestimate. Consequently, many companies are reluctant to enter these markets.

On the other hand, there exist numerous examples of successful entries such as: Siemens (Germany), Alcatel (France, ABB (Sweden/ Switzerland), General Electric (U.S.A.), McDonald's (U.S.A.), Coca Cola and Pepsi Cola (U.S.A.), VW (Germany), Fiat (Italy), Statoil (Norway). Only VW has delivered huge investments, $3 billion in the Czech Republic and $1.5 billion in Eastern Germany. These are only a few examples, so that there are great opportunities and companies should not be reluctant to enter because of some transitional problems. Even if we assume a doubling in the standard of living and completion of some major privatisation schemes by the year 2000, Eastern Europe would still require an investment of $100 billion (Dunning, 1994). Moreover, with the excessive demand, discussed earlier, companies that establish at an early stage would have greater benefits. They should, however, be prepared for a *lean period of 3–5 years*. The investments in these markets by international companies would also have linkage effects on their global marketing and positioning activities.

These marketing efforts should therefore be considered a part of their total international marketing and networking activities. The positive effects on international activities, the support and encouragement expected from the international community, the benefits and other incentives offered by local governments and profit opportunities in the long run are sufficient reasons for companies to consider these markets.

To be successful in these markets the companies should demonstrate *long-term commitment and seriousness*. It is not possible to travel to these markets occasionally and expect to establish successful business operations. It is important for companies to have a long-term representative in these markets. The managers involved in marketing should stay there for longer periods in order to understand the market and culture of the respective countries. We have already discussed that there are some differences in the development and commitment levels of different countries of Eastern Europe and it is not advisable to treat all countries in the same manner. The companies thus have to have innovative approaches.

As far as *entry strategies for doing business in Eastern Europe* are concerned, one has to choose the right alternative for the right reason. The first step is to be clear about why we want to enter that market. There are two basic alternatives. In the first instance, do we want to enter the market in order simply to market our products? On the other hand, do we wish to utilise the low cost of labour and raw materials? In the first case, one can use the traditional entry strategy analysis to determine whether to trade and then whether to manufacture in one's own country and market in these markets through export, agents or distributors. In the case that an attractive enough market is found, one can

start manufacturing in the particular market through a joint venture or wholly owned subsidiary. In the second case, one is looking for a cheap manufacturing facility or raw-material source. In this case, the goods will be exported from there to western or other market places.

When exporting to these countries, there are enormous opportunities due to the excessive demand for all types of Western products, especially consumer goods. However, there are some problems in using this strategy due to the lack of distribution channels and lack of convertible currencies. One way to overcome this problem is to get involved in *barter trade* which is complicated, time-consuming and costly. However, some companies have established their own retailing outlets in the market where they are selling products in local currency as well as in hard currencies. Companies such as IKEA (Sweden) and Statoil (Norway) are good examples. In the case of industrial products, there is enormous demand and even funds (hard currency) available to import these products and technologies. In this case, *trade fairs, exhibitions and frequent visits* are the most useful tools to make customers aware of your products and company. Some companies are getting huge contracts as a result of these fairs and visits. Fiat is a good example; it signed a $1.3 billion contract for an automobile assembly plant in Poland. However, after signing the contract, Fiat set out to find subcontractors to implement the contract. A company signing a significant contract receives a great deal of publicity. This can mean that potential subcontractors make direct contact with the main contractor (Daniels and Radebaugh, 1992).

Joint ventures as a means of market entry have been particularly popular in these markets. As mentioned in the earlier section of this chapter, foreign companies, as well as local organisations, have been very keen to register and start joint ventures. In this case, the evaluation of local partners' contribution is the most difficult aspect. Sometimes the local government is the local partner which leads to contradictory objectives between partners. Quite often, a local partner wants to come up with a contribution in the form of technology or know-how which is obsolete or of no value for the new operations. However, although many East European countries allow wholly owned subsidiaries, foreign companies are more interested in joint ventures. Foreign companies need assistance in handling these markets and bureaucratic environments. The companies have realised the synergetic benefits of these co-operative agreements. When marketing to these countries, a company should consider the following step-by-step approach:

1. Checking priorities.

   Learning about the priorities of the government and business sectors to determine whether the goods or projects at hand are among the priorities of the market.

2. Checking regulations.

   What rules and regulations apply to the import of goods? Are import licenses or other documents necessary? In the case of a joint venture, check all applicable rules and regulations. Is it allowed to have a majority-owned joint venture, property rights, etc.?

3. Checking the local agent/partner.

   Is it difficult to check the validity of the claims made by the local partner or agent? If the claims are valid, how can they be evaluated?

4. Checking the competition.

   It is very important to establish who your competitors are. Local government or another foreign company. It is important to check the potential competitors and what your position would be in the long term. Would you have the same competitive advantage in five years from now?

5. Check to see whether you would be forced to participate in counter-purchasing or bartering. This should be controlled/checked at an early stage in order to avoid surprises. In this case, you should also check the financial position of your counterparts to determine whether they would be able to fulfil their financial obligations.

6. Negotiations.

   It is very important to determine whether the objectives of both parties are complementary. If you can see that the other party has totally different objectives, then you should analyse that situation and determine whether it is acceptable to you. In this case, you should also evaluate whether you would be able to achieve your objectives and commit yourself accordingly.

7. Implementation.

   It is very important to carry out the project whole-heartedly and think in the long term. The potentials and opportunities should be evaluated at every step of implementation and matched with the company's objectives.

When handling these different stages efficiently, companies can get numerous 'spin-off' effects useful for the particular market or for other Eastern European markets. It is also important that after each and every stage companies evaluate their position and commitment. It is better to drop a project than to keep working on it half-heartedly.

In the case of market entry, where the purpose is to make products and sell them in the Western market this represents the best opportunity to participate in these economies in any meaningful way. It is beneficial not only to earn huge profits without the problems of currency convertibility, etc., but also to create wealth in Eastern European economies. Many of these countries have a simple supply of raw material, cheap labour, government incentives and other resources that can provide Western companies with global competitive advantages (Hertzfeld, 1991; Jain and Tucker, 1994). In this type of marketing activity a foreign company must be aware of the pitfalls and crucial factors that may influence the success or failure of such a venture. Firstly, due to excessive demand, price mechanisms are not functioning normally which could lead to overestimated profit expectations. In the long-run, when the gap between supply and demand is filled, market pricing would start functioning automatically. The same is applicable for labour, raw material and component pricing. It is therefore important for companies to realise that factor while selecting sectors to invest in. Secondly, these markets are not, in the long run, typically low-labour-cost economies. The standards of living are improving fast and there is a great chance that within a couple of decades the standards would come quite close to those of Western Europe. The investments in plants and technology, based primarily on low labour costs, could very well backfire in the long run. Finally, sectors that may appear attractive at the moment may not survive in the long run. When the economies are stabilised and standards of living have improved, then these countries might also buy their wine, shoes or garments from the same sources from which Westerners buy theirs. That means that, in spite of excessive demand at the moment, some sectors might not survive the transition period. Consequently, it would no longer be beneficial to produce certain products in Eastern Europe and sell them to Western markets. A long-term analysis and strategy is therefore of great importance. There are of course differences among the countries of Eastern Europe. Some countries offer excellent opportunities for export-oriented investments while others do not. In this instance, factors such as local government attitude and incentives given to foreign investors, investment protection, repatriation of profit, capability and quality of labour force and general economic prospect of the country are also important (Kempe, 1991; Anderson, 1990).

In conclusion, it is very important that companies first evaluate their own vision, strategy and capabilities. Eastern Europe offers great opportunities, but it demands great efforts as well. Moreover, these economies are in transition. This means the companies planning to enter these market must have a long-term prospective and should be able to tolerate a lean period of 3–5 years. Secondly, they should identify the particular market and sector with great care. The market and sector should fit into their global strategies and match their long-term perspective. Finally, the ability to develop a network of relationships with the relevant local authorities, potential partners/agents, local suppliers/distributors is also of utmost importance.

■ References

Anderson, S. (1990), 'The Eastern Bloc Investment Reports Card', *Bloc* (April–May), pp. 10–13.

Van Berendonk, Oosterveer and Associates (1992), *Nederlandse Joint Ventures in Midden- en Oost-Europa: Ervaringen en meningen uit de praktijk*, Eindhoven: Research Report, Van Berendonk, Oosterveer and Associates.

Buckley, P. J. and Ghauri, P. N. (eds) (1994), *The Economics of Change in East and Central Europe: Its Impact on International Business*, London: Academic Press, pp. 373–388.

Cantwell, J. C. (1990), *East–West Business Links and the Economic Development of Poland and Eastern Europe*, Reading: University of Reading, mimeo.

CIA (1988), *Handbook of Economic Statistics*, New York: CIA.

Daniels, J. D. and Radebaugh, L. H. (1992), *International Business, Environments and Operations*, 6th edition, Reading, Mass.: Addison-Wesley.

Edwards, S. (1991), *Stabilization and Liberalization: Policies in Central and Eastern Europe: Lessons from Latin America*, NBER Working Paper Series, 3816, National Bureau of Economic Research, Washington DC.

Franklin, D. and Moreton, E. (1985), 'A Little Late in Learning the Facts', *Economist* (20 April), p. 5.

Havlik, P. (1991), *Dismantling the Command Economy in Eastern Europe*, Boulder, Col: Westview Press.

Hertzfeld, J. M. (1991), 'Joint Ventures: Saving the Soviets from Perestroika', *Harvard Business Review* (January–February), pp. 80–91.

Hood, N. and Young, S. (1994), 'The Internationalization of Business and the Challenge of East European Development', in Buckley, P. J. and Ghauri, P. N. (eds), *The Economics of Change in East and Central Europe: Its Impact on International Business*, London: Academic Press, pp. 321–342.

Jain, S. C. and Tucker, L. R. (1994), 'Market opportunities in Eastern Europe: MNCs Response', in Buckley, P. J. and Ghauri, P. N. (eds), *The Economics of Change in East and Central Europe: Its Impact on International Business*, London: Academic Press, pp. 389–461.

Kase, R. (1992), 'Petrolium Perestroika', *Columbia Journal of World Business*, 26 (4), pp. 16–28.

Kempe, F. (1991), 'East Europe Offers Investors: Big Profits and Big Perils', *The Wall Street Journal* (11 January), p. A6.

Kraljic, A. P. (1990), 'The Economic Gap separating East and West', *Columbia Journal of World Business* (Winter), pp. 14–19.

Lindsay, M. (1992), *Developing Capital Markets in Eastern Europe, a Business Reference*, London: Pinter Publishers.

Palmer, M. (1991), *A Plan for Economic Growth in Central and Eastern Europe*, Luxumbourg: European Parliament, mimeo.

Pear, R. (1990), 'Jobless to Soar in East, CIA says', *New York Times* (17 May), p. A6.

Tietz, B. (1994), 'The Opening up of Eastern Europe: The Implications for West European Business', in Buckley, P. J. and Ghauri, P. N. (eds), *The Economics of Change in East and Central Europe: Its Impact on International Business*, London: Academic Press.

■ Chapter 21 ■

Beyond Relationship Marketing: Flexible and Intelligent Relationship Management Strategy (FIRMS)

K. C. Chan and Michael C. McDermott

■ Introduction

During the 1980s hundred of billions of dollars changed hands as companies restructured themselves, largely through acquisitions and divestments as they sought to become global leaders in their selected line(s) of business. Buying established brands was perceived as offering the quickest and lowest risk route to a position of global leadership. It was also regarded as the key to profitability because brands commanded a premium price and customer loyalty (McDermott and Gray, 1990).

As expected, post-acquisition integration has proven a difficult challenge for many acquiring companies. However, contrary to popular belief in the 1980s (e.g. Saatchi and Saatchi's 'Law of Dominance') even global brands are not immune to competitive pressures. In 1993 Philip Morris reduced the price in the USA of Marlboro, the world's best selling cigarette, because it was losing market share to lower cost rival products. In 1994 Kodak has also had to alter radically its pricing policy to compete against low-cost, non-differentiated products. The whole philosophy underlying branding is to secure customer loyalty, and companies which during the 1980s spent billions of dollars to strengthen their brand portfolios (e.g. BSN, Grand Metropolitan, Guinness, Nestle, Philip Morris, Unilever) are now having to confront an awful reality: consumers throughout the industrialised world are far less loyal to brands than all of these companies believed, as consumers became more cost-conscious for certain products (e.g. soft drinks but not beers).

The plight of these firms, though, lends weight to those who have been highly critical of marketing, and who have predicted a global market of increasingly fickle customers, unless companies undergo a radical rethink of what marketing should be. One such critic is McKenna (1991) who argued that marketing has to brook a major transformation 'from manipulation of the customer to genuine customer involvement; from telling and selling to communicating and sharing knowledge; from last-in-line function to corporate-credibility champion'. He suggests that marketing has evolved from 'tricking the customer to blaming the customer to satisfying the customer – and now to integrating the customer systematically'. The outcome of this metamorphosis is relationship marketing which McKenna discusses in his book *Relationship Marketing: Successful Strategies for the Age of the Customer*.

Christopher *et al.'s* (1991) book, *Relationship Marketing: Bringing Quality, Customer Service and Marketing Together*, like McKenna's stresses the importance of developing good customer relationships. The authors of this chapter obviously agree that developing excellent customer relationships is vital, but it is essential that companies realise that achieving this is impossible without paying *at least* equal attention to other vital relationships.

Kotler (1994) also stresses that in today's turbulent business environment, the winning companies are those that employ excellent marketing practices (see Table 21.1) and which are most successful in 'satisfying, indeed delighting, their target customers'. But just as brand power was seen in the 1980s as a corporate panacea, it is important to recognise in the 1990s that relationship marketing *per se* will not provide companies with the benefits which its proponents claim. Relationship marketing is necessary but not sufficient for business success. It is merely a subset of Value-Oriented Marketing, and it in turn is central to the **Flexible Intelligent Relationship**

Table 21.1. *The marketing excellence review: best practices*

Poor	*Good*	*Excellent*
Product-driven	Market-driven	Market-driving
Mass market-oriented	Segment-oriented	Niche-oriented and customer-oriented
Product offer	Augmented product offer	Customer solutions offer
Average product quality	Better than average	Legendary
Average service quality	Better than average	Legendary
End-product-oriented	Core-product-oriented	Core-competency-oriented
Function-oriented	Process-oriented	Outcome-oriented
Reacting to competitors	Benchmarking competitors	Leapfrogging competitors
Supplier exploitation	Supplier preference	Supplier partnership
Dealer exploitation	Dealer support	Dealer partnership
Price-driven	Quality-driven	Value-driven
Average speed	Better than average	Legendary
Hierarchy	Network	Teamwork
Vertically integrated	Flattened organisation	Strategic alliances
Stockholder driven	Stakeholder driven	Societally driven

Source: P. Kotler, *Winning Through Value-Oriented Marketing*, Senior Managers' Seminar, Marketing Institute of Singapore (28 January 1994).

Management Strategy (FIRMS) model developed by the authors of this chapter.

This chapter begins, though, with a brief examination of the literature on relationship marketing. It will be seen that several prominent authors in this field uphold the great benefits to companies of developing good customer relationships. One might then have expected an enthusiastic recommendation for all enterprises to master relationship marketing. Instead, though, relationship marketing is presented as an attractive *option* for some firms in *certain* industries. Indeed just as too many authors equate global marketing with a tiresome standardisation versus adaptation debate (Hamill, 1992), relationship marketing is in danger of being submerged in a similarly futile debate over its appropriateness for certain industries/businesses.

■ Relationship marketing defined

Pathmarajah (1993) defines relationship marketing as 'the process whereby the seller and the buyer join in a strong personal, professional, and mutually profitable relationship over time'. He characterises such a relationship as having the following properties: effective, efficient, enjoyable, enthusiastic and ethical – the five 'Es'. Companies which are genuinely committed to 'the five Es' are far less common than one may expect, but those who are aim to:

- 'offer the *most value*, personally and professionally;
- become a unique source in helping the buyer build something better, e.g. better peace of mind;
- become a partner with the buyer in his or her objectives; and,
- establish a long-term trusting relationship with the buyer' (Pathmarajah, 1993).

Far too many enterprises continue to disregard Levitt's (1983) advice that they, like their customers, should regard the sale transaction as the start rather than the end of the relationship. Indeed, as Table 21.2 shows, even now too many companies' reaction to the sale is the exact opposite to that of their customers (Mercer, 1992). By and large the majority of companies still practise 'transaction marketing' rather than 'relationship marketing' Pathmarajah (1993) provides a crisp summary of the key differences in these two approaches (see Table 21.3).

At its crudest, transaction marketing is characterised by companies constantly struggling to find new customers because they fail to satisfy existing customers, rather than focusing on retaining the existing customer base by demonstrating an unequivocal commitment to total quality customer care. The former approach inevitably leads quickly to corporate decline, the latter contributes to enduring corporate prosperity.

Table 21.2. *Comparison of seller and buyer reactions when the sale is first made*

Seller	*Buyer*
• Objective achieved	• Judgement postponed; applies test of time
• Selling stops	• Shopping continues
• Focus goes elsewhere	• Focus on puchase; wants affirmation that expectations have been met
• Tension released	• Tension increased
• Relationship reduced or ended	• Commitment made; relationship intensified

Source: D. Mercer, *Marketing*, Oxford: Blackwell Publishers (1992).

Table 21.3. *Contrasting transactional and relationship marketing*

Transactional marketing	*Relationship marketing*
• Do the deal and disappear	• Negotiate a win-win sale situation and stay around, being a resource for better results.
• Push price	• Promote value
• Short-term thinking and acting	• Long-term thinking and acting
• Build the business on deals	• Build the business on relationship
• Getting new customers	• Keeping all customers and clients
• No structure for on-going business	• Structure created to support relationship; special club and memberships for frequent users-buyers
• Selling focused	• Relationship focused for results
• Short-term empathy	• Long-term empathy and rapport
• Incentive for doing the deal	• Incentive for long-term relationships and revenue
• Foundation of sale telling and selling	• Foundation of revenue trust
• Race for a sale result	• Swift, strong, safe and enduring in results through relationship building
• After-sales support and service poor-seen as cost	• After-sales support and service strong-seen as an investment in the relationship
• Product-service focused	• People expectations and perception focused
• Rewards-incentive for 'doing deals'	• Rewards-incentive for maintaining and growing relationship and revenue
• 'The deal is the end'. Pursuit of deal	• The sale-just the beginning. Pursuit of long-term relationship and results

Source: Pathmarajah (1993).

Application of relationship marketing

Faced with such a stark contrast in outcomes, it is essential that businesses practise relationship marketing. However, some customers are more disposed towards relationship marketing than others. By assessing the 'the time horizon within which a customer makes a commitment to a vendor and also the actual pattern the relationship follows over time', Jackson (1985) identifies three types of customer:

- the lost-for-good customer;
- the always-a-share customer; and,
- intermediate types.

The lost-for-good customer makes a series of purchases over time, faces high costs in switching to a new supplier, and views the commitment to a particular supplier as relatively permanent. The buyer adopts this position because switching costs are high. For example, aircraft manufacturers are unlikely to change regularly the type of engines which they choose to fit, and similarly airlines are unlikely to change lightly the type of aircraft which they purchase. Even at a more mundane level, an organisation will have some reluctance in changing its office automation system because of the costs and disruption that ensues.

Jackson argues that since the buyer faces high switching costs, it is looking to form a long-term relationship with the seller. Hence, the seller needs to adopt a similar approach, and be prepared to make a substantial up-front investment to win new or greater commitments from such customers. She thus suggests that 'relationship marketing is apt for the buyer who might be lost for good' (Jackson, 1985, p. 123). In short, the big plus of this type of account is that once won, customer loyalty can be expected, the downside is that if lost, it is unlikely ever to be re-gained.

At the other end of the customer behaviour spectrum, lies the always-a-share customer who purchases regularly, has little loyalty to a particular supplier, and can switch easily from one vendor to another. Both parties recognise such relationships as short-term. For example, if a British firm wishes to send a package by courier to Singapore, it is unlikely to attach any special importance as to which courier operator it last used, but instead obtain quotations from a number of equally acceptable operators. Any operator who can offer immediately an attractive package (i.e. a combination of the marketing mix) has a chance of winning business from always-a-share customers. Thus, Jackson suggests that transaction marketing – marketing that emphasises the individual transaction – is most appropriate for the always-a-share buyer. Table 21.4 summarises the typical characteristics of customers at the end points of the account behaviour spectrum: lost-for-good and always-a-share customers.

Table 21.4.   *Time, account behaviour and marketing approach*

Long Time Horizon	Short Time Horizon
• Typified by lost-for-good customers	• Typified by always-a-share customers
• High switching costs	• Low switching costs
• Substantial investment actions, especially in procedures and lasting assets	• Smaller investment actions
• High perceived exposure	• Lower perceived exposure
• Focus on a technology or a vendor	• Focus on a product or a person
• High importance: strategic, operational, and personal	• Lower importance
Relationship Marketing	**Transaction Marketing**

Source: M. D. Hutt and T. W. Speh, *Business Marketing Management: A Strategic View of Industrial and Organisational Markets*, Fort Worth: The Dryden Press (1992).

Of course, in the real world few customers can be easily pigeon-holed as belonging to either of these two extreme categories. Instead, most customers are in fact 'Intermediate types' (Jackson, 1985). A customer's position within the spectrum of buying behaviour will be determined by a wide range of factors: the characteristics of the product category, the customer's pattern of product usage, and the actions of the customer and the supplier. Such relationships are more applicable for organisational buyers than consumer products, where regular buying is the norm.

Gronroos (1990), like Jackson (1985), suggests that transaction marketing is common in the consumer packaged goods sector, but as a company is forced to become more service-oriented in approach, relationship market increasingly displaces transaction-based marketing (see Figure 21.1). The driving forces behind this displacement are:

- better or more diverse technologies
- growing customer satisfaction
- customer access to more options
- competition

He suggests that all firms are on a continuum with transaction and relationship marketing representing the two extremes with the need for relationship marketing being dependent upon the line of business (e.g. transaction marketing is best suited to commodities). However, while a series of factors may influence the status of a particular product and customer behaviour, it is surely es-

Figure 21.1. *The marketing strategy continuum*

Marketing strategy continuum	Transaction Marketing		Relationship Marketing
Dominating marketing function	Traditional marketing mix dominated		Interactive marketing dominated*
Quality dimension most important for a competitive advantage	Outcome-related technical quality dominating		Process-related functional quality dominating**
Price sensitivity	Customers very price sensitive		Customers much less price sensitive
Interface between marketing and other functions, e.g. operations and personnel	Limited or nonexistent; interface of no significant strategic importance		Substantial; interface of strategic importance
Typical marketing situations continuum	Consumer Packaged Goods Marketing	Consumer Durables Marketing	Industrial Goods Marketing	Services Marketing

Source: C. Grönroos, *Service Management and Marketing: Managing the Moments of Truth in Service Competition*, Lexington, Mass: Lexington Books (1990), p. 146.

sential for companies to acknowledge that their actions are *the* deciding factor. Hence, relationship marketing should not be regarded, as Gronroos (1990) and Jackson (1985) suggest (see Figure 21.1 and Table 21.5), as appropriate for one type of business and not another. Relationship marketing should be applied and developed by all businesses irrespective of size or sector.

Whereas Jackson (1985) tended to present the need for relationship marketing as being determined almost solely by the level of switching costs, and Gronroos (1990) by the element of service-orientation involved, Pathmarajah (1993) rightly suggests that its appropriateness exists so long as it is:

- customised to the customer-client
- culturally comfortable
- delivers value as perceived by the customer-client or prospect; and
- based upon comprehensive understanding of the customer-client problem, needs, wants, and opportunities both organisationally and personally.

Kotler (1994) has also made an important contribution to the issue of relationship marketing.

Table 21.5.   *Relationship marketing and the account behaviour spectrum: advice on using the spectrum*

1.   **To diagnose customers' behaviour, analyse switching costs**

- *What are the investments in money, people, durable asets,or procedures required for the buyer to change?*
- The greater the investment, the closer the account will be the lost-for-good end of the spectrum, and `reltionship marketing' will be most suitable
- *What is the risk involved in changing?*
- The greater the risk, the greater the reluctance to change

2.   **To select a marketing approach, consider the position along the behaviour spectrum**

- Use relationship marketing for buyers near the lost-for-good end of the spectrum
- Use transaction marketing for buyers near the always-share-end of the spectrum
- Use intermediate approaches, for customers in intermediate positions

3.   **To analyse additional possible marketing actions, consider changes along the behaviour spectrum**

- To build switching costs, move the customer towards the relationship marketing end of the spectrum
- To move accounts closer to transaction marketing end of the spectrum, make it easy for the customer to mix and match your products with those of other vendors

4.   **To use the concept of the spectrum successfully, consider the dimension of time**

- Select a time horizon for evaluating marketing actions in light of the time horizons customers use in making commitments to suppliers
- Only make substantial up-front investments, if the customer's commitment can reasonably be expected to be lasting
- Ensure that if market dynamics shift a customer to the lost-for-good end of the spectrum, ensure it is to the advantage of your firm and not that of a rival

Source: Adapted from Jackson (1985).

Figure 21.2. *From transactions to relationship marketing*

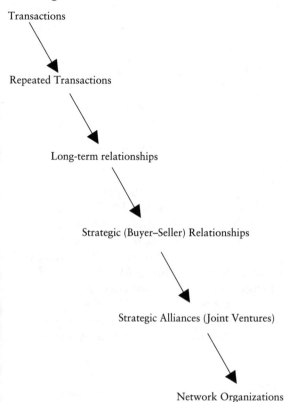

Transactions

Repeated Transactions

Long-term relationships

Strategic (Buyer–Seller) Relationships

Strategic Alliances (Joint Ventures)

Network Organizations

Source: See Table 21.1.

Firstly he has developed a 'stages' model of relationship marketing (see Figure 21.2). He has also developed a classification of company commitment to relationship marketing (see Table

21.6) and then applied that to the nature of business the company is in (see Table 21.7).

Kotler (1994) emphasises that successful enterprises do not settle for being anything other than world-class, and that they recognise the importance of mutually profitable relationship marketing with customers, supplier and distributors. This concept is of major importance but it is yet to be integrated into a model which demonstrates succinctly how to achieve the bundle of benefits (i.e. value-oriented marketing through synergy from other functional areas with value-added chain effect). However he has listed some of the essential aspects (see Table 21.1) of the FIRMS model which is discussed below.

Flexible Intelligent Relationship Management Strategy (FIRMS) defined

Competitive advantage in the 1990s and beyond can be achieved only by those firms which excel in developing a series of world-class relationships with *all* stakeholder groups. FIRMS is a unified theory of strategic corporate management. It unifies workers, suppliers, distributors, and even competitors, in the pursuit of excellence in customer service for profit/market share. It is an holistic people-oriented approach because it recognises that although the world is increasingly driven by high technology, it continues to be influenced and managed by high spirits – by the emotions, values, drive, energy, and persistence of

Table 21.6. *Levels of corporate–customer relationship*

Level	Attitude
Bare bones	The product is all that you need
Reactive	Call me if you need me
Accountable	I'm calling to see if the product is okay
Proactive	I can enhance your use of the product
Partnership	I want to help you succeed in every way

Source: See Table 21.1.

Table 21.7. *Where relationship marketing belongs*

	High Margin	*Medium Margin*	*Low Margin*
Many Customers/ Distributors	Accountable	Reactive	Bare bones
Medium Number of Customers	Proactive	Accountable	Bare bones
Few Customers/ Distributors	Partnership	Accountable	Reactive

Source: See Table 21.1.

individuals. The philosophical core of FIRMS is team working based on principle-centred relationships of **Sincerity, Integrity, and Trust** (SIT). It promotes open communications among functions within the organisation and across organisational boundaries for creative problem solving and quality decision making (see Figure 21.3 for win-win relationships for the business goal of profit/market share). This breakthrough will benefit customers (value for money), workers

(meeting hierarchy of needs), suppliers and distributors (expanding and reliable business) and competitors (setting standards for business excellence). The aim is to create value for all stakeholders by recognising that **Competive Advntage Requires Mutual Advantage** (CARMA).

Figure 3 can be more precisely visualised by the model of a tree. In Figure 21.4 the organization (i.e. the tree) springs from sincerity, integrity, and trust (i.e. the roots), from which grows a clear

Figure 21.3. *Win-win relationships for the business goal of profit/market share*

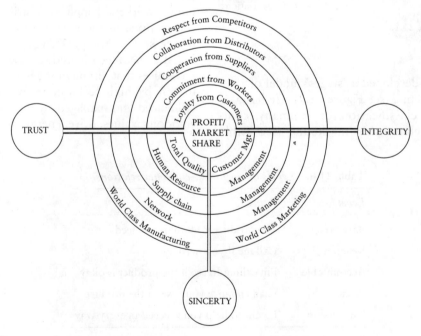

Source: Authors' data.

Figure 21.4. *The tree of total quality business philosophy*

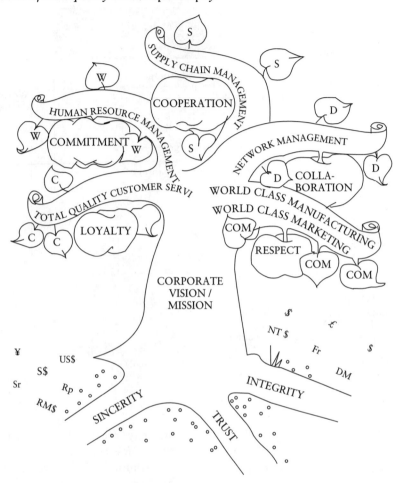

Source: Authors' data.

corporate vision/mission (i.e. the trunk). Other essential features of the organisation include its focus on five key areas (i.e. the branches) which yield benefits (i.e. the fruit). Ultimately, in order for the organisation to grow, reinvestment of profits (i.e. the leaves) is necessary to maintain and sustain competitive advantage (i.e. rich soil).

Engineering often employs a systems approach to analyse a particular situation in terms of the nature of inputs and outputs. It is vital that the latter is measured (i.e. feedback obtained) in order to assess the productivity and suitability of the former. Similarly, a systems approach should be used in any business venture, otherwise it is impossible to measure the effectiveness of inputs in terms of the final output. Hence the FIRMS model incorporates a systems approach for the enterprise as a whole (see Figure 21.5), but more than that, it also provides a systems approach at each of the five levels of the FIRMS model (see Figure 21.6). By doing so, it enables the early identification of a deterioration in any key relationship, and therefore a timely response by the enterprise can avoid any adverse impact. This is precisely why the model is called Flexible Intelligent Relationship Management Strategy.

Figure 21.5.   *Total systems diagram for FIRMS*

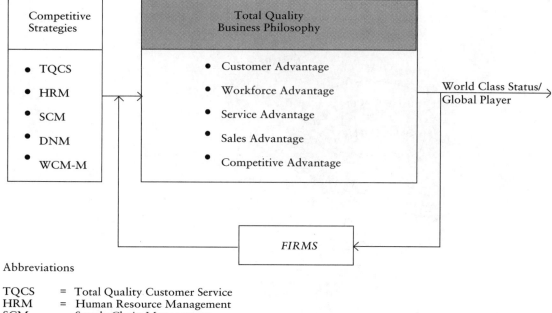

Abbreviations

TQCS   = Total Quality Customer Service
HRM   = Human Resource Management
SCM   = Supply Chain Management
DNM   = Distributor Network Management
WCM–M = World Class Manufacturing/World Class Marketing
FIRMS   = Flexible Intelligent Relationship Management Strategy

Source: Authors' data.

■ The Application of FIRMS

FIRMS offers a unique contribution to the literature by providing a solid framework, a structure for all to analyse and apply to their own enterprise. It overcomes any communication gaps between different stakeholders by uniting them through a 'common language' that enables then to plot their strategies for mutual advantage based upon the framework/strategy of the FIRMS model.

FIRMS has four fundamental attributes. It is an **Adaptive, Integrative, Derivative and Evaluative (AIDE) model** (see Table 21.8).

- *Adaptive*: all enterprises may utilise the model but each can apportion emphasis to different constituent parts and altar the sequence as it sees fit. Adaptiveness is the core of flexibility. Whilst flexibility is the macro aspect, adaptation is the micro agent of change. Any

strategy must adapt to various forces in the domestic and international business-environments. The five strategies in FIRMS are not based on any sequence. Companies can choose their own particular strategy in line with change within the environment and stages of their corporate planning. For example, a new company may have to grapple with the correct mix of the five strategies to achieve customer satisfaction, a competitive workforce, manufacturing/service advantage, market penetration/ market development, market leader/ industrial leader. A company facing a saturated market may focus on world-class manufacturing-marketing to create new products and services offering quality at low cost. Furthermore, the list of techniques is not comprehensive but it is inclusive of the latest developments in all fields of management, and are to be updated continuously.

Figure 21.6. *Systems diagram for the five goals of FIRMS*

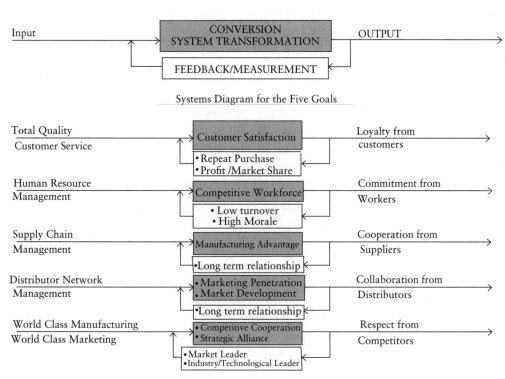

Standard System Diagram

Systems Diagram for the Five Goals

Source: Authors' data.

- *Integrative*: it integrates the essential elements in any business concern. It is holistic because it focuses on all aspects of business management capabilities: of Total Quality Customer Service (TQCS), human resource management, supply chain management, distributor network management, world-class manufacturing and world-class marketing. It is not a piecemeal approach. It looks at all aspects of business management that may impact upon profitability and market share.
- *Derivative*: because of the adaptive and integrative approach a bundle of benefits can be derived (i.e. the outcome of being adaptive and integrative). These are: loyalty from customers, commitment from workers, co-operation from suppliers, collaboration from distributors, respect from competitors – the whole chain of relationships.

- *Evaluative*: it identifies easy-to-measure indicators of excellent corporate performance. These are incidence of repeat purchases and profit/market share; low staff turnover and high morale; long-term relationships with suppliers and distributors; and, competitive co-operation between rivals.

Strategy must be adaptive to the changing environment; management capabilities must be integrated to achieve the company's vision/ mission; the end result is thus derived and open to evaluation. This process is iterative and reiterative in a rapid and dynamic business environment (i.e. a continuous improvement process for breakthrough in innovations (see Figure 21.7). Thus, precisely because it is adaptive, integrative, derivative and evaluative, the authors' model has the essential attributes of being flexible and intelligent.

Table 21.8.   *The route to business goal of profit/market share*

Adaptive	Integrative	Derivative	Evaluative
Competitive Advantage (Strategy)	Management Capabilities (Cause)	Result (Effect)	How do you know you are there? (Measurement)
• Customer Delight	• Total Quality Customer Satisfaction	• Loyalty from Customers	• Repeat Purchase Profit/Market share
• Competive Workforce	• Human resource Management	• Commitment from Workers	• Low Turnover High Morale
• Manufacturing Service Advantage	• Supply Chain Management	• Co-operation from Suppliers	• Long Term Relationship
• Market Penetration Market Development	• Distributor Network Management	• Collaboration from Distributors	• Long Term Relationship
• Beyond World-Class	• World-Class Manufacturing	• Respect from Competitors	• Competitive Cooperation/
• Market Leader	• World-Class Marketing		• Strategic Alliance
• Industrial Leader			

Source: Authors' data.

FIRMS is essentially relationship management. In this respect Western businesses may find this a novel concept, given the formalities and legalities which tend to characterise their relationships with stakeholders, such as suppliers and distributors. This contrasts with Oriental culture where Japanese business practice has a long tradition of 'soft integration' and the Chinese business community rely heavily on 'Guanxi'. Neither of these approaches to inter-company relationships are based on contractual agreements. Both Oriental traditions place great emphasis on building long-lasting relationships and friendships for mutual trust, precisely the proper foundations for business success (Levitt, 1983; Jackson, 1985; Brunner and Koh, 1988; Kirpalani and Robinson, 1989; McKenna, 1991; O'Neil and Bertrand, 1991; Bank, 1992; Hutt and Speh, 1992; Kotler, 1994).

This tradition of emphasising relationships is in stark contrast to the self-centred though ultimately self-destructive approach of many western enterprises. For example, in early 1994 British Aerospace sold off its Rover car business to Germany's BMW allegedly without giving Honda, its Japanese minority shareholder in the business, an opportunity to purchase the division that it had done so much to turn around. Ironically, this divestment arose due to BAe's need for cash after failing to conclude a joint venture with Taiwan Aerospace in 1993. Now BAe's future rests firmly upon its aerospace business where partnerships are so important, but given BAe's treatment of Honda, what company would confidently expect to find a satisfactory relationship with the British company?

Figure 21.7.   *The logic of profit and market share (virtuous circle)*

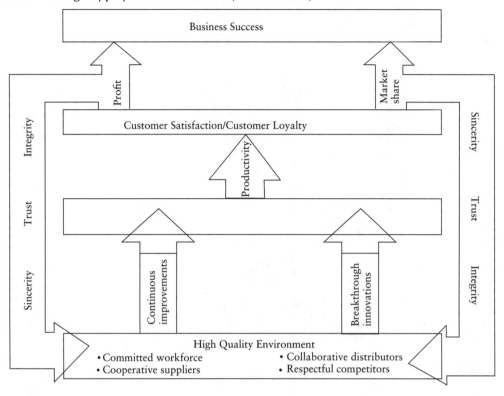

Source: Authors' data.

The principle and values of FIRMS

It has been seen that the essence of FIRMS is relationship management, and the customer represents only one of five critical relationships. If any one of these relationships is weak then it is impossible for that firm to deliver consistently TQCS in the long term. Relationship marketing is just one small element in delivering TQCS (see Figure 21.8) which itself is part of FIRMS.

Through FIRMS, enterprises may seek to establish a win-win outcome in *all* their relationships (e.g. with customers, workers, suppliers, distributors and even competitors) because they adhere to the principle of CARMA. If customers feel shortchanged, workers exploited, suppliers and distributors manipulated, or competitors cheated, then the business lacks the strong foundations necessary for

sustainable competitive advantage. Kotler (1994) also recognises that relationship marketing involves 'not only a company drive to bond better with their consumers', but that winning companies also develop 'mutually profitable relationships with their suppliers and distributors' (p. xxv).

If FIRMS is based upon the principle of CARMA, it in turn is a reflection of the core values underpinning FIRMS, namely SIT.

- *Sincerity* – what you are as a person; you are genuine; inside-out with the most inside part of yourself, your character, your motives. (You mean what you say and you say what you mean.)
- *Integrity* – your self-awareness and self-value lead you to making and keeping promises and commitment. (You say, do and keep to what you mean.)

404

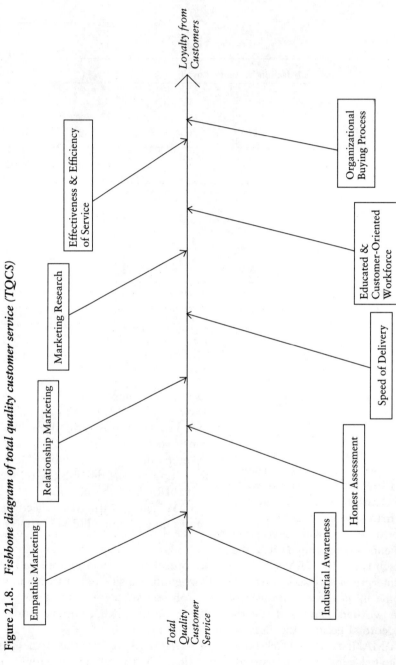

Figure 21.8.   *Fishbone diagram of total quality customer service (TQCS)*

Source: Authors' data.

- *Trust* – you inspire confidence and reliability as a person. (You say what you mean and you do what you say.)

In the real world, these are the roots of success in relationships and in the bottom-line result of business (Chan, 1993; Sonnenberg, 1994). FIRMS establishes two-way openness in each relationship with both parties guided and re-assured by CARMA. This win-win thinking creates relationships characterised by confidence, teamwork and unity of purpose. The alternative is relationships plagued by suspicion, division, and power-struggles. Companies which build relationships based on time-honoured values will build lasting positions in the marketplace, national and/or international and through this prosper. Those which do not, face a dismal future. Hence recent allegations that a leading European car manufacturer poached from a rival a senior executive and his lieutenants, whose main talent is reducing costs through ruthlessly squeezing suppliers, may prove much more harmful than has been imagined precisely because the company's commitment to SIT and CARMA may now be in question.

■ Justification for FIRMS

As industrial companies strive to develop and maintain profitable positions in the global markets of the 1990s, marketing and manu-facturing strategy have moved to centre stage (Webster Jr, 1991; Chaston, 1990; Hayes, 1994). The concept of a customer-focused, market driven business is the core value of many indus-trial companies (Webster Jr, 1991; Wallace, 1992; Kotler, 1994).

In theory, organisations have a hierarchy of inter-related strategies, each formulated at a dif-ferent level of the company. The three major levels of strategy are: corporate strategy, business strategy and functional strategies. In practice, FIRMS merges the strategic issues at the cor-porate level and the business level to ensure minimum communication breakdown/gap at the tactical level. For example this approach is prac-tised by one of Japan's leading machine tool com-panies, Okuma Corporation (see Figure 21.9 and accompanying notes).

Obviously, the world-class firms of tomorrow must aim to improve upon the current specifications for world-class status in marketing (Kotler, 1994) and manufacturing (Hayes, 1994). This strategic intent needs to be driven by a cor-porate desire to develop innovative products through lead-marketing-manufacturing strategy (i.e. lead the customers, create and develop the markets, and manufacture quality products at low cost). The priorities for the application of manufacturing and marketing techniques must be developed in response to corporate needs. The success of world-class companies depend on the common-sense selection and application of these techniques. FIRMS links the manufacturing stra-tegy and the marketing strategy so that an optimal implementation can be achieved and standardised. FIRMS provides the philosophical framework in which the various technologies can actually deliver the considerable benefits they have long promised, but too often fail to achieve.

It is normal at the corporate level, to ask 'Which business should we be in?' and 'What are we good at?' in order to identify the core com-petencies of the company. A company's com-petitiveness derives from its core competencies and its core products (the tangible results of core competitiveness). Core competence (or unique-ness) is the combination of individual tech-nologies and production skills that underlie a company's myriad product lines. Hence, the enterprise must first identify its *core competencies* which meet three requirements: they provide potential access to a wide variety of markets; make a contributions to the customer benefits of the products; and are difficult for competitors to imitate (Prahalad and Hamel, 1990). Undoubtedly, *marketing strategy* has to play a role in strategy formulation at the corporate level.

However, possessing the necessary skills and knowledge is not enough even to ensure attain-ment of current specifications of world-class status, let alone going beyond world-class. Instead it must be accompanied by a focus on its

Figure 21.9.   *Three levels of strategy: the case of Okuma Corporation*

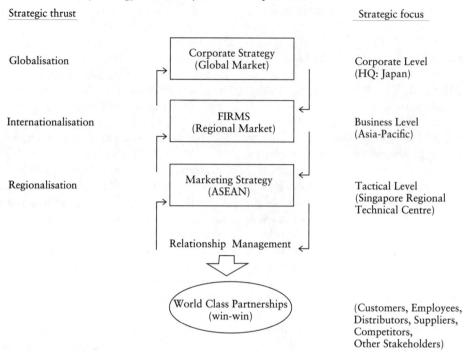

Corporate strategy aims at the global market. This is set at the Corporate Level by headquarters in Japan. The strategic thrust is Globalization.

FIRMS bridges what is planned at the Corporate Level with recommendations from the Business Level – to capture the Regional Market with focus on Asia-Pacific. The strategic thrust is Internationalization, i.e. look for the commonalty for standardisation of product specifications to Achieve economies of scale.

FIRMS adapts what is palnned at the Business Level to what is actually happending at the Tactical or Operational Level to ensure that the expecatios of Headquarters in Japan meet with performance. The Marketing Strategy aims at big market share in ASEAN. To achieve that, the strategic focus is to use Singapore as the Regional Technical Centre for Regionalization, i.e. to control the businesses in ASEAN. With the right strategic focus and strategic thrust as the 3 levels serving the interest of customers, employees, distributors, suppliers, competitors, and other stakeholders.

Source: Authors' data.

core capabilities which hone and harness the company's key business processes and support systems to thereby consolidate its core competencies. The second step is thus to review the architecture of the company (i.e. its manufacturing capabilities to support its core competencies). Undoubtedly, *manufacturing strategy* also has a role to play in strategy formulation at the corporate level.

Competencies and capabilities thus represent two different but complementary dimensions of the paradigm for FIRMS. Both concepts emphasise 'behavioural' aspects of strategy in contrast

of the traditional structural model (see Table 21.9). FIRMS emphasises behaviour (i.e. the organisational practices and business processes in which capabilities are rooted), and focuses attention on the infrastructure that supports capabilities. In the fluid, dynamic and ever-changing business environment, the essence of strategy is the dynamics of corporate behaviour. Virgin is one of the few companies that appear to appreciate this. The majority continue to be hampered by a blinkered focus on product portfolios and the extent of market diversification. The purpose of strategy is to identify and strengthen hard-to-

Table 21.9. *A comparison of the traditional approach to corporate management and the new approach for FIRMS*

Traditional Approach	New Approach – FIRMS
• Piecemeal Approach	• Holistic/Systems Approach
• Hierarchical Management	• Relationship Management
• Unfocused	• Focused (Corporate Vision, Mission, Will)
• Process-Oriented	• People Oriented
• Reactive	• Proactive
• Rational	• Innovative
• Analysis	• Synthesis
• Conservative Mind-Set and Attitude	• Progressive Mind-Set Attitude
• Programmed Learning	• Action/Heuristic Learning
• Individual Effort/Problem Solving	• Collective Effort/Problem Solving
• Stand-Alone Energy	• Multi-Party Synergy
• Trade-off	• Pay-off
• Short-term Profit	• Long-term Market Share/Profit
• Opaque (Functional Barriers)	• Transparent (No Functional Barriers)
• Within Company Boundary	• Across Company Boundary
• Corporate Image	• Corporate Character/Culture
• Win-Lose Relationships	• Win-win Relationships

Source: Authors' data.

imitate organisational capabilities that distinguish a company from it competitors in the eyes of the customers, for capabilities are visible to customers in a way that core competencies rarely are (Stalk, 1992). Whereas core competencies emphasise technology and production expertise at specific points along the value chain, capabilities with their broader base, encompass the entire value chain.

For a company to go beyond world-class status, it has to win the hearts and minds of customers (i.e. delight by exceeding rather than merely satisfying customers' expectations) through leadership in marketing and manufacturing. It has to exploit its core competencies and manufacturing capabilities to produce innovative products which capture the imaginations of its customers. Its desire and drive to compete is based upon its determination to anticipate and satisfy customers' needs by offering a bundle of benefits which represent added value (quality, service, image, etc).

While world-class manufacturing and world-class marketing are the twin pillars of FIRMS (see Figure 21.10), the reinforcements are: total quality customer service (the right focus); human resource management (the right attitude); supply chain management (the right connections); and network management (the right channels).

FIRMS directs and integrates the efforts of disparate groups of people through win-win relationships to maximise profit market share. More importantly, it has the conviction and commitment of top management to drive the

Figure 21.10.   *Synergy in FIRMS*

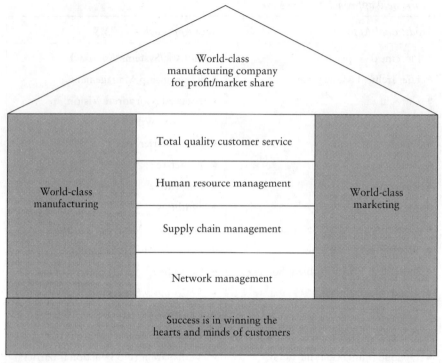

World-class
manufacturing company
for profit/market share

World-class
manufacturing

Total quality customer service

Human resource management

Supply chain management

Network management

World-class
marketing

Success is in winning the
hearts and minds of customers

Source: Authors' data.

company in pursuit of business excellence. It is a common-sense approach because it is built around pragmatism using an AIDE (adaptive, integrative, derivative, and evaluative) strategy:

- Manufacturing and marketing are customer-focused because competitiveness is ultimately judged by current and prospective customers.
- Manufacturing and marketing are integrated because customers' exact requirements are complex. If price alone fulfilled their expectations then Yugo and Aeroflot would replace Toyota and Singapore International Airlines. If quality alone ensured success in the marketplace Sony's Betamax system would have become the world standard for video cassette recorders rather than Matsushita's VHS. If reliable and speedy delivery alone were the main success factor, then Domino's Pizza might usurp McDonald's position in the fast-food industry.

The above examples highlight that customers' requirements are multi-rather than one-dimensional. It is therefore foolhardy for a company to aim simply at becoming a world-class manufacturer. This status by itself confers absolutely no advantage unless the firm is also a world-class marketing company. The opposite is also true. World-class companies are thus by definition world-class at manufacturing *and* marketing. Indeed, it is impossible to see how a firm can possibly be worthy of either one of these epithets if unworthy of the other.

FIRMS is a living system – it is dynamic, responsive, ultimately people-dependent, for people must know *what* to do and *how* to do it. Therefore developing the knowledge and competence of these human resources is essential. It utilises technologies appropriate to the company, its people and the market it serves. It is a people-driven approach based on core values (i.e. SIT) because only a principle-centred relationship (i.e. CARMA) will endure and succeed.

■ The properties of FIRMS

FIRMS attempts to dovetail key business processes and support systems into a new competitive weapon for a strategic edge over competitors. The operative words are 'flexible' and 'intelligent' because it seeks to achieve synergy, the harmonising of the different levels of the enterprise so that the whole is greater than the sum of its parts. It is a win-win relationship, a principle-centred relationship based on the core values of sincerity, trust and integrity. Success in business is in winning the hearts and minds of customers, workers, suppliers, distributors and competitors. It is not easy to achieve. It requires high levels of co-ordination, integration and communications. It takes honed skills because too much emphasis on integration will lead to over-centralisation and control, while too much flexibility will result in poor connectivity and loss of synergy. It is an intelligent heuristic model because it has identified the 'What' in the basics (the 'unchangeables') and it is embedded in time-honoured values. But it also recognises that the environment within which it operates is ever-changing and dynamic and hence the 'How' has to be flexible and adaptive, spurred by the requirements for continuous improvement. The application of common-sense is almost mandatory. The properties of FIRMS are summarised in Table 21.10.

■ Goals of FIRMS

Works by many scholars have reached a similar conclusion about the critical difference in corporate goals between Western enterprises and Asian companies, especially those from Japan; Western corporations focus on short-term profitability while Asian corporations nurse the long-term goal of industry dominance through large market share (i.e. they build barriers to new entrants, they aim to monopolise the market).

While numerous commentators have contrasted Western short-termism with the more patient, market-building long-term perspective of Asian companies there has perhaps been a tendency to overlook the simple fact that for both groups the ultimate goal is identical. They are driven by the profit motive. All business enterprises must make profits if they are to remain in business. Without profits, there cannot be investment in people, process and technology to be a significant player in global industries. Hence, the pursuit of 'profit/market share' through a value-oriented philosophy is central to FIRMS.

There are five strategic goals in FIRMS which represent the human aspect of enterprise:

- Goal 1: Loyalty from customers
- Goal 2: Commitment from workers
- Goal 3: Co-operation from suppliers
- Goal 4: Collaboration from distributors
- Goal 5: Respect from competitors

The focus of Goal 1 in FIRMS is to gain loyalty from customers by ensuring customer satisfaction through TQCS (see Table 21.8). The corporate battle is won through customers' repeat purchases, for only through customer loyalty can the enterprise achieve world-class levels of financial performance. Goals two (commitment from workers), three (co-operation from suppliers), and four (collaboration from distributors) are value-added partnerships with a shared focus, namely working towards serving customers to secure their loyalty. As Figure 21.10 shows, these are represented in the following management areas:

- *Human resource management* to gain commitment from workers which will ensure a competitive work force with low turnover and high morale.
- *Supply chain management* to gain co-operation from suppliers which will ensure manufacturing advantage in the long term.
- *Distributor network management* to gain collaboration from distributors which will ensure market development and market penetration in the long term.

Table 21.10.   *The properties of FIRMS*

Property	Comments
Synergy	The principle of creative co-operation. This is the process of valuing the differences and creating the best possible solution.
Flexibility	The ability to cope with change: versatility: the ease with which the enterprise can respond to change (macro perspective; *the thinking*).
Adaptability	The ability to change with changed circumstances (micro perspective; *the doing*).
Innovativeness	Seeking better ways of serving internal and external customers (moving from maintenance learning to innovative learning).
Wisdom	Learning from mistakes (action learning) and seeking continous improvement (innovative learning through question insight).
Common Sense	The use of innate knowledge and wisdom; practicable understanding; the ordinary capacity to see and take things in the proper light; sound judgement; mental balance (use of left brain/rights brain); heuristic.
Informativeness	The garnering of information about customers' real needs and future needs; knowledge-based database for better quality decision making.
Creative Systems Orientation	Use of the total systems approach for creative problem solving; consideration of the whole (synthesis) rather than the parts (analysis) and finding inter-relationships between these parts and their impact on the whole; study of the main features of all systems to ensure that they are complete and do in fact dovetail one with the other.

Source: Authors' data.

Only a world-class company through the twin pillars of world-class manufacturing and world-class marketing can achieve Goal 5, respect from competitors (see Figure 21.10). World-class companies will restrict competitive co-operation to others in the same league as themselves (e.g. strategic alliances in industries such as airlines where Singapore Airlines partners Swiss Air and Delta). This competitive co-operation accelerates and facilitates expansion of the frontier of world-class status. Thus deprived of world-class partners, today's firms that have failed to achieve world-class status face an even bleaker future as the gap widens between them and their more successful competitors.

FIRMS exhibits the following characteristics:

- the forging of close links with customers
- human resource management policies and practices focused on action learning, team working, workers' participation
- close links with suppliers
- close links with distributors
- a model deriving manufacturing imperatives from marketing imperatives and vice versa.

Unless the enterprise recognises the capability, concept and techniques inherent in each of the five Goals then it cannot meet these targets. A full discussion of each Goal is not provided here, but Table 21.11 summarises the key points.

It is no longer enough for companies to understand and cater for customers' current requirements and wants. They must exceed these to gain competitive advantage in the minds of customers. Only by going beyond merely providing customer satisfaction, can companies build deep customer loyalty. There is a need for a feedback system on what customers, and others who have a stake in the welfare of the enterprise (workers, suppliers, distributors, and competitors), want and expect. The heart of organisational continuous improvement is problem solving around such information.

■ Conclusion

We are entering an organisational era which is fundamentally different from the past, one which is characterised by the shift from the command-and-control organisation to the information-based organisation. These new forms of organisational structure involve fundamental reformation in managerial responsibilities, in communication and information flows, and in interpersonal relationships. As we approach the network form of organisation where small central organisations rely on other companies (for supplies and distributions), the human aspect of business enterprise assumes a central role in the game of competition. Hence, FIRMS, in essence relationship management, is needed to manage the chain of relationships linking customers, workers, suppliers, distributors and even competitors.

The Japanese Zaibatsu (e.g. Mitsui, Mitsubishi, Sumitomo and Yasuda) and South Korea's 'chaebols' (e.g. Daewoo, Hyundai, LG and Samsung) grew not from strength but from weakness. Co-operation was a vehicle for strengthening weak domestic companies and allowing them to compete against much stronger foreign rivals. Information about new technologies and scarce

Table 21.11. *The five levels of Flexible Intelligent Relationship Management Strategy*

	Level 1	*Level 2*	*Level 3*
Output	Loyalty from customers	Commitment from workers	Co-operation from suppliers
Capability	Total quality customer service	Human resource management	Supply chain management
Techniques	• Stages in total quality customer service • Empathic marketing • Relationship marketing • Marketing research • Effectiveness and speed of delivery • Educated and customer-oriented workforce • Honest assessment • Industrial awareness	• Developmental managers in HRM • Creating a corporate family • Lifetime employment • Fostering the spirit of team work • Participative management • Continuous learning • Staff welfare and benefits	• Throughput management • Enabling technologies and standards • Integrated information systems • Identify distinctive competencies • Member of 'extended family' • Management and technological support • Financial clout • Supplier rating system • Awards

Source: Authors' data.

Table 21.11.   (*continued*)

	Level 4	*Level 5*
Output	Collaboration from distributors	Respect from competitors
Capability	Network management	World-class manufacturing World-class marketing
Techniques	<ul><li>Members of an 'extended family'</li><li>Consultancy service</li><li>After-sales service and productive maintenance support</li><li>Market intelligence</li><li>Market coverage and product availability</li><li>Market development and accounts solicitation</li><li>Network management and control</li></ul>	*World-class manufacturing*<ul><li>Materials requirements handling</li><li>Manufacturing resource planning</li><li>Total quality control</li><li>Total quality management</li><li>Just-in-time/Kanban</li><li>Lean production</li><li>Group technology/cellular manufacturing</li><li>Optimised production techniques</li><li>Flexible manufacturing systems</li><li>Computer-integrated manufacturing</li><li>Intelligent manufacturing systems</li><li>Concurrent engineering</li></ul>*World-Class Marketing*<ul><li>Market-driven strategy</li><li>Customer-driven strategy</li><li>Benchmarking</li></ul>

managerial talent was shared; the cost of funds was lower inside a group than outside it; mutual support was forthcoming in bad economic times. The group's trading companies introduced and nurtured new products into foreign markets, until such times as the producing company was strong enough to promote the product itself. Today, such co-operation is necessary especially in, and between, the USA and Europe for precisely the same reason that it was once essential in Asia. However, rather than pursue co-operation to benefit two parties, the common Western response is to resort to costly acquisitions that results in the loss of an independent entity and which traditionally have a very high failure rate. Co-operation is needed in a period of economic recession at the macro level, and loss of competitive advantage at the micro level. It is particularly necessary when the previous two considerations are compounded by an era of radical and turbulent change.

FIRMS is a paradigm for manufacturing companies to cope with change and uncertainty in their search for profit/market share. More importantly, it provides the right perspective. In the midst of relentless competition, the businessmen must anchor their practices in the time-honoured values of sincerity, integrity and trust if they are to survive in the long run in the marketplace. While circumstances may change, values remain constant and the business world is composed of inter-relationships, not things. Clearly then, enterprises must serve the customers and involve fully the stakeholders. The continuity of relationships in the long run will result in continued improvements of systems and processes of working together to serve the customers. This is the strategic intent.

The basic stance of FIRMS is that the quality of human relationships in the corporate world contributes to business success or failure. FIRMS attempts to make manifest or explicit the following intangible psychological factors for value-added partnerships:

- Goal 1 Loyalty from customers (*value for money*)
- Goal 2 Commitment from workers (*meeting hierarchy of needs*)
- Goal 3 Co-operation from suppliers (*expanding and reliable business*)
- Goal 4 Collaboration from distributors (*expanding and reliable business*)
- Goal 5 Respect from competitors (*setting standards for business excellence*)

These goals are inter-linked (see Figure 21.11). Hiccups in any relationship has a chain effect on the ultimate satisfaction of customers' needs. If workers are slothful, or suppliers and distributors pursue self-interest, corporate performance will not and cannot be competitive. Competitors are needed to spur on excellence in performance. FIRMS is a shared vision of excellence and a passion for customers. These are win-win relationships based upon the principle of Competitive Advantage Requires Mutual Advantage (CARMA) to achieve the business goal of profit/market share that are anchored in the sound corporate values of Sincerity, Integrity and Trust (SIT). These time-honoured values give definition to the corporate character.

FIRMS takes a creative systems approach towards the chain of relationships (Flood, 1992). It identifies the stakeholders (i.e. the workers, the suppliers, the distributors and the competitors). These are partners-in-adversity, each with different sets of problems and concerns. Together, they can work towards the common goal of total quality customer satisfaction. Hence, these inter-linking relationships are alive and dynamic, providing a vehicle for constant learning with and from each other to solve the here and now problems amidst the difficulties, the uncertainties and the change.

FIRMS is result-oriented. These partners-in-adversity address the real problems, invite pluralism, generate innovative ideas, and act on realistic and practical solutions. This is action-learning, which is about real people in the real world working on real issues and real problems that have no answers. Thus the need for innovative learning to build on maintenance learning.

Action-learning, learning from experience and life, is the guiding philosophy of FIRMS for world-class performance. Human resource management must address the learner's changing environment. Learning is the challenge of the 1990s, and to be world-class in a period of constant change requires constant learning. Ultimately learning is related to action, for without activity there can be no feedback. Thus the philosophy of action-learning permeates world-class companies which can only achieve this status if they adhere to FIRMS.

Handy (1991) stresses that those who are always learning are those who can ride the waves of change. They regard a changing world as one full of opportunities rather than one where strategy is concerned primarily with damage-limitation to competitiveness. They are the ones most likely to be the survivors in a time of turbulence.

FIRMS is a total business concept and is the way to become the benchmark company of the world because it anticipates the skills needed in the 'age of the customer' (McKenna, 1991).

It is no accident that the emergence of *Relationship Marketing* as a key concept has coincided with the 'discovery' of business ethics, not least by enterprises themselves (e.g. look at the growing number of chairs in business ethics funded by companies). Companies which build relationships based on strong values and ethical principles will establish defensible positions in the market place. The application of strong values and ethical principles will have a direct and positive impact on profitability and market share. Only those businesses which have a *genuine* concern for customers *and* other stakeholders will prosper.

■ References

Aguayo, R. (1990), *Dr. Deming: American Who Taught the Japanese About Quality*, New York: Fireside.

Albrecht, K. (1992), *The Only Thing that Matters: Bringing the Power of the Customer into the Center of Your Business*, New York: Harper Business.

Bank, J. (1992), *The Essence of Total Quality Management*, Hemel Hempstead: Prentice-Hall, pp. 1–19.

Brown, S. A. (1992), *Total Quality Service: How Organizations use it to Create a Competitive Advantage*, Scarborough, Ont.: Prentice-Hall.

Brunner, J. A. and Koh, A. C. (1988), 'Negotiations in the People's Republic of China: An Empirical Survey of American and Chinese Negotiators' Perceptions and Practices', *Journal of Global Marketing* 2 (1).

Chan, K. C. (1993), 'Intelligent Corporate Strategy Beyond World-Class Status', *International Journal of Operations & Production Management* 13 (9), pp. 18–28.

Chaston, I. (1990), *Managing for Marketing Excellence*, London: McGraw-Hill.

Christopher, M., Payne, A. and Ballantyne, D. (1991), *Relationship Marketing*, Oxford: Butterworth-Heinemann.

Davidow, W. H. and Uttal, B. (1989), *Total Customer Service: The Ultimate Weapon*, New York: Harper Perennial.

Day, G., Weitz, B. and Wensley, R. (eds) (1990), *The Interface of Marketing and Strategy*, Greenwich, Conn.: JAI Press.

Fraser-Robinson, J. and Mosscrop, P. (1991), *Total Quality Marketing: What has to Come Next in Sales, Marketing and Advertising*, London: Kogan Page.

Garvin, D. A. (1993), 'Manufacturing Strategic Planning', *California Management Review* 35 (4) Summer, pp. 85–106.

Hayes, R. and Pisano, G. (1994), 'Beyond World-Class: The New Manufacturing Strategy', *Harvard Business Review* (January–February), pp. 77–86.

Heide, J. B. and John, G. (1992), 'Do Norms Matter in Marketing Relationships?', *Journal of Marketing* 56 (April), pp. 32–44.

Hamill, J. (1990), 'Global Marketing', Chapter 6 in *Perspectives on Marketing Management: Volume 2*, (ed.) M. J. Baker, Chichester: John Wiley.

Hutt, M. D. and Speh, T. W. (1992), *Business Marketing Management: A Strategic View of Industrial and Organizational Markets*, Fort Worth: The Dryden Press, pp. 492–493.

Jackson, B. B. (1985a), 'Build Customer Relationships that Last', *Harvard Business Review* (November–December), pp. 120-128.

Jackson, B. B. (1985b), *Winning and Keeping Industrial Customers: The Dynamics of Customer Relationships*, Lexington, Mass.: D. C. Heath.

Kirpalani, V. H. and Robinson, W. R. (1989), 'The China Market and Lessons from Successful Exporters', *Journal of Global Marketing* 2 (4), pp. 81–98.

Kotler, P. (1994), *Marketing Management: Analysis, Planning, Implementation, and Control*, 8th edition, Englewood Cliffs, NJ: Prentice-Hall, pp. 678–681.

Leenders, M. R. and Blenkhorn, D. L. (1988), *Reverse Marketing: The New Buyers–Supplier Relationship*, New York: The Free Press.

Lele, M. M. and Sheth, J. N. (1991), *The Customer is Key: Gaining an Unbeatable Advantage through Customer Satisfaction*, New York: John Wiley.

Levitt, T. (1986), *The Marketing Imagination*, New York: The Free Press, pp. 111–126.

Marconi, J. (1992), 'Relationship Marketing: Understanding the People Business', in *Crisis Marketing: When Bad Things Happen to Good Companies*, Chicago: Probus, pp. 1–41.

McDermot, M. C. and Gray, S. J. (1990), 'International Mergers: The Pursuit of Global Market Leadership', in *Perspective in Industrial Organization*, (eds) Dankbaar, Groenewegen and Schenk, Dordrecht: Kluwer Academic Publishers.

McGregor, D. (1960), *The Human Side of Enterprise*, New York: McGraw-Hill.

McKenna, R. (1991), *Relationship Marketing: Successful Strategies for the Age of the Customer*, Reading, Mass.: Addison-Wesley.

McLaughlin, H. and Thorpe, R. (1993), 'Action Learning – A Paradigm in Emergence: The Problems Facing a Challenge to Traditional Management Education and Development', *British Journal of Management* 4 (1) (March), pp. 19–27.

O'Neal, C. and Bertrand, K. (1991), *Developing A Winning J. I. T. Marketing Strategy: The Industrial Marketer's Guide*, Englewood Cliffs, NJ: Prentice-Hall, pp. 177–195.

Ouchi, W. G. (1982), *Theorgy Z: How American Business Can Meet the Japanese Challenge*, Reading, Mass.: Addison-Wesley.

Pathmarajah, Allen (1991), 'Creativity in Relationship Marketing', *The Singapore Marketer* 1 (1), pp. 14–17.

Payne, A. (1993), *The Essence of Service Marketing*, Hemel Hempstead: Prentice-Hall.

Shani, D. and Chalasani, S. (1993), 'Exploiting Niches using Relationship Marketing', *Journal of Business & Industrial Marketing* 8 (4), pp. 58–66.

Soin, S. S. (1992), *Total Quality Control Essentials: Key Elements, Mehodologies, and Managing for Success*, New York: McGraw-Hill.

Sonnenberg, F. K. (1994), *Managing with a Conscience: How to Improve Performance through Integrity, Trust and Commitment*, New York: McGraw-Hill.

Stalk, G., Evans, P. and Shulman, L. E. (1992) 'Competing Capabilities: The New Rules of Corporate Strategy', *Harvard Business Review* (March–April), pp. 57–69.

Tjosvold, D., Meredith, L. and Wellwood, R. M. (1993), 'Implementing Relationship Marketing: A Goal Interdependence Approach', *Journal of Business & Industrial Marketing* 8(4), pp. 5–17.

Wallace, T. F. (1992), *Customer-Driven Strategy: Winning through Operational Excellence*, Vermont: Oliver Wight Publications.

Webster, F. E. Jr (1991), *Industrial Marketing Strategy*, 3rd edition, New York: John Wiley.

Williams, J. R. (1992), 'How Sustainable is Your Competitive Advantage?', *California Management Review* 34 (3) (Spring), pp. 29–51.

■ Chapter 22 ■

Marketing Theory and Practice in a Postmodern Era

Bernard Cova and Olivier Badot

Introduction: the postmodern, postmodernism and postmodernity

The idea of the present as *postmodern* is now firmly on the agenda for debate. The postmodern has become a concept to be wrestled with, and such a battle-ground of conflicting opinions, that it can no longer be ignored by marketing theory and practice. But diverse and at times conflicting references to *postmodernity* and *postmodernism* are to be found in a growing number of disciplinary fields and across an increasingly broad range of discourses. Consequently, a number of difficulties are encountered in the analysis of modern and postmodern, notably the presence of a constellation of related terms, a lack of specificity associated with the concepts employed, particularly in relation to their historical referents or periodisation, as well as the existence of a number of conceptual distinctions between positive and negative manifestations of respectively modern and postmodern forms (Smart, 1990).

However, the social and philosophical changes characterised by the label of 'postmodern' are considered as major traits of our times by a growing number of European and North-American marketing practitioners and researchers (Brown, 1993; Firat, 1991a, 1991b and 1992; Hirschman and Holbrook, 1992; Ogilvy, 1990; Venkatesh, 1989 and 1992; see also the special issue of the *International Journal of Research in Marketing*, vol. 10, 1993, on 'Postmodernism, Marketing and the Consumer'). In this chapter, we will assume that to speak of **postmodernism** is to refer to a specific **philosophical** perspective replete with epistemological assumptions and methodological preferences (Rosenau, 1991) that proposes a complete rethinking of the general principles of marketing theory (Brown, 1993). Similarly, we will assume that to speak of **postmodernity** is to suggest an epochal shift or break from modernity involving the emergence of a new **social** totality with its own distinct organisation principles (Featherstone, 1991) that addresses the challenge of an aestheticised and tribalised consumption to marketing practice (Badot, Bucci and Cova, 1993).

Postmodernism in arts and science: fragmentation and indeterminacy

Fragmentation, indeterminacy, and intense distrust of all universal or totalising discourses are the hallmark of postmodernist thought in arts (architecture, photography, visual and performing arts...) and science (physics, linguistics, philosophy, social sciences...). 'The rediscovery of pragmatism in philosophy, the shift of ideas about the philosophy of science wrought by Kuhn and Feyerabend, Foucault's emphasis upon discontinuity and difference in history and his privileging of polymorphous correlations in place of simple or complex causality, new developments in mathematics emphasising indeterminacy (catastrophe and chaos theory, fractal geometry), the (re)emergence of concern in ethics, politics, and anthropology for the validity and the dignity of the other, all indicate a widespread and profound shift' (Harvey, 1989, p. 9). In fact, postmodernism haunts especially social science today. In a number of respects, some plausible and some preposterous, postmodern approaches dispute the underlying assumptions of mainstream social science and their research product over the last three decades. The challenges postmodernism poses seem endless. It rejects epistemological assumptions, refutes methodological conventions, resists knowledge claims, obscures all versions of truth, and dismisses policy recommendations (Rosenau, 1991).

The appearance of postmodernism in the social sciences signals more than another novel academic paradigm. Rather, a radically new and different cultural movement is coalescing in a broad-gauged re-conceptualisation of how we experience and explain the world around us. The divergent, even contradictory expositions of postmodernism underline the need to distinguish among its various orientations if we are ever to be able to talk about it all. There are probably as many forms of postmodernism as there are postmodernists. If it were not so clumsy, we could speak of postmodernisms. But within this diversity of postmodern pronouncements two broad, general orientations can be delineated: in

its most extreme formulations ('sceptical postmodernism'), postmodernism is revolutionary, it goes to the very core of what constitutes social science and radically dismisses it; in its more moderate proclamations ('affirmative postmodernism'), postmodernism encourages substantive re-definition and innovation (Rosenau, 1991, p. 4). The sceptical postmodernists, offering a pessimistic, negative, gloomy assessment, argue that the postmodern age is one of fragmentation, disintegration, malaise, meaningless, a vagueness or even absence of moral parameters and societal chaos. They argue that the destructive character of modernity makes the postmodern age one of radical, unsurpassable uncertainty. Although the affirmative postmodernists agree with the sceptical postmodernists' critique of modernism; they have a more optimistic view of the postmodern era. Most affirmatives search for a philosophical and intellectual practice that is non-dogmatic, tentative and non-ideological. These postmodernists do not, however, shy away from affirming an ethic or making normative choices (Rosenau, 1991, pp. 15–16). Both sceptics and affirmatives challenge those versions of modern social science that claim objectivity, causality, a materialist reality, and universal rules of inquiry. Sceptical postmodernists argue that reality is pure illusion: everything is intertextual, not causal or predictive. Their preferred methods include anti-objective, introspective interpretation and deconstruction. Relativism and uncertainty characterise their views. They doubt the value of reason and contend it is impossible to establish standard criteria for judging intellectual production. Affirmative postmodernists also indict modern science. Their own understanding of reality is constructivist or contextualist. Explanation is not only weakly intertextual but also theological. Positive value orientations and specific normative goals openly guide the affirmatives' version of social science. Methodology depends on emotion, intuition, and imagination. Although ambivalent about reason, few affirmatives are, however, willing to abandon it altogether (Rosenau, 1991, p. 23).

The postmodernist epistemological and methodological preferences in social sciences can be delineated as follows (Rosenau, 1991, p. 109–137):

a) While modern social science strives to discover and depict what it calls external reality, postmodernists hold that there are no adequate means for representing it.

b) While modern social science has assumed causality and prediction were essential to explanation, postmodernists consider both uninteresting because, they argue, the requirements of temporal priority and independent, external reality assumed by these concepts are dubious. In a world where everything is related in an absolute interactive way, temporal priority, required by causality, is nearly impossible to establish.

c) While within modern social science, it is often assumed that values should not bias inquiry and that research should be impartial and investigators detached, postmodernists agree that values, normative questions, feelings, and emotions are all part of human intellectual production.

d) While modern social science is guided by general rules of method that direct the conduct of research (its more orthodox practitioners assume that there is but a single method, a self-correcting scientific method that is universal in its application across disciplines), postmodernism is oriented towards methods that apply to a broad range of phenomena, focus on the margins, highlight uniqueness, concentrate on the enigmatic, and appreciate the unrepeatable. All its methods relinquish any attempt to create new knowledge in the modern sense of the word. Therefore, postmodern social science presumes methods that multiply paradox, inventing ever more elaborate repertoires of questions, each of which encourages an infinity of answers, rather than methods that settle on solutions.

e) While modern science specifies precise criteria for evaluating knowledge claims and has guidelines for questioning theories and asserting counterclaims, postmodernists, and especially the sceptical postmodernists, argue

that the very idea of strict evaluative standards goes against the whole postmodernist philosophy of science. 'They disparage modern science's standards and its criteria for evaluating knowledge and all accepted, conventional means to judge the results of intellectual inquiry in any form. They take aim at coherence because false or otherwise wrong versions can hold together as well as right ones. They reject consistency as a criterion, calling for a proliferation of inconsistent theories rather than a weeding out of bad from good theories. Nothing can be proved; nothing can be falsified. They dismiss the possibility of evaluating theory on the basis of data, adding that if theory exists at all it must be liberated from data and observation. Standards are not needed if one gives up the idea of truth-as-a-matter-of-matching-up-facts-to-theory' (Rosenau, 1991, p. 134).

Postmodernity in society: tribalism and linking value

The term postmodernity renders accurately the defining traits of the social condition that emerged throughout the affluent countries of Europe and of European descent in the course of the 20th century, and took progressively its present shape in the second half of this century (Turner, 1990). The term is accurate as it draws attention to continuity and discontinuity as two faces of the intricate relationship between the present social condition and the formation that it preceded and gestated. It brings into relief the intimate, genetic bond that ties the new, postmodern social condition to modernity – the social formation that emerged in the same part of the world in the course of the 18th century, and took its final shape during the 19th (Baumann, 1992a, p. 149). Postmodernity may be interpreted as fully developed modernity; as modernity which goes beyond its false consciousness and comes to understand what it actually was doing all along, i.e producing ambivalence and pluralism, and also reconciles itself to the fact that the purposes which were originally set, e.g. rational order and individual freedom, will never be reached (Baumann, 1992b, p. 134).

Modernity entered history as a progressive force promising to liberate humankind from ignorance and irrationality, but one can readily wonder whether that promise has been sustained. As long as traditional forms of communal mediations have existed (family, village, district, religion...), the modern being has constantly tried to liberate itself from them in order to make the 'enlightened' metaphor of the free subject come true. Modernity in this way opposed the notion of contract, a voluntary and reversible choice made by each individual to associate rationally with others in a specified and limited framework, to the traditional notion of community, an irreversible obligation imposed on each of its members. In the modern view, the individual is primary, he/she exists first as a pre-social being, relations are secondary and essentially instrumental. Differentiation more than communion guides the action of individuals. In order to uproot him/herself from the communal debris of the Middle Ages, the modern being relies on new forms of mediation which are rational and near universal aggregations of impersonal ties, like the nation-state or the social class. Modernity thus opposes personal intimacy, emotional depth, moral commitment, social cohesion and continuity in time of the traditional relations within a community, to the impersonality, the rationality and the universality of modern relations based on a utilitarian and economic approach. The market economy is therefore the strongest force behind the destruction of old communities that can be found. But, in fact 'nous n'avons jamais été modernes', as stated by Latour (1991), and the new and modern mediations have lasted as much because of their contractual basis as thanks to the shared emotion of their members and their 'natural' instinct to recreate the social link. Certain periods of history and certain regions did however come near to attaining the modern social link. It was apparently the case in eighteenth-century England where, as Disraeli writes in no uncertain terms in *Sybil*, 'modern society acknowledges no neighbour', and where isolation between individuals in big cities is extreme. In reaction to this, the nineteenth century appears to have been a period of social recomposition on the basis of modern aggregations. The twentieth century, with its great political and scientific utopias has lived out very intensively the myth of the liberation of the individual. This tension has resulted in the breaking up and 'delegitimisation' of all forms of contractual communities inherited from the two last centuries, and from the so-called uniformisation of behaviour. The individual has never been so free in his/her private and public choices as today, and never so alone and cut off from the community. The present period, sometimes called postmodernity, is therefore one of extreme social dissolution, but also of attempts at recomposition: the modern being, who has finally achieved his/her total liberation from archaic and even modern social links during the eighties, and consequently turned the metaphor of liberty into a reality, is embarking on a reverse movement, seeking social recomposition based on free choice. But this choice concerns emotional groupings more than contractual systems. Free choice and shared emotion: it is the search for the 'irreconcilable community' which characterises our era. If, as Baudrillard writes (1992, p. 151), 'liberty is a critical form, liberation, on the other hand, is a potentially catastrophic form. The former confronts the subject with its own alienation and its transcendence. The latter leads to metastases, to chain reactions, to the disconnection of all the elements and finally to the radical expropriation of the subject'. Liberation is the effective fulfilment of the metaphor of liberty, and in this sense it is also its end. Postmodernity can therefore be said to crown not the triumph of individualism, but the beginning of its end with the emergence of a reverse movement of a desperate search for the social link (see Figure 22.1).

As a consequence, a growing number of sociological studies (Maffesoli, 1988, 1990, 1991, 1992; Featherstone, 1991; Baumann, 1992a and 1992b) advocate that the social dynamics, characteristic of our postmodern era, are made up of a multiplicity of experiences, of representations and of daily-experienced emotions which are very

Figure 22.1.   *The return of community*

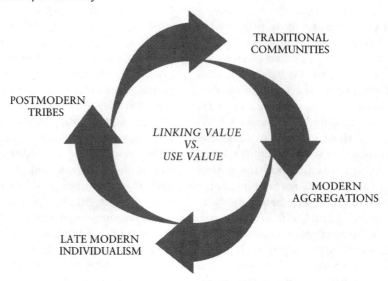

often not properly understood. Whilst such dynamics are, most of the time, explained by individualism, they stress the tribal atmosphere which is developing more and more. Maffesoli thus puts forward an essential paradox (1988, p. 17): 'the constant coming and going between the growing massification and the development of micro-groups which I will call tribes'. The word tribe refers to the re-emergence of quasi-archaic values: a local sense of identification, religiosity, syncretism, group narcissism..., the common denominator of which is the community dimension. These tribes try to revive the community archetype of the district or the village , but they are not communities which are clearly definable in spatial terms; on the contrary, some use all the resources of the latest technical means of communication (micro-computers, Internet, fax) in order to form virtual tribes in which face-to-face encounters or physical co-presence are less and less frequent. Postmodern tribes exist in no other form but the symbolically manifested commitment of their members. They can rely on neither executive powers able to coerce their constituency into submission to the tribal rules (seldom do they have clearly codified rules to which the submission could be demanded), nor on the strength of neighbourly bonds or intensity of reciprocal

exchange (most tribes are deterritorialised, and communication between their members is hardly at any time more intense than the intercourse between members and non-members of the tribe). Postmodern tribes are, therefore constantly in *statu nascendi* rather than *essendi*, brought over again into being by repetitive symbolic ritual of the members but persisting no longer than these rituals' power of attraction (Baumann, 1992a, pp. 157–158). In fact, late modern individualism has moved to a postmodern tribalism (Maffesoli, 1988) made up of successive sincerities favouring the concatenation of little ephemeral emotional entities. Postmodern persons thus evolve from the 'is' (stable identity) to the 'and' (multifaceted) and from 'striving towards' (finality) to 'stretched within' (syntony): free choice and shared emotion. Emotion and social sharing which lead them to the re-integration of rituals and of transcendence in everydayness: the seeking for a relational meaning which is a joint construction of existence is parallel to the rediscovery of the sacred and of traditions (Lipovetsky, 1992, p. 73). In postmodernity, there is a sliding from a *logic of identity to a logic of identification* (Maffesoli, 1991, p. 16). The former was essentially individualist, but the latter is much more collective. The culture of sensation is therefore the consequence of

attraction, the hobby which are held in common and which cement the community constitute ethical vectors. The ethical is a morality with neither obligation nor sanction, with no obligation other than coming together and being a member of a collective body, with no sanction other than being excluded should the interest which brought me into the group come to an end. This is precisely the *ethics of the aesthetic* (Maffesoli, 1991): experiencing something together is a factor socialisation. The postmodern communities taken as a whole are referred to by the term *sociality* which is different from 'social' as it stresses not the mechanical and instrumental function of an individual member of a contractual institution, but the symbolic and emotional role of persons within multiple ephemeral tribes. Contrary to modernity, the person appears in postmodernity to be more secondary, and the social link becomes of primary importance again.

It is remarkable that modernity emphasised essentially the utilitarian value ('use value') of the object, that which enabled the modern individual to be freer and more independent because objects do the work for him. The quality of modern objects is their use value without defect ('the zero defect'). They are designed to serve and to satisfy the needs of the individual. This use value can be functional (material attributes) or symbolic (immaterial attributes) like the so-called 'status symbol', or a combination of the two. What is always at stake is the individual in his/her independence from others. Objects circulate between producers and consumers who have *a priori* no social link. If a minimum social link exists, it is at the service of the economic link, therefore at the service of the individual freed of his/her social obligations. When freed of his/her public obligations (the grocer, the salesman...), the modern individual may choose the obligations he/she wishes in the private sphere. Tradition, for its part, perceived objects more as supporting the social link between persons; so it had above all a 'linking value', before a use value. According to this viewpoint, all that circulates is at the service of the social link. Going to buy a newspaper is, first of all, meeting Michael the newsagent, talking with him for pleasure or out of obligation,

and in addition buying the local paper. And this local paper is the daily link with the spatial community: village, town, region... The modern individual did not want this constraining link. For him/her, the economic sphere had to be completely cut off from the societal sphere. Self service, where 'use value' and not 'linking value' is sold, is his/her ideal. With the neo-tribalism distinguishing postmodernity, a reconfiguration of the use value and the linking value of objects is taking shape (see Figure 22.1). They serve the person in his/her independent individuality and they serve as 'cult-objects' to the ephemeral communities in which he/she participates with others. Cult-objects support the interdependence between persons, either symbolically or instrumentally, an interdependence which was refused and denied by modernity. These objects can thus be found in societal meeting places, in codes of behaviour and dress styles, and above all in the rituals and the emblems of each tribe. They evoke the value system and the taboos which characterise the numerous postmodern tribes, even the most short-lived.

Postmodernism in marketing theory: towards a coherent pluralism of paradigms and methodologies

If, on a superficial level, postmodernism appears to parallel and provide a rationale, albeit a rationale that rejects rationality, for the major elements of marketing theory, the adoption of postmodernism is not without penalty (Brown, 1993). The anti-universalism and anti-foundationalism of postmodernism have very serious implications for marketing theory, the bulk of whose principles are predicated on the archetypal modernist assumptions of analysis, planning and control. Whether it be marketing planning procedures, the product life cycle, SWOT analyses, Maslow's hierarchy of needs, the Howard-Sheth model of consumer behaviour, the trickle down principle of fashion diffusion, the strategic matrices of Ansoff, Porter and the Boston Consulting Group, Copeland's classification of goods, the typologies of retailing institutions, hierarchies of advertising effects, the wheel of retailing or, needless to say, the four P's, the majority of marketing and marketing related conceptualisations are basically modernist in orientation. They represent attempts – admittedly imperfect attempts – to make general statements about marketing phenomena and are thus deemed unacceptable by many postmodernists (Brown, 1993). More, many marketers contend that the recent postmodernist development in the philosophy of science (see p. 417 on the 'sceptical postmodernists') imply that objectivity in marketing research is an illusion, a chimera, or impossible. 'Truth' in marketing theory and research has consequently become the center of a major dispute amongst scholars of the discipline starting with the seminal article of Hunt (1990) in the *Journal of Marketing*, 'Truth in Marketing Theory and Research', followed by critical comments on 'scientific realism' made by Peter (1992), then an alternative perspective proposed by Zinkhan and Hirscheim (1992) and replies by Hunt (1992 and 1993).

In fact, alternative proposals by affirmative postmodernist marketing researchers emphasise essentially the fragmentation and pluralism of marketing theory in a postmodern era:

- fragmentation of marketing theory into many sub-theories concerning diverse areas of interest (Badot and Cova, 1992);
- pluralism of paradigms in marketing theory for the same area of interest (Dholakia and Arndt, 1985).

The fragmentation of marketing theory is a consequence of the proliferation of peripheral marketing which, during the last two decades attempted to apply the basic principles of marketing to market situations that did not fit in with the dominant theory (e.g., the marketing of tangible products from one company to mass consumers in a stable socio-technical context: the U.S.). This could be shifting from product marketing to services marketing, project marketing or even artefact marketing (Figure 22.2). This could

be shifting from a business-to-consumer relation to a business-to-business relation (industrial marketing, reverse marketing, internal marketing or warfare marketing) or even to a business-to-global environment relation (Figure 22.3). This could be shifting from a low-tech/low-touch context to a high-tech (high-tech marketing) or a high touch context (fashion marketing), and reaching at the end of a 'neo-marketing' which characterises the high-tech/high-touch postmodern socio-technical condition (Figure 22.4). In each of these cases of peripheral marketing, the story is quite the same. During a first phase, there is a direct transposition of dominant tools and techniques that results unsatisfactorily in a lot of anomalies; in fact, practitioners resist the dominant marketing theory because they have the feeling it does not match their business reality. In a second phase, there is an attempt to adapt the dominant tools and techniques which often has unsatisfactory results. Finally, in a third phase, there is a complete break with the dominant theory and the construction of an alternative theory or sub-theory. This was typically the case for industrial marketing. Some years ago a number of researchers interested in industrial markets were struck by the fact that the prevailing view in the marketing literature was of a world that didn't tally with their own experience. It just wasn't so (Hakansson, 1982). They knew that there wasn't a neat split in industrial marketing between the active seller and the passive buyer. Often buyers develop an idea of their requirements, seek out, evaluate and persuade a chosen supplier to supply. 'In the markets for cornflakes or soap powder, consumers used to be similar in size and perhaps similar in requirements. In contrast industrial buying companies have pronounced differences in size, power and requirements and there aren't so many of them. They do not buy just because they see an advertisement on television or because a salesman calls. The process is not one of action. It is one of interaction!' (Ford, 1990). These interactions are occurring within the context of relationships between the companies, and these relationships are affected by the pattern of other relationships which surround them: the network. Interactions,

Figure 22.2. *Marketing shifts of object*

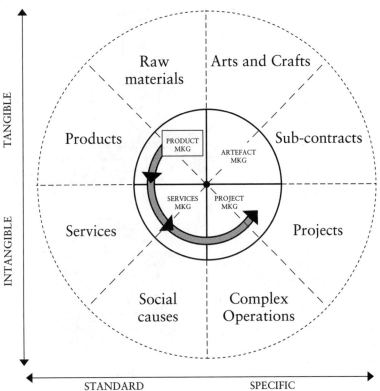

relationships, networks are the basic elements of a specific marketing sub-theory especially developed for industrial markets, that now stands as an alternative to the dominant theory even out of the business-to-business framework; it is known usually under the name of 'relationship marketing'. Peculiarly, the postmodern fragmentation of marketing theory leads sometimes to modern reactions to restore a dominant theory in marketing based on a 'new' approach. This is the case for a long list of new marketing panaceas which starts with the 'new marketing' of Regis McKenna and includes 'relationship marketing' (see Figure 22.5).

The pluralism of paradigm in marketing theory challenges the historical and philosophical foundations of marketing that are clearly embedded in the American notions of capitalism and utilitarianism. It challenges also the traditional micro approach based on the instrumental man

metaphor emphasising purposive decision making. 'Breaking from the paradigmatic provincialism' as proposed by Arndt (1985) has begun to be the key-sentence for affirmative postmodernist marketing researchers. Hirschman and Holbrook (1992) recently presented an overview of what could be the implications of this postmodernist paradigmatic pluralism for consumer research: 'over the past decade, a series of articles has seriously questioned the continued reliance of consumer research on positivistic, neopositivistic, or quasi-positivistic modes of inquiry. Although these challenges do not speak with a unified voice, they share deep concerns over issues related to the nature of knowledge in the study of consumption phenomena' (Hirschman and Holbrook, 1992. p. 1).

An implicit theme running through these postmodernist approaches to research deals with problems of epistemology that arise from ques-

Figure 22.3. *Marketing shifts of relation*

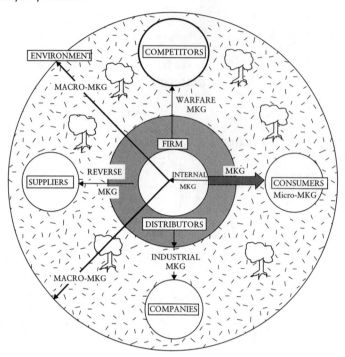

tioning the connection of knowledge to empiricist moorings in a real world. If knowledge does not originate in some reality out there, where does it come from? What rules guide its development, comprehension, description and organisation? Many of those who most oppose the abandonment of neopositivism, logical empiricism, or the received view centre their arguments in the natural fear of scientific anarchy. They argue that relinquishing the metaphysical belief in one world with one truth about one reality precipitates an inevitable free-for-all or free-fall into radical relativism wherein no hope of a scientific consensus exists and no rigorous evaluative criteria remain. Many consumer researchers still shrink from the full implications of just what the implementation of postmodernist methodologies might bring to the field. This lack of confidence receives partial justification from the fact that, with few exceptions, challengers to the neopositivist metaphysics have lacked specificity about how their research programs would actually progress (Hirschman and Holbrook, 1992, p. 2). In consequence, the effort

of Hirschman and Holbrook has been directed toward assisting consumer researchers to make those choices in an informed and personally comfortable manner. They presented a continuum of philosophical concepts regarding the origin and concepts of knowledge relevant to consumer behaviour phenomena. The end points of this epistemological continuum are Material Determinism (e.g., commonsense Empiricism) and Mental Determinism (e.g., pure Rationalism). Between these two extremes lie several philosophies varying in the relative degrees of Material versus Mental Determinism that they attribute to knowledge construction. They also presented a set of research methods aimed at implementing inquiry from the viewpoint of each particular philosophical perspective. The key requirement for validity entails a logical correspondence of the metaphysical assumptions made, on the one hand, with the aims, concepts, and methods employed, on the other (Hirschman and Holbrook, 1992, p. 2–3).

In the same affirmative postmodernist vein, Cova and Salle (1992) have studied the outcomes

Figure 22.4. *Marketing shifts of context*

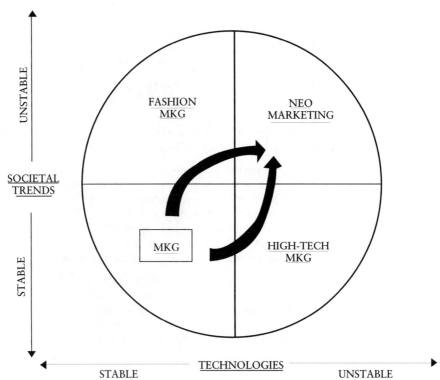

of such a paradigmatic pluralism for industrial buying behaviour research. They argue that an analysis of the different approaches research has adopted towards industrial buying behaviour may very well prove to be an interesting indication of the pluralism of schools of thought that lie behind industrial marketing. During the last twenty years, many alternative paradigms have appeared both in the methods of investigation (the *alternative ways of knowing* of Hunt, 1991) as well as in the in the definition of the object observed (the *alternative objects of knowledge*): the 'inductive' paradigm within the IBB Group of researchers (Industrial Buying Behaviour Group), the 'dyadic' paradigm within the ISBM (Institute for the Study of Business Markets) in the US, the 'interactive' paradigm within the IMP Group (Industrial Marketing and Purchasing Group) in Europe, the 'network' paradigm still within the IMP Group ... This does not claim for the leadership of a particular paradigm, nor for an integra-

tive approach a kind of 'Grand Theory' of industrial buying behaviour, but rather for a 'coherent pluralism' of paradigms and theories as proposed by Bachelard or a 'critical pluralism' as proposed more recently in the field of marketing by Hunt (1991): 'If the partisans of the exact sciences agree on the fruitfulness of a coherent pluralism approach, this approach must *a fortiori* play a role in the understanding of social phenomena' (Maffesoli 1985, p. 178) and in particular of industrial buying phenomena. The fact remains, however, that the scientific community as a whole continues to further its understanding of the complexity of the buying decision-making process in the industrial sector by using approaches that match the phenomenon observed in sophistication and diversity. Thus for a marketing researcher, 'coherent pluralism', in terms of the aims of one's research, one's skills and one's desires, consists in making a deliberate choice amongst the many alternative paradigms (and not

Figure 22.5.   *Postmodern marketing?*

Terminology	Definition	Sources
Micro-marketing	Marketing so finely tuned that, if applied properly, it will speak to customers almost individually	Schlossberg
Maxi-marketing	Direct contact, dialogue and involvement with the individual prospect or customer leading to increased sales and brand loyalty	Rapp and Collins
Database marketing	Direct marketers' (ability) to talk to their audiences as individuals in very large numbers	Davies
New marketing	We are witnessing the emergence of a new marketing paradigm not a 'do more' marketing that simply turns up the volume on the sales spiels of the past but a knowledge and experience-based marketing that . . . finds a way to integrate the customer into the company, to create and sustain a relationship between the company and the customer	McKenna
Wrap-around marketing	Two perennial problems in marketing are getting customers and keeping them. Traditionally, most marketers have spent their time getting customers. But the truth is we ought to start spending more time on the problem of how to retain the customers we have	Kotler
Value-added marketing	Improve existing products and concepts rather than launch new ones	Nilson
Relationship marketing	Has as its concern the dual forces of getting and keeping customers. Traditionally much of the effort of marketing has been directed towards the getting of the customer rather than the keeping of them. Relationship marketing aims to close the loop	Christopher *et al.*
Neo-marketing	The basic rule is break the old rules	Cova and Svanfeldt

Source: S. Brown, 'Postmodern Marketing?', *European Journal of Marketing* (1993).

within one paradigm), of the approach that the researcher considers the most appropriate and not to allow oneself to be prisoner of one dominant model. This may be all the more difficult to achieve, since the researcher may be involved in a particular school of thought, in a militant scientific context that may well restrict the liberty of choice. However, there are many examples at the present time of researchers in the industrial marketing field who, under the influence of the internationalisation of knowledge, have been able to blend together different approaches to their research and different sources of fact and evidence available. This merging of different paradigms and schools encourages the development of 'coherent pluralism' in industrial marketing. And finally, this movement should spread over from research into teaching: not a brilliant lecture in the paradigm itself, but an appraisal of the different approaches and paradigms throughout the discussion of a case study in industrial marketing. This enable the student to understand how each theory, necessarily sub-determined (i.e its predictive value is limited), makes its own contribution to the understanding and the solving of industrial marketing issues (Cova and Salle, 1992).

Postmodernity in marketing practice: towards a societal embeddedness of marketing

The meaning ascribed to objects, often has as much importance as their instrumental functions for the postmodern person. He/she seeks in objects as much their use value (functions and symbols at the service of the individual, and as a mean of differentiation) as their linking value (aesthetics and emotion at the service of the social link between persons, and as a means of de-differentiation). A product's technical functions should not be embellished as in the modern era, rather, the aesthetics are its main function (the aesthetic meaning here, faithful to its etymology, is understood as the fact of experiencing emotions, feelings, common passions, and in a very different areas of social life, and not in its narrow sense of superficial beauty). That the object actually does some 'useful' things – like taking us from A to B, mash potatoes, or keep us warm – is taken from granted. Technological innovation, the hallmark or modernism, is being gradually substituted by aesthetic innovation. Unlike simple modern goods, postmodern objects are transmitted more than they are bought, are thus part of a system of gift-giving, parallel to the exchange system in our society. They then play the role of promoting interaction, of mediators and of societal cement in our postmodern societies. The major marketing problem that companies are facing with postmodernity seems to be that they manufacture products which, on the market, become commodities with a certain use value, but are rarely objects with the potential of having meanings based on their linking value. This can be related to one of the key manifestations of postmodernity, fragmentation, where there is the separation of products from their original function, of the signifier from the signified, and the product from the need (Firat, 1992). The symbolic meaning of products is no longer fixed but free-floating, and each individual may ascribe different cultural meanings to a product depending on the extent to which they share the collective imagination and thus escape from the regime of truth. As each good may have a different meaning for each consumer, then perceptions and emotions may be unique and not reducible to conventional market segmentation techniques. Consequently, marketing needs to develop methodologies for investigating the meaning of consumer goods that elude the artificial limitations of positivist approaches that assume homogeneity of meaning within market segments, and recognise that the consumer may find it difficult to reduce the consumption to simple verbal labels (Elliot, 1993, p. 137).

Therefore, the postmodern challenge for companies seems now to be to develop *societal innovations* (Cova and Svanfeldt, 1993, p. 300), that is to say innovations that are capable of provoking the emergence of new aesthetic and cultural meanings in the societal system. These societal innovations inscribe themselves in a societal context rather than in a market segment. Thus, they constitute a linkage between new socio-cultural trends and tendencies and current technological potentials, by introducing change in a society. Societal innovations renew the relation between products and their users. They result from the recombination of familiar material in unconventional ways and they serve as a means by which a society both encourages and endures change. Apart from their insertion in a societal context, and the fact that they have changed our habits concerning music, transport, computers, domestic life, etc., societal innovations are most often associated with a single firm, such as Swatch throughout Europe, The Body Shop in England or Découvertes Gallimard in France. Microwave ovens can be said to have developed within, and reinforced, a social trend, and they can be said to have changed our habits, but few people would refer to their microwave oven as for instance their Toshiba or their Philips (except maybe ironically). In other words, they are not very cultish as objects – 'My microwave oven is a Toshiba, but my Mac is in fact a PC' – and do not benefit from a status of singularity. Above all, postmodernity clearly advocates against the traditional product/market marriage, based on functional and technical attributes of the product combined with stable illusory segments, and emphasises the flexible dimension of marketing. Postmodern evidences suggest that even niches could be so ephemeral that it could be very difficult to detect them and to serve them. Trends might cross different tribes or different groups at different rates across society. Marketing should help companies to detect emerging aesthetic and cultural trends and to forecast when, where and how these trends might appear across different tribes in order to create new ephemeral markets. The basic strategy is to anchor a brand to a major societal trend, and to use that brand to cover a wide range of products adapted to minor, local and ephemeral trends. The winners would be those companies closest to their tribes and most able to respond to, and even create new trends in society through societal innovations.

Among the postmodern marketing practices, two seem particularly suited to deal with these aesthetic and cultural trends and tribes (Badot, Bucci and Cova, 1993, p. 52):

- Trend-detection;
- Ethno-research.

A societal innovation seems to be the result of the encounter where the culture and competence of the firm perfectly match the currents and stimuli of society. For the company, it is less important to have a technologically perfect product than to 'sniff out' an emerging trend and to stick to it by developing a product which represents the emotional link between this trend and the culture of the company. Successful societal innovations are dependent on both a company-culture stimulating innovation and an understanding, and sensitivity, for the culture (and its manifestations) outside the firm. Societal innovations appear where the internal culture and the know-how of the firm match, and adapt, to the culture outside the firm and its manifestations. The impulse to innovate comes from the external culture (the stimuli) and, when received by a favourable internal culture, can be transformed into societal products or services. Therefore, the company needs to scan the societal environment in order to detect the favourable trends. For that purpose it may be supported by a network of 'experts' of societal trends. These

'experts' may be journalists, professors, stylists, philosophers, non conformists.. and serve as gate-keepers of a sort, reviewing aesthetic, social, and cultural innovations as they first appear in a very diverse areas, judging some as important and others as trivial. It is their responsibility to observe, as best they can, the whirling mass of innovation and decide what is fad and what is fashion, what is ephemeral and what will endure. A Delphi approach can be used to structure their judgements. A societal environmental scanning can also be implemented to feel the possible futures on the basis of the experience of other sectors or other countries.

Management is traditionally searching for a rational and objective approach to innovation, which begins with the ascertainment of consumers' wants and then responds to these by the production of approximate fulfilment. Aesthetics and culture cannot be measured, their expressions and manifestations (such as artifacts and values) can be, but aesthetics or culture themselves have to be interpreted. This means that traditional marketing stands helpless, since its main purpose has been the measurement of different expressions of demand and need. Alternative approaches, used in more peripheral fashion or arts marketing, seem more pertinent. Aesthetic sensibility, cultural background and societal context of users are becoming increasingly important as determining factors behind new product designs. Aesthetics is a very particular expression of social demand, completely different to what can emerge from, for instance, a market survey. The latter can only photograph reality, bringing forward what is, in a way, already obvious. It cannot show the detail, the meeting point between what the general public might want (but has yet to find a way of expressing) and what the producers might offer (but have not yet found an expressional support for), and which constitutes the idea of a new product. In fact, researchers recognise the inherent limitations of verbal reports given by customers in describing their responses to aesthetic and cultural products. Thus, there is a general trend towards increased use of social scientists in the innovation process, and generalists as managers rather than specialists. In

Japan, Sony uses a cultural anthropologist to brief software engineers working on its PC range, and Sharp employs sociologists to study how people live and behave with the objects. Some define this range of methods as 'ethno-research'. These methods make it possible to observe how the meanings resident in objects can be transferred from the object to the consumer/user. Symbolic action, or *ritual* (Bell, 1992), as it is more conventionally called, is a kind of societal action devoted to the manipulation of the aesthetic and cultural meaning for purposes of collective and individual communication and categorisation. Ritual is an opportunity to affirm, evoke, assign, or revise the conventional symbols and meanings of the cultural order. Ritual is to this extent a powerful and versatile tool for the manipulation of aesthetic and cultural meanings. More and more businesses owe their livelihoods to their ability to supply ritual artifacts (cult-objects), or items used in the performance of rituals, to the members of one of the postmodern tribes. The ethnographic observation of these rituals permits the company to understand how meanings move from the object to the consumer/user.

Another common trait of marketing approaches that try to cope with postmodernity is the emphasis on closeness to the customer. Today's marketing restoratives (the so-called 'one-to-one marketing', 'micro-marketing', 'maxi-marketing', 'database marketing', 'relationship marketing', etc.) desire to build, develop and maintain a relationship with the customer as an individual rather than to bombard a mass market (Brown, 1993). However, many of these approaches are too tinged with modern views and fail to deal with the double postmodern movement of aestheticisation and tribalism in everyday life. Believers in 'one-to-one marketing', for example, have got it all wrong for they wish to be close as possible to the consumer without sharing anything with him. They confuse proximity and intimacy. They base everything on customer service; they believe that individuals wish a 'personalised service' in terms of personalisation of functions, while in fact they wish a 'personalised link'. Of course, they do not want to create a link

with all salesmen but find it pleasant and rewarding to be sometimes greeted and recognised in the street. Just as the everyday life objects represent as many links, real or virtual, with other persons encountered. Consumption can therefore be studied as much for its functional and symbolic aspects relative to the individual as for its emotional and aesthetic aspects relative to the link between individuals. Consequently, marketing can be defined less as the launching of a product on a market than as the ascribing of meanings in a society. After having borrowed extensively from economics and psycho-sociology, marketing seems to need to resort to anthropology and ethno-sociology in order to refine its approach. Answering the challenge of postmodernity for marketing practice implies rethinking its essence in the socio-economic paradigm. In any case, marketing activity should no longer be analysed as an independent economic activity but as an activity embedded in a societal context which, at the same time, encompasses it and renders it possible.

■ Conclusion: limits

Often described as the most intellectually demanding challenge facing marketing practitioners and researchers, postmodernism allows us to rethink marketing theory and practice but, we must remember here the limitations of postmodernism and postmodernity. First, we are not sure that postmodernism is fit for globalisation. Postmodernity and postmodernism are social and philosophical traits of the priviledged part of the world and they depend on the high degree of consumption and affluence which is typical of this part of the world. It cannot simply be made into everybody's way of life (Baumann, 1992b, p. 144). Consequently, what we have discussed in this chapter are the possible implications of the postmodern era for marketing theory and practice in Western countries. What might be the future of marketing in other geographic zones (ASEAN for example) would need a completely different approach based on their specific social and philosophical traits. Second, the whole postmodernist philosophy warns us not to be uncritical in our enthusiasm even for the postmodern condition. In fact, negative consequences of extreme postmodernist positions in marketing theory can already be seen in academic conferences where 'anything goes' and 'no one cares' for the work of the other. Everyone, starting from scratch, feels free to reinvent his/her theory without any relationship with previous research. And negative consequences of postmodernity can be detected in the everyday life of our megapolis, where the recomposition by tribes, because of its fragile and ephemeral nature, does not resolve the anguish resulting from the dislocation of former stable community landmarks, and because it is sometimes confronted with pure decomposition which appears barbaric: urban violence and insecurity.

■ References

□ *Marketing*

Arndt, J. (1985), 'The Tyranny of Paradigms: The Case for Paradigmatic Pluralism in Marketing', in Dholakia, N. and Arndt, J. (eds), *Changing the Course of Marketing: Alternative Paradigms for Widening Marketing Theory*, Research in Marketing, Supplement 2, Greenwich: JAI Press, pp. 1–25.

Badot, O., Bucci, A. and Cova, B. (1993), 'Societing: Managerial Response to European Aestheticization', *European Management Journal*, Special Issue EAP 20th Anniversary, pp. 48–56.

Badot, O. and Cova, B. (1992), *Le Néo-marketing*, Paris: ESF.

Brown, S. (1993), 'Postmodern Marketing', *European Journal of Marketing* 27 (4), pp. 19–34.

Cova, B. and Salle, R. (1992), 'Models of Industrial Buying Behaviour: Overview and Rapprochement of New Trends of Research', *Proceedings of the Marketing Science Conference*, London (July).

Cova, B. and Svanfeldt, C. (1993), 'Societal innovations and the postmodern aestheticization of everyday life', *International Journal of Research in Marketing* 10, pp. 297–310.

Dholakia, N. and Arndt, J. (eds) (1985), *Changing the Course of Marketing: Alternative Paradigms for Widening Marketing Theory*, Research in Marketing, Supplement 2, Greenwich: JAI Press.

Elliot, R. (1993), 'Marketing and the Meaning of Postmodern Culture', in Brownlie, D., Saren, M., Wensley, R. and Whittington, R. (eds), *Rethinking Marketing: New Perspectives on the Discipline and Profession*, Coventry: Warwick Business School, pp. 134–142.

Firat, A. F. (1991a), 'The Consumer in Postmodernity', in Holman, R. H. and Solomon M. R. (eds), *Advances in Consumer Research*, Provo: Association for Consumer Research, pp. 70–76.

Firat, A. F. (1991b), 'Postmodern Culture, Marketing and the Consumer', in Childers, T. L. *et al.* (eds), *Marketing Theory and Applications*, Chicago: American Marketing Association, pp. 237–242.

Firat, A. F. (1992), 'Fragmentations in the Postmodern', in, Sherry, J. F. and Sternthal, B. (eds), *Advances in Consumer Research* 19, Provo: Association for Consumer Research, pp. 203–205.

Ford, D. (ed.) (1990), *Understanding Business Markets: Interaction, Relationships, Networks*, London: Academic Press.

Hakansson, H. (ed.) (1982), *International Marketing and Purchasing of Industrial Goods: An Interaction Approach*, Chichester: John Wiley.

Hirschman, C. H. and Holbrook, M. B. (1992), *Postmodern Consumer Research: The Study of Consumption as Text*, Newbury Park: Sage.

Hunt, S. D. (1990), 'Truth in Marketing Theory and Research', *Journal of Marketing* (July), pp. 1–15.

Hunt, S. D. (1991), 'Positivism and Paradigm Dominance in Consumer Research: Towards Pluralism and Rapprochement', *Journal of Consumer Research* 18 (June), pp. 32–44.

Hunt, S. D. (1992), 'For Reason and Realism in Marketing', *Journal of Marketing* 56 (April), pp. 89–102.

Hunt, S. D. (1993), 'Objectivity in Marketing Theory and Research', *Journal of Marketing* 57 (April), pp. 76–91.

Ogilvy, J. (1990), 'This Postmodern Business', *Marketing and Research Today*, 18 (1), pp. 4–21.

Peter, J. P. (1992), 'Realism or Relativism for Marketing Theory and Research: A Comment on Hunt's Scientific Realism', *Journal of Marketing* 56 (April), pp. 72–79.

Venkatesh, A. (1989), 'Modernity and Postmodernity', in Childers, T. L, *et al.* (eds), *Marketing Theory and Practice*, Chicago: American Marketing Association, pp. 99–104.

Venkatesh, A. (1992), 'Postmodernism, Consumer Culture and the Society of the Spectacle', in Sherry, J. F. and Sternthal, B. (eds), *Advances in Consumer*

Research 19, Provo: Association for Consumer Research, pp. 199–202.

Zinkhan, G. M. and Hirscheim, R. (1992), 'Truth in Marketing Theory and Research: An Alternative Perspective', *Journal of Marketing* 56 (April), pp. 80–88.

☐ *Postmodernism, Postmodernity*

Baudrillard, J. (1992), *L'Illusion de la fin*, Paris: Galilée.

Bauman, Z. (1992a), 'A Sociological Theory of Postmodernity', in Beilharz, P., Robinson, G. and Rundell, J. (eds), *Between Totalitarianism and Postmodernity*, Cambridge, Mass.: MIT Press, pp. 149–162.

Bauman, Z. (1992b), 'Modernity, Postmodernity and Ethics', an interview with Zygmunt Bauman by Timo Cantell and Poul Poder Pedersen, *Telos* 93, (Fall), pp. 133–144.

Bell, C. (1992), *Ritual Theory, Ritual Practice*, New York: Oxford University Press.

Featherstone, M. (1991), *Consumer Culture and Postmodernism*, London: Sage.

Harvey, D. (1989), *The Condition of Postmodernity*, Oxford: Basil Blackwell.

Latour, B. (1991), *Nous n'avons jamais été modernes: essai d'anthropologie comparée*, Paris: La Découverte.

Lipovetsky, G. (1992), *Le Crépuscule du devoir*, Paris: Gallimard.

Maffesoli, M. (1985), *La Connaissance ordinaire*, Paris: Méridiens Klincksieck.

Maffesoli, M. (1988), *Le Temps des tribus*, Paris: Méridiens Klincksieck.

Maffesoli, M. (1990), *Au Creux des apprences*, Paris: Plon.

Maffesoli, M. (1991), 'The Ethic of Aesthetics', *Theory, Culture and Society* 8, pp. 7–20.

Maffesoli, M. (1992), *La Transfiguration du politique*, Paris: Grasset.

Rosenau, P. M. (1991), *Post-Modernism and the Social Sciences: Insights, Inroads and Intrusions*, Princeton: Princeton University Press.

Smart, B. (1990), 'Modernity, Postmodernity and the Present' in Turner, B. S. (ed.), *Theories of Modernity and Postmodernity*, London: Sage, pp. 14–30.

Turner, B. S. (ed.) (1990), *Theories of Modernity and Postmodernity*, London: Sage.

Index